SHIPWRECKS & SALVAGE

IN SOUTH AFRICA

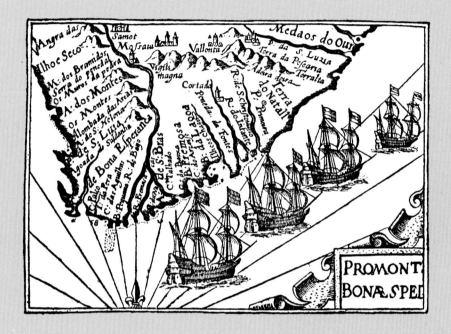

*This book is dedicated to the memory of the hundreds
of people from all nations who have lost their
lives in shipwrecks on the coast of South Africa*

SHIPWRECKS & SALVAGE

IN SOUTH AFRICA

Malcolm Turner

C. Struik
Cape Town

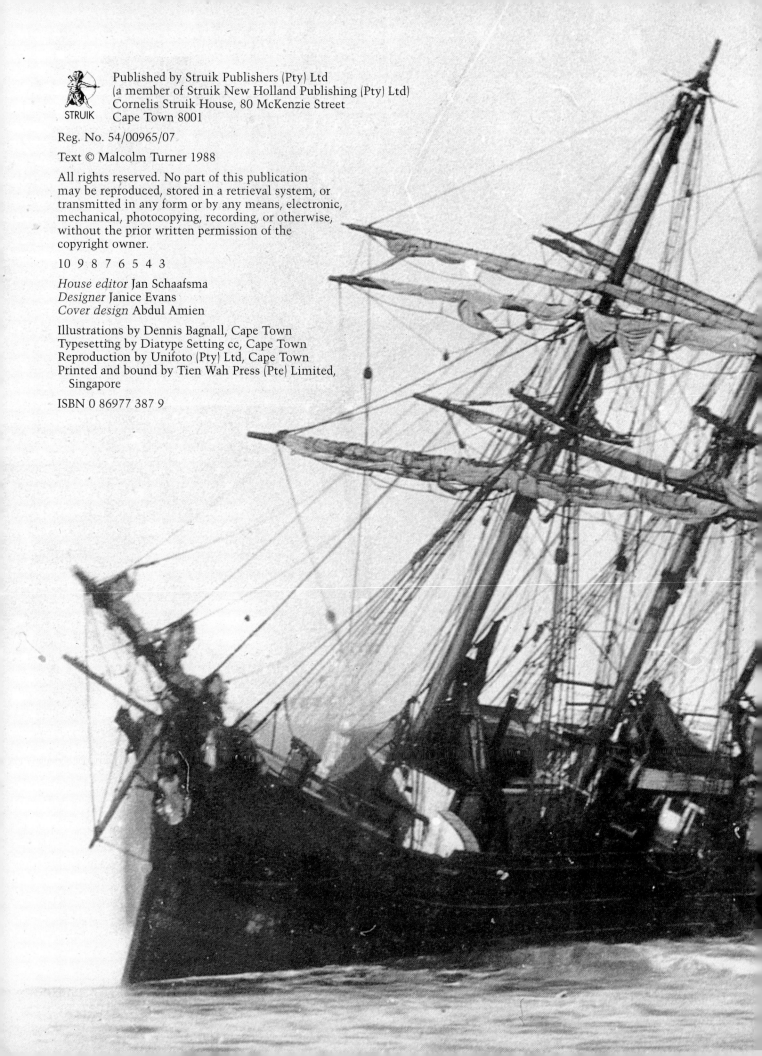

Published by Struik Publishers (Pty) Ltd
(a member of Struik New Holland Publishing (Pty) Ltd)
Cornelis Struik House, 80 McKenzie Street
Cape Town 8001

Reg. No. 54/00965/07

10 9 8 7 6 5 4 3

House editor Jan Schaafsma
Designer Janice Evans
Cover design Abdul Amien

Illustrations by Dennis Bagnall, Cape Town
Typesetting by Diatype Setting cc, Cape Town
Reproduction by Unifoto (Pty) Ltd, Cape Town
Printed and bound by Tien Wah Press (Pte) Limited,
  Singapore

ISBN 0 86977 387 9

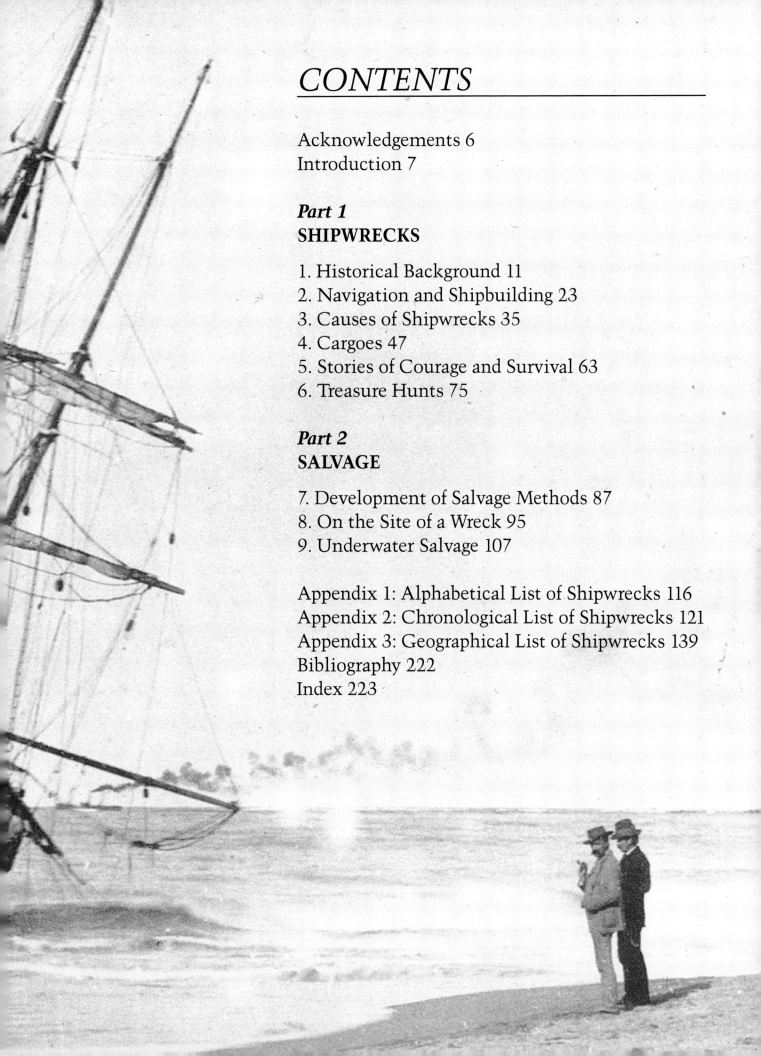

CONTENTS

Endpapers: A huge breaker envelops the wreck of the South African Seafarer, which ran onto the rocks at Green Point on 1 July 1966. (The Argus)

French Title Page: Detail from a Portuguese map of Africa dated 1598.

Title Page: Giant Atlantic winter surf pounds the rust-streaked stern of the wrecked oil tanker Romelia, which ran ashore at Llandudno on 29 July 1977. (M. Turner)

Contents Page: The wooden barque Bridgetown lies stranded on the Back Beach at Durban after being driven ashore on 28 June 1882. The crew were rescued under extremely difficult circumstances by the port lifeboat. (Local History Museum, Durban)

Introduction: Scuba diver Greg Moore descends to the sea-bed in Algoa Bay during a search for shipwrecks. (M. Turner)

Part 1 (pp 8-9): The heat-blistered hulk of the Greek steamer George M. Livanos, which was burnt out after running aground at Green Point on 1 April 1947. (Cape Times)

Chapter 1 (p 10): A painting of Table Bay in 1683 by Aernout Smit, with the Dutch East-Indiaman Africa in the foreground. (William Fehr Collection)

Chapter 2 (p 22): A map of Africa by Abraham Ortelius dated 1570. (William Fehr Collection)

Chapter 3 (p 34): A painting by K. Borrough of the wreck of the Royal Mail Steamer Celt in Celt Bay on 5 February 1875. Note the ensign flown upside-down to signal distress. (Africana Museum)

Chapter 4 (p 46): Silver specie recovered from the wreck of the Dutch East-Indiaman Reigersdaal, wrecked on Springfontein Point on 25 October 1747. (M. Turner)

Chapter 5 (p 62): A contemporary painting of the wreck of the Dutch East-Indiaman Vis at Green Point on 6 May 1740. A copper cauldron, used in the rescue of the crew, can be seen in the background. (South African Library)

Chapter 6 (p 74): A painting by Thomas Luny of the capture on 21 July 1781 of the Dutch East-India fleet in Saldanha Bay by British forces. The large man-of-war in the foreground is the Romney, and the burning Middelburg can be seen in the background. Note that the captured vessels are all flying the British flag. (Africana Museum)

Part 2 (pp 84-85): A view of the salvage camp established opposite the wreck of the Western Knight near The Willows, Port Elizabeth, in 1929. Most of the cargo was recovered by Captain Deric van Delden. (Frank Neave)

Chapter 7 (p 86): The author in a venerable Siebe Gorman 'hard hat' rig. This type of equipment is rarely used today. (Mike Smith)

Chapter 8 (p 94): Diver Simon Gilbert battles against heavy surge as he peers through a brass window-frame on a sunken section of the oil tanker Romelia, which was wrecked at Llandudno on 29 July 1977. (M. Turner)

Chapter 9 (p 106): The salvage vessel Etosha heads for port. On board are bronze cannon and a huge wrought iron anchor recovered from the wreck of the Portuguese East-Indiaman Nossa Senhora de Atalaia do Pinheiro, which went aground in June 1647. (Peter Sachs)

Appendix 2 (p 120): A depiction of the wrecking of the English East-Indiaman Dodington on Bird Island on 17 July 1755. (Africana Museum)

Appendix 3 (p 138): The chaos on the beach after the great north-west gale in Table Bay on 17 May 1865. (Cape Archives)

All reasonable attempts have been made to trace and acknowledge copyright owners of historical photographs used in this book. However, this has not always been possible, and I apologise for any unintentional oversight.

ACKNOWLEDGEMENTS

I would like to thank the many people who offered advice and photographs to help make this book a success, and in particular:

The staff of C. Struik Publishers, without whose help and enthusiasm this book would not have been possible.

Captain C.J. Harris of Fish Hoek, for scanning the manuscript for errors in nautical terminology.

Mark Pratt of *Lloyds Register of Shipping*, London, for his enthusiastic help.

Jen Ferguson of Pinelands, for making available to me the vast nautical library of her late husband, Ronald L. Ferguson.

Peter Sachs of East London, for the use of his unique transparencies of the salvage of the *Nossa Senhora de Atalaia do Pinheiro*.

Reginald Dodds of Milnerton, for assisting me in recording the salvage of the *Merestein* and *Middelburg* wrecks, and for many happy hours underwater.

Mr and Mrs Eric Tompkins of Birmingham, England, for their tireless search for information.

The Ship Society of South Africa, for the use of their large collection of *Lloyds Registers*.

Gill Vernon of the East London Museum, for her help during my search for photographs.

Mrs Harradine of the Africana Room, Port Elizabeth Public Library, for her co-operation.

The staff of the South African Library, Cape Town, for their professionalism and enthusiasm.

The staff of the Cape Archives.

Betty Paap, curator of the William Fehr Collection, Cape Town.

The staff of the Africana Museum, Johannesburg.

The operators of the John Rolfe helicopter.

My wife, Geraldine, for her patience during the long hours spent researching the book, checking the manuscript and reading the proofs.

INTRODUCTION

*T*he purpose of this book is to give as accurate as possible an account of the many shipwrecks that have occurred on the coast of South Africa, as well as the state of underwater salvage in the country; in addition an attempt has been made to perpetuate in photographic form a small sample of the great variety of artefacts and treasures that have been recovered over the years. It will soon be apparent to the reader that very little documentation of finds has been undertaken in South Africa, and that much has been lost through the unprofessional methods employed by many salvage groups over the years, but as there is an international movement to put a stop to indiscriminate salvage operations, it is hoped that our underwater treasures will in future be safeguarded.

This study is the result of more than eight years' work, and covers close on 1 000 wrecks, which can be considered a fair representation of all the major shipwrecks along the South African coast. I have concentrated on vessels which were wrecked close to land, and have therefore not included the many vessels sunk at a distance from the shores of this treacherous coast: that is why the famous *Waratah*, which sank without trace at sea some four nautical miles (8 km) off the east coast in 1909, has not been included. Also excluded are wrecked vessels which were later refloated. In order to keep the study to manageable proportions, I have excluded tugs, steam whalers, fishing-boats, barges, yachts and small vessels under twenty tons. Nor has the Skeleton Coast of Namibia been included, because of its extreme inaccessibility; the book covers the coastline and islands from the Orange River mouth to the Mozambique border. Armchair divers will be able to locate a great number of the wrecks, as approximate latitudes and longitudes have been provided whenever these are known.

MALCOLM TURNER   *Cape Town, November 1987*

Part 1
SHIPWRECKS

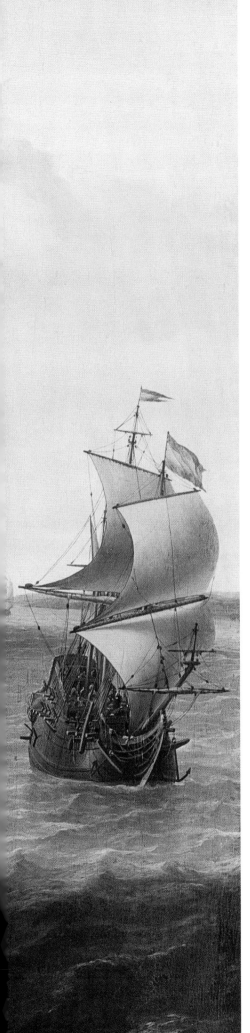

Chapter 1

Historical Background

*I*n 1498 Vasco da Gama opened up the sea route to the East, and in 1505, a mere seven years later, the first recorded wreck on the coast of South Africa occurred when a heavily armed Portuguese sailing vessel loaded with pepper ran ashore at night a little west of Mossel Bay, with the loss of its master, Pero de Mendonca, and the entire crew. Unfortunately the name of this vessel is lost to us – it is known only as the 'Soares Wreck' – and no trace of the wreck itself has been found.

Yet was this in fact the first South African wreck? As far back as 1000 BC the ancient Phoenicians had established themselves as mariners par excellence in the Mediterranean Sea, and it is known that they ventured beyond the Pillars of Heracles, as they called the Straits of Gibraltar, into the Atlantic Ocean. Their fame spread widely, and in about 600 BC the Egyptian pharaoh Necho asked them to undertake a voyage of exploration with the aim of rounding the southern tip of Africa. At the time little was known of the interior of the continent, but as it produced a steady stream of trade goods such as ivory, gold and slaves, it seemed worth an investigation.

Obviously Necho believed that Africa was an island, because his instructions to the Phoenicians were to sail out of the Red Sea and to proceed along the coast of Africa until they reached the Pillars of Heracles, and thereafter home. The Greek historian Herodotus records that the voyage took three years to complete, the Phoenicians stopping every autumn to plant corn and moving on after the harvest. On their return they told Necho that the rising sun, which had consistently been at their left on their voyage down the east coast, had at some point appeared on their right, or starboard side. This observation would seem to indicate that the Phoenicians did round the southern tip of Africa, but even Herodotus himself, though faithfully recording the details of the voyage, remained sceptical about the truth of it.

It is not precisely known for how long Moslem traders have been established on the coast of East Africa – probably from about the 10th or 11th century – but certainly these Arab and Persian traders dominated a large area stretching from North and East Africa and the Levant to India by the time of the first determined Portuguese intrusion in the area. Calicut on the west coast of India was the foremost city on the Malabar Coast, and Malindi, Mombasa and Mozambique on the African east coast were visited regularly by Moslem trading vessels. There is ample evidence in the form of glass beads and Chinese ceramics found as far south as the Iron Age settlement of Mapungubwe in northern Transvaal that these traders penetrated far inland, with gold, ivory and slaves as their goal, and it is quite probable that Moslem vessels rounded the southern tip of Africa from east to west. Legend has it that such a passage took place about 1420, though no recorded proof for this exists.

While Arab dhows regularly criss-crossed the Red Sea and Indian Ocean, only a sketchy picture of that area existed in Medieval Europe, where it was believed that the world consisted of four continents, namely Europe, Africa, Asia and Terra Incognita, a vaguely imagined land mass somewhere in the Southern Hemisphere. Fantastic tales existed about these fabled lands, many passed down from classical times. Somewhere in Africa, for instance, there was reputed to be a river of pure gold emptying into a seething tropical sea in which no man could survive. Somewhere, too, there was a land studded with treasures that were guarded by dragons and legless birds that never came down to land.

One of the most enduring traditions to survive from the 12th century was that of a fabulously wealthy and powerful Christian ruler, Prester John, who was believed to be living somewhere in Africa. Well into the 16th century the hope persisted that if a European power could make contact with him, it would be possible to convert the whole of Africa to Christianity. The Moslem strongholds in North Africa could then be taken in the rear and defeated with his help, and the Moslem stranglehold on the African and Asian markets would in consequence be broken.

Above: *Vasco da Gama, the famed Portuguese explorer. In 1497 he followed the sea-route around the Cape of Good Hope pioneered by Bartolomeu Dias in 1487, and opened up the Eastern trade area to Portuguese vessels. Soon after this voyage, Portugal emerged as the dominant trading nation in the East. (Cape Archives, E319)*
Below: *An illustration from an early Portuguese document recording the loss of four vessels of Pedro Cabral's fleet during a storm off the Cape of Good Hope in 1500. The pioneer explorer Bartolomeu Dias, who captained one of the vessels (see bottom right on the illustration), perished with his caravel. (Cape Archives, M735)*

By the beginning of the 15th century Europe was advancing technologically on many fronts, including navigation and ship-building, and merchants and traders – who for many years had operated successfully from the city-states of Genoa, Pisa, Amalfi and Venice – were more impatient than ever to gain access to the known riches offered by the markets of Africa and Asia. As the overland route was blocked by the Moslem presence, however, an alternative had to be found, and to the rulers of Spain and Portugal the open ocean to the west presented itself as a logical avenue to be explored.

The Portuguese believed that a route to the East could be found round Africa – and the stage was set for a series of pioneering voyages down the west coast of the continent to find it. All it needed was the drive provided by a strong personality, and such a person was the third son of King John I of Portugal. Subsequently known as Prince Henry the Navigator, he had built his reputation during the successful capture and occupation of the strategic Moslem fortress of Ceuta on the shores of Morocco in 1415. Soon he began to gather round him a remarkable group of instrument makers, cartographers, shipbuilders and sailors, all driven by an intense desire to extend their knowledge.

The exploration of the African coast did not pose any physical difficulties for the Portuguese seamen, who were used to operating in the stormy seas off Portugal in their fast and seaworthy caravels, but psychologically they were at a distinct disadvantage, as many of the old Medieval legends persisted and still had a strong hold on the imagination. It was widely believed that life was insupportable at the equator: the tropical sun would burn you to death, and if you survived that, the boiling sea would kill you, not to mention the monsters that lived further south. It was also believed that Africa was joined to Terra Incognita, which meant that there was no passage to India.

Henry's strategy was first to establish outposts on various island groups off the African coast, for instance the Madeiras, the Canaries and the Azores. These were to become important replenishment stations for vessels journeying into the unknown, and also acted as a 'safety net' for vessels blown off course during a storm. As expeditions slowly penetrated further south, the morale of the mariners improved and rapid strides were made. Cape Bojador, which had always presented problems because the trade winds encountered there tended to blow vessels out to sea, was passed in 1434; by 1445 two more important headlands had been passed, namely Cape Blanco and Cape Verde; and in 1473 Lopo Gonçalves crossed the equator without burning to death. By 1483 Diogo Cão had progressed as far south as Cape Cross on the desolate coast of Namibia, leaving a *padrão* or inscribed stone cross on the shore as proof of his presence and in order to claim the land for Portugal. He had opened up more than 2 260 km of coastline, but still it ran seemingly endlessly south.

Then, in 1487, King John II sent out another expedition, led by Bartolomeu Dias. His fleet consisted of three caravels, and his instructions were to try and round the southern tip of Africa, and if possible, to make contact with Prester John. Like all the others, this voyage was shrouded in secrecy in order to deny archrival Spain any advantage in the race to the East, and little is known of the actual route taken. However, we do know that when the fleet was about 380 nautical miles (700 km) northwest of the present-day Cape Peninsula, it was driven out to sea by violent gales. When these subsided, Dias turned east in order to make a landfall on the coast, and when no shore was sighted, turned north, eventually making a landfall near the present-day Mossel Bay, some 400 km east of Cape Point; the fleet then proceeded slowly up the east coast. Although it was apparent to him that he had found the sea route to India, Dias encountered strong opposition from his crew members, and it was with a heavy heart that he turned back after reaching the mouth of the Great Fish River. He stopped at Kwaaihoek, a prominent sandstone headland a little west of the Bushmans River, and erected a *padrão* there to lay claim to the sea route to the East Indies for Portugal.

On the voyage home Dias led the fleet round Cape Point, which he named Cabo Tormentosa, or Cape of Storms, but on his return to Portugal King John renamed it Cabo de Boa Esperança, or Cape of Good Hope, in anticipation of the riches which were to flow from the Indies.

On 8 July 1497 an expedition consisting of two *nãos* – the flagship *São Gabriel* and the *São Raphael* – as well as the caravel *Berrio* and a storeship, under the command of Vasco da Gama, left Lisbon with the instruction to reach the East and open up the trade route round Africa. After a voyage of three months which took them far into the Atlantic, the fleet made a landfall in St Helena Bay, north of the present Cape Town, and here preparations were made to round the Cape, which was done successfully. At Mossel Bay Da Gama reprovisioned the fleet and burned his storeship. Before leaving the bay a *padrão* was erected, but this was pulled down by local Hottentots even as the vessels were sailing out of the bay.

After months at sea the fleet entered the port of Mozambique, where Da Gama made his first contact with Moslem traders – and was surprised to meet with such sophistication: he was greeted by a sultan who treated with contempt the Portuguese trade goods consisting of bracelets, bells, caps and glass beads. Through interpreters Da Gama learned that further north there were large ports where spices, pearls and rubies were traded. A local pilot was hired and the fleet pressed on northwards. At Mombasa, a thriving Arab port, the Portuguese were the object of great suspicion and an attempt was made to capture the *São Gabriel*.

The next port of call was Malindi, and Da Gama was overjoyed to be received courteously by the local sultan. Here he engaged a famous Hindu pilot, Ahmed ben-Madjid, to guide him across the Arabian Sea to India, where he made his landfall near Calicut. To the Arab and Persian merchants of the city the previous isolated appearances of Europeans on the Malabar Coast after having taken the overland route through the Middle East had offered no threat, as they had been too few and their efforts too uncoordinated to present any challenge, but Da Gama's well-equipped and armed fleet was a different story altogether. The Moslem traders reacted with considerable jealousy; trading was made almost impossible and an attempt was even made on the life of Da Gama. But on 29 August 1498 the fleet sailed for Portugal, arriving to a hero's welcome in September 1499.

This was the beginning of a vast Portuguese trade empire that eventually spread its influence throughout the East Indies. At the time the price of spices and other Eastern goods on sale in the markets of Venice was almost thirty times the going price in the East, offering the prospect of huge profits, but first the problem of the Moslem monopoly had to be tackled. Less than six months after Da Gama's triumphant return to Lisbon, King Manuel therefore assembled a huge fleet of 13 heavily armed vessels that were to transport 1 200 men to India, under the leadership of Pedro Alvares Cabral. By this time Portuguese navigators were confident enough of their skills to venture far from the coast of Africa, and the fleet made a landfall on

The riches of the East

Although fantastic tales of the wonders of the East had filtered through to Europe even in Medieval times, they could not be checked by actual observation, and for the most part Europeans remained ignorant about Asia. A few traders had reached India, but attempts by Europeans to penetrate into Asia beyond Syria and Palestine were blocked, first by Persian and then by Moslem rulers. It was not until about 1250 that the widespread Mongol empire, which stretched from China to southern Russia, allowed Christians free passage through all its territories. Various travellers immediately took advantage of this concession, the most famous being Marco Polo, a Venetian merchant, who kept an accurate record of his visit to the court of Kublai Khan; this account became one of the most popular and widely read travel books of the time. In the middle of the 14th century, however, Western access to the East was once more blocked, this time by the Ottoman Turks. Yet it was known that the East was a region of fabulous wealth – if only one could get to it. At about the time of Bartolomeu Dias's journey, King John instructed Pero de Covilhã to go to India via Arabia to report on the routes taken by the Moslem spice ships crossing the Indian Ocean to Africa. Covilhã found his way to Calicut and saw junks bringing spices, porcelain, silks and gems from China and the East Indies, and these goods were then transferred to the holds of merchantmen for shipment to the Persian Gulf and East Africa. He also found that he was by no means the first European visitor to India, and that the craft that sailed regularly down the Red Sea and on to India had also carried Venetian, Genoese, French and Dutch traders. His report no doubt lent urgency to the decision to send Vasco da Gama on his expedition to open up the sea route to the East.

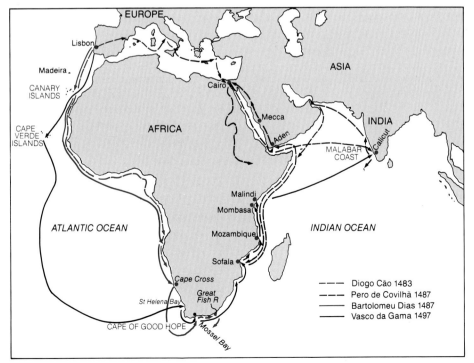

A map showing the approximate routes taken by some of the early Christian explorers during Portugal's drive to discover the sea-route to the East. The East African ports of Sofala, Mozambique, Mombasa and Malindi were found to be dominated by Moslem traders, who had penetrated far into the interior of Africa in search of gold, ivory and slaves. Note that even at this early stage Da Gama felt confident enough of his navigational skills to swing far out into the Atlantic, taking advantage of favourable winds and currents, before sweeping past the Cape of Good Hope.

Top: *A depiction by Charles Bell of Dias erecting his third* padrão *at Angra Pequena. (South African Library)*

Above: *A woodcut depicting the loss of the Portuguese East-Indiaman* Santo Alberto *on the south-east coast of Africa in 1593. (Cape Archives, M736)*

Right, top: *An artist's impression of a Phoenician galley proceeding along the desolate west coast of South Africa in about 600 B.C. after having rounded the Cape of Good Hope. (D. Bagnall)*

Right, centre: *A Portuguese caravel, typical of the tiny vessels in which the early Portuguese explorers searched for, and found, the sea-route around the southern tip of Africa. (D. Bagnall)*

Right, bottom: *A Portuguese* não, *a large, heavily-armed merchant vessel in which the riches of the East were shipped back to Portugal. A larger version of this type of vessel was known as the carrack. (D. Bagnall)*

Opposite: *The Portuguese carrack* São Thomé *under attack by Dutch and English vessels in the Straits of Malacca in 1602. With the appearance of Dutch and English merchants in the East, trade rivalries often led to scenes such as this. (Cape Archives, M48)*

the as yet unclaimed Brazilian mainland before making for the Cape, where four vessels were lost during a storm – including one commanded by Bartolomeu Dias, who perished with his vessel.

At Calicut the local ruler received the Portuguese without enthusiasm, even though they offered him goods as varied as a silver basin, two silver maces, brocaded cushions, tapestries and carpets. Eventually a treaty was signed giving the Portuguese trading rights in Calicut, and a spice cargo was amassed, ready for dispatch to Portugal. However, after loading only two vessels, the Portuguese faced a violent riot in which about 3 000 Moslems stormed the depot, killing 50 Portuguese. In retaliation the Portuguese bombarded the town and then moved south to Cochin, where another agreement with the local ruler was concluded, and here the first Portuguese trading station in the East was established. It was to be the forerunner of an empire based on control of such trading stations and dominance of the sea that was to stretch as far as Macao in China (still a Portuguese possession today), with Goa in India as its centre.

Soon a steady stream of galleons and carracks (eventually to reach the considerable size of 2 000 tons) with valuable cargoes of silver with which to pay for purchases sailed east, to return heavily laden with spices, cloth, Chinese porcelain, diamonds, ivory and slaves.

The period of Portuguese monopoly in the East lasted little more than a hundred years, for by the beginning of the 17th century two great rival trading companies, those of the English and the Dutch, were established. Queen Elizabeth I gave her consent to the first English voyage to the East in 1591: following the Portuguese route, three vessels set off, but only one returned with a full load of pepper. Still, this load was enough to cover the cost of the entire expedition and to turn a handsome profit. The Dutch, too, were gearing up to enter the markets of the East, and the first official Dutch sailing, under Cornelis de Houtman, left Holland in 1595. These two nations established their own trading companies soon afterwards; the English East India Company was granted its charter in 1601, while that of the Dutch East India Company was granted in 1602.

A period of struggle for supremacy in the East ensued. The Portuguese were hampered by the fact that they had failed to spread their influence beyond the confines of their trading posts. Strong religious convictions precluded treaties with heathen rulers, and the Portuguese remained few in numbers; soon these numbers were further whittled down by intermarriages with locals. The key remained control of the sea-lanes, and here the Dutch soon showed the greatest aggression, simply outsailing and out-gunning their rivals. Portuguese influence dwindled, and the English were tolerated by the Dutch only because they were confined to the less profitable Indian trade, with their bases at Surat, Madras and later Calcutta.

The Dutch, on the other hand, were firmly established in the centre of the rich Eastern trade areas such as Indonesia and Java, with their headquarters at Batavia.

The Treaty of Tordesillas

In the late 15th century both Spain and Portugal, with their Atlantic coastlines, ventured beyond the safe confines of Mediterranean trade to open up new routes to the East. Both believed that a sea route could be found to gain access to its riches, but Spain thought that the way lay in sailing west across the Atlantic, while Portugal believed that the route lay around the southern tip of Africa. In 1492 Christopher Columbus set out on behalf of Spain to find the East Indies and reached the present-day Cuba; he then turned back under the mistaken impression that he had reached his goal. His report to Ferdinand and Isabella of Spain convinced them that the sea route to the East had been found, and they immediately decided to safeguard this route by asking the Pope to grant them exclusive rights to trade and conquest across the open sea. Pope Alexander VI, himself a Spaniard, listened sympathetically to their plea, and by the papal bull *Inter Caetera* granted them such rights to trade and conquest to the west of a line drawn from pole to pole about 260 nautical miles (480 km) west of the Azores, while Portugal would enjoy the same privileges east of that line. The king of Portugal immediately objected, and after negotiations between the two countries, a compromise was reached in June 1494. By the Treaty of Tordesillas, later endorsed by the Pope, the dividing line was moved further west, about 325 nautical miles (600 km) from the Azores to longitude 46° 37.00 W. His division of the globe was to prove of immense value to the Portuguese, as the country then undiscovered but now known as Brazil came within their sphere of influence; furthermore, unbeknown to the Spanish, the western passage to the East was blocked by the thin strip of land joining the continents of North and South America.

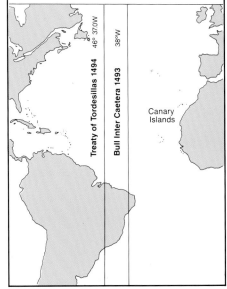

Above: A meeting between Dutch traders and Ceylonese merchants in 1603. The Dutch newcomers to the East soon established large, well-defended trading posts throughout the East Indies. (Cape Archives, M47)
Below: The headquarters of the Dutch East India Company in Amsterdam. (Cape Archives, M64)

Through treaties and gradual conquest they expanded territorially and established a strong permanent presence throughout the East, while hundreds of Dutch East India Company vessels provided a link between the East and the mother country. Over the years, however, the long ocean voyages exacted a heavy toll on lives and equipment, and it was realised that a replenishment station en route would do much to solve this problem. In 1652, therefore, a permanent Dutch presence was established at the Cape under the command of Jan van Riebeeck, and soon the town which developed at the foot of Table Mountain became a port of call for hundreds of vessels from many nations.

The Dutch dominance lasted roughly 150 years. European rivalries and wars weakened the Dutch homeland, and similar struggles in the East also took their toll. In 1795 the Dutch East India Company, which had been in decline for a number of years, was taken over by the Dutch state, and was declared bankrupt soon afterwards. In the meantime Britain had emerged as the strongest force in the East. Its possessions in India proved a boon, and after a fierce struggle with France for supremacy, it took control of the whole of the subcontinent. Its trading influence spread, and soon the tea trade with China came to rival the spice trade of old. At the Cape, too, the British dominance became a reality when a British task force defeated the Dutch defenders in 1795 and took control of the government. Apart from a brief interlude between 1803 and 1806, when Dutch rule was re-established under the Batavian Republic, the Cape was thereafter to remain in British hands. Rapid expansion in the East saw a British Empire which eventually stretched to China and Australia. With time these far-flung possessions became fully-fledged colonies, and a constant stream of shipping carrying Government officials, soldiers, immigrants, supplies, money and other goods needed to rule such a vast number of subjects sailed to and fro past South Africa's shores in countless vessels.

In this period South Africa was not regarded as a particularly desirable colony by either the Dutch or the British metropolitan governments, and the territorial expansion that did take place at the southern tip of Africa was slow, haphazard and unplanned. Despite the fact that hundreds of vessels called at Table Bay, harbour facilities remained primitive – the bay was no more than an anchorage, with people and cargo being transferred to boats for ferrying to the shore; a system that remained in use at some South African harbours as late as the 1860s. Apart from some agricultural produce such as wine (for a while Constantia wine was world famous), wool (which by 1840 had become the most important colonial export and remained so until diamonds overtook it in the 1870s), hides, skins and ostrich feathers, exports from South Africa were virtually non-existent. Although the volume of shipping calling at Cape ports quadrupled between the 1820s and the 1840s, the vessels were for the most part merely passing by on their way to destinations elsewhere.

Yet changes were in the air. In 1820 the first shipload of British immigrants stepped ashore in Algoa Bay, and in subsequent years Port Elizabeth developed as the main port servicing the Eastern Cape area. In 1834 the first of an eventual total of about 15 000 Dutch inhabitants who were no longer prepared to live under the British flag loaded their ox-wagons and departed for the interior, an exodus that has become known as the Great Trek and which led to the establishment of the independent inland republics of the Orange Free State and Transvaal. The coast remained in Britain's hands, however, as Natal was declared British territory in 1843. Here, too, a port slowly developed at Durban.

By the middle of the 19th century the British colonies in Southern Africa had grown to such an extent that demands were made for the establishment of a regular mailship link with Britain, and this was granted when the steamer *Bosphorus* left Plymouth on 18 December 1850, to arrive at Cape Town on 27 January 1851. In November 1857 the *Dane*, the first Union Line mailship, lay at anchor in Table Bay, and in 1872 a competitor, Donald Currie's Castle Line, appeared on the scene. From 1876 the mail contract alternated between these two lines, each of which ran a mailship on alternate weeks, until their amalgamation in March 1900 to form the Union-Castle Line. Their vessels were to remain an established feature of the South African maritime scene until the last mailship was withdrawn in the 1970s.

When diamonds were discovered at Kimberley in 1869 and gold on the Witwatersrand in 1886, the whole picture suddenly changed. South Africa's ports became choked with shipping bringing a flood of adventurers, gamblers, miners, industrialists and bankers to the country, as well as all manner of mining and industrial equipment and machinery, and other imports necessary to keep the wheels of the new industries turning; it was also necessary to export the new riches. Harbour facilities soon became totally inadequate: when the first enclosed harbour at Cape Town, the Alfred Dock, was officially opened on 4 July 1870, it was already too small to accommodate the huge influx of shipping. Consequently expansions were planned and built, and in 1895 the larger Victoria Basin was completed. At Port

The wreck of the Nieuw Haarlem

Of the many vessels wrecked on the coast of South Africa, few have had such a direct influence on its history as the one which on 16 January 1647 set sail in Batavia on a long return voyage to Holland as part of a fleet of Dutch East Indiamen. In March 1647 the *Nieuw Haarlem* was anchored in Table Bay when a strong south-easterly gale sprang up and the vessel was driven ashore a little south of the present Milnerton Beach. The captain continued the journey in another vessel, but a party under the leadership of Leendert Jansz was ordered to remain. They built a temporary fort and lived at the site for about a year before they were eventually rescued by another return fleet, amongst whose number was a young man named Jan van Riebeeck. At the time the long voyages to and from the East were exacting a heavy toll on lives and vessels and the Dutch East India Company had already decided in principle to establish a half-way station on the route. Saldanha Bay, with its magnificent natural harbour, was regarded as a perfect setting, but the lack of fresh water there made it unfeasible, so on their return to Holland the shipwrecked party was asked to report on the possibilities of Table Bay. Their report was favourable, and Van Riebeeck, who was asked to comment on their report, concurred, so the decision was made to establish the half-way station at the Cape. When the first party of Hollanders, led by Van Riebeeck, arrived in 1652 in a fleet consisting of the *Dromedaris*, the *Reiger* and the *Goede Hoop*, a fort was built and extensive gardens laid out. In time a fair-sized town developed in the shadow of Table Mountain, and it has remained a focus for shipping to the present day.

A view of Table Bay in about 1778. Note the Castle, the jetty leading out to sea, and the Company Gardens. These gardens provided the all-important fresh victuals necessary to keep crews in good health.

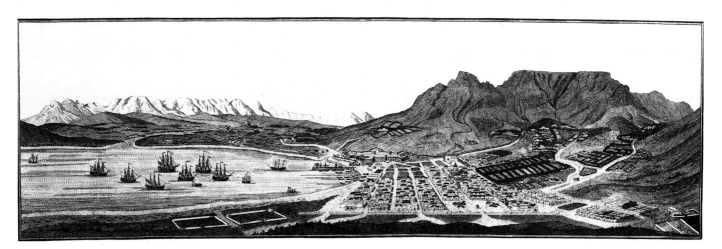

Elizabeth the North Jetty was built in 1881, and this made the loading and unloading of vessels by means of tugs and lighters easier; however, vessels still had to anchor in the bay, where they were largely unprotected against gales. At Durban the sandbar across the entrance to the bay was dredged, but only in 1892 could the *Dunrobin Castle* of 2 783 tons cross the bar and enter the bay. The port was officially declared open for traffic on 26 June 1904 when the *Armadale Castle* of 12 973 tons (at the time one of the biggest steamers in the world) crossed the bar and berthed at E-shed. Almost overnight South Africa had changed from a sleepy British colony relying for its exports mainly on agriculture into the world's most important mining area. Not even the opening of the Suez Canal in 1869 could relieve the pressure of shipping round the shores of the country.

In 1899 South Africa once again became the focus of world attention, but this time for another reason: war broke out between the Boer republics and Britain, and as a result vessels jammed the harbours of Cape Town, Port Elizabeth and Durban, disgorging war material, horses and a total of about 500 000 British troops over the two and a half years that the war lasted. During the war it was not unusual to see vessels tied up two and three abreast in Cape Town harbour, with up to 50 more at anchor in the bay; it often took weeks before a vessel could enter the harbour to be discharged. When the war was over and Britain was firmly in control of the whole country, shipping patterns changed. Instead of viewing South African ports merely as stop-over points on a longer journey, they gradually became destinations in their own right. Because of its close proximity to the new industrial heartland of the Witwatersrand, the port of Durban was the main beneficiary of this activity, eventually becoming Africa's busiest harbour.

The period between the two world wars saw a great expansion of harbour facilities. In 1932 a new basin alongside the Victoria Basin was completed in Cape Town, and an ambitious land reclamation scheme made possible a greatly enlarged Dun-

Opposite, top: *A panoramic view of Table Bay from the slopes of Signal Hill early this century. Much of the seascape in the picture has now been covered by reclamation works. (Cape Archives)*

Opposite, centre: *A similar view taken in 1988. The harbour has been extended far into the bay, and many of the early shipwrecks are now buried beneath reclaimed land. (M. Turner)*

Left: *The Alfred Basin in Cape Town harbour crammed with shipping in 1900. More vessels can be seen in the anchorage in the background, including a dismasted hulk. (Cape Archives, E2865)*

Below: *A view of Table Mountain by Otto Landsberg, showing the anchorage from the new breakwater, under construction in about 1869. (Potchefstroom Museum)*

Above: *A view from the west bank of the Buffalo River, East London. painted in 1884. Two steamers and a sailing vessel lie in the anchorage. The town was first established on the west bank, but with the development of harbour facilities in the river mouth, grew to the fine port city it is today. (Africana Museum)*

Right: *A view of Algoa Bay after the great south-east gale of September 1869. The vessels on the beach include the* Forres, Sarah Black, England, Argali, Gustaf, Sea Snake, Meg Merriles *and* Flash. *Shipping in the anchorage in the bay was particularly vulnerable to these gales, and scores of vessels have broken from their cables and were wrecked on the North End beach. (Cape Archives, AG13421)*

Below: *A view of the Point in Durban Bay taken in 1870. A group of sailing vessels and a paddle steamer lie at anchor in the channel. Note the hulk stranded on the mud bank in the centre of the picture. (National Archives of Zimbabwe)*

The Suez Canal

The notion of a waterway to link the Mediterranean Sea to the Red Sea occupied the minds of men for thousands of years, but always the resources to turn the idea into practice were lacking. The middle of the 19th century, however, saw such an increase in shipping volumes between the East and Europe that the need for such a canal became pressing. In 1854 the Frenchman Ferdinand de Lesseps obtained a concession from the viceroy of Egypt to build the Suez Canal, and it was finally opened on 19 November 1869. In its first year of operation a mere 436 609 tons of shipping passed through, as compared to 81 795 523 tons in 1950 and 267 000 000 in 1966-67. Through the years the canal became of increasing importance to Britain as a direct route to her possessions in the East, especially in times of war, and as a result a convention was signed in 1888 which declared that the canal should be kept open to mercantile vessels and warships without distinction of flag even in wartime. During World War I this convention was adhered to, but since then the canal has often been used as a pawn by warring nations. During World War II the canal was officially open to all nations, but in effect Allied control of the approaches kept Axis shipping out, and in 1956 president Nasser of Egypt sent shock waves throughout the world when he nationalised the canal. The result was an abortive Anglo-French attempt to keep control of the canal by force of arms, and the second in a series of Arab-Israeli wars; during the conflict the canal was blocked for nearly a year when the Egyptians sank vessels in it. During the 1967 Arab-Israeli Six-Day War, too, the canal was closed by sunken hulks and only re-opened on 5 June 1975. In each case the number of vessels using South African ports to take in bunkers and stores increased considerably. Of course the canal has not diverted all shipping from the southern route: many bulk carriers and oil tankers when fully laden have too deep a draught to venture through the canal and use the route round South Africa as a matter of course. When in ballast, however, some of them can sail through Suez.

can Dock, which was completed before World War II. One of its proudest features is the largest graving dock in the Southern Hemisphere, which was completed in 1945 and over the years has attracted a large number of vessels needing repair. At Port Elizabeth work on a breakwater started in 1922, and the first stage of a properly dredged harbour was completed in 1933. At East London work on the present turning basin started in 1927 and was completed ten years later. At Durban, too, constant dredging and the building of piers made possible its development into the first-rate harbour it is today.

During World War II the importance of the Cape sea route was emphasised. Saldanha Bay was a favoured assembly point for convoys, but enemy submarines wreaked havoc among the heavy shipping concentrations, and accounted for 133 merchant vessels and one warship within 860 nautical miles (1 600 km) of the coast between 1939 and 1945. In addition 20 merchant vessels were sunk by raiders and two by mines.

The end of the war heralded a new era of industrial expansion in South Africa, and it became necessary to upgrade harbour facilities further. During periods when the Suez Canal was closed because of war in the Middle East, volumes of shipping round the Cape increased. During the period after the 1967 Arab-Israeli Six-Day War, for instance, it was not uncommon to see up to 17 vessels at a time anchored in Table Bay, waiting for an opportunity to enter the harbour for bunkers or stores. Since then new developments, especially containerization, which drastically cuts down the time a vessel needs to spend in port, and the use of helicopters to provision vessels at sea, have reduced the number of vessels in South Africa's harbours. Furthermore the advent of sophisticated international airlines has robbed the passenger liners of their clientele, resulting in the virtual demise of this elegant form of travel, apart from the occasional luxury cruise liner.

What one is likely to see passing our shores or entering our harbours today are oil tankers too large to travel through the Suez Canal, bulk carriers, container vessels or such specialised vessels as ro-ro ships with their huge ramps which can be lowered onto the quay, refrigerated vessels or the new generation of specialised vessels to service the off-shore oil industry. New harbour developments have also taken note of the latest trends, and tanker basins and container docks have been added to present harbour facilities to accommodate these.

Shipping has indeed come a long way since the Phoenicians rounded our shores in 600 BC — if indeed they did.

The old graving dock in Cape Town harbour, depicted in 1882. Harbour facilities have been greatly improved upon at all South African harbours in recent years. Today, for example, Cape Town harbour boasts two graving docks, one of which is the largest in the Southern Hemisphere, able to accommodate even large bulk carriers.

AFRICAE TABVLA NOVA.

Chapter 2

Navigation and Shipbuilding

*N*avigation is the science of directing a vessel by determining its position, course and distance travelled, and plotting the course to be steered in order to reach a specific destination. When a vessel is sailing within sight of a familiar coastline and it is thus possible to check well-known landmarks regularly, navigation is fairly simple, but it becomes rather more complicated at night, in fog, or well out to sea, where the only fixed orientation points are the sun, moon and stars.

By the beginning of the 15th century many nations routinely crossed large expanses of open sea. The Mediterranean had been criss-crossed for thousands of years and was a major centre of trade by sea, the Chinese were accustomed to long voyages in their seaworthy junks, and Arab traders regularly crossed the Persian Gulf and Indian Ocean. On the other hand the Portuguese discoverers inching their way down the unknown west coast of Africa initially preferred to sail close to the shore, always within sight of land, partly for reasons of security, but also in order to compile information for Prince Henry the Navigator's mapmakers.

They were not completely without navigational aids, however. The compass, which was probably discovered independently in Europe and China in the 10th or 11th century, was in widespread use by the 13th, and by the time the Portuguese discoverers set off on their journeys, it had developed from a magnetised needle floating in a bowl of water on a chip of wood to a pivoted needle swinging above a compass-card marked with the four cardinal winds and the 32 points we know today. It was realised that the needle did not point true north, but so little was known at the time about this magnetic variation that orientation errors were almost inevitable, though acceptably minor. By about 1500, as a further refinement, the compass was mounted in gimbals – rings pivoted at right angles to each other – so that it stayed level no matter how much the vessel pitched or rolled, which reduced errors resulting from wildly swinging needles.

The compass helps in determining a course, but a navigator also needs to know how far he has progressed along that course; as long as he knows how fast the vessel is travelling, this is a fairly simple calculation. At first the determination of a vessel's speed was a matter of guesswork, in which the experience and intuition of the captain played a great role. Pieces of wood were often dropped off the bow and observed as they floated past, and the vessel's speed estimated from such observations. A refinement was the ship's log; this invention from the early 16th century was simply a piece of wood tied to a strong line which was knotted at regular intervals; when the log was streamed astern, the number of knots which ran out over the stern in a given time were counted. Time-keeping was by means of a sand-glass, and it is clear that this method was prone to error. While running before the wind in roughly a straight line, it was fairly easy to keep track of forward progress, but when tacking in zig-zags into the wind, a traverse board had to be used to keep a record of such tacks, which were then averaged out at regular intervals to arrive at the total forward progress for the day.

To determine the vessel's north-south position required an instrument to measure the angle between a known heavenly body and the horizon, which could then be translated into degrees of latitude. In the 15th century the most common instrument in use was the astrolabe, which in its simplest form was a disc marked in degrees, with a swivelling pointer mounted in its centre. Holding the instrument suspended by a ring at the top, the observer sighted through two apertures on the pointer until it aligned with the sun or a chosen star, and then read off the angle at the top end of the pointer, which was then converted to degrees of latitude. Much the same principle was later used in refinements of the astrolabe, namely the cross-staff and back-staff. The former utilised one or more sliding cross-pieces on a horizontal bar: one point of a selected cross-bar was aligned with the horizon and the other with the sun or chosen star. The angle was then read off the horizontal bar. The back-staff utilised a mirror to superimpose an image of the sun on the horizon.

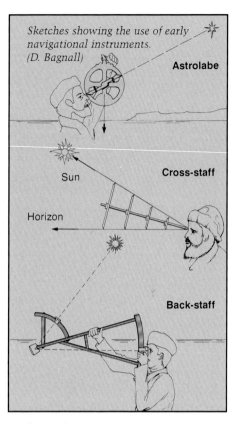

Sketches showing the use of early navigational instruments. (D. Bagnall)

Astrolabe

Cross-staff

Sun

Horizon

Back-staff

Accurate time-keeping, to ensure that sightings are taken at the same time every day, was lacking, and furthermore it was extremely difficult to make proper observations on the deck of a heaving and rolling vessel; the captain often went ashore to take his sightings unhampered by such motions. Yet by the time of Cabral's voyage in 1500 the captains had enough faith in their navigation methods to leave the coast of Africa behind and to swing far out into the Atlantic before sweeping past the southern tip of the continent. The final refinement of such instruments to determine latitude was the sextant, invented in 1731 by John Hadley, which uses a mirror and a ground glass screen to enable the observer to see the sun or star and the horizon simultaneously, which makes the proper alignment extremely accurate.

For a long time the greatest problem of navigation was the determination of longitude, or east-west orientation, as this, too, depended largely on accurate time-keeping in order to compare local time to that at the starting-point, and also to ensure that sightings are taken at the same time each day. The early mariners had to rely on sand glasses that were of dubious accuracy to start with, and became even less so if someone forgot to turn them at the precise point necessary. Pendulum clocks were of little use, as the motion of a vessel tended to upset the pendulum. Matters improved greatly with the development in the 19th century of the chronometer, an extremely accurate time-piece which was normally set to Greenwich Mean Time.

When he suspected that he was nearing the shore, it became of vital importance to the captain of a vessel to know how much water he had under the keel. The instrument used in such circumstances was the sounding line, a solid lead cylinder tapered towards the top and tied to a line which could be lowered to depths of up to 370 m. A concave hollow in the bottom of the lead was often filled with beeswax or tallow, by which means a sample of the bottom sediment could be picked up. By

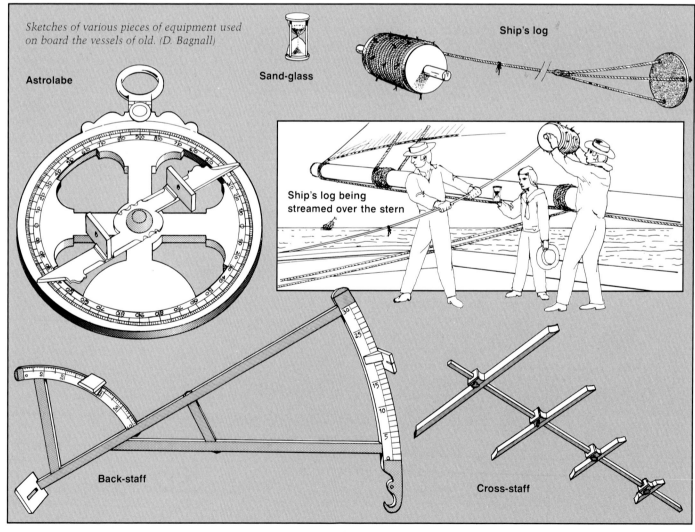

Sketches of various pieces of equipment used on board the vessels of old. (D. Bagnall)

Astrolabe

Sand-glass

Ship's log

Ship's log being streamed over the stern

Back-staff

Cross-staff

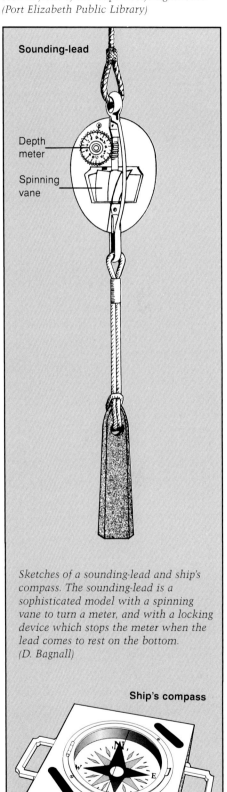

Sounding-lead

Depth meter

Spinning vane

Sketches of a sounding-lead and ship's compass. The sounding-lead is a sophisticated model with a spinning vane to turn a meter, and with a locking device which stops the meter when the lead comes to rest on the bottom. (D. Bagnall)

Ship's compass

comparing the depth and bottom make-up to data marked on a chart, a linesman could often accurately plot his position, even in thick fog. Sometimes the sound of a shout, or the beat of a drum, was timed as it echoed off a cliff, which could give an indication of the vessel's distance from the shore.

Once a captain has used his navigational instruments to determine his position, he will plot this position on a map or chart. The early charts available to the sailors of the 15th and 16th century depended on the accuracy of the information supplied to the map-makers of the time by the early explorers. Free-hand outline drawings of coastlines with headlands, rivers and harbours marked on them existed at an early stage, and many of them were amazingly clear and accurate. To aid navigation they were supplied with a compass rose and criss-crossed with a network of rhumb-lines or loxodromes; to plot a course, a navigator chose as his guideline one of the lines closest to the course he intended to take, and used his dividers to prick a hole in his parchment chart to indicate his present position.

As long as the map or chart covered only a small geographical area, distortion did not play a large role, but as the explorers added more and more information, and maps had to be drawn showing the land surfaces over most of the globe, a problem arose that has not been entirely satisfactorily solved even today: how to represent a round world on flat paper. The most acceptable compromise was found by the Flemish cartographer Gerhardus Mercator, who drew his maps as if the globe were stretched into the shape of a cylinder, with the equator proportionately its true length, but the poles represented as lines of the same length as the equator. On such a map all lines of longitude are parallel; a constant ratio between lines of longitude and latitude is maintained; and distortion within the tropics, where most voyages took place, is relatively minor; in addition a course can be plotted on such a map as a straight line, and so Mercator's projection became the most widely accepted standard.

Vessel types

What makes a schooner different from a sloop, or a barque from a brig? Vessels may be designed with various combinations of masts and sails, and each such combination results in a vessel with its own name. The illustrations and definitions on these pages are included to give the reader an insight into the sometimes bewildering array of vessels mentioned in the text and appendixes.

Barque

Barque
Vessel with three masts; the fore and main masts are square-rigged and the mizen mast fore-and-aft rigged.

Barquentine
Vessel with three masts; the fore mast is square-rigged and the main and mizen masts fore-and-aft rigged.

Brig

Brig
Vessel with two masts; the masts are square-rigged, with additional lower fore and aft sails on a gaff and boom on the main mast.

Brigantine
Vessel with two masts; the fore mast is square-rigged and the main mast fore-and-aft rigged.

Bulk carrier
Large vessel, similar in appearance to an oil tanker. Designed to carry large cargoes of, for instance, ore or grain in bulk.

Coaster
Vessel which trades between ports along the same stretch of coast.

Cruiser
Warship of high speed and medium armament.

Cutter
Vessel with one mast, rigged like a sloop but with a running bowsprit.

Dandy
Sloop with a special rig.

Flute

Flute
Cargo vessel with a round stern, broad beam and flat bottom; inexpensive to build, cheap to man and with a large cargo capacity.

Frigate
Warship, next in size and armament to the Ship of the Line, with 28-60 guns on the main deck, raised quarter deck and forecastle.

Galleon

Galleon
Vessel with three or more masts; the fore and main masts are square-rigged and the aft masts lateen-rigged.

Gunboat
Small vessel with a shallow draught and a relatively heavy armament.

Hoeker
Small Dutch vessel designed to convey cargo from outlying posts to a central warehouse to await shipment in larger cargo vessels.

Ketch
Vessel with two masts; the mizen mast is stepped forward of the rudder.

Liberty ship
Cargo vessel built in great numbers of an all-welded construction during Word War II to make good losses suffered through submarine attacks.

Oil tanker
Large vessel designed to carry crude oil; they have been built to sizes close on 500 000 tons deadweight.

Packet
Small boat used for conveying messages and supplies.

Paddle steamer

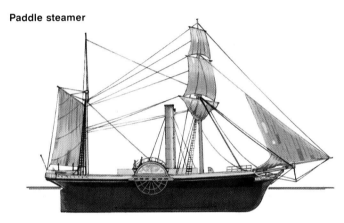

Paddle steamer
Steam vessel propelled by two large wheels amidships on either side of the hull.

Privateer
Armed vessel in private hands authorised by a government to be used against the merchant shipping of a hostile nation.

Schooner

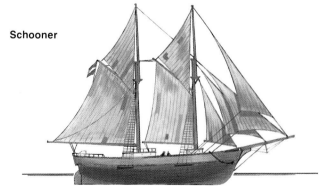

Schooner
Vessel with two or more masts; the masts are fore-and-aft rigged.

Screw steamer
Vessel powered by steam and propelled by means of one or more screw propellers.

Ship

Ship
Vessel with three masts and a bowsprit; the masts are square rigged. Also known as a full-rigged ship.

Ship of the line (3rd rate)

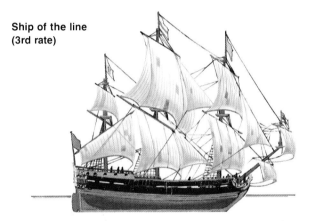

Ship of the Line
Warship mounting at least 64 heavy guns, designed to sail in the navy's line of battle and fight in great fleet engagements.

Sloop
Vessel with one mast; the mast is fore-and-aft rigged with a mainsail and jib and usually a gaff topsail and forestaysail.

Snow
Vessel much like a brig but with a supplementary trysail mast.

Transport
Privately-owned vessel on hire to the military to transport soldiers, supplies and equipment.

Troopship
Vessel used to transport soldiers, supplies and equipment.

Turret steamer
Vessel with sides about 3 m wider below the water-line to increase cargo-carrying capacity and overcome the restrictions of the Suez Canal.

Below: The wooden barque Sayre, *built in 1890 and wrecked on 1 September 1902. Note her carvel-built construction. (Frank Neave)*
Bottom: The lower hull structure of the steamer Kakapo, *wrecked on 25 May 1900. The ribs are a continuation in metal of a method of construction used in wooden vessels. (M. Turner)*
Bottom right: A map by Johannes van Keulen of Table Bay in 1778. Note the pattern of rhumb-lines, an aid in determining a course.

In the 20th century navigational aids received a great impetus with the invention of radio, which made possible wireless communication between vessels at sea and between vessels and the shore; radar, which can draw an electronic picture of the environment in which a vessel finds itself; inertial navigation systems; and satellite systems.

Radio was first used on board vessels towards the end of the 19th century to signal in Morse code, and many shipwrecked mariners owe their lives to the timeous sending and receiving of radio signals to inform rescuers of their plight. The first time that radio was used to summon help to a shipwreck on the coast of South Africa was in the case of the SS *Lisboa*, wrecked on Soldier's Reef south of Cape Columbine in October 1910. Radio became a great boon to navigators with the erection of radio beacons at known positions which sent out constant signals at known frequencies. By using a rotating loop of wire, which picks up a minimum signal when the loop is perpendicular to the source of the signal, it is possible to determine the direction of the beacon. In the same way the direction of a second beacon can be plotted, and the position of the vessel is where these two bearings intersect.

Radar was invented in the 1930s and refined during World War II. Using the device, it is possible to see the outline of the coast, and the positions of other vessels in the vicinity, as glowing projections on a screen. Even though it requires some skill to interpret these outlines accurately, radar has saved countless vessels from shipwreck or collision.

An electronic version of the sounding-lead, an instrument that has served its purpose for centuries, is sonar, which records the time-lapse between the time a sound wave leaves a transducer to the time it bounces back off the sea-bed, thus accurately determining the depth of water under the keel of the vessel. Enertial navigation systems rely on extremely sensitive sensors which record changes in the force of gravity acting on a spinning gyroscope which has been set to remember the direction of this force at the start of the journey. And finally, the space age has made possible the introduction of sophisticated satellite systems in which a vessel is directly linked to one or more satellites orbiting the earth. Signals received from such satellites enable the vessel's navigation officer to plot its position on the ocean to within a few metres.

But for all that, navigators are human. On 25 May 1900, for example, the captain

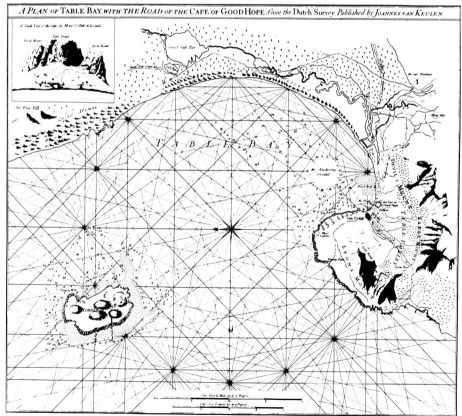

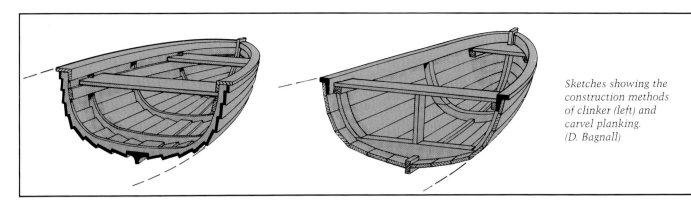

Sketches showing the construction methods of clinker (left) and carvel planking. (D. Bagnall)

of the SS *Kakapo* left Cape Town in bad weather, steamed south, mistook Chapman's Peak for Cape Point, turned to port too soon and ran ashore on Noordhoek Beach. And on 29 July 1985 the MV *Kapodistrias* left Port Elizabeth harbour in fine weather and promptly ran onto Thunderbolt Reef, despite all modern navigational aids and up-to-date charts.

In shipbuilding, too, great changes have come about over the centuries. When man first floated on the water while clinging to a log, he entered a strange and mostly hostile environment, which he slowly learned to conquer. Boatbuilding can be said to have begun when several treetrunks were tied together to form a raft, or one was hollowed out and propelled by a long piece of wood. The Egyptians built boats of bundles of reeds tied together, and some of these were large enough to transport huge obelisks, albeit on the relatively still waters of the Nile.

In the open sea of the Mediterranean it was found necessary to build vessels with keels supporting a framework of ribs over which the hull planking was fastened, in order to provide the strength needed to withstand the rougher sea. The vessels mostly had no decks, and cargo was simply stored inside their often roomy holds. A platform at the rear sufficed as a place where the steersman could stand to control the vessel, using one or more steering oars; a single mast with a sail was enough to propel these vessels. They could not sail into the wind, and oars were often used to manoeuvre in port, or when there was no wind. In parallel with such sailing-vessels, the galley was developed. This was principally a vessel of war and was propelled by one, two or even three banks of oars. The great advantage of these vessels was that they were not dependent on the vagaries of the wind, but their disadvantage lay in their shallow freeboard, which made them unsuitable for use in the rough open ocean.

The fairly unpredictable wind patterns in the Mediterranean eventually led to the development of the lateen rig. One or more masts were fitted with triangular sails fixed directly to long diagonal yards. The advantage of this simple kind of rig is that it is fairly easy to adjust and that boats can sail relatively close to the wind, which cuts down on the number of tacks necessary when sailing into the wind. Its drawback is that the fore-and-aft design places a limit on the number and size of sails that can be carried.

By the 15th century most vessels in the Mediterranean were carvel-built, with flush planking fixed edge to edge to ribs and caulked with pitch. They were difficult to make water-tight, but they had the advantage that they could be built to almost any size.

In northern Europe a separate boat-building tradition developed. Because the Norsemen did not have saws and were thus unable to shape the planking of their boats accurately, they built clinker-built boats, with overlapping planking fastened to internal ribs. These were easy to construct and could be made water-tight with ease, but posed strength problems when built longer than about 30 m. Most northern vessels were designed mainly to run before steady winds and therefore had square rigs, with the sails fastened on crosswise yards. They could not sail so close to the wind, but tacking was easier; furthermore square-rigged vessels could accommodate more than one mast without problems, and as a result the sail area could be broken up into smaller, more manageable units. As a counter to rough seas they were built with high sides and built-up sterns to keep following seas from swamping the vessel.

The Chinese junk

In many respects the Chinese junk was superior to anything Europe could produce up to the 19th century. It is in essence a keelless, flat-bottomed boxlike structure divided into a number of watertight compartments by bulkheads, which makes for great strength and safety. The bow is simply a wedge-shaped addition below the water-line, and the stern is built up to provide accommodation and protection against swamping in following seas. A great innovation is the large rudder, which is placed on the centre-line in a watertight box so that it can be raised or lowered. This allows it to double as a centre-board to prevent sideways slippage in the water. One or more unsupported masts carry square lugsails made of a series of panels, each stiffened by a bamboo batten and fitted with its own sheet. The advantages are that the force of the wind is therefore supported by many sheets, and that the sail can be shortened very quickly by releasing one halyard: the sections of the sail then fold down on top of each other much like a Venetian blind. In addition the entire sail can be close-hauled from head to foot, which enables the vessel to sail very close to the wind. In these craft Chinese sailors roamed wide, and were a common sight in the Indian Ocean by the time of the Portuguese voyages of discovery. Perhaps some of these sailors even gazed at Table Mountain long before Dias did?

Guns at sea

The earliest cannon mounted in vessels at sea were forged, a method whereby wrought-iron bars were formed into a cylinder, heated, hammered and strengthened with iron hoops to form a tube which was open at both ends. They were breech-loaders, that is, the shot was placed in the barrel through a groove at the rear, and the gunpowder charge inside a cylindrical chamber. This chamber or breech-block was then inserted in a bracket in the breech at the rear of the cannon and wedged in position. It became the practice to keep a number of loaded breech-blocks at hand for rapid reloading. All in all it was a somewhat flimsy construction, with many weak points, so only moderate gunpowder charges could be used to fire relatively small shot. The breech-loader with its light weight and quick-loading capabilities became the perfect anti-personnel weapon, and was most often mounted in brackets on the gunwales for use against the enemy on an opposing vessel. Guns mounted in this fashion became known as swivel-guns.

In the 16th century a new method of construction was introduced. Iron or bronze was cast as a solid shape with the rear part wider than the front. The barrel was then drilled out, which made for a much stronger gun, but it did mean that it had to be loaded from the front. As they were much larger than the breech-loaders, these muzzle-loaders were mostly mounted on wooden carriages. By means of wedges they could be layed (the barrel raised or lowered), and by means of tackles they could be trained (turned from side to side); the shock of the recoil was absorbed by heavy tackle. Stone or iron round shot was mainly used, but shot linked by an iron bar or chain was often used to damage an enemy vessel's masts and rigging.

Right: Two bronze breech-loading swivel guns found on the beach opposite the wrecksite of the Dutch vessel Meteren, *wrecked on the Namaqualand coast on 9 November 1723. (M. Turner)*

Below: A sketch of a swivel gun. (D. Bagnall)

Many examples of both these types have been salvaged on the coast of South Africa; the earliest examples were found on the site of the Portuguese vessel *São Bento*, wrecked on the Pondoland coast in 1554. Her armament consisted mainly of bronze breech-loading swivel-guns, although a few large bronze muzzle-loaders were also found. The cannon-balls found consisted of bar-shot coated in lead. The armament of two later Portuguese wrecks, the *Santissimo Sacramento* and the *Nossa Senhora de Atalaia do Pinheiro*, wrecked on the Eastern Cape coast in 1647, are remarkably different: the guns discovered consisted of large bronze and cast iron muzzle-loaders which fired iron round shot. Bronze breech-loading swivel guns have been found in conjunction with bronze and cast iron muzzle-loaders on many Dutch East India Company wrecks, and bar-shot and round cannon-balls are always found on these sites. Breech-loaders have been found on sites as late as that of the *Vis*, which was wrecked on Green Point in 1740. The wreck site of the *Reigersdaal*, which ran aground in 1747, yielded six large bronze muzzle-loaders and more than eight muzzle-loading swivel guns. Many cast iron muzzle-loaders litter the site, and bar shot and round shot has been found in great abundance.

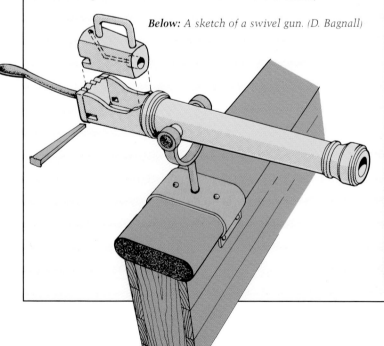

Top: *Bronze cannons from the wreck of the Portuguese East-Indiaman* Nossa Senhora de Atalaia do Pinheiro *on the deck of the salvage vessel* Etosha. *(Peter Sachs)*
Above: *Guns from the* Atalaia *on the quayside in East London. (Peter Sachs)*
Left: *A bronze mortar recovered from the wreck of the Dutch barque* Willem de Zwyger, *wrecked near Arniston on 30 March 1863. (M. Turner)*
Right: *Examples of grape-shot from the* Reigersdaal. *(M. Turner)*
Below: *Sketches showing a muzzle-loading gun and the method of loading it. (D. Bagnall)*

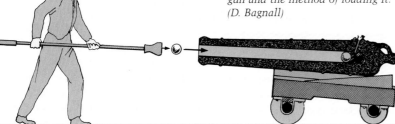

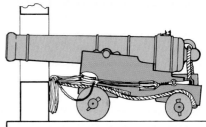

Above, left to right: Engineering or builders' plates from HMS Osprey, *the* Jane Harvey *and the* Western Knight. *(M. Turner)*
***Bottom:** The* Colonial Empire, *which went aground at Cape Recife on 27 September 1917, is a good example of the epitome of sail. (Ferguson Collection)*

Tests for new technologies

Early in the 19th century the idea that a vessel could be built from iron was generally ridiculed – everyone knew that iron couldn't float like wood. In 1818, however, Thomas Wilson successfully built the *Vulcan*, an iron sailing vessel, but iron became popular as a building material only when its strength was graphically demonstrated. In 1834 a storm drove ashore a number of vessels in Britain, among them one built of iron: the steamer *Garryowen*. The wooden vessels were all either badly damaged or totally wrecked, but the *Garryowen* simply refloated itself and proceeded on its way when the storm abated. Within 20 years more vessels were built from iron than from wood.

In the mid 19th century another great debate flared up: whether the future lay with paddle steamers or screw steamers. In itself the paddle-wheel is as efficient at cruising speed as a screw propeller; at slow speed and high thrust, however, it suffers a certain loss of efficiency. Furthermore the rolling motion of a vessel sometimes resulted in a paddle-wheel lifting out of the water, and it was also more prone to damage in rough seas. What really sounded the death-knell of the paddle-wheel, however, was a strange tug-of-war arranged by the British Admiralty between the paddle-wheeler *Alecto* and the screw steamer HMS *Rattler*. Both vessels were of about the same size and power, but, tied stern to stern and each steaming at full power, HMS *Rattler* towed the *Alecto* backwards at about 2 1/2 knots – proof enough for most that screw propellers were superior.

The first Portuguese explorers set out in robust, seaworthy lateen-rigged caravels, used for many years as sturdy fishing craft, and these proved ideal for exploration. They were fast and manoeuvrable, and had a shallow draught, so that they could easily nose into unknown bays and river mouths. For trading, however, larger cargo space was a necessity; the northern and Mediterranean traditions eventually merged and resulted in the large, stable, carvel-built, multimasted *não*, with a combination of square and lateen sails.

Further developments in sailing vessels have been largely extensions and refinements of this theme. Direct steering by means of a tiller was replaced by a whipstaff and then by the wheel; advances in naval gunnery brought with it changes in the tactics of naval warfare. The 'Golden Age of Sail' saw many fine vessels, with the epitome in the late 19th century in the extremely fast clipper ship.

Yet, fine as they were, sailing-vessels are limited as to size, and especially in the fact that they are subject to the mercies of the wind, which may blow too strongly, or not at all. In the late 18th century experiments were underway with a new building material – iron – and a new propulsion method – steam. In 1818 Thomas Wilson of Scotland built the iron sailing vessel *Vulcan*, which remained in service for 60 years, and from about 1850 iron or other metals replaced wood as the most common marine building material. In 1803 Robert Fulton demonstrated a steamboat on the Seine, and in 1807 the *Clermont* steamed up the Hudson at four knots (8 km/h). In 1819 the first passenger paddle steamer, the *Savannah*, crossed the Atlantic. It was helped for most of the way by her sails, which had not yet been done away with, and was also a commercial failure. Off the coast of South Africa, too, such vessels became more common, and the first of this type to be wrecked here was the paddle steamer *Hope* in 1840. At first steamers were propelled by two paddle-wheels at their sides, as it was believed that a vessel would be unmanageable if propelled from the rear; however, this prejudice was eventually overcome and screw steamers – at first with auxiliary sails – rapidly replaced paddle steamers.

Engines became more reliable and eventually sails were done away with altogether. The original reciprocating steam engines were replaced by triple and quadruple expansion engines, in which the steam exhausted from the main high-pressure cylinder passed into two or more others of lower pressure before finally being condensed to water, thus making better use of the steam. In the 1890s the

steam turbine, in which the pressure of the steam turns turbine blades to produce rotary motion, made its appearance and gained favour after initial problems involving the reduction of its high speed to that of the slower-turning screws were overcome through the use of reduction gears. The success of the internal combustion diesel engine on land led to its adaptation to marine vessels, and today the diesel engine is the most common in use. The power plant of the future is undoubtedly the nuclear reactor, although safety and cost factors have somewhat limited their use to date.

Until the 1930s metal-hulled vessels were built from the keel upwards: after the keel was laid, ribs were constructed, floors laid in place and beams attached to the ribs to form a frame to which the hull plates were rivetted. The method did not differ greatly from that used to build a wooden vessel – only the materials had changed. The widespread use of welding during World War II to construct large numbers of merchant vessels – the so-called 'Liberty Ships' – hastened the world-wide adoption of this building method, by which sections of a vessel could be built separately and then brought together to be welded into a whole. Initially the new technology had its share of problems: some of the early welds were found to become quite brittle, especially in cold conditions, and in certain circumstances they sometimes cracked quite rapidly. Since then such problems have been overcome, and the vast majority of vessels today are welded.

A modern vessel is likely to be completely purpose-built. Its hull size and shape, the power plant, the navigation equipment aboard, the method of transporting its cargo – these will have been determined beforehand and all relevant information given to a naval architect, who will have designed a vessel to suit the specific needs of its owners. Whether the owner wants to transport completely assembled motor-vehicles, grain or ore in bulk, oil or general cargo in containers – there is a specialised vessel tailored to his needs; a far cry from the basic designs of the past which simply had to adapt to the task at hand.

Above: The engine-room of the paddle-steamer Great Eastern, *launched on the Thames in 1858. (Illustrated London News)*
Below: *A detail of rivetting on the hull of the Union-Castle liner* Edinburgh Castle, *launched in 1948 at the yard of Harland & Wolff in Belfast. This method of construction has given way to welding. (M. Turner)*

Chapter 3
Causes of Shipwrecks

On 3 February 1552 the richly laden Portuguese galleon *São João* under the command of Manuel de Sousa Sepulvida set sail from the Indian port of Cochin on the Malabar Coast on a voyage home to Lisbon. De Sousa had started late, having been held up while trying to obtain a full load of pepper. He had been able to stow only a third of his vessel's capacity at his previous port of call, which is why he had called at Cochin, but here, too, he encountered difficulties, and eventually he had to sail with only two-thirds of his pepper quota. However, his galleon was well laden with other valuable merchandise, for instance cloth, Chinese porcelain and slaves, and so with due caution he sailed for Portugal.

On 13 April the coastline of Africa was sighted. By checking the sun De Sousa reckoned his vessel to be at latitude 32° S (somewhere off the Transkei coast). He was running well behind schedule, which could be attributed to the bad state of the galleon's sails, her spare sails having been carried away during a storm at the equator. The pilot, André Vas, was steering a course for Cape Agulhas, which they duly sighted, but then they encountered easterly gales which blew them to about 65 nautical miles (120 km) south-west of the Cape of Good Hope by 12 May (see map on p 64). Next, beset by furious westerly gales, the captain, master and pilot agreed that it would be best to run before the storm, back in an easterly direction with the mainsail and foresail set.

About 340 nautical miles (630 km) east of the Cape the wind shifted to the east again, and they resumed their westward voyage in a heavy swell that threatened to sink the galleon at any moment. For three days they travelled on until the wind dropped; then the ship wallowed while the crew tried to make her shipshape, but then the carpenter found that three of the pintles securing the rudder were missing. He told the master, Christovão Fernandes da Cunha, but they decided to keep it secret, as they did not wish to cause alarm.

Unfortunately another violent westerly storm unleashed its fury upon them, the rudder loosened and they luffed, which caused the wind to carry away the mainsail. That left them with only the foresail, which they immediately started to take in, but before they had finished this task, the ship veered round and three huge waves struck her abeam, breaking all the shrouds and backstays on the starboard side and leaving nothing but the three forestays. It was now decided to cut away the mainmast, but while this was being done, it snapped above the upper pulleys and was blown overboard on the starboard side, complete with topsail and shrouds. Shrouds and rigging on the port side were cut away, and everything disappeared over the side. The crew then jury-rigged a mast, using a piece of timber rigged as a storm-sail.

Now the rudder broke in half and was carried away. The ship was rolling badly and taking in vast quantities of water, so it was decided to cut away the foremast too. However, before this could be accomplished, the sea snapped this mast also. The crew then cut away the shrouds, but as the mast went overboard, it carried the bowsprit with it.

Finding themselves without masts, rudder or sails, the captain and his officers decided to construct a makeshift rudder and use some of the cargo of cloth for sails – tasks which took the crew ten days to complete. Though the rudder was not suitable and the vessel was found to be unmanageable, they sailed on until 8 June, when they once again sighted land. It was decided to let the galleon drift shorewards with the wind until they found shallow water, and they finally dropped anchor in about 12 m of water; a boat was launched and another anchor run out towards the land. The wind was now more favourable and they found themselves about two crossbow shots from the shore.

Realising that his vessel must soon go down, De Sousa called the pilot and master and asked them to put him and his wife and children ashore with twenty men, and to remove the provisions, arms and powder from the vessel, as well as some cloth, which could possibly be used for bartering with the native population for food. He

Above: The wreck of the São João. *(Africana Museum)*
Below: Sites of shipwrecks between 1505 and 1796. Note the concentration of outward-bound vessels on the west coast, and homeward-bound vessels on the east coast.
Opposite: The Tantallon Castle *lies aground on Robben Island in 1901.*

intended to build a fort with a barricade of barrels and to construct a caravel from the galleon's timbers by which a message could be sent to Sofala in East Africa.

Three days later the wind increased and large swells began to pound the wretched vessel. The captain, his wife and children and about thirty others had by this time disembarked. On the third trip, however, the landing-boat was smashed and several men were drowned. Those left on board discovered that the seaward anchor cable had parted and they were being held only by the landward anchor; the vessel was starting to run aground. Another forty persons managed to reach the shore in a second boat, but there were were still nearly five hundred people stranded on the *São João* in a rising sea – two hundred Portuguese and the rest slaves.

The galleon was grinding on the rocks and soon broke in half. An hour later each of the two halves broke in two, and the cargo started to float out of the holds. Within four hours the vessel, at that stage the most richly laden galleon that had ever sailed from India, was reduced to small pieces and her vast cargo littered the beach.

De Sousa realised that he could no longer carry out his plan to build a boat; instead he decided to stay next to a fresh-water supply that they had found, build a fort of barrels and chests, and wait for the sick and injured to convalesce before setting out on foot north-eastwards for Delagoa Bay. For twelve days they reconnoitred the area, finding many of the native huts deserted: it seemed as though the local people had fled in fear. Then, on 7 July 1552, they set out on their overland march, and eventually most of them reached Delagoa Bay safely. The surviving Portuguese were later rescued by a trading vessel and taken to Mozambique.

It is not exactly clear where the *São João* was wrecked, but all evidence points to the lower South Coast of Natal as the most likely site, probably a little north-east of the Mtamvuna River near Port Edward, where broken shards of sixteenth-century Chinese porcelain are frequently washed ashore.

This story illustrates many of the reasons why so many vessels were wrecked on the coast of South Africa. Most of the coast is inhospitable, with few navigable rivers or safe natural anchorages apart from Saldanha Bay, which was not used because of a lack of fresh water. Towering rocky cliffs, treacherous hidden reefs and long, open sandy beaches abound, incessantly pounded by heavy surf. Huge waves are a common occurrence off the east coast, and even today it is not uncommon to receive reports of damage sustained even by large vessels as a result of such unex-

Outward-bound wrecks ▲
1 Eiland Mauritius 1644
2 Schollevaar 1668
3 Johanna 1682
4 Gouden Buis 1693
5 Het Huis te Kraaiestein 1698
6 Merestein 1702
7 Meteren 1723
8 Vis 1740
9 Reigersdaal 1747
10 Dodington 1755
11 La Cybelle 1756
12 Colebrooke 1778
13 Nicobar 1783

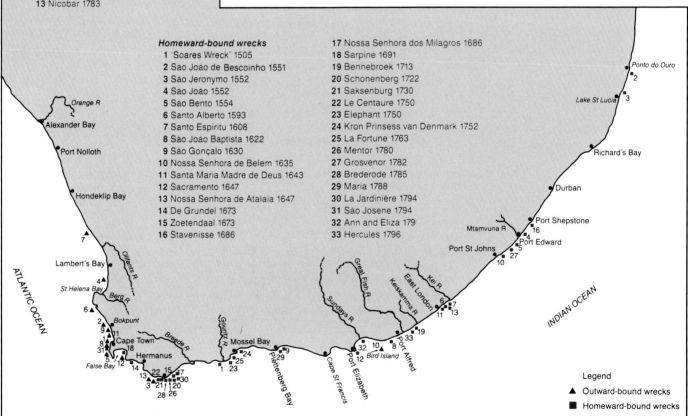

Homeward-bound wrecks
1 'Soares Wreck' 1505
2 São João de Bescoinho 1551
3 São Jeronymo 1552
4 São João 1552
5 São Bento 1554
6 Santo Alberto 1593
7 Santo Espiritu 1608
8 São João Baptista 1622
9 São Gonçalo 1630
10 Nossa Senhora de Belem 1635
11 Santa Maria Madre de Deus 1643
12 Sacramento 1647
13 Nossa Senhora de Atalaia 1647
14 De Grundel 1673
15 Zoetendaal 1673
16 Stavenisse 1686

17 Nossa Senhora dos Milagros 1686
18 Sarpine 1691
19 Bennebroek 1713
20 Schonenberg 1722
21 Saksenburg 1730
22 Le Centaure 1750
23 Elephant 1750
24 Kron Prinsess van Denmark 1752
25 La Fortune 1763
26 Mentor 1780
27 Grosvenor 1782
28 Brederode 1785
29 Maria 1788
30 La Jardinière 1794
31 São Josene 1794
32 Ann and Eliza 179
33 Hercules 1796

Legend
▲ Outward-bound wrecks
■ Homeward-bound wrecks

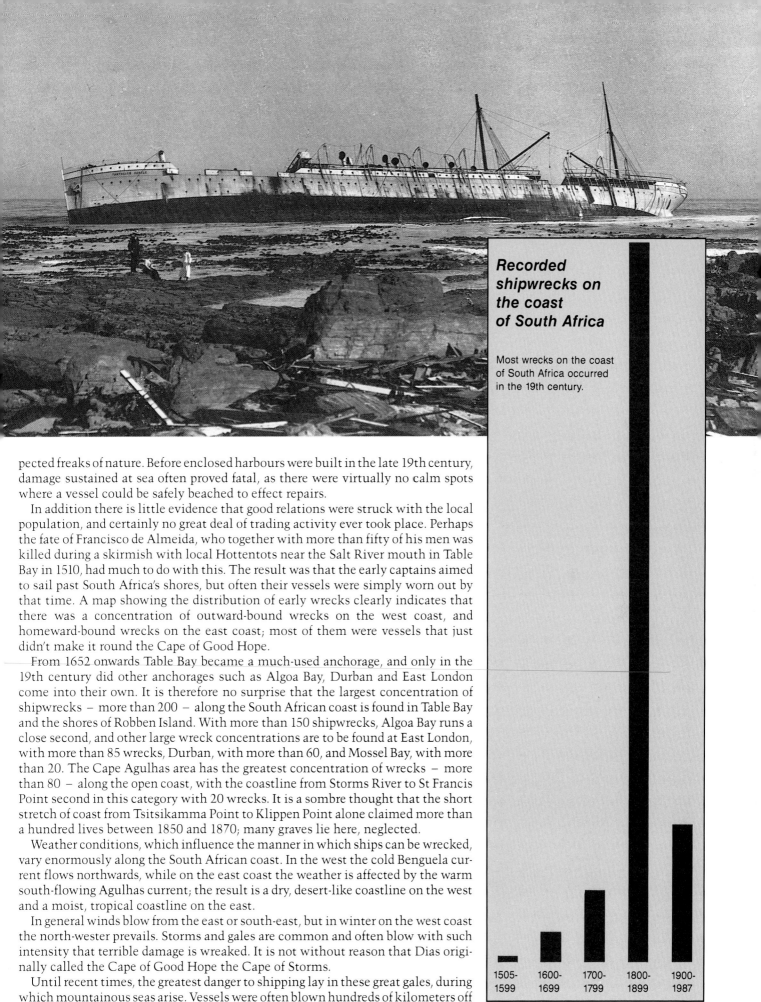

Recorded shipwrecks on the coast of South Africa

Most wrecks on the coast of South Africa occurred in the 19th century.

1505-1599	1600-1699	1700-1799	1800-1899	1900-1987

pected freaks of nature. Before enclosed harbours were built in the late 19th century, damage sustained at sea often proved fatal, as there were virtually no calm spots where a vessel could be safely beached to effect repairs.

In addition there is little evidence that good relations were struck with the local population, and certainly no great deal of trading activity ever took place. Perhaps the fate of Francisco de Almeida, who together with more than fifty of his men was killed during a skirmish with local Hottentots near the Salt River mouth in Table Bay in 1510, had much to do with this. The result was that the early captains aimed to sail past South Africa's shores, but often their vessels were simply worn out by that time. A map showing the distribution of early wrecks clearly indicates that there was a concentration of outward-bound wrecks on the west coast, and homeward-bound wrecks on the east coast; most of them were vessels that just didn't make it round the Cape of Good Hope.

From 1652 onwards Table Bay became a much-used anchorage, and only in the 19th century did other anchorages such as Algoa Bay, Durban and East London come into their own. It is therefore no surprise that the largest concentration of shipwrecks – more than 200 – along the South African coast is found in Table Bay and the shores of Robben Island. With more than 150 shipwrecks, Algoa Bay runs a close second, and other large wreck concentrations are to be found at East London, with more than 85 wrecks, Durban, with more than 60, and Mossel Bay, with more than 20. The Cape Agulhas area has the greatest concentration of wrecks – more than 80 – along the open coast, with the coastline from Storms River to St Francis Point second in this category with 20 wrecks. It is a sombre thought that the short stretch of coast from Tsitsikamma Point to Klippen Point alone claimed more than a hundred lives between 1850 and 1870; many graves lie here, neglected.

Weather conditions, which influence the manner in which ships can be wrecked, vary enormously along the South African coast. In the west the cold Benguela current flows northwards, while on the east coast the weather is affected by the warm south-flowing Agulhas current; the result is a dry, desert-like coastline on the west and a moist, tropical coastline on the east.

In general winds blow from the east or south-east, but in winter on the west coast the north-wester prevails. Storms and gales are common and often blow with such intensity that terrible damage is wreaked. It is not without reason that Dias originally called the Cape of Good Hope the Cape of Storms.

Until recent times, the greatest danger to shipping lay in these great gales, during which mountainous seas arise. Vessels were often blown hundreds of kilometers off

The Cape Town Great Gale of 1865

*I*n May 1865 Cape Town had been experiencing a spell of blisteringly hot north-east berg winds, and gardens and lawns were suffering badly, but on Monday, 15 May a subtle change was felt: the wind started to blow strongly from the west as a cold front approached, and by evening heavy rain was falling. The following night the wind increased to gale force from the north-west, with severe gusts.

On Wednesday, 17 May an extremely heavy sea was running. The vessels in the bay dipped into the giant swells, throwing up huge sheets of spray as they strained at their anchor-cables, and boats put out from shore carrying additional anchors – a common practice at the time.

Then, at 11h00, the anchor-cables of the German brig *Galatea* parted, but she was safely beached beyond the Castle. Soon after the brig *Jane* gave distress signals and joined the *Galatea* on the beach, followed by the cutter *Gem*. Before 14h00 four more vessels had run aground: the barque *Star of the West*, the Danish schooner *Fernande*, the schooner *Clipper* and the barque *Frederick Bassel*. At about 14h00 the cables of the barques *Alacrity* and *Deane* parted and they collided with the steamer *Dane* before running ashore. These vessels were closely followed by the barque *Royal Arthur*, which went ashore near the south wharf, the schooners *Kehrweider*, *Isabel* and *Figilante*, and the brig *Maria Johanna*. By sheer miracle no lives had been lost up to this point.

By now the whole expanse of Table Bay was a sheet of foam, with huge seas breaking 1,5 nautical miles (3 km) from the shore and the north-wester howling at gale force. Parts of the harbour works were badly damaged; trees were uprooted and roofs damaged. By evening the wind abated a little and the Union Company steamer *Athens* tried desperately to escape from the bay, but at 21h00 the wind freshened again and the *Athens* was driven on the rocks near Mouille Point, breaking up rapidly. Crowds of Green Point residents assembled on the beach, but could do nothing to help: cries of anguish came from the doomed men on board, but soon only the pounding of the surf and the howling wind could be heard. Thirty men had died in the ice-cold Atlantic water.

At 22h30 the wooden barque *City of Peterborough*, after dragging her anchors, struck Sceptre Reef near Fort Knokke on Woodstock Beach, and the men on board the stricken vessel were in serious trouble. The rocket brigade had assembled on the shore, but in their zeal they had put too heavy a charge into the line-thrower, so that their first shot went beyond the wreck. A faint cheer could be heard from the men on board. The second shot landed true, but this time no cheering was heard, and when the line was pulled in no one was attached to it. During the delay the whole crew of twenty had been washed into the sea and drowned.

The next day the storm abated a little; the wind veered to the west, but a large swell was still pounding the shore. There was no sign of the *City of Peterborough*, and all that could be seen of the *Athens* were a cylinder and boiler. The whole town was abuzz with news of the tragedy and flags were flown at half-mast. A number of the wrecked vessels were later refloated, but seven were to leave their shattered hulks for ever in Table Bay.

The aftermath of the Great Gale of 1865 in Table Bay, as painted by Otto Landsberg. (Collection B. Kinnes)

course when it was safer simply to batten down and run before the storm, rather than to try to battle one's way through it. When a vessel was blown ashore, it was not uncommon for the entire crew to drown in the surf. As late as 1979 the Greek steel motor-vessel *Evdokia* of 7 144 tons was completely broken up in the space of a few hours in the surf of the Tsitsikamma coast; the waves that night were running up to eight metres high, and all but one of the seven crew members who elected to remain after most had been taken off by helicopter the day before were drowned (see pp 72-73). If this can happen to a large modern steel vessel, one can imagine how long a small wooden barque would last in similar conditions, and how many people were likely to lose their lives, the more so since the crew could rarely swim, and such life-preserving aids as life-jackets were not yet in use.

Even before modern harbours were built, the big bays such as Table Bay, Durban, East London, Algoa Bay, Mossel Bay, Struis Bay and False Bay for the most part provided safe anchorages when the prevailing off-shore winds were blowing, as vessels could normally ride out even the greatest storms in safety. When on-shore winds blew, however, many vessels – completely at the mercy of the wind, as their sails were furled – lost their anchors and were driven ashore in scores. Examples are the series of great south-east gales in Algoa Bay between 1835 and 1903, and the great north-west gales in Table Bay which wreaked havoc amongst shipping from as early as 1692 up until 1902. Most wrecks in Table Bay occurred during these dreaded north-westers, when vessels unable to escape to False Bay were liable to be blown ashore on Woodstock Beach and at the Salt River mouth (see box on p 38).

In Algoa Bay, too, hundreds of vessels have been driven ashore during the various south-east gales which have raged there, and although many were refloated, a vast number were totally wrecked (see box on pp 40-41). Other bays which suffer from easterly gales are East London, Mossel Bay, Struis Bay and False Bay. In general, when vessels were blown ashore in such bays, fewer lives were lost, as many crew members were ashore, and rescue apparatus was often available. In addition the vessels and their cargoes were more easily salvaged, since the bays returned to their sheltered, calm state once the gales abated.

Since sail started to give way to steam towards the end of the 19th century, gales have become much less of a menace to shipping, but until about 1902, when the most destructive gale in South African shipping history occurred in Algoa Bay, gales were by far the most common cause of shipwrecks. Mention must also be made of the reverse of a gale – lack of wind – as this has also been a cause of some shipwrecks, notably those of the *Conch* on 7 November 1847 at Port St Johns, the *Alice Smith* on 21 December 1861, also at Port St Johns, and the *Diligence* on 1 July 1863 at Hondeklip Bay.

Above: The oil-rig standby tug Boltentor *battling through 14-m seas 54 nautical miles (100 km) south of Algoa Bay. Small wooden sailing vessels stood little chance of surviving such conditions unscathed. (M. Turner)*
Below: A lithograph by W.A. Harries depicting Algoa Bay in about 1854. The primitive harbour developments can be seen concentrated at the mouth of the Baakens River. (William Fehr Collection)
Bottom: A surf-boat putting out from the jetty in Algoa Bay during a south-east gale. In the early days such boats were the only way of landing passengers and cargo from vessels at anchor in the roadstead.

The Port Elizabeth Great Gale of 1902

The great gale in Algoa Bay in September 1902 was the greatest tragedy yet experienced by the citizens of Port Elizabeth and the single most destructive shipping disaster in South Africa's history. On Sunday morning, 31 August 1902, 38 vessels were riding at anchor in the bay under a leaden sky. Heavy rain fell during the course of the day, and by evening a south-east gale was blowing, gradually increasing to hurricane force. Just before midnight distress guns could be heard out in the bay and the rocket brigade, who had been on standby, raced down to North End beach to render assistance, but this was a nearly impossible task. Giant foam-flecked waves loomed out of the dark and crashed down on the sand. Ghostly shapes of tall sailing-vessels could be seen in the breakers and on the beach. Before dawn on Monday, 1 September five vessels had lost their anchors and the daylight revealed a scene of chaos – the entire North End beach was covered by a jumble of broken timbers, bales of cargo and crippled sailing-vessels being battered by huge breakers.

Rescue attempts by the watchers proved in the main to be futile. The rocket apparatus at first failed to help; on one vessel many lives were lost while rockets were vainly being fired in her direction. The boats could not be launched because of the big swells and the vast amounts of timber floating in the sea. The greatest deed of bravery ended in tragedy: six men went out along a line to help some sailors, but the line broke and they were all drowned in the surf. The captain's wife aboard one vessel jumped into the sea with her baby and came ashore on a plank to the cheers of the crowd, but she later died from exhaustion, though her baby survived. Another mother jumped into the sea with two children, but both drowned, although she lived.

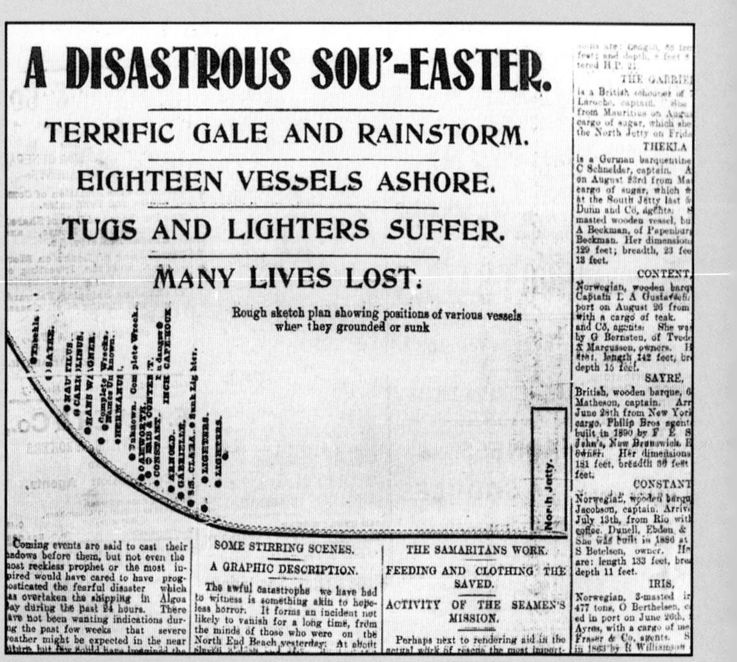

Above: The lead story in the Eastern Province Herald *the day after the great gale. (Eastern Province Herald)*
Below: The Inchcape Rock. *(Frank Neave)*

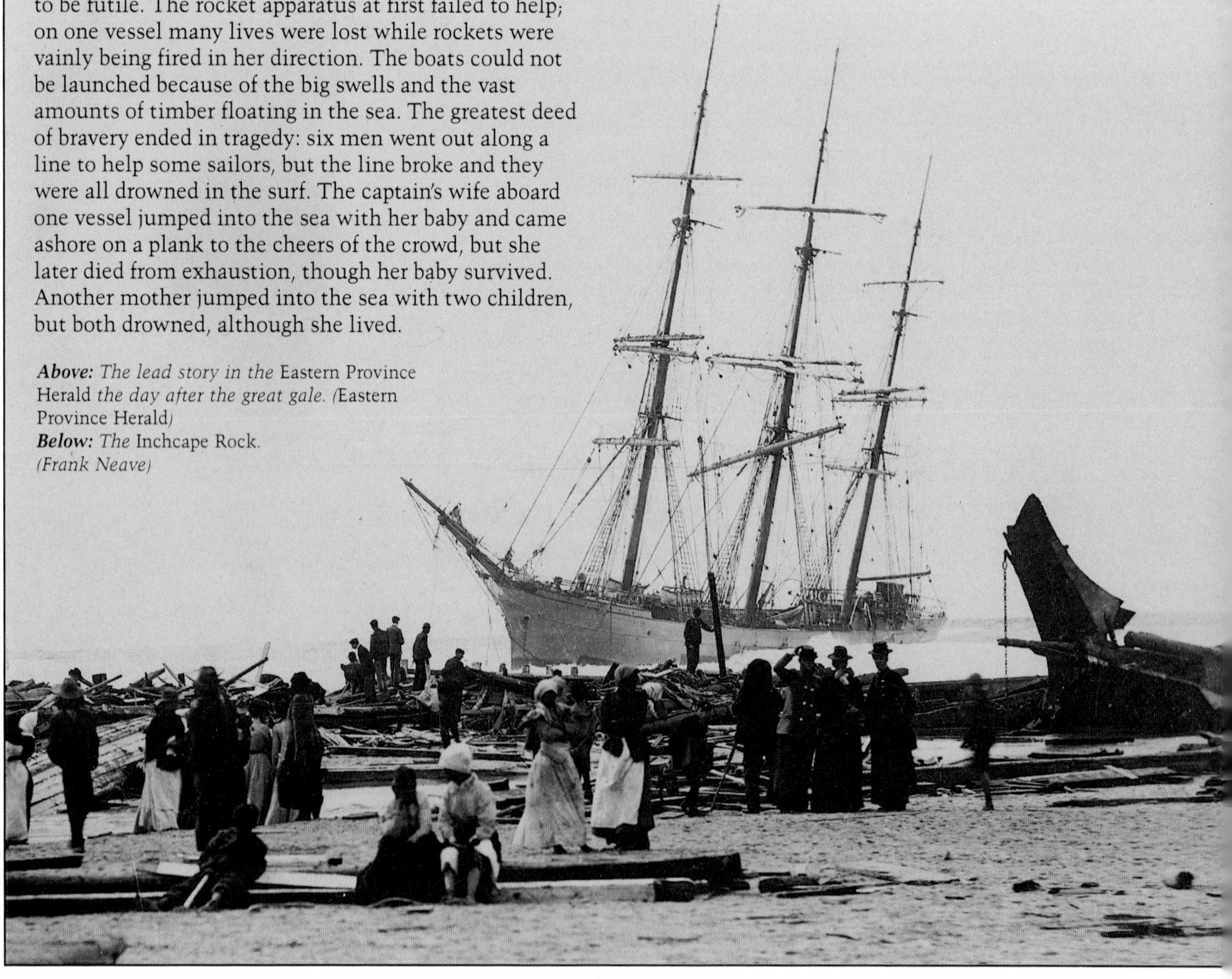

A DISASTROUS SOU'-EASTER.

TERRIFIC GALE AND RAINSTORM.

EIGHTEEN VESSELS ASHORE.

TUGS AND LIGHTERS SUFFER.

MANY LIVES LOST.

Rough sketch plan showing positions of various vessels where they grounded or sunk

The final tally of vessels ashore included nine metal-hulled sailing-vessels, the *Arnold, Cavalieri Michelle Russo, Emmanuel, Hans Wagner, Inchcape Rock, Limari, Nautilus, Oakworth* and *Waimea*; five wooden barques, the *Agostino Rombo, Constant, Content, Hermanos* and *Sayre*; the schooners *Gabrielle, Thekla* and *Iris*; and the wooden tug *Countess of Carnarvon*. There were also a number of lighters and small craft. More than sixty people, including the six rescuers, eventually died in the disaster. About 299 people were saved from the wrecks and were housed in the local Seaman's Institute. The mayor started a relief fund to help those who had suffered in the disaster and messages of sympathy soon poured in from around the world.

September 3rd dawned clear and calm, and a large crowd of mourners gathered at the town hall to witness the departure of the funeral cortège of the first six victims of the great gale for the South End Cemetery. Police kept clear the route, which was lined by a crowd of about 5 000-6 000 and along which all the shops were closed; some were also draped in black. The men who drowned came from many countries, and the coffins were draped in the national flags of the victims. The procession was made up of pall-bearers and mourners, surviving officers and shipmates from the wrecked vessels and others anchored in the bay. The mayor of Port Elizabeth, Mr J.C. Kemsley, councillors, harbour officials, foreign consuls and shipping agents were also part of the cortège, which was so long that the first hearse was close to the top of Walmer Road while the end of the procession had not yet reached the Baakens Bridge. During the next few days many more bodies were washed ashore and funerals became a regular occurrence. A large granite memorial recounting the details of the tragedy was later erected in the cemetery, where it may still be seen.

Top and centre: *Two views of the North End beach. (Frank Neave; Africana Museum)*
Above: *The funeral cortège. (Port Elizabeth Public Library)*

Apart from the wind, the most prominent weather feature of the west coast is the presence of dense fogs which can blanket the coastline in a matter of minutes; many an unwary captain has lost his vessel in foggy but otherwise fine and calm weather. When the fog rolls in, vessels often run onto outlying reefs, islands or rocky promontories, and the chances of a collision also increase greatly. The east coast, too, receives its fair share of fog, and many vessels have come to grief as a direct result of this hazard. A particularly treacherous area lies between Cape St Francis and Storms River mouth on the Tsitsikamma coast. Here wrecks abound – for example, the 5 627-ton Norwegian cargo steamer *Lyngenfjord* and the Greek cargo steamer *Panaghia* of 4 289 tons, wrecked within sight of each other during dense fog in January and February 1938. When sail gave way to steam, fog overtook gales as the most common cause of shipwrecks. Now that radar systems are fitted to most vessels, fog no longer poses the threat it once did, as is evidenced by the noticable reduction in the number of wrecks since World War II, but it remains a factor to be reckoned with.

It is noticable that a very large proportion of wrecks occurred at night, when navigation was particularly difficult in the early days, as instrument sightings could not readily be checked by actual observation of the coast. At the time no lighthouses or other coastal navigation aids existed, and the lights that sometimes emanated from land were often misleading. In the case of the *Vis* (see p 65), for instance, navigators on board saw a light shining in the dark and thought that it must be situated on Robben Island. As it actually shone from the mainland, however, the vessel ran ashore in the dark on 6 May 1740. This problem, too, has been largely eliminated by an extensive and efficient system of lighthouses, and the use of radar.

Faulty navigation and human error was another problem of the early days – and of modern times. Charts, though in general accurate enough, still contained errors, and navigational instruments, too, were never so accurate as to eliminate a margin for error completely. The *Grosvenor* (see pp 68-70) went ashore on the coast of Pondoland on 4 August 1782 because it was realised too late that she was much closer to the shore than calculations had indicated. This error was compounded by the actions of the officer of the watch, who refused to believe the lookouts when they told him they could see breakers ahead, and only took action when it was too late. Similarly the *Dodington* (see pp 65-66) went ashore on Bird Island on 17 July 1755 mainly because of a navigation error, as the vessel was supposed to have been well out to sea at the time. In modern times the only plausible explanation for the wrecking of the *Kapodistrias* on Thunderbolt Reef on 29 July 1985 is human error, as the vessel was equipped with all modern navigational aids, had the most up-to-date charts, and left the harbour in fine, clear weather.

In the early days many vessels were lost because they were 'ill-found' – in a poor state of repair – after many years of use, and overladen with cargo. A wooden vessel needs a lot of attention, and constant maintenance to both hull and rigging is essential, yet quite often the profit motive was stronger than concern for human lives, and as soon as vessels were unloaded they were sent to sea again. Many vessels foundered because of leaks. Most vessels leak, and wooden vessels leaked all the time; normally regular pumping kept the water level in the vessel at an acceptable level, but sometimes the pumps could no longer keep up against the inflow of water. As the cargo was usually stowed in such a way as to make use of every bit of available space, it was often not physically possible to reach the leak in the hull in order to try to halt the inflow of water, and many ships have been lost off the South African coast in this manner. When a vessel came close inshore to try to effect repairs, the inhospitable coast posed as great a danger as the open sea.

Vessels are also lost as a result of military action. South Africa has never been a great naval battlefield, and apart from the *Middelburg*, which sank on 21 July 1781 as the only casualty of the Battle of Saldanha (see pp 75-77), there are few examples of military casualties. Perhaps the *São João Baptista* (see pp 63-65), which ran ashore in October 1622 near the Fish River mouth after being in action against two Dutch vessels, could be included in this category. However, during World War II the importance of the southern sea route was emphasised when German submarines sank many cargo-vessels bringing valuable raw material and war equipment to and from Europe. In addition some vessels carrying war materials were lost when, through fear of submarine attack, they hugged the coast too closely and ran ashore.

Examples are the 6 045-ton Dutch freighter *Meliskerk*, the American liberty ship *Thomas T. Tucker* and the 7 360-ton British cargo vessel *City of Hankow*.

Fire was often a cause of shipwrecks. Fire could overwhelm the old wooden vessels in a matter of minutes, burning the wooden hulls down to the water-line; water would then pour in and the weight of ballast or cargo would pull the vessel down rapidly. Fires were often caused by spontaneous combustion of the cargo, and jute carriers were particularly susceptible. When their tightly packed cargoes became damp during a voyage, ideal conditions were created for spontaneous combustion to take place. Victims of this hazard were the *Freeman Clarke*, which drifted ashore near the Gamtoos River on 18 July 1883 after its cargo of jute cuttings caught alight, and the *Fairholme*, which suffered a similar fate on 1 April 1888 at Buffalo Bay. Other examples are the *William Bayley*, which was run aground at Plettenberg Bay on 11 July 1857 after her cargo caught alight, and the *Charlotte A. Morrison*, whose cargo of rice caught alight in the same way in Algoa Bay on 3 August 1862. Today, giant supertankers ply the coast, yet the same danger exists. The stark reality of disaster was for instance vividly brought home when the burning Spanish tanker *Castillo de Bellver* broke up north of Cape Town in 1983, spilling a vast quantity of crude oil into the sea and causing 'black rain' inland. Only a near-miraculous out-of-season spell of south-east wind which blew the enormous slick in an off-shore direction prevented a major pollution and ecological disaster – but the possibility of such a disaster occurring in the future remains very real.

Piracy was another very great risk in former days. Most of the larger East India Company vessels were well armed with large muzzle-loading cannon, though they did not carry as many guns as a man-of-war. These East-Indiamen used their guns to protect themselves against the pirates who lurked in privateers in the Mozambique Channel and off Madagascar, waiting to plunder the outward-bound, specie-carrying fleets. East-Indiamen usually sailed with their guns primed and ready for action, which is why many cannon recovered from the sea-bed have been found to have cannon-balls in their spouts. The only recorded privateering vessel wrecked on the South African coast, however, was the *Napoléon*, a French privateer armed with cast iron carronades (short cannon of large bore), which was chased ashore near Olifantsbos Point in 1805 by the British navy vessel *Narcissus*.

Above: The diamond recovery vessel Poseidon Cape, *wrecked at Kleinsee on the Namaqualand coast on 27 July 1985. (Keith Grieve)*

Opposite, from top: *The hulk of the stranded coaster* Border, *which ran ashore on 1 April 1947 south of Port Nolloth on the desolate Namaqualand coast (Keith Grieve); The shattered hull of the Brazilian steamer* Piratiny, *wrecked in 1943 south of Kleinsee on the Namaqualand coast (Keith Grieve); The bow of the* Piratiny, *thrown high and dry by decades of Atlantic storms. Note the starboard anchor still in position (Keith Grieve); The twisted remains of the liberty ship* Thomas T. Tucker, *which was wrecked on Olifantsbos Point on 27 November 1942 (P.A. Sargeant); Bronze carronades recovered from the wreck of the Dutch barque* Willem de Zwyger, *which went aground on Martha Point near Arniston on 30 March 1863. Carronades were short, large-caliber naval guns, ideal for short-range battles. The name derives from the Carron iron works in Scotland where this type of gun was first made. The guns were adorned with the insignia of the Batavian Republic (M. Turner).*

Scurvy

The doughty sailors on the early trading voyages to the East faced long continuous periods at sea – often lasting many months. In the absence of modern food preservation methods, food was most often dried or salted, with fresh fruit and vegetables obtainable only when a ship anchored in some sheltered bay and sailors were allowed ashore to buy or barter for fresh foodstuffs. On such long voyages sailors soon began to complain of soreness or stiffness in their joints, swollen and bleeding gums and loosened teeth, bleeding under the skin and wounds that were particularly slow to heal. Many died on board and were buried at sea. The disease from which they suffered was scurvy, caused by a deficiency in vitamin C, which is found especially in citrus fruits. Even though it was noticed that victims soon recovered after a diet containing fresh fruit and vegetables, it was not until 1753 that the Scottish naval surgeon James Lind recognised the link between the disease and a diet lacking sufficient vitamin C, and showed that scurvy could be cured quite rapidly by giving the patient orange, lemon or lime juice to drink. As soon as it became common practice to allow for an adequate vitamin C intake, the disease, which often decimated crews to such an extent that ships became unmanageable, lost its terrors and journeys became much safer.

In a similar vein the long voyages and bad conditions on board the early vessels sometimes led to mutiny, but when an inexperienced crew gained control of a vessel, the danger of shipwreck increased. The case of the Cape slaver *Meermin* is a typical example: In April 1766 she was wrecked near Cape Agulhas after the slaves she was carrying mutinied and tried to return to Madagascar but lost control of the vessel.

The list of causes of shipwrecks would not be complete without mention of scurvy, the disease through which early sailing-vessels often lost several crew members on their long voyages, for the ship's efficiency could be drastically impaired as a result, and disaster sometimes ensued. The Dutch East-Indiamen *Gouden Buis* and *Reigersdaal* provide good examples of the dangers involved.

The *Gouden Buis* left Texel Roads, at the mouth of the Zuider Zee in Holland, on 4 May 1693 with 190 souls on board, and after a long journey scurvy was rife. Unable to man the vessel properly because of this, the captain, Teunis Kornelisz Baanman, was compelled to run her ashore about 20 km north of St Helena Bay on the west coast in November 1693. She had on board a valuable cargo, so when the Governor at the Cape, Simon van der Stel, received news of the stranding he immediately sent a small fleet of salvage vessels to the wreck to recover the 17 money-chests and other cargo and fittings aboard. One of these vessels was the *Dageraad*; she was a 140-ton Cape packet under the command of Jan Tak, and on her way back to Cape Town on a misty January night in 1694 she ran aground on the west point of Robben Island in Table Bay, with the loss of 16 lives. Several chests of money off the *Gouden Buis* went into the sea, and to this day they lie waiting for a team of divers to find them. A small amount of money was salvaged at the time, the last recorded salvage work being undertaken in 1728, when an English team led by the famous early diver John Lethbridge (see p 91) tried to recover the lost chests. Unfortunately the wreck of the *Dageraad* today lies within the prison security area of Robben Island, and if there have been any salvage attempts in recent years they have been kept a close secret.

Similarly, in October 1747 the Dutch East-Indiaman *Reigersdaal* ploughed into a shallow reef off Springfontein Point on the west coast, and took with her eight chests of Spanish-American trade coins. The *Reigersdaal*, under the command of Johannes Band, had left Texel on 31 May 1747 with 297 souls on board. In October she reached Dassen Island, having lost 125 men from scurvy en route. Unable to anchor because of the weather, she lowered a boat to fetch some rabbits and birds from the island. Eventually after much tacking the crew brought the vessel to

Below: The Kapodistrias. *(Colin Urquhart)*

anchor on the north side of Robben Island in Table Bay, and here, because 83 of the surviving men were indisposed with scurvy, the *Reigersdaal* remained at anchor until the next day.

She was in a bad position: the strong south-easterly wind prevented the vessel from reaching the nearby anchorage in Table Bay, so it was decided to weigh anchor and try to return to Dassen Island or else Saldanha Bay. While raising the anchor, the cable parted. The *Reigersdaal* then attempted to sail northwards but the crew were unable to handle her properly and an hour later she ran aground. About 15 men climbed into a boat to try to take a line ashore, but three-quarters of an hour later, when they reached the shore, they saw that their vessel had been smashed to pieces. Some 157 men died in the wreck.

The fact that vessels were often wrecked along the same stretch of coast could be to the mutual benefit of the survivors. There is an interesting interrelationship, for instance, between three different vessels wrecked in the late 17th century on the Natal coast. The *Good Hope*, commanded by John Adams, was a 50-ton English ketch mounting six guns; she had left Gravesend with a crew of 24 and had been trading in Natal for ivory and slaves. On 17 May 1685 she was wrecked on the north shore opposite the Bluff while trying to enter the Bay of Natal. The survivors erected a hut on the Point of the Bluff and started to build a boat. About six weeks later a small 35-ton trader, commanded by a captain Wynnford, arrived and took four men with him. Of the remaining survivors, five stayed on in the shack and continued trading; they accumulated three tons of ivory and explored 80 km into the interior of Natal. The other ten men set off, in the boat that had been completed, on a slaving expedition to Madagascar via Delagoa Bay (Maputo).

Nine months later, on 16 February 1686, a homeward-bound Dutch East-Indiaman, the *Stavenisse*, commanded by Willem Kuif, came to grief near Port Shepstone during a voyage from India, with the loss of eleven lives; 60 survivors made it to the shore. Of these men, 47 began an epic journey to the Cape, and the remaining 13, including the captain, remained at the wreck site to repair a boat, which was unfortunately lost when they tried to launch it. While they were wondering what to do next, two of the English survivors of the *Good Hope* found them and invited the shipwrecked Dutchmen to join them at their hut on the Bluff, and to help them build a further boat.

Eleven months later, on 25 December 1686, the 20-ton English ketch *Bonaventura*, commanded by John Gilford and on a voyage from the Downs (the roadstead off south-east Kent), was wrecked on the Natal coast at Lake St Lucia, with the loss of one life. The nine survivors set out to walk overland to the Cape, but they soon met up with the Dutch and English seamen at the Bay of Natal, and together the combined survivors of the three wrecks built a 25-ton boat which they named the *Centaur*. They loaded it with supplies and were soon safely on their way to the settlement at the Cape.

When the *Centaur* arrived at the Cape, the authorities bought her and sent her back up the coast to look for the overland party from the *Stavenisse*, from whom no word had been received. The *Centaur* reached a point a little east of the Buffalo River, and there its crew found three naked survivors from the *Stavenisse*, who paddled out on a raft and were taken aboard. A further 19 were found living with the indigenous blacks; they, too, were taken on board, after which the *Centaur* sailed back to the Cape. During the next year the galiot *Noord* rescued three more men from the *Stavenisse*, but the rest of the ship's complement were never heard of again.

We have come a long way since Vasco da Gama first opened the sea route to the East. The romantic cargoes carried by the Portuguese and Dutch galleons have been replaced by the more mundane twentieth-century necessities; machinery, motor-cars, spare parts and foodstuffs. Ships today have highly sophisticated computerised navigation systems and, as a result, wrecks are becoming few and far between. Improved anchoring systems as well as well-constructed harbours have minimised the dangers of the gales of the early years. And thanks to the benefits of refrigeration which provide ship's crews with an adequate intake of vitamin C in the form of fresh fruit and vegetables, the health hazard of scurvy with its debilitating effects no longer exists – yet shipwrecks still occur, mainly as a result of human error, as the wrecks of the bulk carriers *Kapodistrias* and *Daeyang Family* of recent times eloquently show.

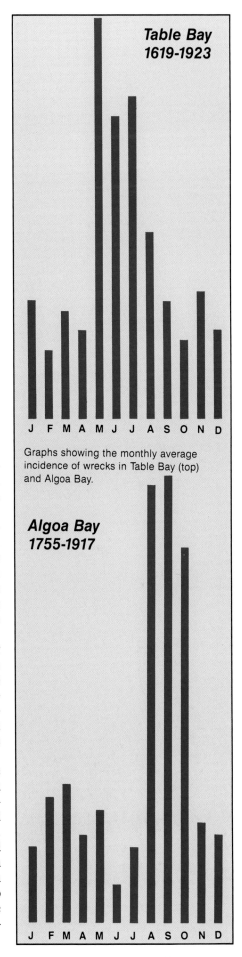

Table Bay 1619-1923

J F M A M J J A S O N D

Graphs showing the monthly average incidence of wrecks in Table Bay (top) and Algoa Bay.

Algoa Bay 1755-1917

J F M A M J J A S O N D

Chapter 4
Cargoes

*T*he Portuguese did not spend so much effort in the 15th century to find the sea route to the East merely out of curiosity: one of the main driving forces was the huge profit to be made from trade. Vasco da Gama was soon disabused of his naive idea that he would be able simply to hand out jingling bells and mirrors to primitive chieftains in exchange for the spices he wanted, and found instead that he was dealing with highly sophisticated and discriminating merchants, who preferred to be paid in coin. Indeed, in the East trade had been a part of life for hundreds of years before the arrival of the Europeans, and Chinese junks were regular visitors to Indian and Middle East ports. The basic pattern for roughly three hundred years of trade between Europe and the East was soon set: outward-bound East-Indiamen from Portugal, Holland, England, France, Denmark and other European countries carried money, trade goods, administrators, soldiers, building-materials, furniture, metals, war material and much more on their voyages round the Cape, while homeward-bound fleets were loaded with spices, slaves, porcelain, cloth, silk, rice, timber, tin and other manufactured and raw materials from the East. Many of the manufactured goods were indeed much sought after in Europe, where nothing comparable could be found, and generally commanded high prices.

Vessels from all these countries have been wrecked on the coast of South Africa, and cargoes of all descriptions have been scattered on the beaches and in among the reefs over the years. Many of these cargoes have of course left no tangible trace, as such perishable goods as tea, cloth, spices, rattan, rice – or slaves – either washed away in the sea or disintegrated soon after being washed ashore. Other cargoes, such as coal, iron or building-blocks, still lie below the waves where the vessels in which they were carried have gone ashore, but are of little commercial value to the salvor, and so attract little attention. Still others, especially the specie carried by so many outward-bound vessels, were of great concern to the companies in whose ships they were stowed, and often attempts were made soon after such vessels were wrecked to recover these cargoes, with varied success. In addition known coin cargoes have been a great temptation to salvors over the years, and as a result much specie has been recovered. Probably very little of great value is therefore left.

To many people the coins or specie carried by early outward-bound East-Indiamen are the most romantic of the cargoes salvaged round our coast. Most of the vessels carrying coins were wrecked on the west coast, when the long voyages from Europe took their toll of men and equipment. A vast number of silver coins have been found, and form a link with the Spanish treasure fleets which sailed across the Gulf of Mexico and the North Atlantic to bring the riches of the New World home to Spain. Of these coins a great number were Spanish pieces-of-eight, and by studying them we can form a clear picture of the evolution of these coins, from the crude 17th-century 'cob' coins found on the outward-bound English East-Indiaman *Johanna* to the beautifully stamped Mexican 'pillar' dollars found at the *Reigersdaal* and *Dodington* sites.

Unfortunately for historians no remains of any outward-bound Portuguese East-Indiamen have been found along the South African coast, but from the knowledge gained from salvage operations on the *Santiago*, wrecked on the Bassa da India atoll in the Mozambique Channel in 1585, we know that such vessels would have carried the Spanish American cob coins which most of the earlier vessels bore.

The earliest cargo of pieces-of-eight found in South African waters is the treasure of the *Johanna*, which was wrecked in 1682 (see p 87). After an early attempt by Olof Bergh and a pearl diver to recover these coins soon after the wrecking, no further recorded salvage was carried out on the shattered hull of the vessel, which still contained more than 23 000 pieces-of-eight and a fair number of silver bullion discs. For three centuries giant waves lashed the site and spread the remains of the vessel over a large area of sea-bed. Then in 1982 a Cape Town diving team headed by Gavin Clackworthy found the remains of the wreck after studying an old map housed in

Early coins

From the many silver coins found on the coast of South Africa, it is possible to trace their development over the years. Many of them were originally minted in the New World, but great numbers made their way into Dutch or English hands after Spanish silver fleets were captured on the high seas. The cob was an irregularly shaped piece of silver, struck in the New World, which usually weighed about 28 g: the name is derived from the Spanish *cabo de barra* ('cut from the bar'). The later cobs were far more angular in design. Once the piece of silver had been cut to the required weight, it was hand-stamped with a rough die depicting the arms of Spain, which controlled the New World silver deposits. These cobs were minted until 1732, when the first milled-edge coins were minted in Mexico City by a machine sent out from Spain for the purpose. The new coins were adorned with two pillars depicting the Straits of Gibraltar, hence the name pillar dollars. These pillar dollars were beautifully stamped with the Crown of Spain, and carried the legend 'By the grace of God King of Spain and the Indies'. The widespread use of the coins are proof of Spain's power in the monetary systems of the world.

Above: Silver cob coins from the Johanna, and *below:* silver pillar dollars from the Reigersdaal. (M. Turner)

the Cape Archives, and most of the remaining cargo was retrieved from beneath the deep sand covering the site. The silver specie recovered by the team consisted of cobs from Mexico and Potosi dated around 1676, and many crude silver discs from the New World.

The next oldest specie wreck found in South Africa is the outward-bound Dutch East-Indiaman *Het Huis te Kraaiestein*, which also carried a cargo consisting of cob money. She was wrecked at Oudekraal on the Cape Peninsula on 27 May 1698 while on a trading mission to the East. Though most of the money she carried was recovered at the time, divers since then have recovered about 1 000 silver cobs. At the time of her wrecking the vessel carried 19 chests of silver pieces-of-eight, 16 of which were taken off by the Cape brigantine *Amy*: three of the chests were unaccounted for, and subsequently lured many salvage parties to the site.

In 1868 two bronze cannon weighing about 3 000 kg each were recovered by Henry Adams and Tom Kehoe. These guns, bearing the insignia of the Zeeland Chamber of the Dutch East India Company and the maker's inscription 'Jasper van Erpecom me fecit 1694', were shipped to England on board the SS *Saxon* in 1870, to be sold as antiques. The early divers also recovered some chinaware, nine tons of lead ingots (weighing 125 kg each) and three silver discs similar to those off the *Johanna*. Many wine-bottles, lead ingots and other items have since been recovered.

In 1702 the Dutch East-Indiaman *Merestein*, also on a trading mission to the East, was wrecked on Jutten Island at Saldanha (see pp 113-115). The spot were she was wrecked was extremely rocky with heavy surf, and the vessel broke up rapidly. An attempt was made in 1728 to salvage her valuable cargo of specie, but to no avail, and it was not until 1971 that her treasure was located and reclaimed. It could have been expected that the *Merestein* would have been carrying a cargo of cob money, but this was not so: the divers who salvaged her found no cobs, but many thousands of 17th-century silver ducatoons from the Spanish Netherlands, and silver riders minted in the United Provinces. These coins were all hand-stamped and had obviously been withdrawn from circulation in Europe. They proved a delight to collectors, as they are works of art in themselves; some were of the highest rarity. A large number of lead ingots were also recovered.

Other Dutch vessels which carried coin cargoes similar to that of the *Merestein* were the *Standvastigheid*, *Rotterdam* and *Zoetigheid*, which were wrecked on 16 June 1722 during a north-west gale in Table Bay; these vessels carried ducatoons and silver bars, most of which were recovered shortly after the gale. Today the wrecks lie buried beneath the Table Bay harbour development.

On the site of the *Dodington*, which was wrecked on Bird Island in Algoa Bay on 17 July 1755 (see pp 65-66), a valuable haul of coins was recently found by divers. After the wrecking the site of the wreck lay undiscovered until the 19th century, when a cast iron cannon was recovered. Nothing more was done at the time, and only a solitary anchor on the shore of the island marked the site of the wreck until 1977, when two well-known Port Elizabeth divers, the late David Allen and Gerry van Niekerk, worked on the site and recovered a noteworthy cargo. The most exciting part of it was a quantity of Spanish American pillar dollars and cobs minted in Mexico City and Potosi. These coins were of a similar type to the ones carried on the *Reigersdaal*, but, unlike the *Reigersdaal* coins, which were being taken East for the purpose of trading, the *Dodington* money was mainly in the hands of the military and was to be used to pay the soldiers of the English East India Company, at that time engaged in a prolonged struggle with the French for supremacy in India.

The *Dodington* was hired specifically to carry stores needed in this struggle, and can therefore not be considered a typical East-Indiaman of the period. In addition to the coins, she was carrying a company of Royal Artillery and in her holds were four bronze field-guns and a large quantity of military stores. The guns sported the crest of King George II, and were in a fine condition. A bronze field-gun was made by A. Schalch in 1748 and a howitzer by R. Gilpin in 1755. In addition there were 30 tons of copper aboard, as well as a number of grindstones, sounding-leads, coal and shot. Salvors have also found an interesting variety of European-manufactured goods such as muskets, pistols, pocket-knives, table-ware, clay pipes, rolls of roofing-lead, multicoloured beads, hand-mirrors, paint, shaving-blade handles, scissors, combs, brass padlocks, brass candlesticks and even a crystal chandelier. From this list one can gain some insight into the needs of the colonies at the time. It is believed that the vessel was also carrying a box of gold coins belonging to Robert Clive of India, but as yet no mention has been made of its having been found on the site.

A great number of interesting finds have been made over the years, but much remains hidden. One wreck that could well bring to light some culturally valuable items is that of the *Colebrooke*: the importance of the wreck is that so much of her military outward-bound cargo remains intact, as does part of her hull.

On 6 January 1778 loading of a large number of lead ingots and some ship's stores into the holds of the *Colebrooke* began at Blackwall in the East India Docks on the Thames, a process which lasted some weeks, and on 3 February she moved to Gravesend to load shot, copper, stores, gunpowder, wine, guns, corn, livestock and military recruits. On 8 March the pilot came aboard, and after the passengers' luggage and some more livestock had been stowed, the crew housed the guns, chained up the ports, raised the top-gallant and set sail for the Downs. In the company of three other vessels she sailed towards Bombay.

On Monday, 24 August Table Bay came into view, but the vessels proceeded south towards Cape Point, which was sighted just after 09h00. They rounded the Point, keeping well clear of the notorious Bellows Rock, but at 11h30 the *Colebrooke* struck hard upon a submerged reef called Anvil Rock. Though she was backed off the rock, her hull was badly damaged and the water was rising rapidly. Pumps were put into operation and a decision was made to sail into the relative safety of False Bay, as it was believed that she would soon sink. There was no way to attend to the hole in the hold as the heavy cargo made access impossible. Nearing Simon's Town, the captain and his officers decided against going into Simon's Bay as the vessel was difficult to steer. Instead they opted for Gordon's Bay at the north-east corner of False Bay, where they planned to anchor.

It was soon realised, however, that the vessel would not reach this destination and it was decided to run her ashore south of Gordon's Bay. The crew tried to jettison the guns, but could not do so as they could not open the ports. The *Colebrooke* fired her guns for the last time to signal her distress and headed for the long white sands of what has become known as Koeëlbaai, 'Koeël' in this case being a distortion of 'Cole'. At 16h00 she struck the beach head-on and immediately slewed around so that her bows pointed out to sea. The boats were lowered, and with the help of the boats from her companion vessels, which had remained in the vicinity, the passengers were taken off.

The Company's packet (letters and other documents) was now placed in the *Colebrooke*'s pinnace with about 20 men, but unfortunately the surf on the beach capsized the boat and several men were drowned. Only on the next day could the remaining crew be taken off by raft. The weather prevented any salvage attempts, and six days later the vessel had broken up.

Only in 1984 did divers begin working on her, but it was soon found that the thick sand and swells on the site guarded her cargo well. Only a small portion of the copper and lead were recovered, and it is tantalising to imagine what awaits discovery if the difficulties presented by the site can be overcome. It is certain that our knowledge of the cargoes carried at the time will be greatly increased.

The Portuguese, Dutch and English were of course not the only nations trading with the East. On 1 July 1782, for instance, the Danish vessel *Nicobar* left Copenhagen on a voyage to Bengal under the command of Andreas Christij. On 19 May 1783, after great hardship, she arrived in False Bay, her crew severely depleted through death as a result of scurvy. Christij approached the Governor of the Cape, Baron Joachim van Plettenberg, and asked him for help in remanning his vessel for the rest of the voyage to Bengal. It was agreed that he could take on board seven Lascars who had survived the wreck of the *Grosvenor* (see pp 68-70), and he was also asked to repatriate two Indian girls from the same wreck.

On 10 July the *Nicobar* left False Bay in the company of another Danish vessel, the *Kroonprins*, but on the following day she ran ashore on a reef close to Cape Agulhas and all but eleven of her crew, including the captain, were drowned. Miraculously one of the Indian girls and some of the Lascars survived their second wreck and were later dispatched to India. Arrangements were made to recover the goods that washed ashore, but before officials from the Dutch East India Company reached the scene of the wreck, it was found that the cargo had been plundered by farmers from the Stellenbosch district.

Cannon

Cannon were not only carried as shipboard armament, but in some instances also as cargo. On the site of the *São Bento*, wrecked in 1554, a bronze gun was found that measured 3 m and was probably being carried as cargo. Crude rings were set into the gun to act as lifting lugs. In the case of the *Santissimo Sacramento* and the *Nossa Senhora de Atalaia do Pinheiro*, wrecked in 1647, bronze cannon cast in the city-state of Macao were beautifully decorated with the arms of Macao, the cannon-maker's name (Manuel Tavares Bocarro) and a rampant lion, the monogram of the Governor of India. A plate, cast into the breeches of some of the guns, states: 'Antonio Telles de Menezes, Governor of India, ordered this gun to be made in the year 1640'. The cascabels on some of the guns sported a clenched fist and framed thumb, others a lotus bud, a seventeenth-century fertility symbol. All the guns were adorned with lifting-lugs fashioned to look like dolphins. The largest of the Bocarro guns, a siege gun carried as cargo, measured 4,69 m, compared with the ship's guns, which measured only 3,23 m.

Above: *A detail of the breech, and* ***below:*** *the coat of arms of Macao on a Bocarro artillery-piece from the* Santissimo Sacramento. *(M. Turner)*

In January 1987 a group of divers exploring the sea-bed opposite the Quoin Point lighthouse found a strange copper plate measuring about 18 cm by 15 cm, with markings in the form of five circular stamps bearing the date 1750 and the legend '2 daler'. What they had found was Swedish copper plate money (*kopperplatmynt*), a large, cumbersome coin minted to represent its value in silver. As the process of salvage is still in progress, little can as yet be said about the cargo the *Nicobar* was carrying, but as it is the first wreck of an outward-bound Danish East-Indiaman yet found on the coast of South Africa, finds of great cultural value are sure to be made. Divers have seen a large number of cast-iron pigs on the sea bottom, and some wine bottles.

The scanty information gleaned from outward-bound wrecks along the South African coast shows that as far as coins are concerned, there was a transition from the angular cob coins on the *Johanna* to a mixture of cob money and milled-edge pillar dollars on the *Reigersdaal* and *Dodington* sites 65 years later. Other cargoes were of course also carried, but not very much is known about these, apart from what can be gleaned from studying the vessels' manifests. An interesting sidenote, however, is that in the case of many of these vessels all that is left is building materials, which many of the lightly laden vessels carried as ballast. Granite building-blocks were found on the site of the *Vis* (see p 65) and building-bricks are known to have been carried by the *Meteren*, which was wrecked north of the Olifants River on 9 November 1723. With much building activity taking place in the East in the form of Company buildings, fortifications and even private dwellings for merchants and the like, it seems an obvious choice to use such materials as ballast. They served a useful double purpose; first in order to stabilise the largely empty outward-bound vessels, and then, when they were removed to make room for the valuable cargoes taken aboard in India or Java, to be used in building activities.

Difficult as it is to write about outward-bound cargoes, it is even more difficult to write about homeward-bound cargoes, as they consisted for the most part of material that disappeared very soon after a wrecking, and very little concrete evidence of such cargoes has remained for salvage divers to find.

A typical Portuguese homeward-bound East-Indiaman was the *São Bento*, which left Cochin on 15 February 1554 under the command of Fernão d'Alvares Cabral. At the time of her wrecking on 21 April 1554 she carried more than 467 persons; 142 were Portuguese and the rest slaves. During the disaster 44 Portuguese and more than 100 slaves lost their lives. The only cargo that has been discovered on the site consisted mainly of broken shards of Chinese porcelain, most of it washed up on the island at the mouth of the Msikaba River where she was wrecked, and some gold rings and Indian gold earrings or 'jhumkas'. Large numbers of cornelian trade beads were also discovered in the vicinity and would probably have constituted a major cargo item. However, it is known that the *São Bento* cargo was packed in 72 wooden crates which washed ashore as the vessel broke up. From survivors' accounts we also know that the vessel carried pepper, coconuts, silk, cotton bales and various spices.

Two later Portuguese merchantmen have recently been salvaged: the *Nossa Senhora de Atalaia do Pinheiro* and the *Santissimo Sacramento*, which left Goa on a voyage to Lisbon in 1647, and parted company during a violent westerly gale. The cargoes of these two vessels are remarkably similar to that of the *São Bento*, although they were wrecked 93 years apart. Many shards of Chinese porcelain have been found, and spices and pepper have come out of the barrels of some of the guns carried as cargo which were found on the site. From the records we know that silks came ashore too. In addition to these items, both vessels included in their cargoes large bronze artillery pieces cast by the famous ordnance-maker Manuel Tavares Bocarro in Macao, but these cannot be considered typical of the homeward-bound cargoes carried by the Portuguese merchantmen.

Homeward-bound 18th-century Dutch East-Indiamen usually carried the same cargoes as those of the Portuguese, who were being crowded out of the markets of the East. The earliest such Dutch vessel found on the coast of South Africa is the *Bennebroek*, which broke up a little to the south-west of the Keiskamma River in Ciskei on 16 February 1713. Apart from her cargo, her story contains so many twists and turns that it is an interesting one to tell.

Opposite, above: Detail of a stamp on a 120-kg lead ingot from the Huis te Kraaiestein, wrecked on 27 May 1698. (M. Turner)
Opposite: Lead ingots from the Reigersdaal, wrecked on 25 October 1747. (M. Turner)
Below, top row, left to right: Blue glass beads found on the beach opposite the wreck of the steamer Kafir, wrecked south of Olifantsbos Point on 13 February 1878 (M. Turner); Spanish-American silver bullion discs and cob coins from the wreck of the English East-Indiaman Johanna, wrecked near Quoin Point on 8 June 1682 (M. Turner); The cascabel of a bronze Bocarro artillery-piece from the wreck of the Portuguese vessel Santissimo Sacramento, wrecked near Port Elizabeth on 1 July 1647. The framed thumb is a sacro-magical fertility symbol (M. Turner); Chinese porcelain figurines from the wreck of the Middelburg, sunk in Saldanha Bay on 21 July 1781 (Reg Dodds).
Below, bottom row, left to right: Swedish copper-plate money (kopperplatmynt) from the wreck of the Danish East-Indiaman Nicobar, wrecked at Quoin Point on 11 July 1783 (M. Turner); Silver ducatoons from the Spanish Netherlands, and silver riders from the United Provinces, recovered from the Dutch East-Indiaman Merestein, wrecked on Jutten Island on 3 April 1702 (M. Turner); Ornate lifting-lugs on a bronze Bocarro artillery-piece from the Sacramento (M. Turner); Chinese export porcelain from the wreck of the Middelburg (M. Turner).

Slaves

Little evidence exists, of course, of the many thousands of souls who were transported in vessels past the coast of South Africa as human cargoes, yet on board the *São João*, one of the earliest Portuguese wrecks on our shores, which came to grief on 11 June 1552, more than 400 slaves were on board, of whom many died during the calamity. The *São Bento*, too, which was wrecked on 21 April 1554 on the island at the Msikaba River mouth, carried more than 300 slaves, of which over a hundred died during the wrecking. Many slavers have been wrecked on our coasts, for example the *La Cybelle*, a French vessel, north of Blouberg Strand on 19 March 1756, and the Portuguese vessel *São Josene* at Camps Bay on 27 December 1794 (with the loss of 200 slaves drowned). In the 19th century an end was made to slavery, and Britain took upon itself the task of trying to eradicate the evil by confiscating vessels on the high seas found to be carrying slaves. Yet even in the mid-19th century we still find slaving vessels being wrecked on our coast. Typical are the Portuguese slaving barque *Diana*, which was taken as a prize by HMS *Mutine* and ran ashore in Table Bay on 7 January 1846 during a north-west gale, and the *Rowvonia*, a Brazilian slaving barque detained by HMS *Pantaloon* which was wrecked in Simon's Bay after her cables parted on 13 January 1850. In the last-mentioned two cases fortunately no lives were lost.

On 22 September 1712 she departed from Ceylon under the command of Jan Hes, with some 150 souls on board, as part of a fleet of five vessels. In her hold was a typical East Indian cargo consisting of spices, silks and a large consignment of Chinese porcelain figurines and bowls, examples of Eastern manufactured goods that were much sought-after in Europe.

A little south-west of Ceylon the fleet encountered a storm and the *Bennebroek*, though undamaged, was parted from the other vessels. A second storm struck, and the vessel – which was only four years old – was badly damaged, with two of her masts broken. When the coastline of South Africa appeared, there was little the crew could do to prevent her running ashore. She struck hard upon a pinnacle of rock and giant swells soon began pounding the vessel to pieces. Many of the passengers and crew, including the captain, were drowned; eventually only about 77 people reached the shore.

A camp was hastily prepared opposite the wreck site. The shipwrecked men stayed there for four days to recover from their ordeal, lengthy discussions were held and it was decided to walk overland to the Cape. They set off in a westerly direction armed with muskets which they had salvaged from the wreck, and after five days of strenuous walking and climbing they arrived at the Great Fish River, which was flowing strongly. Most of the group swam across; those who could not swim had to turn back, however, and eventually this party of non-swimmers arrived at the wreck site again. For about three months they stayed at the camp, living off provisions bartered from the natives in return for iron nails and copper fittings from the pieces of wreckage on the shore.

This supply of trade goods eventually ran out and in desperation they decided once more to attempt the overland route to the Cape, this time heading inland to bypass the many estuaries along their path. After a strenuous journey of nearly a month the hopelessness of their situation became apparent and they were forced once more to return to the wreck site. The survivors now numbered only four and out of sheer desperation they joined a native tribe and lived with them in a kraal for a year.

Luck now played a role, for by sheer chance a longboat belonging to an English vessel, the *Clapham Galley*, found the survivors and took them back to the Cape, where they found that only one survivor from the first party had made it to the Cape. A small Cape vessel, the *Postloper*, was sent to Natal to search for survivors and if possible salvage some of the cargo and equipment from the wreck site, but as they searched too far north, they found nothing. Only in 1783 was the *Bennebroek* site found by members of a relief expedition searching for survivors of the *Grosvenor* wreck. They reported finding seven cast iron cannon lying on the shore a little south-west of the Keiskamma River.

Two hundred and seventy-two years later, in 1985, East London diver Peter Sachs investigated an area where Chinese porcelain shards were regularly being thrown up after storms and discovered a large bronze muzzle-loading cannon and six breech-loading swivel-guns bearing the monogram of the Amsterdam Chamber of the Dutch East India Company. A few fine porcelain pieces have also been found, but unfortunately the heavy surf experienced at the site has damaged most of the cargo. The bronze guns, too, have been badly damaged, but there may be surprises in store for the salvors once the thick overburden on the site has been removed. An interesting find has been more than 50 broken cast iron cannon; it is believed that they were being carried as ballast.

The bankruptcy of the Dutch East India Company at the end of the 18th century brought with it a distinct change in the pattern of cargoes being carried round the Cape. Former trading possessions in the East slowly expanded over the years, as the traders gained control over more and more land in order to safeguard their sources of supply. Eventually possessions that had started out as mere trading stations became colonies – overseas extensions of the metropolitan powers. Britain in particular expanded its influence, and in the 19th century the British Empire, with India as its centre-piece, laid claim to possessions all over the globe. To supply the needs of the growing European populations in the colonies, manufactured goods produced by the factories of Europe became of greater importance, as well as the transporting of people – administrators, soldiers, emigrants, passengers. Two categories of involuntary human cargo at the time were slaves and convicts. Towards the middle of the 19th century, however, forces were gathering to have slavery abol-

no less constant stream of well-clad, healthy, and comfortable-looking peasantry in our streets, induces me to send you the accompanying sketches and communications on that subject.

" Upon reference to notes and papers of my own, and to information afforded me by the emigration agents here, I am disposed to think that about the middle of May the great emigrational torrent ceases to flow from these shores. Look-

ing backward for the last month, I find that, during the week ending April 11 the greatest rush for the season took place. The numbers who left Cork that week could not have fallen far short of 1500 souls, and this with the emigration

EMIGRATION VESSEL.—BETWEEN DECKS.

of the other ports of Limerick, Waterford, Dublin, and even of Belfast, will give us an approach to 5000 weekly leaving the country. Large as this number may appear, it is well known that it is considerably below the mark when the de-

partures for Liverpool are included. One agent informed me that he himself had booked 600 emigrants in four days, and yet he is but one of the many agents who are to be met with not alone in the large towns and seaports, but even

thickly scattered through each petty town and village throughout the country. In England you can have but little conception of the sufferings of the poor Irish emigrant from the time he first announces his intention of leaving home

ished, and Britain took it upon herself to wage a quiet war against this practice. Slaving-vessels from other nations were often captured by British warships and forced into port.

The greatest number of shipwrecks on our shores occurred during the 19th century, most of them British vessels, and they carried virtually every conceivable type of cargo in their holds. Gone are the fairly limited categories of goods carried earlier, as trade became international and took on a complex character. A fairly random sampling of the manifests of vessels wrecked in this period gives an idea of the type of cargoes carried, and highlights certain trends.

During the first half of the 19th century South Africa was still a largely undeveloped British colony, with the bulk of its population engaged in agriculture. To a large extent, however, farming was for own consumption, and in certain areas the colony was not self-sufficient. Evidence of this can be gleaned from two wrecks that occurred on 21 July 1822, when Table Bay was once again lashed by violent northwest gales. Two of the vessels which ran ashore were the *Lavinia*, a snow of 233 tons, and the *Leander*, a brig of 202 tons. Both had completed journeys from London to Cape Town with general cargoes; in addition to these, however, the *Lavinia* carried imports of rice and the *Leander* of wheat – which indicates that the growing colony at the foot of Africa was greatly dependent on Britain for many basic goods. Another item imported in great quantities at the time was coal, and many vessels carrying this commodity have come to grief on the coast, among them the *Udny Castle* on 26 November 1840, the *Queen of Ava* on 29 October 1865, the *Reno* on 8 December 1883, *The Highfields* and the *Verona* on 14 August 1902, and many others. Even after the discovery of rich coalfields in Natal and the Transvaal in the second half of the century, local production evidently had to be supplemented, and only in the 20th century did the country become the important exporter of coal that it is today.

The bewildering array of goods carried by vessels plying the oceans in the 19th century is graphically illustrated by the contrast in the cargoes carried by two vessels wrecked within a few years of each other in the middle of the century. On 13 February 1850 the *Childe Harold*, on a voyage from Bombay to London, was wrecked on Dassen Island. She had on board a cargo of 1 336 pieces of ivory, coffee, coir yarn, gum arabic, gum animé, deer-horns, pearl-shells, shawls and cardamoms, clearly colonial produce which would probably be turned into manufactured articles in the factories of Britain. The *William James*, on the other hand, which came

*Above: A portrayal of the grim conditions between decks on a British emigrant vessel. (*Illustrated London News)
Opposite: Slaves packed on the lower deck of a slaver. (Port Elizabeth Public Library)
Below: Shackles, used to prevent slaves from escaping, found on board the French slaver Vigilante in 1822. (Port Elizabeth Public Library)

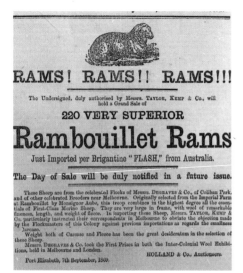

Top: A sale notice advertising rams. (Eastern Province Herald)
Centre: Touch-paper holders from the steamer Maori, *wrecked on 5 August 1909.* (M. Turner)
Above: A container for gorgonzola cheese recovered from the Maori. (M. Turner)

ashore in Table Bay on 10 June 1857, had on board a cargo of five casks of cheese, 17 000 fire bricks, 4 000 slates, 21 tons of coal, ironmongery, lathes, staves, earthenware, stationary, hairpins, salt, vinegar, clothes and ale. Clearly she was on her way from Europe with a cargo bound for the colonies. Consider, too, the cargo of the American ship *Montgomery*, which was on her way from the Philippines to Boston, and was wrecked at Cape Agulhas on 15 March 1847. After the wreck, reports state, the following washed ashore: 42 bales of hides, 150 piculs of rattans, 49 chests of indigo, 13 pieces of ebony, 30 cases of gamboge, 15 cases of gum benjamin, 93 bags of cubebs, 3 133 piculs of sapan wood, 1 060 bales of hemp, 837 coils of cordage, 200 chests of camphor and 490 piculs of gambier. Indeed an exotic variety – and one cannot help but wonder what some of the items would have been used for.

The greatest volume of shipping during the 19th century merely carried cargoes past the Cape to other ports, but in the latter half of the century a change could be detected. Developments in the field of agriculture, mining and industry (after the discovery of diamonds and gold) necessitated a growing volume of shipping for which the Cape and Natal became destinations in their own right. Imports continued and increased, but so did exports, as can be seen from the wrecking of the *Thorne* on 18 May 1831 while on a voyage from Algoa Bay to London with a cargo of colonial produce. It is not specified what this produce was, but wool would in all probability have been at least a part of the cargo. It certainly was in the case of the *Grahamstown* of 327 tons, which was wrecked on 26 May 1864 with a cargo of wool which had been loaded at Algoa Bay for shipment to London, and of the *L'Imperatrice Eugenie*, which was wrecked on Thunderbolt Reef on 6 February 1867 with a similar cargo. Evidence of the growing importance of other forms of trade with South Africa can be found in the case of the *Wilhelmine*, which was wrecked at Mossel Bay on 17 March 1880, and the *Hansa*, wrecked near Danger Point on 3 June 1883. Both vessels were on their way to Mossel Bay with thousands of bags of coffee; such raw materials were necessary to supply a growing processing and manufacturing segment in the economy of South Africa.

Passengers, too, became an important element in shipping. Regular mailship services were introduced towards the middle of the century, and apart from the thousands of passengers steaming past our coast to other destinations, thousands more travelled to or from this country. On 5 February 1875, for instance, RMS *Celt*, an iron steam screw brig commanded by Captain Bird was wrecked without loss of life about 6,5 km west of Quoin Point while on her way to Algoa Bay from London with 98 passengers, mail, and a cargo of coffee, wine and brandy. In another disaster, on 18 April 1911, the pride of Portugal, the liner SS *Lusitania*, was wrecked on Bellows Rock off Cape Point during fog while on a voyage from Lourenço Marques. On board were 25 first-class, 57 second-class and 121 third-class passengers and 475 black labourers, but only eight people died when a boat capsized.

In the 20th century there has been a dramatic reduction in the number of wrecks on the coast of South Africa, due to many factors, for instance better harbour facilities, the construction of a large number of lighthouses, and the introduction of radio and radar. The cargoes carried by shipping to and from South African ports, which have developed into bustling hives of activity, as well as those of vessels passing by, can generally be divided into two categories: raw materials, much of it carried in huge bulk carriers at present, and manufactured goods. The following wrecks can serve as examples of the changing needs of international trade.

On 2 October 1908 the beach at East Beach, East London, was covered in thousands of tins of paraffin after the SS *Valdivia*, on a voyage from New York to China, sank at her moorings after striking a rock off Stalwart Point and holing her bottom. The SS *Maori*, wrecked east of Duiker Point on 5 August 1909, was carrying a cargo including explosives, railway-lines, crockery and water-piping from London to New Zealand. The wreck is still fairly intact and quite accessible, and even today divers recover interesting items of her cargo from the site. Twenty years later the SS *Western Knight* went ashore west of Cape Recife on 8 April 1929, just before reaching her intended destination of Port Elizabeth, with a general cargo which included motorcars, spares and machinery, most of which was salvaged at the time. Clearly South Africa's needs as far as imports is concerned had become quite sophisticated. On 3 May 1932 the SS *Haliartus* was wrecked near Ystervark Point west of the Gouritz River. She had on board 1 200 cases of whisky, 40 cars, oil, machinery, molasses, tyres, tinned foods, clothing and cyanide. The cargo can be considered typical of the mixed goods stowed in the holds of thousands of cargo vessels plying the ocean lanes at the time. Before the age of containerisation the cases, barrels, bales, tins or whatever form of packing employed for the goods would have been stowed in the holds separately, necessitating great numbers of stevedores and crane operators to do the actual loading, careful planning to ensure that the goods to be off-loaded first were loaded last, and expert stowing to ensure that nothing worked loose during a voyage, to pose a threat to the stability of the vessel.

In more modern times much has changed. The accent is on size and volume, and cutting costs through ease of handling, thereby shortening the time a vessel has to stay in port; the result has been the container vessel, the oil tanker and the bulk carrier. South Africa has luckily been spared the ecological disasters faced elsewhere in the world after the wrecking of a fully laden oil tanker on the coast: the closest to it has been the wrecking of the *Esso Wheeling* of 10 172 tons (as compared to the huge modern tankers of up to 500 000 tons) off Quoin Point on 5 November 1948 while in ballast. A more typical wreck of the latter half of the 20th century is that of the MV *Oriental Pioneer*, which was run ashore off Northumberland Point at Cape Agulhas after springing a leak on 22 July 1974 while on a voyage from Maputo. She was a bulk carrier, fully laden with 50 000 tons of iron ore bound for Europe. Other similar bulk carriers were the MV *Kapodistrias*, which ran ashore on the eastern end of Thunderbolt Reef off Cape Recife on 29 July 1985 while fully laden with 7 500 tons of manganese ore, 27 653 tons of sugar, zirconium sand and rutile; and the MV *Daeyang Family*, which was wrecked a little south of Whale Rock in Table Bay with 162 000 tons of iron ore on 30 March 1986.

Above: *A quaint set of animal-headed jugs recovered from the* Maori. *The cargo of this vessel included a large consignment of British-manufactured crockery, much of which has been found, still packed in crates, deep in the silt which has filled the hull. (M. Turner)*

Below: *Stevedores offloading a crate of motor-car components from the fore hold of the wrecked American steamer* Western Knight, *which went aground near Port Elizabeth on 8 April 1929. The well-known salvor Deric van Delden recovered most of her cargo at the time. (Frank Neave)*

The tin wrecks

Tin can today be considered a semi-precious metal and as such it has been the subject of many highly technical and professional salvage attempts over the years. The greatest tin deposits in the world are found in Malaysia and Indonesia, where it is mined by Chinese labourers. The presence of these deposits was known to the Portuguese as long ago as 1511. The Dutch, too, were well situated to gain a foothold in the tin trade, for much of the tin-producing zone (including most of the Straits Settlement of Sumatra and Malaysia, the island of Bangka, off Singapore, and the Batavian area) was within their orbit.

The many tin wrecks along the South African coast have nearly all been successfully salvaged by one highly professional team, the Cape Town divers Tubby Gericke and Brian Clark: together they have recovered a large percentage of all the tin lost along our coast since 1840. Tin is usually cast in ingots of about 45 kg (with lifting-lugs on the sides for easy handling), and a typical tin cargo could weigh up to 280 tons.

A tin ingot has no cultural value, and the salvaged metal has all been sold to eager buyers in industry. The high price received for tin has made the salvage of this metal a highly competitive business. Below is a small selection of the tin wrecks that have been found and salvaged.

Typical of the many tin wrecks is the *L'Aigle*, which was homeward-bound from Sumatra to Marseilles carrying about 70 tons of tin, apart from a cargo of pepper, malacca canes, rattans and coffee, when she was wrecked west of Klippen Point on 16 June 1850. In 1981 she was worked on by Gericke and Clark in a spectacular shallow-water salvage in deep sand which yielded nearly 2 000 ingots.

The *Juno* was a 631-ton Dutch barque on a homeward-bound voyage from Batavia to Rotterdam carrying a medium cargo of tin blocks, coffee, sugar and canes. She was wrecked on 2 March 1852 during thick fog directly below the Cape Agulhas lighthouse. Most of her tin cargo was salvaged by Gericke and Clark, but some of the blocks which they left have been recovered by various other divers over the years.

Below: A block of Malayan tin, weighing 35 kg, recovered from the wreck of the Catharine Jamieson, *which came to grief on Mouille Point on 19 September 1840. (M. Turner)*

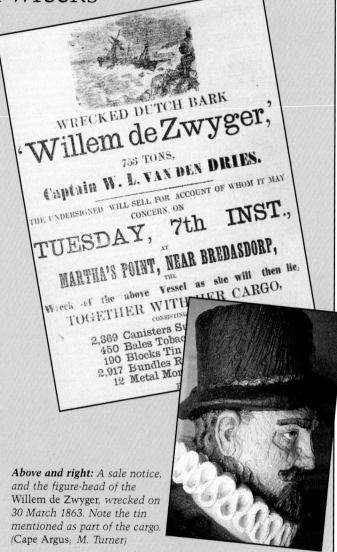

Above and right: A sale notice, and the figure-head of the Willem de Zwyger, *wrecked on 30 March 1863. Note the tin mentioned as part of the cargo. (Cape Argus; M. Turner)*

The *Catharine Jamieson* was a barque of 272 tons on a homeward-bound voyage from Batavia to London and was wrecked on 19 September 1840 on the same side of Mouille Point as the *Athens*. Besides a perishable cargo of coffee, canes and whale-bones she carried about 35 tons of tin blocks. As the area where she was wrecked is fairly sheltered, most of her 989 ingots were probably recovered shortly after the wrecking, but even so she has been well worked by many groups of Cape Town divers, and over the years a considerable amount of tin has been recovered.

The *Borderer* was a 1 062-ton British iron ship on a voyage from Penang to London carrying a cargo of tin blocks, rum, rattans, horns, pepper, hides, sugar and tapioca. She struck the middle blinder of Bulldog Reef off Struis Point, and sank in Struis Bay on 27 October 1868. In 1977 the team of Gericke and Clark undertook the salvage and descended 38 m to recover her cargo. Further salvage work was undertaken in 1985 by a team of divers from the former coastal pollution vessel *Kuswag III*.

Not only vessels engaged in international trade have been wrecked on the coast of South Africa. A vigorous coasting trade was established in the 19th century, with the names of Joseph Barry and C.W. Thesen prominent in the latter half of the century. These vessels, generally small in order to enter the many river ports established to serve local communities before the advent of the railway, carried a great variety of goods. A typical coastal cargo was probably that carried in the 189-ton Cape oak schooner *Albert*, which was wrecked in Struis Bay on 5 February 1857. On a voyage from Cape Town to East London her cargo consisted of 6 logs of teak, 1 log of memel, 9 fir spars, 568 deals, 100 boxes of tea, 13 hogsheads of brandy, 25 boxes of tobacco, brass and ironware, 40 hogsheads of wine, 1 iron barge (in pieces), 3 packages for the 80th Regiment, 18 packages for the 73rd Regiment, 13 packages for the 60th Rifles, 51 packages of furniture, 225 boxes of flour and meal, 50 boxes of soap, 4 quarter cases of vinegar, 21 cases of bottled fruit, cottons, woollens and saddlery. More than a hundred years later a similar miscellany is found when looking at the cargo of the South African coaster SS *Bulwark* of 1 374 tons, wrecked on the Cape Town side of Danger Point on 1 April 1963 while on a voyage from Cape Town to Durban. In this case, apart from a general cargo, fish meal, food in cans, empty drums and liquor were being carried.

Top: *The South African coaster* Horizon, *firmly on the rocks a little south-west of Port St Johns on the Transkei coast in 1967.* (Daily Dispatch)

Above, centre: *Another South African coaster, the* Frontier, *which was wrecked near Kidd's Beach on 27 September 1957.* (Evening Post)

Above: *All that remains of the Union Company steam-coaster* Namaqua, *wrecked at Island Point, south of Hondeklip Bay, on 29 March 1876 is the engine, shaft and propeller. Note the cormorants nesting on the cylinder-heads.* (Keith Grieve)

Left: *The coaster* Bulwark, *her back broken, lies in the kelp beds near Danger Point after running ashore in thick fog on 1 April 1963.* (Cape Argus)

Another local cargo worth mentioning is guano, collected on various rocky islands and islets off the coast. Many vessels carrying this valuable cargo have been wrecked, among them the *Charles*, wrecked on Bird Island in 1845, the *Buffon* and the *Florence*, wrecked on the same island in 1858 and 1883 respectively. On the west coast, too, a number of islands have been regularly visited by guano collectors. On 16 and 17 May 1845, for example, the *Alicia Jane* and the *Eve* ran aground on Paternoster Island. Both vessels had called to load guano and were driven ashore during a north-west gale.

Cargoes therefore are of a bewildering variety, and at one time or another a vessel carrying almost anything one can imagine has been wrecked on the coast of South

Above: *The Liberian oil tanker* Romelia, *wrecked on Sunset Rocks at Llandudno on 29 July 1977. (Argus)*
Bottom: *A contemporary painting of the paddle-steamer* Hope, *wrecked close to Tsitsikamma Point on 11 March 1840. Miraculously no lives were lost. (Africana Museum)*

Below: *Table Mountain forms an impressive backdrop to this view of the giant Korean bulk carrier* Daeyang Family. *The vessel, fully laden with 162 000 tons of iron ore, ran aground a little south of Whale Rock on 30 March 1986. (Argus)*

Africa. The coin cargoes of the early outward-bound East-Indiamen probably fire the imagination of most people, but all the other cargoes have been just as important, though to the modern salvor they do not hold much promise of profits. Concrete evidence of most of the cargoes mentioned does not exist – perhaps the vessel in which they were carried has not been found, or if it has, the cargo it carried has long since disappeared, apart, perhaps, from some evidence such as traces of tea embedded in conglomerate. Yet it must be remembered that in their effort to transport those cargoes from one destination to another, many people have lost their lives when the vessels in which they were travelling were wrecked on our treacherous shores.

Above: *The Greek bulk carrier* Pantelis A. Lemos *hard aground opposite Churchhaven, a little south of Saldanha Bay, in 1978. (James Hellyer)*
Bottom: *Another view of the* Romelia. *Luckily the vessel was in ballast at the time of the disaster. (Herman Potgieter)*

Exports to the East

Interesting trends become apparent if one lists the types of exports to the East carried by vessels that have been wrecked on the coast of South Africa:

17th century
From Holland: Silver specie (Spanish American cob money), Spanish American silver discs, wine, amber, beads, building-bricks, building materials, lead ingots, silver ingots, silverware, mercury, grindstones, taps
From England: Silver specie (Spanish American cob money), Spanish American silver discs, wine

18th century
From Holland: Silver specie (Spanish American cobs and pillar dollars), ducatoons, silver ingots, lead ingots, wine, building-bricks, nails, iron, war material, taps, silverware
From Britain: Silver specie (Spanish American cob money and pillar dollars), lead bars, copper ingots, wine, grindstones, scissors, knives, war material
From Denmark: Silver specie, iron, wine, copper-plate money
From North America: Cotton

19th century
From Britain: Silver specie (Spanish American pillar dollars), zinc, mercury, coal, copper, wine, spirits, beer, timber, wool, mining machinery, creosote, railway material, building-material, pianos, explosives, oil, soap, clothing, cutlery, ironwork
From North America: Flour, machinery, oil, wine, spirits, oats, building-material, tobacco, foodstuffs, timber, explosives, patent medicines
From South America: Coffee, maize, grain

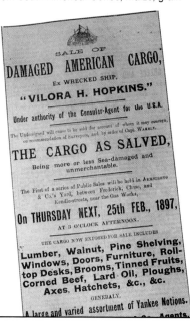

From the Baltic: Timber
From France: Wine, brandy, iron, lead, copper, specie, silverware
From the Netherlands: Gin, wine, furniture
From Germany: Tar, window-glass, explosives, liquor
From Belgium: Bar iron, horse-shoes, matches, glassware

20th century
From Britain: Railway equipment, coal, wine, beer, explosives, motor-cars, copper wire, crockery
From South America: Cattle, sheep, coffee, maize
From North America: Wheat, motor-cars, spare parts, machinery, coal, oil, railway lines, phosphates
From Germany: Chemicals
From France: Wine, brandy
From the Baltic: Timber

Imports from the East

All the materials listed below have been recorded as being on board vessels on their way from the East that have wrecked on the coast of South Africa

16th century
From Cochin: Chinese porcelain, spices, silk, pepper, carpets, gold cloth, cornelian beads, rice, cloth, cambric, diamonds, coconuts, money cowries, cotton

17th century
From Goa: Pepper, Chinese porcelain, spices, silk, bronze cannon, diamonds, turmeric, ebony wood, Indo-Chinese stoneware, saltpetre

Left: A typical cargo. (E.P. Herald)

18th century
From India: Rice, arrack
From Batavia: Pepper, Chinese porcelain, silk, spices, tin, tea, gold bars
From Japan: Porcelain, lacquered goods
From Ceylon: Saltpetre, coffee, pepper

19th century
From Batavia: Coffee, sugar, rice, canes, spice, silk, india-rubber, salt, nuts, tobacco, hides, whale-bones, tin, arrack
From Straits area: Coffee, sugar, rice, rattans, spices, nutmeg, pepper, cork, pearl-shells, india-rubber, tortoise-shell, tobacco, gum, hides, tapioca, gum copal, gambier, tin, rum
From India: Coffee, sugar, rice, saltpetre, cotton, redwood, wool, linseed oil, ivory, grain, rum, indigo, coconut oil, hemp, jute, castor oil, hides, wine, cigars, bar iron, tar, silk, coir rope, horns, drugs, bones, shellac, seeds, teak, wheat, gold specie, sperm oil, gum arabic, gum animé, pearl-shells, ebony, camphor
From the Philippines: Flax, sugar, manila hemp, tobacco, cigars, canes, hides, camphor, indigo, ebony, gum benjamin, gambier, gamboge, cubebs, Japan wood
From China: Tea, cotton, wool, fibre, cassia, silk, seeds, copper, tobacco, spices, lacquered goods, grass cloth fibre
From Japan: Silk, lacquered goods, tea, straw hats
From Pacific Islands: Copra, tortoise-shell
From Celebes: Rattans, pearl-shell, gum copal, tortoise-shell, coffee, tobacco, india-rubber, gutta-percha, cajaput, macassar oil, cork, spices
From Burma: Rice, cotton, teak
From Siam: Rice, cassia, stick-lac, Japan wood
From Borneo: Timber, guano
From Ceylon: Cotton, coffee, coconut oil, cinnamon oil, tea
From Indian Ocean islands: Sugar, rice, rum,

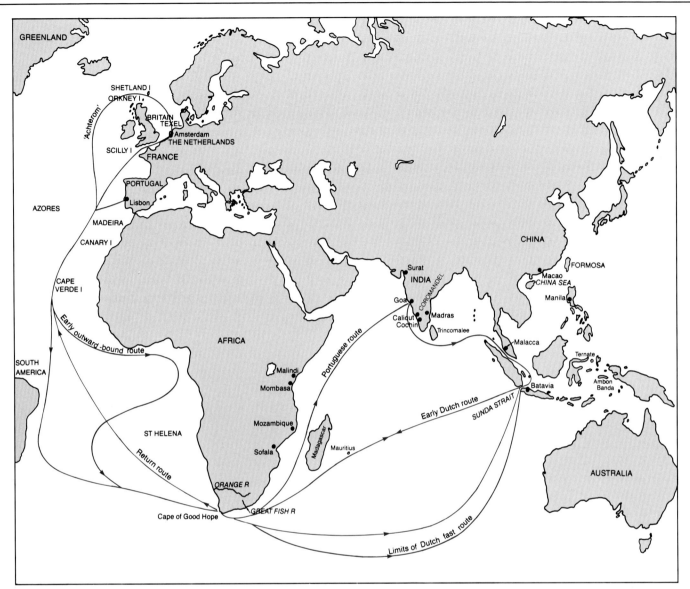

Above, left: *Cutlery from the* Trafalgar.
(M. Turner)
Above: *A map of the main trade routes.*
Right: *Tins of paraffin from the* Valdivia.
(Africana Museum)

dates, cotton, cloves, coconuts (copra), cigars, molasses, coffee, nutmegs, tortoise-shell
From Australia: Sleepers, copper, wheat, flour, mutton, wool, rabbits, gold
From Zanzibar: Hides, gum, cocoa, ivory
From South Africa: Wool, barley, brandy, hides, aloes, goatskins, sheepskins, copper, horns, ivory, ostrich feathers, spermaceti

20th century

From Japan: Paraffin, machinery, clothing
From Australia: Jarrah wood, wool, nickel, wheat, flour, butter, sugar
From South Africa: Lead, copper, nickel, tin plate, iron ore, sugar, manganese ore, coal, fruit, fish, molasses
From Burma: Rice, teak
From Indian Ocean islands: Sugar

Chapter 5

Stories of Courage and Survival

$\mathcal{W}$henever the subject of shipwrecks is broached, the human element is invariably found to have played an important part. The tribulations endured by the survivors of the wreck of the *São João* were repeated often, a common thread being the desire of the survivors to reach some place where they were reasonably sure that they would be rescued by some other vessel. In the early days Delagoa Bay (today Maputo) or the Arab trading port of Sofala was the goal chosen by most, although in the case of the *Nossa Senhora de Belem*, which was wrecked a little north-east of Port St Johns on 24 July 1635, the survivors intended to make for Luanda and built two boats, one of which eventually reached its destination 48 days after setting out on its voyage.

More typical is the story of the *São João Baptista*, which ran ashore near the Fish River mouth in October 1622. Under the command of Pedro de Moraes Sarmento she left the harbour of Goa on 1 March 1622 on her return journey to Lisbon in the company of the flagship *Nossa Senhora do Paraiso* carrying Commodore Nuno Alvares Botelho. She was obviously an old and ill-found ship, as her rudder had been taken from an old wreck lying in Goa. Her armament was also old and inadequate, consisting of only 18 cannon of very small calibre. Perhaps no wonder that she began to leak badly after only 15 or 20 days at sea. Though the pumps were worked to full capacity, a constant level of water was observed in the holds.

The vessel managed to battle on, however, but in the night of 17 July contact was lost with the flagship. The *Baptista* sailed on alone for two days, but then, at about 35° 30.00 south latitude, she encountered two outward-bound Dutch East-Indiamen, the *Wapen van Rotterdam* and the *Mauritius*. At this stage the rivalry for domination of the trade routes between these two nations had spilled over into open warfare; the Portuguese therefore immediately readied their vessel for battle.

Cannon fire was soon exchanged, and during the first two days of the battle 20 Portuguese lost their lives; in desperation a barricade of cloth from the vessel's cargo was erected in an effort to protect them from the devastating Dutch cannon fire. The Dutch concentrated on the stern castle, ripping a hole two metres below her waterline, blasting away the rudder, and leaving gaping holes in the hull. In addition her mainmast and bowsprit were shot away.

During the running battle the vessels proceeded as far south as 42°, with the Dutch remaining in close attendance, though it was clear that the *Baptista* was close to foundering. As the Portuguese drifted helplessly, they encountered snowstorms, during which many of the slaves aboard died of exposure, leaving the Portuguese to work the pumps. It was decided to jury-rig a sail, and for many days the vessel was helplessly driven before the wind, with the crew fearing that she would go to the bottom at any moment.

On 29 September the crew saw land, according to their instruments at about 33° south latitude; by morning they had drifted further down the coast and found themselves just outside the breakers, which naturally posed another great danger. Two anchors were released and the vessel came to a halt in about 14 m of water.

Sixteen armed men were sent ashore immediately to reconnoitre the area; their report must have been favourable, for during the next few days the crew, passengers and valuables were landed from the vessel, but not without difficulty, for 18 people were drowned when a boat capsized in the surf. On 3 October the alarm was raised when a large group of natives was seen to approach the camp site, but fortunately they did not prove hostile, and soon the Portuguese were engaged in a brisk bartering trade.

The survivors stayed at the wreck site for more than a month, during which time they built a church covered with canvas and hung inside with Chinese cloth and decorations of gold and other rich objects from the vessel's cargo. Various options were considered to escape from their precarious position, including the building of a boat from the vessel's timbers, but it was realised that the heavy surf at the ship-

Right: A map tracing the approximate courses followed by the Portuguese vessels São João (see Chapter 3) and São João Baptista before they were wrecked. The most probable overland routes taken by the survivors are also shown.
Below, from top to bottom: Contemporary woodcuts depicting the wrecking of the São João near Port Edward on 11 June 1552 (Africana Museum) and the Santo Alberto on 24 March 1593 (Africana Museum); Two South African Air Force helicopters hover over the stricken cargo vessel South African Seafarer during rescue operations in July 1966 (Cape Argus).

wreck site would make it nearly impossible to launch such a boat. In early October the captain therefore ordered that the hull be burned, mainly in order to retrieve most of the nails, which proved to be good bargaining counters.

On 6 November a properly formed caravan consisting of 279 shipwrecked Portuguese set off on the long walk to Sofala, which they had chosen as their destination. During their journey the party was often harassed by natives who stole their cattle, but the Portuguese, too, often displayed a cruelty that we would find difficult to understand today. In one instance they callously killed the son of a chief, and in another a hapless seaman, Sebastião de Moraes, was beheaded because he was thought to have been the ringleader of a group responsible for stealing a packet of jewellery.

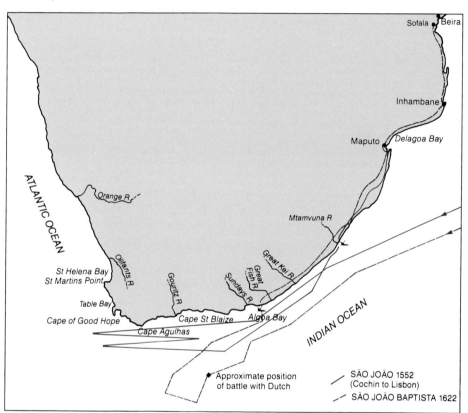

By 21 November the party was suffering severely from fatigue. Some of the women had been carried all the way in litters, paying for the privilege, but this was not enough to persuade the sailors not to leave a young girl behind to the mercy of the elements. As the party advanced, more and more women, children or wounded members were either told to walk, or, if they could no longer keep up, were left behind at native kraals to fend for themselves as best they could.

Having successfully negotiated the Zululand coast, the bedraggled survivors stayed for some time in Delagoa Bay, where a native chief by the name of Inyaka Sangane inhabited the island which today bears his name. The party was taken across Delagoa Bay by boat and then continued on their overland march, once more suffering harassment by the native population. Eventually they reached Inhambane in Mozambique, a port known to be visited by Dutch traders, who called there from time to time to ship ivory and supplies. However, no vessel had called at the port for more than two years, so it was decided to send an advance party to Sofala, which was known to be inhabited by Arab traders. This advance party eventually reached Sofala on 28 July 1623, and had to pay a heavy bribe to arrange for a boat to be sent back to Inhambane to fetch the rest of the party. And yet the tribulations of the shipwrecked Portuguese were not yet over, for soon after leaving Inhambane the rescue boat was wrecked as well. When the surviving Portuguese eventually reached the fortress of Sofala, they were travelling in canoes.

The last stages of their journey were, first, to the port of Mozambique, where they marched in procession behind a wooden cross, chanting the litanies, and finally to Goa. Out of the original 279 survivors of the shipwreck of the *São João Baptista*, only 28 made it back to the port where their voyage had started.

In the early days rescue methods were rather primitive, and consisted mainly of trying to establish a link between the stricken vessel and the shore by means of a rope or cable – but sometimes one must applaud the ingenuity displayed. For instance, a graphic account has been left us of the last moments of the *Vis*, a 650-ton Dutch East-Indiaman built in 1732 at the Enkhuizen shipyard, which left Texel roads in Holland on a voyage to Batavia on 8 January 1740 under the command of Jan Sikkes.

On 5 May 1740 she arrived in the roadstead in Table Bay in pitch darkness, her lookout spotting a light which he presumed to be shining from Robben Island, and, after a bearing had been taken, she sailed on to find an anchorage. Since the light actually emanated from the mainland, however, the *Vis* was, unbeknown to its crew, slowly making for the rocks of Green Point.

Early in the morning of 6 May she struck hard amongst the breakers a little south of the present-day Green Point lighthouse. At daylight the Governor of the Cape, Hendrick Swellengrebel, and other officials arrived at the wreck site to oversee the rescue of the passengers and crew, and, possibly of greater urgency to them, the money-chests belonging to the Company which were an important part of her cargo. A fairly strong swell was running and there was no possibility of getting near the *Vis* from land or sea; the people aboard were therefore forced to help themselves.

A meeting of ship's officers was held and it was decided to try to get a line to the shore. An empty cask was attached to a thin line and thrown into the sea; the cask was eventually washed on to the rocks, where someone on the shore took hold of it and brought it in. Those on the wreck then tied a thick cable to their end of the line and signalled to the shore party to pull it ashore; and in this way a strong cable was rigged up between the wreck and a pole which had been driven into the ground ashore.

Next a large copper cooking-cauldron from the vessel's galley was slung by its rings on to the cable, and two ropes were attached by means of which the cauldron could be pulled back and forth above the water. The crew and passengers then began their evacuation of the wreck, two at a time, by clambering into the cauldron and being drawn swiftly to safety by willing helpers on the shore. More than 150 people were saved in this manner before disaster struck. The ship's steward and his assistant climbed into the cauldron, taking with them a young boy; the steward had foolishly decided to bring his money and had crammed his pockets full of heavy silver ducatoons. On the way to the shore one of the rings on the cauldron, burdened with this load, broke off and all three people were tipped into the sea. The cable was immediately slackened and the assistant steward and the boy managed to save themselves by holding on to it – but the steward, weighted down by all the heavy coins in his pockets, sank like a stone and drowned.

By this stage more than a thousand spectators had gathered opposite the wreck. The broken cauldron was pulled back to the ship and the ring repaired in a workshop on board. A few hours later the rescue effort was resumed, though it was decided not to risk bringing the heavy money-chests ashore this way. With the *Vis* lying right in amongst the rocks and waves lashing around her hull, it was obvious that salvage boats could only approach the wreck at their peril, and the captain and some crew members were compelled to stay on board and guard the money-chests until the sea calmed.

The next morning dawned fine, with a flat sea, and no time was wasted. The Governor offered a reward to a boat crew to row out to the wreck and recover the money-chests. Eventually all the chests were safely on shore under the guard of some Company soldiers. The following day the *Vis* took a severe battering by the sea and broke open along her entire length. All the light cargo drifted out of her shattered holds and washed ashore, to be collected by eager sailors.

If a vessel was wrecked on the coast, it was always possible for the survivors to attempt an overland trek back to civilisation, but if the shipwreck occurred on an island, the only possible option, of course, was to build a boat from the timbers of the wrecked vessel. One such example is provided by the *Dodington*, a 499-ton vessel on hire to the English East India Company, which sailed from the Downs, off south-east Kent, on 22 April 1755 on her way to India as part of a fleet of vessels sent

The South African Seafarer

Often one finds an interesting correlation between wrecks. A twist was added to the tale of the *Vis* when on 1 July 1966 the 8 101-ton steel freighter *South African Seafarer* ran aground very close to the final resting place of the *Vis*. In place of the cauldron method of rescuing those on board, modern-day aids in the form of three Air Force helicopters were used. Time and again the determined pilots risked the strong winds to hover above the wreck while huge waves crashed against the side of the stricken vessel, reaching up as if to swamp the aircraft above. One after the other those on board were slowly winched to the safety of the helicopters, which then made for the shore and off-loaded the bedraggled passengers and crew under the gaze of the large crowd who had gathered to watch the spectacle. In the days following the wreck, chemicals from the *Seafarer*'s hold spilled into the sea and killed the dense kelp which had hidden the site of the *Vis* for some 226 years, and soon after divers discovered her large cast iron cannon and main cargo of building-blocks on the sea-bed. And although the Dutch East India Company's money-chests had been removed at the time, the modern divers eventually recovered more than 1 000 silver riders from the site.

A crew-member from the South African Seafarer *is led to safety. (Cape Argus)*

The Bounty survivors

One of the great stories of survival at sea is that of the crew members who were put in a boat after the famous mutiny on the *Bounty* on 28 April 1789, to fend for themselves as best they could. The mutineers under Fletcher Christian allowed Captain William Bligh and 19 others to step into the vessel's launch, but they were allowed only the basics needed for survival; a compass, sextant, some tools, a set of nautical tables, four cutlasses, a few gourds of water, ships' biscuit and some chunks of salt pork. After a near-disastrous visit to the island of Tofua, during which one man was killed by the natives, it was decided to make for Timor in the East Indies rather than for some South Seas island. Against the greatest odds the men made their way across the Pacific, braving storms, hunger, thirst and boredom, with Bligh constantly exhorting his men to keep faith, overseeing the distribution of the rations with an iron hand, and meticulously keeping track of his daily navigational sightings. On 28 May they had reached the Great Barrier Reef off Australia and had sailed through a gap to reach land on Restoration Island at the northern tip of Queensland. By this stage tempers in the boat were short, but Bligh managed to assert his authority. After passing through the Endeavour Straits and into the Arafura Sea, the exhausted men entered a critical phase, and at one stage Bligh thought that many of the men would die. Yet on 14 June the boat entered Coupang harbour under oars as the guns from the Dutch fort boomed out in salute. Against all odds Bligh had brought his men to safety.

Detail of the breech of a bronze field gun from the wreck of the Dodington. *The 'M' monogram is that of John, the second Duke of Montagu. (M. Turner)*

out to support the war effort there. This was a time when the French and English East India Companies were engaged in a prolonged struggle for supremacy in India, and therefore, to support the English war effort, the *Dodington* carried, in addition to her general cargo, a company of Royal Artillery and some infantry, as well as a large quantity of military stores and four bronze field-guns sporting the crest of George II, King of England.

After an uneventful journey of about three months the *Dodington* encountered a storm as she approached Algoa Bay. There was a westerly gale blowing, with squalls, and the main topsail was treble-reefed, as her master, Captain James Sampson, attempted to make her more manageable. At about midnight the forward lookout saw breakers dead ahead and to leeward. The helmsman swung the wheel in an attempt to turn the vessel, but it struck the south-eastern corner of Bird Island with great force – much to the crew's surprise, as they had estimated their position to be at least 230 nautical miles (430 km) to seaward!

The ship rapidly broke up and about 247 people lost their lives as they were thrown into the boiling sea. Once ashore, the 23 survivors searched for and found clothing, which they were very glad of as the weather was extremely cold. On a few occasions, over the next few days, they boarded the wreck and recovered a fair amount of equipment and tools, and they also found one of the vessel's treasure-chests and a box of silver plate. For seven months the survivors stayed on the island and lived off fish, and gannet and penguin eggs, as well as provisions which washed ashore from the wreck. In search of provisions some of the survivors made a journey by boat to the mainland, some 4 nautical miles (8 km) distant, but they were driven away by the hostile Xhosa tribes on the shore, and one of their number was lost. The ship's carpenter, meanwhile, had worked hard, and constructed a vessel called the *Happy Deliverance* from the *Dodington*'s timbers. This boat was launched in a gully on the east side of the island on 17 February 1756.

A mild westerly breeze was blowing, and after waiting for high tide, the *Happy Deliverance* headed out – but almost immediately she grounded on a reef. Fortunately she could be pulled off at once; she was then brought to anchor while provisions such as water, salt pork, bread and two live pigs where loaded aboard. The next day she set sail for Delagoa Bay under the command of Evan Jones, the chief mate.

Their progress was slow, thwarted by a heavy head current and easterly winds; often they would come to anchor and fish if it seemed as if they were losing headway. At one stage they became so despondent at their lack of progress that they decided to turn around and make for the Cape of Good Hope; however, they changed their minds when the boat was almost swamped by following seas. Their progress up the east coast may have been slow, but at least it was sure, and they were not lacking in provisions, for they were able to barter with the native settlements they passed along the way for meat and wood.

On 15 March the *Happy Deliverance* crossed a bar and entered a large river full of hippopotamus – probably the Mzimvubu River, at the mouth of which lies the present-day Port St Johns. They stayed here for two weeks, successfully bartering with the natives and exploring the river. By 5 April they had reached the mouth of the St Lucia River; after waiting at anchor for the heavy surf over the bar to subside, they entered the estuary – not without incident, for they grounded on a sandbank, fortunately without sustaining any damage. Here they stayed for nearly two weeks, bartering with the natives for meat.

On 18 April, once again after waiting for the heavy surf over the bar to subside, the *Happy Deliverance* sailed across it safely and proceeded on her voyage to her destination – but without nine of the crew members, who had refused to risk their lives in the surf and had elected instead to walk the rest of the way to Delagoa Bay. After a total voyage of just over two months, the boat sailed into Delagoa Bay on 20 April, and to their delight they found the British vessel *Rose Galley* at anchor. The captain, Edward Chandler, who was trading in the area, agreed to give the *Dodington* survivors a passage to Madagascar.

The treasure recovered from the *Dodington* was handed to Chandler for safekeeping, and he issued Jones with a receipt. After further bargaining Chandler also agreed to buy the *Happy Deliverance*, and shortly afterwards both vessels sailed to Madagascar, where the *Dodington* survivors were transferred to the British vessel *Carnarvon* and eventually taken to Madras in India.

Tales of personal heroism on the coast of South Africa abound. For example, on 10 June 1692, when the 222-ton Dutch East India Company yacht *Hogergeest* ran aground while on a homeward voyage, a heroic rescue was effected. While the vessel was at anchor in Table Bay, a north-west gale sprang up, during which the vessel's anchor cable parted. Helpless, the vessel ran aground in heavy surf at the mouth of the Salt River, and the crew were unable to reach the shore. Despite all the dangers, a Dutch seaman by the name of Jochem Willemsz volunteered to swim out to the wreck with a line tied to his waist. After battling through the ice-cold surf, he finally reached the wreck. Here he was pulled aboard, and a stronger line attached to the one he brought aboard was hauled in and made fast. A raft was then launched, with two lines secured to it – one leading to the shore, and one to the wreck, in order to make it possible to pull it to and fro between the wreck and the shore. Within a short time all the crew had left the wreck and most of them survived, thanks to the heroism of Jochem Willemsz.

Unfortunately there were also occasions when the safety of the sailors was considered to be of secondary importance to the recovery of money. This occurred, for instance, in the case of the *Jonge Thomas*. Outward-bound vessels were always a great source of concern to the Dutch East India Company: the valuable chests of specie were of consuming interest to pirates and plunderers and often, when a vessel was wrecked, the Company would hang anyone found interfering with the cargo that washed ashore.

On 20 October 1772 the *Jonge Thomas*, commanded by Barend de la Maire, left Texel on a voyage to Batavia. She arrived in Table Bay on 29 March 1773, reporting 70 deaths and 41 sick, who were sent to hospital. Two months later, on the morning of 1 June 1773, her anchor cables parted during a north-west gale and she ran ashore near Woodstock Beach. The Company immediately set up a salvage camp to recover

Above: *Detail of the breech of a field-gun from the* Dodington. *(M. Turner)*
Below: *A painting of the wreck of the* Hogergeest. *(Africana Museum)*

A lithograph depicting the heroic rescue attempt by Wolraad Woltemade and his horse during the great north-west gale in Table Bay on 1 June 1773 when the vessel Jonge Thomas *was wrecked with great loss of life. (South African Library)*

Another horseback rescue

When thinking of shipwrecks and individual heroism displayed during the rescue of survivors, the name of Wolraad Woltemade always comes to mind. Yet his rescue was by no means the only one effected on horseback. In 1817 the Rose family, with two sons and four daughters, emigrated to South Africa and settled in an attractive cottage on the slopes of Table Mountain. Four years later, on 4 January 1821, a north-westerly gale struck Table Bay and early in the morning three vessels ran aground: the *Indian Packet*, the *Emma* and the *Dorah*. Although a heavy surf lashed the coast, distress guns could be heard above the sound of the wind. The youngest son, Francis, a moral, hard-working lad aged about 17, was woken by his father and the two of them rushed to the beach to see if they could render any assistance. Soon afterwards Francis came back to the cottage to fetch his favourite horse, and after shouting assurances to his anxious mother he rode down to the scene of one of the wrecks and proceeded to rescue the whole crew by riding into the surf and bringing them ashore one by one. On his last trip back from the wreck, however, the strain told on horse and rider, and Francis was drowned.

any cargo that might wash ashore, but little attempt was made to rescue the sailors stranded on the rapidly disintegrating vessel.

Early in the morning an elderly German, Wolraad Woltemade, a dairy farmer in the employ of the Company, set out on horseback to the wreck site to take his son, a corporal on duty at the salvage camp, a bottle of wine and a loaf of bread for breakfast. When he arrived at the scene of the disaster he was so deeply upset by the cries for help emanating from the shattered vessel that he rode his horse into the waves and started to bring the men ashore, two at a time. He made seven trips to the wreck and saved 14 people this way, but on the eighth trip his exhausted horse was dragged under when too many people held on to its bridle and tail. He was drowned, too, and his body was washed ashore the next day, but his heroism has earned him a deserved place in South African folk history.

Soon after his brave attempt an edict was issued stating that anyone coming near the wreck would be hanged, and a gibbet was erected on the spot. This effectively deterred anyone from helping the remaining crew, and eventually 138 people were to drown in the ice-cold surf. Perhaps another reason why the Company did not want too many people near the wreck was because the *Jonge Thomas* was not supposed to have been in Table Bay at that time in the first place; because of the well-known danger of the north-westerly gales in winter, a standing instruction ordered all vessels to anchor in False Bay during the winter months. In fact it was many months before a report on the wrecking of the *Jonge Thomas* was sent to Company headquarters in Amsterdam.

The Dutch East India Company, on hearing a report from the survivors of the part played by Wolraad Woltemade, made a substantial reward to his wife and sons, and later also honoured him by naming a vessel after him. This was the 1150-ton East-Indiaman *Held Woltemade*, but it remains a sad reflection on this great trading power that the value of boxes of money and cargo could be regarded as greater than human life. Ironically it was the *Held Woltemade* that in 1781 unwittingly betrayed the position of the Dutch merchant fleet in Saldanha Bay to the British warship *Active* and so brought about the Battle of Saldanha Bay which was to end so calamitously for the Dutch (see pp 75-77).

Probably the best-known of the homeward-bound English East India Company vessels wrecked on our coast is the *Grosvenor*, a 729-ton merchantman that sailed from Trincomalee in Ceylon on 13 June 1782, under the command of Captain John Coxon, after a successful trading mission in the East. She had an uneventful voyage until 4 August 1782, when she came to grief on the rocks of the Pondoland coast.

Her problems had begun two days earlier. The wind began blowing strongly from the south-west and the sky became very overcast, preventing the officers of the watch from making an accurate observation. Captain Coxon himself had reckoned the vessel to be at least 240 nautical miles (450 km) from the nearest land, but in actual fact the stormy weather had carried the vessel off-course and she was dangerously near the shore.

During the last night watch John Hynes was in the crow's-nest with some others when he saw breakers ahead; they hastened to inform the officer of the watch, a young and inexperienced man who laughed and insisted that they were well away from the shore. Fortunately one of the look-outs also informed Captain Coxon of the danger, and he at once ordered the helmsman to alter course – but it was too late, for almost immediately the *Grosvenor*'s keel struck a reef with tremendous force. This brought everyone on deck, the passengers in a state of near-panic. The wells were sounded, but as yet there was no water in the holds; it was found that the stern was high up on the rocks.

Now the wind changed and started blowing directly off-shore, and the officers feared that this would blow the badly damaged vessel out to sea, where she might sink. Though the masts had been cut away, she started taking in vast quantities of water. The rapidly disintegrating hull had been driven to within one cable's length of the shore and it was realised that she could not be saved from total disaster.

Chaos ruled on the deck. The more rational of the crew set about making a raft by which they hoped to reach the shore with the women, the children and the sick. Three men, one of whom died in the attempt, swam to the shore with the deep-sea line and managed to attach a hawser to the rocks. A huge crowd of Pondos had by this time accumulated on the shore to witness the drama being played out on the rocks, and some of them helped with the hawser. The raft was now completed and launched, but almost immediately the cable which surrounded it snapped and the raft was upset, throwing into the water the four men who had climbed onto it – three of whom were drowned. The yawl and the jollyboat had already been smashed to pieces and the only means of preserving life was now to use the hawser which ran from the wreck to the rocks. It was a case of every man for himself; several people reached the shore by clambering hand-over-hand along this cable, but 15 others died in the attempt.

Soon after this, the ship broke in two just before the mainmast and by a miracle the wind veered back to the west; this saved the lives of many who had climbed on to the poop deck, for the deck split in two and the starboard quarter floated into shallow water. The remaining hull structure effectively blocked off the incoming water to some degree, and all the women and children were deposited safely on shore, the only further deaths being those of the cook's mate and a black man who was too drunk to leave the wreck.

As darkness fell, the Pondos returned to their villages. The survivors lit several fires which they had made from fragments of wood, and the scattered provisions which had been washed ashore provided a meal. Two tents were made from the vessel's sails and the women were soon housed in these, while the men combed the shore looking for useful items of flotsam.

The next morning, 5 August 1782, the Pondos returned to the wreck site and carried away what they liked. The brazen attitude of these tribesmen caused the women a great deal of anxiety; they feared that they, too, would be carried off, but their fears were unfounded. The next day was spent collecting whatever further useful articles could be found, as by this time the survivors realised that they would have to walk to the Cape. A quick tally of the available stores showed them to have two casks of flour, a tub of pork and some arrack; the captain wisely decided to pour this liquor away as he feared that the natives could become aggressive if they were to drink it. He called a meeting, and, after dividing the provisions, asked if there was any objection to his leading an overland journey to the Cape. The survivors agreed to this plan. The captain had estimated that it would take 15 days to reach the nearest Dutch settlement, but unfortunately he did not take into consideration the many rivers which lay in their path.

The party eventually set out on the westward march on 7 August 1782, leaving behind an old soldier who was lame; he intended to make his own way home at a later date. While they were walking along, some of the natives followed them,

Top: A painting by an unknown artist of the wrecking of the transport vessel Abercrombie Robinson *and the convict vessel* Waterloo *during a violent north-west gale in Table Bay on 28 August 1842. No lives were lost on the* Abercrombie Robinson, *but, due to the extremely rotten state of her timbers, 190 people drowned on the ageing* Waterloo. *(Africana Museum)*
***Above:** A boat leaving the wreck of the* Abercrombie Robinson.

taking every opportunity to plunder what they could and occasionally throwing stones. After a few kilometres they met a runaway slave from the Cape who was fluent in Dutch; he was accompanied by about thirty natives with red-painted faces and hair tied up in conical form. The slave's name was Trout, and when he heard of the wreck and of their intention to walk to the Dutch settlements at the Cape, he warned them of the great dangers that they would encounter and refused their request to be their guide.

The survivors pressed on for five days, during which time they were constantly harassed by the natives, who only left them at the approach of night. On their journey they passed many indigenous villages, which they carefully avoided. One day in a deep gully they met three natives armed with spears. These men threatened Captain Coxon by holding the blades to his throat, whereupon the captain lost his temper, grabbed one of the spears from its owner and broke it. The aggressors seemed nonplussed and left them, but the next day, when the survivors were near a large village, they saw the three men accompanied by three or four hundred tribesmen, all armed with spears. The tribesmen stopped the party of survivors, began stealing their belongings and eventually started to beat them. Believing that their lives were threatened, Coxon and his men put the women and children to one side and were soon engaged in a running battle, though there were only eighty or ninety of them against the tribesmen. Many were wounded on both sides, but amazingly no one was killed. The English managed to position themselves favourably and eventually a truce was declared – whereupon they presented the locals with some buttons cut from their jackets. The natives then retired and were seen no more.

Yet this was by no means the last of the tribulations of Captain Coxon and his party. They spent nights of terror listening to wild animals circling their camp. They were harassed by other indigenous inhabitants, who stole their tinder-box, flint and steel, so that they were now forced to carry a burning torch in order to be assured of fire. The increasingly aggressive natives also stole the men's watches and the diamonds which had been concealed in the ladies' hair. Any attempt to resist such harassment brought on fresh insults and even blows.

The sailors now started complaining about the delays caused by travelling with the women and children, and it soon became apparent that the party would have to split up. Which is what happened: the sailors, who were stronger and more mobile, made it back to the Cape, and it is a tribute to the Dutch – who were on a war footing with Britain at this stage – that a party was sent out from the Cape to search for the missing survivors, including the captain, women and children. Most of them were, however, never seen again.

Personal courage in the face of utmost danger can take many forms. Obeying strict military discipline in the face of certain death is one. In the case of the wrecking of the crowded British troop transport *Abercrombie Robinson* in Table Bay in 1842, cool courage and chivalry played a great role in preventing the possible loss of hundreds of lives. The vessel had left Dublin Bay on 2 June 1842 under the command of Captain J. Young, carrying a complement of more than 600 troops of the 91st and 27th regiments, as well as more than 80 women and children. On 27 August she lay at anchor in Table Bay, as did the *Waterloo*, a British convict ship on her way to Tasmania with 219 male convicts, 30 guards of the 99th regiment and 19 women and children on board.

By 05h00 on 28 August the wind that had sprung up the day before had reached gale force. The *Abercrombie Robinson*'s anchor cables parted, and she went aground close to the Salt River mouth. A strict code of discipline was observed on board and urgent plans were made to get the women and children ashore as soon as possible. A line was taken ashore by means of one of the vessel's boats, and at the same time surfboats which had been sent to the scene set out from the shore and began evacuating the women and children from the rapidly disintegrating wreck. Not until the last of them was safely ashore did the first of the men disembark.

The souls on board the ageing and unseaworthy *Waterloo* were, however, not so fortunate. Just after 10h00 she, too, ran ashore, about 500 m from the *Abercrombie Robinson*, but with a great loss of life. The *Waterloo* was an old vessel, having been built in 1815, and her hull was in an extremely poor state of repair. Soon after hitting the shore the power of the surf broke the vessel into four pieces, and most of the people on board were thrown into the sea, where nearly 200 were drowned. It is a sad reflection on the British authorities of the time that the lives of these people, whose crimes were mainly of a petty nature, could be endangered in such a way by placing them aboard such an unseaworthy vessel.

A decade later a similar scene to that which had played itself out on the *Abercrombie Robinson* occurred, and perhaps because so many lives were lost, it has become rather better known, even moving William Makepeace Thackeray to write in May 1852: 'I can fancy a future author taking for his story the glorious action off Cape Danger, when, striking only to the powers above, the *Birkenhead* went down, and when, with heroic courage and endurance, the men kept to their duty on deck.'

The story of the last voyage of the 1 400-bm iron paddle steamer *Birkenhead*, designed and built by Lairds on the River Mersey in 1845, begins in late December 1851 when she sailed from Cork in Ireland under the command of Captain Robert Salmond, carrying a complement of 23 officers and 469 drafted men to aid Lieutenant-General Sir Harry Smith in the Eighth Frontier War being waged at the Cape. She had eight water-tight compartments and two engines, built by George Forrester & Co, and was originally designed as a frigate, but was later converted to a troopship by the addition of a poop deck.

She put into Madeira, Sierra Leone and St Helena for coal and provisions, and eventually arrived at Simon's Town on 23 February 1852 after a voyage of more than

Top: An etching of the last moments of the Waterloo. *In contrast to the calm scene aboard the* Abercrombie Robinson, *the chaos on the* Waterloo *is graphically illustrated. (William Fehr Collection)*

Above: A plaque erected on Danger Point in 1936 by the Navy League of South Africa in memory of the many lives lost during the wrecking of HMS Birkenhead *on 26 February 1852. (P.A. Sargeant)*

Left: A painting of the Birkenhead *down by the head off Danger Point. (Africana Museum)*

WRECK OF H. M. STEAMER "BIRKENHEAD."

OFFICIAL INFORMATION.

Colonial Office, 28th Feb., 1852, 10 o'clock, A.M.

THE following Documents, received from Commodore WYVILL, are published, as affording some relief to public anxiety.

(Signed) JOHN MONTAGU,
Secretary to Government.

"*Castor*," Simon's Bay, 27th February, 1852.

To His Excellency Lieut.-General
SIR HARRY G. W. SMITH, Bart.,
Governor and Commander-in-Chief,
&c., &c., &c.

Sir,—It is with much pain I have to inform Your Excellency of the total loss of Her Majesty's Steam Ship *Birkenhead*, at 2 o'clock on the morning of the 26th instant, near to Point Danger,—and I regret to add that from the statement given by Dr. Culhane, Assistant Surgeon of the ship, it would appear that only about 70 persons are saved out of 630 souls, nine of whom have landed, but the other are in two Boats and had proceeded seaward, to be picked up by a sailing Vessel.

I have dispatched the *Rhadamanthus* to the scene of this fearful disaster to afford all possible relief, and to search for the missing Boats.

As it is possible they may be compelled to effect a landing, I would be glad if your Excellency gave instructions to the Resident Magistrates and Field-Cornets, on the Coast, to keep a look out for them, and render every necessary assistance.

I beg to enclose Dr. Culhane's statement.

And have the honour to be,
Sir,
Your Excellency's most obedient Servant,
C. WYVILL, Commodore.

Since writing the above, the *Rhadamanthus* has towed in the Schooner *Lioness*, which vessel picked up one hundred and sixteen in number, are at present on board the *Castor*, and the *Rhadamanthus* has again proceeded to the scene of the wreck. Nothing had been heard of the other two boats. Dr. Bowen, Staff-Surgeon, reports that several of the Soldiers reached the land on rafts.

Copy.—C. WYVILL.

Statement of Dr. CULHANE, of Her Majesty's late Steam Ship "Birkenhead."

That Her Majesty's steam ship "*Birkenhead*" struck the ground at about two a.m. on the morning of the 26th February, somewhere near Point Danger, and in twenty minutes after filled, and went down. The quarter boats were lowered, and about 65 persons got into them; the gig was also down. Whilst getting the paddle-box boats out, the heave of the ship in sinking washed them away. Many were drowned below before they could effect their escape to the upper deck. Dr. Culhane and eight men landed, in the gig, near Port D'Urbin, where Mr. Phillipson has a store, about thirty miles from the wreck. Nothing had been heard of the other two boats, except that they pulled out to sea, to get picked up by a sailing vessel.

List of the Persons saved from the "Birkenhead" by the three Boats.

OFFICERS.
Dr. Culhane, Assistant-Surgeon.
Mr. Richards, Master's Assistant.
Mr. Renwick, 1st Class Assistant-Engineer.
Mr. Hire, Clerk.

SEAMEN AND STOKERS.
John Bowen, Henry Cheeseman,
Thos. Dunn, Able Stone,
George Till, John McCabe,
John Smith, Wm. Chase,
Chas. Noble, George Kelly,
Thos. Daley, Martin Niole,
Thos. Longmaid, Robt. Finn,
John Ashbolt, George Windsor,
Geo. Randall, Wm. Bushe,
John Klog, John Lewis,
Thos. Dew, John Wood.

MARINES.
John Drake, Sergt., Thomas Daniels,
Wm. Northoven, Prvt., John Cooper.

BOYS.
W. Gale, Chas. Mathews, J. R. Howard.
Total—Thirty-three in number.

SOLDIERS.
2nd Regt.	60th Rifles.
John Moore,	Wm. Burlow,
Ml. Malay,	Thos. Nutall,
P. Peters,	Thos. Smith,
John Peters,	Wm. Sooter.
Thos. Chadwick,	
Robt. Page,	73rd Regt.
Hy. Double,	Sergt. Kilberry,
Wm. Vernon,	Wm. Bushe,
Jas. Gildeo,	Thos. Cash,
Benj. Worill,	Jas. Fitzpatrick,
Pk. McCrery.	Wm. Halfpenny,
	Pk. May,
6th Regt.	Ml. O'Brien,
Sergt. Teile,	Pk. Lynch,
W. Bushe,	John Sullivan,
Wm. Clark,	Wm. Wood.
Thos. Coa,	
Jas. Goldin,	74th Regt.
John Herrich,	Sergt. Harold,
Jas. Wade,	Wm. Boyce,
Wm. Welch.	Chas. Ferguson,
	Jas. Henderson,
12th Regt.	D. Kirkford,
Dl. Waters,	Walter Taylor,
Thos. Sangaw,	John Smith,
John Irvin,	Chas. Walker,
Jas. Johnson,	Dl. Shaw.
Robt. Dolan,	
John Yale,	91st Regt.
John Simon,	John Stanley,
Pk. Ward.	Dd. Carey,
	Pk. Mullins,
43rd Regt.	Pk. Cunnynham,
John Herin,	John Cougham.
Ed. Ambrose,	
Jas. West.	91st Regt.
	John Lamb,
45th Regt.	John Wamsley,
Adam Keating.	Fred. Winterbottom.

LADIES AND WOMEN.
Mrs. Darkins, Mrs. Gwichar,
Mrs. Nesbit, Mrs. Spruce,
Mrs. Mullins, Mrs. Hudson,
Mrs. Montgomery.
13 Children.
Mr. Bowen, Staff Surgeon.
Total—1 Officer and 62 soldiers.
7 Women and 13 children.

Above: The official newspaper report on the wrecking of HMS Birkenhead. An indication of the importance of her mission can be gained from the number of regiments represented.
Below: An Air Force helicopter of No 16 Squadron, Port Elizabeth, hoists aboard a crew member from the doomed Greek cargo vessel Evdokia. (Evening Post)

50 days, during which four women passengers had died, three in childbirth and one of consumption. The next two days were spent preparing the vessel for the resumption of her voyage; 350 tons of coal and provisions were loaded on board. The government dispatches for Sir Harry Smith were received and the vessel left Simon's Town at 18h00 on 25 February on her voyage to Algoa Bay and East London to land the soldiers.

The sea was flat and the weather fine as the *Birkenhead* steamed across False Bay at 8,5 knots, with Seaman Thomas Coffin at the wheel. The rhythmic thump of the paddle-wheels lulled to sleep the men, including the commander and master, who were down below. In the holds were 350 double-barrelled carbines of a revolutionary new design intended for the use of the 12th Lancers, and a large cargo of wine, no doubt eagerly awaited on the frontier. Bales of fodder and some officers' horses were stowed on deck, as very little space was available below.

At about 02h00 a violent shock was felt and in an instant the lower deck flooded, drowning many unfortunate men in their bunks. All the surviving officers and men went up on deck. Being the senior officer on board, Lieutenant-Colonel Seton of the 74th Foot took charge of all military personnel; he immediately summoned his officers around him and stressed the importance of maintaining order and discipline.

The men were commanded to stand drawn up in line and to await orders, while about sixty men were sent to the pumps. Distress rockets were fired, but there was no help at hand. At this stage the captain made a grave mistake in ordering the *Birkenhead* to be put astern, an action which caused the hull to rip open further. The sudden inrush of water swamped the boiler fires, and the vessel began to break up; in its collapse the funnel killed the men working at the paddle-box boat.

The teams who were in charge of the boats were frustrated to find that most of the lowering equipment would not function, as a result of a lack of maintenance and the thick layer of paint that clogged the mechanisms. Eventually two cutters and a gig were launched and the women and children were rowed away from the wreck to safety. The horses were cut loose and thrown overboard. Captain Salmond now shouted to the men that everyone who could swim must save himself by jumping into the sea and making for the boats – but the soldiers, not wishing to endanger the lives of those already in the boats, stood firm.

The *Birkenhead* disintegrated rapidly. Twenty-five minutes after she had struck the rocks, only the topmast and topsail yard were visible above the water, with about fifty men clinging to them. The bow broke after twelve minutes, then the vessel broke in two abaft the engine-room, whereafter the stern sank immediately.

The sea was full of men desperately clawing for anything that could float. Death by drowning came quickly to most of them, but some of the men – and the horses – were taken by Great White sharks (Blue Pointers); and even today the locals in Gansbaai call this shark the 'Tommie-haai' (Tommy shark), after the Tommys who died. Those who made it to the shore had to run the gauntlet of the thick kelp which lined the coast: many were tangled in the fronds of this weed and drowned miserably only metres from the shore.

The next morning the schooner *Lioness* found one of the *Birkenhead*'s cutters in Walker Bay. An hour later, after saving the second boat crew, she made straight for the scene of the disaster and reached the wreck that afternoon, saving as many as possible. The gig, meanwhile, had landed near Hermanus and a rider was on his way to the Cape to report the tragedy. It was later reported that of the 638 people aboard the *Birkenhead*, only 193 were saved.

Modern aids have of course cut down drastically on the numbers of shipwrecks on our coast, yet they still occur. On Monday, 11 June 1979 snow fell on the mountain ranges of the Cape, and offshore the sea was lashed by rain and westerly gales blustering up to 50 knots. On board the 7 144-ton Greek steel motor freighter *Evdokia*, lightning lit up the sky and large hailstones smashed onto the deck. Formerly named the *Himeji Maru* and then the *Atlantic Darby*, the *Evdokia* was built in Japan in 1956, and was on her way to Rio de Janeiro from Durban and East London with a cargo of 1 974 tons of copper ingots, 90 tons of nickel plates, rolls of tinplate and newsprint.

During the day the radio operator on board started sending out distress signals: the *Evdokia*'s no 5 hold was flooded; she was lying low in the water; she was listing heavily to port and she was in danger of sinking at any moment. Although the

Left: *On 12 June 1979 the* Evdokia *ran aground at the base of steep cliffs and broke up almost immediately, with the loss of six lives. The broken stern and upended bridge protruding from the surf in the Tsitsikamma Coastal National Park were the only signs to be seen of the vessel. (Colin Urquhart)*

pumps were working at full capacity, they could not cope with the inrush of water.

The vessel's position was reported as being about 17 km east of Plettenberg Bay, and the Cape Town-based salvage tug *Albatross* immediately set out to the rescue, though it was realised that it would be many hours before she would be able to reach the scene. That afternoon, fearing for the lives of the men on board, Captain Patsiatzis requested the services of a helicopter to take off the crew. Two South African Air Force helicopters immediately took off in the foul weather, at great risk to the pilots.

In the meantime it had been decided to try and steer the *Evdokia* to the relative safety of an anchorage in Plettenberg Bay, and Patsiatzis and six crew members decided to stay on board as a skeleton crew while the remaining 16 crew were taken off by the helicopters. This was accomplished under extremely difficult circumstances, and the *Evdokia* was left to battle through mountainous seas in the direction of Cape St Francis.

The next day a massive air search was mounted, but no trace of the vessel could be found. Only on the morning of 13 June was a large oil slick surrounded by debris found floating off the Tsitsikamma coast, and it was presumed that the *Evdokia* had sunk. Later that morning, however, two Air Force helicopters found the shattered remains of the vessel at the base of towering cliffs a little to the east of the Storms River mouth. A figure was seen clinging to the rocks, and a rescuer was winched down from one of the helicopters to save the man, who turned out to be Hitolio Castro Ibanez, the third engineer.

He was the only survivor of the seven people who had decided to remain on board, and he later told of how the captain had decided to run the vessel ashore to save the lives of the crew, as he feared that she was about to sink at any moment; he had thought the shore opposite them was sandy. The *Evdokia* had run ashore at 18h15 on the 12th and had begun to break up almost immediately. Policemen were airlifted on to the rocks to try and find any other survivors, but six people had drowned in the most violent modern shipwreck on the coast of South Africa. Within a matter of hours the incredible power of the waves had broken up the ship totally.

Courage can take on many forms, as we have seen, and certainly a recurring theme amongst the tale of shipwrecks is the drive of the survivors to make it back to safety. Many – the fittest – did, but one must spare a thought for those who died in the attempt, and also for the captains of vessels who often had to make choices that were in the interests of those for whom they felt a responsibility, even though it meant that they themselves perished.

The wreck of the Jane Davie

Three hours after leaving Durban on Sunday, 26 May 1872, the German steamer *Bismarck*, under the command of Captain Staats, encountered the tail end of a cyclone which had left a heavy and confused sea running. During the approach to East London on Tuesday he saw a sailing vessel lying with her bow inshore amongst the breakers, but as there did not seem to be anyone on board, he proceeded on his way. At the port confusion reigned, for the storm had taken its toll. Six sailing vessels (the *Elaine*, *Emma*, *Martha*, *Queen of May*, *Refuge* and *Sharp*) and the steamer *Quanza* were all ashore. A signal from the shore was then received, asking for assistance for a vessel in distress to the east. The *Bismarck* immediately returned to the place where the vessel ashore had been spotted and, on coming closer, saw that it was a British iron schooner, the *Jane Davie*. Men were clinging to the rigging, but her mainmast was gone and it was clear that the vessel was beginning to break up. A volunteer crew from the *Bismarck* manned the vessel's starboard lifeboat, but it was clear that they would not be able to come close to the *Jane Davie*, so the *Bismarck* returned to East London. On Wednesday, 29 May the port lifeboat, under the command of the harbour-master, George Walker, made it out to the *Bismarck*, which then towed the boat to the scene of the disaster, where Captain Le Gallais, his wife and two-year-old child, and 17 crew members were rescued. The captain's wife was eight months pregnant, and she and her child had been lashed to a stanchion for three nights and two days to prevent them from being swept overboard. On board the *Bismarck* Mrs Le Gallais fainted and was immediately taken to a cabin and attended to. Her child, however, besides complaining of the cold, was none the worse for wear and was soon running up and down the decks.

*I*t is true that many vessels bearing valuable cargoes have been wrecked on the coast of South Africa, and that many attempts have been made to recover all or part of such cargoes. While it is a temptation to speak of treasure hunts when dealing with such salvage operations, especially when specie is involved, the term must, however, be used with great circumspection. In the case of the *Vis*, for instance, we have seen that most of the treasure in the form of specie aboard the vessel was salvaged fairly soon after the wrecking, and this salvage left very little 'treasure' to be hunted (see p 65). In other cases vessels were reputed to be carrying treasure, while in fact this was not so. The concept of what actually constitutes treasure must also be critically examined. Would one for instance consider the value of a modern cargo such as the copper which was recently salvaged from the *Evdokia* or the *Cariboo*, or the tons of tin recovered from various tin wrecks, to be treasure, or would treasure necessarily have to be a hoard of gold, jewels and silver? If the latter, then treasure hunters are in for a lean time.

It is quite probable that diligent research may throw up a number of wreck sites where interesting finds could still be made — but here the problem arises of finding the correct wreck site. Some, like that of the *Birkenhead*, are well-documented and relatively easy to trace; some, like that of the *Grosvenor*, have attracted the attention of many treasure hunters, but have failed to yield any significant finds; and some, like that of the *Middelburg*, have been reworked after earlier expeditions have done their worst — and still yielded finds that where worth while, though on a small scale. What is without doubt, however, is that the merest hint of a possible treasure is enough to quicken the pulse of many, and that treasure hunters have been prepared to speculate — and lose — large amounts of money in chasing after rainbows, as the sorry tale of the *Dorothea* graphically demonstrates.

Many misconceptions abound, too, about the nature of a wreck site and the valuables that one is likely to find. The schoolboy idea of the classic sunken galleon with all sails set, containing beckoning treasure-chests protected by a glowering octopus persists right into adulthood, and someone who has dived on wrecks is often asked: What do you do with the human remains that you find? Is it dark inside the wrecks? How do you protect yourself from sharks? The raising of the well-preserved hulls of the *Vasa*, which sank in 1628 in 35 m of water in Stockholm harbour, and of the *Mary Rose*, recently raised in the Solent, have done much to strengthen this naive notion of a shipwreck, for both hulls were largely intact. This was, however because they had come to rest in calm waters and had been buried in soft mud and sand, where the rough and dangerous surf conditions found on most wreck sites were absent. The truth is, however, that in most cases very little concrete evidence of the wrecked vessel is to be seen at a wreck site.

One of the most noteworthy of modern South African finds was that of the *Middelburg*, which sank in Saldanha Bay in 1781. It provides a good example of what can be regarded as a treasure hunt, even though the 'treasure' which was recovered consisted not of gold or silver coins, but mainly of Chinese porcelain.

Early in 1781 the Governor at the Cape, Baron Joachim van Plettenberg, received word from Europe that Holland, France and Spain had united with the American colonies in a war against Britain. He realised that the position of the settlement at the Cape was very vulnerable: should a British task force arrive before the much-needed reinforcements that had been promised, an entire fleet of homeward-bound merchantmen and their valuable Eastern cargoes then at anchor in Table Bay could well fall into British hands. In order to protect the vessels against this possibility, he ordered them to proceed to the safe anchorage of Saldanha Bay in May 1781.

The commodore of the East-Indiaman fleet was Captain Gerrit Harmeyer, of the vessel *Hoogkarspel*, and he was ordered to set the whole fleet of five vessels on fire should they be discovered by the British. The order was passed on to the commanders of the other four vessels, the *Middelburg*, *Honkoop*, *Parel* and *Dankbaar-*

The Middelburg *treasure*

The following pieces of china were recovered from the *Middelburg* after the Dodds brothers worked on the wreck in 1969. Most of the items were auctioned in Cape Town and Johannesburg in 1972 and were eagerly bought.

9 glazed Chinese figurines
2 white vases
9 white saki bowls
10 copper-glazed blue and white bowls
8 blue and white bowls
16 copper-glazed bowls
1 blue and white plate
8 blue and white crocus pots
2 white saucers
1 small blue and white octagonal bowl
5 white cups
9 copper-glazed blue and white saucers
1 octagonal blue and white cup and saucer
13 copper-glazed blue and white cups
10 copper-glazed cups
7 copper-glazed saucers
13 blue and white saucers
51 blue and white tea-cups
4 white lids surmounted by Chinese lions
2 blue and white vase-lids surmounted by blue Chinese lions
2 white lids
6 large blue and white lids
8 small blue and white lids
1 white rain or tear-drop vase with Chinese animal mounted on lid

Captain Charles Gardiner of the South African Salvage Association, flanked by two of his divers during salvage operations on the wreck of the Middelburg in Saldanha Bay in 1906. The desolate rocks of Hoedjies Point can be seen in the background. Apart from the Middelburg, Captain Gardiner was involved in many other salvage attempts, notably on the Dorothea in 1898. (Cape Times Weekly)

heid, but only the captain of the *Middelburg*, Van Gennep, and his first mate, Abraham de Smidt, made any serious attempt at preparations to obey the instructions.

During the next few weeks the vessels remained at anchor in Hoedjies Bay. Although the fleet was supposedly on standby in case of emergency, the crews in fact relaxed and went hunting. François le Vaillant, a French naturalist later to become famous for his books on his travels in South Africa and for his paintings of birds, had placed all his possessions (including his priceless collection of natural history specimens) on board the *Middelburg*, which he had joined in Table Bay after shipping out from Holland on the *Held Woltemade*, which had left Texel on 19 December 1780 and soon after her arrival had also been sent to Saldanha Bay to hide from the British. No doubt he was delighted at this opportunity to study the fauna and flora of the desolate bay.

In early June the French admiral Pierre André de Suffren arrived at the Cape, bringing the reinforcements necessary for its defence against a British attack. He then sailed on to India to engage the British there, satisfied that the Cape was in safe hands. A despatch was sent to Saldanha Bay to inform Harmeyer that the reinforcements had arrived and that he was to await a naval escort before proceeding on his journey home. On 28 June 1781 the *Held Woltemade* sailed out of the bay to continue on her voyage to Ceylon. Three days later she met a frigate flying the French flag, which signalled her for information. The unsuspecting Dutch officers told the captain of the vessel all about the Dutch merchantmen lying at anchor in Saldanha Bay – and then watched in dismay as the French flag was hauled down to be replaced by the British one. The vessel was the British man-of-war *Active*, under the command of Captain MacKenzie, and the furious Dutchmen had no choice but to surrender in the face of primed British cannon. The East Indiaman and her valuable cargo were eventually taken to Plymouth as a prize of war.

Active then rejoined the British task force under the command of Commodore George Johnstone, and on 21 July 1781 the British fleet sailed into Saldanha Bay flying French flags. When the bored Dutch sailors first saw the fleet arriving they were jubilant, as they thought that these were the long-awaited reinforcements due to escort them safely home to Holland. As the fleet passed Marcus Island, however, the French flags were hauled down and British flags run up. Led by the *Romney*, the fleet then attacked and British cannon-balls ripped into the unprepared Dutch merchantmen.

In great panic the Dutch sailors belatedly tried to carry out the emergency orders, but only the more alert *Middelburg* crew was successful. Blazing furiously, she was towed in towards Hoedjies Point; her crew abandoned her and soon after she blew up when the flames reached her powder-store. The British sailors were able to extinguish the fires on the other vessels, which were taken as prizes by the British commodore, but the *Middelburg* sank like a stone, her valuable homeward-bound cargo destined to be buried beneath the soft sand. The loss of an outward-bound and five homeward-bound vessels was a serious financial loss to the Dutch East India Company and no doubt contributed towards its bankruptcy.

Salvage operators soon became interested in the sunken cargo. The first recorded salvage attempt was begun in 1788, when a burgher of Cape Town, Gerrit Munnik, brought up a few pieces of china, and the next occurred a century later in 1888, when Captain Teague recovered large quantities of tin and china. The wreck site was next visited in 1895 by Captain Lea and Charles Adams; during this attempt the diver Karl Ericsen recovered about 300 items of china. In 1906 an expedition under Captain Gardiner engaged in salvage operations; during the course of this attempt the diver, William Smith, used explosives, ostensibly to kill a huge octopus, and in consequence much of the china on the site must have been damaged. Still, this expedition recovered three cannon, china cups, saucers, vases and tea-chests. In 1907 Captain Gardiner returned with a salvage vessel, the *Alfred Nobel*, and continued to work on the wreck. On their return to Cape Town the team was very secretive and only showed some muskets, cutlasses and boarding-pikes they had found; it was also reported that plates bearing the Dutch East India Company insignia had been recovered from the wreck.

The best-documented salvage attempt was begun in July 1969 when the brothers Billy and Reggie Dodds of Cape Town decided to salvage the remaining *Middelburg* cargo. They had found the wreck two years previously, but had decided to keep it a

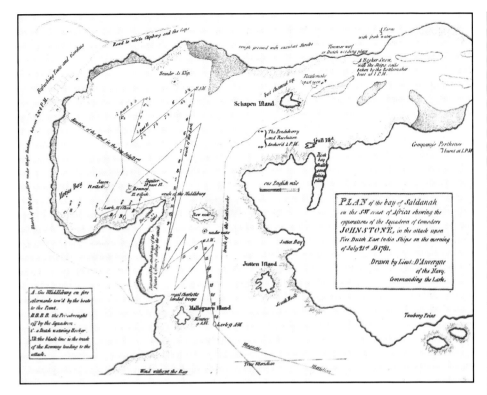

secret until they were ready to mount a proper salvage operation. Anchoring their boat over the site, they spent the next two weeks removing the overburden from the hull by means of a powerful air-lift (see p 108), fed by a compressor parked on the nearby headland. They found that the *Middelburg*'s timbers were in good condition and most of her lower hull structure was intact. After having removed the sand right down to the lowest part of the keel, the remaining hull was found to be over 30 m long.

During the excavation 198 intact pieces of Ch'ien Lung china (1736-1795) were found, including tea-cups, a fine tear-drop vase and nine Chinese mandarin figurines. These figurines were found in close proximity to each other on top of the hull, covered with sand. When the sand was removed, it seemed as if they were gazing up at the moon – on the day the first men stepped onto its surface. The china needed no elaborate cleaning and was in perfect condition; later it was sold at auction to collectors. In addition to the china they found many cast iron cannon (one of them mosaic-ed with broken porcelain shards), conglomerated tea and the vessel's pig-iron ballast. As soon as the brothers left the site, the sand gradually began to shift back and once again covered the timbers. Recently a breakwater has been built out from Hoedjies Point and this has caused a sandy beach to build up over the site; at low tide one can walk dry-shod over her resting-place. Perhaps one day her hull will be excavated and put on display in Saldanha: she is certainly worthy of such attention.

Legends about treasure abound, and even though most have virtually no basis in fact, the mere possibility of quick riches is enough to send pulses racing. The alleged 'treasure' of coins and other valuable items that supposedly went down with the English East Indiaman *Grosvenor* in 1782 has become such a legend – and almost certainly an exaggerated one. Most homeward-bound vessels like the *Grosvenor* did not carry hoards of coins aboard, apart, possibly, from personal fortunes amassed by officials returning to Europe after a spell of duty in the East.

Yet over the years stories have been told and retold of how the *Grosvenor* wreck lay intact beneath the sand loaded with jewels, bars of gold and silver, and even the fabulous 'Peacock Throne' of the great Moguls, said to be worth £6 500 000. Many people have believed these stories, but even though they have put into operation some of the most imaginative yet impractical ideas for recovering the alleged riches, it is clear that no great treasure was ever recovered from the site.

The only notable success on the *Grosvenor* site, in fact, was accomplished by Captain Sidney Turner and Lieutenant Beddoes of the Natal Pioneers in 1880 when,

Above, left: A contemporary map of Saldanha Bay, annotated to explain the movements of the various vessels involved in the Battle of Saldanha on 21 July 1781. (Cape Archives)
Below: Curious onlookers examine an encrusted cannon recovered from the wreck of the *Middelburg* during salvage operations in 1906. (Cape Times Weekly)

Top: The Directorate of the Grosvenor Treasure Recovery Company. The leader of the expedition, Capt Jameson, is seated in the centre, with Harry Lyons on his right.
Above, centre: *The mouth of the tunnel which was dug in an abortive attempt to reach the famed treasure aboard the* Grosvenor. *The tunnel filled with water and the attempt was abandoned. (Ferguson Collection)*
Above: *Rocks and wire rope are all that remain of a failed attempt to build a coffer dam around the wreck of the* Grosvenor. *(Ferguson Collection)*

after blasting the site, they recovered cannon and some coins. And in 1896 Alexander Lindsay, a local trader, dredged pools close to the site and found 340 gold and silver coins beneath the gravel and sand.

Over the next 75 years many attempts have been made to recover the reputed treasure. One such occurred shortly after the Anglo-Boer War, when Alexander Lindsay and his partner, B. Malraison, a solicitor on the Rand, attempted a salvage, but the operation ended in complete failure. A few years later, in 1907, Harry S. Lyons, a journalist of Barberton, became chairman of a syndicate known as the '*Grosvenor* Treasure Recovery Company', which used divers and a dredger to locate and explore the wreck. They recovered some gold star-pagodas, Venetian ducats and many pieces of silver, but in the process one of the divers lost his life.

In 1921 the 'Webster Syndicate' was established. Its members sold shares for one shilling each and canvassed the whole country for funds, to their credit explaining that the venture was a gamble, though they made a point of mentioning the vast treasures that were reputed to be in the wreck. The gullible public soon parted with enough money for the company to make a start, and the syndicate embarked on what is perhaps the most outlandish salvage attempt ever carried out.

Engineers were employed to dig a 150-metre tunnel from the shore towards the supposed site of the wreck, with the purpose of salvaging the cargo by moving to and from the site by this means. By 1923 the tunnel was over 120 m long, even though the exact position of the wreck had still not been pinpointed. At this point divers went into operation and marked with bouys the site where, according to the chairman of the syndicate, the *Grosvenor* lay. The tunnel was aimed in the direction of these bouys, but shortly afterwards became flooded. Nothing daunted, the syndicate actually started another tunnel, but after excavating for 70 m they ran out of money and abandoned the site. An American named Pitcairn purchased all the plant and machinery from the bankrupt 'Webster Syndicate' in 1927, and after installing better machinery dug yet another tunnel, but this one, too, was later abandoned. At some stage an attempt at salvage was also made by building a stone coffer dam around the site, presumably with the intent to pump out the water inside its protection in order to gain access to the site, but this attempt was likewise abandoned.

The peak of fantasy was reached in 1964 when a 33-year-old Belgian, Guido de Backer, floated a £200 000 salvage company with the aim of building a revolutionary steel-lined tunnel with a hydraulically operated door, designed by Jan Haalmeyer, a Dutch engineer. After the sand covering the wreck had been pumped out through the tunnel, divers, led by Manganelli, a famous French aquanaut, were to leave the door and enter the hold of the *Grosvenor* – but the plan never materialised.

One of the shareholders, a German by the name of Helmuth Frevel, sued De Backer for £4 500, which he claimed he had paid for shares in the salvage company. Frevel stated that he had received neither shares in the company nor a refund when the tunnel attempt was abandoned. In the Johannesburg Regional Court there was an uproar when it was recounted that while on a business trip to Europe, De Backer had washed his socks in champagne and had bathed in champagne, wine and beer. Frevel, it was revealed, had himself participated in these ablutions, though he had limited himself to bathing in beer!

In 1968 a further salvage attempt was made when three Germans leased a 4,8 km stretch of the coast and erected a fence around a camp site, protected by Pondo guards. The leader of the team was none other than Frevel, convinced that the other attempts had been concentrated in the wrong area and that he would be successful. He hired a professional diver from Durban to find the real site, but the expedition failed to find any treasure, and after many months of fruitless activity they left the site. Now rusty machinery, abandoned tunnels and the remains of the coffer dam stand as monuments to the faith that human beings can place in a legend.

Another famous wreck that has been the subject of persisting legend is that of the *Birkenhead*, which struck Birkenhead Rock near Danger Point and sank in 1852; a large consignment of gold coins was reputed to have been lost on the wreck, even though no official proof existed that it was loaded aboard. The only concrete evidence of the loss of money came from a survivor, Colour Sergeant O'Neill of the 91st Foot (a survivor also of the wrecking of the *Abercrombie Robinson* ten years previously), who claimed that immediately after the wrecking he was paid in Spanish

Left: *'Women and children first.' A painting immortalising the heroic action of the gallant men aboard HMS Birkenhead.*
Below: *Notice advertising the sale of the Birkenhead wreck by public auction.*
Below, centre: *A cap badge of the 43rd Light Infantry, one of many recovered from the site of the wreck of HMS Birkenhead over the years. (M. Turner)*
Bottom: *Bronze window parts recovered from the stern section of HMS Birkenhead. The wreck has been intensively worked on by salvors over the years. (M. Turner)*

WRECK OF H.M. STEAMER
"BIRKENHEAD,"
WRECKED OFF DANGER POINT,
Near the Farm of Sir Robt. Stanford.

ON MONDAY MORNING next, the 29th instant, will be sold, by Public Auction, on the Beach of DANGER POINT, the above Vessel, as she lies in the Sea, with RIGGING, SPARS, YARDS, &c., &c., STORES and PROVISIONS, and whatever may be on Board.

ALSO,
WEARING APPAREL,
Consisting of Naval and Military Clothes, Shirts, Shoes, Stockings, and whatever may have been washed on Shore from the above Wreck.

R. J. JONES, Auctioneer.

dollars, which led him to believe that the normal gold payment was lost in the disaster. Perhaps the real seeds for the tale of the legendary treasure were sown a year earlier, in 1851, when the *Birkenhead* had arrived in Algoa Bay with a large pay-packet for the army. It is true that a note found in the British Archives refers to a large consignment of gold stored secretly in the powder-room of the *Birkenhead* – but this gold has never been recovered.

What is certain is that at the time of the wrecking the Admiralty did not appear to be worried about the loss of the *Birkenhead*, as she was sold by public auction by agents of the Admiralty at the Cape. The first attempt at salvage occurred early in 1854, when a team of divers led by A.H. Adams worked on the wreck and found papers and engraved silverware belonging to Colonel Seton, which were returned to his family. In addition many other items were found, but unfortunately no record of them was kept.

Towards the end of the century the government gave permission to a Mr Bandmann at the Cape to dive for the £240 000 in gold reputed to be on board, but it was made clear than any relics belonging to the officers or men on board the *Birkenhead* were to be handed over to their relatives, and any treasure found was to be split up

The sailing notice of the Birkenhead, *and the official notice of her wrecking.* (South African Commercial Advertiser)

Unfound treasure

Many of the wrecks on the coast of South Africa are known to have been carrying valuable cargoes, but for various reasons not all of these have been salvaged. Some lie buried deep beneath the sand, some lie in restricted areas closed to divers, and in many cases the records are so vague that it seems likely that the wrecks will be found only by chance. However, the following is a list of wrecks that could, if found, prove worthwhile to the salvor.

HNMS **Amsterdam**: Wrecked in Algoa Bay in 1817. Believed to have been carrying a valuable consignment of 'rare treasure from Java for the king of the Netherlands'. The wreck lies in deep sand.

Brederode: Lost in the vicinity of Cape Agulhas in 1785. Believed to have been carrying a large cargo of tin and Chinese porcelain. May lie in deep water.

Dageraad: Wrecked on the west point of Robben Island in 1694. Was carrying chests of specie salvaged from the *Gouden Buis*. Lies within a restricted area.

Nieuw Haarlem: Wrecked in Table Bay in 1647. Was carrying a large cargo of Chinese porcelain. Lies in sand. Shards of Chinese porcelain have been found on the beach a little north of the Milnerton lighthouse.

RMS **Kafir**: Wrecked a little south of Olifantsbos Point in 1878. Was carrying a box of specie belonging to the Portuguese government.

Nossa Senhora dos Milagros: Wrecked in Struis Bay in 1686. Was carrying a large amount of jewellery. Probably lies in deep sand.

São Gonçalo: Wrecked in Plettenberg Bay in 1630. Was carrying a large amount of Chinese porcelain. Probably lies buried beneath deep sand.

Timor: Wrecked on the southern tip of Robben Island in 1856. Was carrying a cargo of tin. Some was salvaged soon after the wrecking, but much probably remains. Lies within a restricted area.

SS **Waldensian**: Wrecked on Struis Point in 1862. The Christy Minstrels were on board, and one of their number, Mr Joe Brown, lost a silver belt encrusted with precious stones.

Musquash	Duncan	Dobie & Co	For Sale
Onward	Claydon	A. Croll	
Osprey	Way	Phillips & King	Algoa Bay
Adderley	Herbert	Broadway & Co	Mossel Bay
Sans Pareille	Bawden	R. P. Dobie	
CUTTER.			
Fox	Bruce	Granger & Co	

Sailed out of Simon's Bay.

Feb. 10. H.N.M.S. *Zwaluw*, Ct. Noorduyn, to Texel.
25. H.MS. *Grecian*, Hon. Keane, to Cruising.
25. H.M. St. *Birkenhead*, Salmond, Esq., to East London.
25. *Zoe*, Cameron, to Akyab.
26. H.M. St. *Styx*, Comr. Hall. to East London.

Vessels in Simon's Bay.

Vessels.	Commanders.	Agents.	Destination
SHIPS.			
H. M. S. Se-ringapatam	J.T. Russel R.N., Master comnd.	—	(Hulk)
H. M. S. Castor	Cmre Wyvill	—	
Schoon Ver-bond (Dt.)	Schuymer	Thomson & Co	Amsterdam
H. M St. Rha-damanthus	Belam, Esq.	—	
H.M.Bg.Pickle	Lt. Campbell	—	
BARKS.			
Sovereign	King	Dickson & Co	London
Holland (Dt.)	Dekker	Thomson & Co	
Sir John Falstaff	Rowell	Thomson & Co	Portsmouth

Arrived in Port Elizabeth.

February 18.—*Wanderer*, brig, 174 tons, N. Glendining, from Table Bay 10th February, to this port. Cargo sundries. Passengers, Mrs. Brown, family, and servant

el adjourned till 12 o'clock on Thursday.

WRECK OF H. M. STEAMER "BIRKENHEAD."

OFFICIAL INFORMATION.

Colonial Office, 28th February, 1852,
10 o'Clock A.M.

The following Documents, received from Commodore WYVILL, are published, as affording some relief to public anxiety.

(Signed) JOHN MONTAGU,
Secretary to Government.

" *Castor*," Simon's Bay, 27th February, 1852.
To His Excellency Lieut.-General
SIR HARRY G. W. SMITH, Bart.,
Governor and Commander-in-Chief,
&c., &c., &c.

Sir,—It is with much pain I have to inform Your Excellency of the total loss of Her Majesty's Steam Ship *Birkenhead*, at 2 o'clock on the morning of the 26th instant, near to Point Danger—and I regret to add that from the statement given by Dr. Culhane, Assistant Surgeon of the ship, it would appear that only about 70 persons are saved out of 630 souls, nine of whom have landed, but the other are in two Boats and had proceeded seaward, to be picked up by a sailing Vessel.

I have dispatched the *Rhadamanthus* to the scene of this fearful disaster to afford all possible relief, and to search for the missing Boats.

As it is possible they may be compelled to effect a landing, I would be glad if your Excellency gave instructions to the Resident Magistrates and Field-Cornets, on the Coast, to keep a look-out for them, and render every necessary assistance.

I beg to enclose Dr. Culhane's statement.
And have the honour to be,
Your Excellency's most obedient Servant,
C. WYVILL, Commodore.

Since writing the above, the *Rhadamanthus* has towed in the Schooner *Lioness*, which vessel picked up the two Boats mentioned. The sufferers, one hundred and sixteen in number, are at present on board the *Castor*, and the *Rhadamanthus* has again proceeded to the scene of the wreck. I annex a list of persons saved. Dr. Bowen, Staff-Surgeon, reports that several of the Soldiers reached the land on rafts.

Copy,—C. WYVILL.
Statement of Dr. CULHANE, *of Her Majesty's late Steam Ship* "*Birkenhead.*"

in the proportion of one-third to the government and two-thirds to the salvor – even though the authorities at this stage had no knowledge of any money lost on the *Birkenhead*. The salvage attempt ended in failure.

Various divers continued to search her remains; in recent times one of these was the well-known Cape personality Tromp van Diggelen, who began diving operations in June 1958. His team reported that the bow and most of the midships section were badly broken up and overgrown, and that the large paddle-wheels still stood upright on the sea-bed; the stern section could, however, not be found. Van Diggelen and a group of businessmen formed the 'Birkenhead Syndicate' to try and find the treasure on board, but they managed to recover only some anchors and a variety of copper and brass fittings to cover their costs. The gold, the ship's bell and the stern section eluded them.

Since then many amateur and professional divers, including the Cape diver Brian Clark, have continued to recover items from the wreck. Explosive charges have been employed, but no gold has been reported. Then, in January 1985, a group of divers announced in the press that they had identified the stern section in 30 m of water not far from Birkenhead Rock, and in early 1986 a newly formed company, the 'Depth Recovery Unit' of Johannesburg, began excavating the wreck. A small saturation diving system (see p 89) was mounted on board the tug *Causeway Adventurer*, but it could not be used because of the heavy swells on site. The expensive salvage operation, aimed at the gold and backed up by extensive press coverage, had little success; the few gold coins found were obviously from an officer's chest and not part of the legendary treasure. Earlier divers had by this time removed most of the bronze artefacts from the site, so in all little of value was found and the expedition soon sank into obscurity as press coverage dried up.

For sheer persistence coupled with the greatest folly, and for the greatest effort for the least return, few examples can top the various attempts at reaching the supposed gold hoard aboard the *Dorothea*. The story is littered with broken dreams, and begins towards the end of the last century.

In 1896 a vessel then named the *Ernestine* off-loaded a general cargo from Hamburg in Cape Town harbour. In the process it was discovered that acid had spilled into her hold and had eaten into her hull, causing her to leak badly. She was repaired and sold to a Mr Camp of East London for £800. Her next voyage took her to the South Sea Islands, where she was loaded with copra to be taken to Antwerp, and on her subsequent outward-bound voyage she brought a cargo of Baltic railway sleepers to Lourenço Marques (the present Maputo). On entering Delagoa Bay she struck a reef and the captain was compelled to run her ashore to prevent her from sinking. Her cargo was off-loaded, and she was condemned and sold to a Mr Pitt as a hulk.

The *Ernestine* lay mouldering on a river bank until a Johannesburg firm headed by Dr Kelly bought her, supposedly for fishing purposes. She was renamed the *Dorothea*, was registered under the American flag and was patched up by Captain George Vibert before she left for Durban under the command of Captain Harold Mathisson for more thorough repairs to be effected. On her departure a rumour started to circulate that she was carrying 120 000 ounces of illicit Transvaal gold that Dr Kelly's syndicate had supposedly been buying up.

Not surprisingly, the *Dorothea* soon started to leak badly, and in the night of Monday, 31 January 1898 she was abandoned at sea about 4 nautical miles (8 km) east of Cape Vidal, and ran ashore at that cape soon afterwards. On the strength of the rumours of the gold aboard, various salvage groups showed an interest in her almost immediately. Three months after the wrecking the salvage vessel *Alfred Nobel*, under the command of Captain Charles Gardiner, was chartered by the Natal Government to investigate. The salvors found the wreck with only the masts showing above the water, but bad weather prevented them from doing any work on her.

In 1899 the next expedition arrived in a small steam fishing-boat, the *Nidaros*, under the command of Captain Wakeford, who two years previously had lost his vessel *Clan Gordon* on the Tenedos Reef on the Zululand coast. The salvage operation was financed by a syndicate of the original owners of the *Dorothea* and some leading Durban shipping men and was well equipped, with a surf-boat, diver and experienced crew. They found the wreck, and the diver descended and began his search. To his great excitement he discovered some bars of yellow metal, but these proved to be copper. On their second visit to the wreck, disaster struck when a large wave hit the work-boat and it capsized. The diver, Captain Wakeford and two other men were drowned. No gold was reported found, but one cannot help but wonder whether the original owners would have taken such risks and have gone to such expense if the wreck had been completely worthless.

Another salvage attempt followed soon afterwards when in July 1899 the tug *Hansa*, commanded by the same Captain Vibert who had repaired the *Dorothea* at Lourenço Marques, sailed for the wreck; it was arranged that a land party would occupy a shore base. When the *Hansa* reached the wreck, she lowered a surf-boat, but it capsized and was lost. She then sailed back to Durban to fetch another boat, but on her return to the wreck site the weather was found to be too bad to start operations, so this attempt was shelved until the following year.

Even the outbreak of the Anglo-Boer War did not interrupt the treasure-hunters; in December 1899 the *Countess of Carnarvon*, a 29-ton wooden tug (later to be wrecked in Algoa Bay during the Great South-East Gale of 1902) was chartered to proceed to the wreck by a syndicate headed by Mr Hall. She was commanded by Captain J.P. Nansson, and some experienced divers accompanied the expedition. The group recovered some 'curios', which fired the imagination of further groups, and in July 1901 yet another salvage attempt was made, this time from the salvage vessel *Fenella* under the command of the self-same Captain Vibert. Among those on board were a number of policemen to oversee the salvage operation. Close on the heels of this expedition came the next hopeful: In December 1903 the Hon. Thomas Hassall left Durban harbour on board the steam-tug *Ulundi*. He had obtained Government support and in addition to the tug he had hired an expert diver, but he was soon back home, counting his losses.

The most tragic attempt to recover the *Dorothea* treasure took place in August 1904, when the *Penguin*, a small steamer commanded by J. Jorgenson and carrying a well-equipped salvage party led by a Scandinavian, C.E. Frees, foundered nearly 7 nautical miles (13 km) from the shore off the Mhlatuze River. The sinking cost the lives of eleven men, yet this did not deter the promotors of the expedition. At the end of October 1904 they sent a second vessel, the *Good Hope*, to Cape Vidal; supported by a large land party housed in tents on the beach, they began to work on the wreck. In the meantime others had been busy drumming up support for yet another expedition, and in December 1904 the '*Dorothea* Treasure Trove Syndicate', headed by Sir Edward Murray, was formed in the Transvaal; they believed that the gold was packed in twelve boxes and three leather bags and cemented below the main mast of the wreck. Unfortunately, however, no gold was ever reported found by this group.

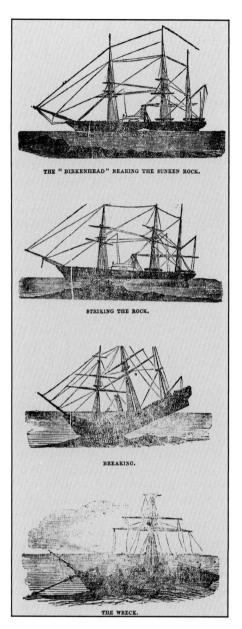

THE " BIRKENHEAD " NEARING THE SUNKEN ROCK.

STRIKING THE ROCK.

BREAKING.

THE WRECK.

Above: A depiction of four stages during the wrecking of the Birkenhead. *(Illustrated London News)*
Below: A photograph believed to be that of the Dorothea *shortly after she wrecked on 31 January 1898, reputedly with a fortune in gold aboard.*

Many more companies have come and gone – all of them bankrupted. The largest, the S.A. Salvage Company, was worth £25 000 and planned to salvage not only the treasure of the *Dorothea*, but also that of other wrecks, including the *Middelburg*, and they intended using Captain Gardiner and the *Alfred Nobel*. Yet another syndicate was formed in 1908, calling themselves 'The *Dorothea* Barque Treasure Trove Syndicate Limited', headed by S.E. Hall, who had organised the *Countess of Carnarvon* expedition in 1899. He hired a crack diver, S. Abrahamson, and they stayed at the site for six weeks in the summer of 1908, but nothing was reported as having been found.

After this feverish burst of activity the wreck was largely forgotten for many years. Then, in 1962 and 1966, teams of divers once more tried to get at the gold, but nothing was revealed. Even today divers periodicaly visit the site.

A common thread in all these attempts, not only on the *Dorothea*, but on the *Grosvenor* and *Birkenhead* as well, is the immense amount of effort and money that was expended for so little return. Unless one of the expeditions actually found a hoard of gold and quietly removed it without telling anybody – possible, perhaps, but highly unlikely – then people were prepared, time and again, to risk their savings and their lives in a chase after rainbows. It is probable that treasure does exist somewhere, but it will need diligent research, a professional approach and a lot of luck for this to be discovered one day – and as has been amply demonstrated, the chances of failure are much higher than the chances of success. Still, human nature being what it is, more treasure-hunting attempts are likely to be reported in the newspapers in years to come.

Left: A white teardrop vase recovered by the Dodds brothers from the wreck of the Middelburg. (M. Turner)
Below: Rusty machinery at the site of the wreck of the Grosvenor *stands as mute testimony to the gullibility of men who believed in the legend of a vast treasure lost beneath the sand. (Peter Sachs)*

The treasure of the Fame

While many men have spent long years and huge amounts of money searching for real or imagined treasures, one of the more successful recoveries of treasure on the coast of South Africa was the result of an accidental discovery. In 1965 the Bell brothers, George and James, were looking for perlemoen in the dense kelp beds opposite Graaff's Pool in Sea Point when they came across the scattered remains of an old sailing-ship in the deep rocky gullies. The two began excavating and recovered a large number of British and Indian gold and silver coins. The latter included Spanish-American silver portrait-dollars and silver Indian rupees, and in addition copper Indian coins and British pennies were found. The site also yielded silver spoons and forks, gold jewellery and watch-cases, nails and a broken ship's bell. The remains proved to be those of the 629-ton British vessel *Fame* which was wrecked on 14 June 1822 while leaving Table Bay on her way to Britain from India. On board were a number of prominent people returning home after a spell of duty in the East, among them Francis Farewell: after the wrecking he decided to stay on at the Cape, and eventually established a trading post in the Bay of Natal, the start of what eventually became the city of Durban. The following gold coins were recovered by the Bell brothers:

British: guineas, one-third guineas, sovereigns, half sovereigns
English East India Company: mohurs, half mohurs, one-third mohurs, one-quarter mohurs
Madras: two pagodas, one pagodas
Hindustani: one-quarter mohurs, one-eighth mohurs
Murshidabad: one mohurs, half mohurs
Arcot: one mohurs
Mysore: one pagodas, one fanams
Travancore: one fanams

A gold English East India Company mohur recovered from the Fame. (M. Turner)

Part 2

SALVAGE

Chapter 7

Development of Salvage Methods

For many years salvage operations on the coast of South Africa consisted of little more than pitching a tent opposite the site of a wreck, posting guards to keep away unwanted visitors, and collecting anything that may have washed ashore. Obviously only a small amount of cargo could be saved this way, as only cargo light enough to float would eventually wash up, and much of value, for instance specie, tin, lead and copper was consequently lost. Gradually this passive method of salvage gave way to more active methods, and the use of these in South Africa closely followed the development of various pieces of diving gear and techniques overseas. For the purpose of this chapter it must, however, be kept in mind that only wrecks actually on the coast are included in the book, which means that some devices, such as the diving bell, which is used exclusively for deep-sea recoveries, were never successfully used in salvage operations on vessels included in the text.

One of the earliest recorded active salvage operations in South Africa took place a mere thirty years after the establishment of the permanent Dutch East India Company settlement at the Cape. On 18 June 1682 three weary English sailors arrived at the Castle in Table Bay with the news that their vessel, with a crew of a hundred on board, had been wrecked ten days earlier a little east of Quoin Point at a place known to-day as 'Die Dam'. Ten or eleven of the crew had drowned, but the rest had saved themselves on rafts. The captain, Robert Brown, had been left at a Hottentot camp they had passed; he had fallen ill and had been shown great kindness by the Hottentot chief Klaas.

The *Johanna*, a vessel of 550 tons launched in 1671 and mounting 36 cast iron guns, was named after the Johanna Islands in the Comoros Group. She had left the Kentish Downs on 24 February 1682 on a voyage to Bengal in the company of four other East-Indiamen: the *Williamson*, *Nathaniel*, *Samson* and *Welvaert*, and prior to the wrecking she had completed five successful voyages to the East. On board was a vast treasure in silver bullion and pieces-of-eight, being carried to the English factories in the Bay of Bengal in 70 chests.

The Dutch, who showed the wrecked Englishmen great kindness, sent a wagon to the kraal of the Hottentot chief to fetch Captain Brown. Soon afterwards the Governor, Simon van der Stel, learnt that the *Johanna* was carrying specie, and a secret party headed by Olof Bergh, assisted by a certain Calcoen, was sent to the scene of the wreck to attempt to salvage any money or other valuables which may have washed ashore or which could be reached in the hull. They arrived at the wreck site 22 days after the disaster and scouted the beach, where they came across four badly decomposed bodies; after burying these they walked along the beach and were delighted to find some 600 pieces-of-eight scattered among the rocks. A little further along they found a broken money-chest which had, they suspected, been plundered by the Hottentots. A copper kettle, pipes and liquor were also collected and stowed in a tent opposite the wreck.

A few days later a carpenter and a Malay pearl-diver by the name of Pay Mina were sent by wagon to assist them. The pearl-diver set to work and eventually more than 9 000 pieces-of-eight were delivered to Van der Stel, who was doubtless highly pleased. Subsequently a small Cape yacht, the *Jupiter*, was also sent from the Cape to help recover as much of the *Johanna's* equipment as possible. Three months later Bergh arrived back at the Castle with a wagon-load of salvaged items, including the ship's bell.

The limitations of a diver who could stay underwater for three or four minutes at the most were obvious. When a gale hit Table Bay in 1722 and wrecked a complete outward-bound fleet of Dutch merchant vessels – the *Lakenman*, *Rotterdam*, *Schotse Lorrendraaier*, *Standvastigheid* and *Zoetigheid* – much specie was lost in the process, and this caused the Company much concern. Fortunately this time they could call on something of greater use than a pearl-diver to help them recover

Opposite top: *Salvage work in progress on the cargo of the wrecked turret steamer* Clan Monroe *in 1905. (Cape Archives, GA 6539)*
Top: *Two customs officials outside their temporary customs post opposite the wreck of the* Winton *in Table Bay in 1934. (Cape Times)*
Above, centre: *The motor vessel* Winton, *wrecked a little north of the Milnerton lighthouse, Table Bay on 28 July 1934. (Cape Times)*
Above: *A dramatic photograph of the* Winton *burning. (Cape Times)*

some of the specie. In England Jacob Rowe had patented a workable diving-barrel in 1720, and a rival diver, John Lethbridge, had invented a similar machine in 1715. In 1749 Lethbridge described this revolutionary machine in the *Gentleman's Magazine* in the following words:

'It is made of wainscot perfectly round, about six feet in length, about two foot and a half diameter at the head, and about eighteen inches diameter at the foot, and contains about thirty gallons; it is hoop'd with iron hoops without and within to guard against pressure. There are two holes for the arms, and a glass about four inches diameter, and an inch and a quarter thick to look thro', which is fixed in the bottom part, so as to be in a direct line with the eye, two air-holes upon the upper part, into one of which air is conveyed by a pair of bellows, both which are stopt with plugs immediately before going down to the bottom. At the foot part there's a hole to let out water. Sometimes there's a large rope fixed to the back or upper part, by which it's let down, and there's a little line called the signal line, by which the people above are directed what to do, and under it is fix'd a piece of timber as a guard for the glass. I go in with my feet foremost, and when my arms are got thro' the holes, then the head is put on, which is fastened with scrues. It requires 500 wheight to sink it, but take but 15 pound wheight from it and it will buoy upon the surface of the water. I lie straight upon my breast all the time I am in the engine, which hath many times been more than six hours, being frequently refreshed upon the surface by a pair of bellows. I can move it about 12 foot square at the bottom, where I have stayed many times 34 minutes. I have been ten fathom deep many a hundred times, and have been 12 fathom, but with great difficulty.'

The Dutch East India Company showed great interest in Lethbridge and his machinery, and at their request he worked on the outward-bound Dutch East-Indiaman *Slot Ter Hoge*, wrecked in November 1724 on the Portuguese island of Porto Santo, with a fair amount of success. The Company then decided to bring Lethbridge to the Cape from England to try to recover the money lost during the gale of 1722, and in September 1727 he and his diving-barrel arrived at the Cape on board the *Valkenisse*.

Lethbridge's first task after arriving at the Cape was to work on the vessels *Rotterdam* and *Zoetigheid*, and to recover what specie he could. In the relatively calm, protected waters of Table Bay he had a fair amount of success, retrieving seven cannon and 200 bars of silver off the *Rotterdam*, and more than 2 000 silver ducatoons off the *Zoetigheid*.

So pleased were the Company directors that in 1728 they allowed him to proceed to Jutten Island in Saldanha Bay to try to recover the *Merestein* treasure; the Company had been greatly perturbed by the vessel's loss in 1702 (see pp 113-115). However, after many months in the area and only a few dives to his credit, the great swells at the wreck site forced Lethbridge to give up after recovering only a few ducatoons.

Although the diving-barrel method of salvage met with considerable success, it, too, had severe limitations, aspecially as regards manoeuvrability. This problem was largely overcome in the 1820s, when a great leap forward was made in diving techniques with the development of the diving helmet or 'hard hat'. For the first time a diver could move freely on the sea-bed while a constant supply of air was fed to him, enabling him to spend long hours on the work-site. Two of the first helmet divers were Charles Deane and his brother John, who undertook salvage work on the *Mary Rose* and the *Royal George* in the Solent in the 1830s. The famous salvage of German battleships scuttled in Scapa Flow at the end of World War I was undertaken by helmet divers, who were capable of great depths in their cumbersome gear. The record is held by a Royal Navy diver, P.O. Wookey, who reached a depth of over 184 m in 1956.

In South Africa helmet diving equipment was used with great success when, soon after the wrecking of the *Jupiter T.* at Cape Padrone in 1875, helmet divers recovered most of her cargo of tin; and at the *Grosvenor* site, where cannon were successfully recovered, but only after a long wait for flat sea conditions. On the other hand, in the 1880s divers waited for three months to recover the tin off the *L'Aigle* and eventually had to give up because the heavy seas prevalent at this typical surf-line wreck-site tended to throw the divers around too much. Helmet divers had their greatest success in deeper water, for instance in the recovery of copper off the *Hypatia*, a cargo vessel wrecked on Whale Rock in Table Bay in 1929.

It was not until the mid-twentieth century that surf-line wrecks began to yield their treasures. This was made possible by the development after World War II of the breathing valve by Jacques Cousteau and Émile Gagnan, which made self-contained underwater breathing apparatus (scuba) the most popular diving system in use. At present a further refinement of the system is the 'hookah', which eliminates the compressed-air cylinders normally carried on the diver's back and instead consists of a motor-driven, low-pressure compressor which feeds a constant stream of purified air to the diver through a flexible tube. As long as the diver does not work below the safe depth of ten metres (see pp 99-101), he is immune to any ill-effects from decompression sickness and can remain submerged and hard at work, often for up to six hours at a stretch.

Numerous shallow-water wreck sites on the South African coast have been worked using these methods, and indeed even some sites that are considerably deeper. The deepest salvage carried out by modern free divers in South Africa was that of the *Borderer*, lying in 38 m of water in Struis Bay, when the team of Brian Clark and Tubby Gericke successfully raised a large number of tin blocks from the wreck in 1977.

At present a number of modern diving systems are in use throughout the world. Diving-bells, which had been used as early as 1687 by the William Phipps expedition to recover many tons of silver ingots and pieces-of-eight from the homeward-bound Spanish galleon *Nuestra Senora de la Conception* which had been wrecked off Haiti on the legendary Silver Shoal in 1641, are still in use today. When the depth exceeds 50 m, a mixture of helium and oxygen is released into the bell at working depth. When the pressures inside and outside the bell are equal, the hatch at the bottom drops open, and a diver can exit and enter as he wishes.

A great breakthrough has been the development of the saturation method, by which divers are slowly compressed to a little above working depth in a master chamber on board the salvage vessel and are thereafter lowered to the sea-bed and raised again in a diving-bell. Working on a shift basis, divers can stay in this closed system for periods of up to a month at a time, after which only one decompression period is needed. The use of the saturation technique is extremely expensive, however, and it stands to reason that it cannot be used on deep sites unless it is known that the results will make it worthwhile. A saturation system was set up for the latest salvage attempt on the *Birkenhead*. However, the heavy turbulence on the bottom made its use unfeasible.

Below: The salvage of blister copper from the steamer Hypatia *in 1929. (George Young)*
Bottom: *Recovery of cargo from the wreck of the Dutch coaster* Nolloth. *(Ferguson Collection)*

Right: An Oceaneering 'Sam' suit or atmospheric diving system about to be lowered 130 m to the sea-bed from the oil-rig Sedco K. *(M. Turner)*
Below: Scuba diver Simon Gilbert exploring the wreck of the oil tanker Romelia *at Sunset Rocks. The wreck occurred on 29 July 1977 and the site has become a popular Cape diving venue. (M. Turner)*
Bottom: A saturation diving system mounted on the deck of the salvage tug Causeway Adventurer. *This unit was specially designed for use on the wreck site of HMS* Birkenhead. *(M. Turner)*

John Lethbridge

*I*n the year 1715 John Lethbridge, a wool merchant living at 83 Wolborough Street, Newton Abbot, England, found himself in financial difficulties; he was 39 and had seven children to support. Pondering various ways of making money, it occurred to him that vast treasures were lying under the sea, and that a man could become rich by salvaging these. In his own words he 'was prepossessed that it might be practicable to contrive a machine to recover wrecks lost in the sea; and the first step I took towards it was going into a hogshead, upon land, bung'd up tight, where I stayed half-an-hour without communication of air; then I made a trench, near a well, at the bottom of my orchard in this place in order to convey a sufficient quantity of water to cover the hogshead, and then try'd how long I could live under water without air-pipes or communication of air'. The primitive experiment was a success, and his next step was to approach a cooper in Stanhope Street, London, to build him a diving-barrel with holes for his arms and a glass plate 'an inch and a quarter thick' in the bottom for him to look through. The air supply inside the barrel could be replenished by means of a bellows, after which the hole was bunged tight and the barrel lowered under water. In order to impress the English East India Company with the possibilities of his machine, Lethbridge arranged a demonstration in April 1720, which is decribed as follows: 'Last Tuesday, Wednesday & Thursday, Mr. Lethbridge of Devonshire, the famous Diver, was let down into the Thames near Whitehall-Stairs, in an Engine, & kept under Water half an hour; he took with him Meat & Drink, and had his Dinner under Water; he had also Fire in the Engine, & baked a Cake, bored several Holes in a Piece of Wood, besides other Performances, in a small Quantity of Air, without the Use of Air-Pipes.' The Company showed little interest, however, and Lethbridge was forced to team up with Jacob Rowe, who in 1720 had patented a similar diving-barrel. On the Isle of May the two had considerable success on the wreck of the English East-Indiaman *Vansittart*, from which they recovered 27 chests of silver, 868 slabs of lead, 64 iron cannon and 11 anchors. Word of his prowess reached the Dutch East India Company, who contracted him to recover specie from vessels wrecked in Table Bay in 1722. However, they first sent him to work on the *Slot ter Hoge*, wrecked on Porto Santo in 1724, and in 1727 his attempt at salvaging the sunken fleet in Table Bay resulted in the recovery of considerable amounts of silver, and other items. Other salvage operations followed, and as late as 1757 Lethbridge, who was then more than eighty years old, was still petitioning the English East India Company to allow him to mount an operation to salvage the treasure on board the *Dodington*, which had been wrecked on Bird Island near Algoa Bay, but this was turned down. On 11 December 1759 an entry was made in the parish register of Wolborough which read: 'Buried Mr. Lethbridge, inventor of a most famous diving engine, by which he recovered from the bottom of the sea, in different parts of the globe, almost £100,000 for the English and Dutch merchants which had been lost by shipwreck.' A simple statement on the life of a truly remarkable and courageous 'wrackman'.

A page from the resolutions of the Council of Policy of the Dutch East India Company, dated 9 March 1728, concerning the salvage attempt on the Merestein *by John Lethbridge. (M. Turner)*

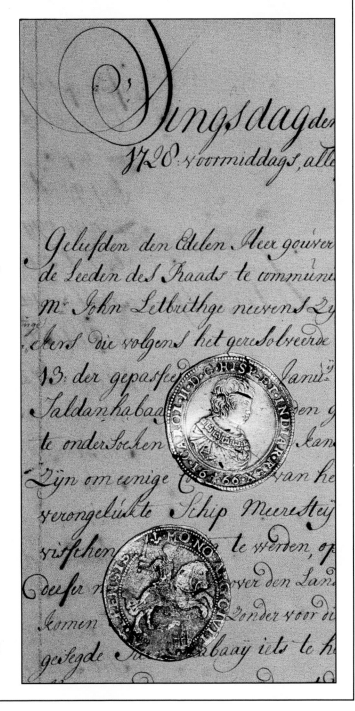

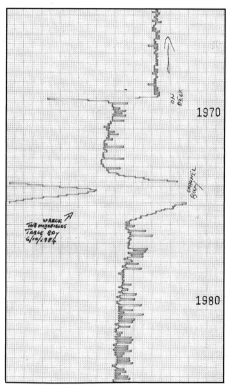

An old concept in deep diving technology has lately been revived and is now being used commercially on many oil-fields and by a growing number of scientific organisations. The atmospheric diving system is a modern-day advancement on the system used by John Lethbridge in the 18th century. The contemporary atmospheric diving suit (ADS) is available in a variety of different models, all with a cast alloy body and segmented arms. The 'Wasp' suit has sets of thrusters and can be controlled by the operator much like an underwater helicopter. The 'Jim' and 'Sam' suits have segmented legs which enable the operator to walk about on the sea-bed. The suits are cumbersome and the most menial of tasks takes much longer than a free diver would, but the operator can stay submerged up to six hours before recharging his oxygen supply, and he does not need to waste time decompressing, as he is operating at atmospheric pressure inside the armoured walls of the suit.

The ADS suits are fitted with oxygen tanks and the atmosphere is constantly being circulated and filtered of carbon dioxide. The operator adds oxygen when necessary, so he has to surface only to recharge the oxygen supply. The suits are attached to the surface by means of an electro-mechanical cable and are equipped with lights and communications. These suits are used regularly to descend to depths of 300 m and, though limited in their applications, can be used at a fraction of the cost of putting saturation divers into the water.

ADS suits and saturation diving teams have operated off various oil-search vessels along the South African coast and will be used more and more in the future to recover cargoes from deep-water sites. The cost savings made possible by the use of ADS suits will enable salvors to investigate cargoes which saturation teams have up until now considered uneconomical.

Salvaging the cargo from a wreck has therefore become much less a question of luck, and can be properly planned beforehand. The range of diving equipment available to the modern salvor is so wide that he should have no problem in choosing the best system for his particular needs, but before he can put his equipment to use, he first has to locate and identify his wreck. Apart from accidental discoveries by spearfisherman and the like, proper research is undoubtedly the best way of starting a search, as the salvor will then gain some insight into the cargo a vessel was carrying, and know roughly where the wreck occurred. When the approximate location of a wreck has been ascertained, the modern salvor has a number of further advantages over his earlier colleagues.

Some offshore wrecks like the *Paris Maru* and the *Haleric* are clearly marked on charts, and by the use of radar they are easily located, but old vessels wrecked on long, open stretches of coast are almost impossible to find without the help of

Top: *An example of a magnetometer readout, in this case indicating the position of the wreck of* The Highfields *in Table Bay. (M. Turner)*

Above: *A view of the inside of a diving bell. (M. Turner)*

Right: *Modern equipment such as this is necessary to monitor and control a saturation diving system. (M. Turner)*

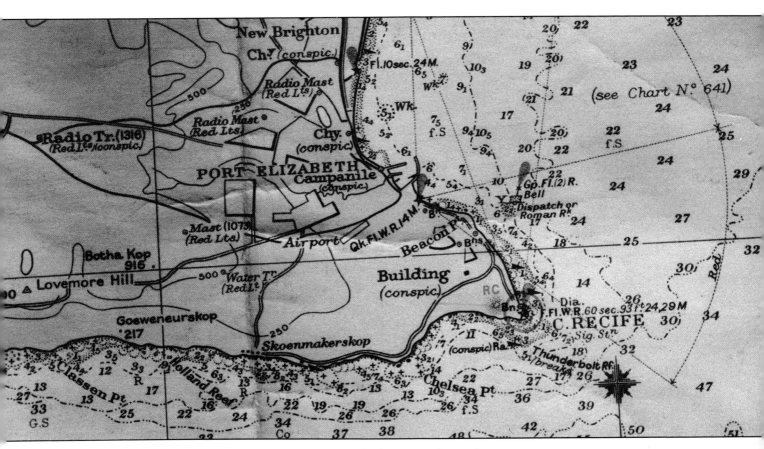

Above: A chart of the Port Elizabeth area, with a number of wreck sites marked. (M. Turner)
Below: Notice of a sale of diving equipment in May 1857. (Cape Argus)

sophisticated and expensive electronic equipment. Recently large numbers of divers worldwide have started to use proton magnetometers for this purpose, and the results speak for themselves. The magnetometer was developed for use in geological surveys; when towed behind a boat it registers any anomalies interfering with the normal magnetic readings received from the earth's crust. It is thus possible to find anchors, cannon and large pieces of ferrous metal, even when they are buried under thick sand and mud. Another piece of equipment often used is the hand-held metal detector, which indicates the presence of both ferrous and non-ferrous metals.

South African wrecks found by these methods include the *Reigersdaal*, *Borderer*, *Arniston*, *Jupiter T.* and *The Highfields*. One of the most recent success stories was the discovery of the *Johanna* in 1982 by Gavin Clackworthy of Cape Town, and his team. The wreck was extremely difficult to find because the salvors had available only very misleading maps, and it is doubtful whether she would have been located at all without the aid of a metal detector. The wreck eventually yielded more than 23 000 Spanish-American silver cobs and 27 bullion discs of silver varying in weight from four to seventeen kilograms – a good return on the investment made in the instrument.

Other modern devices which will play an important role in future salvage operations are the side-scan sonar, which is ideal for looking for large intact wrecks in deep, flat areas, and the sub-bottom profiler, which tells the operator what is lying beneath a sandy or muddy bottom. All these highly sophisticated instruments provided invaluable assistance in the modern search for the *Mary Rose*.

Salvage has come a long way from the time tents were pitched opposite wreck sites and a patient watch was kept for anything that may float ashore. From the first pearl divers to the modern saturation diver who is now capable of interventions at more than 550 m there is almost a quantum leap, and with ever more sophisticated electronic equipment coming on the market to assist the salvor in finding and identifying wrecks, some spectacular discoveries are sure to be made in the future. And once these wrecks have been found and identified, the salvor can choose from a wide range of equipment tailored specifically to his particular needs. Indeed a far cry from a diver such as John Lethbridge groping about the sea bottom from within the confines of his primitive contraption.

Chapter 8

On the Site of a Wreck

*T*he inexperienced diver who visits a wreck site for the first time and expects to see a complete, intact vessel is bound to be disappointed. Recent images of the *Titanic*, lying on the bottom of the ocean in an almost pristine state, have reinforced the false perception of a shipwreck, but it must be kept in mind that the *Titanic* came to rest at a depth where she was for the most part undisturbed by strong currents and wave action. Apart from the woodwork, which has largely disappeared through the action of marine organisms, the only deterioration of the hulk was caused by the impact when it hit the bottom of the ocean, and thereafter slow oxidation and encrustation, while the wrecks described in this book mostly occurred in shallow water on the open coast, where the power of the waves in bad weather can be awesome, as we have seen in the case of the *Evdokia* (see pp 72-73).

Still, the first time I saw a submerged shipwreck was an unforgettable experience. While working for the Port Elizabeth dolphinarium, a colleague and I headed along the coast west of the city to the site of the SS *Western Knight*, an American cargo vessel which went ashore in 1929. Both of us were experienced divers, but we had never dived on a shipwreck before, so we had no idea what to expect or where to begin. A piece of wreckage lying on the shore above the water-line at least gave us a clue as to the whereabouts of the wreck, so we decided to set out from there.

We soon came upon her remains – large, tangled chunks of steel from the hull lay scattered about, heavily encrusted with calcium deposits and seaweed and mostly uninteresting. Further out we saw more signs of wreckage and then suddenly came upon two large boilers standing upright on the sea-bed. We swam past metres of gleaming copper steam-pipes, bronze valves and a huge steam-engine lying on its side and covered with marine growth, then came upon the drive shaft snaking across the sea-bed and finally the huge bronze propeller looming in front of us. As a memento of that dive I recovered a brass porthole surround from the site.

Since that first experience I have spent many hours underwater in all conditions, exploring dozens of wrecks, and each one is different. Even on the site of one wreck, for instance that of HMS *Osprey*, a small Royal Navy gunboat which ran aground on the Tsitsikamma coast west of the Cape St Francis lighthouse (see box), one is likely to meet with many different underwater conditions, depending on the weather. During the more than 24 hours I have spent diving on her, I have encountered calm, clear perfection, but also bad days when a diver is thrown about like chaff in the wind; it can be a frightening experience suddenly to hurtle across the sea-bed and be hurled against a jagged piece of iron, a cannon or an anchor. The first warning one has of an approaching wave is the abrupt darkness as white water rolls overhead; this is then followed by heavy turbulence as the force of the wave billows down to the floor of the sea, often with enough force to throw up sand and sediment, or even roll around boulders.

Often after heavy storms shipwrecks give up more of their secrets as artefacts and coins that had lain covered in crevices and potholes are exposed; on the site of the *Osprey* I found silver brooches and Japanese coins, trinkets perhaps captured from the pirates in the China Sea being taken home by sailors after their spell of duty in the East.

The state of preservation of a wreck depends on many factors, one of the most important of which is the material from which the vessel was built. It is rare to find a wooden sailing vessel intact, an exception being the *Middelburg*, which came to rest on a sandy bottom in sheltered water. The sand slowly engulfed her bottom timbers, which have remained largely preserved. However, a wooden vessel wrecked in heavy surf on a rocky shore would naturally be smashed to pieces and scattered very quickly, leaving little evidence behind; furthermore wood is more prone to attack by underwater organisms which cause further serious deterioration of the wooden structure. Metal objects such as cannon and anchors are often the only indication of the site of such a wreck.

Below: *The first two photographs show the American cargo steamer* Western Knight *soon after being wrecked on a rocky shore (Frank Neave), and what remains after being pounded by the surf (R. Ferguson). In contrast, the British steamer* Kakapo *came ashore on the beach near Noordhoek, and the sand has preserved her lower hull structure very well (Stephen Goodson).*

One is likely to find more physical remains of a metal-hulled vessel, but its more robust construction is no guarantee that it will still be in one piece. Often the might of the waves leaves only the most solid of structures intact, such as the engine-block, boilers, drive-shaft and propeller. In shallow water oxidation of the iron parts takes place quite rapidly, and mostly only objects made of more resistant metal such as copper or brass remain recognisable. In many cases such wrecks have been extensively worked by salvors eager to reach the non-ferrous fittings, and the chances are that they used heavy explosive charges to blow her apart to make this task easier, leaving wreckage scattered on the sea-bed.

Another factor to take into account is the exact site in which a vessel came to rest. In sheltered water waves do not cause so much damage, but on the open coast a vessel can be pounded into fragments in a very short space of time. Usually a vessel breaks into two or more parts quite rapidly, and these parts then slowly deteriorate over the years until very little visible evidence is left. In general wrecks in sheltered bays have withstood the force of the waves better, but even within the same bay conditions at the sites of two wrecks quite close to each other can differ so widely that the one is well-preserved while the other is hardly recognisable.

The bottom on which the vessel has come to rest also plays an important part. Sand is generally a good preservative. In the first place it is often fairly flat, which allows the vessel to come to rest on an even keel, which means that its weight is distributed evenly. The wave action then tends to swirl the sand around, so that it slowly engulfs the hulk. Sand further helps in the preservation of the wreck in that it excludes much of the oxygen that so often contributes greatly to the rapid breaking down of a structure, and also inhibits the marine growths and organisms that aid the process.

A rocky bottom is likely to cause the rapid breaking up of a vessel, as the jagged edges and unevenness of the site cause the weight of the vessel to be unevenly distributed, leading to stresses that cause it to fracture. Even in relatively calm water a rocky bottom is likely to cause more damage than sand, as the vessel cannot become buried and will be exposed to the deterioration processes of oxidation and marine organisms.

A diver, whether an amateur on a sight-seeing trip or a professional intent on working on a wreck, will be well advised to acquaint himself with the local conditions at the site he intends to visit before he attempts his first dive.

Generally speaking there are some noticable differences between conditions on the east coast and those on the west coast. A diver contemplating working for long periods in the Atlantic must ensure that he is adequately protected from the biting cold sea conditions he is likely to experience. The best suit to use is a 7 mm long john covered by a 7 mm long-sleeved jacket. Boots and hood are essential, as is a pair of gloves. With this type of insulation a reasonably fit diver should be able to stay in the water for at least five hours. On the east coast, where the water is considerably warmer, a 5 mm suit is usually quite adequate.

The strength and direction of the wind is often a good indication of the bottom conditions one is likely to encounter. After a south-westerly gale on the east coast the water becomes extremely warm and clear, as the clear water from the Mozambique/Agulhas current is blown inshore. The reverse happens when the easterly gales blow, as these winds tend to blow the clear water away from the coast, which allows the cold, dirty bottom water to well up to the surface. When this happens, fish accustomed to warm water are often stunned and wash up on the beaches.

In the Atlantic the surface water tends to be very rich in plankton and is usually a dirty green in colour; in contrast the bottom water is crystal clear and ice-cold. When the summer easterly gales blow offshore they tend to blow the dirty, warm surface water out to sea and the cold, clear bottom water wells up. This phenomenon is most noticable along the southern Cape Peninsula; one can expect clear, flat water conditions along the Atlantic coast within hours of a south-easterly gale. It is interesting to note that the water on the west coast in fact tends to be warmer during the winter than during the summer, as the north-westerly gales during winter blow the warm but dirty surface water towards the shore.

An obvious limitation placed on any open-coast surf-line salvage operation is wave action; diving teams usually have to live near the site to take full advantage of the few flat days on which they can work with safety. On the east coast the best

HMS Osprey vs the pirate junks

In 1866, while on a tour of duty in the Far East, the Royal Navy steam gunboat HMS *Osprey*, in the company of HMS *Opossum*, left Hong Kong on a mission to seek and destroy a number of troublesome Chinese pirate junks. On board were a Chinese mandarin and a native merchant who had been robbed by the pirates, and it was hoped that they would be able to identify the perpetrators. The two gunboats proceeded to Quang-Chow-Wang, but the junks had disappeared. They then steamed to the island of Hainan, where, off the village of Yu-Lin-Kan, a fisherman reported the presence of a fleet of twelve pirate junks in the next bay, which was called Sama Bay. Arriving on the scene, the gunboats found not twelve but 22 junks, some from Macao and some from Cochin China, many extremely large and mounting more than ten cannon ranging in size from 9 to 32 pounds. Although the gunboats had only six guns between them, as opposed to the 54 of their opponents, they were forced into action as the pirate junks started firing at them as soon as they entered the bay. For two hours fire was exchanged, the *Opossum* managing to get much closer to the enemy because of her shallower draught, but the fight remained inconclusive. It was then decided to land a shore party of about 60 men from the two vessels, which was done against stiff opposition. This party attacked the pirates occupying the village, who fled in panic to the junks – but in the meantime this refuge had been neutralised. The junks were then boarded and they and their cargoes of opium and other valuable merchandise were set on fire. In all 21 junks were destroyed in the engagement, and over 700 pirates killed.

On her way back to England the next year, HMS *Osprey* found herself off the coast of South Africa under sail and 'easy' steam. The sea was rough and a heavy south-westerly gale with rain squalls reduced visibility considerably. Just before dawn on 30 May 1867 a sharp 'grating, grazing, hollow' sound was heard 'like Vulcan's file', and it was realised that they had run ashore, the vessel having struck amidships. The stricken vessel, pounded by heavy surf, was eventually washed over a reef, landing in a gully 100 m wide. When morning dawned land could be seen about 200 m away and it was discovered that they had run aground about 3 km west of the Cape St Francis lighthouse. A boat was launched with some difficulty and Lieutenant Richard Meade and two men climbed in to try and get a line ashore, but the boat capsized. The two sailors swam back to the vessel, but Meade struck out for the shore with the line, which unfortunately became entangled among the rocks. Eventually, after a hard struggle, he managed to make the line fast to some rocks, and all but one of the 83 officers and men aboard were saved from the stricken vessel. On land the shipwrecked men were rendered all assistance by Mr Mostert, a farmer who lived nearby, and on 6 June they arrived at Port Elizabeth in five bullock wagons.

HMS Osprey *(foreground) and HMS* Opossum *destroying pirate junks in Sama Bay.* (Illustrated London News)

Top: *Scuba diver Norman Denton explores the wreck of the Greek factory trawler* Athina, *which went ashore off Robberg beach on 1 August 1967. The wreck has been submerged for a number of years and is lying on a sandy bottom. (M. Turner)*
Above, centre: *A cannon rises to the surface suspended by two lifting bags or camels. (Peter Sachs)*
Above: *The steep cliffs of the Tsitsikamma coast below which the Greek freighter* Evdokia *met her end in 1979. The heavy ground swells experienced on this stretch of coast caused the rapid disintegration of her hull. (M. Turner)*
Opposite: *Giant surf pounds the half-submerged wreck of the* Athina. *This section of beach rarely experiences swells of this velocity, and her hull is largely intact. (M. Turner)*

months are normally January and February, when there is little trouble with the south-westerly winds which tend to throw up the swells. Cold fronts are normally associated with south-westerly winds which can whip up the sea into a boiling cauldron in a matter of hours, and in such conditions the salvors must be content to sit and wait until the sea calms. On the east coast easterly winds are normally not a great threat to divers at open-coast wreck sites, but in many bays they tend to blow up tremendous swells, which usually subside as soon as the offshore winds start to blow. Big storm swells, however, can travel thousands of nautical miles, and a wreck site is sometimes pounded by large breakers for weeks on end even though the weather at the salvage site is fine, with no sign of wind. Such swells which have travelled vast distances are called ground swells.

In this respect the west coast is more predictable than the east coast, where swells seem to be prevalent no matter how good the weather. On the Atlantic coast working conditions are often completely flat and salvors frequently have the advantage of three good days in a row, especially in summer when the easterly winds blow.

Swell conditions need not necessarily mean that diving is impossible. Where the shoreline drops steeply, as it docs at the site of the *Merestein* on Jutten Island, the surf bounces back from the shore and in the process tends to neutralise the effect of the oncoming waves to some degree. Divers can therefore work in larger swell conditions; divers can work at the *Merestein* site even if the swells are 1,5 m high. A diver working at the base of a large rock is likely to experience the same effect.

In contrast conditions at the site of the *Reigersdaal* are vastly different. This wreck lies on a shallow off-shore reef at Springfontein Point, and here the swells break on the reef and run far inshore. Divers find that any swell over a metre high causes them to be thrown around violently and in some cases to be heaved bodily over the reef.

Two such contrasting sites are found also on the east coast. The *Lyngenfjord* lies at the base of a high cliff at the Tsitsikamma River mouth where the waves tend to bounce back off the steep rock face, neutralising the incoming waves to a certain extent. This wreck site, too, can be visited without too much discomfort even if the swells are running 1,5 m high, but at Sardinia Bay near Port Elizabeth the *Zeepaard* lies on a shallow off-shore reef over which the waves break and run a long way inshore. The sea has to be extremely flat for a diver to be able to venture out to the outer reef area of the *Zeepaard*.

Anybody who intends diving on a shallow surf-line wreck site, especially from a boat, must be well versed in the sea-bed conditions which cause ocean swells to break. If the depth of the water is more than 4 m, both boat and divers should be safe, as only extremely large ground swells will ever break at this depth. On the other hand, if one intends to work off a boat at a shallow site such as that of the *Merestein* or the *Dodington*, where any ground swell of more than 1,5 m should be considered enough to make work impossible, a good knowledge of local sea-bed conditions is essential.

The skipper of a boat arriving at the site of a wreck should spend at least 20 minutes circling the area in which he intends to drop anchor in order to ascertain where the larger sets of swells are breaking. When he is quite sure where the swells are breaking, he should anchor far enough away to stay out of danger. Waves will only break where the water is shallow enough, and the boat will be safe in the deeper water outside the area of breaking swells. A fairly heavy anchor should be used to prevent the boat from dragging towards the shore as the bigger swells come in. The tide should also be considered, and if it is ebbing, the boat should be anchored a little further out, as the swells will also break further and further out as the water becomes shallower.

On an ideal diving day only occasional white water action should be seen on the tips of the shallowest reefs. If the swells are breaking in deep water, it is best simply to pack up and go home, as the diving boat and the equipment on board will be in jeopardy in such conditions.

The site of the *Reigersdaal* can be particularly treacherous; often large ground swells race in from a perfectly flat sea, and many divers have narrowly missed losing their boats. Perhaps the example of the Cape Town salvage expert James Bell will serve as a warning: he and his colleagues were busy stripping brass pipes from inside a condensor housing on the *City of Hankow*, a British cargo vessel wrecked in thick fog a little north of Saldanha Bay on 18 December 1942, when, unbeknown to them as they worked inside the safety of the steel walls of the housing, the sea picked up. When they emerged from the housing and returned to the surface, they found that the wreck site was being pounded by giant swells. It was only with luck that they reached their diving boat unscathed, and managed to race for shelter.

At the site of the *Lyngenfjord*, too, divers engaged in towing a 1 800-kg propeller blade out to sea with the aid of lifting-bags were surprised by a sudden three- to four-metre set of ground swells; as their ski-boat climbed up the face of a wave the tow-rope snapped, the blade and lifting bags washed into a gully and were lost. In another instance two divers working on the site of HMS *Osprey* had anchored their boat over the shallow site on an extremely flat day and were hard at work on the wreck when a slight movement in the water made them decide to surface. To their horror they saw their diving-boat surfing down the face of a two-metre wave; fortunately the anchor rope held and they were able to beat a hasty retreat, minutes away from disaster. The worst accident of this type occurred on the site of the *Dodington*, when divers from Port Elizabeth lost their boat and all their equipment and had to be rescued from Bird Island by helicopter.

Divers constantly have to be conscious of two very real dangers if they are going to work at depths deeper than ten metres for any length of time: the bends, and nitrogen narcosis. The cause of the bends is very simple; a diver who ventures below the safe depth of ten metres is subject to great pressure from the water, which causes the gas from his breathing supply to accumulate in his bloodstream. If he returns to normal pressure too quickly, the accumulated gas in his blood-stream comes out of solution and forms bubbles, which can lodge anywhere in his circulation and form an obstruction to the flow of blood. Should this occur in the tiny blood-vessels of the brain, the effect is similar to a stroke; in certain circumstances instant death can occur, and in others permanent crippling.

Above: *A scuba diver displays his find. (M. Turner)*

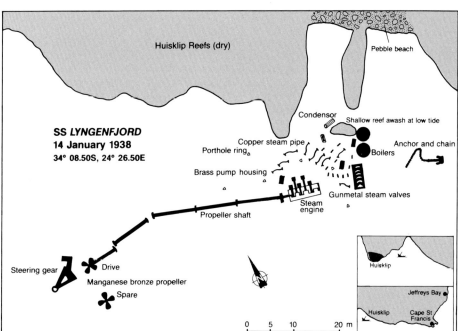

SS *LYNGENFJORD*
14 January 1938
34° 08.50S, 24° 26.50E

Above: *The veteran salvor Sam Pettersen, flanked by two associates, travels in an aerial conveyance rigged up between the shore and the wrecked steamer Lyngenfjord during salvage operations at Huisklip on the Tsitsikamma coast in 1938. (John Munnik)*
Above, right: *A site plan showing the remains of the Lyngenfjord after more than forty years of violent surf action. Very little shell plating is visible on the site.*
Below: *The wrecked Norwegian cargo steamer Lyngenfjord, her stern broken off, lies at the base of a hill at Huisklip on the Tsitsikamma coast after running aground on 14 January 1938. Only a small part of her cargo was saved. (Frank Neave)*

The solution to the problem is simple; a diver who has run into decompression time must return to the surface in a pre-arranged pattern of stops of certain lengths at certain depths. This allows the gas in his bloodstream to be safely dissipated through the lungs without forming the deadly bubbles. In planning a dive this factor must always be kept in mind; the deeper a dive, the more gas is absorbed, the more time must be spent decompressing, and the less time can be spent actually working on the bottom.

In some cases it may even be worth while to situate a compression chamber near to the wreck site. If a diver finds that he has to surface suddenly because of an emergency of some sort, he can be placed inside this chamber, which is then compressed to the same pressure as the depth at which he was working, and then slowly brought to surface pressure, with the same effect as the decompression stops underwater.

Salvage attempts have been restricted to certain depth limits not only by the decompression problem, but also by the phenomenon known as nitrogen narcosis. When nitrogen is breathed under high pressure it can have a narcotic effect on the diver which can result in a severe loss of judgement. The recognised safety depth for compressed-air diving is 50 m, and any intervention below this depth should be carried out with gas mixtures such as heliox (in which helium replaces the nitrogen in the breathing mixture).

To operate effectively along the coast of South Africa the salvage diver requires some basic equipment without which he is not likely to achieve satisfactory results. Wrecks that are worth investigating have often occurred in extremely remote positions and sometimes large tracts of beach have to be traversed before boats can be launched within range of these sites. Four-wheel drive vehicles are therefore essential, especially if boats have to be launched and recovered from sandy beaches, and in order to prevent them from sinking into the soft sand, they should be equipped with wide tyres.

Boats must be of rugged construction and should be fitted with two powerful motors in order to enable them safely to negotiate the heavy surf conditions found on the coast. As such boats are normally heavily laden with equipment, the extra power is essential to provide the necessary speed. The most important equipment on board such a boat is the breathing apparatus. Because of the short duration of the air supply, aqualungs are of little use to the professional diver. Most serious wreck divers therefore mount a low-pressure compressor on their boats, as this can be used to feed a constant stream of air to one or two divers through reinforced hoses which lead from the compressor to a down stream demand valve. To allow the diver enough free movement around the wreck site, the hose should be at least 70 m long. In addition the compressor can be used to drive small pneumatic tools such as chipping hammers, and to inflate 'camels' or lifting-bags.

On older wreck sites very little of the actual wreck is normally visible, and a metal detector becomes an invaluable tool to provide clues to the whereabouts of valuables buried beneath sand and boulders. Where large deposits of conglomerate or matrix occur, these have to broken up in order to remove the artefacts inside. Even though explosive charges are frowned upon in academic circles because of the damage that may be caused, they are often the only means by which conglomerate can be broken up. An alternative is the use of pneumatic chipping hammers or chisels, but the possibility of damage is not lessened. A diver should always keep handy a high-tensile steel bar with which to move heavy boulders or other objects; such object may also be moved by means of lifting-bags. Lastly it is a good idea to have an underwater camera available to record interesting finds *in situ*. Such photographs form a visual record of a salvage operation, can be of great assistance to institutions such as museums, and can also be used to illustrate possible articles in publications concerning the operation.

Decompression tables

When diving below the generally accepted safe limit of 10 m, divers should, during their ascent, stop at certain levels for certain periods of time to allow the accumulated gas in their blood-stream to dissipate safely. Tables showing these depths and times are called decompression tables. The example below is adapted to the depths sometimes encountered on the wreck sites mentioned in this book.

Depth (metres)	Duration of dive (minutes)	Stoppage at different depths (minutes)		
		9m	6m	3m
12	165			5
	195			10
	225			15
	255			20
	330			25
	390			30
	660			35
15	105			5
	120			10
	135			15
	145			20
	160			25
	170		5	25
	190		5	30
18	70	5		
	80	5		5
	90	5		10
	100	5		15
	110	5		20
	120	5		25
	130	5		30
21	55			5
	60		5	5
	70		5	10
	75		5	15
	85		5	20
	90		5	25
	95	5	5	25

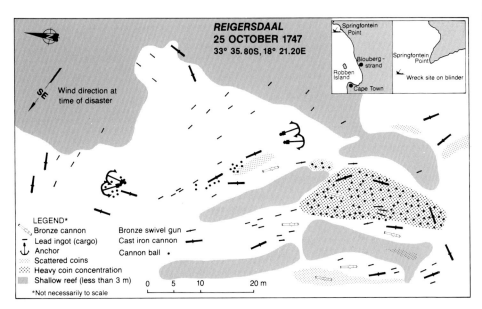

REIGERSDAAL
25 OCTOBER 1747
33° 35.80S, 18° 21.20E

Springfontein Point
Blouberg-strand
Robben Island
Cape Town
Springfontein Point
Wreck site on blinder

Wind direction at time of disaster

LEGEND*
Bronze cannon
Lead ingot (cargo)
Anchor
Scattered coins
Heavy coin concentration
Shallow reef (less than 3 m)
Bronze swivel gun
Cast iron cannon
Cannon ball
0 5 10 20 m
*Not necessarily to scale

A site plan showing the remains of the Reigersdaal after more than 230 years of violent surf action. The site was blanketed in kelp, black mussels and red bait pods. Diving is possible on the site only on a few selected days of the year, but the site has nevertheless been scoured by a large number of divers eager to recover the valuable silver specie the vessel carried.

As we have seen, conditions at wreck sites differ greatly. In order to give the potential diver a better understanding of such conditions, some actual sites are described below in more detail:

The *Reigersdaal*, an outward-bound Dutch East-Indiaman of 850 tons, was wrecked on the rocky reef which juts out from Springfontein Point on 25 October 1747. She had on board a large hoard of silver specie which was in mint condition at the time the vessel was wrecked. The wreck site (at 33° 35.80S, 18° 21.20E), was discovered in 1979 by the crack South African salvage team of Brian Clark and Tubby Gericke, who despite an intense search failed to find the vast treasure which the ship was known to have carried. However, they did manage to salvage six large bronze muzzle-loading cannon adorned with beautiful curved lifting-lugs in the shape of dolphins; the cannon were lifted with the help of a helicopter. Although the cannon were unfortunately worn a little smooth as a result of years of wave action, it was still possible to make out the crest of the Amsterdam Chamber of the Dutch East India Company they bore. The salvors also removed some of the 30-ton cargo of lead bars, and then went on to a more profitable wreck site.

Word of the wreck's whereabouts spread among the Cape Town diving community, and soon many rival teams of divers were searching for the treasure – and one day it was discovered lying in a deep gully, covered by cannon-balls. The large, concreted pile of silver coins was broken up by a rather destructive explosive charge, and feverish divers began filling bags with handfuls of perfectly preserved pieces-of-eight, silver Mexican pillar dollars in denominations of eight and four reals dated from 1732-1744, and a fair number of Guatemalan, Mexican, Potosi and Lima silver cobs. A tragic accident occurred, however, when a diver was pulled down by the weight of his salvage bag.

No one knows for sure how many coins were recovered altogether, but it must have been in the region of 20 000; one large pile was removed, like the cannon, with the aid of a helicopter. In addition the divers discovered four more bronze muzzle-loading swivel-guns with the Amsterdam Chamber's insignia. These guns were in perfect condition, still mounted in their iron frames, and are possibly the best-preserved bronze cannon ever found on the coast of South Africa.

The *Reigersdaal* is a fine example of an open-coast surf-line wreck. In the same matrix in which the coins were found, the divers found only small traces of hull timber; the rest had been broken up by the heavy surf and had been washed ashore, mainly at Silverstroom Strand. Besides the coins, lead and bronze cannon, many other items were found at the site, including anchors, cannon-balls, cast iron muzzle-loading cannon, silver and pewter buckles, silverware, clay pipes, wine-bottles, bricks, brass pins, grape-shot, navigational instruments and sounding-leads, one of which weighed 27,5 kg.

To compare the difference in preservation of two wrecks in close proximity to each other as a result of dissimilar swell conditions, the *Maori* and *Oakburn* can serve as excellent examples. The wrecks were of more or less the same size, have been submerged for a similar period and were wrecked in the same bay, yet the one is extremely well preserved, while little can be seen of the other.

The *Maori*, a 5 317-ton British steamer, was wrecked on 5 August 1909 and lies at 34° 01.90S, 18° 18.90E, blanketed in kelp in 20 m of water right inside the bay at Duiker Point on the Cape Peninsula in such a position that only during the worst storms can waves break on her. Her hull is about 30 per cent intact, and in one place her sides soar up from the sea-bed to a height of about eight metres; in some places a diver can swim underneath her keel. In her aft hold one can still see her cargo of railway-lines stowed in their original position, and in her fore hold a cargo of water-

pipes is visible. Her reciprocating steam-engine still stands upright, and divers have found crates containing chinaware and liquor stowed in position; over the years many glass bottles and fine pieces of English porcelain have been recovered by divers. The *Maori* is a good example of a sheltered-water wreck which has remained remarkably intact; divers from the famous research vessel *Calypso* have visited her and described her as the best-preserved wreck of her vintage that they had seen.

In contrast the *Oakburn*, which was wrecked on 21 May 1906 at 34° 02.20S, 18° 18.70E, lies at more or less the same depth as the *Maori*, but broadside on to the giant swells which roll in from the Atlantic Ocean. Little kelp grows on the site. When one dives on the wreck it is difficult to imagine that this jumbled mass of wreckage was once a fine steel steamer; her cargo of railway-lines lies scattered amongst the boulders, and her engine, boilers and other unidentifiable machinery are spread over a wide area. Little is to be discerned of her hull plating, and her other cargo of glassware, ceramics and medicines is mostly smashed to pieces.

The *Paquita*, a 484-ton German iron barque, ran ashore on the east bank of the Knysna Heads on 19 October 1903 at 34° 04.60S, 23° 03.60E. She filled with water almost immediately, but her upper works remained above the surface of the water for many months, during which time salvors removed most of her fittings; more recently divers have recovered wooden dead-eyes from the rigging, as well as brass portholes from the remains of her hull. The site of her wrecking is sheltered from the great Indian Ocean ground-swells, and it is amazing how well she has stood up to the many years of immersion, apart from the damage that was done when her hull was blown open with explosives. The rough outline of her hull can still be made out and in some places one can swim inside the hull with ease. Large, delicate sea-fans and sponges grow on her iron plates in profusion.

The only regular water movement that affects the site is the extremely strong tidal surge that races in and out of the Heads when the tides turn; indeed one must wait for the slack tide before venturing on to the *Paquita*, which is another typical calm-water wreck site.

A fine example of an open-coast gale site is that of the *L'Aigle*, a 700-ton French wooden barque wrecked on 16 June 1850 during a south-westerly gale at the centre of a large sandy bay west of Wreck Point on the Tsitsikamma coast at 34° 10.70S, 24° 33.20E. When she was visited in recent years, little could be seen on the sea-bed apart from her huge cargo of tin, which occasionally showed through the sand; once the pile of ingots was removed, however, her lower hull structure was found to be fairly intact, having been held in place by the heavy cargo. The interesting thing is that large pieces of hull-frame lie well above the high-water mark, testimony to the extremely heavy surf encountered on this stretch of coast.

The *Santissimo Sacramento* was a homeward-bound Portuguese merchant vessel which came to grief west of Port Elizabeth in 1647. The site, at 34° 02.15S, 25° 31.20E, is a typical open-coast type and the wreck is culturally important, as very little is known about the Portuguese vessels which plied the oceans at the time of her wrecking. The site was known for many years mainly because of a solitary bronze cannon in a rock pool which was discovered by Colonel Robert Gordon in 1778. It became a legend in the area, and eventually the bay in which it lay was called Cannon Bay.

Since before World War II salvors have shown a great deal of interest in the wreck, and eventually in 1951 the well-known Port Elizabeth salvor H.G. Harraway removed the cannon from the site with the aid of a team of oxen; today it stands outside the Port Elizabeth Museum. In the years thereafter spearfishermen, among them the late Tony Dicks, found some more bronze cannon opposite the site of the one removed by Harraway. These became a talking point among divers at the Dolphin Underwater Club in Port Elizabeth, and many divers spoke vaguely of salvage.

In 1977 two rival teams of divers removed more than 40 bronze cannon from the sea-bed over a period of two months. One team consisted of Brian Clark, Peter Mason and Brian McFarlane on board the fishing-vessel *Gavin*, and the other of the late David Allen, Gerry van Niekerk, Gert Botha and the late Arthur Perry on board the *Etosha*. Two of the cannon are now on display in the Port Elizabeth Museum and Art Gallery. The cannon were mostly badly eroded, but one was found in perfect condition, and promptly named the Miracle Cannon – it had come to rest between two cast iron cannon which had acted as anodes, and the consequent weak electri-

Opposite, top to bottom: Artefacts recovered from the wreck of the Reigersdaal: *A bronze muzzle-loading swivel-gun (the crest of the Amsterdam chamber of the Dutch East India Company on the breech is shown); Silver coins and a silver buckle; A pewter and silver spoon; A deep-sea sounding-lead weighing 27,5 kg. (M. Turner)*
Top: *The bell of the* Maori. *(M. Turner)*
Above, centre: *A brass porthole ring recovered from the* Maori. *(M. Turner)*
Above: *A span of oxen drags ashore a bronze cannon (first discovered by Col Robert Gordon in 1778) from the wreck of the* Santissimo Sacramento *in 1951. The salvage work was initiated by Mr H.G. Harraway of Port Elizabeth. (Port Elizabeth Museum)*

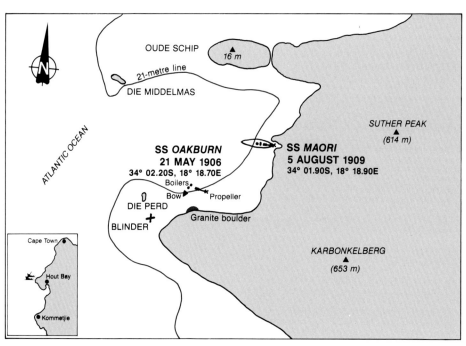

From top to bottom: Salvors removing fittings from the Paquita *shortly after her wrecking (Frank Neave); Cannon from the* Sacramento *on the salvage vessel (Evening Post); The stern of the* Maori *shortly after she ran aground, with members of the crew awaiting rescue (Argus Weekly); The* Oakburn *hard aground and down by the head (Hout Bay Museum).*

Top right: *A site map showing the close proximity of the wrecks of the* Maori *and* Oakburn *to each other. Note the good state of preservation of the former compared to the latter. The wrecks are popular diving venues.*

cal interaction between the different metals had prevented any great metal loss.

Seventeen cast iron cannon can still be seen on the site of the wreck, much of which is covered with shifting sand. The intense competition between the rival groups of salvors had an unfortunate consequence in that the site was not properly worked. Cannon and anchors should always be left on the wreck site till last, so that all buried artefacts can be removed and a systematic search completed, but this was not done in the case of the *Sacramento*. As a direct consequence of the negative publicity this activity received, the South African authorities eventually passed legislation to protect similar sites from indiscriminate salvage.

The *Sacramento* had left Goa in the company of another Portuguese vessel, the *Nossa Senhora de Atalaia do Pinheiro*. On Easter day the *Atalaia* fired a seven-gun salute in honour of the Commodore on board the *Sacramento*, and in the process began leaking badly. In mid-June a violent south-westerly gale unleashed its fury on the two vessels and they parted company. The *Atalaia* was leaking badly and was brought to anchor off the coast north-east of East London, but broke up during a heavy swell. Her final resting place is at 32° 48.60S, 28° 08.70E, a little further up the coast close to the Cefane River east of East London. In 1980 salvage was carried out on the *Atalaia* by Peter Sachs and Sean Mitchley of East London, and they removed 23 bronze cannon from the site. Two of the cannon, of a similar type to that carried by the *Sacramento*, are now housed in the East London Museum. Peter Sachs is at present further investigating the wreck site in conjunction with the Museum, and many artefacts are being found on the site and also at the survivors' camp which was discovered opposite the wreck site.

An enormously destructive south-easterly gale hit Port Elizabeth in September 1902, and one of its victims was the *Inchcape Rock*, a 1 599-ton iron sailing-ship which was wrecked at 33° 56.00S, 25° 37.10E on 2 September 1902 after she had entered the bay to off-load a cargo of wheat from Portland in the U.S.A. As the wreck lies within the shelter of the bay in a calm area that is affected only by the worst south-east gales and the occasional large ground-swell (comparable to that of the *Maori*), she is amazingly well preserved. When the normal prevailing south-west wind blows, this area of the bay becomes dead flat and the surf almost non-existent.

When one dives on the *Inchcape Rock*, which seems complete from the air, the bow area is what strikes one first. At low tide the bowsprit can be seen above the water, and up to about a third of the way down her length her sides are still intact. On the sea-bed her masts lie perfectly preserved, and some of the rigging-cables can even be seen. As one moves towards her midships section the hull becomes more flattened until the stern is reached; here the complete stern counter with its steering gear can be seen lying on its side.

Near the *Inchcape Rock*, at 33° 56.20S, 25° 37.10E, lies the hull of the 2 312-ton steel screw steamer SS *Queen Victoria*, which was run aground on 18 August 1896, and her hull is in an even better state of preservation. In the North End beach area of Algoa Bay there are many other well-preserved hulks apart from these, but few of them are of great cultural value.

Much has been written about the *Grosvenor*, a typical homeward-bound English East-Indiaman which was wrecked on 4 August 1782 at 31° 22.40S, 29° 55.00E, and she is undoubtedly the most historically famous of all South African shipwrecks. The site lies at the mouth of a gully on the point to the north-east of the Tezani River in Pondoland, and it can be visited only on a few selected days of the year when the mountainous seas prevalent in the area subside. The site is a typical open-coast surf-line wreck; little is to be seen with the exception of a few cast iron cannon, cannon-balls, iron pigs and pieces of lead. Most of the site lies beneath shifting sand, and only with great difficulty and expertise will her remaining artefacts be recovered.

The wreck was first investigated closely by commercial salvors in 1880 when Captain Sydney Turner and Lieutenant Beddoes of the Natal Pioneers blasted the site and removed the cast iron cannon which showed at low tide. Amongst the many iron pigs scattered among the rock crevices they encountered the red matrix which later divers also found on the sites of the *Reigersdaal* and *Merestein* wrecks, and from it recovered about 800 gold and silver coins. The site was virtually forgotten until early in this century when various syndicates attempted to recover a reputed fortune from the site without much success (see pp 77-78). Recently many divers have investigated the site anew and have found a fair number of artefacts. Although the site has little of cultural value to offer, it represents an interesting piece of South African history.

One of the oldest wrecks yet salvaged along the South African coast, and one of the most important culturally, is that of the *São Bento*, which came to grief at 31° 19.60S, 29° 59.00E on 21 April 1554. She was a typical homeward-bound Portuguese East-Indiaman of the mid-sixteenth century when Portuguese influence in the East was at its peak. The site, the existence of which was known for years as a result of the broken Ming pottery shards and cornelian trade beads which regularly washed ashore, lies on the island at the mouth of the Msikaba River between Port Edward and Port St Johns. The site, covered by an overburden of gravel and stones, is in an open, rocky area and only small traces of red matrix can be seen.

Salvage work was first carried out in the 1960s when a team of divers from Kokstad salvaged a small bronze breech-loading swivel-gun from the site, which was at first mistakenly identified as that of the *Grosvenor*. When a salvage team headed by Chris Auret began salvage work on her, however, her Portuguese origins were confirmed; research into the account of her wrecking removed all doubt, as the island locality was mentioned. By the mid-1970s the team had removed 18 fine bronze cannon from the site and it was found that in contrast to the cannon from the *Sacramento*, which were mainly field guns, the *São Bento* cannon were mostly naval types, of which little was known at the time. The cannon, adorned with beautiful Portuguese crests as well as the divided globe insignia depicting the Treaty of Tordesillas (see p 15), and with bronze lifting-rings, have been preserved for posterity in various South African museums.

The little-publicised exploration of the *São Bento* can perhaps be considered a model of historical salvage. Many interesting lead-coated cannon-balls of various sizes, a few gold coins and some jewellery have been recovered, but many coins, artefacts and pottery shards probably still lie buried. Fortunately the salvors had the sense to leave four bronze cannon on the sea-bed to mark the wreck site's outer limits.

The sites referred to above show how various wrecks appear to the diver. The wreck of the Dutch East Indiaman *Reigersdaal* is perhaps the most interesting because of the rich haul of well-preserved silver coins recovered from the site, but from a commercial point of view the cargo of tin from the *L'Aigle* is most impressive – and she also bears testimony to the ocean's awesome power. The *Maori, Queen Victoria, Paquita*, and *Inchcape Rock* are significant because of their good state of preservation, while the Portuguese wrecks the *São Bento, Sacramento* and *Nossa Senhora de Atalaia* have provided us with valuable insights into a little-known period of history. Finally the *Grosvenor* site still fires the imagination and awakens visions of the romance and tragedy that often accompanies shipwreck disasters.

Top to bottom: The British iron ship Inchcape Rock *(Eastern Province Herald); A depiction by George Carter of the wreck of the* Grosvenor *(South African Library); Iron cannon-balls coated with lead from the* São Bento *(M. Turner).*

Chapter 9

Underwater Salvage

*O*ften in underwater salvage operations the most difficult part is finding the wreck itself, and the older the site, the greater the problems encountered by the salvor in this regard. Some wrecks, it is true, are discovered by spearfishermen who accidentally stumble on them while pursuing their quarry; the *Zeepaard*, *Fame*, *Sacramento* and *Nicobar* are examples, but clearly this is no reliable basis for salvage.

More modern wrecks are generally easier to find. In many cases there are detailed newspaper reports and photographs of the wrecking and the wreck site. Once the rough area in which the disaster took place is known, the rocks nearby can be searched at low tide for such remains as anchors, shell plating, copper sheeting or broken glass. As an example, the *President Reitz* was found through the large amount of twisted steel lying opposite the wreck site, and the British gunboat HMS *Osprey*, the *Cape Recife* and the *Western Knight* were similarly found. Examples of wrecks found through newspaper research are the *Lyngenfjord*, which was pinpointed by means of an aerial photograph taken at the time of its wrecking, and the *Panaghia*, which was found through an article in a newspaper which described it as lying within sight of the *Lyngenfjord*.

Older wrecks present greater problems, as there is likely to be far less concrete evidence pointing to their existence, but divers came across the Portuguese galleons *Nossa Senhora de Atalaia* and *São Bento* and the Dutch East Indiaman *Bennebroek* when investigating sites where shards of Chinese porcelain and trade beads regularly wash ashore.

Research is normally the starting point in any search for a historical wreck, and archival sources and old maps often provide valuable clues as to the general whereabouts of such wrecks. Modern aids such as side-scan sonar and especially proton magnetometers have proved invaluable in giving clues to metallic masses on the sea-bed, but the actual identification of a wreck usually depends on an inspection on site and correlating the evidence found with archival research.

Once a wreck has been found and identified, the next step is to apply for the necessary permissions to proceed with a salvage operation. Formerly anyone in possession of a valid salvage permit issued by the Department of Customs could take anything he liked off any wreck along the coast, and was only required to pay a small percentage of the value of the items found to the Department. At present, if a wreck is more than fifty years old, in addition to the salvage permit an excavation permit issued by the South African National Monuments Council is required. The Council discusses the salvor's application at its regular meetings and decides whether the applicant, who must be affiliated to a museum, is a trustworthy, well-intentioned salvor who will respect the historical value of the wreck site on which he intends working. If the Council agrees to the permit, it is issued in the applicant's name and grants him sole salvage rights on the wreck, subject to a number of conditions. The usual agreement is that the co-operating museum receives a percentage of all finds, that the salvor must keep proper records of such finds, and that the salvor must grant museum researchers the opportunity to study these finds as soon as possible. Furthermore, no salvage may be undertaken until the proper notice has been given in the *Government Gazette*.

The new dispensation for the salvor allows him to go about his business without having to remove all valuable cargo with undue haste, as any other diver who tries to pirate the site risks prosecution. The salvor is thus able to plot and evaluate the entire site systematically before recovering items of historical and commercial value. All such finds are handed to museum researchers who document and record them, after which they are handed back to the salvor. With this system it is hoped that the mistakes of the past will not be repeated, but obviously a great deal of trust is placed in the salvor, who has a responsibility to all other divers not to damage the relations between divers and museum officials any further.

Below: A ceramic container for mineral water recovered from the wreck of the Dutch corvette Zeepaard, *which came to grief near Port Elizabeth on 29 March 1823. The maker's inscription identifies it as a product of the Selters Mineral Works in Germany, a company still operating today. (M. Turner)*
Below, centre: A French naval flintlock pistol recovered from the wreck of the Zeepaard. *(M. Turner)*
Bottom: A sale notice concerning the wreck of the British transport vessel Arniston, *wrecked at Waenhuiskrans on 30 May 1815. (Cape Town Gazette)*

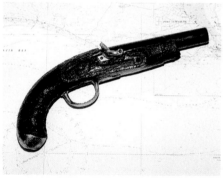

PUBLIC SALE.

THE undersigned, (authorized by His Excellency The Governor and Commander in Chief), will expose to Public Sale, on Monday, Tuesday, and Wednesday, the 7th, 8th, and 9th of August next, on account of Government, and those interested therein, a quantity of Goods, saved from the Wreck of the Transport Ship *Arniston*, consisting of:—

122 Casks, containing Wine, Arrack, &c.
580 empty ditto, of different sorts.
5 Ps. of the Wreck of said Ship, one of which is laying in Sea.
1 Bellows.
2 Casks Pitch, and various pieces of Cordage, and Rattans.
Further, whatever else may be offered for Sale on the above days.
The Sale will commence at 10 o'clock in the morning of each day, and be held on the Beach near the Eilands Valley.
Caledon, 23th July, 1815.
  J. H. FROUENFELDER, V. Mr.

Once the required permissions have been obtained, the next step on a wreck site west of Cape Agulhas would probably involve a kelp-cutting programme, as this thick, fleshy sea-weed blankets most west coast sites so thoroughly that it is all but impossible to work without first clearing it.

On sites of historic value, a thorough preliminary survey should be made, without removing any artefacts that may be found. After such a survey has been made, the salvor should try to lay out a rough grid system of nylon rope or interlocking metal tubing over the whole site. Not only will this be of benefit to the museum in its subsequent evaluation of artefacts, but it is also of great help to the salvor himself, especially in the sandy conditions in which so many wrecks are found.

Ideally plastic numbers are placed in each square in the grid and a helper in the support boat catalogues each find in a register with its particular grid number so that a museum can later reconstruct the site on paper. Sometimes wave and bottom conditions are such that a grid system is impractical, as it may take a tremendous pounding during heavy surf action. Over some areas of a wreck there could be as little as 0,6 m of water, even at high tide; on the site of the wreck of the Dutch corvette *Zeepaard*, which lies on an offshore reef in Sardinia Bay, for instance, a cast iron carronade is actually visible above the water at low tide, and the sea would have to be exceptionally flat to excavate in that area effectively. However, any alternative system which allows the salvor to plot his finds accurately is acceptable. It must be remembered that a hole dug in the sandy bottom of the sea fills up again within hours of the diver's leaving the site, and the grid allows the salvor to orientate himself when he returns on the next calm day, which can be up to three weeks later.

It must be remembered that the long time spent on archaeological sites on land in recovering artefacts from a dig are not practical underwater. Neither is any laborious dating procedure necessary, as a wreck site is a time capsule, in which all the articles were deposited at one known time. A rough grid simply enables the diver and the museum to understand how a vessel broke up and in which area a certain article was found. In practice it is good policy to work in the blocks closer to the shore on calm days as these are normally shallower, and to work the deeper blocks when there is a stronger ground swell.

Grid systems were used with great success during the excavations of the wrecks of the British transport vessel *Arniston* at Arniston (or Waenhuiskrans) in 1982, the *Johanna* at 'Die Dam' in 1983, and also during the salvage of a large number of tin ingots off the *L'Aigle* in 1981 by Tubby Gericke and Brian Clark, an operation which can be considered the most technically advanced and difficult salvage yet carried out on the South African coast. The cargo lay beneath shallow, surf-line sand-banks and the grid allowed the salvors to keep track of the areas which had been cleared of ingots; this saved the team a great deal of money and time.

Many different types of deposits are likely to be found on any wreck site. The deeper crevices on the site will contain sand and shingle deposits, some of them up to a metre deep, and the only way to clean out these holes is to deploy an air-lift. This is a flexible pipe, preferably at least 150 mm in diameter, which extends from the sea-bed to the surface. By means of a compressor, which may be situated in the salvage vessel or ashore, air is fed into the mouth of the pipe underwater, controlled by a quarter-turn valve. The other end of the pipe should be at least 5 m from the excavation area in order to prevent a constant stream of debris falling back into the hole.

The air-lift works on the principle of air expansion: the air enters the submerged mouth at ambient pressure – that is, the same pressure as that of the surrounding water – and as it rushes up the pipe towards the surface it expands rapidly. This upward rush of air brings about a strong inflow of water into the pipe, and all the loose debris is carried up with it. Larger pieces of material such as stones, large shells and artefacts will lodge in the submerged mouth, and after the air supply has been cut off they can be removed and placed safely at a distance from the hole. Very heavy artefacts will all lie on bedrock, and only when the overburden has been completely removed will the diver find these.

In certain circumstances a sand-blower (originally devised for use off the coast of Florida by divers salvaging gold and silver from a sunken Spanish fleet) can be used to remove sand overburden in a fraction of the time necessary for more conventional sand-removal systems to accomplish this. In essence the sand-blower consists of a hood fitted over the powerful propeller of a custom-built craft in such a way

Legislation

Shipwrecks and salvage on the coast of South Africa are regulated mainly by two Acts, namely the *Merchant Shipping Act*, No. 57 of 1951, and the *National Monuments Act*, No. 28 of 1969, as amended.

Merchant Shipping Act

The relevant part of this Act is Chapter VII, comprising Section 293-306. Provision is made, *inter alia*, for the appointment of salvage officers, whose powers and duties are set out; this includes the power to suppress plunder and disorder by force. Various aspects concerning compensation for salvage services rendered are also set out. A noteworthy provision is that no-one may board a vessel without the permission of the person in charge of the vessel, and that any attempt at an unauthorised boarding may be repelled by force. Another is that anybody has the right of access to a stricken vessel for the purposes of rendering assistance, or for salvage. If no access road is available, for instance, an owner of land opposite the wreck site may not deny access to the wreck across his land. This right of access includes the right to set up a camp, and to store salvaged material from the wreck. Care must be taken, however, to cause as little damage as possible.

National Monuments Act

The relevant part of this Act is Section 12, which deals mainly with wrecks older than 50 years, and has the object of controlling indiscriminate and destructive salvage operations through a permit system. The National Monuments Council will issue such a permit only if the applicant agrees to certain conditions, namely:

1. The applicant must satisfactorily complete the application form whereby he agrees to the conditions laid down by the National Monuments Council.
2. The applicant must have a salvage license from the Department of Customs and Excise.
3. As the wreck is a protected historical site, the salvage work must be undertaken in an approved scientific manner to ensure that the maximum historical information is recovered from the site about the ship's construction, equipment, cargo and so forth. The method used should be that of a marine archaeological excavation.
4. The applicant must with his application submit the exact situation of the wreck as well as evidence regarding the identity of the ship and how and when it was lost. As soon as the applicant has positively identified the wreck he should inform the National Monuments Council to ensure that a salvage permit has not already been issued for the wreck.
5. The applicant must also submit a letter of agreement between himself and the museum, approved by the Council, with which he intends to collaborate and which should be able to receive, preserve, store and identify the salvaged material.
6. The salvor, who must personally be in charge of the salvage operation, is required to keep a register of all the salvaged material in accordance with his salvage license, and also a salvage logbook to be written up daily. The logbook will record the salvage methods used, the location of the objects found, features of the wreck, and so forth. It must be available at all times for inspection by representatives of the Council.
7. The salvor must submit a quarterly report to inform about what progress, if any, has taken place since his previous report. Such a report must include a detailed list of acquisitions from the wreck, plans, and so forth. If no work has been done, this must also be reported. Within a year of the termination of the permit, the salvor must submit a final report to the Council. Copies of published reports must also be lodged with the Council.
8. A plan of the wreck site must be prepared before any objects are removed and all finds must be related to a grid system or to fix-points. If possible the site should be photographed.
9. All salvaged material must be recorded and placed in custody of the museum for storage and preservation and may not be disposed of until studied and shared. An exception to this rule is cargo accepted by the museum to be of no historical or cultural value.
10. The museum, in consultation with the Council and the salvor, will then decide on the division of the salvaged material between the museum and the salvor. The museum may demand a maximum of 50% of the salvaged goods but the salvor may give the museum a bigger share if he so chooses. The modus operandi for the sharing is that the objects or lots will be chosen alternatively by the museum and the salvor, the museum having the first choice.
11. The salvor is responsible for all costs involved in the salvage operation, as well as the transport of the salvaged material to the museum. In addition, the salvor is also responsible for the payment of all duties and royalties on his share of the salvaged material to the nearest Controller of Customs and Excise.
12. In the case of dispute the Council will nominate two assessors or arbitrators from which the salvor may select one. Arbitration in terms of the Arbitration Act, No. 42 of 1965, will be the final means of settling any dispute.

The function of the permit system is to safeguard wrecks by requiring that those who investigate them have a legitimate reason for doing so, are competent, employ a methodology which ensures the greatest amount of information recovery possible, will report to the Council the results of their undertaking in a satisfactory manner and within reasonable time, and have provided for the conservation, in perpetuity, of all recovered objects and associated data and records.

Top: *A broken Chinese porcelain bowl embedded in conglomerate recovered from the wreck of the Dutch East-Indiaman* Middelburg, *which blew up and sank in Saldanha Bay on 21 July 1781. (M. Turner)*
Above, centre: *A silver Mexican pillar dollar or piece of eight conglomerated onto a clay brick recovered from the wreck of the Dutch East-Indiaman* Reigersdaal, *which ran aground on Springfontein Point on 25 October 1747. Note the clay pipe-stem protruding to the right of the coin. (M. Turner)*
Above: *Modern treasure in the form of a pile of copper ingots recovered from the wreck of the* Evdokia, *stacked on the deck of the salvage vessel* Ocean Pride. *Each ingot weighed about 118 kg. (M. Turner)*

that it directs downward the propeller wash, which then blows away the sand over-burden covering a wreck. The first sand-blower deployed on the coast of South Africa was built by Tubby Gericke and Brian Clark to recover the cargo of tin from the site of the wreck of the *L'Aigle*. The same sand-blower was later used on the site of the *Johanna* wreck with great success, and more than 23 000 cob coins, as well as many pieces of pewter-ware, musket balls and clay pipes were recovered from below the sand.

Potholes often contain many articles such as bottles, ceramics and wooden items in near-perfect condition, as even violent surf-action would not have been able to break them up. Gold coins found in these circumstances will be in pristine, shiny condition, but silver coins will probably be badly oxidised, often losing up to 80 per cent of their original thickness. The only way such coins will be recovered in good condition will be if they were coated in thick, hard matrix. The matrix is usually at its best when iron articles such as cannon balls lie in close proximity, as, by a process of electrolysis, iron oxide will have been deposited on the articles. In the open areas of a reef the deepest crevices are normaly coated with a deposit of the matrix, and here the best-preserved artefacts are likely to be found, especially in an area where the vessel's stern was broken up.

The best way to remove these deposits is to employ a light explosive charge to break them up into manageable chunks, which can then be easily loaded into the work-boat and taken home to be processed at leisure. Open reef deposits are unlikely to contain intact fragile artefacts such as porcelain and glass, and a light explosive charge is not likely to do damage to copper, gold and silver objects. On the other hand the usual hammer-and-chisel method could cause some damage, as the salvor does not know what is hidden inside the matrix conglomerate.

Pewter, silver spoons, bronze cannon, coins and brass and copper artefacts have been successfully removed from matrix by blasting, but it must be remembered that too violent a charge will cause damage: many valuable artefacts were destroyed on the *Reigersdaal* by the incorrect use of explosives.

A proper salvage operation can take more than a year to complete. Only after all deposits, potholes and crevices have been thoroughly explored should any bronze guns be removed. Cast iron guns are not usually worth removing as highly sophisti-cated and expensive conservation procedures are necessary to prevent them from flaking and crumbling away. Only if they are culturally important should they be taken from the site and then only if proper preservation facilities are available. Cast iron cannon and anchors should, however, be marked on the grid and, before the diving party leaves the site, should be rolled over and the area beneath them exca-vated. Many well-preserved coins and other articles have often been found beneath cannon. Before a site is finally left, a metal detector survey should be carried out to find any remaining artefacts.

Bronze cannon may be towed out to deep water with the aid of lifting 'camels' (bouyant air-bags made of reinforced plastic) and placed on a marked dump site to await the salvage boat. Use nylon rope to secure them as this prevents damage to crests, markings and so on. Under no circumstances should bronze cannon be sent to scrapyards; even in a badly eroded state they are objects of beauty. Recently helicopters have been used to salvage bronze cannon from wreck sites; this was first successfully attempted in 1978, when a carronade was removed by helicopter from the *Zeepaard*.

The salvage of a modern metal steamer site can be considered a purely commer-cial venture, and no archaeological procedures need to be followed. The salvor is mainly involved in removing non-ferrous metal such as brass and copper from the site, and this is sold as scrap metal. Various articles of a vessel's equipment, such as portholes, bells and name-plates, have collector appeal, and a ready market exists for them. The main sources of non-ferrous metals on such salvage sites are the propeller, condensors, pump housings, valves and the network of copper steam-pipes found in older engine-rooms.

A metal steamer site is best worked with heavy explosive charges, as the blasting loosens all metal on the site and removes oxidised iron from the brass articles. After a blast the brass gleams and can easily be located and salvaged – but great care must be taken since the metal plates become razor-sharp following the blast. Many tons of brass and copper can be recovered from a typical steamer wreck. The Portuguese

liner *Lisboa*, wrecked near Cape Columbine in 1910, has the reputation of yielding the largest supply of scrap metal recovered on the South African coast. Over the years many groups of salvors have worked on her, and each time good hauls have been made.

Propellers are a fine source of scrap metal. Bronze propellers are of two types: the earlier models had each individual blade bolted on to an iron boss, for instance the propellers found on the *Western Knight, Hypatia, Cariboo* and *Cape Recife*, but most of the later propellers were of solid bronze, for instance those of the *Lyngenfjord* and the *President Reitz*.

Propellers are usually salvaged with the help of explosives. The first step is to blow the propeller off the shaft; this is done by placing charges between the stern frame and the boss. The charge should knock the propeller off the shaft, after which charges can be placed inside the hollow boss and each blade broken loose. The older, bolted types are broken up in much the same way, the only difference being that the iron boss must be broken on the shaft. The individual blades can then be towed out to deeper water with the aid of lifting-bags and salvaged by a large salvage boat.

Once an article of cultural value has been removed from a wreck site, it needs to be restored to a condition as close to its original state as possible. Some articles removed from a wreck will be in near-perfect condition, and to be restored these will simply need to be soaked in fresh water and then dried out. Bottles, ceramics, gold coins and brass and copper artefacts are often found in this state. Other items make good museum exhibits when left with a small portion of their original concretion attached; the romance of the sea is captured when they are displayed alongside articles that have been cleaned and restored. When an artefact is found to be damaged, it is best to leave it uncleaned, but those in a perfect state should be cleaned as this enables one to see all the details of their workings or ornamentation.

The most common articles found on old shipwreck sites are usually made of copper, brass or lead. Their degree of preservation is linked to the sea-bed conditions in which they are found. Large banks of matrix must first be broken up, preferably by employing a small explosive charge. The smaller chunks of matrix are then loaded into the boat and should be kept in a bath of water, as once they dry out they

Top: A way to find shipwreck sites is to walk along the beach at low tide looking for broken porcelain, beads, glass, metal plating or timber. This iron stay and timber spiked with a copper nail comes from an unknown wreck and was found on Thys Point near Cape St Francis. (M. Turner)
Above: Bernard Moore rests after a 1 700-kg manganese bronze propeller blade was loaded onto a truck on the beach at Huisklip. The blade was recovered from the wreck of the Lyngenfjord, *wrecked in 1938. (M. Turner)*

Top: Silver coins in the process of being cleaned by electrolysis. (M. Turner)
***Above, centre:** A selection of artefacts from the* Reigersdaal. *(M. Turner)*
***Above:** A selection of silver coins and a silver spoon from the* Reigersdaal *after cleaning. (M. Turner)*

tend to set like concrete and are then extremely difficult to break up. The wet matrix is tapped lightly with a flat-headed hammer and carefully crushed. As the artefacts are recovered from the matrix, they are dropped into a bucket of fresh water in order to enable the salts to leach out.

Different materials need different conservation methods. If one suspects that very fine and delicate objects are encased in the lumps of matrix, it is a good idea to have the lumps X-rayed before attempting to break them open. Lead artefacts are usually badly corroded, and conservation is of little use; but if the lead artefact is well-preserved, a solution of hydrochloric acid (HCL) can be used to remove any matrix or lead oxide clinging to it. Brass is also best cleaned with hydrochloric acid, but here a stronger solution can be used; a 100 per cent application of HCL does no harm to brass provided that the article is not left in the acid too long. Gold artefacts and coins are usually found in a perfect state of preservation and it is normally necessary only to remove the matrix. A dilute solution of hydrochloric acid will serve the purpose; a violent bubbling reaction will be seen when the matrix and acid come into contact with each other. After an article has been cleaned in acid, it is advisable to drop it into an alkaline solution afterwards to neutralise the acid and to prevent any further chemical reaction from taking place. All metal objects should be treated in an electrolytic bath to remove salts and other corrosive chemicals. Untreated bronze often suffers from 'bronze disease', which appears as a green verdigris and which slowly eats away the metal. The correct cleaning of artefacts is a specialised science and no fixed methods can be adopted.

Silver is the most difficult material to clean satisfactorily. Even if it is found encased in matrix, it will still be coated with a thin layer of silver oxide, and this is not easy to remove without damaging the surface of the article. A silver article removed from its protective layer of matrix must be dipped into a 100 per cent hydrochloric acid bath; once again a violent reaction will be seen as the HCL attacks the lime and iron oxide encrustations that make up a typical matrix deposit. The article must be left to soak in the acid until all reaction has stopped; it is then washed thoroughly in a soap solution. The silver article should now be clear of most oxides or matrix encrustations, and details such as hallmarks or, in the case of coins, crests and dates, will be visible; however, the silver oxide layer will still be attached and will be seen as a black coating that clogs all details on the article.

To remove this oxide the article must be placed in an alkaline solution and an electric current of 12 volts passed through it. The article must be attached to the negative terminal of a car battery and the positive terminal attached to a stainless steel plate: article and plate should be about 5 cm apart. When the current is switched on, a stream of bubbles will be seen rising from the article; this breaks up the oxide and eventually repels it. After a few seconds large pieces of black oxide will be seen falling off the article and the solution will soon be discoloured. No more than ten coins should be cleaned in a litre of solution before it is changed.

After about a minute the article must be removed from the electrolytic bath and washed in a strong detergent – it will now be a dull silver colour. To bring out the original lustre of the piece, use a toothbrush and detergent, but do so with care, as too vigorous a cleaning will detract from the article's antique appeal. Coins cleaned in this way have proved acceptable to numismatists and in many cases have shown only about 1 per cent silver loss after being immersed for more than 250 years at a wreck site. Coins from the *Merestein*, some of which were already more than a hundred years old when the vessel was wrecked in 1702, were found to have only pre-wrecking wear and tear visible, while the *Reigersdaal* coins were in exceptional condition after 232 years of immersion at a shallow surf-line wreck site.

A study of various salvage attempts on different wreck sites shows that no one single method can be recommended. The older wrecks have great cultural value, and it is essential that they be worked with great care and professionalism. In the past too many valuable sites have been damaged and too much material lost. Some of the blame for this should be borne by the museums, as many salvors, genuinely interested in their finds, have approached museums for help, only to be told bluntly to leave the wrecks alone. A working relationship built up with the divers would have enabled museums to put on display a great number of interesting artefacts from wrecks. The care shown by the early divers who salvaged the *Fame*, the *Merestein* and the *Middelburg* has been largely overlooked by critics of the wreck-diving fraternity, which has even donated many valuable artefacts to museums.

In order to show how many of the points touched on thus far are carried out in practice, a study of one of the most valuable and interesting salvages to date, that of the *Merestein*, can serve as a good example.

On 3 April 1702 the *Merestein*, an outward-bound Dutch East-Indiaman on a trading mission to the East heavily laden with specie, was wrecked on Jutten Island at the entrance to Saldanha Bay; many members of her crew were sick with scurvy and she was hoping to pick up fresh victuals. As she entered the bay, the look-out sighted heavy surf breaking off Jutten Island and a warning was shouted by the watchman. A south-westerly wind was blowing and the order was given to sail the ship into the wind; the sails were consequently shortened, but the vessel failed to answer her helm properly. The captain, Jan Subbing, ordered an anchor to be dropped, but this failed to steady the vessel, and he ordered another. At this point the sails filled with wind and the chief mate suggested that the anchor lines be cut, so that the vessel could be brought about. However, Subbing first called a council of his officers, but as a result of the delay the vessel ran aground on the south-west corner of the island, and only 99 of her crew of 200 managed to save themselves.

The sea was extremely rough, and when morning came, nothing of the *Merestein* showed above the water. The survivors gazed at the wreck site from the safety of the island, but all they could see were a few planks floating over her grave. Word was sent to the Governor at the Cape, Willem Adriaan van der Stel, and when he heard that a huge treasure had been lost in the disaster, he sent a search party to the island to try to locate the exact spot were the vessel had been wrecked, with a view to salvaging the treasure at a later date. The vessel dispatched to the scene of the disaster was the *Wezel*, and on board was the first mate of the *Merestein*. By using a sounding-lead it was established that the *Merestein* had at first proceeded over a sandy bottom, but within 200 m of the island an extremely rocky bottom was encountered; this, as well as heavy breakers, made it impossible for the *Wezel* to proceed any closer. A report was submitted to Van der Stel in which it was stated, under oath, that it would never be possible to recover any treasure off the wreck and that it was unlikely that any of it would be washed ashore, due to the steep nature of the shoreline.

The Dutch East India Company was much perturbed by the loss of this treasure. When they contracted the famed English diver John Lethbridge in 1727 to recover as much specie as he could from various wrecks at the Cape, he was allowed, at his request, to proceed to Jutten Island after completing salvage operations in Table Bay. In the relatively calm waters off Cape Town he had had some success with his diving-barrel, but on Jutten Island his attempts were foiled by the heavy surf conditions; after spending some time waiting for suitable conditions, he gave up. Thereafter the wreck lay undisturbed for a long time; even though the *Merestein* treasure was mentioned in many a book on South African shipwrecks, no serious attempt was made to salvage it.

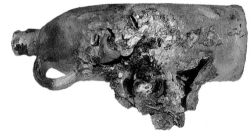

Above, from top to bottom: *Various artefacts in different stages of cleaning: Silver coins from the* Reigersdaal *(M. Turner); A flintlock pistol from the* L'Alouette *(M. Turner); A mineral water bottle from the* Zeepaard *(M. Turner); A brass porthole from the* Maori *(M. Turner).*

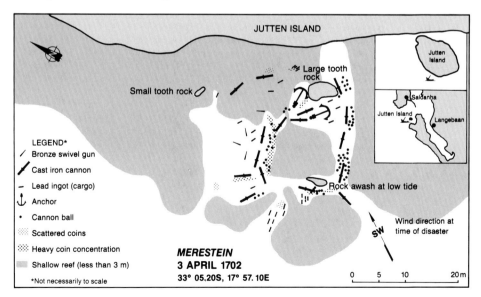

Left: *A map of the site of the Dutch East-Indiaman* Merestein, *which was wrecked on Jutten Island on 3 April 1702.*

JUTTEN ISLAND

Large tooth rock

Small tooth rock

Jutten Island

Saldanha

Jutten Island

Langebaan

LEGEND*
/ Bronze swivel gun
↗ Cast iron cannon
– Lead ingot (cargo)
⚓ Anchor
• Cannon ball
Scattered coins
Heavy coin concentration
Shallow reef (less than 3 m)
*Not necessarily to scale

Rock awash at low tide

Wind direction at time of disaster

SW

MERESTEIN
3 APRIL 1702
33° 05.20S, 17° 57.10E

0   5   10   20m

Top: *Brass furniture from a flintlock firearm recovered from the* Merestein. *(M. Turner)*
Above, centre: *Coins and a pewter plate from the* Merestein. *(M. Turner)*
Above: *A view of Jutten Island, where the* Merestein *was wrecked. (M. Turner)*

In recent times the most significant signs of the wreck were a large number of lead ingots from her cargo scattered in the deeper crevices, as well as some badly eroded muzzle-loading cast iron cannon concreted on to the rocks and covered in marine growth. A few bronze breech-loading swivel-guns could also be seen.

The first team of divers to attempt a serious salvage of the wreck arrived at the island in 1971. The leader of this group was Bobby Hayward of Cape Town, a well-known commercial diver with a great interest in history. The rough location of the site was known, as coins occasionally washed up and were picked up by the personnel employed to gather guano on the island; they were well aware of the presence of the wreck. Unaided by modern search aids such as magnetometers or metal detectors, the diving team found the exact location of the site after a search of only a few hours. An attempt was made to obtain sole rights to the wreck through an action in the Supreme Court, but the application was turned down, and this left the site open to exploitation by rival groups.

The *Merestein* is typical of a wreck on an open-coast surf-line site. The wreck site on the south-west side of the island is in an extremely exposed area which is completely at the mercy of the huge ground swells that periodically pound the shore. Very little timber from her hull has been found, and this is understandable, as the hull completely disintegrated in the heavy surf at the time of her wrecking, the timber being washed ashore on the island and on the beaches in the vicinity. Some idea of the velocity of the wave action on the site can be gained by noting the position of a cast iron cannon on the island, high above the water line. Furthermore the site is blanketed with red-bait pods and in the deeper crevices kelp covers the rocks.

The salvage party began systematically searching through the gullies and crevices and discovered banks of red matrix consisting of lime, iron oxide and broken glass carpeting the bottom of the deeper crevices. They had to wait patiently for flat conditions and during the few calm days allowed them they blasted and chipped away at the beds of conglomerate, and, to their amazement, found encased in it the legendary silver treasure of the *Merestein*.

The only coins which had survived in a perfect state of preservation were those which were completely embedded in the concretion. After cleaning, these coins proved the *Merestein* to be the most important coin wreck found on the South African coast. Ducatoons, silver riders and Dutch schillings dating back to the late 16th century were found in great numbers. The coins which had not been encased in the matrix were badly corroded; some were worn paper-thin, of interest only to scrap metal dealers. Besides the silver coins, a few gold ducats were found, but not in great quantities.

News of the find soon leaked out and much to the consternation of the Hayward team the Dodds brothers, who had been working at the site of the *Middelburg*, began salvage operations on the *Merestein* site, as they were legally quite entitled to do. An uneasy truce was arranged, and both teams feverishly worked to salvage as much as possible. Even though they salvaged great quantities of coins, not all were found. Over the years many other groups of divers have worked on the site, and even today coins are still to be found. The total number of coins recovered must be in the region of 15 000, but the only documented lists of coins are those contained in the catalogues for the 1972 Johannesburg and Cape Town auction sales of treasure recovered by the Dodds brothers.

Apart from the fact that on the whole the financial rewards of this recovery of treasure were disappointing, the greatest tragedy of the salvage operation at this and most other sites along the coast of South Africa was the intense competition between the rival groups of salvors. The greatest emphasis was placed on the recovery of the treasure, and little attempt was made to recover the other valuable artefacts which were uncovered. The bronze guns and lead ingots were removed, but many other objects such as pewter spoons and plates, clay pipes and candlesticks were largely ignored in the rush for silver. Furthermore the authorities showed little interest in obtaining a representative collection for display, for instance in Saldanha, and thereby lost a great opportunity.

One can but hope that the mistakes of the past will serve as lessons for the future. Overhasty action benefits nobody, while due caution will ensure that finds of undoubted cultural value will be preserved for future generations to enjoy.

Coins recovered from the Merestein

The following is a selection of the large variety of coins recovered from the site of the *Merestein*:

Rijksdaalder
30 stuivers, Utrecht 1687

Ducatoons
Philip IV
  Antwerp, 1631, 1633-1640, 1642,
    1644-1665
  Brussels, 1632-1640, 1642, 1644,
    1647-1665
  Flanders, 1631-1632, 1639, 1647-1659,
    1662, 1664-1665
  Tournay, 1633, 1649
Charles II
  Antwerp, 1666-1668, 1670, 1672-1673,
    1679, 1683-1684
  Brussels, 1666, 1668-1671, 1673, 1676,
    1678-1680, 1683-1684, 1686 (inscribed
    edge)

Flanders, 1666-1667, 1670, 1673, 1694
Albert & Isabella
  Antwerp, 1619
Philip of Tournay
  1633, 1649
Maximilian of Bavaria
  1668, 1671

Half Ducatoons
Philip IV
  Antwerp, 1647-1648, 1651-1652,
    660-1661
  Brussels, 1651, 1661, 1663
  Flanders, 1661
Charles II
  Antwerp, 1666, 1668, 1676

Silver Riders
  Campen, 1659-1662, 1664, 1666-1670,
    1676-1677, 1679, 1680
  Deventer, 1662, 1664, 1666
  Gelderland, 1659-1660, 1662, 1666-1670,
    1672, 1674, 1676-1677, 1679-1681
  Holland, 1659, 1661, 1668, 1672-1676,
    1678, 1692, 1694
  Overijssel, 1660, 1664, 1666, 1668, 1670,

1672-1673, 1676-1680
  Utrecht, 1659-1662, 1666-1668, 1670,
    1674, 1679-1680, 1692
  West Friesland, 1653, 1659-1666, 1668-
    1670, 1672-1674, 1676-1677, 1679
  Zeeland, 1659-1660, 1662, 1664, 1668
  Zwolle, 1659-1661, 1668-1670, 1677

Half Silver Riders
  Overijssel (Various dates)

Schillings
  Campen, 1670, 1675, 1683
  Deventer (Various dates)
  Friesland, 1582, 1621, 1622, 1624
  Gelderland (Various dates)
  Groningen, 1691
  Holland, 1601
  Schipschillings (Various dates)
  Utrecht, 1601, 1677
  West Friesland, 1600-1601, 1629, 1656,
    1661, 1674, 1678-1680, 1682, 1689
  Zeeland, 1610, 1624, 1668
  Zwolle, 1675, 1678-1679

Dubbel Stuivers (Various dates)

A selection of silver coins recovered from the wreck of the Merestein. *(M. Turner)*

Appendix 1

Alphabetical List of Shipwrecks

Please note: The name of a wrecked vessel is followed by the year of wrecking and Geographical Region (see Appendix 3) in brackets

A

A.H. Stevens 1862 (13)
Abbotsford 1843 (29)
Abdul Medjid 1871 (29)
Abeona 1900 (28)
Abercrombie Robinson 1842 (9)
Active 1845 (25)
Addison 1722 (9)
Adelaide 1866 (37)
Adele 1888 (18)
Adelfotis 1956 (19)
Admiral Cockburn 1839 (16)
Adolphus 1819 (24)
Adriatic 1822 (9)
Africaine 1841 (32)
African Adventure 1830 (37)
African Belle 1873 (32)
Agnes 1882 (25)
Agostino Rombo 1902 (29)
Akbar 1863 (7)
Alacrity 1865 (9)
Albatross 1863 (15)
Albatross 1874 (17)
Albatross 1881 (29)
Albert 1857 (20)
Albert Juhl 1876 (33)
Albinia 1851 (29)
Alcestis 1892 (19)
Alert 1840 (29)
Alfred 1830 (9)
Alfredia 1887 (35)
Alice Smith 1861 (35)
Alicia Jane 1845 (3)
Alma 1877 (29)
Alma 1878 (33)
Almira Coombs 1878 (29)
Amana 1889 (32)
Amatola 1852 (33)
Ambleside 1868 (36)
Amelia Mulholland 1850 (29)
America 1900 (9)
Amersham 1869 (21)
Amsterdam 1817 (29)
Amwell 1852 (29)
Amy 1722 (9)
Andreas Riis 1888 (29)
Ann Staniland 1876 (33)
Ann and Eliza 1796 (30)
Annabella 1856 (37)
Anne 1818 (9)
Anne 1859 (15)
Anne Marie 1872 (29)
Annie Benn 1872 (23)
Annie S. 1875 (33)
Antelope 1837 (9)
Antipolis 1977 (14)
Antonie 1864 (33)

Anubis 1799 (9)
Apollo 1823 (10)
Arab 1850 (9)
Arabia 1858 (12)
Arabian 1859 (29)
Arago 1858 (7)
Araminta 1889 (29)
Argali 1869 (29)
Arion 1854 (21)
Ariosto 1854 (37)
Armenia 1902 (7)
Arniston 1815 (21)
Arnold 1902 (29)
Arosa 1976 (1)
Ashlands 1900 (31)
Ashleigh Brook 1890 (8)
Ashmount 1905 (32)
Asiatic 1850 (29)
Asphodel 1878 (34)
Atbara 1902 (33)
Athens 1865 (11)
Athina 1967 (25)
Atlantic 1835 (29)
Atlas 1859 (21)
Atlas 1896 (7)
Aurora 1902 (33)
Avala 1939 (19)
Avenhorn 1788 (9)

B

Ballarat 1864 (29)
Barbadoes 1861 (29)
Barbara Gordon 1853 (19)
Barrys I 1848 (20)
Barrys II 1857 (21)
Basileia 1859 (29)
Bato 1806 (16)
Belleisle 1849 (21)
Benefactress 1870 (16)
Bengal 1840 (7)
Benjamin 1800 (16)
Bennebroek 1713 (32)
Bernicia 1861 (13)
Berwick 1827 (26)
Betsy and Sara 1839 (30)
Bia 1917 (15)
Bierstadt 1877 (33)
Birkenhead 1852 (17)
Bismarck 1873 (32)
Bittern 1848 (13)
Blackaller 1846 (29)
Bodiam Castle 1852 (20)
Bonanza 1894 (33)
Bonaventura 1686 (38)
Border 1947 (1)
Borderer 1868 (20)

Bosphorus 1867 (26)
Brederode 1785 (19)
Breidablik 1872 (37)
Bridgetown 1882 (37)
Brighton 1881 (33)
Brilliant 1880 (29)
Briseis 1859 (32)
Britannia 1826 (2)
British Duke 1888 (26)
British Peer 1896 (6)
British Settler 1850 (4)
British Tar 1850 (37)
Brunswick 1805 (16)
Bruydegom 1674 (5)
Buffalo 1889 (32)
Buffon 1858 (31)
Bulli 1884 (3)
Bulwark 1963 (17)
Burnham 1840 (37)

C

C. Boschetto 1888 (29)
C.P. 1874 (20)
Calcutta 1881 (35)
Caledonian 1878 (9)
Calpe 1831 (9)
Cambusnethan 1897 (30)
Camphill 1913 (19)
Candian 1831 (9)
Cape Breton 1835 (29)
Cape of Good Hope 1881 (21)
Cape Recife 1929 (27)
Caprera 1884 (29)
Cariboo 1928 (32)
Carl zu den Drei Greiffen 1875 (33)
Carlotta B. 1886 (15)
Carrie Wyman 1886 (33)
Caterina Doge 1886 (15)
Catharine Jamieson 1840 (11)
Catherine 1846 (32)
Catherine 1883 (29)
Catherine Isabella 1845 (1)
Catherine Scott 1878 (29)
Cavalieri Michelle Russo 1902 (29)
Celt 1875 (17)
Cerberus 1821 (7)
Chancellor 1854 (21)
Chandois 1722 (9)
Chanticleer 1848 (32)
Charles 1845 (31)
Charles Jackson 1884 (37)
Charlotte 1854 (29)
Charlotte A. Morrison 1862 (29)
Charmer 1877 (18)
Chartley Castle 1851 (7)
Chasseur 1859 (29)
Chieftain 1848 (10)
Childe Harold 1850 (8)
Christabel 1857 (9)
Christina 1882 (25)
Chub 1945 (3)
Circassia 1894 (35)
City of Hankow 1942 (4)
City of Lima 1883 (37)
City of Lincoln 1902 (9)
City of Peterborough 1865 (9)
Clan Gordon 1897 (38)
Clan Lindsay 1898 (35)
Clan Macgregor 1902 (21)

Clan Monroe 1905 (14)
Clan Stuart 1914 (16)
Clansman 1882 (33)
Clara 1880 (29)
Claudine 1849 (21)
Clipper 1873 (1)
Clyde 1879 (18)
Clymping 1881 (33)
Cockburn 1823 (16)
Cockburn 1850 (9)
Colebrooke 1778 (16)
Colonial Empire 1917 (28)
Columba 1880 (33)
Columbia 1796 (9)
Columbine 1829 (3)
Compage 1874 (33)
Conch 1847 (35)
Congune 1872 (37)
Conservative 1843 (6)
Constant 1902 (29)
Constantia 1868 (33)
Content 1902 (29)
Coquette 1874 (33)
Cottager 1845 (6)
Countess of Dudley 1877 (33)
County of Pembroke 1903 (29)
Courier 1846 (37)
Courier 1852 (9)
Craigellachie 1900 (32)
Crixea 1872 (33)
Cruiser 1872 (29)
Crusader 1868 (33)
Crusader 1910 (31)
Crystal Palace 1862 (9)

D

Daeyang Family 1986 (13)
Dageraad 1694 (13)
Dane 1865 (28)
Dauntless 1883 (33)
Dauphin 1830 (5)
Deane 1865 (9)
Defence 1857 (7)
Defiance 1871 (36)
Delhi 1843 (29)
Dennia 1864 (23)
Derby 1895 (27)
Diadem 1851 (25)
Diana 1846 (9)
Dido 1853 (10)
Die Heimath 1881 (33)
Diligence 1863 (1)
Discovery 1816 (9)
Doncaster 1836 (19)
Dorah 1821 (9)
Doris 1850 (29)
Dorothea 1898 (38)
Dorothys 1836 (25)
Dorthea 1888 (29)
Draga 1880 (37)
Drei Emmas 1888 (29)
Drei Thürme 1854 (20)
Drie Gebroeders 1792 (16)
Drietal Handelaars 1789 (16)
Duchess of Buccleugh 1850 (19)

Duinbreek 1737 (9)
Duke of Northumberland 1838 (20)
Dundrennan 1895 (20)
Dunlop 1838 (9)

E

E. A. Oliver 1873 (20)
E. B. Lohe 1872 (29)
Eagle Wing 1879 (19)
Earl of Hardwicke 1863 (37)
East London Packet 1855 (29)
Eastern Province 1865 (19)
Eastern Star 1880 (37)
Edie Waters 1876 (17)
Edith Smith 1871 (31)
Edward 1809 (20)
Eiland Mauritius 1644 (9)
Elaine 1872 (33)
Elda 1903 (29)
Eleanor 1839 (37)
Elephant 1750 (22)
Elise 1878 (33)
Elise 1879 (20)
Elise Linck 1902 (33)
Elite 1870 (32)
Eliza 1863 (10)
Eliza and Alice 1870 (27)
Elizabeth 1817 (1)
Elizabeth 1819 (9)
Elizabeth 1839 (32)
Elizabeth Brown 1872 (29)
Elizabeth Rowell 1843 (29)
Elizabeth Stevens 1888 (29)
Ellen 1861 (20)
Ellen Browse 1877 (33)
Ellida 1888 (17)
Elpida 1893 (33)
Emelia 1877 (18)
Emile Marie 1874 (33)
Emilia 1898 (29)
Emma 1821 (9)
Emma 1872 (33)
Emma 1880 (33)
Emma 1888 (32)
Emmanuel 1902 (29)
Emu 1817 (24)
Enchantress 1849 (11)
Enfants Nantais 1876 (37)
England 1869 (29)
Equator 1856 (20)
Erfprins van Augustenburg 1790 (9)
Erin 1872 (23)
Espero 1902 (36)
Essex 1832 (29)
Esso Wheeling 1948 (19)
Esterias 1865 (32)
Etheldreda 1865 (21)
Etta Loring 1878 (9)
Eurydice 1857 (29)
Euterpe 1876 (33)
Evdokia 1979 (26)
Eve 1845 (3)
Evelyn 1863 (17)

F

Fairfield 1842 (9)
Fairfield 1852 (36)

Fairholme 1888 (24)
Fame 1822 (14)
Fanny 1851 (9)
Fascadale 1895 (36)
Feejee 1837 (29)
Felix Vincidor 1841 (16)
Feniscowles 1819 (12)
Fernande 1865 (9)
Fidela 1873 (28)
Fidia D. 1889 (36)
Fijenoord 1736 (9)
Fingoe 1874 (33)
Finland 1887 (32)
Flamingo 1833 (16)
Flash 1869 (29)
Flora 1737 (9)
Flora 1821 (13)
Flora 1854 (29)
Florence 1859 (1)
Florence 1883 (31)
Florie 1874 (33)
Flower of the Arun 1870 (33)
Flying Fish 1855 (1)
Flying Scud 1880 (29)
Foam 1851 (33)
Forest Grove 1887 (31)
Forfarshire 1864 (13)
Forres 1869 (29)
Forresbank 1958 (35)
Fountain 1872 (28)
Frances Burn 1849 (29)
Frances Watson 1830 (29)
Francis Spaight 1846 (9)
Francisca 1882 (33)
Fratelli Arecco 1883 (37)
Fredheim 1897 (24)
Freeman Clarke 1883 (28)
Frida 1882 (1)
Friends Goodwill 1840 (3)
Frigga 1862 (9)
Frontier 1957 (32)
Frontier I 1926 (35)
Frontier II 1938 (35)
Fusilier 1865 (36)
Fynd 1946 (19)

G

Gabrielle 1902 (29)
Galatea 1846 (23)
Galera 1892 (23)
Galloway 1882 (28)
Gambia 1871 (29)
Gazelle 1879 (37)
General Nott 1876 (33)
Gentoo 1846 (20)
George 1831 (17)
George Henry Harrison 1851 (25)
George M. Livanos 1947 (12)
Gerhardine 1888 (29)
Gertrud Woermann 1903 (1)
Ghika 1847 (33)
Gilbert Henderson 1847 (29)
Gitana 1857 (9)
Gladiator 1860 (30)
Gleam 1882 (1)
Gloria Deo 1882 (19)
Goede Hoop 1692 (9)
Goel No. 1 1976 (13)
Gondolier 1836 (13)

Good Hope 1685 (37)
Good Hope 1819 (29)
Good Intent 1822 (9)
Gothenburg 1796 (12)
Gouda 1722 (9)
Gouden Buis 1693 (2)
Goudriaan 1737 (9)
Governess 1859 (29)
Gowan 1830 (29)
Grace 1822 (19)
Grace Peile 1872 (37)
Graf Wedell 1880 (37)
Grahamstown 1864 (9)
Greystoke Castle 1896 (21)
Grosvenor 1782 (35)
Gustaf 1869 (29)
Gustav Adolph 1902 (17)

H

H.D. Storer 1878 (37)
Haarlem 1728 (9)
Haddon Hall 1913 (4)
Haleric 1933 (3)
Haliartus 1932 (22)
Hamilla Mitchell 1844 (1)
Hamlet 1927 (6)
Hannah 1799 (9)
Hans Wagner 1902 (29)
Hansa 1883 (17)
Harmonie 1891 (28)
Harmony 1826 (24)
Harriet 1848 (21)
Harry Mundahl 1901 (36)
Hawthorn 1889 (37)
Hector 1852 (36)
Hektor 1913 (18)
Helen 1842 (10)
Helen 1858 (24)
Helene 1905 (33)
Henry Douse 1867 (33)
Hercules 1796 (32)
Hermann 1874 (29)
Hermanos 1902 (29)
Hermes 1901 (7)
Hero 1861 (29)
Herschel 1852 (7)
Het Huis te Kraaiestein 1698 (14)
Heworth 1823 (29)
Hogergeest 1692 (9)
Hohenzollern 1876 (33)
Holland 1786 (15)
Hoop 1784 (10)
Hope 1840 (26)
Hope 1880 (33)
Hopefield Packet 1869 (14)
Horizon 1967 (35)
Horwood 1845 (29)
Hotbank 1873 (28)
Howard 1840 (9)
Huma 1855 (33)
Hunter 1805 (9)
Hydra 1867 (37)
Hypatia 1929 (13)

I

Ianthe 1890 (1)
Idomene 1887 (35)
Iepenrode 1737 (9)

Il Nazerino 1885 (13)
Ilva 1866 (29)
Imerina 1885 (18)
Imogen 1867 (33)
Inchcape Rock 1902 (29)
Iris 1902 (29)
Isaac 1847 (19)
Isabel 1844 (29)
Isabella 1857 (9)
Ismore 1899 (3)
Ispahan 1886 (17)
Israel 1847 (9)
Itzehoe 1911 (28)
Ivy 1878 (36)

J

Jacaranda 1971 (35)
Jack Tar 1840 (29)
Jaeger 1619 (9)
James Gaddarn 1882 (37)
James Gibson 1874 (34)
James Shepherd 1851 (21)
Jane 1818 (9)
Jane 1888 (25)
Jane Davie 1872 (33)
Jane Harvey 1888 (29)
Japarra 1856 (19)
Jeanne 1878 (9)
Jefferson 1798 (9)
Jessie 1829 (19)
Jessie Smith 1853 (1)
Jim Crow 1846 (29)
Johan 1882 (33)
Johanna 1682 (19)
Johanna 1848 (29)
Johanna 1881 (29)
Johanna Wagner 1862 (16)
John 1803 (17)
John 1821 (7)
John and James 1844 (17)
John Bagshaw 1842 (9)
John Witt 1850 (29)
Jonge Thomas 1773 (9)
Jonquille 1866 (1)
Jorawur 1887 (29)
Josephine 1855 (28)
Juliana 1839 (10)
Juno 1852 (20)
Jupiter T. 1875 (30)
Justitia 1848 (32)

K

Kadie 1865 (21)
Kaffir 1890 (33)
Kafir 1878 (15)
Kakapo 1900 (14)
Kapodistrias 1985 (28)
Kate 1834 (29)
Kate 1849 (23)
Kate 1862 (9)
Katherine Gwladys 1854 (31)
Katwijk aan den Rijn 1786 (16)
Kehrweider 1865 (9)
Kent 1856 (9)
Khedive 1910 (34)
Kilbrennan 1907 (32)
King Cadwallon 1929 (33)
King Cenric 1903 (23)

King George IV 1824 (21)
Kingston 1852 (13)
Knysna Belle 1876 (7)
Kolstrop 1883 (18)
Krimpenerward 1867 (29)
Kron Prinsess van Denmark 1752
    (23)

L

L'Aigle 1834 (15)
L'Aigle 1850 (26)
L'Alouette 1817 (15)
L'Atalante 1805 (9)
L'August 1858 (27)
L'Éclair 1821 (7)
L'Éole 1829 (35)
L'Imperatrice Eugenie 1867 (28)
L'Uranie 1800 (28)
La Camille 1836 (16)
La Ceres 1776 (9)
La Cybelle 1756 (6)
La Fortune 1763 (22)
La Jardinière 1794 (20)
La Lise 1840 (20)
La Maréchale 1660 (9)
La Pénélope 1788 (16)
La Rozette 1786 (15)
La Souvénance 1871 (19)
Lada 1888 (29)
Lady Head 1859 (28)
Lady Holland 1830 (8)
Lady Kennaway 1857 (33)
Lady Leith 1848 (28)
Lady McDonald 1876 (29)
Lady Pryse 1880 (23)
Laetitia 1874 (32)
Lakenman 1722 (9)
Lakmé 1896 (28)
Lancastria 1880 (13)
Laura 1843 (29)
Lavinia 1822 (9)
Le Centaure 1750 (19)
Le Cygne 1840 (9)
Le Napoléon 1805 (15)
Le Paquebot Bordelais 1847 (37)
Le Protie 1839 (16)
Le Victor 1782 (9)
Leading Star 1880 (36)
Leander 1822 (9)
Lebu 1899 (28)
Ligonier 1842 (29)
Lilla 1897 (32)
Limari 1902 (29)
Linneus 1834 (18)
Lion 1878 (1)
Lisboa 1910 (4)
Lizzie 1874 (1)
Lockett 1884 (33)
Locust 1824 (21)
Lola 1879 (37)
Lord George Bentinck 1861 (37)
Lord Hawkesbury 1796 (20)
Lord of the Isles 1873 (33)
Losna 1921 (32)
Louisa Dorothea 1882 (23)
Louise 1901 (24)
Louise Scheller 1882 (16)
Lucy 1864 (17)
Lucy Johnson 1862 (9)

The Table Bay Great Gale
of 1865. (Cape Archives,
M785)

Luna 1830 (24)
Luna 1880 (37)
Lunaria 1861 (33)
Lusitania 1911 (15)
Lyme Regis 1859 (29)
Lyngenfjord 1938 (26)
Lyttelton 1874 (29)

M

Mabel 1877 (37)
Mackay 1871 (20)
Madagascar 1858 (32)
Magneten 1872 (25)
Magnolia 1859 (24)
Malabar 1858 (7)
Malmesbury 1930 (4)
Malta 1818 (9)
Malton 1841 (17)
Manhegan 1887 (1)
Maori 1909 (14)
Marengo 1876 (33)
Margareth 1846 (29)
Maria 1788 (25)
Maria 1790 (9)
Maria 1837 (29)
Marie Élise 1877 (21)
Marietta 1862 (9)
Mariner 1860 (12)
Maron Neil 1885 (33)
Martha 1826 (21)
Martha 1845 (23)
Martha 1848 (29)
Martha 1872 (33)
Martlet 1870 (32)
Mary 1824 (23)
Mary 1825 (37)
Mary 1844 (29)
Mary 1853 (23)
Mary Ann 1850 (29)
Mary Ann 1888 (29)
Mary Emily 1889 (37)
Mary Stewart 1842 (11)
Medusa 1863 (33)
Meermin 1766 (20)
Meg Merriles 1869 (29)
Melbourne 1862 (22)
Meliskerk 1943 (35)
Memento 1876 (32)
Mentor 1780 (20)
Merestein 1702 (5)
Meridian 1828 (17)
Meteren 1723 (1)
Middelburg 1781 (5)
Middenrak 1728 (9)

Midge 1874 (25)
Miles Barton 1861 (21)
Milford 1875 (26)
Minerva 1850 (36)
Minnie 1874 (21)
Modesta 1892 (29)
Momina Zino 1874 (21)
Mona 1846 (29)
Montagu 1847 (14)
Montgomery 1847 (20)
Mulgrave Castle 1825 (12)
Munster Lass 1863 (24)

N

Namaqua I 1876 (1)
Namaqua II 1889 (1)
Nancy 1848 (23)
Nant-Y-Glo 1872 (33)
Natal 1852 (1)
Natal 1888 (29)
Natal Star 1874 (33)
Nautilus 1826 (9)
Nautilus 1902 (29)
Nebo 1884 (36)
Nederlandsche Vlag 1870 (26)
Nepaul 1850 (23)
Newark Castle 1908 (38)
Newport 1857 (9)
Niagara 1872 (27)
Nicobar 1783 (19)
Nicoline 1875 (29)
Nieuw Haarlem 1647 (9)
Nieuw Rhoon 1776 (9)
Nightingale 1722 (9)
Nimrod 1851 (9)
Noatun 1892 (30)
Nolloth 1965 (15)
Noord(ster) 1690 (27)
Norfolk 1850 (31)
North-East 1872 (19)
North-Wester 1839 (37)
Nossa Senhora D'Guia 1819 (9)
Nossa Senhora de Atalaia do
    Pinheiro 1647 (34)
Nossa Senhora de Belem 1635
    (35)
Nossa Senhora dos Milagros 1686
    (20)
Nukteris 1897 (16)
Nundeeps 1868 (33)
Nuovo Abele 1874 (34)

O

Oakburn 1906 (14)
Oaklands 1860 (29)
Oakworth 1902 (29)
Obell 1916 (35)

Octopus 1906 (38)
Oldenburg 1799 (9)
Olga R. 1885 (11)
Olive 1878 (33)
Onaway 1892 (36)
Onni 1890 (7)
Onward 1858 (17)
Oosterland 1697 (9)
Orange 1692 (9)
Orange Grove 1829 (29)
Orchomene 1892 (29)
Orient 1907 (33)
Oriental Pioneer 1974 (20)
Osmond 1859 (21)
Ospray 1855 (21)
Osprey 1865 (33)
Osprey 1867 (27)
Oste 1859 (7)
Otto 1860 (21)
Ourimbah 1909 (28)
Ovambo Coast 1958 (5)
Ovington Court 1940 (37)

P

Pacquet Real 1818 (9)
Padang 1828 (16)
Paddenburg 1737 (9)
Palatinia 1911 (33)
Palestine 1846 (29)
Palmer 1840 (10)
Panaghia 1938 (26)
Pantelis A. Lemos 1978 (6)
Paquita 1903 (24)
Paragon 1840 (14)
Paralos 1880 (15)
Parama 1862 (16)
Paris Maru 1934 (29)
Pati 1976 (28)
Paz 1884 (29)
Pembroke Castle 1890 (1)
Pénélope 1809 (9)
Perimede 1860 (2)
Perseverance 1826 (13)
Pescadora 1839 (4)
Petronella 1878 (29)
Peusamento 1879 (37)
Philia 1880 (23)
Philip Dundas 1828 (29)
Phoenix 1829 (16)
Phoénix 1881 (24)
Piccadilly 1877 (17)
Pioneer 1862 (37)
Piratiny 1943 (1)
Pisa 1879 (17)
Piscataqua 1865 (11)
Ponda Chief 1878 (37)
Port Douglas 1897 (28)
Port Fleetwood 1846 (20)

Portsmouth 1866 (29)
Poseidon 1889 (29)
Poseidon 1902 (23)
Poseidon Cape 1985 (1)
President Reitz 1947 (26)
Prince Albert 1844 (25)
Prince of the Seas 1866 (28)
Prince Rupert 1841 (10)
Prince Woronzoff 1859 (29)
Princeport 1885 (18)
Princess Alice 1872 (37)
Prins Willem I 1819 (9)
Produce 1974 (36)

Q

Quanza 1872 (33)
Queen 1863 (37)
Queen of Ava 1865 (8)
Queen of Ceylon 1882 (37)
Queen of May 1872 (33)
Queen of Nations 1889 (33)
Queen of the Thames 1871 (21)
Queen of the West 1850 (26)
Queen Victoria 1896 (29)
Queenmoor 1934 (28)

R

R.A.C. Smith 1898 (30)
R.P. Buck 1877 (19)
Racer 1879 (19)
Rangatira 1916 (13)
Rastede 1858 (7)
Redbreast 1878 (9)
Reflector 1851 (2)
Reform 1842 (9)
Refuge 1872 (33)
Reigersdaal 1747 (6)
Reistad 1897 (29)
Reno 1883 (10)
Resolution 1846 (29)
River Plate 1878 (17)
Robert 1847 (16)
Robilant 1890 (4)
Rodenrijs 1737 (9)
Roma 1892 (30)
Romelia 1977 (14)
Rosalie 1881 (32)
Rosalind 1869 (1)
Rosebud 1859 (2)
Rosebud 1888 (23)
Rotterdam 1722 (9)
Rover 1863 (7)
Rowvonia 1850 (16)
Royal Albert 1850 (9)
Royal Arthur 1865 (9)
Royal Saxon 1851 (9)
Royal William 1837 (10)
Rubens 1865 (7)
Rubia 1901 (32)
Ruby 1866 (23)
Runnymede 1866 (26)
Rusholme 1923 (1)
Ryvingen 1902 (9)

S

SA Oranjeland 1974 (33)
Sabina 1842 (28)

Saint Antonio 1842 (14)
Saint Austell 1870 (32)
Saint Clare 1871 (37)
Saint Lawrence 1876 (3)
Saksenburg 1730 (20)
Saldanha Bay Packet 1847 (9)
San Antonio 1824 (9)
San Antonio 1903 (29)
Sandvik 1888 (33)
Sandwich 1853 (7)
Santa Maria Madre de Deus 1643 (33)
Santissimo Sacramento 1647 (28)
Santo Alberto 1593 (34)
Santo Espiritu 1608 (34)
Santos 1874 (23)
São Bento 1554 (35)
São Gonçalo 1630 (25)
São Jeronymo 1552 (38)
São João 1552 (36)
São João Baptista 1622 (30)
São João de Bescoinho 1551 (38)
São Josene 1794 (14)
Sappho 1864 (7)
Sarah 1822 (9)
Sarah Black 1869 (29)
Sarah Charlotte 1860 (9)
Sarah Phillips 1871 (33)
Sarpine 1691 (16)
Saxon 1896 (38)
Sayre 1902 (29)
Sceptre 1799 (9)
Sceptre 1925 (20)
Schmayl 1883 (33)
Schollevaar 1668 (6)
Schonenberg 1722 (20)
Schotse Lorrendraaier 1722 (9)
Schuilenburg 1756 (14)
Scotland 1860 (20)
Sea Eagle 1856 (13)
Sea Gull 1843 (29)
Sea Rover 1868 (33)
Sea Snake 1869 (29)
Sea Wave 1879 (33)
Seafield 1882 (33)
Seaforth 1844 (32)
Seagull 1894 (23)
Seatrader 1971 (2)
Sebastian 1863 (37)
Sedwell Jane 1893 (29)
Seenymphe 1885 (37)
Seier 1910 (24)
Sévere 1784 (7)
Shantung 1868 (33)
Sharp 1872 (33)
Shepherd 1874 (9)
Shepherdess 1859 (28)
Sierra Leone 1799 (9)
Simon 1871 (29)
Sincapore 1830 (11)
Sir Henry Pottinger 1860 (9)
Sir James Saumarez 1831 (9)
Sir John S. Aubyn 1843 (32)
Sir William Heathcote 1841 (21)
Snorre Straulassen 1875 (32)
'Soares Wreck' 1505 (22)
Sophia 1846 (29)
Sophia 1853 (15)
South African Seafarer 1966 (12)
South American 1889 (20)

South Easter 1872 (33)
Southport 1878 (37)
Sovereign 1841 (24)
Sparfel 1869 (20)
Speedy 1842 (9)
Spy 1851 (28)
Sri Rezeki 1971 (21)
St Claire 1838 (5)
St Helena 1851 (25)
St Mungo 1844 (20)
Stabroek 1728 (9)
Standvastigheid 1722 (9)
Star Beam 1880 (33)
Star of Africa 1880 (15)
Star of the East 1859 (29)
Star of the East 1861 (22)
Star of Wales 1874 (37)
Stavenisse 1686 (36)
Stella 1876 (29)
Sterreschans 1793 (9)
Strathblane 1890 (28)
Stuart Star 1937 (33)
Suffren 1845 (37)
Surprise 1880 (37)
Susan 1846 (29)
Susan 1862 (9)
Susan Crisp 1857 (25)
Susan Pardew 1872 (23)
Swallow 1863 (28)
Swea 1852 (10)
Swiftsure 1847 (25)
Swona 1946 (19)
Sybille 1901 (2)
Sydostlandet 1942 (37)

T

Tancred 1879 (37)
Tantallon Castle 1901 (13)
Tarleton 1818 (9)
Taurus 1872 (29)
Tentonia 1869 (29)
Tevere 1878 (30)
The Highfields 1902 (10)
Thekla 1902 (29)
Therese 1861 (33)
Theresina 1878 (37)
Thermopylae 1899 (12)
Thomas T. Tucker 1942 (15)
Thorne 1831 (13)
Thunderbolt 1847 (28)
Ticino 1908 (1)
Timavo 1940 (38)
Timor 1856 (13)
Tonga 1875 (36)
Trafalgar 1839 (14)
Transvaal 1874 (37)
Trekboer 1844 (29)
Trichera 1905 (36)
Trygve 1897 (38)
Tugela 1868 (37)
Two Brothers 1903 (29)

U

Udny Castle 1840 (12)
Uitenhage Packet 1819 (29)
Umhlali 1909 (15)
Umsimkulu 1883 (21)
Umvolosi 1890 (32)

Unity 1859 (15)
Univers 1877 (29)
Urania 1835 (29)

V

Valdivia 1908 (33)
Valleyfield 1862 (12)
Venerable 1840 (20)
Verona 1902 (17)
Veronica 1886 (1)
Verulam 1874 (33)
Victoria 1737 (9)
Vigilant 1853 (33)
Vigor 1884 (37)
Ville D'Obéron 1854 (29)
Vilora H. Hopkins 1897 (29)
Vis 1740 (14)
Volo 1896 (30)
Volunteer 1869 (1)
Voorzichtigheid 1757 (9)
Vrouw Ida Alida 1818 (16)

W

Waddinxveen 1697 (9)
Wagrien 1874 (37)
Waif 1874 (25)
Waimea 1902 (29)
Waldensian 1862 (20)
Wallarah 1891 (8)
Walsingham 1828 (9)
Waterloo 1821 (16)
Waterloo 1842 (9)
Waterloo 1848 (32)
Wayfarer 1903 (29)
Welcombe 1885 (32)
West Indian 1851 (29)
Westenhope 1871 (31)
Western Knight 1929 (28)
Western Star 1874 (33)
Westerwijk 1737 (9)
Wheatlandside 1878 (29)
Wigrams 1859 (29)
Wigtonshire 1885 (21)
Wild Rose 1872 (33)
Wilhelmine 1880 (23)
Willem de Zwyger 1863 (21)
William Bayley 1857 (25)
William Forster 1851 (28)
William James 1857 (9)
William Shaw 1873 (35)
Windsor Castle 1876 (8)
Winifred & Maria 1817 (9)
Winton 1934 (7)
Witch of the Waves 1859 (29)
Wolseley 1888 (29)
Woodbridge 1816 (9)

Z

Zalt Brommel 1856 (9)
Zambesi 1882 (37)
Zeeland 1793 (9)
Zeepaard 1823 (28)
Zennia 1880 (37)
Zephyr 1889 (29)
Ziba 1879 (37)
Zoetendaal 1673 (20)
Zoetigheid 1722 (9)

Chronological List of Shipwrecks

Please note:
1. Letters in brackets immediately following a vessel's name indicate its nationality of ownership, as follows:

Am	– United States of America	Ger	– Germany
Au	– Australia	Gr	– Greece
Aus	– Austria	Ind	– Indonesia
B	– England or Britain	It	– Italy
		Ir	– Ireland
Bel	– Belgium	Kor	– Korea
Bra	– Brazil	Lib	– Liberia
Can	– Canada	Nor	– Norway
Chi	– China	P	– Portugal
CR	– Costa Rica	Prus	– Prussia
Cyp	– Cyprus	Rus	– Russia
D	– Netherlands	SA	– South Africa
Dan	– Denmark	Sp	– Spain
Fr	– France	Swe	– Sweden
		Yug	– Yugoslavia

2. An asterisk (*) following a vessel's name indicates that the vessel in question is mentioned in the main text.
3. Where this is known, an indication of the circumstances of a wrecking is given in brackets at the end of an entry.
4. Entries *in italics* indicate wider historical perspectives.

15th CENTURY

1488

Bartolomeu Dias rounds the Cape of Good Hope

1494

Treaty of Tordesillas divides the globe between Portugal and Spain

1498

Vasco da Gama opens up the sea route to the East

16th CENTURY

1503

Antonio de Saldanha explores Table Bay

1505

'Soares wreck' (P)*: West of Mossel Bay (night)

1509

Portuguese overcome Moslem sea power at Battle of Diu

1511

Tin mines of Malacca ceded to Portugal

1521

Ferdinand Magellan reaches the Philippines during circumnavigation of the globe

1551

São João de Bescoinho (P): Ponta do Ouro

1552

June	São Jeronymo (P): North of Richards Bay (storm)
11 June	São João (P)*: Near Port Edward (disabled)

1554

21 April	São Bento (P)*: On island at Msikaba River mouth (disabled)

São Bento. (Africana Museum)

1577

Sir Francis Drake sets out on circumnavigation voyage

1581

Portugal incorporated into Spanish Empire

1588

Spanish Armada sets sail for England

1593

24 March	Santo Alberto (P): Possibly near East London (disabled)

1595

First official Dutch trading voyage to the East

17th CENTURY

1601

English East India Company chartered; first English East India Company fleet calls at Table Bay

1602

Dutch East India Company chartered

1604

French East India Company chartered

1608

Santo Espiritu (P): Possibly near Haga-Haga, north-east of East London

1611

King James Bible published

1616

Danish East India Company chartered

1619

27 July   Jaeger (Dan): Woodstock Beach, Table Bay (north-west gale – first recorded Danish wreck on South African coast)

1622

October   São João Baptista (P)*: Between Woody Cape and Kei River (after action with Dutch)

1630

July   São Gonçalo (P)*: Plettenberg Bay (put into bay after developing a leak)

1635

24 July   Nossa Senhora de Belem (P)*: North-east of the Mzimvubu River (disabled)

1642

English civil war starts

1643

Santa Maria Madre de Deus (P): Possibly near Bonza Bay, East London

1644

7 February   Eiland Mauritius (D): Salt River mouth, Table Bay (first recorded Dutch wreck on South African coast)

1647

25 March   Nieuw Haarlem (D)*: Milnerton, Table Bay (south-east gale)

June   Nossa Senhora de Atalaia do Pinheiro (P)*: Near Cefane River (disabled)
1 July   Santissimo Sacramento (P)*: Schoenmakerskop (disabled)

1652

The Dutch establish a replenishment station at the Cape

1653

Start of Cromwell's rule in England

1657

First Free Burghers granted land at the Cape

1660

19 May   La Maréchale (Fr): Salt River mouth, Table Bay (north-west gale – first recorded French wreck on South African coast)

1666

Construction of Castle begins

1668

31 May   Schollevaar (D): North of Bokpunt, West Coast (north-west gale)

1673

20 February   De Grundel (D): East of Cape Hangklip
23 August   Zoetendaal (D): Struis Bay

1674

9 April   Bruydegom (D): Saldanha Bay

1679

Simon van der Stel appointed Cape Governor

1682

8 June   Johanna (B)*: Die Dam, Quoin Point (night – first recorded English wreck on South African coast)

1685

Edict of Nantes revoked by Louis XIV
17 May   Good Hope (B)*: Durban

1686

16 February   Stavenisse (D)*: Natal South Coast, near Port Shepstone
16 April   Nossa Senhora dos Milagros (P)*: Near Cape Agulhas (night)
25 December   Bonaventura (B)*: St Lucia Bay

1687

Divers salvage treasure from Nuestra Senora de la Conception off Haiti

1690

16 January   Noord(ster) (D)*: Klippen Point

1691

Sarpine (P): Near Gordon's Bay, False Bay (south-east gale)

1692

5 June   North-west gale, Table Bay
Orange (B)
Goede Hoop (D)
10 June   Hogergeest (D)*: Table Bay (north-west gale)

1693

November   Gouden Buis (D)*: North of St Helena Bay (scurvy)

Gouden Buis. *(Africana Museum)*

1694

Bank of England founded
20 January   Dageraad (D)*: Western point of Robben Island (mist)

1697

24 May   North-west gale, Table Bay
Oosterland (D)
Waddinxveen (D)

1698

27 May   Het Huis te Kraaiestein (D)*: Oudekraal, Cape Peninsula (mist)

1699

Willem Adriaan van der Stel becomes Governor at the Cape

18th CENTURY

1700

War of the Spanish Succession following death of Charles II of Spain

1702

3 April   Merestein (D)*: South-west corner of Jutten Island (south-west wind)

1705

Thomas Newcomen constructs an improved steam pump

1711

St Paul's Cathedral completed

1713

Peace of Utrecht; Philip V of Spain reigns over Holland
16 February — *Bennebroek* (D)*: A little south-west of Hamburg, near East London

1719

Daniel Defoe publishes Robinson Crusoe

1722

16 June — North-west gale, Table Bay
Lakenman (D)*
Rotterdam (D)*
Schotse Lorrendraaier (D)*
Standvastigheid (D)*
Zoetigheid (D)*
Addison (B)
Chandois (B)
Nightingale (B)
Amy (D)
Gouda (D)
20 November — *Schonenberg* (D): Skoonbergbaai, east of Cape Agulhas (fine weather)

1723

9 November — *Meteren* (D)*: North of the Olifants River (scurvy)

1727

John Lethbridge begins diving in Table Bay

1728

3 July — North-west gale, Table Bay
Middenrak (D)
Stabroek (D)
4 December — *Haarlem* (D): Salt River, Table Bay (north-west gale)

1730

8 January — *Saksenburg* (D): Off Cape Agulhas

1734

31 November — *De Hoop* (D): Dassen Island (north-west wind)

1736

1 July — *Fijenoord* (D): Table Bay

1737

21 May — North-west gale, Table Bay
Rodenrijs (D): Near Salt River mouth
De Buis (D): Salt River mouth
Duinbreek (D)
Goudriaan (D)
Flora (D)
Paddenburg (D)
Victoria (D)
Westerwijk (D)
Iepenrode (D)

1740

6 May — *Vis* (D)*: Green Point, Table Bay (night)

1745

Town of Swellendam proclaimed

1747

25 October — *Reigersdaal* (D)*: Springfontein Point (scurvy, south-east gale)

1750

19 January — *Le Centaure* (Fr): A little west of Cape Agulhas (fine weather)
8 August — *Elephant* (Dan): Gouritz River (scurvy)

1752

9 June — *Kron Prinsess van Denmark* (Dan): Mossel Bay (disabled)

1755

17 July — *Dodington* (B)*: Bird Island, Algoa Bay (south-west gale, night)

1756

19 March — *La Cybelle* (Fr)*: North of Blouberg, Table Bay
3 June — *Schuilenburg* (D): Camps Bay area

1757

8 June — *Voorzichtigheid* (D): Table Bay (north-west gale)

1759

British Museum opened

1762

Catherine the Great rules Russia

1763

11 September — *La Fortune* (Fr): Visbaai, near Gouritz River

1766

9 April — *Meermin* (D)*: Cape Agulhas (mutiny)

1769

James Watt patents the improved steam engine

1773

'Boston Tea Party'
1 June — *Jonge Thomas* (D)*: Table Bay (north-west gale)

1775

American War of Independence starts

Jonge Thomas. *(Cape Archives, M744)*

1776

American Declaration of Independence
31 January — *Nieuw Rhoon* (D): Table Bay (beached near the Castle, south-east gale)
15 October — *La Ceres* (Fr): Table Bay (north-west gale)

1778

France Allies herself with America
24 August — *Colebrooke* (B)*: Koeëlbaai, False Bay (disabled)

1779

First Frontier War

1780

5 January — *Mentor* (D): On reef off Cape Agulhas (storm)

1781

Battle of Saldanha
21 July — *Middelburg* (D)*: Hoedjies Point, Saldanha Bay (naval action)

1782

4 August — *Grosvenor* (B)*: A little north-east of the Tezani Stream, Pondoland (south-west gale, night)
24 September — *Le Victor* (Fr): Table Bay (north-west gale)

Grosvenor. *(Africana Museum)*

1783

American colonies become independent
11 July   *Nicobar* (Dan)*:
                 On Quoin Point

1784

27 January   *Sévere* (Fr): Blouberg,
                 Table Bay
30 June   *Hoop* (D): Mouille Point,
                 Table Bay

1785

3 May   *Brederode* (D)*:
                 Cape Agulhas

1786

Graaff-Reinet founded
11 May   HNMS *Holland* (D): Near
                 Olifantsbos Point, Cape
                 Peninsula (night)
19 August   *La Rozette* (Fr): South of
                 Olifantsbos Point, Cape
                 Peninsula (mutiny)
7 October   *Katwijk aan den Rijn* (D):
                 Simon's Bay

1787

Second Frontier War starts

1788

7 May   *Avenhorn* (D): Table Bay (north-
                 west gale)
23 August   *Maria* (D): Near Robberg,
                 Plettenberg Bay (south-east
                 gale)
16 October   *La Pénélope* (Fr): Muizenberg

1789

French Revolution starts; Bastille stormed
16 May   *Drietal Handelaars* (D):
                 Swartklip in False Bay (south-
                 east gale)

1790

12 April   *Erfprins van Augustenburg*
                 (Dan): Table Bay
                 Maria (It): Table Bay

1792

2 June   *Drie Gebroeders* (D):
                 Simon's Bay
                 (disabled, run ashore)

1793

22 May   North-west gale, Table Bay
                 Sterreschans (D)
                 Zeeland (D)

1794

                 La Jardinière (Fr): Struis Bay
27 December   *São Josene* (P)*: Camps Bay

1795

*Battle of Muizenberg; first British Occupation of
the Cape; Dutch East India Company taken over
by Dutch state*

1796

8 March   *Gothenburg* (Swe): Green
                 Point, Table Bay
April   *Ann and Eliza* (B): Algoa Bay
May   *Lord Hawkesbury* (B):
                 Soetendalsvlei (mutiny)
4 June   *Columbia* (Am): Table Bay
16 June   *Hercules* (Am): Bira River,
                 Kaffraria (leaking, grounded)

1798

9 May   *Jefferson* (Am): Table Bay

1799

*Napoleon overthrows Directory and becomes
First Consul; 5th Frontier War starts*
5 November   Great north-west gale,
                 Table Bay
                 Sceptre (B)
                 Anubis (Am)
                 Hannah (Am)
                 Oldenburg (Dan)
                 Sierra Leone (B)

Sceptre. *(South African Library)*

19TH CENTURY

1800

*First South African newspaper, The Cape Town
Gazette, started*
22 September   *Benjamin* (B): Gordon's Bay,
                 False Bay
October   *L'Uranie* (Fr): Seekoei River,
                 St Francis Bay (scurvy)

1803

Batavian Republic resumes control of the Cape
16 September   *John* (B): Near Danger Point

1804

Napoleon crowns himself Emperor of France

1805

Battle of Trafalgar
19 September   *Brunswick* (B): Simon's Town
                 (prize ship, south-east gale)
3 November   North-west gale, Table Bay
                 Hunter (Am)
                 L'Atalante (Fr):
                 Charlotte battery
25 December   *Le Napoléon* (Fr)*: Olifantsbos
                 Point, Cape Peninsula (naval
                 action)

1806

*Battle of Blaauwberg; Second British
occupation of the Cape*
8 January   HNMS *Bato* (D): Long Beach,
                 Simon's Town (burnt on
                 purpose)

1809

16 April   *Pénélope* (Fr): Table Bay (prize
                 vessel)
                 Edward (B): Struis Bay

1811

Fourth Frontier War starts

1812

War between United States and Britain

1814

*Lord Charles Somerset appointed Governor of
the Cape*

1815

Battle of Waterloo
30 May   *Arniston* (B)*: At Arniston
                 (storm)

1816

July   *Discovery* (B): Black River
                 mouth, Table Bay
5 November   *Woodbridge* (B): Table Bay

1817

11 February   *Emu* (B): Knysna Lagoon
                 (disabled)
6 June   *L'Alouette* (Fr): Olifantsbos
                 Point, Cape Peninsula (fog)
August   *Winifred & Maria*: Table Bay
December   *Elizabeth*:
                 Olifants River mouth
16 December   HNMS *Amsterdam* (D)*:
                 Amsterdamhoek,
                 Algoa Bay
                 (disabled and run ashore)

1818

Fifth Frontier War starts
March   *Malta* (B): Paarden Island,
                 Table Bay
17 April   *Tarleton* (B): Table Bay
18 May   *Jane* (B): Table Bay (north-west
                 gale)
                 Pacquet Real (P): Table Bay
                 (north-west gale)
July   *Anne* (B): Paarden Island, Table
                 Bay
10 November   *Vrouw Ida Alida* (D): St James,
                 False Bay

1819

2 May   *Nossa Senhora D'Guia* (P):
                 Table Bay (north-west gale)
26 July   *Prins Willem I* (D): Table Bay
                 (disabled)
30 August   *Good Hope* (SA): Algoa Bay
                 (south-east gale)
                 Uitenhage Packet (SA): Algoa
                 Bay (south-east gale)

7 October	*Elizabeth* (B): Paarden Island, Table Bay (missed stays)	
21 October	*Feniscowles* (B): Green Point, Table Bay (night)	
December	*Adolphus*: Knysna	

1820

First British Settlers land in Algoa Bay

1821

Greek War of Independence starts

4 January	Great north-west gale, Table Bay
	Emma (B)*
	*Dorah**
5 February	*L'Éclair* (Fr): Table Bay (night)
10 March	*Cerberus* (B): Blouberg, Table Bay (night)
25 October	*Waterloo* (B): Fish Hoek, False Bay
16 November	*Flora* (D): Robben Island, Table Bay (night)
4 December	*John*: Blouberg, Table Bay (missed stays)

1822

4 June	*Grace* (B): A little east of Quoin Point (fire)
14 June	*Fame* (B)*: Graaff's Pool, Sea Point, Table Bay (north-west gale)
9 July	*Sarah* (B): Table Bay (north-west gale)
20 July	*Adriatic* (B): Table Bay (north-west gale)
21 July	Great north-west gale, Table Bay
	Good Intent (SA)
	Lavinia (B)*
	Leander (B)*

1823

18 March	*Heworth* (B): Algoa Bay
29 March	HNMS *Zeepaard* (D)*: Holland Reef, Sardinia Bay (fog, night)
3 April	HM Schooner *Cockburn* (B): Muizenberg Beach (south-east gale)
16 April	*Apollo* (B): Below the Mouille Point battery, Table Bay (night)

1824

The British settle in Port Natal; South African Commercial Advertiser and South African Journal first published; Moshoeshoe founds Basotho nation

9 July	*Mary* (B): Mossel Bay
16 July	*King George IV* (B): Sebastian Bay (abandoned)
4 August	*San Antonio*: Table Bay
2 September	*Locust* (SA): Breede River (sank)

1825

4 September	*Mulgrave Castle* (B): Green Point (fine weather)
1 October	*Mary* (B): Durban

1826

Cape of Good Hope Gazette first published

12 March	*Perseverance* (B): Whale Rock, Table Bay
13 March	*Harmony* (B): Knysna Heads

31 March	*Nautilus* (B): Table Bay	
24 September	*Martha* (B): Martha Point, east of Arniston	
22 October	*Britannia* (B): Britannia Bay, near Cape St Martin (disabled)	

1827

30 June	*Berwick* (B): A little west of Algoa Bay

1828

Death of Shaka

19 May	*Meridian* (B): East side of Silversands Bay, Cape Hangklip
14 June	*Walsingham*: Opposite the Military Hospital, Table Bay (night)
29 June	*Padang* (D): Muizenberg, False Bay (night)
16 August	*Philip Dundas*: Algoa Bay (south-east gale)

1829

Stephenson's Rocket runs between Liverpool and Manchester

31 March	*Columbine* (B): 1,5 km north of Cape Columbine lighthouse
12 April	*L'Éole* (Fr): 48 km south-west of Bashee River
19 July	*Phoenix* (B): Phoenix Shoal, Simon's Town
7 October	*Jessie* (B): Jessie se Baai, Quoin Point (west gale, mist)
11 November	*Orange Grove*: Algoa Bay (south-east gale)

1830

13 January	*Frances Watson* (B): Algoa Bay (south-east gale)
January	*African Adventure* (P): Durban
13 February	*Lady Holland* (B): Dassen Island (night)
5 March	*Dauphin* (Am): Saldanha Bay
27 June	*Luna* (B): Knysna
4 July	*Alfred*: Table Bay (north-west gale)
9 October	*Gowan* (B): Algoa Bay (south-east gale)
1 December	*Sincapore* (B): Near Green Point lighthouse (night)

1831

Graham's Town Journal first published

13 May	*George*: Vicinity of Dyer Island (north-east gale)
18 May	*Thorne* (B)*: Robben Island, Table Bay (fog)
16, 17 July	Great north-west gale, Table Bay
16 July	*Calpe* (B)
	Sir James Saumarez
17 July	*Candian* (B)

1832

Great Reform Act adopted in Britain

22 June	*Essex* (B): Algoa Bay

1833

Slavery abolished by British Government

16 August	*Flamingo*: Buffels Bay, False Bay (fire)

1834

Sixth Frontier War starts; Great Trek starts

16 January	*Linneus*: Vicinity of Dyer Island
15 February	*L'Aigle* (Fr): Slangkop area, Cape Peninsula (night)
5 October	*Kate*: Algoa Bay (south-east gale)

1835

1 October	Great south-east gale, Algoa Bay
	Atlantic (B): (night)
	Urania (SA): (night)
	Cape Breton (B)

1836

7 February	*Gondolier* (B): Robben Island, Table Bay
14 July	*Dorothys* (B): Plettenberg Bay
17 July	*Doncaster* (B): Near Quoin Point
18 October	*La Camille* (Fr): Strandfontein, False Bay

1837

11 March	*Maria* (B): Algoa Bay (south-east gale)
10 August	*Feejee* (B): Algoa Bay (south-east wind)
18 August	*Antelope* (B): Table Bay (night)
20 September	*Royal William* (B): Near Mouille Point battery, Table Bay (night)

1838

Battle of Blood River

14 March	*St Claire*: Saldanha Bay area (south-east gale)
25 August	*Duke of Northumberland* (B): Northumberland Point, Cape Agulhas (midnight)
24 November	*Dunlop* (Ir): Woodstock Beach, Table Bay (night)

1839

4 January	*Pescadora* (P): On reef of rocks at the mouth of Saldanha Bay
10 January	*Le Protie* (Fr): Strandfontein, False Bay (night)
19 January	*Juliana*: On Mouille Point near the Battery, Table Bay
21 February	*Trafalgar* (B): Off Rocklands Beach, Table Bay (night)
19 April	*Betsy and Sara* (D): A little west of the Bushmans River mouth
31 May	*North-Wester*: Durban
27 July	*Admiral Cockburn* (B): Muizenberg
28 July	*Eleanor*: Inner Bank, Durban
8 November	*Elizabeth* (B): Bira River mouth (night)

1840

12 January	*Jack Tar*: Algoa Bay (south-east gale)
6 February	*Friends Goodwill*: Near St Helena Bay or Paternoster
22 February	*Venerable*: Struis Bay (night)
9 March	*La Lise* (Fr): Struis Bay (night)

11 March	PS *Hope* (SA)*: Near Tsitsikamma Point (fire, fog – first wreck of steamer on the coast of South Africa)
1 April	*Paragon*: A little west of Green Point lighthouse, Table Bay (north-west gale)
29 May	*Burnham* (B): Durban
16 July	*Howard* (B): Near the Castle, Table Bay (north-west gale)
8 August	*Le Cygne* (Fr): Paarden Island, Table Bay (night)
19 August	*Palmer* (B): Near Mouille Point, Table Bay (night)
4 September	*Alert*: Algoa Bay (south-east gale)
17 September	*Bengal* (B): Blouberg, Table Bay (night)
19 September	*Catharine Jamieson**: Mouille Point, Table Bay (night)
26 November	*Udny Castle* (B)*: Green Point lighthouse, Table Bay (night)

1841

15 April	*Sir William Heathcote* (B): Breede River
5 May	*Africaine*: Near Kowie River
28 July	*Felix Vincidor*: Muizenberg, False Bay (night)
4 September	*Prince Rupert* (B): Mouille Point battery, Table Bay (night)
14 October	*Malton* (B): Walker Bay (evening)
29 December	*Sovereign*: Knysna Heads

1842

British take control of Port Natal

2 March	*Ligonier* (SA): Algoa Bay (south-east gale)
29 March	*Saint Antonio*: Chapmans Bay
29 May	*Helen* (B): Mouille Point, Table Bay (night)
13 July	*Speedy* (B): Near Imhoff battery, Table Bay (north-west gale, night)
7 August	*Sabina* (Sp): Cape Recife (night)
28 August	North-west gale, Table Bay
	Abercrombie Robinson (B)*: Salt River mouth
	Waterloo (B)*: Salt River mouth
9 September	North-west gale, Table Bay
	Fairfield (Am): (night)
	John Bagshaw (B): Near the south wharf
	Reform (B)
3 November	*Mary Stewart* (Ger): Between the two lighthouses, Table Bay (fog)

1843

31 January	PS *Sir John S. Aubyn*: Kowie River (fouled)
14 March	*Conservative* (B): 10 km south of Saldanha Point
25 August	South-east gale, Algoa Bay
	Delhi (B): (night)
	Elizabeth Rowell (B): (night)
	Laura (B)
	Sea Gull (B)
12 October	*Abbotsford* (B): Algoa Bay (south-east gale)

1844

Cape of Good Hope & Port Natal Shipping & Mercantile Gazette started

4 March	*Mary*: Algoa Bay (south-east gale)
18 August	*Seaforth* (B): Port Alfred (becalmed)
21 August	South-east gale, Algoa Bay
	Isabel (Bra): (night)
	Trekboer: (night)
24 August	*Prince Albert*: Plettenberg Bay (south-east gale, night)
1 September	*John and James*: Danger Point (night)
20 September	*St Mungo* (B): St Mungo Point, near Cape Agulhas (fog)
8 December	*Hamilla Mitchell* (B): Near Oranjemund

1845

27 March	*Horwood* (B): Algoa Bay (south-east gale)
8 April	*Cottager* (B): South of Saldanha Bay
16, 17 May	North-west gale
16 May	*Alicia Jane**: Paternoster Island
17 May	*Catherine Isabella*: Elephants Rock
	*Eve**: Paternoster Island
30 August	*Martha*: 3 km from the landing place in Mossel Bay (south-east gale)
9 September	*Active* (B): Plettenberg Bay (disabled)
15 November	*Charles**: Bird Island, Algoa Bay (sank)
17 December	*Suffren* (Fr): Durban (north-east gale)

1846

Seventh Frontier War (War of the Axe) starts

7 January	North-west gale, Table Bay
	Diana (P)*: Imhoff battery
	Francis Spaight (B): Woodstock Beach
25 March	South-east gale, Algoa Bay
	Blackaller (B)
	Jim Crow (B): (night)
	Susan (B): (night)

Francis Spaight. *(Africana Museum)*

29 April	*Gentoo* (Am): Northumberland Point, Struis Bay (night)
27 August	*Courier* (B): Durban (west wind)
15 September	*Port Fleetwood* (B): Struis Bay
3 October	*Catherine* (B): Waterloo Bay (south-west gale)
10 October	*Galatea* (B): Mossel Bay (south-east gale, night)
28, 29 October	South-east gale, Algoa Bay
28 October	*Mona*
	Palestine
29 October	*Margareth*
	Resolution
	Sophia

1847

3 February	HMS *Thunderbolt* (B): Baakens River mouth, Algoa Bay (disabled, beached)
12 February	*Robert* (B): Gordon's Bay, False Bay (south-east gale)
6 March	*Isaac*: West of Struis Bay
15 March	*Montgomery* (Am)*: Cape Agulhas (south-east gale, night)
16 March	*Gilbert Henderson* (B): Algoa Bay (south-east gale)
30 March	*Montagu* (SA): Chapmans Bay (capsized)
9 April	*Israel* (Am): Salt River mouth, Table Bay (north-west gale, night)
28 June	*Le Paquebot Bordelais* (Fr): Durban
8 August	*Swiftsure*: Plettenberg Bay (north-north-west gale, night)
17 October	*Ghika* (SA): Esplanade rocks, East London
7 November	*Conch**: Port St Johns (becalmed)
21 November	*Saldanha Bay Packet*: Imhoff battery, Table Bay (north-west gale)

South African Commercial Advertiser

1848

Gold discovered in California

18 January	*Bittern* (B): North-west point of Robben Island, Table Bay (south-east gale, night)
27 February	*Lady Leith*: Thunderbolt Reef, Cape Recife (south-east gale)
1 March	*Chanticleer* (SA): East bank, Kowie River
8 March	*Harriet* : Lee bank, Breede River
4 April	*Barrys I* (B): Struis Bay (south-east gale, night)
5 April	*Nancy*: Mossel Bay (south-east gale)
	South-east gale, Algoa Bay
	Johanna (B)
	Martha (B)

	Waterloo (SA): Between Kowie and Fish rivers (Cawoods Bay) (south-east gale)
6 June	*Chieftain*: Mouille Point, Table Bay (night)
28 September	*Justitia*: Waterloo Bay

1849

21 February	*Claudine* (B): Martha Point (fog)
25 March	*Frances Burn* (B): Algoa Bay (south-east gale, night)
15 July	*Belleisle* (B): St Sebastian Bay (south-east gale, night)
16 July	*Kate*: Mossel Bay (south-east gale, night)
24 August	*Enchantress* (B): Between Green Point and Mouille Point, Table Bay

1850

Eighth Frontier War starts

13 January	*Rowvonia* (Bra)*: Simon's Bay (parted anchor during south-east gale)
11 February	*Nepaul* (B): Swart River mouth at Sedgefield (south-west gale)
13 February	*Childe Harold* (B)*: South-east point of Dassen Island (night)
16 February	*Amelia Mulholland* (B): Algoa Bay (south-east gale)
1 June	*Arab*: Near the hospital lines, Table Bay (north-west gale)
	British Settler (SA): Jacobs Bay, near Saldanha Bay (north-west gale)
9 June	*Asiatic* (B): Algoa Bay (south-east gale)
13 June	*Duchess of Buccleugh* (B): Near Quoin Point (disabled)
16 June	Great south-west gale
	L'Aigle (Fr)*: About 4 km west of Klippen Point
	Queen of the West (B): West of Wreck Point
25 June	*Royal Albert* (B): Table Bay (north-west gale)
4 July	*Minerva* (B): Point of the Bluff, Durban (night)
16 September	*Cockburn* (B): Table Bay (north-west gale)
23 September	*Norfolk* (SA): Seal Island, off Bird Island, Algoa Bay
29 September	*British Tar* (B): Durban (east-north-east gale)

Minerva. (J. Sanderson)

17 October	South-east gale, Algoa Bay
	Doris
	John Witt (B)
	Mary Ann (B)

1851

31 January	*James Shepherd* (B): Near Still Bay
17 April	*Reflector* (B): St Helena Bay (disabled)
17 July	*William Forster*: Thunderbolt Reef, Cape Recife (night)
24 July	*Nimrod* (B): Paarden Island, Table Bay (north-west gale, night)
29 July	*Fanny*: Imhoff battery, Table Bay (north-west gale)
21 August	*Spy* (B): St Francis Bay (south-east gale)
13 September	*Albinia* (B): Algoa Bay (south-east gale)
	Foam (B): East London (east wind)
13-15 September	South-east gale, Plettenberg Bay
13 September	*St Helena*
15 September	*George Henry Harrison*
1 October	*Royal Saxon* (B): Paarden Island, Table Bay (night)
8 October	*Chartley Castle* (B): Milnerton, Table Bay (night)
4 December	*Diadem*: Plettenberg Bay (south-east gale)
	West Indian (B): Algoa Bay (south-east gale)

1852

Sand River Convention grants independence to South African Republic (Transvaal); Napoleon III becomes Emperor of France

24 January	*Herschel* (B): Rietvlei, Table Bay (night)
26 February	HMS *Birkenhead* (B)*: Birkenhead Rock, Danger Point (night)
2 March	*Juno* (D)*: Cape Agulhas (fog)
4 March	*Natal*: Espiegle Bay, Port Nolloth (south-east gale)
18 May	*Courier*: Near Imhoff battery, Table Bay (north-west gale)
28 May	*Amatola*: East London
27 July	*Hector* (B): South Coast, Natal (disabled)
13 August	*Bodiam Castle* (B): Struis Point
14 August	*Amwell*: Algoa Bay (south-east gale)
7 September	*Fairfield* (B): South Coast, Natal
10 November	*Swea* (Swe): Mouille Point, Table Bay (night)
23 December	*Kingston* (Am): South-west point of Robben Island, Table Bay (night)

1853

Commander Perry opens Japan to East-West trade

16 February	*Mary*: Mossel Bay (south-east gale)
7 March	*Sophia* (B): White Sands, south of Hout Bay
10 April	*Dido* (B): Mouille Point, Table Bay (night)
5 May	*Barbara Gordon* (B): East of Quoin Point (midnight)

10 August	*Sandwich* (B): Rietvlei, Table Bay
23 August	*Jessie Smith* (B): Alexander Bay (parted anchor)
11 December	*Vigilant* (B): East London (south-east gale)

1854

Bloemfontein Convention grants independence to the Orange Free State; Cape Colony granted representative government

27 February	*Katherine Gwladys* (B): Bird Island, Algoa Bay
7 April	*Arion* (Ger): Breede River mouth
31 July	*Ariosto* (Am): Durban
12 September	*Chancellor* (B): Martha Strand, near Arniston
20 September	*Charlotte* (B): Algoa Bay (south-east gale)
9 October	*Ville D'Obéron* (Fr): Algoa Bay (disabled)
30 December	*Flora*: Algoa Bay (south-east gale)
	Drei Thürme (Ger): Struis Point (south-east gale, night)

Charlotte. (Illustrated London News)

1855

4 April	*Flying Fish*: Port Nolloth
13 April	*Ospray*: St Sebastian Bay
17 May	*Josephine*: 16 km west of Cape Recife
24 October	*East London Packet*: Algoa Bay
27 October	*Huma*: East London

1856

Natal established as a separate colony; Henry Bessemer invents his converter to make pig iron into steel

21 January	*Annabella* (B): Durban
7 February	*Equator* (B): Struis Bay
30 July	*Kent* (B): Paarden Island, Table Bay
3 October	*Japarra* (D): Quoin Point
20 November	*Sea Eagle* (Am): Murrays Bay, Robben Island, Table Bay (south-east gale)
3 December	*Zalt Brommel* (D): Near Mouille Point, Table Bay
22 December	*Timor* (D)*: Robben Island, Table Bay (south wind)

1857

Cape Argus first published

5 February | *Albert* (SA)*: Struis Bay (disabled)
17 February | *Eurydice* (B): Algoa Bay (south-east gale)
5 March | *Defence* (B): Near Milnerton, Table Bay (night)
7 May | *Barrys II* (SA): Breede River, Port Beaufort (south-west wind)
5 June | *Newport*: Table Bay (north-west gale)
7 June | North-west gale, Table Bay
| *Gitana*
| *Isabella*
10 June | North-west gale, Table Bay
| *Christabel* (B)
| *William James* (B)*
11 July | *William Bayley* (B)*: Plettenberg Bay (fire)
28 September | *Susan Crisp* (B): Plettenberg Bay (south-east gale)
25 November | *Lady Kennaway* (B): East London (south-east gale)

1858

14 January | *Onward*: Caledon district
22 January | *L'August* (Fr): Near Cape St Francis (gale)
26 February | *Buffon* (Fr)*: Roman Rock, Bird Island, Algoa Bay
5 March | *Rastede*: Rietvlei, Table Bay (south-east gale)
10 May | *Arabia* (Am): Green Point, Table Bay
11 September | *Helen* (SA): East Head, Knysna
4 November | *Malabar* (It): Rietvlei, Table Bay
30 November | *Arago* (Ger): Rietvlei, Table Bay (south-east gale)
4 December | SS *Madagascar* (SA): Madagascar Reef (struck reef, beached, night)

1859

Charles Darwin completes the Origin of Species
18 January | *Atlas* (D): Near Martha Duinen
16 March | *Briseis* (B): Fountain Rocks, Port Alfred (abandoned)
20 March | *Oste* (Ger): White Sands, near Blouberg, Table Bay (south-east wind, night)
26 April | *Lady Head* (B): Near Kromme River, Cape St Francis
30 May | *Shepherdess* (B): Thunderbolt Reef, Cape Recife
3 June | *Anne*: Near Olifantsbos Point (fog)
13 June | *Osmond* (Dan): Breede River
25 June | *Rosebud*: Lamberts Bay
24 July | *Magnolia* (B): Knysna Heads
5 September | *Unity* (B): Near Cape Point
3 October | South-east gale, Algoa Bay
| *Chasseur* (Fr)
| *Basileia* (B)
| *Witch of the Waves*: (night)
16 October | South-east gale, Algoa Bay
| *Star of the East*
| *Arabian*
| *Prince Woronzoff* (B)
| *Lyme Regis* (B)
| *Governess*
| *Wigrams* (B)
11 December | *Florence*: Port Nolloth

1860

Table Bay Dock building commenced; civil war breaks out in Transvaal; first Indian labourers arrive in Natal

19 January | *Otto* (Rus): Otterbaai, Struis Point
20 March | *Oaklands* (B): Algoa Bay
27 June | *Scotland* (B): Struis Bay (night)
3 July | *Sarah Charlotte* (B): Table Bay (north-west gale)
4 July | *Sir Henry Pottinger* (B): Table Bay (north-west gale)
3 August | *Mariner* (B): Green Point, Table Bay
4 August | *Perimede* (B): North of St Helena Bay (disabled)
12 November | *Gladiator* (B): Near Cape Padrone

Cape of Good Hope Shipping & Mercantile Gazette

1861

3 January | *Lord George Bentinck* (B): Durban (north-east wind)
3 February | *Hero* (Am): Algoa Bay (south-east gale)
8 February | *Miles Barton* (B): Near Miles Barton Reef, Arniston area
10 April | *Star of the East* (B): Near Ystervark Point
16 June | *Bernicia* (B): Robben Island, Table Bay (north-west gale)
1 September | *Ellen* (B): Struis Point
12 September | South gale, East London
| *Therese* (SA): West Bank (night)
| *Lunaria* (B): West Bank (night)
| *Barbadoes* (B): Algoa Bay (south gale)
21 December | *Alice Smith* (SA)*: Port St Johns (becalmed)

1862

First French annexations in Cochin China

19 January | *Frigga* (Dan): Near Milnerton (south-easter)
7 February | *A.H. Stevens* (Am): Robben Island, Table Bay (fog)
15 June | *Valleyfield* (B): Green Point, Table Bay (fog)
17 July | *Johanna Wagner* (Prus): Strandfontein, False Bay
3 August | *Charlotte A. Morrison* (Am)*: Algoa Bay (fire, night)
8 August | North-west gale, Table Bay
| *Crystal Palace* (B): Sceptre Reef (collision)
| *Kate* (B): (collision)
| *Marietta*
20 September | *Lucy Johnson* (Am): Table Bay (night)
| *Susan* (B): Table Bay

9 October | *Parama* (Am): Simon's Bay, False Bay (south-east gale)
13 October | SS *Waldensian* (B)*: Struis Point (night)
23 October | *Pioneer* (B): Durban
4 November | *Melbourne* (B): Ystervark Point (west gale)

1863

12 January | *Akbar* (B): Rietvlei, Table Bay (south-east wind)
22 February | *Rover* (SA): White Sands, Blouberg, Table Bay (fog)
30 March | *Willem de Zwyger* (D): Martha Point
10 April | SS *Albatross* (SA): Albatross Rock, Cape Peninsula (sank)
19 April | *Munster Lass*: East side of Knysna Heads
1 July | *Diligence* (SA)*: Hondeklip Bay (becalmed)
6 August | *Eliza* (Ger): Mouille Point, Table Bay (north-east wind)
16 August | *Queen* (B): Durban (north-east wind)
26 September | North-east gale, Durban
| *Sebastian* (B)
| *Earl of Hardwicke* (B)
10 November | *Medusa* (B): East London
26 November | *Swallow* (B): West of Cape Recife
18 December | *Evelyn* (SA): Danger Point (north wind)

1864

16 February | *Lucy* (SA): Danger Point (south-east gale)
15 March | *Sappho* (B): Blouberg, Table Bay (south-east gale, night)
26 May | *Grahamstown* (B)*: Table Bay (fire)
15 September | *Forfarshire*: Whale Rock, Table Bay
18 October | *Antonie* (Ger): West Bank, East London (south-east gale, night)
19 October | *Ballarat* (B): Algoa Bay (south-east gale, night)
| *Dennia* (B): Mossel Bay (south-east gale)

1865

10 May | *Rubens* (B): Rietvlei, Table Bay (south-east gale, night)
17 May | Great north-west gale, Table Bay
| *Fernande* (Dan)*
| *Alacrity* (B)*
| *Deane* (B)*
| *Royal Arthur* (B)*
| *Kehrweider* (Ger)*
| RMS *Athens* (B)*: Between Green Point and Mouille Point (night)
| *City of Peterborough* (B)*: Sceptre Reef (night)
25 May | *Fusilier* (B): Durban (north-east wind)
26 June | SS *Eastern Province* (B): Near Quoin Point
19 July | *Piscataqua* (Am): Between Green Point and Mouille Point, Table Bay
23 September | *Osprey* (B): East London (south-east gale)

29 October	*Queen of Ava* (B)*: Dassen Island
17 November	SS *Kadie* (SA): Breede River
1 December	*Etheldreda* (B): Martha Strand
	RMS *Dane* (B): Thunderbolt Reef, Cape Recife (south-west wind)
4 December	*Esterias*: Port Alfred

1866

First Transatlantic cable is layed; Alfred Nobel patents dynamite

13 January	*Ruby* (B): Mossel Bay (south-east wind)
6 February	*Runnymede* (B): Wreck Point, a little west of Klippen Point (abandoned)
8 February	*Adelaide* (B): Durban (east gale)
14 March	*Portsmouth* (Am): Coega River mouth, Algoa Bay (north-west gale)
18 April	*Prince of the Seas* (B): 13 km west of Cape Recife (west gale, night)
16 July	*Jonquille* (SA): Hondeklip Bay
16 August	*Ilva* (B): Algoa Bay

1867

Karl Marx completes first volume of Das Kapital; first diamond discovered at Hopetown

6 February	*L'Imperatrice Eugenie* (B)*: Thunderbolt Reef, Cape Recife
30 May	HMS *Osprey* (B)*: West of Cape St Francis lighthouse (south-west gale, night)
12 August	*Krimpenerward* (D): Algoa Bay (south-east gale, disabled)
	Henry Douse (B): East London (south-east gale)
21 October	SS *Bosphorus* (B): Near Tsitsikamma Point (night)
20 November	*Imogen* (B): East London (south-east gale)
13 December	*Hydra* (Ger): Durban (south-west gale)

SALE OF THE WRECK OF
H.M. Ship "Osprey."
The Undersigned, being duly authorised, will sell
On Wednesday, the 12th instant,
At 12 o'clock precisely,
On the Beach, where she now lies, about 12 miles West of Cape St. Francis,
The HULL, MASTS, SPARS, SAILS,
And whatever else might be washed up of H.M.S. "Osprey."
W. & R. METELERKAMP, Auctioneers.
Humansdorp, June 8, 1867.

Eastern Province Herald

1868

3 February	*Tugela* (B): Durban (night)
20 July	South-west gale, East London
	Sea Rover (B)
	Shantung (B)
	Constantia (B)
29 August	South-East gale, East London
	Nundeeps (B)
	Crusader

30 August	*Ambleside* (B): Natal South Coast (south-east wind)
27 October	*Borderer* (B)*: Struis Bay (sank)

1869

Suez Canal opened

2 January	*Hopefield Packet* (SA): Camps Bay
25 June	*Rosalind* (B): Port Nolloth (night)
7 August	*Tentonia* (Ger): Algoa Bay
4 September	*Sparfel* (Fr): Struis Point
18, 19 September	South-east gale, Algoa Bay
18 September	*Forres* (B)
	Sarah Black (B): (night)
	England (B)
19 September	*Argali* (SA)
	Gustaf (Swe): (disabled)
	Sea Snake (Swe): (disabled)
	Meg Merriles (B)
	Flash
	Amersham (B): Near Arniston (south-east gale)
11 October	*Volunteer*: Hondeklip Bay

1870

2 May	*Saint Austell* (B): Port Alfred (gale)
26 June	*Elite* (Ger): Kowie River, Port Alfred (beached)
22 July	*Nederlandsche Vlag* (D): Near Tsitsikamma Point (south-west gale)
12 August	*Martlet* (B): Port Alfred
21 September	*Eliza and Alice*: Mosterts Hoek, Cape St Francis
31 October	*Flower of the Arun* (B): East London (south-east gale)
19 November	*Benefactress* (Am): The Strand, False Bay (disabled)

1871

Verdi completes his opera Aïda*; German Empire established; France forms its Third Republic*

1 January	SS *Westenhope* (B): Bird Island, Algoa Bay (night)
13 January	*Simon*: Algoa Bay (south-east gale)
20 February	*Abdul Medjid* (B): Algoa Bay (south-east gale)
18 March	SS *Queen of the Thames* (B): Near Ryspunt (night)
19 May	*La Souvénance* (Fr): Quoin Point
27 May	SS *Gambia* (B): Algoa Bay (fouled)
13 September	*MacKay* (B): Off Struis Point
6 October	*Defiance* (B): 3 km north of Mzimkulu River (fog)
15 October	*Sarah Phillips* (B): East London
20 October	*Saint Clare* (B): Durban (north-east wind)
2 December	*Edith Smith* (SA): Bird Island, Algoa Bay

1872

20 March	*Fountain*: Thunderbolt Reef, Cape Recife
26 April	*Nant-Y-Glo* (B): East London (south-east gale)
28 April	*Susan Pardew* (B): Mossel Bay
26 May	Great south-east gale, East London

	Elaine (B)*: East of East London
	*Emma**
	*Martha**
	SS *Quanza**: Quanza Beach (night)
	Queen of May (B)*: West of East London
	Refuge (B)*
	Sharp (B)*: (night)
	Jane Davie (B)*: North-east of East London
29 June	*South-Easter* (B): East London

Eastern Province Herald

30, 31 July	North-east gale, Durban
30 July	*Grace Peile* (B)
31 July	*Princess Alice* (B)
	Breidablik (Nor)
4 September	*Niagara* (Fr): Slang River, Oyster Bay (disabled)
25 September	*Wild Rose* (B): Orient Beach, East London (south-east gale)
16 October	*Congune*: Durban (sank)
27 November	*Crixea* (B): East London (south-east gale)
	South-east gale, Mossel Bay
	Annie Benn (SA)
	Erin
	South-east gale, Algoa Bay
	Taurus (Fr)

Great Gale at Durban in July 1872. (Africana Museum)

	Anne Marie (Fr)
	Cruiser (B)
	E.B. Lohe (Ger)
29 November	*Magneten* (Nor): Plettenberg Bay (south-east gale)
31 December	*Elizabeth Brown* (B): Algoa Bay (south-east gale)
	North East (B): Vicinity of Quoin Point (south-east gale)

1873

	Clipper: Hondeklip Bay (east wind)
14 January	*E.A. Oliver* (B): Struis Bay (disabled)
31 January	SS *Bismarck* (Ger)*: South-west of Keiskamma River (fog)
7 April	SS *Fidela* (B): Cape Recife (fog)
25 April	*Hotbank* (B): Shark River, Algoa Bay (disabled)
12 September	*African Belle* (SA): Port Alfred
26 October	*Lord of the Isles*: East London
9 December	*William Shaw* (SA): Port St Johns

1874

24 March	*Albatross* (Nor): Danger Point (night)
25 March	*Waif* (B): Plettenberg Bay
1 May	*Lizzie* (B): North of Port Nolloth (parted anchor)
10 June	*Minnie*: Breede River
18 July	*Laetitia* (Ger): Port Alfred (parted anchor)
	Santos (Ger): Mossel Bay
19 July	Gale, East London
	Natal Star (B)
	Fingoe (SA)
9 August	*Shepherd* (B): Table Bay
11 September	*Hermann* (Dan): Algoa Bay (south-east gale)
5 October	*C.P.* (Fr): Struis Bay
19 November	*Midge* (B): Plettenberg Bay (south-east gale)
	Lyttelton: Algoa Bay (south east gale)
25 November	*Momina Zino* (It): Klippe-strand, east of Arniston (mist)
5, 6, 7 December	South-west gale, East London
5 December	*Western Star* (B)
	Coquette
	Compage (B)
6 December	*Nuovo Abele* (It): Cintsa River, East London area
	Florie (B)
7 December	*James Gibson* (B): Near Cape Henderson, north-east of East London
	Emile Marie: North-east of East London
	Verulam (B): West Bank
7, 8 December	South gale, Durban
7 December	*Star of Wales* (B)
8 December	*Transvaal* (B)
	Wagrien (Ger)

1875

Great Britain purchases controlling shares in Suez Canal; First Afrikaans Language Movement starts

5 February	RMS *Celt* (B)*: Celt Bay, west of Quoin Point
19 April	*Jupiter T.* (Aus)*: East of Cape Padrone (night, fog)

16 May	*Tonga* (B): Winkelspruit, Natal South Coast (north-east wind)
15 July	*Snorre Straulassen* (Nor): West of Port Alfred (south-west gale)
12 October	*Milford* (B): Near Tsitsikamma Point (abandoned)
16 October	*Carl zu den Drei Greiffen* (Ger): East London (south-east wind)
11 December	*Annie S.* (B): East London
23 December	*Nicoline* (Ger): Algoa Bay (south-east gale)

1876

Nikolaus Otto develops the four-stroke internal combustion engine

4 February	*Albert Juhl*: Orient Beach, East London
5 February	*Memento* (B): Near Cove Rock, East London (south-east wind)
9 February	*Lady McDonald* (B): Algoa Bay
1 March	*Edie Waters* (Am): Celt Bay
29 March	SS *Namaqua I* (B): Island Point, south of Hondeklip Bay
19 June	*Knysna Belle* (SA): Rietvlei, Table Bay
14 September	*Enfants Nantais* (Fr): Durban (east-north-east wind)
18 September	*Stella* (Nor): Algoa Bay (south-east gale)
19 October	*Marengo* (B): East London (south-east wind)
	RMS *Windsor Castle* (B): Dassen Island
1 November	South-west gale, East London
	Hohenzollern (Ger): Blind River
	Euterpe (B): East Beach
8 November	SS *Saint Lawrence* (B): Paternoster Point
28 November	*Ann Staniland* (B): East London (disabled)
10 December	*General Nott* (B): East London (north-west gale)

1877

Ninth (last) Frontier War starts

3 February	*Bierstadt* (Am): Nahoon Point, East London (north-west gale)

East London Dispatch

	Emelia (B): North-east side of Dyer Island (north-west gale)
4 April	*R.P. Buck* (Am): West of Cape Agulhas (fog)
23 August	South-east gale, Algoa Bay
	Alma (Ger)
	Univers (Fr)
	Countess of Dudley (Au): Orient Beach, East London (east breeze)
24 August	*Charmer* (B): North-west point of Dyer Island
26 October	*Ellen Browse* (Ger): East London (south-east gale)
	Mabel (B): Durban (east-north-east gale)
6 November	*Marie Élise* (Fr): Klippestrand
26 November	*Piccadilly* (SA): Near Celt Bay

1878

Ninth Frontier War ends

30 January	*Wheatlandside* (B): Algoa Bay (disabled)
13 February	RMS *Kafir* (B)*: South of Olifantsbos Point, Cape Peninsula (fine weather)
16 February	South gale, East London
	Elise (Ger): (night)
	Olive (B): (night)
3 March	*Ponda Chief* (B): Durban
27 March	*Ivy* (B): Ivy Point, Natal South Coast
8 April	*Catherine Scott* (B): Algoa Bay
9 April	*Theresina* (B): Durban (east-north-east gale)
13 May	*River Plate*: Near Buffelsjacht River
16 July	South-east gale, Algoa Bay
	Almira Coombs (Am)
	Petronella (D): (disabled)
19, 20, 22 July	North-west gale, Table Bay
19 July	*Caledonian* (B): Woodstock Beach (leaking)
	Jeanne (Fr): Salt River mouth
20 July	*Redbreast* (B)
22 July	*Etta Loring* (Am): Woodstock Beach
2 August	*H.D. Storer* (Am): Durban (east-north-east gale)
23 August	*Southport* (B): Durban (east-north-east gale)
12 October	*Tevere* (B): Near Woody Cape, Algoa Bay (south-west gale)
15 October	*Asphodel* (B): Near Cape Morgan (south-west gale)
20 October	*Lion* (SA): Port Nolloth (south-east gale)
26 October	*Alma* (Ger): Near Gonubie River mouth (south-west gale)

1879

Anglo-Zulu War starts

27 January	*Racer* (B): East of Quoin Point
22 February	*Eagle Wing* (B): Quoin Point (gale)
13 March	North-east gale, Durban
	Ziba (Am)
	Gazelle (Am)
30 March	*Lola* (Swe): Durban (north-east wind)
3 April	SS *Clyde* (B): North-east of Dyer Island (fine weather)
2 May	*Tancred* (B): Durban (east wind)
12 June	*Elise* (Ger): Struis Bay (south-west gale)
18 August	*Pisa* (It): Bot River area

8 October	*Sea Wave* (B): West Bank, East London (gale, night)
19 October	*Peusamento* (P): Durban

1880

First Anglo-Boer War starts

11 January	*Philia* (B): Mossel Bay (south-east gale)
18 January	*Paralos* (Fr): Cape Point area (sank)
17 March	*Wilhelmine* (Ger)*: Mossel Bay (south-east gale)
5 May	*Brilliant* (Ger): Algoa Bay (south-east breeze)
21 July	*Zennia* (Ir): Durban (south wind, night)
25 August	East gale, Durban *Eastern Star* (B) *Surprise* (Nor)

Natal Mercury

29 August	*Star of Africa* (SA): Albatross Rock, Cape Peninsula (sank, night)
1 September	*Flying Scud* (B): Algoa Bay (south-east gale)
2 September	*Luna* (B): Durban (south-east gale)
24 October	*Graf Wedell* (Ger): Durban (east wind, night)
1 November	*Draga* (Aus): Durban (north-east wind)
4 November	*Star Beam*: East London (south-east gale)
5 November	South-east gale, East London *Columba* (Rus) *Hope* *Clara* (Am): Algoa Bay (south-east gale)

Natal Mercury

6 November	*Lady Pryse* (B): Mossel Bay (south-east gale)
	Leading Star (B): Mzimkulu River (night)
18 November	*Emma* (Ger): East London (south-west gale)
31 December	*Lancastria* (B): Robben Island, Table Bay (south-east gale)

1881

30 January	*Rosalie*: Port Alfred
15 February	*Johanna* (D): Algoa Bay (south-east gale)
5 April	*Phoénix* (Fr): Noetzie River, east of Knysna
25 July	South-west gale, East London *Brighton* (B): Nahoon Point *Clymping* (B): East Beach *Die Heimath*: Beyond Bats Cave
28 July	*Calcutta* (Am): A little south-west of Xora River
25 November	*Cape of Good Hope*: Port Beaufort
16 December	*Albatross* (Ger): Algoa Bay (south-east gale)

Albatross. *(P.E. Public Library)*

1882

27 January	*James Gaddarn* (B): Durban (east-north-east gale)
20 February	*Johan* (Swe): East London (south-east gale)
3 March	*Queen of Ceylon* (B): Durban (north-east wind)
4 April	*Gleam* (B): Port Nolloth (heavy surf)
12 May	*Francisca* (It): East London (beached)
28 May	*Christina* (SA): Plettenberg Bay *Agnes* (SA): Plettenberg Bay
29 May	*Seafield* (B): East London (south-west gale) *Louisa Dorothea* (Ger): Mossel Bay (south-east gale)
31 May	*Clansman* (B): East London (south-east gale)
6 June	*Louise Scheller* (Ger): Cape Hangklip (north-west gale)
28 June	*Bridgetown* (B): Durban (north-east wind)
29 June	*Gloria Deo* (It): Ratel River area
11 October	*Galloway* (B): Cape Recife (night)
25 October	*Frida* (Swe): Port Nolloth (south-east gale)
10 December	*Zambesi* (D): Durban (east wind)

1883

Paul Kruger elected President of the Z.A.R.

19 April	*Florence* (B)*: Stag Island, Algoa Bay
11 May	*Kolstrop* (Ger): Dyer Island (night)
3 June	*Hansa* (Ger)*: Vicinity of Danger Point (night, north-west wind)
16 June	SS *Umsimkulu* (B): Breede River, Port Beaufort
18 July	*Freeman Clarke* (Am)*: Gamtoos River mouth (fire)
21 July	*City of Lima* (B): Durban (east-north-east wind)
22 August	*Fratelli Arecco* (It): Durban (east-north-east wind, night)
28 September	*Dauntless* (Am): East London (south-east breeze)
24 October	*Schmayl* (Am): East London (south-east gale)
25 October	*Catherine* (Ger): Algoa Bay (south-east gale)
8 December	*Reno* (It)*: Mouille Point, Table Bay

1884

Charles Parsons develops a steam turbine

4 January	*Lockett* (B): West Bank, East London (south-east gale)
5 May	SS *Bulli* (Au): Paternoster Point (fog)
20 May	SS *Nebo* (B): Aliwal Shoal, Natal South Coast (fine weather)
9 June	*Vigor* (Nor): Durban (east wind)
23 August	*Caprera* (Am): Algoa Bay (south-east gale)
26 August	*Charles Jackson* (B): Durban
8 October	*Paz* (B): Algoa Bay (south-east gale)

1885

Bismarck calls Berlin Conference on Africa

7 January	*Wigtonshire* (B): East of Arniston (midnight)
16 March	*Princeport* (B): Dyer Island
5 September	*Maron Neil*: Orient Beach, East London (parted anchor)
18 October	SS *Imerina* (B): Dyer Island (fog)
30 October	*Olga R.* (Aus): Mouille Point, Table Bay
16 November	SS *Welcombe* (B): East of Great Fish Point
2 December	*Il Nazerino* (It): Robben Island, Table Bay
12 December	*Seenymphe* (Ger): Durban (east wind, night)

1886

Gold discovered on the Witwatersrand

8 February	*Veronica* (B): Port Nolloth (south-east gale, sank)
3 June	*Caterina Doge* (It): Near Cape Point
7 August	*Carlotta B.* (It): Olifantsbos, Cape Peninsula
14 August	*Carrie Wyman* (Am): East London
1 December	*Ispahan* (B): Near Cape Hangklip (fog)

1887

13 January	*Forest Grove* (B): Doddington Rock, Bird Island, Algoa Bay
2 February	*Jorawur* (B): Algoa Bay (south-east gale)
26 April	SS *Finland* (B): Near Great Fish Point
10 July	SS *Alfredia*: Port St Johns
26 August	*Manhegan* (B): South of Hondeklip Bay
14 November	*Idomene* (B): Qora River, Mazeppa Bay (night)

1888

John Dunlop produces his pneumatic tyre

12 January	*Mary Ann* (B): Algoa Bay (parted anchor)
26 March	*Sandvik* (Swe): East London
31 March	*Emma* (Nor): Peddie district
1 April	*Fairholme* (B)*: East side of Buffalo Bay, Knysna (fire, abandoned)
8 May	*Gerhardine* (Ger): Coega River mouth, Algoa Bay
21 May	*Adele*: Dyer Island
4 June	*Ellida* (Nor): Danger Point (north-west gale)
27 August	*Jane* (B): Near Forest Hall, Plettenberg Bay (south-east gale)
30 August	*Rosebud* (B): Mossel Bay (south-east gale)

Dorthea. *(P.E. Public Library)*

	Great south-east gale, Algoa Bay
	Dorthea (Dan)
	Drei Emmas (Bel)
	Wolseley (B)
	Natal (Swe)
	Lada (Aus)
	Jane Harvey (B)
	Elizabeth Stevens (B)
	C. Boschetto (It): (disabled)
	Andreas Riis (Nor)
13 November	*British Duke* (B): West of Klippen Point

1889

19 January	*Araminta* (B): Algoa Bay (south-east gale, night)
31 May	SS *Namaqua II* (B): Port Nolloth (beached)
8 June	*Queen of Nations* (B): Bats Cave, East London (parted, disabled)
18 July	*Fidia D.* (It): Mkomaas River (east gale, disabled)
19 July	PS *Buffalo* (SA): Port Alfred (sank in river)

19 August	*Hawthorn* (B): Durban (north-east gale)
29 August	*Mary Emily* (Ger): Durban (east gale, night)
17 September	*South American* (Am): Struis Bay (fog)
25 September	*Amana* (B): Near Fish River mouth
16 October	*Zephyr* (Nor): Algoa Bay (south east gale)
30 October	*Poseidon* (Nor): Algoa Bay (south-east gale)

1890

23 January	SS *Strathblane* (B): Chelsea Point, near Port Elizabeth (beached)
5 February	SS *Robilant* (It): Near Saldanha Bay (fog, sank)
7 February	*Onni* (Rus): Blouberg, Table Bay (fine weather, night)
12 April	SS *Umvolosi*(B): Near Kleinmond
24 May	SS *Ashleigh Brook* (B): Dassen Island (night)
18 July	*Ianthe* (B): Cliff Point, north of Olifants River
7 December	SS *Kaffir* (B): East London
26 December	*Pembroke Castle* (B): South of Hondeklip Bay (fog)

1891

1 August	SS *Wallarah* (B): Boom Point, Dassen Island (fog)
22 October	*Harmonie* (Nor): Cape Recife

1892

9 January	*Orchomene* (B): Algoa Bay (beached)
3 February	*Onaway* (B): Durban (night)
28 February	SS *Alcestis* (B): Cape Agulhas (sank)
22 June	*Noatun* (Nor): Near Cape Padrone (westerly storm)
19 August	*Roma* (B): Near Cape Padrone (night)
25 August	*Galera* (Nor): Danger Point, Mossel Bay (south-east gale)
26 August	*Modesta* (Nor): Algoa Bay (south-east gale)

1893

29 September	*Elpida* (Nor): East London
2 October	*Sedwell Jane* (B): Algoa Bay (south-east gale)

1894

11 March	*Seagull* (Nor): Mossel Bay (south-east gale)
10 November	*Circassia* (Nor): Near Qora River mouth
22 December	*Bonanza* (Am): Orient Beach, East London

1895

Jameson Raid fails

7 February	*Fascadale* (B): South of Mbizane River (night)
6 April	*Dundrennan* (B): Struis Point (fog)
27 April	*Derby* (Nor): Thys Bay, Cape St Francis (disabled)

1896

29 January	SS *Saxon* (P): Near Kosi Bay
6 March	*Volo* (Nor): Near Bushmans River mouth
8 June	*Greystoke Castle* (B): Near Martha Point
18 August	SS *Queen Victoria* (B)*: North End, Algoa Bay (beached)
2 September	*Lakmé* (Nor): Thunderbolt Reef, Cape Recife (sank)
9 October	*Atlas* (Nor): Blouberg Beach, Table Bay
9 December	*British Peer* (B): A little south of Grotto Bay, West Coast

1897

Zululand annexed to Natal; Rudolf Diesel patents the diesel engine

31 January	*Reistad* (Nor): Algoa Bay (south-east wind, collision)
7 February	*Vilora H. Hopkins* (Am): Algoa Bay (south-east gale)
5 May	*Cambusnethan* (B): Near Woody Cape, Algoa Bay (south-west gale, night)
10 June	*Trygve* (Nor): Zinkwazi River, Natal
19 June	*Port Douglas* (B): Cape Recife (night)
23 June	*Fredheim* (Nor): Coney Glen, Knysna (north-west wind)
7 August	*Nukteris*: Buffels Bay, near Cape Point (night)
17 October	SS *Clan Gordon* (B)*: Natal North Coast
28 November	*Lilla* (B): Kowie River (good weather, broke tow)

1898

31 January	*Dorothea* (Am)*: Cape Vidal (abandoned at sea)
20 March	SS *Clan Lindsay* (B): Mazeppa Bay
16 May	*R.A.C. Smith* (Am): 13 km east of Sundays River mouth (disabled, night)
17 July	*Emilia* (P): Algoa Bay (disabled, sank)

1899

Anglo-Boer War starts; Boxer Rebellion breaks out in China; Sigmund Freud makes public his Interpretation of Dreams

17 May	*Lebu* (Nor): Cape Recife
12 September	SS *Thermopylae* (B): Green Point, Table Bay (night)
3 December	SS *Ismore* (B): Near Cape Columbine lighthouse (south-east gale, night)

Thermopylae.

20TH CENTURY

1900

10 May	SS *Craigellachie* (B): East of Riet Point
25 May	SS *Kakapo* (B)*: Chapmans Bay (north-west gale, night)
29 May	*America* (B): Woodstock Beach, Table Bay (fire)
5 July	SS *Ashlands* (B): Bird Island (night)
4 September	*Abeona* (B): Thunderbolt Reef, Cape Recife

Kakapo. *(Stephen Goodson)*

1901

Queen Victoria dies and Edward VII ascends the throne; first message sent over Marconi's Transatlantic wireless telegraph

16 January	HMS *Sybille* (B): South of Lamberts Bay (night)
31 January	*Harry Mundahl* (SA): Near Port Shepstone (dawn)
4 May	*Rubia* (Nor): South of East London

Tantallon Castle. *(Robert Pabst)*

7 May	RMS *Tantallon Castle* (B): North-western point of Robben Island (fog)
12 May	SS *Hermes* (B): Milnerton Beach, Table Bay (north-west gale)
17 October	*Louise* (Nor): East of the Knysna Heads (south-west wind)

1902

Treaty of Vereeniging signed

30 May	*Ryvingen* (Nor): Near the Mole on Woodstock Beach, Table Bay (night)
	SS *Clan Macgregor* (B): Near Ryspunt
9 June	*Armenia* (It): Blouberg, Table Bay (disabled)

10 June	South-east gale, East London
	Atbara (Nor): Marina Beach
	Aurora (Swe): Blind River
	Elise Linck (Ger): Blind River
28 June	*Gustav Adolph* (Nor): Palmiet River, near Kleinmond
14 August	North-west gale, Table Bay
	SS *City of Lincoln* (B): Salt River mouth
	The Highfields (B)*: (collision, sank)
	Verona (Nor)*: Near Cape Hangklip (north-west gale)
19 August	*Espero* (It): North of Port Shepstone (gale)
1, 2 September	Great south-east gale, Algoa Bay
1 September	*Hans Wagner* (Ger)*
	Arnold (Ger)*
	Cavalieri Michelle Russo (It)*
	Constant (Nor)*
	Content (Nor)*
	Emmanuel (Ger)*
	Hermanos (Nor)*
	Limari (Swe)*
	Thekla (Ger)*
	Waimea (Nor)*
	Gabrielle (B)*
	Agostino Rombo (It)*
	Nautilus (Ger)*
	Oakworth (B)*
	Iris (Ger)*
	Sayre (B)*
2 September	*Inchcape Rock* (B)*: (night)
	Poseidon (Nor): Mossel Bay (south-east gale, night)

1903

Wright brothers make the first aeroplane flight

23 August	SS *Gertrud Woermann* (Ger): South of Port Nolloth (fog)
19 October	*Paquita* (Ger)*: Knysna Heads
14 November	*King Cenric* (Nor): Mossel Bay (south-east gale)
	South-east gale, Algoa Bay
	County of Pembroke (B)
	Elda (Nor)
	Wayfarer (Nor)
	Two Brothers (Nor)
	San Antonio (It)

San Antonio. *(Frank Neave)*

1904

Russo-Japanese War starts

1905

Trans-Siberian railway completed; Albert Einstein presents his Theory of Relativity

| 5 April | SS *Ashmount* (B): Near Stalwart Point |

1 June	*Trichera* (Swe): Natal South Coast (night)
1 July	SS *Clan Monroe* (B): Slangkop lighthouse, Cape Peninsula (night)
10 October	*Helene*: East London (night)

1906

Bambatha rebellion breaks out in Natal

| 21 May | SS *Oakburn* (B)*: Near Duiker Point (fog) |
| 15 October | SS *Octopus* (B): Near Ballito Bay, Natal (storm) |

1907

| 28 March | SS *Kilbrennan* (B): East of Kowie (sank) |
| 29 July | *Orient* (Rus): Orient Beach, East London |

1908

12 March	SS *Newark Castle* (B): Richards Bay (abandoned)
2 August	*Ticino* (It): South of Port Nolloth
2 October	SS *Valdivia* (B)*: East London (disabled, sank)

1909

Blériot makes the first aeroplane flight across the English channel

5 August	SS *Maori* (B)*: Duiker Point (drizzle, fog)
15 September	SS *Umhlali* (SA): Olifantsbos Point, Cape Peninsula (beached, night)
26 November	SS *Ourimbah* (B): Chelsea Point (fog)

1910

Union of South Africa comes into being

25 February	SS *Crusader* (B): East Reef, Bird Island, Algoa Bay
23 May	*Seier* (Nor): Buffalo Bay (beached)
16 August	SS *Khedive* (Ger): Near Kei Mouth
23 October	SS *Lisboa* (P)*: Soldiers Reef, Cape Columbine (south-east gale)

1911

7 March	SS *Palatinia* (B): East Beach, East London (sinking, beached)
18 April	SS *Lusitania* (P)*: Bellows Rock, Cape Point (midnight, fog)
24 May	SS *Itzehoe* (Ger): Cape Recife (night)

Itzehoe. *(P.E. Public Library)*

1913

1 February	SS *Haddon Hall* (B): North of Saldanha Bay
23 March	SS *Hektor* (Nor): Dyer Island (fog)
27 March	SS *Camphill* (B): Cape Agulhas (mist)

1914

First World War starts; South African Rebellion breaks out

21 November	SS *Clan Stuart* (B): Glencairn, False Bay (south-east gale, night)

Clan Stuart. *(Cape Archives, G360)*

1916

31 March	SS *Rangatira* (B): North-western corner of Robben Island (fog)
29 December	SS *Obell* (B): South-west of Bashee River

1917

Russian Revolution starts

18 September	SS *Bia* (Swe): Olifantsbos Point, Cape Peninsula (beached, night)
27 September	*Colonial Empire* (B): Cape Recife - last sailing cargo ship wrecked on South African coast

Colonial Empire. *(P.E. Public Library)*

1918

First World War ends

1920

Brand and Van Ryneveld fly from London to Cape Town

1921

28 November	SS *Losna* (Nor): Near Fish River

1922

Great Miners' Strike on the Witwatersrand

1923

24 March	SS *Rusholme*: South of Port Nolloth

1925

22 May	SS *Sceptre* (B): Struis Bay (night)

1926

J.L. Baird demonstrates the first television

20 November	SS *Frontier I* (SA): Port St Johns

1927

7 April	SS *Hamlet* (SA): South Head, Saldanha Bay (mist)

1928

South African national flag adopted

24 November	SS *Cariboo* (B)*: East of Stalwart Point (sank)

1929

Great Wall Street crash; Great Depression starts

20 February	SS *Cape Recife* (B)*: Cape St Francis lighthouse (fog)
8 April	SS *Western Knight* (Am)*: Near The Willows, west of Cape Recife (mist)
11 September	SS *King Cadwallon* (B): East London (fire, abandoned)
29 October	SS *Hypatia* (B)*: Whale Rock, Table Bay (fog)

King Cadwallon.

1930

9 September	SS *Malmesbury* (B): Jacobs Reef, near Saldanha Bay (fog)

1932

South Africa abandons the gold standard

3 May	SS *Haliartus* (B)*: West of Gouritz River (fog)

1933

Adolf Hitler becomes Chancellor of Germany

5 April	SS *Haleric* (B)*: South-west of Cape St Martin (sank)

Paris Maru. *(P.E. Public Library)*

1934

15 January	SS *Paris Maru* (Jap)*: North End Beach, Algoa Bay (disabled, sank)
28 July	MV *Winton* (B): Milnerton Beach, Table Bay (night)
7 September	SS *Queenmoor* (B): Chelsea Point (fog)

1937

17 December	SS *Stuart Star* (B): Hood Point, East London (fog)

1938

14 January	SS *Lyngenfjord* (Nor)*: West of Tsitsikamma Point (fog)
17 February	SS *Panaghia* (Gr)*: Near Tsitsikamma Point (fog)
7 April	MV *Frontier II* (SA): Shixina Point, Transkei Coast

1939

Second World War starts

3 February	SS *Avala* (Yug): Quoin Point (mist)

Ovington Court. *(A.L. Russell)*

1940

June	SS *Timavo* (It): North of Leven Point, Zululand (military action)
25 November	SS *Ovington Court* (B): South Beach, Durban (north-east gale)

1942

6 April	HMSAS *Sydostlandet* (SA): Durban (gale, night)

27 November   SS *Thomas T. Tucker* (Am)*: Olifantsbos Point, Cape Peninsula (fog)
18 December   SS *City of Hankow* (B)*: North of Saldanha Bay (fog)

1943

10 January   SS *Meliskerk* (D)*: A little north-east of Port St Johns
              SS *Piratiny* (Bra): A little south of Kleinsee

1944

Allied invasion of Normandy

1945

First atomic bomb dropped; Second World War ends
2 November   SS *Chub* (SA): South of Cape St Martin

1946

10 December   SS *Swona* (SA): Quoin Point (north-west gale, disabled)
              SS *Fynd* (SA): Quoin Point (fouled)

1947

1 April   SS *George M. Livanos* (Gr): Green Point, Table Bay
           MV *Border* (B): South of Port Nolloth (fog)
27 November   SS *President Reitz* (SA)*: West of Tsitsikamma Point (fog)

1948

Berlin Air Lift; D.F. Malan becomes Prime Minister
5 November   SS *Esso Wheeling* (Am)*: Quoin Point (midnight)

Esso Wheeling. (Cape Argus)

1950

Korean War starts

1956

Royal Navy diver reaches 184m in standard diving equipment
30 December   SS *Adelfotis* (Cr): Quoin Point (fog, south-east wind)

1957

Soviet Union launches Sputnik I

27 September   SS *Frontier* (SA): East London area

1958

23 July   MV *Ovambo Coast* (SA): Marcus Island, Saldanha Bay (fog)
10 November   MV *Forresbank* (B): North-east of Mtakatye River, Transkei coast (fire)

1961

South Africa becomes a Republic; Yuri Gagarin becomes the first man in space

1963

1 April   SS *Bulwark* (SA)*: Danger Point (fog)

1965

30 April   MV *Nolloth* (D): Olifantsbos Point, Cape Peninsula (beached)

1966

H.F. Verwoerd assassinated; Rhodesia declares UDI
1 July   SS *South African Seafarer* (SA)*: Green Point, Table Bay (north-west gale, night)

South African Seafarer. (Cape Argus)

1967

12 May   MV *Horizon* (SA): South-west of Port St Johns
1 August   MFV *Athina* (Gr): Robberg Beach, Plettenberg Bay (beached, night)

1969

First man lands on the moon

1971

6 April   MV *Sri Rezeki* (Ind): Stilbaai area (fog)
3 June   MV *Seatrader* (Lib): Cape St Martin (fog)
18 September   MV *Jacaranda* (Gr): North-east of Kei River mouth (disabled)

1974

22 July   MV *Oriental Pioneer* (Chi)*: Cape Agulhas (beached)
11 August   MV *Produce* (Nor): Aliwal Shoal, south of Natal (sank)
13 August   MV *SA Oranjeland* (SA): East London (north-east gale)

S.A. Oranjeland. (Marius Garb)

1975

Working dive to 329 metres by Comex divers, followed by dive to 464 metres; Mozambique and Angola become independent

1976

27 January   MV *Goel No. 1* (Can): Robben Island, Table Bay
29 February   MV *Pati* (Cyp): Thunderbolt Reef, Cape Recife (fog)
16 June   SS *Arosa* (Cyp): South of Kleinsee, West Coast

1977

28 July   SS *Antipolis* (Gr): South of Oudekraal, Cape Peninsula (north-west gale, broke tow)
29 July   SS *Romelia* (Lib): Sunset Rocks, Llandudno, Cape Peninsula (north-west gale, broke tow)

1978

17 March   MV *Pantelis A. Lemos* (Gr): Opposite Churchhaven (night, fog)

1979

12 June   MV *Evdokia* (Gr)*: Tsitsikamma Park, east of Storms River (south-west gale, night)

1985

27 July   MV *Poseidon Cape* (SA): Kleinsee (gale)
29 July   MV *Kapodistrias* (Gr)*: Thunderbolt Reef, off Cape Recife (fine weather)

1986

30 March   MV *Daeyang Family* (Kor)*: A little south of Whale Rock, Table Bay

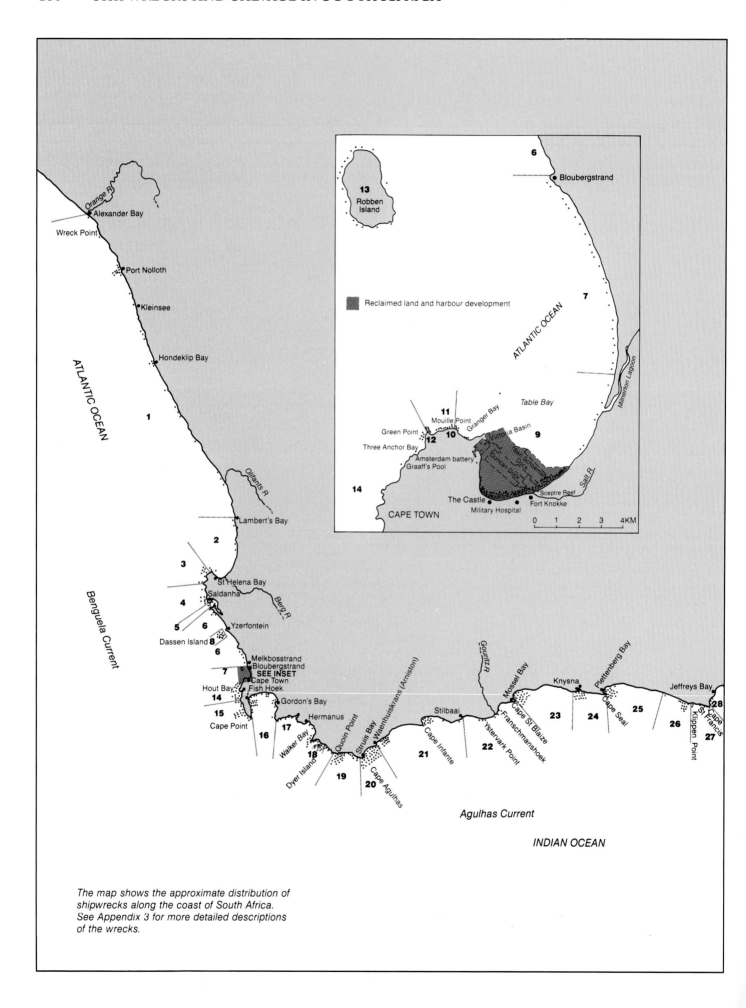

The map shows the approximate distribution of
shipwrecks along the coast of South Africa.
See Appendix 3 for more detailed descriptions
of the wrecks.

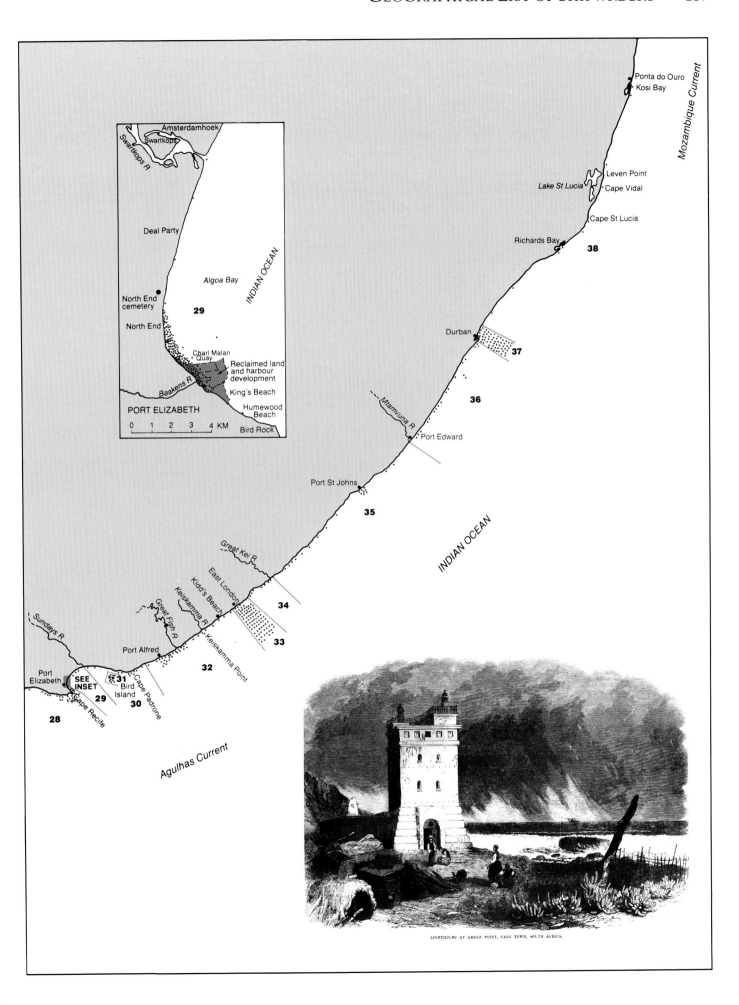

Ponta do Ouro
Kosi Bay

Mozambique Current

Leven Point
Lake St Lucia
Cape Vidal

Cape St Lucia

Richards Bay
38

Durban
37

36

Mtamvuna R
Port Edward

Port St Johns

35

Great Kei R

INDIAN OCEAN

East London
Kidd's Beach
34

Keiskamma R
33

Keiskamma Point
32

Great Fish R
Port Alfred

Sundays R

Port Elizabeth
SEE INSET
Bird Island
29
30
31
Cape Padrone

Cape Recife
28

Agulhas Current

Inset: PORT ELIZABETH

Amsterdamhoek
Swartkops
Swartkops R

Deal Party

Algoa Bay

INDIAN OCEAN

North End cemetery
29

North End

Charl Malan Quay
Reclaimed land and harbour development
King's Beach
Baakens R
Humewood Beach

PORT ELIZABETH

0 1 2 3 4 KM

Bird Rock

LIGHTHOUSE AT GREEN POINT, CAPE TOWN, SOUTH AFRICA.

Geographical List of Shipwrecks

Please note: Wrecks are listed alphabetically within each of 38 coastal regions, from the Orange River mouth to Ponta do Ouro. (See map on pp 136-137)

1. Orange River mouth to Lambert's Bay

A dry, inhospitable stretch of coast, most of which is restricted diamond territory. The Atlantic water is cold due to the Benguela current which flows northward. The sea is usually turbid and the shore is pounded by heavy ground swells. The underwater vegetation consists of vast kelp beds in which crayfish are found in large numbers. The land is hot and dry with a scant covering of semi-desert vegetation, and is sparsely populated. The main commercial activities are fishing and the recovery of alluvial diamonds. The chief settlements along the coast are Alexander Bay, which is an important diamond mining centre, Port Nolloth, from where copper ore from the rich Namaqualand copper mines is exported, and Hondeklip Bay, a centre of the crayfishing and fishing industry. Jonquille Rock at Hondeklip Bay is named after the Cape schooner Jonquille wrecked there in 1866.

SS **Arosa** (ex *Atlantic General*)
30° 02.50S, 17° 10.00E

Cypriot freighter of 7 669 tons, built in 1956. Wrecked 40 km south of Kleinsee on 16 June 1976 while on a voyage in ballast from Lagos to dry-dock in Cape Town for repairs. She lies in a restricted diamond area, and is still visible on the rocks (1987).
Argus, 17, 21 June 1976
Lloyds Register of Shipping, 1976-77

MV **Border** (ex *Albion*)

British motor coaster of 205 tons, built in 1927 by N.V. Noord Nederl. Schips., Groningen, registered in Durban, owned by the Coastal Steamship Co, and commanded by Capt R.C. Armitage. Wrecked 80 km south of Port Nolloth on 1 April 1947 in dense fog while on a voyage from Cape Town to Port Nolloth with a 200-ton cargo of explosives, petrol and general cargo. No lives were lost. She was engaged in a weekly return service from Cape Town to Port Nolloth.
Cape Argus, 5 April 1947
Lloyds Register of Shipping, 1946-47

Catherine Isabella

Schooner commanded by Capt N. Nicholson. Wrecked at Elephants Rock, north of the Olifants River, on 17 May 1845 when her cables parted during a north-west gale. One man was drowned.
Cape Town Mail, 31 May 1845
Shipping Register, Cape Archives, C.C. 2/16
South African Commercial Advertiser 4, 7 (sale notice) June 1845

Clipper

Coasting schooner. Wrecked on the rocks at Hondeklip Bay in 1873 during an east wind while leaving the bay.
Shipping Register, Cape Archives, C.C. 3/7/2/2

Diligence

Cape schooner commanded by Capt Carstens. Wrecked on the rocks at Hondeklip Bay on 1 July 1863 after becoming becalmed while on a voyage to Cape Town.
Shipping Register, Cape Archives, C.C. 3/7/2/1

Elizabeth

Wrecked at the Olifants River mouth, a little north of Doringbaai, in December 1817.
Cape Town Gazette, 27 December 1817 (sale notice)

Florence

Schooner of 80 tons, commanded by Capt J. Bradston. Wrecked on the rocks at the entrance to Port Nolloth on 11 December 1859. Most of her cargo was saved.
Shipping Register, Cape Archives, C.C. 2/18

Flying Fish

Schooner of 80 tons, commanded by Capt J. Iceton. Wrecked at Port Nolloth on 4 April 1855 after striking rocks while attempting to enter the bay.
Shipping Register, Cape Archives, C.C. 2/18

Frida

Swedish barque of 407 tons, commanded by Capt Granland. Wrecked at Port Nolloth on 25 October 1882 during a south-east gale with a cargo of timber for the Cape Copper Mining Company.
Shipping Register, Cape Archives, C.C. 3/7/2/3

SS **Gertrud Woermann**

German South West Africa Line steel screw steamer of 1 743 tons, built in 1885 by Act. Ges. 'Vulcan', Stettin, and commanded by Capt Parow. Wrecked 19 km south of Port Nolloth on 23 August 1903 in fog while on a voyage from South West Africa to Port Nolloth with passengers, a crew of 34, mail and general cargo. No lives were lost.
Cape Times, 25 August 1903
Lloyds Register of Shipping, 1901-02

Gleam

British composite iron and wood barque of 292 tons, built in 1859 in London. Ran ashore at Port Nolloth on 4 April 1882 while attempting to move to a safer anchorage in a heavy swell. She was waiting to enter the port and had anchored too close to the reef. Five lives were lost.
Cape Argus, 18 April 1882
Lloyds Register of Shipping, 1882-83

Hamilla Mitchell

British wooden brig of 175 tons, built in 1837 at Arbroath. Wrecked south of Cape Voltas, south of Oranjemund, on a reef near Wreck Point (Soco Reef?) on 8 December 1844. One boy was drowned while crossing the Orange River.
Lloyds Register of Shipping, 1844-45
South African Commercial Advertiser, 14 December 1844

Ianthe

British wooden barque of 380 tons, built in 1858 by A. Stephens & Son, Dundee, and commanded by Capt R.V. Clay. Wrecked at Cliff Point, a little to the north of the Olifants River, on 18 July 1890 while on a voyage from Port Nolloth to Swansea with a cargo of copper ore. Three lives were lost.
Lloyds Register of Shipping, 1890-91
Shipping Register, Cape Archives, C.C. 3/7/2/4

Jessie Smith

British wooden brig of 226 tons, built in 1845 at Yarmouth, and commanded by Capt W. Baxter. Wrecked at Alexander Bay on 23 August 1853 after her anchor cables parted. Four men were drowned.
Lloyds Register of Shipping, 1852-53
Shipping Register, Cape Archives, C.C. 2/18

Jonquille

Cape wooden schooner of 47 tons, built in 1859 by Thackray, Sunderland. Wrecked on Jonquille Rock on 16 July 1866 while entering Hondeklip Bay. No lives were lost.
Cape Argus, 28 July 1866
Lloyds Register of Shipping, 1866-67

Lion

Cutter of 60 tons. Wrecked at 06h00 on 20 October 1878 during a south-east gale after entering Port Nolloth while on a voyage from St Helena Bay to Walvis Bay in ballast. No lives were lost.
Cape Argus, 26 October 1878

Lizzie

British wooden brigantine of 205 tons, built in 1873 by McDonald, Prince Edward Island, registered in Swansea and commanded by Capt J. Jones. Ran aground 3,2 km north of Port Nolloth on 1 May 1874 after her cables parted while on a voyage from London with a general cargo.
Lloyds Register of Shipping, 1874-75
Shipping Register, Cape Archives, C.C. 3/7/2/2

Manhegan

Sydney-based British wooden barque of 1 143 tons, built in 1876 by J. Pascal, Camden, USA, and commanded by Capt A. C. Paulsen. Wrecked 32 km south of Hondeklip Bay on 26 August 1887 while on a voyage from Hong Kong to New York. No lives were lost.
Lloyds Universal Register of Shipping, 1887-88
Shipping Register, Cape Archives, C.C. 3/7/2/4

Meteren

Dutch hoeker of 190 tons, built in 1719 at the Enkhuizen Yard for the Amsterdam Chamber of the Dutch East India Company, and commanded by Willem van Turenhout. Ran ashore 30 km north of the Olifants River on 9 November 1723 after anchoring there due to the death of six crew members from scurvy while on an outward-bound voyage from Texel, which she had left on 24 May 1723 with a crew of 29 and a cargo of bricks. Five people were drowned. Two bronze breech-loading swivel guns bearing the Dutch East India Company monogram, and a large cast iron muzzle-loader, were dug up on the beach.
Cape Archives, V.C. 22. Translated into English in *Précis of the Archives of the Cape of Good Hope, Journal, 1699-1732*, H.C.V. Leibbrandt, 1896
Dutch-Asiatic Shipping Outward Voyages, 1595-1794, The Hague, 1979

SS **Namaqua I**

Union Company iron screw coaster of 352 tons, built in 1872 by Oswald, Sunderland, and commanded by Capt Gibbs. Wrecked at Island Point south of Hondeklip Bay on 29 March 1876. No lives were lost. She traded between Table Bay and Port Nolloth carrying copper ore.
Lloyds Register of Shipping, 1876-77
Shipping Register, Cape Archives, C.C. 3/7/2/2

SS **Namaqua II**

British coaster of 182 tons, built in 1872 by J.

Fullerton & Co, Paisley, owned by Berrys of Cape Town, and commanded by Capt H.J. Hanson. Beached on 31 May 1889 after striking rocks in the channel at Port Nolloth.
Argus Annual 1892
Lloyds Register of Shipping, 1890-91
Shipping Register, Cape Archives, C.C. 3/7/2/4

Natal

Schooner of 97 tons. Wrecked in Espiegle Bay, Port Nolloth, on 4 March 1852 during a south-east gale. No lives were lost.
Cape Town Mail, 23 March 1852

Pembroke Castle

British iron barquentine of 410 tons, built in 1863 by A. Stephen & Sons, Glasgow, and commanded by Capt D. Thomas. Wrecked near the Groenrivier, south of Hondeklip Bay, on 26 December 1890 in thick fog while on a voyage from the River Plate to Port Nolloth in ballast. No lives were lost.
Lloyds Register of Shipping, 1890-91
Shipping Register, Cape Archives, C.C. 3/7/2/4

SS **Piratiny** (ex *Carla*)
30° 09.00 S, 17° 10.00 E

Brazilian cargo steamer of 5 187 tons, built in 1921 by Cant. Nav. Triestino Monfalcone. Wrecked south of Kleinsee in 1943 while on a voyage from Brazil to Cape Town with a general cargo.
Lloyds Register of Shipping, 1942-43

MV **Poseidon Cape** (ex *Shearwater Cape*, ex *Seaforth Cape*, ex *Tiko*)
29° 40.00S, 17° 02.00E

Twin-screw diamond recovery vessel of 1 340 tons, built in 1967 by A.G. 'Weser'werk Seebeck, Bremerhaven. Ran ashore at Kleinsee on 27 July 1985 during a gale after moving inshore to lay anchors while on her first operational voyage for Dawn Diamonds, fully equipped with a saturation diving system. Her crew of 26 were rescued by helicopter. No lives were lost. The wreck was stripped of equipment by a professional salvage company.
Argus, 27 July 1985
Lloyds Register of Shipping, 1985-86

Rosalind

British wooden schooner of 160 tons, built in 1861 by Hall, Sunderland, and commanded by Capt J. Akester. Wrecked at Port Nolloth on 25 June 1869 at night while on a voyage from London to Port Nolloth with a cargo of railway iron and material for the Cape Copper Mining Company. No lives were lost.
Lloyds Register of Shipping, 1869-70
Shipping Register, Cape Archives, C.C. 3/7/2/2

SS **Rusholme** (ex *Flora*, ex *Bagger No. 1*)

Twin-screw coasting steamer of 272 tons, formerly a lighter, built in 1904 in Germany. Wrecked 45 km south of Port Nolloth on 24 March 1923 while on a voyage to Saldanha Bay after her first trip to Port Nolloth with wheat and general cargo. No lives were lost. She had once been engaged in salvage work on the wrecked steamer *Losna* (1921) and was being used in the coasting trade to and from Saldanha Bay.
Cape Argus, 26 March 1923
Lloyds Register of Shipping, 1923-24

Ticino (ex *M.E. Watson*)

Italian iron sailing ship of 1 718 tons, built in 1883 by Richardson, Duck & Co, Stockton. Wrecked 8 km south of Port Nolloth on 2 August 1908 with a crew of 22 and a cargo of coal and coke. No lives were lost.
Lloyds Register of Shipping, 1908-09
Shipping Register, Cape Archives, C.C. 3/7/2/6 (customs report)

Veronica

British wooden barque of 344 tons, built in 1860 by Brocklebank, Whitehaven, and commanded by Capt Kite. Foundered at Port Nolloth on 8 February 1886 after striking the barque *Marquis of Worcester* during a south-east gale while on a voyage to Swansea with a full cargo of copper ore. No lives were lost.
Lloyds Register of Shipping, 1885-86
Shipping Register, Cape Archives, C.C. 3/7/2/3

Volunteer

Schooner commanded by Capt S. Jackson. Wrecked on Espiegle Rock at Hondeklip Bay on 11 October 1869 at the start of a voyage from Hondeklip Bay to Port Nolloth. No lives were lost.
Shipping Register, Cape Archives, C.C. 3/7/2/2

2. Lambert's Bay to Cape St Martin Point

A dry, inhospitable stretch of coast which is often visited by tourists and holiday-makers. The Atlantic water is cold due to the Benguela current which flows northward. The sea is usually turbid, and with the exception of St Helena Bay the shore is pounded by heavy ground swells for most of the year. The underwater vegetation consists of vast kelp beds in which crayfish are found in large numbers. The land is hot and dry with a scant covering of semi-desert vegetation, but is well populated. The main commercial activities are farming, the collection of guano and fishing. The chief settlements along the coast are Lambert's Bay, which gained fame when, during the Boer War, HMS Sybille exchanged fire with Gen J.B.M. Hertzog's men in the only 'naval engagement' of

the war. Sybille Park in the town is named after this wreck. The port is a major fish-canning and crayfish-packing centre. Velddrif is a fishing centre at the mouth of the Berg River, and Stompneus Bay a fishing village in St Helena Bay. Britannia Reef, Rock, Point and Bay in St Helena Bay are all named after the British vessel Britannia *wrecked there in 1826.*

Britannia
32° 43.00S, 17° 57.00E

British vessel. Struck the reef since known as Britannia Blinder in St Helena Bay on 22 October 1826 and was beached in Britannia Bay near Cape St Martin while on a voyage from England to India with passengers and a cargo of copper, wine and beer, most of which was salvaged.
Shipping Register, Cape Archives, C.C. 2/11

Gouden Buis

Dutch ship, built in 1692 at the Enkhuizen yard for the Enkhuizen Chamber of the Dutch East India Company, and commanded by Teunis Kornelisz Baanman. Wrecked about 20 km north of St Helena Bay in November 1693, after most of her crew contracted scurvy and were thus unable to man the ship properly, while on an outward-bound voyage from Texel, which she had left on 4 May 1693 with 190 souls and a cargo of 17 chests of specie, wine and beer. Most of the cargo and specie was saved, but was subsequently lost on the west coast of Robben Island when the recovery vessel *Dageraad* was wrecked.
Cape Archives, V.C. 13
Dutch-Asiatic Shipping Outward Voyages, 1595-1794, The Hague, 1979
Ongeluckig of Droevig Verhaal van t' Schip De Gouden Buys, Sillerman and Thysz, Amsterdam, 1718 (Cape Archives, V.C. 94)

Perimede

British wooden brig of 315 tons, built in 1854 at Prince Edward Island, and commanded by Capt Purnish. Wrecked 11 km north of the Berg River on 4 August 1860 while on a voyage from England via Madeira. Although she had been repaired in Cadiz, she was still leaking, and the captain was compelled to run her ashore. Most of her cargo was saved. No lives were lost.
Cape Argus, 11 August 1860
Lloyds Register of Shipping, 1860-61
Shipping Register, Cape Archives, C.C. 3/7/2/1

Reflector

British wooden barque of 374 tons, built in 1840 at Sunderland, and commanded by Capt T. Maning. Wrecked on a reef on 17 April 1851 after having put into St Helena Bay as a result of a leak sprung while on a voyage from Table Bay to Hull. No lives were lost.
Lloyds Register of Shipping, 1851-52
Shipping Register, Cape Archives, C.C. 2/17

Rosebud

Schooner. Wrecked at Lambert's Bay on 25 June 1859 while on a voyage from East London to Table Bay.
Cape Argus, 22 October 1859
Cape of Good Hope Shipping and Mercantile Gazette, 7 September 1859
Cape Weekly Chronicle, 7 October 1859

MV Seatrader (ex *Wiltrader*, ex *Igadi*)
32° 42.70S, 17° 55.60E

Liberian motor vesssel of 5 562 tons, built in 1949, and commanded by Capt Vladimir Kutle. Wrecked a little north of the Cape St Martin lighthouse on 3 June 1971 in fog while on a voyage from Antwerp to Kuwait with a general cargo, including 10 000 tons of reinforcing steel. No lives were lost.
Argus, 3, 4 June 1971 (photographs)
Lloyds Register of Shipping, 1971-72

Seatrader. (Cape Times)

HMS Sybille
32° 10.10S, 18° 18.60E

British twin-screw 2nd class steel cruiser of 3 400 tons, built in 1890 by R. Stephenson & Co, Newcastle, and commanded by 1st Lieut Holland (Capt Hugh Williams being ashore). Wrecked opposite Steenbokfontein, south of Lambert's Bay, on 16 January 1901 at night in heavy seas after she stood out from Lambert's Bay during a storm and drifted south with the current; furthermore lights on a farm were mistaken for those of Lambert's Bay. One man was killed by the impact when she ran ashore. The *Sybille* was the guardship at Lambert's Bay and was involved in the only 'naval engagement' of the Boer War when she exchanged fire with Gen J.B.M. Hertzog's men. She has been extensively worked on for her non-ferrous fittings and is reputed to have had a box of gold sovereigns on board. Some of her guns, which consisted of two 6-inch, six 4,7-inch and eight 6-pounder guns, were salvaged at the time.
Cape Argus, 17, 18 January 1901

3. Cape St Martin Point to Cape Columbine

A dry stretch of coast often visited by tourists and holiday-makers. The Atlantic water is cold due to the Benguela current which flows northward. The sea is often clear and suitable for diving, especially during the summer months. The underwater vegetation consists of vast kelp beds in which crayfish are found in great numbers. The land is hot and dry in summer with a scant covering of semi-desert vegetation, but is well populated. The main commercial activities are farming and fishing. The chief settlement along the coast is Paternoster, which is an important centre for the crayfishing industry. Off the coast there are many reefs and islands which are a hazard for the unwary mariner. Place names associated with shipwrecks are Kraletjiesbaai at Cape Columbine, named after the beads which washed ashore after the wrecking of the Columbine in 1829; and Soldatebaai, named after the soldiers who came ashore after the wrecking of the Ismore in 1899.

Alicia Jane

Brig commanded by Capt T. Foales. Wrecked on Paternoster Island on 16 May 1845 after her cables parted during a north-west gale. She was intending to load guano. No lives were lost.
Eastern Province Herald, 28 May 1845
Sam Sly's African Journal, 29 May 1845 (sale notice)
Shipping Register, Cape Archives, C.C. 2/16

SS Bulli
32° 44.10S, 17° 52.10E

Australian steel screw steamer of 277 tons, built in 1884 in Glasgow, and commanded by Capt C.W. McConachy. Wrecked near Seal Island on Paternoster Point on 5 May 1884 in dense fog while on a voyage from Glasgow to Sydney in ballast. No lives were lost.
Cape Argus, 10 May 1884
Lloyds Register of Shipping, 1884-85
Shipping Register, Cape Archives, C.C. 3/7/2/3

SS Chub
32° 44.10S, 17° 54.40E

South African coasting steamer of 172 tons, built in 1897 by Lobnitz & Co, Renfrew. Wrecked 3 km south of Cape St Martin on 2 November 1945 while on a voyage from Port Nolloth to Cape Town. No lives were lost. The *Chub* once belonged to Capt Van Delden and was used in an abortive attempt to refloat the *Paris Maru* (1934) in Algoa Bay. She can still be seen amongst the kelp at the northern point of Great Paternoster Point (1987). She has been extensively worked on for her non-ferrous metal.
Cape Argus, 8 November 1945 (photograph)
Lloyds Register of Shipping, 1945-46

Columbine
32° 49.00S, 17° 51.90E

British wooden snow of 280 tons, built in 1824, and commanded by Capt Tuit. Wrecked 1,5 km north of the Cape Columbine lighthouse on 31 March 1829 while on a voyage from London to New South Wales with a cargo of British-manufactured goods. No lives were lost. A small amount of cargo was saved at the time of her wrecking, but most was salvaged in 1974. Kraletjiesbaai is named after the beads (krale) which wash ashore from this wreck.
Cape of Good Hope Government Gazette, 10 April, 17 July (sale notice) 1829
Lloyds Register of Shipping, 1829
Shipping Register, Cape Archives, C.C. 2/12
South African Commercial Advertiser, 8 April 1829

Wreck of the COLUMBINE.
THE Beams, Planks, Timbers, &c. of the above Vessel, are for private Sale in Lots, at St. Martin's Point, until the 6th August next.
Cape Town, 16th July, 1829.   T. & J. SINCLAIR.

Cape of Good Hope Government Gazette

Eve

Brig commanded by Capt J. Coath. Wrecked on Paternoster Island on 17 May 1845 after her cables parted during a north-west gale. No lives were lost. She was intending to load guano.
Eastern Province Herald, 28 May 1845
Sam Sly's African Journal, 29 May 1845
Shipping Register, Cape Archives, C.C. 2/16
South African Commercial Advertiser, 24 May 1845

Friends Goodwill

Cutter. Wrecked near St Helena Bay (Paternoster?) on 6 February 1840. No lives were lost. The cargo was saved.
Shipping Register, Cape Archives, C.C. 2/15

SS Haleric (ex *Warsparrow*)
32° 43.60S, 17° 53.10E

British steamer of 5 169 tons, built in 1918 by Palmers & Co, Newcastle, owned by the Bank Line, managed by Andrew Weir, and commanded by Capt Mann. Sank 4 km south-west of Cape St Martin lighthouse on 5 April 1933 after striking Cape St Martin in fog while on a voyage from England to Australia in ballast to load wheat.
Cape Argus, 5, 6 April 1933 (photographs)
Lloyds Register of Shipping, 1932-33

SS Ismore
32° 49.30S, 17° 50.70E

British four-masted single-screw transport steamer of 7 744 tons, built in 1899 by Barclay, Curle & Co, Glasgow. Wrecked a little north of the Cape Columbine lighthouse at 02h50 on 3 December 1899 during a south-east gale while on her maiden voyage from Liverpool to Table Bay with 500 people on board, including the 10th Hussar Regiment and 63rd Royal Artillery, as well as 350 horses. All the men were landed at Soldate Bay, but most of the horses were lost.
Cape Argus, 4, 5, 6 December 1899
Lloyds Register of Shipping, 1899-1900

SS Saint Lawrence
32° 44.50S, 17° 53.20E

Iron steam troopship of 2 090 tons, built in 1874 by Laing, Sunderland, and commanded by Capt Hyde (RNR). Wrecked on Great Paternoster Point inside the Great Paternosters on 8 November 1876. She was on hire from the Temperley Line and was on a voyage to Cape Town with the 2nd Battalion of the 3rd Buffs (411 men, 43 women and officers) and a crew of 67, a cargo of 9 mountain guns (lost), 50 tons of gunpowder and £1 000 worth of Government stores. No lives were lost.
Cape Times, 10, 13, 14 November 1876

Saint Lawrence. (Illustrated London News)

Eastern Province Herald, 10 November 1876
Illustrated London News, 16 December 1876
   (picture)
Lloyds Register of Shipping, 1876-77
Shipping Register, Cape Archives, C.C. 3/7/2/2

4. Cape Columbine lighthouse to Saldanha Bay North Head

A dry stretch of coast often visited by fishermen and divers. The Atlantic water is cold due to the Benguela current which flows northward. The sea is often clear and suitable for diving, especially during the summer months. The underwater vegetation consists of vast kelp beds in which crayfish are found in great numbers. The land is hot and dry in summer, but receives good rains during the winter months. There is a scant covering of semi-desert vegetation and the coast is sparsely populated. The main commercial activities are fishing and farming. Off the coast there are many reefs and islands which are a hazard for the unwary mariner. The area close to the entrance to Saldanha Bay is a restricted military zone. Soldiers Reef at Cape Columbine is named after the soldiers who came ashore after the wrecking of the Saint Lawrence *in 1876.*

British Settler

Iron schooner of 73 tons, built in 1844 in Britain for the Kowie Shipping Company, and commanded by Capt W.A. Train. Wrecked in Jacobs Bay near Saldanha Bay on 1 June 1850 during a north-west gale while on a voyage from the Kowie River to London with a cargo of wool. There were no survivors; the bodies of a woman and child were washed ashore.
Cape Town Mail, 22 June 1850
Shipping Register, Cape Archives, C.C. 2/17

SS City of Hankow
33° 01.80S, 17° 53.40E

British cargo vessel of 7 360 tons, built in 1915 by W. Gray & Co, West Hartlepool, and owned by the Ellerman Line. Wrecked a little north of Saldanha Bay on 18 December 1942 in dense fog

City of Hankow. *(George Young)*

with a cargo of 8 000 tons of military equipment, most of which was salvaged at the time. She has been extensively worked on for her non-ferrous fittings. The navy put a ban on diving on her because of the great amount of ammunition on board.
Lloyds Register of Shipping, 1942-43

SS Haddon Hall
32° 59.50S, 17° 52.00E

British steel screw steamer of 4 177 tons, built in 1895 by Palmers & Co, Newcastle, owned by the Ellerman Harris Line, and commanded by Capt O'Parry. Wrecked a little north of Danger Bay (north of Saldanha Bay) on 1 February 1913 while on a voyage from Liverpool to Cape Town and coastal ports with a cargo of motor-cars, tramcar frames, rails, sleepers and copper wire. Three crew members were drowned.
Cape Times, 4, 5 February 1913
Lloyds Register of Shipping, 1911-12

SS Lisboa
32° 53.00S, 17° 49.90E

Portuguese twin-screw mail-steamer of 7 700 tons, built in 1910 by D & W Henderson & Co, Glasgow, owned by Empreza Nacional de Navegacao, Lisbon, and commanded by Capt Menezes. Wrecked on Soldiers Reef near the SS *Malmesbury* (1930) on 23 October 1910 during a south-east gale while on a voyage from Lisbon to Lourenço Marques (Maputo) with a crew of 300 and a cargo of specie, mail, bulls and olive oil. Seven people were drowned. During this disaster wireless telegraphy was used for the first time along the South African coast to save the crew of a wrecked vessel. The wreck was heavily plundered by the locals.
Cape Argus, 24, 25 (photograph) October 1910
Lloyds Register of Shipping, 1910-11

SS Malmesbury
32° 57.30S, 17° 51.80E

British steel cargo vessel of 5 173 tons, built in 1928 by R. Duncan & Co, Port Glasgow, and commanded by Capt Ellis. Wrecked on Jacobs

Malmesbury. *(Cape Times)*

Reef south of Cape Columbine on 9 September 1930 in fog while on her maiden voyage from Cardiff to Table Bay in ballast to load maize. She lies near the *Lisboa* (1910) and has been extensively worked on to recover her non-ferrous fittings.
Cape Argus, 10, 11 September 1930 (photographs)
Cape Times, 11 September 1930 (aerial photograph)
Lloyds Register of Shipping, 1930-31

Pescadora

Portuguese schooner, owned by the Lisbon Fishing Company. Wrecked on a reef of rocks near the entrance to Saldanha Bay on 4 January 1839. No lives were lost.
Cape of Good Hope Government Gazette, 11 January, 1 February (sale notice) 1839

SS Robilant

Italian iron screw brig of 5 085 tons, built in 1883 by Oswald, Mordaunt & Co, Southampton, and commanded by Capt A. Longobardo. Struck Jacobs Reef near Saldanha Bay on 5 February 1890 in dense fog and sank within two hours while on a voyage from New York to Yokohama with a cargo of 137 000 cases of paraffin oil. No lives were lost.
Lloyds Register of Shipping, 1890-91
Shipping Register, Cape Archives, C.C. 3/7/2/4

5. Saldanha Bay and Islands

This stretch of coast consists of a large sheltered lagoon which forms a perfect natural harbour, but due to a lack of fresh water it was never developed into a major port. The bay supports a thriving fishing industry, and there is a Naval presence as well as a large, well-populated town. The water is not as cold as in the open sea, due to the warming effect of the sun, but is nevertheless cold. The water is usually clear. The bottom is flat and sandy, and rocky reefs protrude in places. Kelp beds, in which crayfish are found in large numbers, abound. The land is hot and dry in summer but good rains fall in the winter months, and the vegetation consists of small semi-desert bushes. The main commercial activities are fishing, farming, tourism, the collection of guano and the export of iron ore from the mines of the Northern Cape. The bay is a playground for watersport enthusiasts, and nature-lovers can enjoy bird-watching on the Langebaan lagoon. The main settlements around the bay are Saldanha, a thriving town, and Langebaan, which is chiefly a residential area. The bay is dotted with islands, for instance Skaap, Meeuw, Marcus, Malgas and Jutten Island.

Bruydegom

Small Cape vessel sent to Saldanha Bay for provisions. Struck a rock between Meeuw and

Skaap islands at the entrance to Langebaan Lagoon on 9 April 1674 while waiting for the right wind so as to return to Table Bay with a cargo of shells and limestone; she then drifted into the lagoon and sank near Kraal Bay.
Cape Archives, V.C. 7. Translated into English in *Précis of the Archives of the Cape of Good Hope, Journal, 1671-1674 and 1676*, H.C.V. Leibbrandt, 1902

Dauphin

American whaler commanded by Capt Bery Hussey. Drifted ashore at Saldanha Bay on 5 March 1830 and became a total wreck, though her cargo was saved. No lives were lost.
Cape of Good Hope Government Gazette, 12 March 1830
Shipping Register, Cape Archives, C.C. 2/12

Merestein
33° 05.20S, 17° 57.10E

Dutch pinnace of 826 tons, built in 1693 at the Amsterdam Yard for the Amsterdam Chamber of the Dutch East India Company, and commanded by Capt Jan Subbing. Wrecked on the south-west corner of Jutten Island at the entrance to Saldanha Bay on 3 April 1702 during a south-west wind while on an outward-bound voyage from Texel, which she had left on 4 October 1701 with a large cargo of coins. A hundred and one lives were lost. Most of the coins were salvaged in 1971, and her bronze cannon and cargo of 125-kg lead bars were also recovered. The wreck lies within the harbour area of Saldanha Bay and diving is only allowed with the permission of the Port Captain. Her remains are scattered on the island shore at depths ranging from 3 to 6 m.
Cape Archives, V.C. 16. Translated into English in *Précis of the Archives of the Cape of Good Hope, Journal, 1699-1732*, H.C.V. Leibbrandt, 1896
Dutch-Asiatic Shipping Outward Voyages, 1595-1794, The Hague, 1979

Middelburg
33° 01.60S, 17° 57.80E

Dutch East-Indiaman of 1 150 tons, built in 1775 at the Zeeland Yard for the Amsterdam Chamber of the Dutch East India Company, and commanded by Capt Van Gennep. While on a voyage from China, which she had left on 15 January 1781 with a full cargo of Oriental goods, including Chinese porcelain, tea, silk, aniseed and tin, she was set on fire by her crew to prevent her capture by the British, who surprised a Dutch fleet in Saldanha Bay on 21 July 1781, and eventually sank off Hoedjies Point in Saldanha Bay. The wreck has been worked on by various groups of salvors, most successfully by the Dodds brothers in 1969.
Cape Archives, V.C. 33
Dutch-Asiatic Shipping Homeward Voyages, 1597-1795, The Hague, 1979

MV **Ovambo Coast** (ex *Ovambo*, ex *Walvis*, ex *Springbok*, ex *Wijnhaven*, ex *Jantje*)
33° 02.70S, 17° 58.30E

South African coaster of 217 tons, built in 1939, owned by Thesens, and commanded by Capt W.M. Baird. Wrecked on Marcus Island in Saldanha Bay on 23 July 1958 in fog with a cargo of fish-oil bound for Cape Town.
Lloyds Register of Shipping, 1958-59
Cape Argus, 24 July 1958

Ovambo Coast. (Cape Times)

St Claire

Wrecked in the vicinity of Saldanha Bay on 14 March 1838 during a south-east gale. Several lives were lost.
South African Commercial Advertiser, 21 March 1838

6. Saldanha Bay South Head to Bloubergstrand

A dry stretch of coast often visited by divers, fishermen and holiday-makers. The Atlantic water is cold due to the Benguela current which flows northward. The water is often clear and suitable for diving, especially during the summer months. The underwater vegetation consists of large kelp and mussel beds in which crayfish are found in great numbers. The land is hot and dry in the summer months, but receives good rain in the winter months. The vegetation consists of semi-desert scrub, and the area is well populated. The main commercial activities are farming, fishing, tourism, the collection of guano and the generation of electricity at the Koeberg nuclear power station. Three islands, Vondeling, Dassen and Seal Ledges, are found off-shore. The main settlements along the coast are Yzerfontein, a small holiday settlement with a small harbour, and Melkbosstrand, a small residential and holiday settlement.

British Peer
33° 30.40S, 18° 18.70E

British iron ship of 1 478 tons, built in 1865 by Harland & Wolff, Belfast, owned by the Nourse Line, and commanded by Capt Jesse Jones. Wrecked a little south of Grotto Bay on the West Coast (Kabeljou Bank) on 9 December 1896 while on a voyage from London to Table Bay with a cargo of Dutch gin, tea, coffee, crockery, machinery, pianos and building materials. Many lives were lost; seven bodies were buried at the wreck site. Many tons of lead sheeting, as well as the bell, were salvaged in 1979. Building-bricks from her cargo still wash ashore.
Cape Argus, 10, 11, 12 December 1896
Lloyds Register of Shipping, 1896-97

Conservative

British snow of 225 tons, built in 1840 at Sunderland, and commanded by Capt G. Lind. Wrecked on the beach about 10 km south of Saldanha Point (Saldanha Bay) on 14 March 1843 while on a voyage from Liverpool to Table Bay with a cargo of soap, clothing, cutlery and Government mail, much of which was saved. Six bodies were washed up, but the rest of the crew were never found. Mystery surrounds the wrecking of this vessel.
Cape of Good Hope Government Gazette, 24 March 1843 (sale notice)
Lloyds Register of Shipping, 1843-44
Shipping Register, Cape Archives, C.C. 2/15
South African Commercial Advertiser, 5 April 1843 (sale notice)

SALE OF THE WRECK AND CARGO OF THE BRIG "*CONSERVATIVE*," ON FRIDAY, 31ST INST.

IT is intended, should a sufficient number of Tickets be taken, to start the PHŒNIX steamer, on THURSDAY, the 30th INST., at 9 A.M. to SALDANHA BAY with Passengers, and to return on the following Saturday.
  Tickets, including refreshments, 3 Guineas each. The holders of the first forty Tickets taken, to have the choice of berths in rotation.

Cape of Good Hope Government Gazette

Cottager

British snow of 273 tons, built in 1838 at Newcastle, and commanded by Capt J. Young. Wrecked on rocks 6 km south of the entrance to Saldanha Bay on 8 April 1845 while on a voyage to Table Bay in ballast. Two lives were lost.
Lloyds Register of Shipping, 1845-46
Shipping Register, Cape Archives, C.C. 2/16
South African Commercial Advertiser, 23 April 1845

SS **Hamlet**

South African coaster of 328 tons, built in 1906 by Earle's Co, Hull, and commanded by Capt Charles Dumaresq. Wrecked on the South Head at Saldanha Bay on 7 April 1927 in mist while on a voyage from Table Bay to the Irvin & Johnson

whaling-station with a cargo of coal, timber and provisions. No lives were lost. She belonged to the Kerguelen sealing fleet.
Cape Times, 8, 9, 11, 12 (photograph), 23 April (enquiry) 1927
Lloyds Register of Shipping, 1927-28

La Cybelle

French slave ship of twelve guns. Wrecked a little north of Blouberg Strand in Table Bay on 19 March 1756 while on a voyage from the coast of Guinea (West Africa) to Mauritius with a cargo of slaves. She had entered the bay for water. No lives were lost.
Cape Archives, V.C. 28

MV **Pantelis A. Lemos**
33° 10.00S, 18° 01.50E

Greek bulk carrier of 35 545 tons, built in 1973 by Brodogradiliste, owned by the Somelas Corporation, registered in Piraeus, and commanded by Capt Lemos Vasilios. Ran aground opposite Churchhaven at 03h00 on 17 March 1978 in thick fog while on a voyage from Europe to Fremantle in ballast to load iron ore. She had a crew of 26 and was due to stop at Cape Town for bunkers.
Argus, 17, 18 March 1978 (photographs)
Lloyds Register of Shipping, 1978-79

Pantelis A. Lemos. (Argus)

Reigersdaal
33° 35.80S, 18° 21.20E

Dutch vessel of 850 tons, built in 1738 at the Amsterdam Yard for the Amsterdam Chamber of the Dutch East India Company, and commanded by Johannes Band. Wrecked on an offshore reef at Springfontein Point on 25 October 1747 after drifting from her anchorage during a south-east gale while on an outward-bound voyage from Texel, which she had left on 31 May 1747 with eight chests of specie and a cargo of lead ingots. 157 lives were lost. She was salvaged in 1979; about 20 000 silver coins, as well as bronze guns and a cargo of lead ingots, were recovered. The wreck lies in shallow water on the northern tip of an offshore reef and her anchors and a number of badly corroded cast iron cannon can clearly be seen.
Cape Archives, V.C. 26
Dutch-Asiatic Shipping Outward Voyages, 1595-1794, The Hague, 1979

Schollevaar

Dutch hoeker of 90 tons, built in 1667 at the Rotterdam Yard for the Rotterdam Chamber of the Dutch East India Company, and commanded by Capt Romboutz Hackert. Wrecked a little north of Bokpunt on the west coast at dawn on 31 May 1668 during a north-west gale while on an outward-bound voyage from the Maas, which she had left on 24 December 1667 with a large amount of liquor, distilled water, nails and anchors. The captain and one sailor died. The crew blamed the captain for the disaster; the chief mate and a sailor were sent to Batavia in irons, charged with mutiny. Her boat washed up at the Salt River mouth in Table Bay.
Cape Archives, V.C. 5. Translated into English in *Précis of the Archives of the Cape of Good Hope, Journal, 1662-1670*, H. C. V. Leibbrandt, 1901
Dutch-Asiatic Shipping Outward Voyages, 1595-1794, The Hague, 1979

7. Bloubergstrand to Milnerton lighthouse

A dry stretch of coast often visited by divers, fishermen and holiday-makers. The Atlantic water is cold due to the Benguela current which flows northward. The water is often clear and suitable for diving, especially during the summer months. The underwater vegetation consists of large kelp beds and a large section of sandy bottom, and crayfish are found in abundance. The land is hot and dry in summer, but receives good rain during winter. The shoreline is built up.

Akbar

British wooden ship of 809 tons, built in 1852 at Sunderland, and commanded by Capt A. Hutton. Wrecked at Rietvlei in Table Bay 4 km south of the *Rover* (1863) on 12 January 1863 during a south-east wind while on a voyage from Siam to London with a cargo of rice, cassia, sticklac and Japan wood. No lives were lost. Most of her cargo was saved by the steamer *Albatross*, which was wrecked on Albatross Rock in April 1863.
Cape Argus, 13, 15 January 1863
Lloyds Register of Shipping, 1862-63
Shipping Register, Cape Archives, C.C. 3/7/2/1

Arago

German barque of 630 tons, commanded by Capt J. C. Kolling. Wrecked at Rietvlei in Table Bay on 30 November 1858 during a south-east gale while on a voyage from Memel (a fortified Prussian sea-port) to Batavia with a cargo of timber. No lives were lost. A court of enquiry found that the captain was drunk at the time.
Cape Argus, 28, 29 December 1858
Shipping Register, Cape Archives, C.C. 2/18

Armenia

Italian barque, commanded by Capt Schaffina.

Ran ashore during a storm on 9 June 1902 after she had collided with a vessel at the start of a voyage from Table Bay to Delaware in ballast and had anchored off Blouberg. No lives were lost.
Eastern Province Herald, 12 June 1902

Atlas

Norwegian wooden ship of 1 296 tons, built in 1875 by D. O. Blaisdell, Bath, Maine, and commanded by Capt J. L. Marchussen. Wrecked on Blouberg Beach, Table Bay, on 9 October 1896 while on a voyage from Rangoon to the English Channel with a cargo of teak. No lives were lost.
Cape Argus, 10 October 1896
Lloyds Register of Shipping, 1896-97
Shipping Register, Cape Archives, C.C. 3/7/2/5

Bengal

British barque of 765 tons, commanded by Capt A. Carson. Wrecked near Blouberg Beach in Table Bay on 17 September 1840 after entering the bay at night while on a voyage from Calcutta to London with a cargo of saltpetre and redwood, part of which was saved at the time. No lives were lost.
Shipping Register, Cape Archives, C.C. 2/15

Cerberus

British ship of 372 tons, built in 1816 in Sunderland, and commanded by Capt Renoldson. Wrecked at Blouberg in Table Bay on 10 March 1821 at night while on a voyage from Ceylon to London.
Cape Town Gazette, 17, 24 March 1821
Lloyds Register of Shipping, 1821
Shipping Register, Cape Archives, C.C. 2/10

Chartley Castle

British wooden barque of 382 tons, built in 1842 at Teignmouth, and commanded by Capt A. McLean. Wrecked at Milnerton on 8 October 1851 at night after a voyage from London to Table Bay with a cargo of coal. No lives were lost. Her bell is in the Simon's Town Museum.
Lloyds Register of Shipping, 1851-52
Shipping Register, Cape Archives C.C. 2/17

Defence

British wooden ship of 608 tons, built in 1844, and commanded by Capt W. Pearson. Wrecked between the Salt River mouth and Rietvlei, opposite the salt pans, on 5 March 1857 after entering Table Bay at night while on a voyage from Manila to Cork with a cargo of 20 000 bags of sugar and 1 500 bags of Manila hemp. No lives were lost.
Cape Argus, 7, 11, 18, 21 March 1857
Lloyds Register of Shipping, 1857-58
Shipping Register, Cape Archives, C.C. 2/18

Hermes. *(Cape Archives, A2918)*

SS **Hermes**
33° 52.00S, 18° 29.20E

Houston Line transport steamer of 3 400 tons, built in 1899 by J. Blumer & Co, Sunderland, and commanded by Capt Grose. Wrecked on Milnerton Beach on 12 May 1901 when she dragged her anchors during a north-west gale after a voyage from Argentina to Cape Town with eleven passengers and a cargo of Government stores, livestock and forage. Two female passengers in the lifeboat were drowned. The wreck lies shoreward of the *Winton* (1934), a little north of the Milnerton lighthouse.
Cape Argus, 13, 14, May 1901
Lloyds Register of Shipping, 1901-02

Herschel

British wooden snow of 221 tons, built in 1839 at Dysart, and commanded by Capt J. McNeill. Wrecked near Rietvlei in Table Bay at 22h30 on 24 January 1852 after a voyage from Dundee to Table Bay with a cargo of coal. No lives were lost.
Cape Town Mail, 27 January 1852
Lloyds Register of Shipping, 1852-53
Shipping Register, Cape Archives, C.C. 2/17

John

Schooner commanded by Capt Kincaid. Wrecked at Blouberg in Table Bay on 4 December 1821 when she missed stays after a voyage from Plettenberg Bay to Table Bay with a cargo of spice and coffee, which was saved. No lives were lost.
Cape Town Gazette, 4 December 1821
Shipping Register, Cape Archives, C.C. 2/9

Knysna Belle

Cape wooden schooner of 66 tons, built in 1863, and commanded by Capt Carstens. Wrecked at Rietvlei in Table Bay on 19 June 1876. No lives were lost.
Lloyds Register of Shipping, 1876-77
Shipping Register, Cape Archives, C.C. 3/7/2/2

L'Éclair

French ship, commanded by Capt Pronck. Wrecked on the north-east side of Table Bay at night on 5 February 1821 while on a voyage from Batavia to Antwerp. Six lives were lost.
Shipping Register, Cape Archives, C.C. 2/9

Malabar

Sardinian ship of 650 tons, commanded by Capt M. D. Michelle. Wrecked at Rietvlei in Table Bay on 4 November 1858 while on a voyage from London to Aden with a cargo of coal.
Shipping Register, Cape Archives, C.C. 2/18

Onni

Russian wooden barque of 826 tons, built in 1871, and commanded by Capt H. J. Galenius. Wrecked at Blouberg on 7 February 1890 at night in fine weather after entering Table Bay while on a voyage from West Hartlepool with a cargo of coal for the Gas Light Company. No lives were lost.
Lloyds Register of Shipping, 1890-91
Shipping Register, Cape Archives, C.C. 3/7/2/4

Oste

German brigantine of 120 tons, registered in Hanover. Wrecked at Whitesands near Blouberg, Table Bay, on 20 March 1859 at night during a south-east wind while on a voyage from Hanover to Sydney, Singapore and China with a cargo of tar, window-glass and sundries.
Cape Argus, 22 March 1859
Cape Town Gazette, 22 March 1859 (sale notice)
Shipping Register, Cape Archives, C.C. 2/18

Rastede

Barque of 462 tons, commanded by Capt J. Froboshe. Wrecked at Rietvlei in Table Bay on 5 March 1858 during a south-east gale after entering the bay while on a voyage from Newcastle with a cargo of coal. No lives were lost.
Shipping Register, Cape Archives, C.C. 2/18

Rover

South African brig, commanded by Capt Furness. Wrecked at Whitesands near Blouberg, Table Bay, on 22 February 1863 in thick fog while leaving the bay. No lives were lost. The wreck lies 4 km north of the *Akbar* (1863)
Cape Argus, 24, 26 February (sale notice) 1863
Shipping Register, Cape Archives, C.C. 3/7/2/1

Rubens

British wooden ship of 403 tons, built in 1853 at Aberdeen, and commanded by Capt A. Roberts. Wrecked near Rietvlei on 10 May 1865 at night during a south-east gale after entering Table Bay while on a voyage from Liverpool to Algoa Bay with a general cargo. No lives were lost.
Lloyds Register of Shipping, 1864-65
Shipping Register, Cape Archives, C.C. 3/7/2/1
South African Advertiser and Mail, 11 May 1865

Sandwich

British wooden brig of 150 tons, built in 1810 at Falmouth, and commanded by Capt J. Creighton. Wrecked 3 km north-east of the Salt River near Rietvlei in Table Bay on 10 August 1853 after entering the bay while on a voyage from Akyab, Burma, to London with a cargo of rice. One man died of exposure in the lifeboat.
Lloyds Register of Shipping, 1853-54
Shipping Register, Cape Archives, C.C. 2/18

Sappho

British wooden barque of 374 tons, built in 1840 in Greenock, and commanded by Capt Hildreth. Wrecked at Blouberg Beach at night on 15 March 1864 during a south-east gale after entering Table Bay while on a voyage from Shanghai to London with a cargo of 600 tons of tea. No lives were lost.
Cape Argus, 17 March 1864
Lloyds Register of Shipping, 1864-65
Shipping Register, Cape Archives, C.C. 3/7/2/1

Sévere

French man-of-war of 64 guns. Wrecked at Bloubergstrand in Table Bay on 27 January 1784 while on a voyage from Mauritius to France with a regiment of soldiers. No lives were lost.
Cape Archives, V.C. 34

MV **Winton**
33° 52.20S, 18° 29.28E

British motor vessel of 4 388 tons, built in 1928 by W. Hamilton & Co, Port Glasgow, and commanded by Capt C. J. Mordaunt. Wrecked a little north of the Milnerton Beach lighthouse in Table Bay on 28 July 1934 at night while on a voyage from Australia to Britain with 6 000 tons

of wheat, which caught fire by spontaneous combustion and burnt out the vessel. She lies a little north and to seaward of the *Hermes* (1901).
Cape Argus, 30 July 1934 (photograph)
Lloyds Register of Shipping, 1934-35

8. Dassen Island

A large island lying offshore opposite Yzerfontein. It is home to a large number of Cape jackass penguins. The water is cold due to the Benguela current which flows northward. The underwater vegetation consists of kelp beds in which crayfish are found. The vegetation on land is sparse and heavy deposits of guano are found. The only commercial activity is the collection of guano and the trapping of crayfish. There are many offshore reefs and pinnacles which are a hazard to the unwary mariner. Waterloo Bay was named after the schooner Waterloo, wrecked between the Kowie and Fish rivers in 1848, which often called at Dassen Island to load penguin eggs.

SS **Ashleigh Brook** (ex *Abana*)

British iron screw steamer of 2 863 tons, built in 1882 by M. Pearse & Co, Stockton, and commanded by Capt W. Burgers. Wrecked close to the *Wallarah* (1891) on Dassen Island at 02h30 on 24 May 1890 while on a voyage from Barry Dock, Cardiff, to Rockhampton, Queensland, with a cargo of coal. No lives were lost.
Cape Argus, 24 May 1890
Lloyds Register of Shipping, 1890-91
Shipping Register, Cape Archives, C.C. 3/7/2/4

Childe Harold

British full-rigged wooden ship of 463 tons, built in 1825 at Ipswich, and commanded by Capt J. Byres. Wrecked on the south-east point of Dassen Island at 01h00 on 13 February 1850 while on a voyage from Bombay to London via Table Bay with a cargo of 1 336 pieces of ivory, coffee, coir yarn, gum arabic, gum animé, deer-horns, pearl-shells, shawls and cardamoms. The captain drowned while trying to carry a line ashore.
Cape Town Mail, 2 March 1850
Lloyds Register of Shipping, 1850-51
Shipping Register, Cape Archives, C.C. 2/17

De Hoop

Dutch galiot, owned by the Dutch East India Company. Wrecked on Dassen Island on 31 November 1734 during a north-west wind. Part of her equipment was saved by the *Fijenoord*, which was wrecked in Table Bay in 1736.
Cape Archives, V.C. 24

Lady Holland
33° 24.80S, 18° 04.30E

British ship of 455 tons, built in 1811, and com-

manded by Capt J. Snell. Wrecked on a reef off the north-west point of Dassen Island at 22h00 on 13 February 1830 while on a voyage from London to Calcutta. Part of her cargo was saved. No lives were lost.
Cape of Good Hope Government Gazette, 19 February 1830
Lloyds Register of Shipping, 1830
Shipping Register, Cape Archives, C.C. 2/12
South African Commercial Advertiser, 17, 24 February 1830

Queen of Ava

British wooden barque of 422 tons, built in 1853 at Sunderland, and commanded by Capt J. Petherick. Wrecked on the north side of Dassen Island on 29 October 1865 while on a voyage from Cardiff to Table Bay with a cargo of coal. The captain and crew landed on Dassen Island and were brought to Table Bay by cutter. No lives were lost.
Cape Argus, 2 November 1865
Lloyds Register of Shipping, 1865-66
Shipping Register, Cape Archives, C.C. 3/7/2/1
South African Advertiser and Mail, 2 November 1865

SS **Wallarah**
33° 24.80S, 18° 04.20E

Blue Anchor-Line steamer of 3 505 tons, built in 1891 by the Sunderland Shipbuilding Company, and commanded by Capt F. H. Ekins. Wrecked close to the *Ashleigh Brook* (1890) on the north-west tip of Dassen Island (Boom Point) at 04h45 on 1 August 1891 in heavy fog while on her maiden voyage from London to Melbourne with a general cargo, including mercury and pianos. No lives were lost. The mercury was recovered at the time.
Cape Argus, 6 August 1891 (sale notice)
Lloyds Register of Shipping, 1891-92
Shipping Register, Cape Archives, C.C. 3/7/2/4

Cape Argus

RMS **Windsor Castle**
33° 25.40S, 18° 04.30E

Iron passenger liner of 2 623 tons, built in 1872 by R. Napier of Glasgow, and commanded by Capt William Hewitt. Wrecked near the Triangles to the west of Dassen Island on 19 October 1876 while on a voyage to Cape Town. No lives were lost.

Windsor Castle. (Illustrated London News)

Illustrated London News, 2 December 1876
Lloyds Register of Shipping, 1876-77
Shipping Register, Cape Archives, C.C. 3/7/2/2

9. Milnerton lighthouse to Mouille Point

Most of the original coastline of this area, known as Table Bay, has been covered by reclamation works and many of the shipwrecks which occurred here are today buried beneath harbour developments, roadworks and buildings. Cape Town was first settled by the Dutch East India Company in 1652 and is today the largest city in the Cape Province. The city boasts a large, modern harbour and has been described as one of the most beautiful cities in the world, with Table Mountain as its most impressive feature. The water is cold due to the Benguela current which flows northward. In summer the sea becomes extremely clear, especially after a strong south-easterly gale. Crayfish are found in large numbers, especially in the harbour. The climate is Mediterranean, with hot and dry summers and cold and wet winters. The prevailing winds are south-east in the summer and north-west in the winter.

Abercrombie Robinson
33° 54.90S, 18° 27.95E

British wooden transport ship of 1 425 tons, launched in 1825 in London, and commanded by Capt J. Young. Wrecked about 500 m from the *Waterloo* (1842) at the Salt River mouth in Table Bay at 05h00 on 28 August 1842 during a north-west gale after a journey from Dublin Bay, which she had left on 2 June 1842, to Table Bay. No lives were lost. She lies buried beneath reclaimed land. Her bell was found in the Dutch Reformed church, Caledon, in 1986.
Lloyds Register of Shipping, 1842-43
Shipping Register, Cape Archives, C.C. 2/15
South African Commercial Advertiser, 31 August, 3 September 1842

Addison
33° 54.90S, 18° 27.95E

English East-Indiaman of 400 tons. Went ashore, capsized and broke up at the Salt River mouth in Table Bay on 16 June 1722 during a north-west gale while on a homeward-bound journey from Bengal. Of her crew of 80, only 10 were saved.

She lies buried beneath reclaimed land.
Cape Archives, V.C. 22. Translated into English in *Précis of the Archives of the Cape of Good Hope, Journal, 1699-1732*, H.C.V. Leibbrandt, 1896
Hardy, Charles, *A Register of Ships in the Service of the English East India Company*, 1800

Adriatic

British snow of 193 tons, built in 1810 in Sunderland, and commanded by Capt W. Rutter. Wrecked in Table Bay on 20 July 1822 during a north-west gale after a voyage from London with a cargo of sundries. One man was drowned.
Cape Town Gazette and African Advertiser, 27 July 1822
Lloyds Register of Shipping, 1822
Shipping Register, Cape Archives, C.C. 2/10

Alacrity
33° 55.50S 18° 26.75E

British wooden barque of 317 tons, built in 1856 at Sunderland, and commanded by Capt Gouch. Wrecked beyond the Military Hospital in Table Bay on 17 May 1865 during a north-west gale after a voyage from London with a general cargo. No lives were lost. She lies buried beneath reclaimed land.
Lloyds Register of Shipping, 1865-66
Shipping Register, Cape Archives, C.C. 3/7/2/1

Alfred

Wooden barque of 267 tons, commanded by Capt J. D. Jackson. Wrecked in Table Bay on 4 July 1830 during a north-west gale while on a voyage from the Downs off south-east Kent to Mauritius via Table Bay with a cargo of sundries.
Shipping Register, Cape Archives, C.C. 2/12
South African Commercial Advertiser, 7 July 1830

America
33° 54.95S, 18° 27.00E

British iron barque of 1 280 tons, built in 1877 by A. McMillan & Son, Dumbarton, and commanded by Capt R.H. Reay. Caught fire in the anchorage in Table Bay after a voyage from London with a general cargo including oil, was towed to Woodstock Beach, pumped full of water and then abandoned on 29 May 1900. The *Ryvingen* collided with her in 1902. She lies within the new harbour.
Cape Argus, 29, 30 May 1900
Lloyds Register of Shipping, 1900-01

Amy
33° 55.45S, 18° 25.70E

Cape brigantine. Went ashore against the Castle in Table Bay alongside the *Chandois* (1722) on

America. *(Cape Archives, E8856)*

16 June 1722 during a north-west gale. No lives were lost. She lies buried beneath reclaimed land.
Cape Archives, V.C. 22. Translated into English in *Précis of the Archives of the Cape of Good Hope, Journal, 1699-1732*, H.C.V. Leibbrandt, 1896

Anne

British ship of 310 tons, built in 1811 in Durham, and commanded by Capt John Colvell. Wrecked at Paarden Island in Table Bay in July 1818 after a voyage from the Downs, off south-east Kent.
Cape Town Gazette, 11 July 1818 (sale notice)
Lloyds Register of Shipping, 1819
Shipping Register, Cape Archives, C.C. 2/9

Antelope
33° 55.50S, 18° 26.40E

British schooner of 107 tons, built in 1800 at Cowes, and commanded by Capt J. Adams. Wrecked near the jetty in Table Bay at 24h00 on 18 August 1837 after a voyage from Rio de Janeiro with a cargo of coffee. She had loaded a cargo for St Helena. She lies buried beneath reclaimed land.
Lloyds Register of Shipping, 1837-38
Shipping Register, Cape Archives, C.C. 2/14
South African Commercial Advertiser, 23 August 1837

Anubis

American ship, commanded by Capt Isaac Bridges. Wrecked in Table Bay on 5 November 1799 during a north-west gale while on a voyage from India to Boston with a cargo of cotton. No lives were lost.
Cape Archives, B.O. 161

Arab
33° 55.50S, 18° 26.40E

Barque of 378 tons, built in 1829 at Dumbarton, and commanded by Capt T. Baker. Wrecked near the hospital lines in Table Bay on 1 June 1850

when her cables parted during a north-west gale while on a voyage from Mauritius to London with a cargo of sugar and rum. She had put into the bay for water. No lives were lost. She lies buried beneath reclaimed land.
Cape Town Mail, 8 June 1850
Lloyds Register of Shipping, 1850-51
Shipping Register, Cape Archives, C.C. 2/17

Avenhorn

Dutch ship of 880 tons, built in 1780 at the Hoorn Yard for the Dutch East India Company, and commanded by Capt A. Arend Thobiasz. Wrecked in Table Bay on 17 May 1788 during a north-west gale while on a homeward-bound voyage from Batavia (Jakarta), which she had left on 4 November 1787, arriving at the Cape on 22 January 1788. No lives were lost. She lies buried beneath reclaimed land.
Cape Archives, V.C. 34
Dutch-Asiatic Shipping Homeward Voyages, 1597-1795, The Hague, 1979

Caledonian
33° 55.00S, 18° 27.60E

British wooden barque of 607 tons, built in 1861 at Dumbarton, and commanded by Capt W. Thomas. Wrecked on Woodstock Beach in Table Bay on 19 July 1878 during a north-west gale while on a voyage from Cardiff to Java with a cargo of coal. She had put into Table Bay after springing a leak and making 8 inches of water per hour. The captain and three crew members were drowned. She lies buried beneath reclaimed land.
Lloyds Register of Shipping, 1878-79
Shipping Register, Cape Archives, C.C. 3/7/2/3

Calpe

British brig of 165 tons, built in 1828, and commanded by Capt S. Eales. Wrecked in Table Bay on 16 July 1831 during a north-west gale while on a voyage from Dartmouth in South Devon with a cargo of sundries.
Lloyds Register of Shipping, 1831
Shipping Register, Cape Archives, C.C. 2/12
South African Commercial Advertiser, 20 July 1831

Candian

British barque of 226 tons, built in 1826, and commanded by Capt F. Reid. Wrecked on an off-shore reef in Table Bay on 17 July 1831 during a north-west gale while on a voyage from Bordeaux to Mauritius with a cargo of wine and brandy. No lives were lost.
Lloyds Register of Shipping, 1831
Shipping Register, Cape Archives, C.C. 2/12
South African Commercial Advertiser, 20 July 1831

Chandois
33° 55.45S, 18° 25.70E

English East-Indiaman of 440 tons. Wrecked close to the Castle in Table Bay, next to the *Amy*, on 16 June 1722 during a north-west gale while on a homeward-bound voyage from Bengal. Of her crew of 70, two were drowned. She lies buried beneath reclaimed land.
Cape Archives, V.C. 22. Translated into English in *Précis of the Archives of the Cape of Good Hope, Journal, 1699-1732*, H.C.V. Leibbrandt, 1896
Hardy, Charles, *A Register of Ships in the Service of the English East India Company*, 1800

Christabel
33° 55.45S, 18° 26.00E

British wooden barque of 335 tons, built in 1845 at Workington, and commanded by Capt N. Tyack. Wrecked at the Castle in Table Bay on 10 June 1857 when her cable parted during a north-west gale after a voyage from London with a cargo of sundries. The crew were taken off by lifeboat. She lies buried beneath reclaimed land.
Lloyds Register of Shipping, 1857-58
Shipping Register, Cape Archives, C.C. 2/18

SS City of Lincoln (ex *Solis*, ex *Massachusetts*, ex *Manhattan*)
33° 54.90S, 18° 27.95E

British iron screw steamer of 3 182 tons, built in 1866 by Palmers & Co, Newcastle, and commanded by Capt Neale. Wrecked at the Salt River mouth in Table Bay on 14 August 1902 when her cables parted during a north-west gale after a voyage from the River Plate with a cargo of cattle and sheep. No lives were lost. She lies buried beneath the container berth.
Cape Argus, 15 August 1902
Lloyds Register of Shipping, 1901-02

City of Lincoln, *with* Ryvingen *in the background. (Cape Archives, E155)*

City of Peterborough
33° 55.30S, 18° 26.50E

British wooden barque of 331 tons, built in 1852 at Sunderland, and commanded by Capt Joseph Wright. Wrecked on Sceptre Reef in Table Bay at 22h30 on 17 May 1865 during a north-west gale while preparing for a voyage to London with a cargo of wool and wine. All crew were lost. Sceptre Reef was buried when the Royal Cape Yacht Basin was constructed.
Lloyds Register of Shipping, 1865-66
Shipping Register, Cape Archives, C.C. 3/7/2/1
South African Advertiser and Mail, 17 May 1865 (sale notice)

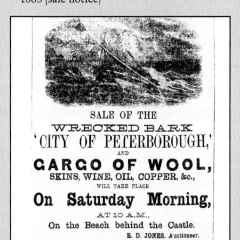

SALE OF THE
WRECKED BARK
'CITY OF PETERBOROUGH,'
AND
CARGO OF WOOL,
SKINS, WINE, OIL, COPPER, &c.,
WILL TAKE PLACE
On Saturday Morning,
AT 10 A.M.,
On the Beach behind the Castle.
R. D. JONES, Auctioneer.

South African Advertiser and Mail

Cockburn
33° 54.90S, 18° 27.95E

British wooden barque of 294 tons, built in 1840 at Leith, and commanded by Capt J. Young. Wrecked near the Salt River in Table Bay on 16 September 1850 when her cables parted during a north-west gale after a voyage from Liverpool with a cargo of sundries. Some of the passengers and crew were drowned. She lies buried beneath reclaimed land.
Cape Town Mail, 21 September 1850
Lloyds Register of Shipping, 1850-51
Shipping Register, Cape Archives C.C. 2/17

Columbia

American vessel, commanded by Capt Frankling. Wrecked in Table Bay on 4 June 1796 while on a voyage from Mauritius to Philadelphia with a cargo of coffee.
Cape Archives, B.O. 194

Courier
33° 55.50S, 18° 26.40E

Schooner of 136 tons, commanded by Capt F. P. Bide. Wrecked near the Imhoff battery in Table Bay on 18 May 1852 when her cables parted during a north-west gale. No lives were lost. She lies buried beneath reclaimed land.
Shipping Register, Cape Archives C.C. 2/18

Crystal Palace
33° 55.30S, 18° 26.50E

British wooden barque of 480 tons, built in 1852 at Teignmouth, and commanded by Capt J. Marley. Wrecked on Sceptre Reef in Table Bay on 8 August 1862 during a north-west gale while on a voyage from London to Simon's Town with Government stores. No lives were lost. She lies buried beneath reclaimed land. Her hulk was struck by the barque *Kate* (1862).
Cape Argus, 12, 21, 29 August 1862
Lloyds Register of Shipping, 1862-63
Shipping Register, Cape Archives, C.C. 3/7/2/1

De Buis
33° 54.90S, 18° 27.95E

Dutch ship of 600 tons, built in 1727 at the Enkhuizen Yard for the Hoorn Chamber of the Dutch East India Company, and commanded by Hendrik Orsel. Wrecked at the Salt River mouth in Table Bay on 21 May 1737 during a north-west gale while on a homeward-bound voyage from Batavia, which she had left on 6 February 1737 with a cargo of Eastern goods, arriving at the Cape on 11 May 1737. There were only five survivors. She lies buried beneath reclaimed land.
Cape Archives, V.C. 25
Dutch-Asiatic Shipping Homeward Voyages, 1597-1795, The Hague, 1979

Deane

British wooden barque of 200 tons, built in 1851 in London, and commanded by Capt Bradner. Wrecked in Table Bay on 17 May 1865 during a north-west gale after a voyage from New York with a general cargo. No lives were lost.
Lloyds Register of Shipping, 1864-65
Shipping Register, Cape Archives, C.C. 3/7/2/1

Diana
33° 55.50S, 18° 26.40E

Portuguese slaving barque of 270 tons, under the command of Lieut Mends (RN). Ran ashore at the Imhoff battery in Table Bay on 7 January 1846 when her cables parted during a north-west gale after a voyage from Pemba, Zanzibar, with a cargo of slaves. No lives were lost. She had been taken as a prize by HMS *Mutine*. She lies buried beneath reclaimed land.
Sam Sly's African Journal, 9 January 1846
Shipping Register, Cape Archives, C.C. 2/16

Discovery
33° 55.50S, 18° 26.75E

British ship of 300 tons, built in Bombay of Malabar teak, and commanded by Nathaniel Fish. Wrecked at the Black River mouth in Table Bay, opposite Fort Knokke, in July 1816 while on a voyage from Calcutta via Mauritius. She lies buried beneath reclaimed land.
Cape Town Gazette, 3 August 1816 (sale notice)

Dorah

Commanded by Capt John Akin. Wrecked at Paarden Island in Table Bay on 4 January 1821 during a north-west gale while on a voyage from Calcutta with a cargo of bar iron and tar.
Cape Town Gazette, 6 January 1821 (sale notice)
Shipping Register, Cape Archives, C.C. 2/9

Duinbreek
33° 55.28S, 18° 27.28E

Dutch ship of 800 tons, built in 1727 at the Zeeland Yard for the Zeeland Chamber of the Dutch East India Company, and commanded by Jan van Thiel. Wrecked a little south of the Salt River mouth in Table Bay on 21 May 1737 during a north-west gale while on a homeward-bound voyage from Batavia, which she left on 6 February 1737 with a cargo of Eastern produce, arriving at the Cape on 16 May 1737. Only a few lives were saved. She lies buried beneath reclaimed land.
Cape Archives, V.C. 25
Dutch-Asiatic Shipping Homeward Voyages, 1597-1795, The Hague, 1979

Dunlop
33° 55.10S, 18° 27.20E

Irish ship of 332 tons, built in 1806, and commanded by Capt J. M'Griffney. Wrecked on Woodstock Beach at 02h00 on 24 November 1838 as she was entering Table Bay while on a voyage from Liverpool to Hobart with a cargo of sundries. No lives were lost. She lies buried beneath reclaimed land.
Cape of Good Hope Government Gazette, 30 November 1838
Lloyds Register of Shipping, 1838-39
Shipping Register, Cape Archives, C.C. 2/14
South African Commercial Advertiser, 23 January 1839

Eiland Mauritius
33° 54.89S, 18° 27.90E

Dutch East Indiaman, built at the Amsterdam Yard for the Amsterdam Chamber of the Dutch East India Company, and commanded by Capt Pieter Theunisz. Struck a reef below Lions Heads after entering Table Bay on 7 February 1644 while on an outward-bound voyage from Texel Roads, which she had left on 4 October 1643 in company with the *Tijger*, *Vrede* and *Harinck*. She was pulled off on 12 February but ran ashore at the Salt River mouth. Her cargo, specie and cannon were taken off, and the crew sailed to Batavia on board the *Tijger* and the *Vrede*. She lies buried beneath reclaimed land.
Dutch-Asiatic Shipping Outward Voyages, 1595-1794, The Hague, 1979

Elizabeth

British vessel of 502 tons, commanded by Capt

T. Harrison. Wrecked near Paarden Island in Table Bay on 7 October 1819 after missing stays while on a voyage from Bombay to London with a cargo of cotton, coffee, castor oil, camphor, gums, rice, sugar and drugs.
Cape Town Gazette and African Advertiser, 9, 23 October (sale notice), 6 November (sale notice) 1819
Lloyds Register of Shipping, 1820

Emma

British ship of 467 tons, built in 1813 in India of teak, and commanded by Capt C. Baumgardt. Wrecked in Table Bay on 4 January 1821 during a north-west gale while on a voyage from Portsmouth to Madras. No lives were lost.
Cape Town Gazette, 13 January 1821 (sale notice)
Lloyds Register of Shipping, 1821
Shipping Register, Cape Archives, C.C. 2/9

Erfprins van Augustenburg

Danish East-Indiaman, wrecked in Table Bay on 12 April 1790 while on an outward-bound voyage with 36 chests of money, which were saved. No lives were lost.
Cape Archives, C. 186

Etta Loring
33° 55.00S, 18° 27.20E

American barque of 716 tons, commanded by Capt Loring. Wrecked in Table Bay on 22 July 1878 after dragging her anchors off Woodstock Beach during a north-west gale while on a voyage from Philadelphia to Japan with a cargo of oil. No lives were lost. She had put into Table Bay for repairs and was ready for sea. She lies buried beneath reclaimed land.
Shipping Register, Cape Archives, C.C. 3/7/2/3

Fairfield
33° 55.50S, 18° 26.40E

American barque of 198 tons, commanded by Capt G. Holmes. Wrecked near the hospital lines in Table Bay at 01h00 on 9 September 1842 when her anchor cables parted during a northwest gale after a voyage from Boston with a cargo of sundries. No lives were lost. She lies buried beneath reclaimed land.
Shipping Register, Cape Archives, C.C. 2/15
South African Commercial Advertiser, 14 September 1842

Fanny
33° 55.50S, 18° 26.40E

Brig of 217 tons, commanded by Capt F. Bristow. Wrecked near the South Jetty (Imhoff battery) in Table Bay on 29 July 1851 during a north-west gale after a voyage from Glasgow with a cargo of sundries. No lives were lost. She lies buried beneath reclaimed land.

Cape Monitor, 31 July 1851
Shipping Register, Cape Archives, C.C. 2/17

Fernande
33° 55.50S, 18° 26.40E

Danish schooner of 86 tons, commanded by Capt Giles. Wrecked beyond the Castle in Table Bay on 17 May 1865 during a north-west gale while on a voyage from Rio de Janeiro to Singapore with a general cargo. She had put into the bay for supplies. No lives were lost. She lies buried beneath reclaimed land.
Shipping Register, Cape Archives, C.C. 3/7/2/1

Fijenoord
33° 54.90S, 18° 27.95E

Dutch brigantine of 160 tons, owned by the Rotterdam Chamber of the Dutch East India Company. Wrecked near the Salt River mouth in Table Bay on 1 July 1736. Only one life was lost. She had been used by the Lethbridge salvage expedition to the *Merestein* (1702) in 1728, and also for salvage work on the *De Hoop*, wrecked on Dassen Island in 1734. She lies buried beneath reclaimed land.
Cape Archives, V.C. 24
Dutch-Asiatic Shipping Outward Voyages, 1595-1794, The Hague, 1979

Flora
33° 54.90S, 18° 27.95E

Dutch ship of 850 tons, built in 1730 at the Amsterdam Yard for the Amsterdam Chamber of the Dutch East India Company, and commanded by Gerrit Pik. Wrecked near the Salt River mouth in Table Bay on 21 May 1737 during a north-west gale while on a homeward-bound voyage from Batavia, which she had left on 2 January 1737, arriving at the Cape on 29 April 1737. Only six out of her complement of 140 were saved. She lies buried beneath reclaimed land.
Cape Archives, V.C. 25
Dutch-Asiatic Shipping Homeward Voyages, 1597-1795, The Hague, 1979

Francis Spaight
33° 54.90S, 18° 27.70E

British barque of 368 tons, built in 1835 at Sunderland, and commanded by Capt H. Pattison. Wrecked on Woodstock Beach in Table Bay near the *Waterloo* (1842) on 7 January 1846 when her cables parted during a north-west gale while on a voyage from Manila to London with a cargo of sugar, hemp, tobacco, cigars and rattans. She had put into the bay for refreshments. The captain and 14 crew were drowned when their boat capsized in the surf. She lies buried beneath reclaimed land.
Cape of Good Hope Government Gazette, 9 January 1846
Lloyds Register of Shipping, 1846-47
Shipping Register, Cape Archives, C.C. 2/16

Frigga

Danish barque, commanded by Capt Herbeck. Went ashore near Milnerton in Table Bay on 19 January 1862 during a south-east gale after entering the bay while on a voyage from Copenhagen to Singapore with a cargo of deal.
Cape Argus, 21 January 1862 (sale notice)
Shipping Register, Cape Archives, C.C. 3/7/2/1

Gitana
33° 55.50S, 18° 26.40E

Schooner of 90 tons, commanded by Capt W. Brabner. Wrecked below the Imhoff battery in Table Bay on 7 June 1857 after her cables parted during a north-west gale. The crew were taken off by a breeches-buoy attached to a parapet of the battery. She lies buried beneath reclaimed land.
Cape Argus, 10, 17 June 1857, 20 February 1858 (sale notice)
Shipping Register, Cape Archives, C.C. 2/18

Goede Hoop
33° 54.90S, 18° 27.95E

Dutch pinnace of 1 177 tons, built in 1688 at the Amsterdam Yard for the Amsterdam Chamber of the Dutch East India Company, and commanded by Anthonie Pronk. Wrecked near the Salt River mouth in Table Bay on 5 June 1692 during a north-west gale while on a homeward-bound voyage from Ceylon, which she had left on 28 February 1692, arriving at the Cape on 7 May 1692. Most of her cargo was saved. She lies buried beneath reclaimed land.
Cape Archives, V.C. 12
Dutch-Asiatic Shipping Homeward Voyages, 1597-1795, The Hague, 1979

Good Intent

Coasting schooner. Wrecked in Table Bay on 21 July 1822 during a north-west gale.
Cape Town Gazette and African Advertiser, 27 July 1822

Gouda

Dutch hoeker of 220 tons, built in 1719 at the Amsterdam Yard for the Amsterdam Chamber of the Dutch East India Company. Wrecked in Table Bay on 16 June 1722 during a north-west gale. No lives were lost.
Cape Archives, V.C. 22. Translated into English in *Précis of the Archives of the Cape of Good Hope, Journal, 1699-1732*, H. C. V. Leibbrandt, 1896

Goudriaan
33° 54.90S, 18° 27.95E

Dutch flute of 630 tons, built in 1719 at the Delft Yard for the Delft Chamber of the Dutch East

India Company, and commanded by Jurriaan Zeeman. Wrecked at the Salt River mouth in Table Bay on 21 May 1737 during a north-west gale while on a homeward-bound voyage from Batavia, which she had left on 6 February 1737, arriving at the Cape on 6 May 1737. Most of her crew died. She lies buried beneath reclaimed land.
Cape Archives, V.C. 25
Dutch-Asiatic Shipping Homeward Voyages, 1597-1795, The Hague, 1979

Grahamstown
33° 55.50S, 18° 26.40E

British wooden barque of 327 tons, built in 1862 by Thompson, Sunderland, and commanded by Capt F.C. Wale. Burnt out in Table Bay and went ashore behind the Military Hospital on 26 May 1864 while on a voyage from Algoa Bay to London with a cargo of wool. She had put into the bay after spontaneous combustion had set fire to the cargo. She lies buried beneath reclaimed land.
Cape Argus, 28 May 1864
Lloyds Register of Shipping, 1864-65
Shipping Register, Cape Archives, C.C. 3/7/2/1

Haarlem
33° 54.90S, 18° 27.95E

Dutch ship of 850 tons, built in 1720 at the Amsterdam Yard for the Amsterdam Chamber of the Dutch East India Company, and commanded by Anthonie Biermans. Wrecked near the Salt River mouth in Table Bay on 4 December 1728 during a north-west storm while on an outward-bound voyage from Texel Roads, which she had left on 7 February 1728 with 13 chests of specie, arriving at the Cape on 7 June 1728. She had run ashore on 3 July 1728 during a north-west gale, but was re-floated and repaired, and the specie was taken off. Only 16 crew were saved. She lies buried beneath reclaimed land, close to the *Stabroek* (1728) and the *Nightingale* (1722).
Cape Archives, V.C. 23. Translated into English in *Précis of the Archives of the Cape of Good*

Cape of Good Hope Government Gazette

Hope, Journal, 1699-1732, H. C. V. Leibbrandt, 1896
Dutch-Asiatic Shipping Outward Voyages, 1595-1794, The Hague, 1979

Hannah
33° 55.45S, 18° 25.70E

American brig, commanded by William Wyman. Wrecked under the Castle in Table Bay on 5 November 1799 during a north-west gale while on a voyage from India to Boston. No lives were lost. She lies buried beneath reclaimed land.
Cape Archives, B.O. 161

Hogergeest
33° 54.90S, 18° 27.95E

Dutch yacht (or pinnace) of 222 tons, built in 1681 at the Amsterdam Yard for the Dutch East India Company, and commanded by Jakob ter Huisen. Wrecked near the Salt River mouth in Table Bay on 10 June 1692 during a north-west gale while on a homeward-bound journey from Batavia, which she had left on 6 March 1692, arriving at the Cape on 23 May 1692. Only a few of her crew were drowned, thanks to the heroic action of a Dutch seaman, Jochem Willemsz, who swam a line out to the wreck. She lies buried beneath reclaimed land.
Cape Archives, V.C. 12
Dutch-Asiatic Shipping Homeward Voyages, 1597-1795, The Hague, 1979

Howard
33° 55.45S, 18° 25.70E

British barque of 197 tons, built in 1833 at Dumbarton, and commanded by A. Bisset. Wrecked near the Castle in Table Bay on 16 July 1840 during a north-west gale after a voyage from Port au Prince to Table Bay with a cargo of coffee, part of which was saved. No lives were lost. She lies buried beneath reclaimed land.
Cape of Good Hope Government Gazette, 17, 24 July (sale notice) 1840
Lloyds Register of Shipping, 1840-41
Shipping Register, Cape Archives, C.C. 2/15

Wrecked Barque 'Howard.'

A PUBLIC SALE will be held on SATURDAY next, the 25th current, (TO-MORROW,) at ONE o'Clock, (for the benefit of the concerned,) on the Beach, opposite the New Hospital, of the HULL, MASTS, SPARS, &c. of the above vessel, as she now lays Stranded.

Likewise such SAILS, RIGGING, and other Appurtenances, as may be laying on the beach. As also, such of the Cargo *then* on board, consisting of COFFEE and LOGWOOD.

After which, in the neighbourhood of the Jetty, Two ANCHORS of about 12 Cwt. each, and Two New CHAINS of 40 and 90 fathoms. And at the Queen's Warehouse, such of her STORES and PROVISIONS as may be there deposited.

Hunter

American ship of 188 tons mounting four cannon, commanded by Capt B. Cartwright. Wrecked in Table Bay on 3 November 1805 during a north-west gale while on a voyage from Rio de Janeiro to Mauritius with provisions.
Cape Archives, B.R. 537

Iepenrode
33° 54.90S, 18° 27.95E

Dutch ship of 650 tons, built in 1731 at the Amsterdam Yard for the Amsterdam Chamber of the Dutch East India Company, and commanded by Dirk Elsberg. Wrecked at the Salt River mouth in Table Bay on 21 May 1737 during a north-west gale while on a homeward-bound voyage from Batavia, which she had left on 1 January 1737, arriving at the Cape on 20 May 1737. She broke up rapidly and many lives were lost. She lies buried beneath reclaimed land.
Cape Archives, V.C. 25
Dutch-Asiatic Shipping Homeward Voyages, 1597-1795, The Hague, 1979

Isabella
33° 55.50S, 18° 26.40E

Brigantine of 104 tons, commanded by Capt J. Glover. Wrecked at the South Jetty near the Imhoff battery in Table Bay on 7 June 1857 when her cables parted during a north-west gale after a voyage from Plettenberg Bay. The crew were taken off by the port lifeboat. She lies buried beneath reclaimed land.
Cape Argus, 20 February 1858 (sale notice)
Shipping Register, Cape Archives, C.C. 2/18

Israel
33° 54.90S, 18° 27.95E

American whaler of 357 tons, commanded by Capt W. Bowman. Wrecked near the Salt River mouth in Table Bay at 23h00 on 9 April 1847 when her cables parted during a north-west gale, with a cargo of 245 barrels of oil, which was saved. She had come from the whaling grounds to take on water. No lives were lost. She lies buried beneath reclaimed land.
Cape Town Mail, 17 April 1847
Shipping Register, Cape Archives, C.C. 2/16

Jaeger (ex *Prinsens Jagt*)
33° 55.00S, 18° 27.50E

French yacht, under the command of Hans Lindenow. Wrecked near Woodstock Beach in Table Bay on 27 July 1619 during a north-west gale. She lies buried beneath reclaimed land. In November 1618 a fleet of Danish warships and merchantmen had set out from Copenhagen on a voyage to Goa; on the way two French vessels were captured on suspicion of piracy, and one of them, the *Prinsens Jagt*, was renamed the *Jaeger*. On 8 July 1619 the fleet anchored off Robben Island, and eight English vessels were sighted at anchor in the roads. In the night of 27 July the *Jaeger* ran aground. The English loot-

ed the wreck, but were chased off by the Danish sailors. Subsequently the English boat capsized and some of the English sailors lost their lives.
Schlegels Sammlung, Royal Library, Copenhagen

Jane
33° 55.45S, 18° 25.70E

British snow of 200 tons, built in 1806 in Denmark, and commanded by Capt William Berridge. Wrecked opposite the Castle in Table Bay on 18 May 1818 during a north-west gale while on a voyage from the Downs off south-east Kent. She lies buried beneath reclaimed land.
Cape Town Gazette, 18 May 1818
Lloyds Register of Shipping, 1818
Shipping Register, Cape Archives, C.C. 2/9

Jeanne
33° 54.90S, 18° 27.95E

French schooner of 181 tons, commanded by Capt Burnie. Wrecked at the Salt River mouth in Table Bay on 19 July 1878 during a north-west gale while on a voyage to Algoa Bay via Mossel Bay with a cargo of coffee, wine and brandy. The crew were saved by means of rocket apparatus. She lies buried beneath reclaimed land.
Graham's Town Journal, 22 July 1878
Shipping Register, Cape Archives, C.C. 3/7/2/3

Jefferson

American ship, commanded by Capt Benjamin Hooper. Wrecked in Table Bay on 9 May 1798 while on a voyage from Boston to Mauritius with a cargo of sundries.
Cape Archives, B.O. 194

John Bagshaw
33° 55.50S, 18° 26.40E

British ship of 416 tons, built in 1835 at Liverpool, and commanded by Capt N. Reddington. Wrecked near the south wharf in Table Bay on 9 September 1842 when her cables parted during a north-west gale while on a voyage from Calcutta to London with a cargo of silk, indigo and jute. No lives were lost. She lies buried beneath reclaimed land.
Cape of Good Hope Government Gazette, 16 September 1842
Lloyds Register of Shipping, 1842-43
Shipping Register, Cape Archives, C.C. 2/15

Jonge Thomas
33° 54.90S, 18° 27.95E

Dutch ship of 1 150 tons, built in 1764 at the Amsterdam Yard for the Amsterdam Chamber of the Dutch East India Company, and commanded by Barend de la Maire. Wrecked near the Salt River mouth in Table Bay on 1 June 1773 during a north-west gale while on an outward-bound voyage from Texel, which she left on

Israel. (Africana Museum)

20 October 1772, to Batavia, arriving at the Cape on 29 March 1773. Out of the crew of 271, 138 were drowned. A burgher at the Cape, Wolraad Woltemade, rescued 14 crew members on his horse, but died in the attempt. Later a new vessel, *De Held Woltemade*, was named in his honour. The *Jonge Thomas* lies buried beneath reclaimed land.
Cape Archives, V.C. 31
Dutch-Asiatic Shipping Outward Voyages, 1595-1794, The Hague, 1979
Thunberg, C.P., *Travels in Europe, Africa and Asia* (4 Vols), London, 1795

Kate
33° 54.90S, 18° 27.95E

British wooden barque of 904 tons, built in 1848 at Quebec, and commanded by Capt Loutitt. Wrecked a little east of the Salt River mouth in Table Bay on 8 August 1862 during a north-west gale with a cargo of sundries. She struck the *Crystal Palace* (1862). No lives were lost. She lies buried beneath reclaimed land.
Cape Argus, 12, 21 August 1862
Lloyds Register of Shipping, 1862-63
Shipping Register, Cape Archives, C.C. 3/7/2/1

Kehrweider

German schooner of 180 tons, commanded by Capt Havenberg. Wrecked alongside the *Figilante* in Table Bay on 17 May 1865 during a north-west gale after a voyage from Knysna with a cargo of timber. No lives were lost. The *Figilante* was refloated and renamed the *Ruby*; she was totally wrecked at Mossel Bay in 1866.
Shipping Register, Cape Archives, C.C. 3/7/2/1

Kent

British full-rigged wooden sailing ship of 815 tons, built in 1846 at Sunderland, and commanded by Capt Victor Howes. Wrecked at Paarden Island in Table Bay on 30 July 1856 while on a voyage from Madras to London with a general cargo and ivory.
Cape Monitor, 9 August 1856
Lloyds Register of Shipping, 1856-57
Shipping Register, Cape Archives, C.C. 2/18

L'Atalante
33° 55.42S, 18° 27.00E

French frigate, commanded by Capt Gaudin. Wrecked at the Charlotte battery in Table Bay on 3 November 1805 during a north-west gale after she had been brought from Simon's Bay to Table Bay. One man was lost. The French survivors of this wreck are mentioned in the Articles of Capitulation by which the Batavian Republic handed control of the Cape to the British. She lies buried beneath reclaimed land.
Cape Archives, B.R. 537, B.R. 593 (articles)
Kaapsche Courant, 9 November 1805, 11 January 1806

La Ceres
33° 54.90S, 18° 27.95E

French ship. Wrecked at the Salt River mouth in Table Bay on 15 October 1776 during a north-west gale while on a homeward-bound voyage from Pondicherry with a cargo of coffee-beans and saltpetre. No lives were lost, but very little cargo was saved. She lies buried beneath reclaimed land.
Cape Archives, V.C. 32

La Maréchale
33° 54.90S, 18° 27.95E

French ship, commanded by Capt Simon Vesron. Wrecked near the Salt River mouth in Table Bay on 19 May 1660 during a north-west gale while on a voyage from Nantes to Madagascar. She had a crew of 180. Some of her cannon were salvaged and used in land fortifications. She lies buried beneath reclaimed land.
Cape Archives, V.C. 3

Lakenman

Dutch flute of 600 tons, built in 1718 at the Enkhuizen yard for the Enkhuizen Chamber of the Dutch East India Company, and commanded by Herman Branus. Wrecked in Table Bay on 16 June 1722 during a north-west gale while on an outward-bound voyage from Texel, which she had left on 15 December 1721, arriving at the Cape on 6 June 1722. One crew member was drowned. Ten boxes of specie (approximately 35 000 pieces) were recovered at the time.
Cape Archives, V.C. 22. Translated into English in *Précis of the Archives of the Cape of Good Hope, Journal, 1699-1732*, H. C. V. Leibbrandt, 1896
Dutch-Asiatic Shipping Outward Voyages, 1595-1794, The Hague, 1979

Lavinia
33° 55.45S, 18° 25.70E

British snow of 233 tons, built in 1815 at Sunderland, and commanded by Capt A. Keith. Wrecked near the Castle in Table Bay on 21 July 1822 during a north-west gale after a voyage from London to Table Bay with a cargo of rice and sundries. She lies buried beneath reclaimed land.
Cape Town Gazette and African Advertiser, 27 July 1822 (sale notice)
Lloyds Register of Shipping, 1822
Shipping Register, Cape Archives, C.C. 2/10

Le Cygne

French ship of 318 tons, commanded by Capt W. Le Breton. Wrecked at Paarden Island in Table Bay at 21h00 on 8 August 1840 while on a voyage from Granville, a French fortified seaport, to Mauritius with a cargo of mules. One man was lost.
Shipping Register, Cape Archives, C.C. 2/15

Le Victor
33° 54.90S, 18° 27.95E

French corvette of 16 guns, commanded by Capt Renard. Wrecked near the Salt River mouth in Table Bay on 24 September 1782 during a north-west gale while on a voyage from Cadiz to Mauritius. Most of her crew of 90 were saved. She lies buried beneath reclaimed land.
Cape Archives, V.C. 33

Leander
33° 55.45S, 18° 25.70E

British brig of 202 tons, built in 1813 in Whitehaven, and commanded by Capt Middleton. Wrecked near the Castle in Table Bay on 21 July 1822 during a north-west gale after a voyage from London with a cargo of wheat and sundries. The captain and one seaman were drowned. She lies buried beneath reclaimed land.
Cape Town Gazette and African Advertiser, 27 July , 3 August (sale notice) 1822
Lloyds Register of Shipping, 1822
Shipping Register, Cape Archives, C.C. 2/10

Lucy Johnson
33° 55.50S, 18° 26.40E

American barque of 263 tons, commanded by Capt Johnson. Wrecked near the Military Hospital in Table Bay on 20 September 1862 at night after her cables parted with a cargo of flour and pork. No lives were lost. She lies buried beneath reclaimed land.
Cape Argus, 23 September 1862
Cape Chronicle, 26 September 1862
Shipping Register, Cape Archives, C.C. 3/7/2/1

Malta

British snow of 166 tons, built in 1802, and commanded by Capt J. Lindsey. Wrecked at Paarden Island in Table Bay in March 1818 while on a voyage from the Downs with a cargo of earthenware, glass-ware, clothing and ironware.
Cape Town Gazette, 14 March 1818 (sale notice)
Lloyds Register of Shipping, 1818

Maria

Italian barque. Wrecked in Table Bay on 12 April 1790. No lives were lost.
Cape Archives, C. 186

Marietta
33° 55.30S, 18° 27.50E

Brigantine of 133 tons, commanded by Capt Boisso. Ran ashore opposite Woodstock Church on 8 August 1862 during a strong north-west gale when she was struck by a heavy sea and her cables parted. No lives were lost. She lies buried beneath reclaimed land.
Shipping Register, Cape Archives, C.C. 3/7/2/1

Middenrak

Dutch vessel of 600 tons, built in 1717 at the Amsterdam Yard for the Amsterdam Chamber of the Dutch East India Company, and commanded by Capt Hendrick Jurriaan van Beek. Wrecked a little north of the Salt River mouth in Table Bay on 3 July 1728 during a north-west gale while on an outward-bound voyage from Texel, which she had left on 7 February 1728, arriving at the Cape on 25 May 1728. All 116 of her crew were drowned, and all the specie aboard was lost. Two of John Lethbridge's divers, Richard Boone and William Holditch, worked on this wreck in September 1728, but they only recovered two anchors. She lies close to the reclaimed land at the container berth.
Cape Archives, V.C. 23. Translated into English in *Précis of the Archives of the Cape of Good Hope, Journal, 1699-1732*, H. C. V. Leibbrandt, 1896
Dutch-Asiatic Shipping Outward Voyages, 1595-1794, The Hague, 1979

Nautilus

British brig of 163 tons, built in 1812, and commanded by Capt W. Tripe. Wrecked in Table Bay on 31 March 1826 while on a voyage from London to Mauritius with a cargo of sundries. No lives were lost.
Lloyds Register of Shipping, 1826
Shipping Register, Cape Archives, C.C. 2/11

Newport
33° 55.50S, 18° 26.40E

Brigantine of 116 tons, commanded by Capt J. C. Ahier. Wrecked in Table Bay on 5 June 1857 when her cables parted during a north-west gale while on a voyage from St Helena with a cargo of sundries. She was wrecked near the *William James* (1857). She lies buried beneath reclaimed land.
Cape Argus, 13 June 1857
Shipping Register, Cape Archives, C.C. 2/18

Nieuw Haarlem
33° 53.60S, 18° 28.80E

Dutch ship of 500 tons, built at the Amsterdam Yard for the Amsterdam Chamber of the Dutch East India Company, and commanded by Pieter Pietersz. Wrecked on a sandy shore near Milnerton 2,4 km from Table Bay Roads on 25 March 1647 during a south-east gale while on a homeward-bound voyage from Batavia, which she had left on 16 January 1647, arriving at the Cape on 25 March 1647, with a cargo of spices. The shipwrecked mariners stayed at the Cape for about a year and built a fort; when they were eventually repatriated to Holland, they reported favourably on the Cape, and the Dutch East India Company consequently decided to establish a refreshment station there.
Cape Archives, V.C. 284 (ex The Hague)
Dutch-Asiatic Shipping Homeward Voyages, 1597-1795, The Hague, 1979

Nieuw Rhoon
33° 55.16S, 18° 25.85E

Dutch East-Indiaman of 1 150 tons, built in 1764 at the Zeeland Yard for the Amsterdam Chamber of the Dutch East India Company, and commanded by Capt Jakob Koelders. Hit a reef (Whale Rock) at Robben Island on 31 January 1776 during a south-east gale and was later beached near the jetty in Cape Town in order to save her cargo. She was on a homeward-bound voyage from Ceylon, which she had left on 22 November 1775. Her remains were found in 1971 while the foundations of the new Civic Centre were being dug.
Cape Archives, V.C. 32
Dutch-Asiatic Shipping Homeward Voyages, 1597-1795, The Hague, 1979

Nightingale
33° 55.42S, 18° 27.20E

English East-Indiama of 480 tons. Wrecked a little south of the Salt River mouth in Table Bay, close to the *Stabroek* (1728) and the *Haarlem* (1728), on 16 June 1722 during a north-west gale while on an outward-bound voyage. One man was drowned. Her cargo of specie was saved. She lies buried beneath reclaimed land.
Cape Archives, V.C. 22. Translated into English in *Précis of the Archives of the Cape of Good Hope, Journal, 1699-1732*, H. C. V. Leibbrandt, 1896
Hardy, Charles, *A Register of Ships in the Service of the English East India Company*, 1800

Nimrod

British wooden ship of 469 tons, built in 1812 at Ipswich, and commanded by Capt J. Lawson. Wrecked near Paarden Island in Table Bay on 24 July 1851 at night when her cables parted during a north-west gale after a voyage from Liverpool with a cargo of sundries. No lives were lost.
Cape Argus, 13 July 1865
Lloyds Register of Shipping, 1851-52
Shipping Register, Cape Archives, C.C. 2/17

Nossa Senhora D' Guia

Portuguese brig, commanded by Capt R. Peach. Wrecked in Table Bay on 2 May 1819 during a north-west gale while on a voyage from Macao and Batavia to Rio de Janeiro with a cargo of tea, sugar and cinnamon.

Cape Town Gazette and African Advertiser

> On Monday next the 24th inst.
> Will be Sold by PUBLIC VENDUE,
> PART of the Cargo of the Portuguese Brig
> *Nora Senhora D'Guia*, consisting of Tea,
> Sugar, Cinnamon, &c. more or less damaged, or
> liable to damage, which was saved from the
> Wreck of the said Brig.
> Custom House, 18th May, 1819.

Cape Town Gazette and African Advertiser, 22 May 1819 (sale notice)
Shipping Register, Cape Archives, C.C. 2/9

Oldenburg

Danish man-of-war of 64 guns. Wrecked in Table Bay next to the *Sierra Leone* (1799) on 5 November 1799 during a north-west gale. No lives were lost.
Cape Archives, B.O. 161

Oldenburg. *(Cape Archives, M754)*

Oosterland
33° 54.90S, 18° 27.95E

Dutch vessel of 1 123 tons, built in 1685 at the Zeeland Yard for the Amsterdam Chamber of the Dutch East India Company. Wrecked at the Salt River mouth in Table Bay on 24 May 1697 during a north-west gale while on a homeward-bound voyage from Ceylon (Sri Lanka), which she had left on 17 February 1697 with a cargo which included diamonds. She broke up quickly. She lies buried beneath reclaimed land.
Cape Archives, V.C. 14
Dutch-Asiatic Shipping Homeward Voyages, 1597-1795, The Hague, 1979

Orange
33° 54.90S, 18° 27.95E

English East-Indiaman. Wrecked near the Salt River mouth in Table Bay on 5 June 1692 during a north-west gale. She broke up rapidly and some crew members were drowned. She lies buried beneath reclaimed land.
Cape Archives, V.C. 12

Pacquet Real
33° 55.45S, 18° 25.70E

Portuguese slaving brig, commanded by Capt I. P. de Souza. Wrecked near the wharf in Table Bay on 18 May 1818 during a north-west gale while on a voyage from Mozambique to San Salvador in the Bahamas with 167 slaves on board. There was a heavy loss of life. She lies buried beneath reclaimed land.

Cape Town Gazette, 23 May 1818
Shipping Register, Cape Archives, C.C. 2/9

Paddenburg
33° 54.90S, 18° 27.95E

Dutch vessel of 850 tons, built in 1732 at the Amsterdam Yard for the Amsterdam Chamber of the Dutch East India Company, and commanded by Capt Arie van Veurden. Wrecked near the Salt River mouth in Table Bay on 21 May 1737 during a north-west gale while on a homeward-bound voyage from Batavia, which she had left on 2 January 1737, arriving at the Cape on 27 April 1737. Most of the crew were saved. She lies buried beneath reclaimed land.
Cape Archives, V.C. 25
Dutch-Asiatic Shipping Homeward Voyages, 1597-1795, The Hague, 1979

Pénélope

French prize vessel. Wrecked near Milnerton in Table Bay on 16 April 1809.
Cape Town Gazette and African Advertiser, 29 April (sale notice), 17 June (sale notice) 1809

Prins Willem I

Dutch brig, commanded by Capt John Eber. Wrecked in Table Bay on 26 July 1819 after putting into the bay in distress as a result of having been struck by lightning on 20 May 1819 while on a voyage from Batavia to Amsterdam.
Shipping Register, Cape Archives, C.C. 2/9

Redbreast
33° 55.50S, 18° 26.75E

British wooden barque of 312 tons, built in 1863 by Dalton, Grimsby, and commanded by Capt A. Walsh. Wrecked at Fort Knokke in Table Bay on 20 July 1878 during a north-west gale after a voyage from Port Pine with a cargo of wheat, which had been discharged. No lives were lost. She lies buried beneath reclaimed land.
Cape Argus, 23 July 1878
Lloyds Register of Shipping, 1878-79
Shipping Register, Cape Archives, C.C. 3/7/2/3

Reform
33° 55.50S, 18° 26.40E

British brig of 131 tons, built in 1830 at Maryport, and commanded by Capt R. I. Cloyde. Wrecked at the Imhoff battery in Table Bay on 9 September 1842 when her cables parted during a north-west gale after a voyage from Algoa Bay with Government stores. No lives were lost. She lies buried beneath reclaimed land.
Lloyds Register of Shipping, 1842-43
Shipping Register, Cape Archives, C.C. 2/15
South African Commercial Advertiser, 14 September 1842

Rodenrijs
33° 54.90S, 18° 27.95E

Dutch vessel of 650 tons, built in 1735 at the Rotterdam Yard for the Rotterdam Chamber of the Dutch East India Company, and commanded by Capt Jan van Heemstede. Wrecked near the Salt River mouth in Table Bay on 21 May 1737 during a north-west gale while on a homeward-bound voyage from Batavia, which she had left on 6 February 1737, arriving at the Cape on 7 May 1737. Six men died. She lies buried beneath reclaimed land.
Cape Archives, V.C. 25
Dutch-Asiatic Shipping Homeward Voyages, 1597-1795, The Hague, 1979

Rotterdam

Dutch vessel of 800 tons, built in 1716 at the Rotterdam Yard for the Zeeland Chamber of the Dutch East India Company, and commanded by Gerrit Fiers. Wrecked in Table Bay on 16 June 1722 during a north-west gale while on an outward-bound voyage from Rammekens, which she had left on 3 March 1722, arriving at the Cape on 13 June 1722. Only 45 men were saved. The hull was blown up shortly after the disaster and some of her money-chests were recovered. The English diver John Lethbridge removed seven cannon and 200 silver bars from this wreck in 1727. After Lethbridge's departure from the Cape, divers using Lethbridge's equipment recovered 330 ducatoons, 12 iron cannon and 14 grindstones. She lies close to the *Schotse Lorrendraaier* and *Standvastigheid*, which came ashore during the same gale.
Cape Archives, V.C. 22. Translated into English in *Précis of the Archives of the Cape of Good Hope, Journal, 1699-1732*, H. C. V. Leibbrandt, 1896
Dutch-Asiatic Shipping Outward Voyages, 1595-1794, The Hague, 1979

Royal Albert
33° 55.50S, 18° 26.40E

British wooden barque of 407 tons, built in 1840 at Sunderland, and commanded by Capt J. Whiteside. Wrecked near the Military Hospital in Table Bay on 25 June 1850 when her anchor cables parted during a north-west gale after a voyage from London with a cargo of sundries. All the crew were saved by lifeboat at great risk. She lies buried beneath reclaimed land.
Cape Town Mail, 29 June 1850
Lloyds Register of Shipping, 1850-51
Shipping Register, Cape Archives, C.C. 2/17

Royal Arthur
33° 55.50S, 18° 26.40E

British wooden barque of 301 tons, built in 1855 at Lynn, and commanded by Capt McDougal. Wrecked near the south wharf in Table Bay on 17 May 1865 during a north-west gale while on a voyage from Mauritius to London with a cargo

Royal Albert. *(Cape Archives, E3364)*

of sugar. No lives were lost. She lies buried beneath reclaimed land.
Lloyds Register of Shipping, 1864-65
Shipping Register, Cape Archives, C.C. 3/7/2/1

Royal Saxon

British wooden barque of 322 tons, built in 1847 at Leith, and commanded by Capt J. Millar. Wrecked at Paarden Island on 1 October 1851 at night while entering Table Bay after a voyage from London with a cargo of coal. No lives were lost.
Lloyds Register of Shipping, 1851-52
Shipping Register, Cape Archives, C.C. 2/17

Ryvingen (ex *Tenasserim*)
33° 55.00S, 18° 27.20E

Norwegian iron barque of 1 504 tons, built in 1866 by Harland & Wolff, Belfast, and commanded by Capt Tonnesen. Wrecked near the mole on Woodstock Beach just after midnight on 30 May 1902 when her cables parted during a north-west gale with a cargo of coal, 600 tons of which was recovered by Ambrose Carrol. She struck the sunken hulk of the *America* (1900) on her way to the beach. No lives were lost.
Cape Argus, 30 May 1902
Lloyds Register of Shipping, 1901-02

Saldanha Bay Packet
33° 55.50S, 18° 26.40E

Schooner. Sank off the old lighthouse near the Imhoff battery in Table Bay on 21 November 1847 during a north-west gale while on a voyage to Waterloo Bay with a general cargo. There were no survivors. She lies buried beneath reclaimed land.
Shipping Register, Cape Archives, C.C. 2/16
South African Commercial Advertiser, 24 November 1847

San Antonio
33° 55.50S, 18° 26.40E

Brig of 141 tons, commanded by Capt J. Ward. Wrecked near the Military Hospital in Table Bay on 4 August 1824 during a gale after a voyage from Calcutta with a cargo of sundries. No lives were lost. She lies buried beneath reclaimed land.
Cape Town Gazette and African Advertiser, 7 August 1824
Shipping Register, Cape Archives, C.C. 2/11

Sarah
33° 54.90S, 18° 27.95E

British ship of 600 tons, built in 1810 in Bristol, and commanded by Capt J. Norton. Wrecked near the Salt River mouth in Table Bay on 9 July 1822 during a north-west gale while on a voyage from Bombay to London with a cargo of coffee and sundries. Three men died. She lies buried beneath reclaimed land. It is interesting to note that she is registered in the appendix dealing with licenced India vessels in *Lloyds Register* as 498 tons. This was a common practice adopted by the English East-India Company at the time, in order to save on duties on vessels above 500 tons.
Cape Town Gazette, 13 July 1822
Lloyds Register of Shipping, 1822
Shipping Register, Cape Archives, C.C. 2/10

Sarah Charlotte
33° 55.50S, 18° 26.40E

British wooden brig of 207 tons, built in 1840 at Mistly, and commanded by Capt J. Eagle. Wrecked near the Military Hospital in Table Bay on 3 July 1860 when her cables parted during a north-west gale after a voyage from London. She lies buried beneath reclaimed land.
Cape Chronicle, 6 July 1860
Cape of Good Hope Shipping and Mercantile Gazette, 6 July 1860
Lloyds Register of Shipping, 1860-61
Shipping Register, Cape Archives, C.C. 3/7/2/1

Sceptre
33° 55.30S, 18° 26.50E

British 3rd rate ship of the line of 1 398 bm (64 guns), built in 1781 by Randall at Rotherhithe on the Thames, and commanded by Capt Valentine Edwards. Wrecked on Sceptre Reef opposite Fort Knokke in Table Bay on 5 November 1799 during a north-west gale. Out of her crew of 411 only 42 survived. She broke up rapidly due to her excessive state of decay. She lies buried beneath reclaimed land.
Cape Archives, B.O. 161

Schotse Lorrendraaier

Dutch frigate, built for the Zeeland Chamber of the Dutch East India Company, and commanded by Adriaan Hijpe. Wrecked in Table Bay on

Sceptre. *(Cape Archives, M755)*

16 June 1722 during a north-west gale while on an outward-bound voyage from Rammekens, which she had left on 3 March 1722, arriving at the Cape on 13 June 1722. Many lives were lost. She was wrecked close to the *Rotterdam* (1722) and the *Standvastigheid* (1722).
Cape Archives, V.C. 22. Translated into English in *Précis of the Archives of the Cape of Good Hope, Journal, 1699-1732*, H. C. V. Leibbrandt, 1896
Dutch-Asiatic Shipping Outward Voyages, 1595-1794, The Hague, 1979

Shepherd
33° 54.80S, 18° 25.60E

British wooden barque of 424 tons, built in 1862 by Davison, Sunderland, and commanded by Capt Armstrong. Wrecked when she drifted on to the new breakwater in Table Bay on 9 August 1874 while entering the bay after a voyage from London with a general cargo. No lives were lost. Little of the cargo was saved, and the crew lost all their personal effects. She lies buried beneath reclaimed land.
Cape Argus, 11, 13, 15, 25 August, 19 November (sale notice) 1874
Lloyds Register of Shipping, 1874-75
Shipping Register, Cape Archives, C.C. 3/7/2/2

Sierra Leone

British whaler. Ran aground next to the *Oldenburg* (1799) in Table Bay on 5 November 1799 during a north-west gale while on a voyage from the southern whaling grounds to London. No lives were lost.
Cape Archives, B.O. 161

Sir Henry Pottinger
33° 54.90S, 18° 27.95E

British barque of 586 tons, built in 1844, and

commanded by Capt P. Guest. Wrecked near the Salt River mouth in Table Bay on 4 July 1860 when her cables parted during a north-west gale while on a voyage from Aden to Wanks River, Honduras, in ballast. She lies buried beneath reclaimed land.
Cape Chronicle, 6 July 1860
Cape of Good Hope Shipping and Mercantile Gazette, 6 July 1860 (sale notice)
Lloyds Register of Shipping, 1860-61
Shipping Register, Cape Archives, C.C. 3/7/2/1

Sir James Saumarez
33° 55.50S, 18° 26.40E

Brig of 100 tons, commanded by Capt P. Machon. Wrecked near the Military Hospital in Table Bay on 16 July 1831 during a north-west gale after a voyage from Rio de Janeiro with a cargo of sundries. She lies buried beneath reclaimed land.
Shipping Register, Cape Archives, C.C. 2/12
South African Commercial Advertiser, 20 July

Speedy
33° 55.45S, 18° 25.70E

British schooner of 115 tons, built in 1834 at Nova Scotia, and commanded by Capt J. Adams. Wrecked near the Imhoff battery in Table Bay at 21h00 on 13 July 1842 when her cables parted during a north-west gale after a voyage from St Helena in ballast. She lies buried beneath reclaimed land.
Lloyds Register of Shipping, 1842-43
Shipping Register, Cape Archives, C.C. 2/15

Stabroek
33° 55.42S, 18° 27.20E

Dutch ship of 900 tons, built in 1722 at the Amsterdam Yard for the Zeeland Chamber of the Dutch East India Company, and commanded by Barend van der Zalm. Wrecked a little south of the Salt River in Table Bay on 3 July 1728, close to the *Nightingale* (1722) and the *Haarlem* (1722), during a north-west gale while on an outward-bound voyage from Rammekens, which she had left on 24 January 1728, arriving at the Cape on 9 June 1728. Two men died. All the specie aboard (15 boxes) were saved at the time. The English divers Richard Boone and William Holditch working for John Lethbridge dived on her in 1728 and recovered barrels of nails, 39 lead ingots and 69 iron ingots. She lies buried beneath reclaimed land.

Cape Archives, V.C. 23. Translated into English in *Précis of the Archives of the Cape of Good Hope, Journal, 1699-1732*, H. C. V. Leibbrandt, 1896
Dutch-Asiatic Shipping Outward Voyages, 1595-1794, The Hague, 1979

Standvastigheid

Dutch ship of 888 tons, built in 1706 at the Amsterdam Yard for the Zeeland Chamber of the Dutch East India Company, and commanded by Jan Kole. Wrecked in Table Bay on 16 June 1722 during a north-west gale while on an outward-bound voyage from Rammekens, which she had left on 3 March 1722, arriving at the Cape on 13 June 1722 with chests of silver bars and coins. Many lives were lost. The hulk was blown up shortly after the disaster and some of her money-chests were recovered. She lies close to the *Schotse Lorrendraaier* (1722) and the *Rotterdam* (1722).

Cape Archives, V.C. 22. Translated into English in *Précis of the Archives of the Cape of Good Hope, Journal, 1699-1732*, H. C. V. Leibbrandt, 1896
Dutch-Asiatic Shipping Outward Voyages, 1595-1794, The Hague, 1979

Sterreschans
33° 55.45S, 18° 25.70E

Dutch hoeker of 850 tons, bought in 1789 by the Amsterdam Yard for the Amsterdam Chamber of the Dutch East India Company, and commanded by Johan Ernst van Ollenhausen. Wrecked near the Castle in Table Bay on 22 May 1793 during a north-west gale while on an outward-bound voyage to Batavia. No lives were lost. She lies buried beneath reclaimed land.

Cape Archives, C. 218
Dutch-Asiatic Shipping, 1595-1795, The Hague, 1979

Susan
33° 55.50S, 18° 26.40E

British schooner of 80 tons, commanded by Capt G. Murison. Ran ashore close to the Military Hospital in Table Bay on 20 September 1862 when her cables parted while preparing for a voyage to Walvis Bay. She drove well up the beach and the crew dropped from the jib boom on to the land. The cargo was saved. The vessel

was insured for £600. She lies buried beneath reclaimed land.
Shipping Register, Cape Archives, C.C. 3/7/2/1

Tarleton
33° 55.45S, 18° 25.70E

British ship of 298 tons, built in 1790 at Liverpool, and commanded by Capt John Jefferson. Wrecked at the Castle in Table Bay on 17 April 1818 after a voyage from Rio de Janeiro. She lies buried beneath reclaimed land.
Cape Town Gazette, 2 May 1818 (sale notice)
Lloyds Register of Shipping, 1818
Shipping Register, Cape Archives, C.C. 2/9

Victoria
33° 55.00S, 18° 27.20E

Dutch brigantine (Cape packet) of 160 tons, built in 1724 at the Hoorn Yard for the Hoorn Chamber of the Dutch East India Company. Wrecked on Woodstock Beach in Table Bay on 21 May 1737 during a north-west gale. Nearly all the crew were saved. She lies buried beneath reclaimed land.
Cape Archives, V.C. 25
Dutch-Asiatic Shipping, 1595-1795, The Hague, 1979

Voorzichtigheid
33° 54.90S, 18° 27.95E

Dutch provision ship of 850 tons, built in 1743 at the Delft Yard for the Enkhuizen Chamber of the Dutch East India Company. Wrecked at the Salt River mouth in Table Bay on 8 June 1757 during a north-west gale with a cargo of rice. No lives were lost. She lies buried beneath reclaimed land.
Cape Archives, V.C. 28
Dutch-Asiatic Shipping, 1595-1795, The Hague, 1979

Waddinxveen
33° 54.90S, 18° 27.95E

Dutch ship of 751 tons, built in 1691 at the Rotterdam Yard for the Enkhuizen Chamber of the Dutch East India Company, and commanded by Thomas van Willigen. Wrecked near the Salt River mouth in Table Bay on 24 May 1697 during a north-west gale while on a homeward-bound voyage from Batavia, which she left on 15 January 1697, arriving at the Cape on 20 May 1697. Only four men were saved. She lies buried beneath reclaimed land.
Cape Archives, V.C. 14
Dutch-Asiatic Shipping Homeward Voyages, 1597-1795, The Hague, 1979

Walsingham
33° 55.50S, 18° 26.40E

Ship of 185 tons, built in 1795, and commanded

by Capt R. Bourke. Wrecked opposite the Military Hospital in Table Bay on 14 June 1828 at night after a voyage from St Helena in ballast. She lies buried beneath reclaimed land.
Cape of Good Hope Government Gazette, 20 June 1828 (sale notice)
Lloyds Register of Shipping, 1828
Shipping Register, Cape Archives, C.C. 2/12
The Colonist, 17 June 1828

Waterloo
33° 54.90S, 18° 27.95E

British convict ship of 414 tons, built in 1815 at Bristol, and commanded by Capt H. Ager. Wrecked at the Salt River mouth in Table Bay, near the hospital lines, on 28 August 1842 during a north-west gale while on a voyage from the Downs off south-east Kent to Tasmania. She had put into the bay for water. She broke up in half an hour as her hull was in an extremely rotten state, and 190 people died, of which 143 were convicts, 18 women and children, 15 soldiers and 14 crew. She was wrecked 500 m from the *Abercrombie Robinson* (1842) and near the *Francis Spaight* (1846). She lies buried beneath reclaimed land.
Lloyds Register of Shipping, 1842-43
Shipping Register, Cape Archives, C.C. 2/15
South African Commercial Advertiser, 31 August, 3 September 1842

Westerwijk
33° 54.89S, 18° 27.96E

Dutch vessel of 850 tons, built in 1735 at the Amsterdam Yard for the Amsterdam Chamber of the Dutch East India Company, and commanded by Wouter Bos. Wrecked near the Salt River in Table Bay on 21 May 1737 during a north-west gale while on a homeward-bound voyage from Batavia, which she had left on 6 February 1737, arriving at the Cape on 7 May 1737. Only a few lives were lost. She lies buried beneath reclaimed land.
Cape Archives, V.C. 25
Dutch-Asiatic Shipping Homeward Voyages, 1597-1795, The Hague, 1979

William James
33° 55.50S, 18° 26.40E

British wooden barque of 293 tons, built in 1855 at Sunderland, and commanded by Capt G. Singleton. Wrecked close to the *Newport* (1857) at the Imhoff battery in Table Bay on 10 June 1857 during a north-west gale with a cargo of 5 casks of cheese, 17 000 fire bricks, 4 000 slates, 21 tons of coal, ironmongery, lathes, staves, earthenware, stationery, hairpins, salt, vinegar, clothes and ale. No lives were lost. She lies buried beneath reclaimed land.
Cape Argus, 25 July 1857 (sale notice)
Lloyds Register of Shipping, 1857-58
Shipping Register, Cape Archives, C.C. 2/18

Winifred & Maria
33° 55.45S, 18° 25.70E

Coasting brig, commanded by Capt Brown. Wrecked near the wharf in Table Bay in August 1817 after having arrived in the bay on 21 August 1817 from Algoa Bay with a cargo of sundries. She lies buried beneath reclaimed land.
Cape Town Gazette, 6 September 1817 (sale notice)

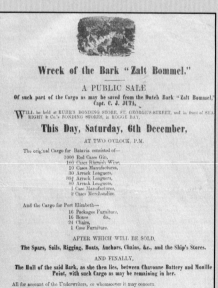

Cape Town Gazette

Woodbridge

British wooden ship of 522 tons, built of teak. Wrecked in Table Bay on 5 November 1816 while on a voyage from the Baltic with a cargo of wood. No lives were lost.
Cape Town Gazette, 9, 23 November (sale notice) 1816

Zalt Brommel
33° 54.85S, 18° 25.60E

Dutch emigrant barque of 642 tons, commanded by Capt C.J. Juta. Wrecked between Mouille Point and the Chavonnes battery on 3 December 1856 as she was leaving Table Bay while on a voyage from Rotterdam to Batavia with a cargo including gin, wine and furniture, most of which was saved. No lives were lost. She lies buried beneath reclaimed land.
Cape Monitor, 6 December (sale notice), 13 December (enquiry) 1856
Shipping Register, Cape Archives, C.C. 2/18

Cape Monitor

Zeeland

Dutch East India Company ship of 1 150 tons, commanded by Albert Tjerksz. Wrecked in Table Bay on 22 May 1793 during a north-west gale while on a homeward-bound voyage from China, which she had left on 3 December 1792, arriving at Table Bay on 8 April 1793. No lives were lost.
Cape Archives, C.217, C.218
Dutch-Asiatic Shipping Homeward Voyages, 1597-1795, The Hague, 1979

Zoetigheid

Dutch flute of 600 tons, built in 1718 at the Delft Yard for the Delft Chamber of the Dutch East India Company, and commanded by Capt Abraham van der Ceel. Wrecked in Table Bay on 16 June 1722 during a north-west gale while on an outward-bound voyage from Goeree, which she left on 23 December 1721, arriving at the Cape on 13 June 1722. Half of the crew died. More than 2 000 ducatoons were recovered from this wreck by the English diver John Lethbridge in 1727. Prior to Lethbridge's attempt the hulk had been blown up, but nothing was recovered. A chest containing 81 staves of silver was recovered later.
Cape Archives, V.C. 22. Translated into English in *Précis of the Archives of the Cape of Good Hope, Journal, 1699-1732*, H. C. V. Leibbrandt, 1896
Dutch-Asiatic Shipping Outward Voyages, 1595-1794, The Hague, 1979

10. Mouille Point

Dominated by the Merchant Navy Academy General Botha, Mouille Point is the meeting point between the reclaimed area of Table Bay and the original coastline. Many of the shipwrecks on Mouille Point are buried beneath reclaimed land. The old lighthouse which operated on Mouille Point is now obsolete. The water is cold due to the Benguela current which flows northward. In summer the sea becomes extremely clear, especially after a strong south-easterly gale. Crayfish are abundant in the thick kelp beds and the area and its shipwrecks are often visited by divers. The climate is Mediterranean, with hot and dry summers and cold and wet winters. The prevailing winds are south-east in summer, and north-west in winter.

Apollo

British ship of 694 tons, built in 1812, and commanded by Capt George Tennent. Wrecked below the Mouille Point battery in Table Bay on 16 April 1823 in good weather at night while on a voyage from Calcutta to London with a cargo of wheat, rice and indigo. A man died when a gun exploded when fired to signal the disaster.
Cape Town Gazette and African Advertiser, 19 April 1823
Lloyds Register of Shipping, 1823
Shipping Register, Cape Archives, C.C. 2/10

Chieftain

Brig of 147 tons, built in 1841 at Dumbarton, and commanded by Capt J. N. Miller. Wrecked near the Mouille Point lighthouse at 03h00 on 6 June 1848 after a voyage from Mauritius to Table Bay with a cargo of sugar and rum. No lives were lost.
Lloyds Register of Shipping, 1848-49
Shipping Register, Cape Archives, C.C. 2/17
South African Commercial Advertiser, 7 June 1848

Dido (ex *Louise & Eliza*)

British barque of 248 tons, built in 1847 at Toulon, and commanded by Capt E. Evans. Wrecked on Mouille Point at 21h00 on 10 April 1853 after entering the bay while on a voyage from Fremantle to London with a cargo of wool. No lives were lost.
Cape Monitor, 16 April 1853
Lloyds Register of Shipping, 1853-54
Shipping Register, Cape Archives, C.C. 2/18

Eliza

German brig of 264 tons, commanded by Capt Aikmann. Wrecked on Mouille Point in Table Bay on 6 August 1863 during a north-east wind after a voyage from Bremen with a general cargo. She had put in to Table Bay for orders. The crew were taken off by lifeboat without loss of life.
Cape Argus, 8 August 1863
Shipping Register, Cape Archives, C.C. 3/7/2/1

Helen

British barque of 307 tons, built in 1835 at Sunderland, and commanded by Capt H. Henderson. Wrecked on Mouille Point at 22h00 on 29 May 1842 after a voyage from St Helena to Table Bay. No lives were lost.
Cape of Good Hope Government Gazette, 3 June 1842
Lloyds Register of Shipping, 1842-43
Shipping Register, Cape Archives, C.C. 2/15

Hoop

Dutch flute of 800 tons, bought by the Amsterdam Yard for the Amsterdam Chamber of the Dutch East India Company, and commanded by Sijbrand Sax. Wrecked on Mouille Point in Table Bay on 30 June 1784 while on a homeward-bound voyage from Batavia, which she had left on 15 December 1783 with 40 men. One man was drowned.
Dutch-Asiatic Shipping Homeward Voyages, 1597-1795, The Hague, 1979

Juliana

Barque of 549 tons, commanded by Capt F. W. Lodge. Wrecked near the Mouille Point battery

on 19 January 1839 after entering Table Bay while on a voyage from the Downs, off south-east Kent, to Sydney with 241 passengers and a cargo of sundries. No lives were lost.
Cape Archives, M.151
Shipping Register, Cape Archives, C.C. 2/14
South African Commercial Advertiser, 20 January 1839

Palmer

British brig of 283 tons, built in 1836 at Sunderland, and commanded by Capt J. Francis. Wrecked near Mouille Point on 19 August 1840 at night after a voyage from the Downs, off south-east Kent, to Table Bay with a cargo of sundries, part of which was saved. No lives were lost.
Cape of Good Hope Government Gazette, 25 September 1840 (sale notice)
Lloyds Register of Shipping, 1840-41
Shipping Register, Cape Archives, C.C. 2/15

Prince Rupert

British barque of 322 tons, built in 1827 in London, and commanded by Capt Ramage. Wrecked at the Mouille Point battery at 21h00 on 4 September 1841 after entering the bay while on a voyage from London to New Zealand with a cargo of sundries. No lives were lost.
Cape of Good Hope Government Gazette, 1 October 1841
Cape Town Mail, 11 September 1841
Lloyds Register of Shipping, 1841-42
Shipping Register, Cape Archives, C.C. 2/15

Reno

Italian barque of 648 tons, built in 1875 by Fava, Voltri, and commanded by Capt Schiaffiro. Wrecked on Mouille Point on 8 December 1883 after a voyage from Cardiff to Table Bay with a cargo of coal. No lives were lost.
Lloyds Register of Shipping, 1883-84
Shipping Register, Cape Archives, C.C. 3/7/2/3

Royal William

British ship of 451 tons, built in 1830 at Whitby, and commanded by Capt D. Fraser. Wrecked near Leesars Fishing near the Mouille Point battery on 20 September 1837 after entering Table Bay between 20h00 and 21h00 while on a voyage from Portsmouth to Calcutta via Madras with a cargo of sundries.
Lloyds Register of Shipping, 1837-38
Shipping Register, Cape Archives, C.C. 2/14

Swea

Swedish barque of 344 tons, commanded by Capt L. Altin. Wrecked near the Mouille Point lighthouse at 02h00 on 10 November 1852 after

entering Table Bay while on a voyage from Hartlepool to Colombo with a cargo of coal. No lives were lost.
Shipping Register, Cape Archives, C.C. 2/18

The Highfields
33° 53.00S, 18° 25.30E

British four-masted steel barque of 2 280 tons, built in 1892 by Richardson Duck & Co, Stockton, and commanded by Capt E.R. Dunham. Lost north of Mouille Point on 14 August 1902 after a voyage from Cardiff to Table Bay with a cargo of coal. She hit the SS Kaiser and sank. Nineteen lives were lost. She lies in 25 m of water and is fairly intact, but diving on her is very dangerous due to the heavy shipping activity in this area.
Cape Argus, 15, 16 August 1902
Lloyds Register of Shipping, 1901-02

11. Mouille Point to Green Point

A stretch of rocky shoreline, with the bottom covered in thick kelp beds. The engine block of RMS Athens, wrecked in 1865, can be seen protruding from the surf (1987). The water is cold due to the Benguela current which flows northward. The land is densely populated and the seabed and its wrecks are often visited by divers. The climate is Mediterranean, with hot and dry summers and cold and wet winters. The prevailing winds are south-east in the summer and north-west in the winter.

RMS Athens
33° 53.85S, 18° 24.57E

Union Company iron steam screw barque of 739 tons, built in 1856 by Denny, Dumbarton, and commanded by Capt David Smith. Wrecked between Mouille Point and Green Point on 17 May 1865 at night after her boiler fires were extinguished by heavy seas during a north-west gale while trying to steam out of Table Bay. She had been lying at anchor while preparing for a voyage to Mauritius. All 30 people aboard were drowned. She lies on the same spot as the Piscataqua (1865), and the site can be identified by her engine-block, which is visible (1987).
Lloyds Register of Shipping, 1865-66
Shipping Register, Cape Archives, C.C. 3/7/2/1
South African Advertiser and Mail, 17 May 1865 (sale notice)

Athens. (Cape Archives, E4486)

South African Advertiser and Mail

Catharine Jamieson
33° 53.89S, 18° 24.68E

Wooden barque of 272 tons, built in 1838 at Bremerhaven, and commanded by Capt A. Hutchinson. Wrecked on the Mouille Point side of the Athens (1865) between Green Point and Mouille Point on 19 September 1840 at night after entering Table Bay while on a voyage from Batavia, Java, to London with a cargo of coffee, 2 959 bundles of rattans, whale-bones and 35 tons of tin (in 989 ingots of 35 kg each), part of which was saved. No lives were lost. Most of the tin has now been recovered.
Graham's Town Journal, 8 October 1840
Lloyds Register of Shipping, 1840-41
Shipping Register, Cape Archives, C.C. 2/15

Enchantress

British wooden schooner of 142 tons, built in 1834 at Ipswich, and commanded by Capt W. Spurgin. Wrecked between Green Point and Mouille Point in Table Bay on 24 August 1849 while on a voyage from Plymouth to Natal with a cargo of sundries. No lives were lost.
Lloyds Register of Shipping, 1849-50
Shipping Register, Cape Archives, C.C. 2/17
South African Commercial Advertiser, 25 August 1849

Mary Stewart
33° 53.90S, 18° 24.50E

German ship of 500 tons, commanded by Capt L. Henrichen. Wrecked between the two lighthouses in Table Bay on 3 November 1842 in thick fog as she left the bay while on a voyage from Hamburg to Batavia via Table Bay with a cargo of sundries. No lives were lost.
Cape of Good Hope Government Gazette, 4, 11 November 1842 (sale notice)
Shipping Register, Cape Archives, C.C. 2/15
South African Commercial Advertiser, 9 November 1842

Olga R.
33° 53.85S, 18° 24.65E

Austrian wooden barque of 674 tons, built in 1874 at Buccari, and commanded by Capt G. Makulicich. Wrecked at Mouille Point east of the *Athens* (1865) on 30 October 1885 after a voyage from New York to Cape Town with a general cargo. No lives were lost. Little is to be seen of her today, apart from a few copper nails, etc.
Lloyds Register of Shipping, 1885-86
Shipping Register, Cape Archives, C.C. 3/7/2/3

Piscataqua
33° 53.85S, 18° 24.53E

American ship of 890 tons. Wrecked between Mouille Point and Green Point on 19 July 1865 as she was leaving Table Bay while on a voyage from Cardiff to Basiland. No lives were lost. The wreck and cargo were sold for £565. She lies in the same spot as the *Athens* (1865).
Cape Argus, 22 July 1865
Shipping Register, Cape Archives, C.C. 3/7/2/1

Sincapore

British snow of 271 tons, built in 1826, and commanded by Capt M. Tait. Wrecked near the Green Point lighthouse or Mouille Point at 21h00 on 1 December 1830 after entering Table Bay while on a voyage from Mauritius to Greenock.
Cape of Good Hope Government Gazette, 3, 10 December 1830
Lloyds Register of Shipping, 1830
Shipping Register, Cape Archives, C.C. 2/12
South African Commercial Advertiser, 4 December 1830

12. Green Point

A prominent rocky outcrop dominated by a large lighthouse. On the seabed in front of the lighthouse there are dense kelp beds. The water is cold, due to the Benguela current which flows northward. The land is densely populated and the seabed and its wrecks are often visited by divers. The climate is Mediterranean, with hot and dry summers and cold and wet winters. The prevailing winds are south-east in summer and north-west in winter.

Arabia

American barque of 382 tons, commanded by Capt J. Wallis. Wrecked on the rocks at Green Point on 10 May 1858 while on a voyage from Zanzibar to America with a cargo of hides, gum, cocoa and ivory.
Shipping Register, Cape Archives, C.C. 2/19

Feniscowles

British ship of 359 tons, built in 1818 at Shields,

Arabia.

and commanded by Capt W. Humble. Wrecked at Green Point at 22h30 on 21 October 1819 while on a voyage from Calcutta to Liverpool. No lives were lost.
Cape of Good Hope Government Gazette, 20 July 1820 (sale notice)
Lloyds Register of Shipping, 1819
Shipping Register, Cape Archives, C.C. 2/9

SS George M. Livanos
33° 53.95S, 18° 23.90E

Greek steamer of 5 482 tons, built in 1938 by W. Gray & Co, West Hartlepool, and commanded by Capt Jean Menis. Wrecked and burnt out opposite the Green Point lighthouse on 1 April 1947 while on a voyage from Newcastle, New South Wales, to Antwerp via Le Havre with a cargo of 27 000 bales of wool and 1 300 tons of nickel ore, most of which was recovered. No lives were lost.
Cape Argus, 1 April 1947 (photograph)
Lloyds Register of Shipping, 1946-47

George M. Livanos. (Cape Times)

Gothenburg

Swedish East-Indiaman, commanded by Capt Carl Trutiger. Wrecked on Green Point on 8 March 1796 while on an outward-bound voyage from Gothenburg to Bombay.
Cape Archives, B.O. 147, B.O. 160, B.O. 194

Mariner

British barque of 487 tons, commanded by Capt Farmer. Wrecked on the rocks at Green Point on 3 August 1860 as she was heading out of Table Bay while on a voyage from Plymouth to St

Helena. No lives were lost, but the captain shot himself.
Cape Argus, 21 August 1860
Cape Chronicle, 10 August 1860
Shipping Register, Cape Archives, C.C. 3/7/2/1

Mulgrave Castle

British ship of 405 tons, built in 1813, and commanded by Capt J. Ralph. Wrecked on Green Point in Table Bay on 4 September 1825 in fine but hazy weather while on a voyage from Gravesend to Calcutta via Madras with a cargo of sundries, four horses and 46 dogs. No lives were lost.
Cape Town Gazette, 16 September 1825
Lloyds Register of Shipping, 1825
Shipping Register, Cape Archives, C.C. 2/11

SS South African Seafarer (ex *Clan Shaw*, ex *Steenbok*)
33° 53.80S, 18° 23.80E

South African freighter of 8 101 tons, built in 1950 at Greenock, and commanded by Capt Ian Branch. Wrecked directly in front of the Green Point lighthouse and against the wreck of the *George M. Livanos* (1947) at 01h00 on 1 July 1966 during a north-west gale. The crew and passengers were taken off by helicopter, and no lives were lost. Very little of the cargo, which included 190 drums of tetra-ethyl lead, was saved. She has often been visited by divers and has been extensively worked on for her non-ferrous fittings.
Cape Argus, 1, 2 July 1966 (photographs)
Lloyds Register of Shipping, 1966-67

SS Thermopylae
33° 53.95S, 18° 23.95E

Aberdeen Line steel screw barquentine of 3 711 tons, built in 1891 by Hall, Russell & Co, Aberdeen, and commanded by Capt W. Philip. Wrecked in front of the Green Point lighthouse in Table Bay on 12 September 1899 at night while on a voyage from Australia to England with a cargo of gold specie (£100 000 in gold sovereigns were saved from the wreck at the time), frozen rabbits and mutton. The famous Australian racehorse Chesney was aboard the vessel. No lives were lost. She is often visited by divers. She lies a little to the east of the *South African Seafarer* (1966) and the *George M. Livanos* (1947).
Cape Argus, 12 September 1899
Lloyds Register of Shipping, 1899-1900

Udny Castle

British snow of 287 tons, built in 1839 at Sunderland and commanded by Capt Turnbull. Wrecked near the Green Point lighthouse at 02h00 on 26 November 1840 while entering Table Bay after a voyage from Liverpool with a cargo of coal. No lives were lost.

Cape of Good Hope Government Gazette, 27 November 1840
Lloyds Register of Shipping, 1840-41
Shipping Register, Cape Archives, C.C. 2/15

Valleyfield

British wooden barque of 400 tons, built in 1851 at Quebec, and commanded by Capt Burton. Wrecked on Green Point on 15 June 1862 in fog while entering Table Bay after a voyage from Liverpool with a general cargo. Nine people, including the captain, were drowned.
Cape Argus, 17 June, 9 September 1862
Lloyds Register of Shipping, 1862-63
Shipping Register, Cape Archives, C.C. 3/7/2/1

13. Robben Island and Whale Rock

This island dominates the centre of Table Bay and is a restricted area, due to the presence of a maximum-security prison on the island, which also harbours a well-established settlement and a lighthouse. The island is surrounded by dense kelp beds and is well known as a venue for illegal crayfish diving at night. Wreck divers have had to operate clandestinely due to the security regulations and as a result few finds have been recorded. Whale Rock is a large submerged pinnacle just outside the island security area and is often visited by divers. The water is cold due to the Benguela current which flows northward. The prevailing winds are south-east in the summer and north-west in the winter. Rangatira Bay is named after the steamer Rangatira *wrecked there in 1916.*

A. H. Stevens

American ship of 999 tons, commanded by Capt Talbot. Wrecked on the north-west tip of Robben Island close to the *Bernicia* (1861) on 7 February 1862 in fog while on a voyage from Maulmein, Burma, to Falmouth. The wreck and cargo was sold for £3 500.
Cape Argus, 8 February 1862
Shipping Register, Cape Archives, C.C. 3/7/2/1

Bernicia

British wooden barque of 548 tons, built in 1848 at Sunderland, and commanded by Capt Pierce. Wrecked on the north-west point of Robben Island (Shell Bay) on 16 June 1861 during a north-west gale after a voyage from London to Cape Town with a cargo of wine, spirits, beer, timber and general cargo. Six passengers and one crew member drowned. She lies close to the *A.H. Stevens* (1862).
Cape Argus, 20 June 1861 (sale notice)
Cape Chronicle, 21 June 1861
Cape of Good Hope Shipping and Mercantile Gazette, 21 June, 12 July 1861
Lloyds Register of Shipping, 1861-62
Shipping Register, Cape Archives, C.C. 3/7/2/1

Bittern

British wooden snow of 348 tons, built in 1842 at North Shields, and commanded by Capt T. E. Foss. Wrecked on the north-west point of Robben Island at 02h30 on 18 January 1848 during a south-east gale after entering Table Bay while on a voyage from Shields to Madras with a cargo of coal. No lives were lost.
Cape of Good Hope and Port Natal Shipping and Mercantile Gazette, 21 January 1848
Lloyds Register of Shipping, 1848-49
Shipping Register, Cape Archives, C.C. 2/17

MV Daeyang Family (ex *Emerald Transporter*, ex *Adria Maru*)
33° 50.80S 18° 22.90E

Korean ore-carrier of 183 583 tons, built in 1972 by Mitsui Shipbuilding and Engineering Co, Ichihara, and commanded by Capt Hee Man Yoo. Wrecked a little south of Whale Rock in Table Bay on 30 March 1986 when her anchors dragged and she drifted onto the reef while on a voyage from Brazil to Korea with a cargo of 162 000 tons of iron ore. The crew were rescued by helicopter and no lives were lost. Her bunker fuel was salvaged by the vessel *Oranjemund* to prevent pollution, but the cargo was abandoned.
Cape Times, 31 March 1986
Lloyds Register of Shipping, 1986-87

Dageraad

Cape packet of 140 tons, built in 1692 at the Zeeland Yard for the Zeeland Chamber of the Dutch East India Company, and commanded by Jan Tak. Wrecked on the west point of Robben Island on 20 January 1694 in mist. She broke up quickly and 16 lives were lost. She was proceeding from St Helena Bay to Cape Town with salvaged treasure and other goods from the outward-bound vessel *Gouden Buis*, which ran ashore north of St Helena Bay in 1693. Seventeen chests of specie were loaded on to her; three were recovered at the time. Two English divers, assistants to John Lethbridge, tried to work on this wreck in 1728, but without much success.
Cape Archives, V.C. 13, V.C. 94
Dutch-Asiatic Shipping, 1595-1795, The Hague, 1979

Flora

Dutch schooner, commanded by Capt H. Blom. Wrecked on a reef on the south point of Robben Island on 16 November 1821 at night while on a voyage from Batavia to Amsterdam with a cargo of coffee and sugar.
Cape Town Gazette, 21 November 1821
Shipping Register, Cape Archives, C.C. 2/9

Forfarshire
33° 50.05S 18° 22.85E

Ship of 611 tons. Wrecked on Whale Rock on

15 September 1864 after entering Table Bay while on a voyage from Liverpool to Calcutta with a cargo of coal. No lives were lost. The captain had died and the first officer was in charge.
Shipping Register, Cape Archives, C.C. 3/7/2/1

MV Goel No.1 (ex *Thorarinn*, ex *Inge Vinke*)
33° 49.25S, 18° 22.60E

Canadian geophysical research ship of 787 tons, built in 1961. Wrecked on the south tip of Robben Island on 27 January 1976 while leaving the bay. No lives were lost. She was on charter to the Paul Getty Organisation to make a detailed study of offshore deposits along the Cape coast.
Argus, 28 January 1976
Lloyds Register of Shipping, 1976-77

Gondolier

British brig of 226 tons, commanded by Capt R. Rhodes. Wrecked on Robben Island on 7 February 1836 after entering Table Bay while on a voyage from Liverpool to Calcutta via Madras with a general cargo, part of which was saved.
Lloyds Register of Shipping, 1836-37
Shipping Register, Cape Archives, C. C. 2/13
South African Commercial Advertiser, 17 February 1836 (advertisement)

Goel No. 1. *(George Young)*

SS Hypatia
33° 50.10S, 18° 22.90E

British Houston Line steamer of 5 728 tons, built in 1902 by Palmers & Co, Newcastle, and commanded by Capt Chrichton. Wrecked on Whale Rock in Table Bay on 29 October 1929 in fog while on a voyage from Beira to New York with a cargo of blister copper and chrome ore. No lives were lost. Her bell was recovered in the 1960s and her propeller was salvaged in 1974. The diver Olaf Pedersen died on the wreck after recovering 1 000 tons of copper over a three-year period.
Cape Times, 30 October 1929
Lloyds Register of Shipping, 1929-30

Il Nazerino

Italian barque of 938 tons, commanded by G. Rassi. Wrecked on a reef on the north-west point of Robben Island (Shell Bay) on 2 December 1885

after a voyage from Cardiff to Table Bay with a cargo of 1 500 tons of coal.
Cape Argus, 3 December 1885 (sale notice)
Shipping Register, Cape Archives, C.C. 3/7/2/3

Kingston

American barque of 214 tons, commanded by Capt J. Sterling. Wrecked on the south-west point of Robben Island at 03h00 on 23 December 1852 while entering Table Bay after a voyage from Baltimore with a cargo of flour. Five people were drowned, including the captain's wife and children.
Cape Monitor, 8 January 1853
Shipping Register, Cape Archives, C.C. 2/18

Lancastria

British wooden barque of 321 tons, built in 1856 by Pallion, and commanded by Capt Macintosh. Wrecked on Robben Island on 31 December 1880 when her cable parted during a south-east gale after a voyage from Sunderland to Table Bay with a cargo of coal. Two lives were lost.
Cape Argus, 4 January 1881
Lloyds Register of Shipping, 1880-81
Shipping Register, Cape Archives, C.C. 3/7/2/3

Perseverance
33° 50.15S, 18° 22.88E

British ship of 353 tons, built in 1825, and commanded by Capt J. Best. Wrecked on Whale Rock in Table Bay on 12 March 1826 while on a voyage from London to Madras with a cargo of sundries, including zinc and mercury, some of which was saved at the time. No lives were lost. The remainder of the cargo was salvaged in 1970; about 2,5 tons of mercury and about 30 tons of zinc were recovered.
Cape Town Gazette, 17, 24, 31 March 1826
Lloyds Register of Shipping, 1826
South African Commercial Advertiser, 12, 15 March 1826

SS Rangatira
33° 48.30S, 18° 21.50E

British Shaw Savill and Albion twin-screw cargo and emigrant steamer of 7 465 tons, built in 1910 by Workman, Clarke & Co, Belfast. Wrecked on the north-west corner of Robben Island on 31 March 1916 in dense fog while on a voyage from London to Hobart with a general cargo, most of which was saved. She was to have put into Table Bay for bunkers.
Cape Argus, 1 April 1916
Lloyds Register of Shipping, 1915-16

Sea Eagle

American barque of 625 tons, commanded by Capt A. N. Williams. Wrecked in Murrays Bay on Robben Island on 20 November 1856 during

Rangatira.

a south-east gale while on a voyage from Boston to Calcutta with a cargo of machinery.
Cape of Good Hope Shipping and Mercantile Gazette, 21 November 1856
Shipping Register, Cape Archives, C.C 2/18

RMS Tantallon Castle
33° 47.50S, 18° 21.65E

Union Castle Line single-screw mailship of 5 636 tons, built in 1894 by Fairfield, Glasgow, and commanded by Capt De la Cour Travers. Ran aground on the north-west tip of Robben Island at 15h00 on 7 May 1901 in dense fog while on a voyage from Southampton with a general cargo. No lives were lost. She lies close to the *Rangatira* (1916).
Cape Argus, 8 May 1901
Lloyds Register of Shipping, 1901-02

Tantallon Castle. *(Robert Pabst)*

Thorne

British ship of 251 tons, built in 1819, and commanded by Capt W. Poole. Wrecked on Robben Island on 18 May 1831 in thick fog while leaving Table Bay while on a voyage from Algoa Bay to London with a cargo of colonial produce, part of which was saved.
Lloyds Register of Shipping. 1831
Shipping Register, Cape Archives, C.C. 2/12

Timor

Dutch barque of 441 tons, commanded by Capt F. Agema. Wrecked between Whale Rock and Robben Island on 22 December 1856 after missing stays during a south wind while on a voyage from Batavia with a cargo of coffee and tin blocks. By 10 January 1857 112 blocks of tin had been recovered from the wreck.
Cape Argus, 7 January, 14 February (sale notice) 1857
Cape Monitor, 24 December 1856 (sale notice)
Cape of Good Hope Shipping and Mercantile Gazette, 9 January 1857
Shipping Register, Cape Archives, C.C. 2/18

14. Green Point to Slangkop lighthouse

This stretch of coastline includes some of the most beautiful scenery and beaches in South Africa. The most prominent features are the beaches of Clifton and Camps Bay, the Twelve Apostles mountain range, Llandudno, Sandy Bay, Hout Bay, Chapman's Peak and Kommetjie. The land is well populated, especially in the Sea Point and Camps Bay area. The sea is cold due to the Benguela current which flows northward. The seabed vegetation consists of large kelp beds in which crayfish are found. The area is often visited by divers. The vegetation on land consists of Cape fynbos, including large numbers of proteas and heather. The prevailing winds are south-east in summer and north-west in winter. Geldkis at Oudekraal is named after a money-chest supposedly lost after the wrecking of the Het Huis te Kraaiestein in 1698.

SS Antipolis
33° 59.00S, 18° 21.45E

Greek tanker of 24 119 tons, built in 1959 by Harima Zosensho, registered in Piraeus and owned by Marceloso Cia Naviera, S.A. Ran ashore a little south of the *Huis te Kraaiestein* (1698) at Oudekraal on the Cape Peninsula on 28 July 1977 after her tow-cable snapped while being towed to a breakers' yard in Taiwan by the Japanese tug *Kiyo Maru 2*. Her upper works were cut up for scrap down to the waterline. The *Romelia* broke from the same tow.
Argus, 29 July 1977
Cape Times, 29 July 1977 (photographs)
Lloyds Register of Shipping, 1977-78

SS Clan Monroe
34° 08.70S, 18° 19.00E

Turret screw steamer of 4 853 tons, built in 1897 by W. Doxford & Sons, Sunderland, and commanded by Capt Brown. Wrecked a little north of the Slangkop lighthouse at Kommetjie on 1 July 1905 at night while on a voyage from Liverpool to Delagoa Bay with a general cargo including cyanide, dynamite and gun cotton. No lives were lost, as her crew were saved by rocket apparatus.
Cape Times, 3 July 1905
Lloyds Register of Shipping, 1901-02
Shipping Register, Cape Archives, C.C. 3/7/2/6

Fame
33° 54.50S, 18° 23.30E

British wooden sailing ship of 629 tons, built in 1817 in Calcutta of teak, and commanded by Capt William Clark. Wrecked a little south of Graaff's Pool in Sea Point, Table Bay, on 14 June 1822 during a north-west gale while on a homeward-bound voyage from Bengal and Madras to London with a large number of Indian and British gold coins aboard. Most of these were recovered in 1965.
Cape Town Gazette, 22 June 1822

Lloyds Register of Shipping, 1822
Shipping Register, Cape Archives, C.C. 2/10
South African Numismatic Journal, Number 4,
  November 1967

Het Huis te Kraaiestein
33° 58.85S, 18° 21.70E

Dutch ship of 1 154 tons, built in 1697 at the
Zeeland Yard for the Zeeland Chamber of the
Dutch East India Company, and commanded by
Jan van de Vijver. Wrecked on the rocks in the
bay at Oudekraal on the Cape Peninsula on
27 May 1698 in thick mist as she was trying to
find her way into Table Bay. She was on her
maiden voyage outward-bound from Wielingen,
which she had left on 1 February 1698, with a
cargo of 19 chests of pieces-of-eight (approximately 57 000 pieces). No lives were lost. Three
chests of treasure disappeared and the name
'Geldkis' (money-chest) appears on maps of the
area.
Cape Archives, V.C. 14
Dutch-Asiatic Shipping Outward Voyages,
  1595-1794, The Hague, 1979

Hopefield Packet

Coasting schooner. Wrecked at Camps Bay on
the Cape Peninsula on 2 January 1869 while on
a voyage to Dyer Island with part of her cargo of
stores.
Cape Argus, 5, 7 (sale notice) January 1869
Shipping Register, Cape Archives, C.C. 3/7/2/2

SS Kakapo
34° 07.35S, 18° 20.10E

British steamer of 1 093 tons, built in 1898 by
Grangemouth Dockyard Co, Grangemouth, and
commanded by Capt P. Nicolayson. Ran ashore
on the southern end of Chapman's Bay beach on
25 May 1900 at night during a north-west gale
after having left Cape Town in bad weather and
mistakenly having identified Chapman's Peak
as Cape Point. She was on her maiden voyage
from Swansea to Sydney in ballast with a crew of
20. No lives were lost. She lies high and dry
above the high-tide line (1987), and her boilers
have become something of a tourist attraction
on the lonely Chapman's Bay beach.
Cape Times, 26 May 1900
Lloyds Register of Shipping, 1899-1900

Kakapo. *(Stephen Goodson)*

Maori. *(George Young)*

SS Maori
34° 01.90S, 18° 18.90E

British steam cargo vessel of 5 317 tons, built in
1893 by Swan & Hunter, Newcastle, owned by
the Shaw Savill Company, and commanded by
Capt G. Nicole. Wrecked in the big bay to the
east of Duiker Point on the Cape Peninsula on
5 August 1909 in thick fog and drizzle while on
a voyage from London to New Zealand with
a crew of 53 and a mixed cargo of British-
manufactured goods, including explosives,
railway-lines, crockery and water-piping. A boat
with 15 crew members made for Chapman's Bay,
but six were drowned when it capsized in surf;
altogether 32 lives were lost. She had left Table
Bay at midnight after having put in for coal. She
lies in about 20 m of water a little west of the
Oakburn (1906), which sank on the eastern corner of the bay. She has been extensively worked
on for her non-ferrous fittings and is a favourite
weekend venue for diving clubs. A large amount
of intact crockery has been recovered over the
years and the hull remains in fairly good shape.
Her bell is in the Hout Bay museum.
Cape Argus, 5, 6, 7 August 1909
Cape Times, 6 August 1909
Lloyds Register of Shipping, 1909-10
Shipping Register, Cape Archives, C.C. 3/7/2/7

Montagu

Schooner of 20 tons, built on the Kowie River.
Wrecked close to the farm Slangkop on the
south end of Chapman's Bay near Kommetjie on
30 March 1847 while on a voyage from Table Bay
to the Kowie River with a cargo of 84 bags of
meal, 25 bags of sugar, 35 bags of coffee, 25 bags
of rice, 100 bags of oats, 1 bag of mails, 22 deals,
2 bars of iron, 3 bars of steel, 2 casks of pitch,
2 casks of tar and 2 bales of oakum. There were
no survivors. She was seen bottom-up and later
washed ashore, and the cargo was plundered.
She was one of the first vessels to be built in the
Eastern Province.
Cape of Good Hope Government Gazette, 6
  May 1847
Eastern Province Herald, 10 April 1847
Shipping Register, Cape Archives, C.C. 2/16

SS Oakburn
34° 02.20S, 18° 18.70E

British steel cargo steamer of 3 865 tons, built in
1904 by Russell & Co, Port Glasgow, and commanded by Capt J. J. Crosthwaite. Wrecked in
the big bay east of Duiker Point on the Cape
Peninsula on 21 May 1906 in fog while on a
voyage from New York to Sydney with a general
cargo, including 1 000 tons of steel railway-lines,
railway equipment, glassware, 'American notions', sewing machines, paper, oil and musical
instruments. Two Chinese seamen were
drowned. She lies in about 20 m of water on the
eastern side of the *Maori* (1909) and is a lot more
broken up than the *Maori*. She has been extensively worked on.
Cape Times, 22, 23, 24 May 1906
Lloyds Register of Shipping, 1905-06
Shipping Register, Cape Archives, C.C.
  3/7/2/6

Paragon

Ship of 376 tons, commanded by Capt D. Ogilvy.
Wrecked a little west of Green Point in Table Bay
at 19h30 on 1 April 1840 during a north-west
gale after entering the bay while on a voyage
from Mauritius to London with a cargo of sugar.
No lives were lost.
Cape of Good Hope Government Gazette, 3
  April 1840
Shipping Register, Cape Archives, C.C.
  2/15
South African Commercial Advertiser, 4 April
  1840

SS Romelia (ex *Zodiac*, ex *Varbergshus*)
34° 00.65S, 18° 19.90E

Derelict Liberian tanker of 20 421 tons, built in
1959 by Kieler Howaldtswerke, registered in
Monrovia and owned by the Soc. Pacifica Marina, S.A. Ran ashore at Sunset Rocks near Llandudno on the Cape Peninsula on 29 July 1977

when the tow-cable to the Japanese tug *Kiyo Maru 2* broke during a north-west gale while on her way, with the *Antipolis*, to a breakers' yard in Taiwan. Her stern section is still clearly visible on the rocks (1987).
Argus, 29 July 1977 (photograph)
Cape Times, 30 July 1977 (photograph)
Lloyds Register of Shipping, 1977-78

Saint Antonio

Slaving brig. Wrecked in Chapmans Bay on 29 March 1842 while on a voyage from Rio de Janeiro. She had been detained by HMS *Partridge*. No lives were lost.
Graham's Town Journal, 14 April 1842
Shipping Register, Cape Archives, C.C. 2/15

São Josene

Portuguese slaving ship. Wrecked at Camps Bay on 27 December 1794 with a cargo of 500 slaves from Mozambique. Of this number, 200 were drowned.
Cape Archives, C. 649, B.O. 147

Schuilenburg

Cape vessel of 300 tons, built in 1747 at the Amsterdam Yard for the Amsterdam Chamber of the Dutch East India Company. Wrecked near Camps Bay on 3 June 1756 during a north-west gale while on a voyage from Table Bay to False Bay with provisions.
Cape Archives, V.C. 28
Dutch-Asiatic Shipping Outward Voyages, 1595-1794, The Hague, 1979

Trafalgar
33° 54.45S, 18° 23.60E

British wooden emigrant ship of 364 tons, commanded by Capt R. E. Baxter. Ran ashore on the south-west point of Rocklands Bay in Sea Point, Table Bay, at 23h30 on 21 February 1839 after becoming becalmed on entering the bay. She was on a voyage from Liverpool to Sydney with passengers (9 cabin and 28 steerage) and a cargo of sundries. One woman, Mrs Troy, was killed when a mast fell; her husband lost £1 000 in cash on the wreck. The wreck is identified by the large mound of cast iron ingots on the site, and was worked on in 1981; silverware bearing the captain's initials has been found, as have a number of coins.
Shipping Register, Cape Archives, C.C. 2/14
South African Commercial Advertiser, 23, 27 February, 2 March 1839

Vis
33° 54.20S, 18° 23.85E

Dutch ship of 650 tons, built in 1732 at the Enkhuizen Yard for the Dutch East India Company, and commanded by Jan Sikkes. Wrecked a little

to the south of the Green Point lighthouse in Table Bay on 6 May 1740 at night while on an outward-bound voyage from Texel Roads, which she had left on 8 January 1740. One man was lost. Her cargo of specie was saved. Many Dutch silver riders have been recovered from this site, as well as a few bronze breech-loading swivel-guns. Her cargo of granite blocks (measuring about 1 m x ,5 m) and also many large cast iron muzzle-loading cannons litter the site.
Cape Archives, V.C. 25
Dutch-Asiatic Shipping Outward Voyages, 1595-1794, The Hague, 1979

15. Slangkop lighthouse to Cape Point lighthouse and Bellows Rock

Beautiful and unspoilt, this is the last stretch of true Atlantic coastline. The Agulhas and Benguela currents meet off Cape Point. The land is well populated, apart from the southern tip of the peninsula, which has been proclaimed a nature reserve. The sea is cold due to the Benguela current which flows northward. The seabed vegetation consists of dense kelp beds in which large numbers of crayfish are found, and the area is often visited by divers. The vegetation on land consists of fynbos, including many species of proteas and heather. The prevailing winds are south-east in summer and north-west in winter. Two large reefs, Bellows Rock and Anvil Rock, pose a threat to mariners off this point. Place names associated with shipwrecks are Albatross Rock, named after the tug Albatross wrecked there in 1863, and Italiaanse Kerkhof, a little north of Olifantsbos Point, named after the crew members of the Caterina Doge *who were buried there in 1886.*

SS Albatross

Steam screw tug of 74 tons, commanded by Capt Johnson. Wrecked on Albatross Rock near Olifantsbos Point on 10 April 1863 and sank 12 minutes after striking while on a voyage from Simon's Bay to Table Bay with a cargo of cotton. The crew all landed in Hout Bay. Albatross Rock derives its name from this wreck.
Cape Argus, 11, 20 April 1863
Shipping Register, Cape Archives, C.C. 3/7/2/1

Anne

Schooner of 96 tons, commanded by Capt T. Armson. Wrecked near Olifantsbos Point on 3 June 1859 in thick fog while on a voyage from Rio de Janeiro to Table Bay.
Cape Argus, 7 June 1859
Cape Weekly Chronicle, 10 June 1859
Shipping Register, Cape Archives, C.C. 2/18

SS Bia
34° 16.15S, 18° 22.95E

Swedish freighter of 3 344 tons, built in 1905 by

Hawthorn Leslie & Co, Newcastle. Struck Albatross Rock and was beached a few hundred metres north of Olifantsbos Point at 22h30 on 18 September 1917 while on a voyage from Scandinavia to the Persian Gulf with a cargo of timber. Four men died.
Cape Argus, 19, 20, 21 September 1917
Lloyds Register of Shipping, 1917-18

Bia. *(Cape Archives, G354)*

Carlotta B.

Italian wooden barque of 759 tons, built in 1874 by Briasco, Sestri Ponente, and commanded by Capt N. L. Rolandi. Wrecked at Olifantsbos Point on 7 August 1886 while on a voyage from Cardiff with a cargo of 1 079 tons of coal for the Union Steamship Company. No lives were lost.
Lloyds Register of Shipping, 1886-87
Shipping Register, Cape Archives, C.C. 3/7/2/4

Caterina Doge

Italian wooden barque of 856 tons, built in 1875 by Patrone, Voltri, and commanded by Capt Filippe. Wrecked at Matroosdam, Cape Point, on 3 June 1886 while on a voyage from Cardiff to Table Bay with a cargo of 1 326 tons of coal. Five crew members were drowned and lie buried at Italiaanse Kerkhof, a little north of Olifantsbos Point.
Lloyds Register of Shipping, 1886-87
Shipping Register, Cape Archives, C.C. 3/7/2/4

HNMS Holland

Dutch frigate, commanded by Capt Willem Silvester. Wrecked near Olifantsbos Point on 11 May 1786 at night while on a voyage from Holland to Java. Eight lives were lost.
Cape Archives, V.C. 34

RMS Kafir
34° 17.80S, 18° 24.00E

Union Company iron steam-coaster of 982 tons, built in 1873 by Key, Kinghorn, and commanded by Capt Ward. Beached about 400 m north of the Brightwater houses, about 3 km south of Olifantsbos Point, on 13 February 1878 during a west breeze in fine weather after striking Albatross Rock while on a voyage from Table Bay to Mozambique and East Africa with passengers, mail and a package of specie. Four men were drowned, one of whom was an Arab who had crossed Africa with H. M. Stanley and was

present at his meeting with David Livingstone; he had been left at the Cape due to poor health.
Cape Argus, 14, 16 (sale notice), 19, 21 February (enquiry) 1878
Cape Standard & Mail, 14, 16 (sale notice), 19, 21 February (enquiry) 1878
Cape Times, 13 (sailing notice), 15 (sale notice), 20, 21 February (enquiry) 1878
Lloyds Register of Shipping, 1878-79
Shipping Register, Cape Archives, C.C. 3/7/2/3

L'Aigle

French whaler. Ran aground near Slangkop Beach at about 21h00 on 15 February 1834. Three men were drowned, including the third officer. She had caught only one whale.
South African Commercial Advertiser, 19 February 1834

L'Alouette
34° 16.20S, 18° 22.80E

French ship (king's transport), commanded by Lieut Claude Rigodit. Hit Albatross Rock off Olifantsbos Point at 06h00 on 6 June 1817 in heavy fog during a voyage from Rochefort-sur-Mer, a French naval fortress and arsenal, which she had left on 3 April 1817, to Réunion with passengers, 70 seamen and a cargo of Government supplies including wine, iron, lead, copper, gold and silver specie, silver spoons and forks, jewellery, glass, porcelain, clothing for the troops, swords, firelocks, pistols, muskets and mathematical instruments. One child was drowned. Six-livre silver coins, gold-plated instruments, copper and pewter tankards, pistols, muskets,

Cape Town Gazette

> By Permission of His Excellency Lord
> **CHARLES HENRY SOMERSET.**
> ## Public Sale,
> ON Thursday the 26th June 1817, at the Oliphants Bosch, of a quantity of Masts, Yards, Sails, Cordage, &c. being part of the Wreck of the French Ship LALOUETTE, stranded at that place; at the same time will be sold, the said Ship as she lays on the Klipbank — The Sale will be held by the Captain and Commissioner of the Ship, assisted by the undersigned.
> The Cargo shipped in France, consists of the following, viz. Iron, Copper, Lead, a great variety of new Cordage and Sails for the use of the Ship, and for two Boats for landing Goods at the Government Stores at Bourbon, four new 13 inch Cables, four ditto of a less size, a variety of new Cordage and Sails, three Anchors, six 6 lbr. Guns, three Boats, bolts of Canvas, a large quantity of Provisions, viz. Flour in cask, salted Pork and Beef, Biscuit, red Wine, Brandy, Oil, &c. laid in for a voyage of eight months, for 85 persons; between 5 a 6000 lbs. in gold and silver Specie, silver Spoons, Forks, and some Jewellery; 50 cases, containing, Glass, Porcelain, Goods for the Government of Bourbon, such as Cloths, Clothes for the Troops, Swords, Firelocks, Pistols, various Mathematical Instruments, Secretaries and Trunks belonging to the Captain and Officers of the Ship.
> F. DE LETTRE, ⎫ Agents.
> C. LIND, ⎭

firelocks, and many other articles have been recovered. The site lies on a rocky bank a fair way offshore, a little inshore from the *Umhlali* (1909), off the small beach a little north of the *Thomas T. Tucker* (1942), and is identified by the large number of cast iron pigs scattered towards the shore.
Cape Town Gazette, 14, 21 June (sale notice), 30 August (sale notice) 1817

La Rozette

French brig, commanded by Capt La Bordes. Wrecked near a little cove called Platboom near Brightwaters, south of Olifantsbos Point, on 19 August 1786 after the crew mutinied and ran her aground while on a voyage from Bordeaux to Mauritius with a general cargo.
Cape Archives, V.C. 34

Le Napoléon
34° 15.90S, 18° 23.00E

French privateer. Driven ashore at Olifantsbos on 25 December 1805 after being chased by the British navy frigate *Narcissus*. The French subjects from this wreck are mentioned in the Articles of Capitulation by which the Batavian Republic handed control of the Cape to Britain.
Cape Archives, B.R. 593 (articles)
Kaapsche Courant, 28 December 1805, 11 January 1806

SS Lusitania
34° 23.40S, 18° 29.65E

Portuguese twin-screw liner of 5 557 tons, built in 1906 by Sir Raylton Dixon & Co, owned by Empreza Nacional De Navegacao, Lisbon, and commanded by Capt Faria. Wrecked on Bellows Rock off Cape Point at 24h00 on 18 April 1911 in fog while on a voyage from Lourenço Marques (Maputo) with 25 first-class, 57 second-class and 121 third-class passengers, and 475 African labourers. On 20 April she slipped off the rock into 37 m of water. Out of 800 people on board, eight died when a boat capsized.
Cape Argus, 19, 20 April 1911
Lloyds Register of Shipping, 1911-12

MV Nolloth (ex *Reality*, ex *Leuvehaven*, ex *Alpha*)
34° 16.70S, 18° 23.40E

Dutch coaster of 347 tons, built in 1936 at Waterhuizen, and commanded by Capt A. van der Luit. Wrecked 500 m south of Olifantsbos Point on 30 April 1965 after striking Albatross Rock. She plied between Table Bay and Durban and had on board a general cargo, including liquor, most of which was salvaged at the time. Her crew were rescued by helicopter. She was on charter to African Coasters. She was cut up and demolished in 1966.
Cape Argus, 1 May 1965
Lloyds Register of Shipping, 1964-65

Lusitania. *(Cape Times Weekly)*

Paralos

French barque of 362 tons, commanded by Capt Pasco. Struck Bellows Rock off Cape Point on 18 January 1880 and sank two hours later while on a voyage from Borneo to Falmouth with a cargo of guano. No lives were lost.
Graham's Town Journal, 19 January 1880
Shipping Register, Cape Archives, C.C. 3/7/2/3

Sophia

British wooden brigantine of 165 tons, built in 1848 at Nova Scotia, owned by Norden & Co, and commanded by Capt J. Poe. Wrecked near the white sands 16 km south of Hout Bay on 7 March 1853 while on a voyage from Table Bay to Port Philip in Australia. No lives were lost.
Cape Monitor, 12 March 1853
Lloyds Register of Shipping, 1853-54
Shipping Register, Cape Archives, C.C. 2/18

Star of Africa

Cape iron barque of 431 tons, built in 1876 by Duthie, Aberdeen, and commanded by Capt W. Barron. Struck Albatross Rock at 03h30 on 29 August 1880 and sank almost immediately while on a voyage from Calcutta to Table Bay with a general cargo of Eastern produce, including rice, wool packs and grain bags. Out of a crew of 16, only two were saved; the captain and his wife were also drowned.
Cape Argus, 30, 31 August, 2 September (sale notice) 1880
Lloyds Register of Shipping, 1880-81
Shipping Register, Cape Archives, C.C. 3/7/2/3

SS **Thomas T. Tucker**
34° 16.50S, 18° 22.80E

American liberty ship of 7 176 tons, built in 1942 by the Houston Shipbuilding Corporation, Texas. Struck Albatross Rock on 27 November 1942 in fog and was beached at Olifantsbos Point while on her maiden voyage from New Orleans to Suez with a cargo of war materials, most of which was saved. Parts of her hull can be seen clearly on the Point (1987).
Lloyds Register of Shipping, 1943-44

Thomas T. Tucker. *(Ferguson Collection)*

SS **Umhlali**

Steamer of 3 388 tons, built in 1904 by Sir J. Laing & Son, Sunderland, owned by Bullard King & Co, and commanded by Capt J. L. Richards. Struck Albatross Rock at 22h30 on 15 September 1909 and was beached at Olifantsbos Point while on a voyage from London to Durban with 47 passengers and a general cargo. A baby was drowned during the lowering of a lifeboat. The wreck site lies near the SS *Bia* (1917) and the *Thomas T. Tucker* (1942).
Cape Argus, 17 September 1909
Lloyds Register of Shipping, 1909-10
Shipping Register, Cape Archives, C.C. 3/7/2/7

Unity

British wooden brig of 190 tons, built in 1848 at Whitehaven, and commanded by Capt S. Rich. Wrecked on Bellows Rock off Cape Point on 5 September 1859 while on a voyage from Table Bay to East London. Two lives were lost. Pieces from her wreckage washed up in Saldanha Bay.
Cape Argus, 22 October 1859
Cape of Good Hope Shipping and Mercantile Gazette, 30 September 1859
Cape Weekly Chronicle, 23 September, 7 October 1859
Lloyds Register of Shipping, 1859-60
Shipping Register, Cape Archives, C.C. 2/18

16. Cape Point lighthouse to Cape Hangklip

A stretch of coastline encompassing False Bay, in which the water is usually a few degrees warmer than on the Atlantic side of the

Peninsula, depending on the wind conditions. The whole area from Cape Point to Cape Agulhas can be considered a transitional area between the effects of the warm Agulhas current and the cold Benguela current. Dense kelp beds abound, but the kelp is of a much thinner variety than on the Atlantic side. Fish life is more prolific due to the warmer sea conditions. The sea is normally clear, with small surf conditions, and is often visited by divers. The bay is home to a large number of sharks, the most prominent being the Great White sharks found mainly in the vicinity of Seal Island, which is populated by a large number of Cape fur seals. The most prominent settlement is Simon's Town, South Africa's chief naval base. Diving is prohibited in the navy area. The northern side of the bay consists of a large expanse of golden beach dominated by the Strand, a seaside resort. Gordon's Bay is a well-populated residential town with a well-appointed harbour. The coastline from Gordon's Bay to Cape Hangklip consists of a spectacular scenic drive along the mountainside. The vegetation consists of Cape fynbos, including many species of proteas and heather. The prevailing winds are south-east in the summer and north-west in the winter. Place names associated with shipwrecks are Koeëlbaai, a distortion of the 'Cole' in Colebrooke, wrecked there in 1778, and Phoenix Shoal at Simon's Town, named after the English vessel Phoenix wrecked there in 1829. Many of the wrecks in the Muizenberg Beach area have been engulfed in deep sand and are in a remarkable state of preservation.

Admiral Cockburn

British whaling barque of 350 tons, built in 1809 in Philadelphia, and commanded by Capt Lawrence. Wrecked on Muizenberg beach on 27 July 1839 while entering False Bay with a cargo of 1 039 barrels of sperm-whale oil, which was saved. No lives were lost among the 80 crew.
Cape of Good Hope Government Gazette, 9 August 1839
Lloyds Register of Shipping, 1839-40
Shipping Register, Cape Archives, C.C. 2/15

HNMS Bato
34° 11.00S, 18° 25.60E

Dutch warship of 800 tons and 74 guns. Set on fire and sunk off Long Beach, Simon's Town, on 8 January 1806, the same day that the Battle of Blaauwberg began. The Batavian Republic forces at the Cape capitulated to the British forces two days later. The wreck has been worked on and cannon from the site stand outside the Simon's Town Post Office.
Cape Archives, V.C. 80

Benefactress

American barque of 540 tons, commanded by Capt Elridge. Run ashore at the Strand (Louwrens River) on 19 November 1870 after striking a rock

off Agulhas while on a voyage from Yokohama to New York with a cargo of tea. No lives were lost.
Cape Argus, 22 November 1870
Shipping Register, Cape Archives, C.C. 3/7/2/2

Benjamin

British sloop. Wrecked at Gordon's Bay on 22 September 1800 during a gale while proceeding from False Bay to Table Bay.
Cape Town Gazette, 4 October 1800

Brunswick
34° 11.50S, 18° 25.60E

English East-Indiaman of 1 200 tons, commanded by Capt James Grant. Ran aground at Simon's Town on 19 September 1805 after losing three anchors during a south-east gale. While on a howeward-bound voyage with a cargo of cotton and sandal-wood, she was captured by the French Admiral Linois in the Indian Ocean and brought to Simon's Town.
Cape Archives, B.R. 537
Hardy, Horatio Charles, *A Register of Ships in the Service of the English East India Company*, 1813

SS **Clan Stuart**
34° 10.20S, 18° 25.90E

British turret steamer of 3 594 tons, built in 1900 by W. Doxford & Sons, Sunderland, and owned by the Clan Line. Went ashore at Glencairn at 02h00 on 21 November 1914 when she dragged her anchors during a south-east gale after a voyage from St Helena with a cargo of coal. Her steam engine block can be seen protruding from the sea near Simon's Town (1987).
Cape Times, 21, 23 November 1914
Lloyds Register of Shipping, 1914-15

HM Schooner **Cockburn** (ex Steamer *Braganza*)

Purchased by the Royal Navy in Rio de Janeiro in 1822 and commanded by Lieut Jones (RN). Wrecked on Muizenberg beach on 3 April 1823 when her cables parted during a south-east gale after a voyage from Delagoa Bay to Simon's Bay. No lives were lost.
Cape Town Gazette and African Advertiser, 12 April 1823
Shipping Register, Cape Archives, C.C. 2/10

Colebrooke
34° 13.60S, 18° 50.30E

English East-Indiaman of 723 tons and 26 guns, built by Perry, launched in 1770, and commanded by Capt Arthur Morris. Run ashore in the vicinity of Koeëlbaai on 24 August 1778 after striking Anvil Rock off Cape Point while on an outward-bound voyage from the Downs, off

south-east Kent, which she had left in March 1778 in the company of the *Asia*, *Gatton* and *Royal Admiral*, to Bombay with a cargo of lead, copper and military supplies. Several lives were lost. She was worked on in 1984, when lead and copper was recovered. The wreck lies in deep sand.
Cape Archives, V.C. 32
East India Office, London, *Logbook of the Colebrooke*, 10R L/Mar/B/532C
Hardy, Charles, *A Register of Ships in the Service of the English East India Company*, 1800

Drie Gebroeders

Dutch flute of 828 tons, on hire to the Amsterdam Chamber of the Dutch East India Company, and commanded by Jan Roelofsz de Groot. Beached in Simon's Bay on 2 June 1792 after springing a leak and putting into False Bay while on a homeward-bound voyage from Batavia, which she had left on 22 February 1792. Most of her cargo was saved.
Cape Archives, C. 208 (Commission of Enquiry)
Dutch-Asiatic Shipping Homeward Voyages, 1597-1795, The Hague, 1979

Drietal Handelaars

Dutch ship of 502 tons, on hire to the Amsterdam Chamber of the Dutch East India Company, and commanded by Kornelis de Vries. Went to pieces on the rocks at Swartklip on 16 May 1789 after dragging her anchors during a southeast gale while on a homeward-bound voyage from Batavia, which she had left on 27 February 1789 with a cargo of Eastern produce. No lives were lost.
Cape Archives, V.C. 34
Dutch-Asiatic Shipping Homeward Voyages, 1597-1795, The Hague, 1979

Felix Vincidor

Schooner of 140 tons, under the command of Capt W. Boothby (RN). Run ashore at Muizenberg beach on 28 July 1841 at night while on a voyage from St Catherines on Lake Ontario to Simon's Bay with a cargo of wine and spirits. No lives were lost. She was detained by HMS *Clio*.
Shipping Register, Cape Archives, C.C. 2/15

Flamingo

Schooner commanded by Capt Lingard. Wrecked in Buffels Bay after catching alight on 16 August 1833.
Shipping Register, Cape Archives, C.C. 2/12
South African Commercial Advertiser, 21 August 1833 (sale notice)

Johanna Wagner

Prussian barque, commanded by Capt Kempl. Wrecked at Strandfontein near Muizenberg on 17 July 1862 while on a voyage from Batavia to Amsterdam with a cargo of sugar, gall-nuts, india-rubber, tobacco and tin. No lives were lost.
Cape Chronicle, 18, 25 July 1862
Shipping Register, Cape Archives, C.C. 3/7/2/1
South African Advertiser and Mail, 19 July (sale notice and account of wrecking), 6 August (enquiry) 1862

South African Advertiser and Mail

Katwijk aan den Rijn

Dutch hoeker of 750 tons, bought in 1774 by the Amsterdam Yard for the Amsterdam Chamber of the Dutch East India Company. Wrecked in Simon's Bay on 7 October 1786. No lives were lost.
Cape Archives, V.C. 34
Dutch-Asiatic Shipping Outward Voyages, 1595-1794, The Hague, 1979

La Camille

French brig. Wrecked near Farmer Peck's Farm at Strandfontein in False Bay on 18 October 1836 while on a voyage from Réunion with a cargo of sugar, coffee, nutmegs, cloves and tortoiseshell. No lives were lost.
South African Commercial Advertiser, 22 October 1836 (sale notice)

La Pénélope

French frigate of 40 guns. Wrecked on Muizenberg beach on 16 October 1788 with a cargo of military supplies. Most of her crew were saved.
Cape Archives, V.C. 34

Le Protie

French whaling brig of 187 tons, commanded by Capt A. Lory. Wrecked near Farmer Peck's Farm at Strandfontein on 10 January 1839 after trying to enter Simon's Bay at night while on a voyage from Nantes to the whaling grounds with whale-oil on board. No lives were lost.
Shipping Register, Cape Archives, C.C. 2/14
South African Commercial Advertiser, 16 January 1839 (sale notice)

Louise Scheller

German barque of 408 tons, commanded by Capt H. Klocking. Wrecked at Cape Hangklip on 6 June 1882 during a north-west gale after putting into Simon's Bay to restow her cargo while on a voyage from New York to Singapore with a cargo of paraffin oil. The lower tier having leaked out, it was decided to restow at Table Bay. No lives were lost.
Cape Argus, 13 June 1882
Shipping Register, Cape Archives, C.C. 3/7/2/3

Nukteris
34° 19.00S, 18° 27.80E

Schooner, owned by a Mr Auret. Wrecked on the north side of Buffels Bay on 7 August 1897 at night while she was trying to sail out of the bay to Cape Town with a cargo of lime from Cape Point. Four men were drowned.
Cape Argus, 9 August 1897

Padang

Dutch ship of 430 tons, built in 1821, and commanded by Capt G. Ogg. Wrecked on Muizenberg beach at 22h00 on 29 June 1828 while on a voyage from Padang, Sumatra, to Antwerp with a cargo of coffee and spices.
Cape of Good Hope Government Gazette, 4 July 1828 (sale notice)
Lloyds Register of Shipping, 1828
Shipping Register, Cape Archives, C.C. 2/12
South African Commercial Advertiser, 31 December 1828

Parama

American barque, commanded by Capt May. Wrecked opposite the blockhouse in Simon's Bay on 9 October 1862 after her cables parted during a south-east gale with a cargo of coal, two boilers and two chimneys. No lives were lost.
Shipping Register, Cape Archives, C.C. 3/7/2/1
South African Advertiser and Mail, 15 October 1862 (sale notice)

Phoenix
34° 11.40S, 18° 27.00E

British ship of 500 tons, built in 1810, and commanded by Capt T. Cuzins. Wrecked a little seaward of Phoenix Shoal in Simon's Bay on 19 July 1829 while on a voyage from Ceylon with passengers and a cargo of sundries, part of which was saved. No lives were lost. She was armed with two cast iron cannon. Her iron ballast can be seen on the reef, while her stern lies buried in sand.

Cape of Good Hope Government Gazette, 24 July 1829 (sale notice)
Lloyds Register of Shipping, 1829
Shipping Register, Cape Archives, C.C. 2/12
South African Commercial Advertiser, 22 July 1829

Robert

British ship of 595 tons, built in 1843 at New Brunswick, and commanded by Capt N. R. Sayer. Run ashore at Mosterd Bay near Gordon's Bay on 12 February 1847 during a south-east gale after springing a leak while on a voyage from Maulmein, Burma, to London with a cargo of teak. No lives were lost.

Lloyds Register of Shipping, 1847-48
Shipping Register, Cape Archives, C.C. 2/16
South African Commercial Advertiser, 17 February 1847

Rowvonia

Brazilian slaving barque of 300 tons, commanded by Lieut Montgomerie (RN). Wrecked in Simon's Bay on 13 January 1850 after her cables parted during a south-east gale while on a voyage from Quilimane, Mozambique, with a cargo of slaves. No lives were lost. She had been detained by HMS *Pantaloon*.

Cape Town Mail, 26 January 1850
Shipping Register, Cape Archives, C.C. 2/17

Sarpine

Portuguese man-of-war, commanded by Ignatius

Cape Town Gazette

PUBLIEKE VERKOOPING,
Van het Wrak, drie zware Touwen,
een Kabeltouw en eenige enden
Touwwerk, Wanden, Stagen en
verdere Tuigagie, diverse Zei-
len, verscheide Rondhouten,
als : Stengen, Raas en
Blokken, eenige Water-
vaten en Duigen, 1
Barkas, 1 Sloep ;
Zoo mede kopere Ketels en Kombuisge-
reedschap, wat Yzer- en Houtwerk,
Van het Hollandsche Schip
VROUWE IDA ALIDA,
GESTRAND BY MUIZENBURG,
Voor Rekening der Assuradeurs, of
die het mag aangaan.
Op aanstaande Dingsdag den 8 dezer, zullen
per publieke Venditie op het Strand by Muizenburg, de bovengem. Goederen verkocht wor-
den ; als mede het Wrak van het gem. Schip,
zoo als hetzelve aldaar gestrand legt, met de
inhetzelve zich nog bevindiende Goederen, de-
welke calculatief zouden bestaan in 88 vaten
Tamarinde, omtrent 2000 zakken Koffy, 3000
zakken Ryst en 1000 bossen Bindrottings, doch
waarvan een gedeelte kan weggespoeld of an-
derzints door het breken van vaten of zakken
verlooren zyn geraakt.
VOLSTREKT ZONDER RESERVE.

Ferreira. Wrecked near the Hottentots Holland, possibly near Gordon's Bay, in 1691 during a south-east gale while on a voyage from China and Japan with ambassadors for Lisbon. Only five people were saved.

Africana Notes and News, Vol 6, p 49 (original archival source missing)

Vrouw Ida Alida

Dutch ship, commanded by Capt C. Sipkes. Wrecked near St James on 10 November 1818 while on a voyage from Batavia to Amsterdam with a cargo of spices, coffee, rhubarb and comfits.

Cape Town Gazette, 14, 28 November (sale notice) 1818

Waterloo
34° 08.20S, 18° 26.20E

British wooden brig of 215 tons, built in 1815 at Sunderland, and commanded by Capt D. T. Lyon. Wrecked on Fish Hoek beach on 25 October 1821 while loading oil. Part of her cargo was saved. She was from Portsmouth.

Cape Town Gazette, 3 November 1821 (sale notice)
Lloyds Register of Shipping, 1821
Shipping Register, Cape Archives, C.C. 2/10

17. Cape Hangklip to Buffelsjacht River

A beautiful, unspoilt stretch of coast with many points, reefs and sandy beaches. The water is normally fairly warm, but can be icy cold when dominated by water from the Benguela current. The seabed vegetation consists of kelp beds with very few crayfish, but large numbers of perlemoen (abalone). The land is well populated, mainly by retired people and farmers, and the seabed is often visited by divers. The vegetation on land consists of Cape fynbos including many species of proteas and heather. Prominent settlements are Bettys Bay, Kleinmond, Hermanus and Gansbaai. The most dangerous hazards to mariners are Danger Point, which claimed HMS Birkenhead in 1852, and Dyer Island. The main commercial activities are farming and fishing. Place names associated with shipwrecks are Birkenhead Rock, named after the troopship Birkenhead wrecked there in 1852, and Celt Bay, west of Quoin Point, named after the steamer Celt wrecked there in 1875.

Albatross

Norwegian schooner of 117 tons. Wrecked on Danger Point at 02h00 on 24 March 1874 during a fresh south-easterly wind while on a voyage from Knysna to Cape Town with a cargo of wood. The crew left the wreck in boats and landed on Dyer Island.

Cape Argus, 31 March 1874
Shipping Register, Cape Archives, C.C. 3/7/2/2

HMS Birkenhead (ex HMS *Vulcan*)
34° 38.60S, 19° 17.30E

British iron paddle-frigate of 1 400 bm, built in 1845 by Laird, converted to a troopship in 1848, and commanded by Capt R. Salmond. Piled up on Birkenhead Rock off Danger Point on 26 February 1852 at night while on a voyage from Simon's Town to East London with troops for the Frontier War. 445 lives were lost. The wreck has secured a place in history due to the gallantry of her men, who, in the face of great danger, allowed the women and children to escape in the boats before attempting to save themselves – the 'Birkenhead Drill'. Legends of a vast military pay-packet in gold coin have drawn many divers to the site. She lies in about 35 m of water on the west side of the rock.

Addison, A.C., *The Story of the Birkenhead*, 1902
Addison, A.C. and Matthews W.H., *A Deathless Story*, 1906
Shipping Register, Cape Archives, C.C. 2/17
South African Commercial Advertiser, 28 February, 3 March 1852

SS Bulwark (ex *Ruta*, ex *Finland*, ex *Mahmoudiéh*)
34° 37.40S, 19° 17.70E

South African coaster of 1 374 tons, built in 1920 by Caledon Shipbuilding & Engineering Co, Dundee, and commanded by Capt P. A. Potgieter. Wrecked 500 m to the Cape Town side of Danger Point and 150 m offshore on 1 April 1963 in thick fog while on a voyage from Cape Town to Durban with 350 tons of general cargo, fishmeal, food in cans, empty drums and liquor. No lives were lost.

Cape Argus, 1 April 1963 (photograph)
Lloyds Register of Shipping, 1962-63

RMS Celt
34° 44.00S, 19° 35.60E

Iron steam screw brig of 2 112 tons, built in 1865 by the Millwall Shipbuilding Co, London, owned by the Union Company, and commanded by Capt Bird. Wrecked 6,5 km west of Quoin Point (Celt Bay) on 5 February 1875 while on a voyage from London to Algoa Bay with 98 passengers, mail and a cargo of coffee, wine and brandy. No lives were lost.

Cape Argus, 11, 12 February 1875
Lloyds Register of Shipping, 1875-76
Shipping Register, Cape Archives, C.C. 3/7/2/2

De Grundel

Dutch hoeker of 90 tons, built in 1668 at the Delft Yard for the Delft Chamber of the Dutch East India Company. Wrecked a little to the east of Cape Hangklip near Bettys Bay on 20 February 1673 while on a voyage from Batavia to Mauritius with a cargo of 'necessaries'. She had lost her way and was trying to reach the Cape after being shot at in Madagascar by the French, and

losing four men killed and the captain wounded. No lives were lost during the wrecking.
Cape Archives, V.C. 6. Translated into English in *Précis of the Archives of the Cape of Good Hope, Journal, 1671-1674 and 1676*, H. C. V. Leibbrandt, 1902
Dutch-Asiatic Shipping Homeward Voyages, 1597-1795, The Hague, 1979

Edie Waters

American schooner. Wrecked in Celt Bay on 1 March 1876 after her cables parted.
Cape Argus, 4, 7 March (sale notice) 1876
Shipping Register, Cape Archives, C.C. 3/7/2/2

Ellida

Norwegian barque of 309 tons, commanded by Capt Christoffersen. Wrecked on Danger Point on 4 June 1888 during a north-west gale while on a voyage from New York to Natal with a general cargo, most of which was saved. The crew were landed by basket.
Shipping Register, Cape Archives, C.C. 3/7/2/4

Evelyn

Cape wooden schooner of 101 tons, built in 1859 in Newhaven, and commanded by Capt J. Murison. Wrecked on Sunbeam Rock on Danger Point on 18 December 1863 during a northerly wind while on a voyage to Natal with a cargo of sundries. Four lives were lost. The vessel was employed in trade between the Cape and Natal; due to a sore throat the captain had left the vessel in the care of the second officer, the first officer being incapacitated.
Cape Argus, 2, 7 January 1864
Shipping Register, Cape Archives, C.C. 3/7/2/1

George

Cutter. Wrecked in the vicinity of Dyer Island on 13 May 1831 during a north-east gale.
Shipping Register, Cape Archives, C.C. 2/12
South African Commercial Advertiser, 21 May 1831

Gustav Adolph

Norwegian wooden barque of 757 tons, built in 1879 at Arendal and commanded by Capt A. Gjeruldsen. Wrecked near the Palmiet River mouth, near Kleinmond, on 28 June 1902 while on a voyage from Fremantle to Cape Town with a cargo of timber. The captain and three men were drowned.
Cape Times, 1, 2 July 1902
Lloyds Register of Shipping, 1901-02

Hansa

German brig of 295 tons, commanded by Capt E.

Schilthase. Wrecked in the vicinity of Danger Point on 3 June 1883 at night during a north-west wind while on a voyage from Rio de Janeiro to Mossel Bay via Table Bay with a cargo of 6 000 bags of coffee. Six of the nine crew members were drowned, including the captain.
Eastern Province Herald, 15 June 1883
Shipping Register, Cape Archives, C.C. 3/7/2/3

Ispahan
34° 23.40S, 18° 51.70E

British iron full-rigged ship of 1 436 tons, built in 1876 by Richardson, Duck & Co, Stockton, and commanded by Capt D. Fergusson. Wrecked on the east side of Holbaai Punt near Doringbaai (Cape Hangklip) on 1 December 1886 in dense fog while on a voyage from Calcutta to London with a cargo of 2 000 tons of wheat, bone dust, rape seed, poppy seed and linseed. No lives were lost. She has been dived on and her bell has been recovered.
Cape Argus, 4, 6 December 1886
Lloyds Register of Shipping, 1886-87
Shipping Register, Cape Archives, C.C. 3/7/2/4

John

British coasting brig, commanded by Capt Richard Kelly. Wrecked between Kleinriviermond and Franskraal on 16 September 1803 while on a voyage to Algoa Bay. Only five men were saved. The missionary Irwin was among those drowned, and a printing-press on the way to Bethelsdorp was lost. A bronze cannon recovered in this area is believed to have come from this wreck.
Kaapsche Courant, 1 October 1803

John and James

Barque commanded by Capt J. Elliot. Wrecked on Danger Point at 22h00 on 1 September 1844 while on a voyage from Calcutta and Mauritius to London via St Helena. The crew took to the boats and no lives were lost.
Cape of Good Hope Government Gazette, 15 September 1844 (sale notice)
Shipping Register, Cape Archives, C.C. 2/16

Lucy

Cape brig of 186 tons, commanded by Capt Dahl. Wrecked at Birkenhead Rock in the vicinity of Danger Point on 16 February 1864 at night during a south-east gale while on a voyage from Table Bay to East London. No lives were lost.
Cape Argus, 23 February 1864
Shipping Register, Cape Archives, C.C. 3/7/2/1

Malton

British snow of 295 tons, built in 1839 at Sunderland, and commanded by Capt Thomas Fox. Wrecked in Walker Bay on 14 October 1841 after

sunset while on a voyage from Bombay to London with a cargo of cotton. No lives were lost. Walker Bay had been mistaken for Table Bay.
Cape of Good Hope Government Gazette, 22 October 1841
Lloyds Register of Shipping, 1841-42
Shipping Register, Cape Archives, C.C. 2/15
South African Commercial Advertiser, 23 October 1841

Meridian
34° 22.50S, 18° 52.90E

British brig of 144 tons, built in 1818, and commanded by Capt J. Kerr. Wrecked on the east side of Silversands Bay near Cape Hangklip on 19 May 1828 while on a voyage from Singapore and Batavia to Table Bay with a cargo of sundries, including sugar, coffee, pepper, sago, tamarinds, coconut oil, cassia, brown and white nankeens, segara, rattans, rice, sugar candy, tobacco and red fish. No lives were lost. She had arrived in Simon's Bay for repairs on 5 May 1828 after being damaged in a storm. Part of her cargo was removed and she departed on 12 May 1828 for Table Bay for further repairs. She was found in 1985; six cast iron cannon and two anchors are evident on the site.
Cape of Good Hope Government Gazette, 27 May 1828 (sale notice)
Lloyds Register of Shipping, 1828
Shipping Register, Cape Archives, C.C. 2/12
The Colonist, 27 May 1828

Onward

Schooner of 99 tons, commanded by Capt J. Tosh. Wrecked near Zoetfontein in the Caledon district on 14 January 1858 while on a voyage from Cape Town to Mauritius. No lives were lost.
Shipping Register, Cape Archives, C.C. 2/18

Piccadilly

Cape wooden brig of 163 tons, built in 1863 by Taylor, Sunderland. Wrecked in a cove near Celt Bay on 26 November 1877. She had been chartered to salvage teak from the wreck of the British ship *Charmer* wrecked on the north-west point of Dyer Island in 1877. No lives were lost.
Cape Argus, 15, 29 December 1877
Lloyds Register of Shipping, 1877-78
Shipping Register, Cape Archives, C.C. 3/7/2/2

Pisa (ex *F. Caffarena*)

Italian wooden barque of 640 tons, built in 1873 by Rolla, Genoa, and commanded by Capt G. B. Isola. Wrecked near the Bot River on 18 August 1879 after striking a reef off Cape Agulhas while on a voyage from Rangoon to Falmouth with a cargo of 10 000 bags of rice. No lives were lost.
Lloyds Register of Shipping, 1879-80
Shipping Register, Cape Archives, C.C. 3/7/2/3

River Plate

34° 44.60S, 19° 35.70E

Schooner. Wrecked near Buffelsjacht, west of Quoin Point, on 13 May 1878 while trying to make the Buffelsjacht River. No lives were lost.
Shipping Register, Cape Archives, C.C. 3/7/2/3

Verona

Norwegian barque of 700 tons. Abandoned off Cape Hangklip in a sinking condition and driven ashore on 14 August 1902 during a north-west gale while on a voyage from Glasgow to Table Bay with a cargo of coal.
Cape Argus, 16 August 1902
Eastern Province Herald, 18 August 1902

18. Dyer Island

Lying a little east of Danger Point, this island is surrounded by reefs and pinnacles. It is home to a large population of Cape fur seals, and Great White sharks are found in the vicinity in large numbers. The shark attacks during the wrecking of HMS Birkenhead were probably made by such sharks. The seabed vegetation consists of large kelp beds, and the water is normally warm and clear. The area is rarely visited by divers.

Adele

Schooner of 69 tons, commanded by Capt Pleuss. Wrecked on Dyer Island on 21 May 1888 after her cables parted. The crew were brought to Simon's Town by naval boat, without loss of life. She was intending to load guano.
Cape Argus, 31 May 1888
Shipping Register, Cape Archives, C.C. 3/7/2/4

Charmer

British wooden full-rigged ship of 1 024 tons, built in 1854 in the USA. Wrecked on the north-west point of Dyer Island on 24 August 1877 while on a voyage from Maulmein, Burma, to Amsterdam with a cargo of teak. No lives were lost.
Cape Argus, 30 August 1877
Cape Times, 24 August 1877
Lloyds Register of Shipping, 1877-78
Shipping Register, Cape Archives, C.C. 3/7/2/2

SS Clyde (ex *City of Poonah*)

Iron screw-steamer of 1 480 tons, built in 1870 by Connell, Glasgow, owned by the Temperley Line, used for transporting troops, and commanded by Capt A. H. Luckhurst. Wrecked on a reef 1 km north-east of Dyer Island on 3 April 1879 in fine weather while on a voyage from England to Natal with troops and a cargo of Government mail, stores and munitions for use in the Zulu War. No lives were lost, but the mail and cargo was lost.

Lloyds Register of Shipping 1879-80
Shipping Register, Cape Archives, C.C. 3/7/2/3

Emelia

British schooner of 106 tons, built in 1867 in Spain, and commanded by Capt Andrews. Wrecked on the north-east side of Dyer Island on 3 February 1877 during a north-west gale after a voyage from Table Bay to load guano. No lives were lost.
Lloyds Register of Shipping, 1877-78
Shipping Register, Cape Archives, C.C. 3/7/2/2

SS Hektor

Norwegian steel steamship of 3 856 tons, built in 1905 by J. L. Thompson & Sons, Sunderland. Wrecked on Dyer Island on 23 March 1913 in fog while on a voyage from Baltimore to Australia with a cargo of rails.
Cape Argus, 25 March 1913
Lloyds Register of Shipping, 1911-12

SS Imerina

British iron screw steam-coaster of 241 tons, built in 1881 by Campbeltown Shipbuilding Co, owned by the Cape Shipping Co, and commanded by Capt F. Airth. Wrecked on Dyer Island on 18 October 1885 in dense fog while on a voyage from Table Bay to Port Elizabeth with a general cargo, including wheat. She sank 20 minutes after striking, but no lives were lost.
Cape Argus, 20 October 1885
Lloyds Register of Shipping, 1885-86
Shipping Register, Cape Archives, C.C. 3/7/2/3

Kolstrop

German brigantine of 190 tons, commanded by Capt Frahm. Wrecked on a reef off Dyer Island on 11 May 1883 at night while on a voyage from Antwerp to Shanghai with a general cargo consisting of bar iron, horse-shoes, matches and glassware. The captain and crew were picked up by the cutter *Volunteer* and taken to Struis Bay. No lives were lost.
Cape Argus, 24 May 1883
Eastern Province Herald, 30 May 1883
Shipping Register, Cape Archives, C.C. 3/7/2/3

Linneus

Barque commanded by Capt Smith. Wrecked on a reef off Dyer Island on 16 January 1834 while on a voyage from Liverpool to Bombay. The cargo was saved.
South African Commercial Advertiser, 25 January 1834 (sale notice)

Princeport

British wooden ship of 1 269 tons, built in 1874

South African Commercial Advertiser

by Norris, Nova Scotia, and commanded by Capt R. Fletcher. Wrecked on Dyer Island on 16 March 1885 while on a voyage from Calcutta to New York with a cargo of jute. No lives were lost.
Cape Argus, 17, 24 March, 2, 4 April 1885
Lloyds Register of Shipping, 1884-85
Shipping Register, Cape Archives, C.C. 3/7/2/3

19. Buffelsjacht River to Cape Agulhas

A beautiful unspoilt stretch of coastline with many reefs, points and sandy beaches. The water is normally fairly warm, but can be icy cold when dominated by water from the Benguela current. The seabed vegetation consists of sparse beds of kelp. Cape Agulhas, the most southerly tip of Africa, can be considered the most easterly limit of South African kelp. Perlemoen (abalone) is found in great abundance in these beds. The land is sparsely populated, but the seabed is often visited by spearfishermen. The vegetation on land consists of low shrub and fynbos. The most prominent hazard to shipping is Quoin Point with its offshore reefs. The main commercial activities are farming and fishing. The prevailing winds are south-east in summer and south-west in winter. Jessie se Baai at Quoin Point is named after the British ship Jessie wrecked there in 1829.

Adelfotis. (Cape Argus)

SS Adelfotis (ex *Agelef*, ex *Tovelil*, ex *Monica Seed*)

34° 47.30S, 19° 38.50E

Costa Rican screw steamer of 2 310 tons, built in 1925 by the New Waterway Shipbuilding Co,

Schiedam, owned by the Agelef Shipping Co, and commanded by Capt P. Caloudis. Wrecked on a reef 1 km south of Quoin Point on 30 December 1956 in heavy fog and a moderate southeast wind while on a voyage from Bremerhaven to Bombay via Maputo with 3 330 tons of ammonium sulphate in 50-kg bags. No lives were lost.
Cape Argus, 31 December 1956 (photograph)
Cape Times, 31 December 1956 (photographs)
Lloyds Register of Shipping, 1956-57

SS Alcestis

British steel screw steamship of 1 850 tons, built in 1890 by Mackie & Thomson, Glasgow, and commanded by Capt Duff. Struck a sunken wreck 2,5 km off Cape Agulhas and sank on 28 February 1892 while on a voyage from England to Mauritius with a general cargo including Government stores, explosives and railway material.
Eastern Province Herald, 2 March 1892
Lloyds Register of Shipping, 1891-92

SS Avala
34° 47.10S, 19° 38.00E

Yugoslav cargo screw steamer of 6 403 tons, built in 1929 by W. Doxford & Sons, Sunderland, and commanded by Capt Joseph Sikic. Wrecked 1 km offshore on the Cape Town side of Quoin Point on 3 February 1939 in mist while on a voyage from Cardiff to Rangoon with a cargo of beer, wine and 11 000 tons of coal. No lives were lost.
Cape Argus, 3 February 1939 (photographs)
Cape Times, 4 February 1939 (photogarphs)
Lloyds Register of Shipping, 1939-40

Barbara Gordon
34° 46.50S, 19° 41.50E

British wooden barque of 338 tons, built in 1836 at Sunderland, and commanded by Capt J. Lilley. Wrecked on a reef east of Quoin Point near the Ratel River at midnight on 5 May 1853 while on a voyage from Adelaide to Swansea and London with a cargo of 181 bales of wool and

Avala. (George Young)

338 tons of copper ore. Five passengers and one seaman were drowned.
Cape Town Mail, 14, 17 May 1853 (sale notice)
Lloyds Register of Shipping, 1853-54
Shipping Register, Cape Archives, C.C. 2/18

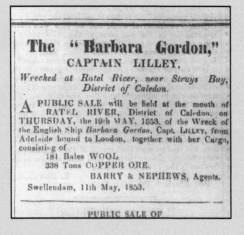

The "Barbara Gordon,"
CAPTAIN LILLEY,
Wrecked at Ratel River, near Struys Bay, District of Caledon.

A PUBLIC SALE will be held at the mouth of RATEL RIVER, District of Caledon, on THURSDAY, the 19th MAY, 1853, of the Wreck of the English Ship *Barbara Gordon*, Capt. LILLEY, from Adelaide bound to London, together with her Cargo, consisting of
181 Bales WOOL
338 Tons COPPER ORE.
BARRY & NEPHEWS, Agents.
Swellendam, 11th May, 1853.

PUBLIC SALE OF

Cape Town Mail

Brederode

Dutch East-Indiaman of 1 150 tons, built in 1780 at the Amsterdam Yard for the Amsterdam Chamber of the Dutch East India Company, and commanded by Capt Gottlieb Mulder. Ran on to a reef off Cape Agulhas and was wrecked on 3 May 1785 while on a homeward-bound voyage from China, which she had left on 27 January 1785. Twelve lives were lost and 80 saved. The cargo was also lost. She most probably lies on the west side of Cape Agulhas.
Cape Archives, V.C. 34
Dutch-Asiatic Shipping Homeward Voyages, 1597-1795, The Hague, 1979

SS Camphill
34° 50.00S, 19° 59.20E

British steel screw steamship of 3 988 tons, built in 1906 by Ropner & Son, Stockton. Wrecked west of the Cape Agulhas lighthouse on 27 March 1913 in thick mist while on a voyage from Bassein, Burma, to Buenos Aires with a cargo of rice. Three men died when the main steam-pipe burst.
Cape Argus, 27, 28 March 1913
Lloyds Register of Shipping, 1911-12

Doncaster

British barque of 235 tons, built in 1825 in London, and commanded by Capt G. Pritchard. Wrecked about 21 km west of Cape Agulhas in a small, rocky, kelp-fringed bay about 1 km in extent near the Ratel River on 17 July 1836 while on a voyage from Mauritius to London with troops and passengers. All lives were lost; 38 bodies of men, women and children were interred after being found on the beach.
Cape of Good Hope Government Gazette, 5 August, 2 September 1836
Graham's Town Journal, 18 August 1836
Lloyds Register of Shipping, 1836-37
South African Commercial Advertiser, 30 July, 27 August 1836

Duchess of Buccleugh

British wooden barque of 404 tons, built in 1843 at Shields, and commanded by Capt W. Bell. Run ashore on a sandy beach close to the Ratel River at Quoin Point on 13 June 1850 after losing her rudder while on a voyage from Calcutta to London with a cargo of indigo, rice, sugar and silk. No lives were lost.
Cape Town Mail, 15 June 1850
Lloyds Register of Shipping, 1850-51
Shipping Register, Cape Archives, C.C. 2/17

Eagle Wing

British wooden schooner of 175 tons, built in 1868 by Moore, Dartmouth, and commanded by Capt W. Blake. Wrecked at Quoin Point on 22 February 1879 during a gale. Four of the seven crew members were drowned.
Lloyds Register of Shipping, 1878-79
Shipping Register, Cape Archives, C.C. 3/7/2/3

SS Eastern Province
34° 46.60S, 19° 47.80E

British iron screw steamer of 784 tons, built in 1864 by Laing, Sunderland, owned by the Diamond Steamship Co, and commanded by Capt Wilson. Wrecked on the rocks near Mr Van Breda's farm Visch Vlei near Quoin Point on 26 June 1865 while on a voyage from Port Eliza-

beth to Falmouth. No lives were lost, but part of her cargo was lost.

Cape Argus, 13 July 1865
Lloyds Register of Shipping, 1865-66
Shipping Register, Cape Archives, C.C. 3/7/2/1
South African Advertiser and Mail, 28 June, 19, 20, 22, 31 July 1865

SS **Esso Wheeling**
34° 46.80S, 19° 37.70E

American T2 tanker of 10 172 tons, built in 1944 by the Alabama Dry Dock & Shipbuilding Co, Mobile, owned by the Standard Oil Company, and commanded by Capt William White. Wrecked on a reef off Quoin Point at 24h00 on 5 November 1948 while on a voyage from Santos to Abadan in ballast. No lives were lost.

Cape Argus, 5 November 1948 (photograph)
Lloyds Register of Shipping, 1948-49

SS **Fynd** (ex *Toureau*)
34° 46.60S, 19° 38.40E

Salvage vessel of 167 tons, built in 1911 by Porsgrund Mek. Vaerks, Porsgrund, and owned by the salvage expert Capt Van Delden. Ran aground on 10 December 1946 after a line got caught around her propeller while trying to pull the salvage vessel *Swona* off Quoin Point. No lives were lost. She was employed to ferry cargo from the *City of Lincoln*, which had run aground on 9 November 1946, but which was later pulled off.

Cape Argus, 11 December 1946
Lloyds Register of Shipping, 1946-47

Gloria Deo

Italian barque of 977 tons, commanded by Capt Schiappacassa. Wrecked on a reef in the vicinity of the Ratel River on 29 June 1882 while on a voyage from Singapore and Rangoon to Falmouth with a cargo of rice and rattans. No lives were lost.

Cape Argus, 3, 5 July 1882
Shipping Register, Cape Archives, C.C. 3/7/2/3

Grace

British ship of 250 tons, built in 1811 at Ipswich, and commanded by Capt Robert Lethbridge. Ran ashore east of Quoin Point on 4 June 1822 after catching fire and being abandoned while on a voyage from Port Jackson to London with a cargo of wool and grain oil. No lives were lost.

Cape Archives, C.O. 2640, No 53
Lloyds Register of Shipping, 1822

Isaac

Sloop commanded by Capt Davies. Wrecked west of Struis Bay on 6 March 1847. No lives were lost.

Cape of Good Hope and Port Natal Shipping & Mercantile Gazette, 26 March 1847

Japarra

Dutch barque of 465 tons, commanded by Capt I. T. Kley. Wrecked on Quoin Point on 3 October 1856 while on a voyage from Holland to Table Bay. Eleven bodies were buried.

Shipping Register, Cape Archives, C.C. 2/18

Jessie
34° 46.70S, 19° 38.40E

British ship of 274 tons, built in 1826, registered in London and commanded by Capt Thomas Winter. Wrecked on the rocks at Jessie se Baai at Quoin Point on 7 October 1829 at night during a westerly gale with big swells and mist while on a voyage from London to Algoa Bay and Mauritius via Table Bay with passengers and a general cargo including wine, corn, spirits and horses. Many lives were lost. The survivors took to the boats and eventually came ashore 11 km west of the Breede River. Parts of her hull came ashore at the Ratel River.

Cape of Good Hope Government Gazette, 13 November 1829 (advertisement)
Lloyds Register of Shipping, 1829
Shipping Register, Cape Archives, C.C. 2/12
South African Commercial Advertiser, 24 October 1829 (poem 'Loss of *Jessie*')
South African Library Manuscript Collection, M.S.B. 527

South African Commercial Advertiser

LINES ON THE LOSS OF THE JESSIE, BARK, *Off Cape L'Aguillas, on the night of* Wednesday, *Oct.* 7, 1829.

How late as to the fav'ring breeze
  Her dazzling canvas proudly bent,
The gallant Jessie swam the seas,
  All eyes admiring as she went!

Of fair friends who on shore remain,
  White hands are wav'd and 'kerchiefs float;
And eyes at length are stain'd in vain
  To mark the forms on which they float.

Hope's visions dance before their sight;
  No damp of fear the voy'gers feel;
Quick o'er the waters, blue and bright,
  Their bosoms bound, as bounds their keel.

Then little thought they yon bright sun,
  That glitter'd on their heaving stem,
When that day's glad career was run,
  Would rise no more for some of them.

Night came: a tempest swept the deep;
  The fitful moon all feebly shone;
An anxious watch the seamen keep;
  The freshning gale impels them on.

One moment—and before the blast
  The gallant bark sublimely rode;
Another—and above her mast
  The welt'ring billows fiercely flow'd.

And where are they—the thirty souls
  Whom late that vanish'd vessel bore?
The sullen wave above them rolls,—
  Yet some have reach'd the distant shore.

And there they sit forlorn, and bend
  O'er the wild wave their eager view,
If more the ruthless sea might send
  To join them, of that fated crew.

In vain:—no more may reach the land;
  The inmost chambers of the main
The fairest of that once gay band
  Within their gloomy bounds detain.

No more their hearts' warm pulses bound—
  The young, the beautiful, the gay;
Now not a rock in ocean's round,
  More senseless and more cold than they!

Unheard of them, their dirge forlorn
  Is sung by night winds moaning loud—
Themselves the sport of tempest borne,
  Wrapt in a wave their restless shroud!

Cape Town.   W. C.

Johanna
34° 46.20S, 19° 42.10E

English East-Indiaman of 550 tons, commanded by Capt Robert Brown. Wrecked on the outside reef at 'Die Dam', a little east of Quoin Point early in the morning on 8 June 1682 while on an outward-bound voyage from the Downs, off south-east Kent, which she had left on 24 February 1682 in the company of the *Williamson*, *Nathaniel*, *Welvaert* and *Samson*. Her cargo consisted of 70 chests of pieces-of-eight and silver bullion for the English factories in Bengal. Olof Bergh, a Dutch East India Company official, recovered some specie at the time, but the wreck then lay untouched until 1982, when 23 000 cob coins and 300 kg of silver bullion in the form of 27 silver discs were recovered. Forty-four cast iron cannon litter the site, which is in a sandy area.

Cape Archives, V.C. 9

La Souvénance

French barque of 796 tons, commanded by Capt Brunettau. Wrecked at Quoin Point on 19 May 1871 while on a voyage from Pondicherry, India, to the West Indies with 400 Indian emigrants, 20 crew and a cargo of jute. All lives were lost.

Cape Argus, 23, 27 May (sale notice) 1871
Shipping Register, Cape Archives, C.C. 3/7/2/2

Le Centaure
34° 48.10S, 19° 55.20E

French ship. Wrecked a little west of Cape Agulhas on 19 January 1750 in fine weather while on a voyage from Mauritius to France. Four hundred passengers and crew eventually reached Cape Town.

Cape Archives, V.C. 26

Nicobar
34° 46.80S, 19° 38.30E

Danish East-Indiaman, commanded by Capt Andreas Christij. Wrecked on Quoin Point on 11 July 1783 while on an outward-bound voyage from Copenhagen, which she had left on 1 July 1782, to Bengal. Only eleven people survived the wrecking. She had arrived in False Bay on 19 May 1783 after a disasterous voyage during which many of her crew members had died. After negotiating with the Dutch East India Company she took on board two Indian girls and seven lascars who had survived the *Grosvenor* wreck (1782). She sailed from False Bay on 10 July in the company of the *Kroonprins*. Soon after the wreck occurred, it was looted by some farmers from the Stellenbosch district. The wreck site was discovered in 1987 and a large amount of Swedish copper plate money (kopperplatmynt) was recovered. Twelve cast iron muzzle-loading cannon litter the site.

Cape Archives, V.C. 33, C. 165

North-East

British iron barque of 1 022 tons, built in 1863 at Chester, and commanded by Capt J. L. Fawkes. Wrecked in the vicinity of the Ratel River, near Quoin Point, on 31 December 1872 during a south-east gale with a cargo of 355 000 cigars, 43 cases of pearl shells, 128 bales of hides, 17 424 bags of sugar and 5 070 bales of hemp or jute. No lives were lost.
Lloyds Register of Shipping, 1872-73
Shipping Register, Cape Archives, C.C. 3/7/2/2

R. P. Buck

American barque of 926 tons, commanded by Capt F. A. Curtis. Wrecked 24 km west of Cape Agulhas near the Ratel River on 4 April 1877 in thick fog while on a voyage from Robalingo to Falmouth with a cargo of sugar. No lives were lost.
Shipping Register, Cape Archives, C.C. 3/7/2/2.

Racer

British wooden brigantine of 249 tons, built in 1874 by Keefe, Prince Edward Island, and commanded by Capt J. Moody. Wrecked 14,5 km east of Quoin Point on 27 January 1879 while on a voyage from Mossel Bay in ballast. No lives were lost.
Lloyds Register of Shipping, 1878-79
Shipping Register, Cape Archives, C.C. 3/7/2/3

SS Swona
34° 46.50S, 19° 38.40E

Salvage vessel of 313 tons, built in 1925 by Smiths Dock Co, Middlesbrough, and owned by the salvage expert Capt Van Delden. Wrecked on Quoin Point on 10 December 1946 after she lost her propellor and anchored to await assistance; a north-west gale caused her cables to part and she ran aground. No lives were lost during the wrecking. She was being used to ferry cargo from the *City of Lincoln*, which had run aground on 9 November 1946, but which was later refloated. Capt Van Delden was killed during salvage work when a hatch-cover on board the *City of Lincoln* blew off.
Cape Argus, 11 December 1946
Lloyds Register of Shipping, 1946-47

20. Cape Agulhas to Struis Point

This stretch of coastline is dominated by the long white beach of Struis Bay, which is a popular holiday venue. The area is well-populated and many divers visit the reefs off Cape Agulhas, mainly in pursuit of fish. The water is normally warm and clear, influenced by the Agulhas current which flows westward. The underwater reefs are sparsely vegetated but reef fish are found in great abundance. The vegetation on land consists of low scrub. The most hazardous area for shipping is the Agulhas Point area, where reefs jut out into the sea. The prevailing winds are south-east in summer and south-west in winter. Place names associated with shipwrecks are Northumberland Point at Cape Agulhas, named after the English East-Indiaman Duke of Northumberland *wrecked there in 1838;* Skoonbergbaai, *named after the Dutch East Indiaman* Schonenberg *wrecked there in 1722;* Soetendalsvlei, *named after the Dutch East-Indiaman* Zoetendaal *wrecked nearby in 1673; and St Mungo Point and Bay at Cape Agulhas, named after the British barque* St Mungo *wrecked there in 1844.*

Albert

Cape oak schooner of 189 tons, built in 1844 in Dundee, and commanded by Capt J. Morton. Wrecked in Struis Bay on 5 February 1857 after striking a reef off Danger Point while on her way from Table Bay to East London with a cargo of 6 logs of teak, 1 log of memel, 9 fir spars, 568 deals, 100 boxes of tea, 13 hogsheads of brandy, 25 boxes of tobacco, brass and ironware, 40 hogsheads of wine, 1 iron barge (in pieces), 3 packages for the 80th Regiment, 18 packages for the 73rd Regiment, 13 packages for the 60th Rifles, 51 packages of furniture, 225 boxes of flour and meal, 50 boxes of soap, 4 quarter cases of vinegar, 21 cases of bottled fruit, cottons, woollens and saddlery. No lives were lost, and part of the cargo was saved.
Cape Argus, 11, 14, 25 February, 21 March 1857
Lloyds Register of Shipping, 1856-57
Shipping Register, Cape Archives, C.C. 2/18

Barrys I

British wooden schooner of 149 tons, built in 1841 at Hull, and commanded by Capt J. Dixon. Wrecked in Struis Bay on 4 April 1848 at night after her cables parted during a south-east gale with a cargo of 300 bales of wool and 400 muids of grain. No lives were lost.
Cape Town Mail, 15 April 1848
Lloyds Register of Shipping, 1848-49
Shipping Register, Cape Archives, C.C. 2/17

Bodiam Castle

British wooden schooner of 182 tons, built in 1847 at Rye, and commanded by Capt E. Hilder. Wrecked on Struis Point on 13 August 1852 while on a voyage from Algoa Bay to London via Table Bay. The captain, four men and a boy were drowned.
Lloyds Register of Shipping, 1852-53
Shipping Register, Cape Archives, C.C. 2/18

Borderer
34° 42.60S, 20° 14.40E

British iron ship of 1 062 tons, built in 1864 by Lawrie, Glasgow, and commanded by Capt J. Laback. Struck the middle blinder of the reef off Struis Point on 27 October 1868 during a wester-ly wind and sank in 38 m of water while on a voyage from Penang to London with a cargo of rum, rattans, pepper, hides, sugar, horns, tapioca and a large cargo of tin ingots. A boat-load of her crew were drowned. Most of the tin was salvaged in 1977.
Cape Standard, 31 October, 12 November 1868
Lloyds Register of Shipping, 1868-69
Shipping Register, Cape Archives, C.C. 3/7/2/2
South African Advertiser and Mail, 6 November 1868

C.P.

French barque. Wrecked at Struis Bay on 5 October 1874 after her cables parted. She broke up within half an hour and seven men died.
Cape Argus, 8 October 1874
Shipping Register, Cape Archives, C.C. 3/7/2/2

Drei Thürme

German brig of 200 tons, commanded by Capt C. Sienan. Wrecked on Struis Point at 02h00 on 30 December 1854 during a south-east gale while on a voyage from Zanzibar to the West Coast of Africa. Two crew members were drowned.
Shipping Register, Cape Archives, C.C. 2/18

Duke of Northumberland
34° 48.10S, 20° 03.90E

English East-Indiaman (ship) of 608 tons, built in 1831 at Newcastle, and commanded by Capt G. Wood. Wrecked on Northumberland Point, a little east of Cape Agulhas, at 24h00 on 25 August 1838 while on a homeward-bound voyage from Madras to London with a 600-ton cargo of silks, indigo, cotton, ebony, redwood, coffee and iron. No lives were lost, but her cargo could not be saved.
Cape of Good Hope Government Gazette, 31 August 1838
Lloyds Register of Shipping, 1838-39
South African Commercial Advertiser, 5 September 1838

Dundrennan

British iron ship of 1 950 tons, built in 1880 by Oswald Mordaunt & Co, Southampton, and commanded by Capt H. A. Palmer. Wrecked on Struis Point on 6 April 1895 in fog while on a voyage from Chittagong to Dundee with a cargo of jute. Twenty-five men, including the captain, were lost.
Cape Argus, 8 April 1895
Lloyds Register of Shipping, 1895-96

E. A. Oliver

British ship of 692 tons, commanded by Capt C. H. Gale. Struck Struis Point and was beached in Struis Bay on 14 January 1873 while on a voyage from Shanghai to New York with a cargo

of 15 035 packages of merchandise, 19 bales of straw hats, 1 case of silk and 2 cases of curios and tea. No lives were lost.
Cape Argus, 4 March 1873 (sale notice)
Shipping Register, Cape Archives, C.C. 3/7/2/2

Edward

British ship. Wrecked in Struis Bay between Soetendalsvlei mouth and Skoonbergbaai 8 km east of Cape Agulhas in 1809. The crew and cargo were saved.
Moodie, D., *The Record*, Part 5, p 29
Theal, G.M., *Records of the Cape Colony*, Vol 7, p 131

Elise

German schooner of 122 tons, commanded by Capt T.C. Rittmann. Wrecked in Struis Bay on 12 June 1879 during a south-west gale while on a voyage to Table Bay with a cargo of 400 bags of grain. No lives were lost.
Shipping Register, Cape Archives, C.C. 3/7/2/3

Ellen

British wooden barque of 309 tons, built in 1848 in Belfast, and commanded by Capt Sullivan. Wrecked on Struis Point on 1 September 1861 while on a voyage from Colombo with a cargo of 217 bales of cotton, coffee, cinnamon oil and curios. No lives were lost.
Cape Chronicle, 13 September 1861
King William's Town Gazette, 13 September 1861
Lloyds Register of Shipping, 1861-62
Shipping Register, Cape Archives, C. C. 3/7/2/1

Equator

British composite wood and iron brig of 235 tons, built in 1845 at Liverpool, and commanded by Capt A. R. Henderson. Wrecked in Struis Bay on 7 February 1856.
Cape of Good Hope Shipping and Mercantile Gazette, 8 February 1856
Lloyds Register of Shipping, 1855-56
Shipping Register, Cape Archives, C.C. 2/18

Gentoo

American ship commanded by Capt Hollis. Wrecked on Northumberland Point, Struis Bay at 22h00 on 29 April 1846 while on a voyage from Calcutta to Boston with a cargo of indigo, shellac, saltpetre and hides. Seven lives were lost. Among the survivors were a number of servant girls who had been engaged by wealthy Cape Town citizens. They soon drifted into prostitution, and to this day prostitutes are called 'gentoos' by the Cape Malays.
Shipping Register, Cape Archives, C.C. 2/16
South African Commercial Advertiser, 6 May 1846 (sale notice)

Juno
34° 50.00S, 20° 01.00E

Dutch barque of 631 tons, commanded by Capt W. J. Chevalier. Wrecked on the point of Cape Agulhas, directly under the lighthouse, at 13h00 on 2 March 1852 in dense fog while on a voyage from Batavia to Rotterdam with a cargo of coffee, sugar, rattans and tin blocks. Five passengers were drowned.
Shipping Register, Cape Archives, C.C. 2/17

La Jardinière

French ship commanded by Nicholas Boudin. Wrecked in Struis Bay in 1794 while on a homeward-bound voyage from Bombay. The captain was charged with having abducted a slave from the Cape during a previous voyage and releasing him in Bombay.
Cape Archives, C.J. 651

La Lise

French ship commanded by Captain Le Cacheuf. Wrecked in Struis Bay on 9 March 1840 at night while on a voyage from Mauritius to Bordeaux. She came ashore near St Mungo Point. Twenty men drowned, including her captain and mate.
Shipping Register, Cape Archives, C.C. 2/15
South African Commercial Advertiser, 18 March 1840
South African Library Manuscript Collection, M.S.B. 190

Lord Hawkesbury

British whaler under the command of the French. She had been taken as a prize off the coast of Brazil and was on her way to Mauritius. In May 1796 she was run ashore near Soetendalsvlei near Cape Agulhas by one of the three English sailors who had remained on board to help the 13 Frenchmen – he had the helm at the time. No lives were lost, but the French prize crew were then taken prisoner by the British.
Cape Archives, B.O. 48, B.O. 146, B.O. 147, B.O. 160, 1/STB 10/9

Mackay

British wooden barque of 384 tons, built in 1864, registered in Liverpool, and commanded by Capt E. Williams. Wrecked off Struis Point on 13 September 1871 while on a voyage from Algoa Bay to Cape Town with a cargo of wool. No lives were lost.
Lloyds Register of Shipping, 1871-72
Shipping Register, Cape Archives, C.C. 3/7/2/2

Meermin

Dutch hoeker of 450 tons, built in 1759 at the Amsterdam Yard for the Amsterdam Chamber of the Dutch East India Company, and used by the Cape authorities. Wrecked at Cape Agulhas on 9 April 1766 after the 140 slaves she was carrying from Madagascar tried to take control of the vessel in order to return home.
Cape Archives, V.C. 30
Dutch-Asiatic Shipping Homeward Voyages, 1597-1795, The Hague, 1979

Mentor

Dutch vessel of 1 150 tons, built in 1774 at the Amsterdam Yard for the Dutch East India Company, and commanded by Johan de Korte. Wrecked on a reef off Cape Agulhas on 5 January 1780 during a heavy storm while on a homeward-bound voyage from Batavia, which she had left on 27 October 1779. Only two men survived.
Cape Archives, V.C. 33
Dutch-Asiatic Shipping Homeward Voyages, 1597-1795, The Hague, 1979

Montgomery

American ship commanded by Capt Constant. Wrecked at Agulhas Point at 21h00 on 15 March 1847 during a south-east gale while on a voyage from Manila to Boston. No lives were lost. The following cargo washed ashore: 42 bales of hides, 150 piculs of rattans, 49 chests of indigo, 13 pieces of ebony, 30 cases of gamboge, 15 cases of gum benjamin, 93 bags of cubebs, 3 133 piculs of sapan wood, 1 060 bales of hemp, 837 coils of cordage, 200 chests of camphor and 490 piculs of gambier.
Shipping Register, Cape Archives, C.C. 2/16
South African Commercial Advertiser, 24 March 1847 (sale notice)

Nossa Senhora dos Milagros

Portuguese East-Indiaman commanded by Don Emmanual de Silva. Wrecked near Cape Agulhas on 16 April 1686 at night while on a homeward-bound voyage from Goa, which she had left on 27 January 1686 with Jesuit priests, three ambassadors from the King of Siam and a cargo of pepper and saltpetre on board. Many people lost their lives and the survivors tried to reach Cape Town. Olof Bergh stole jewels from this wreck and was sentenced to three years imprisonment on Robben Island.
Cape Archives, V.C. 10

MV Oriental Pioneer
34° 48.50S, 20° 05.30E

Chinese bulk carrier of 58 926 tons, built in 1966 by Sasebo Heavy Industries, Japan, and commanded by Capt H. R. Chizen. Run ashore off Northumberland Point at Cape Agulhas on 22 July 1974 after springing a leak while on a voyage from Maputo to Europe fully laden with 50 000 tons of iron ore. She has been a landmark (1987) ever since.
Argus, 23 July 1974
Lloyds Register of Shipping, 1974-75

Oriental Pioneer. *(Ferguson Collection)*

Port Fleetwood

British wooden schooner of 180 tons, built in 1840 in Aberdeen, and commanded by Capt R. Vidler. Wrecked on a sandy beach in Struis Bay on 15 September 1846 after her anchor cables parted with a cargo of 7 600 ox and buffalo hides and 6 500 goat skins. No lives were lost. This was her second accident, as she had previously struck the bar at the Breede River on 5 January 1845.
Lloyds Register of Shipping, 1846-47
Shipping Register, Cape Archives, C.C. 2/16
South African Commercial Advertiser, 3 October 1846 (sale notice)

Saksenburg

Cape provision-ship of 610 tons, built in 1723 at the Amsterdam Yard for the Amsterdam Chamber of the Dutch East India Company. Wrecked off Cape Agulhas on 8 January 1730 after leaking so badly that the crew were obliged to jettison her guns, while on a voyage from Batavia to the Cape with a cargo of rice. Out of 88 people on board, only seven were saved.
Cape Archives, V.C. 23. Translated into English in *Précis of the Archives of the Cape of Good Hope, Journal, 1699-1732*, H.C.V. Leibbrandt, 1896
Dutch-Asiatic Shipping, 1595-1795, The Hague, 1979

SS Sceptre (ex Ary)

British cargo vessel of 5 280 tons, built in 1921 by Craig, Taylor & Co, Stockton, and commanded by Capt Newman. Wrecked on the rocks 900 m offshore off Northumberland Point, 8 km from Cape Agulhas, on 22 May 1925 at night while on a voyage from Cardiff to Mauritius with a cargo of coal. The crew were saved in the boats.
Cape Argus, 23, 25 May 1925
Lloyds Register of Shipping, 1924-25

Schonenberg

Dutch East-Indiaman of 800 tons, built in 1717 at the Amsterdam Yard for the Amsterdam Chamber of the Dutch East India Company, and commanded by Albert van Soest. Wrecked in Skoonbergbaai near Cape Agulhas on 20 November 1722 while on a homeward-bound voyage from Batavia in the company of the *Anna Maria*. She ran ashore in fine weather due to the negligence of her officers. No lives were lost.
Cape Archives, V.C. 22. Translated into English in *Précis of the Archives of the Cape of Good Hope, Journal, 1699-1732*, H.C.V. Leibbrandt, 1896
Dutch-Asiatic Shipping Homeward Voyages, 1597-1795, The Hague, 1979

Scotland

British ship of 969 tons, commanded by Capt Bolase. Wrecked on Montgomery Point on 27 June 1860 at night after having put into Struis Bay while on a voyage from Aden to Pensacola in ballast. No lives were lost, and most of the baggage was saved.
Shipping Register, Cape Archives, C.C. 3/7/2/1

South American

American wooden ship of 1 694 tons, built in 1876 in Boston, Massachusetts, and commanded by Capt Connolly. Wrecked at Struis Bay on 17 September 1889 in thick fog while on a voyage from Hsito to New York with a cargo of sugar. No lives were lost.
Eastern Province Herald, 27 September 1889
Lloyds Universal Register of Shipping, 1889-90
Shipping Register, Cape Archives, C.C. 3/7/2/4

Sparfel

French schooner. Wrecked on the rocks at Struis Point on 4 September 1869. There were no survivors.
Shipping Register, Cape Archives, C.C. 3/7/2/2

St Mungo
34° 49.40S, 20° 01.75E

British barque of 355 tons, built in 1839, and commanded by Capt W. H. Lamond. Wrecked on St Mungo Point, 1 km east of Cape Agulhas, at 05h00 on 20 September 1844 during calm but foggy weather while on a voyage from Calcutta to Newcastle, England, with a cargo of sugar, rice, linseed, castor oil, jute, 1 800 ox and buffalo-hides and teak. Only seven, including the captain, out of a total crew of seventeen survived.
Lloyds Register of Shipping, 1844-45
Shipping Register, Cape Archives, C.C. 2/16

Venerable

Brig commanded by Capt McKay. Wrecked in Struis Bay on 22 February 1840 at night while on a voyage from Mauritius to Cork with a cargo of 6 091 bags of sugar, all of which was lost. No lives were lost.
Shipping Register, Cape Archives, C.C. 2/15

SS Waldensian

Rennies iron screw steamer of 369 tons, built in 1856 at Greenock, and commanded by Capt W. A. Joss. Wrecked on Bulldog Reef on Struis Point on 13 October 1862 at night during a light south-east wind while on a voyage from Durban to Cape Town with the Christy Minstrels and eight Dutch ministers on board. Mr Joe Brown of the Christy Minstrels lost a silver belt encrusted with precious stones earned in recognition of his work. The *Waldensian* was a sister ship to the *Madagascar*, wrecked at the Bira River in 1858. No lives were lost.
Cape Argus, 21 (sale notice), 23 October (enquiry), 20 November, 6 December 1862
Lloyds Register of Shipping, 1862-63
Shipping Register, Cape Archives, C.C. 3/7/2/1

Zoetendaal

Dutch flute of 448 tons, built in 1669 at the Zeeland Yard for the Enkhuizen Chamber of the Dutch East India Company, and commanded by Jan Block. Wrecked in Struis Bay on 23 August 1673 while on a homeward-bound voyage from Batavia, in the company of the *Gooiland*, with a cargo of rice. Four crew were drowned.
Cape Archives, V.C. 6. Translated into English in *Précis of the Archives of the Cape of Good Hope, Journal, 1671-1674 and 1676*, H. C. V. Leibbrandt, 1902
Dutch-Asiatic Shipping Homeward Voyages, 1597-1795, The Hague, 1979

21. Struis Point to Still Bay

A long stretch of coastline consisting of reefs and sandy beaches. The area is sparsely populated and is not often visited by divers. The water is normally warm and clear, due to the Agulhas current which flows westward. The surf is normally heavy and divers must wait for good conditions. The seabed is sparsely vegetated, but reef fish are found in abundance. The vegetation on land consists of shrub interspersed with sand dunes. The most prominent features along this stretch of coast are: Waenhuiskrans (Arniston), a popular tourist resort, and Witsand (Port Beaufort), a small settlement at the mouth of the Breede River. The most hazardous area for shipping is Bulldog or Saxon Reef, which juts out to sea off Waenhuiskrans. The area from Waenhuiskrans to the east includes a restricted military zone. A number of place names are associated with local shipwrecks. Arniston (Waenhuiskrans) is named after the British transport Arniston wrecked there in 1815; Atlas Reef east of Arniston after the Dutch barque Atlas wrecked there in 1859; Martha Point, Reef and Duinen, also east of Arniston, after the British brig Martha wrecked there in 1826; Miles Barton Reef east of Arniston after the British transport Miles Barton wrecked there in 1861; Otterbaai at Struis Point after the Russian barque Otto wrecked there in 1860; Ryspunt east of Arniston after the cargo from a wrecked vessel which washed ashore here and lay more than a metre deep in places; and Skipskop after a figurehead used for many years by a local farmer as a scarecrow.

Amersham

British barque of 781 tons, commanded by Capt Huliman. Wrecked near Arniston on 19 September 1869 during a south-east gale while on a voyage from Akyab, Burma, to Cork with a cargo of rice. No lives were lost.
Eastern Province Herald, 24 September 1869
Shipping Register, Cape Archives, C.C. 3/7/2/2

Arion

German brig of 162 tons, commanded by Capt R. Kayser. Wrecked on the east side of the Breede River on 7 April 1854 after her cables parted. No lives were lost.
Shipping Register, Cape Archives, C.C. 2/18

Arniston
34° 41.40S, 20° 14.60E

British transport ship of 1 498 tons and 22 guns, built in 1794 on the Thames, requisitioned by the Navy, and commanded by Capt George Simpson. Wrecked at Arniston on 30 May 1815 during a storm while on a voyage from Ceylon (Sri Lanka) to England with Viscount and Lady Molesworth and many invalid soldiers on board. Only six out of 378 people were saved. The wreck was worked on in 1982 and many arte-

facts were recovered, including star pagodas, rupees, mercury and jewellery.
Cape Town Gazette, 29 July 1815 (sale notice)
Lloyds Register of Shipping, 1815

Atlas

Dutch barque of 745 tons, commanded by Capt B. Bakker. Wrecked near Martha Duinen (Atlas Reef) in the Bredasdorp district on 18 January 1859 while on a voyage from Batavia to Amsterdam with a cargo of rice, sugar, hides and cane. No lives were lost.
Shipping Register, Cape Archives, C.C. 2/18

Barrys II

Schooner commanded by Capt Hunter. Wrecked after crossing the bar at Port Beaufort (Breede River) on 7 May 1857 during a south-west wind while on a voyage to London via Table Bay with a cargo of 280 bales of wool, 141 muids of barley, 73 muids of beans, 46 casks of brandy, 40 hides, 16 cases of aloes, 1 672 goatskins and 2 562 sheepskins. The captain and two women were drowned when the boat capsized. She lies at the same place as the *Sir William Heathcote* (1841) and close to the *Osmond* (1859).
Cape Argus, 13, 16, 20 May (sale notice) 1857
Shipping Register, Cape Archives, C.C. 2/18

Cape of Good Hope and Port Natal Shipping and Mercantile Gazette, 20 July 1849
Lloyds Register of Shipping, 1849-50
Shipping Register, Cape Archives, C.C. 2/17

Cape of Good Hope

Brigantine of 107 tons, commanded by Capt R. Nelson. Wrecked while entering Port Beaufort (Breede River) on 25 November 1881 after a voyage from Montevideo with a cargo of grain. No lives were lost.
Cape Argus, 30 November 1881 (sale notice)
Shipping Register, Cape Archives, C.C. 3/7/2/3

Chancellor

British wooden ship of 864 tons, built in 1848 in New Brunswick, and commanded by Capt J. Turner. Wrecked at Martha Strand near Arniston on 12 September 1854 while on a voyage from Bombay to London. Two crew members were drowned.
Cape of Good Hope Shipping and Mercantile Gazette, 15 September 1854
Lloyds Register of Shipping, 1854-55
Shipping Register, Cape Archives, C.C. 2/18

Cape Argus

WRECK "BARRYS."

PORT BEAUFORT.

A PUBLIC SALE,

FOR ACCOUNT OF WHOM IT MAY CONCERN, WILL BE HELD AT THE MOUTH OF THE "BREEDE RIVER" PORT BEAUFORT,

ON FRIDAY, THE 22ND INSTANT,

Of the Wrecked Schooner "BARRYS," as she now lies, with her MASTS, YARDS, GEAR, &c.; also such Cargo as may be saved and found damaged, originally consisting of—

280 Bales Wool,	1672 Goatskins,
141 Muids Barley,	2562 Sheepskins,
73 Muids Beans, &c.,	40 Hides,
46 Casks Brandy,	16 Cases Aloes.

BARRY & NEPHEWS.

Belleisle

British wooden brigantine of 135 tons, built in 1848 at Nova Scotia, and commanded by Capt J. Dixon. Wrecked on the rocks at St Sebastian Bay on 15 July 1849 at night during a south-east gale while on a voyage from Table Bay to Port Beaufort with a cargo of 724 bars and 64 bundles of iron, 200 bags of sugar, 158 bags of coffee, 158 bags of rice, 22 casks of fish, wine, beer, gin, cheese, cotton, tea, medicine, timber, hats, furniture, 8 casks of hardware, 15 boxes of tin plates and 10 kg of horse-shoes. No lives were lost.

SS Clan Macgregor
34° 36.30S, 20° 20.50E

Clan Line screw steamer of 4 526 tons, built by A. McMillan & Son, Dumbarton. Wrecked near the *Queen of the Thames* (1871) and the *Wigtonshire* (1885) at Martha Point (near Ryspunt) on 30 May 1902 while on her maiden voyage from Durban to New York. No lives were lost.
Cape Times Weekly, 4, 25 June, 16 July 1902
Lloyds Register of Shipping, 1901-02
Shipping Register, Cape Archives, C.C. 3/7/2/6

Clan Macgregor. *(J.A. Parker)*

Claudine

British wooden barque of 452 tons, built in 1811 in Calcutta, and commanded by Capt W. Black. Wrecked near Martha Point on 21 February 1849 in fog while on a voyage from Calcutta to London via Table Bay with a cargo of sugar, rice, rum, indigo, coffee, hemp, jute, castor oil, hides, wine, saltpetre and cigars. No lives were lost.
Cape Town Mail, 3 March 1849 (sale notice)
Lloyds Register of Shipping, 1849-50
Shipping Register, Cape Archives, C.C. 2/17

Etheldreda

British wooden barque of 327 tons, built in 1858 at Sunderland, and commanded by Capt Winsborrow. Wrecked 32 km east of Struis Bay at Martha Strand on 1 December 1865 while on a voyage from Samarang, Java, with a cargo of sugar. No lives were lost.
Lloyds Register of Shipping, 1865-66
Shipping Register, Cape Archives, C.C. 3/7/2/1
South African Commercial Advertiser and Mail, 4 December 1865

Greystoke Castle

British iron ship of 1 878 tons, built in 1886 by R. Williamson & Son, Workington, and commanded by Capt W. Griffiths. Wrecked south of Martha Point on 8 June 1896 while on a voyage from Rangoon to Buenos Aires with a cargo of rice. No lives were lost.
Cape Times, 10 June 1896
Lloyds Register of Shipping, 1896-97

Harriet

Schooner commanded by Capt W. Messum. Wrecked on the lee bank while leaving the Breede River on 8 March 1848 at the start of a voyage to Waterloo Bay with a cargo of grain. She was copper-fastened and had 10-12 tons of lead in her bottom. No lives were lost.
Cape of Good Hope and Port Natal Shipping and Mercantile Gazette, 24 March 1848
Shipping Register, Cape Archives, C.C. 2/17

James Shepherd

British wooden barque of 365 tons, built in 1850 in London, and commanded by Capt J. Hoare. Wrecked near Still Bay on 31 January 1851 while on a voyage from Mauritius to London via Table Bay. No lives were lost.

Lloyds Register of Shipping, 1850-51
Shipping Register, Cape Archives, C.C. 2/17

SS **Kadie**
34° 24.40S, 20° 51.00E

Iron screw steamer of 199 tons, built in 1859 by Denny, Dumbarton, owned by Barry Brothers, and commanded by Capt Fowler. Wrecked on the west bank while entering the Breede River on 17 November 1865. No lives were lost. She traded between Port Beaufort and Cape Town and other ports.
Lloyds Register of Shipping, 1865-66
Shipping Register, Cape Archives, C.C. 3/7/2/1

King George IV

British ship of 470 tons, built in 1820, and commanded by Capt Prissick. Abandoned at sea after a storm and ran ashore on a sandy beach in Sebastian Bay 5 km north-east of 'Klein Fountain' on 16 July 1824 while on a voyage from Mauritius to London with a cargo of sugar, cotton and cloves. No lives were lost.
Cape Town Gazette and African Advertiser, 24 July 1824
Lloyds Register of Shipping, 1824

Locust

Colonial government brig commanded by Godfry Saunders. Filled with water, was abandoned and sold after being careened at the Breede River on 2 September 1824. An attempt was being made to repair her damaged keel.
Cape Town Gazette, 18, 25 September (sale notice) 1824

Marie Élise

French barque commanded by Capt Portal. Wrecked at Klippestrand near Arniston on 6 November 1877 while on a voyage from Réunion to Belleisle with a cargo of 500 tons of sugar. No lives were lost.
Cape Times, 12 (sale notice), 13 November 1877

Cape Times

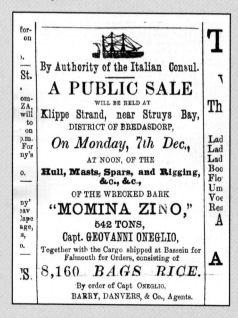

Martha

British brig of 206 tons, built in 1823, and commanded by Capt J. Dobson. Wrecked at Martha Point, east of Arniston, on 24 September 1826 while on a voyage from Mossel Bay to Cape Town with a cargo of stinkwood logs.
Lloyds Register of Shipping, 1826
South African Commercial Advertiser, 7 October 1826

Miles Barton

British wooden transport ship of 1 034 tons, built in 1853 at St Johns, and commanded by Capt J. Shelford. Wrecked near Miles Barton Reef, east of Arniston, on 8 February 1861 while on a voyage from Hong Kong with 320 men of the 3rd Regiment under the command of Maj King. No lives were lost.
Cape Argus, 16 February 1861 (sale notice)
Lloyds Register of Shipping, 1860-61
Shipping Register, Cape Archives, C.C. 3/7/2/1

Minnie

Schooner of 78 tons, commanded by Capt C. Hofman. Wrecked on the bar of the Breede River on 10 June 1874 after a voyage from Table Bay with a general cargo, most of which was saved.
Shipping Register, Cape Archives, C.C. 3/7/2/2

Cape Argus

Momina Zino

Italian barque of 542 tons, commanded by Capt Giovanni Oneglio. Wrecked at Klippestrand, east of Arniston, near the *Queen of the Thames* (1871), on 25 November 1874 in mist and rain while on a voyage from Bassein to Falmouth for orders with a cargo of 8 160 bags of rice. Four lives were lost.
Cape Argus, 28 November, 3 December (sale notice) 1874

Osmond

Danish brig of 207 tons, commanded by Capt J. Harboe. Wrecked close to *Barrys* (1857) on the bar at the Breede River on 13 June 1859. She had been chartered by Barry & Nephew to take a cargo of wool to London.
Cape Weekly Chronicle, 24 June 1859
Shipping Register, Cape Archives, C.C. 2/18

Ospray

Schooner of 71 tons, commanded by Capt J. W. Hunter. Wrecked in St Sebastian Bay on 13 April 1855 after her cables parted.
Shipping Register, Cape Archives, C.C. 2/18

Otto
34° 41.30S, 20° 14.20E

Russian barque of 548 tons, commanded by Capt Blomguitt. Wrecked in Otterbaai on Struis Point on 19 January 1860 while on a voyage from Maulmein, Burma, to Cork with a cargo of teak. No lives were lost.
Shipping Register, Cape Archives, C.C. 3/7/2/1

SS Queen of the Thames
34° 36.00S, 20° 20.50E

Australian Royal Mail Line iron screw steamer of 2 491 tons, built in 1870 by Napier, Glasgow, and commanded by Capt MacDonald. Wrecked at Klippestrand near Ryspunt at 01h00 on 18 March 1871 while on her maiden voyage from Melbourne to Britain with 200 passengers and a cargo of 2 500 bales of wool, 12 000 bags of copper ore, £7 000 worth of gold dust, and preserved meats. A bush-fire had been mistaken for the Agulhas lighthouse. Four people were drowned. Everything of value was stripped off her at the time as she stood high and dry for some time. She lies close to the *Momina Zino* (1874) and near the *Clan Macgregor* (1902). The *Wigtonshire* (1885) is also in the vicinity.
Lloyds Register of Shipping, 1870-71
Shipping Register, Cape Archives, C.C. 3/7/2/2

Sir William Heathcote

British brig of 149 tons, built in 1833 at Sunderland, and commanded by Capt J. Morrison. Wrecked on the sand bank opposite Mrs Dunns while coming out of the Breede River on 15 April 1841. No lives were lost. She lies close to the *Barrys* (1857).
Graham's Town Journal, 29 April 1841
Lloyds Register of Shipping, 1841-42
Shipping Register, Cape Archives, C.C. 2/15

MV Sri Rezeki (ex *Hunzeborg*)
34° 26.10S, 21° 20.00E

Indonesian cargo vessel of 397 tons, built in 1961, and commanded by Capt C. van Beelen.

Sri Rezeki. (Argus)

Wrecked on the rocks at Jongensfontein, 11 km west of Stilbaai, on 6 April 1971 in dense fog while on a voyage from Amsterdam to Durban with a cargo of 6 motor vehicles and 4 elevators.
Argus, 6, 7 April 1971 (photographs)
Lloyds Register of Shipping, 1971-72

SS Umsimkulu

British iron steam coaster of 176 tons, built in 1882 in Paisley, and commanded by Capt F. W. Gardner. Wrecked while leaving the Breede River at Port Beaufort on 16 June 1883. No lives were lost. She was engaged in coastal trade between Natal and Cape Town.
Eastern Province Herald, 20 June 1883
Lloyds Register of Shipping, 1883-84
Shipping Register, Cape Archives, C.C. 3/7/2/3

Wigtonshire

British iron barque of 899 tons, built in 1880 by Russell & Co, Port Glasgow, and commanded by Capt R. W. Furneaux. Wrecked at Klippestrand near Arniston at 24h00 on 7 January 1885 while on a voyage from Calcutta to London with a cargo of jute. No lives were lost. She lies near the *Queen of the Thames* (1871) and the *Clan Macgregor* (1902).
Cape Argus, 9 January 1885
Lloyds Register of Shipping, 1884-85
Shipping Register, Cape Archives, C.C. 3/7/2/3

Willem de Zwyger
34° 36.60S, 20° 19.80E

Dutch barque of 753 tons, commanded by Capt W. L. van den Dries. Wrecked on Martha Point on 30 March 1863 while on a voyage from Batavia to Holland with a cargo of 190 blocks of tin, 12 bronze carronades and mortars, 2 369 canisters of sugar, 450 bales of tobacco and 2 917 bundles of rattans. No lives were lost. Her cargo

was recovered in 1978 and her figurehead can be seen in the Bredasdorp Museum.
Cape Argus, 2, 4 April (sale notice) 1863
Shipping Register, Cape Archives, C.C. 3/7/2/1

22. Still Bay to Cape St Blaize Point

A long, rocky stretch of coast consisting of low rocky reefs interspersed with sandy beaches. The water is normally warm and clear, influenced by the Agulhas current which flows westward, but is pounded by heavy ground swells. The reefs are sparsely vegetated, but reef fish are found in great abundance. The land is sparsely populated and few divers visit the area. The vegetation on land consists of low scrub. The most prominent features along the coast are the Gouritz River mouth, Cape Vacca and Vleespunt. The most hazardous area for shipping is Ystervark Point. The main commercial activity is farming. The prevailing winds are south-east in summer and south-west in winter. Kanonpunt, east of the Gouritz River mouth, is named after cannons believed to have come from the French man-of-war La Fortune, *wrecked there in 1763.*

Elephant

Danish ship commanded by Capt Andries Evertsz Grimstra. Run ashore on purpose close to the Gouritz River on 8 August 1750 while on a homeward-bound voyage from Tranquebar, India, in an effort to save the lives of the desperately sick crew. She was trying to reach Mossel Bay. No lives were lost; her crew of 65 walked to Cape Town.
Cape Archives, V.C. 26

SS Haliartus (ex *Dennistoun*)
34° 23.60S, 21° 41.70E

Houston Line steamer of 5 294 tons, built in 1919 by J. Redhead & Sons, South Shields, and commanded by Capt J. H. Malpas. Wrecked near Ystervark Point, west of the Gouritz River, on 3 May 1932 in dense fog with a cargo of 1 200 cases of whisky, 40 cars, oil, machinery, molasses, tyres, tinned foods, clothing and cyanide. Some of the cargo was salvaged by Capt Van Delden at the time.
Cape Argus, 4 May 1932
Lloyds Register of Shipping, 1931-32

Haliartus. (Dias Museum, Mossel Bay)

La Fortune

French man-of-war. Wrecked opposite the fresh-water spring near Kanonpunt in Visbaai in the Gouritz area on 11 September 1763 while on a voyage from Réunion. No lives were lost. The crew of 441 soldiers and sailors went overland to Cape Town. A cannon is wedged in the rocks and can be seen at very low tide. The vessel anchored at the water-spring to replenish her stocks. All valuables were removed from the wreck at the time. The name 'Franschmanshoek' in the area derives from the Frenchmen who came ashore from the wreck.
Cape Archives, V.C. 29

Melbourne

British wooden ship of 1 170 tons, built in 1853 at Quebec, owned by Wilson & Slaters, Fenchurch Street, London, and commanded by Capt R. Whitehill. Struck rocks 70 m from the shore and wrecked on the rocks at Buffelshoek, 15 km west of the Gouritz River (probably Ystervark Point) on 4 November 1862 during a westerly gale while on a voyage from Shanghai to London with a cargo of 900 tons of tea, 366 bales of cotton, 40 bales of grass cloth fibre, 92 bales of wool, 179 bales of cassia, 13 bales of silk, 5 bales of seeds, 3 bales of copper, 1 box of laquered ware, 6 cases of tongues, 49 boxes of tobacco and spices, worth £120 000. Three lives were lost. A box of goods washed ashore at Brandfontein.
Cape Argus, 11 (sale notice and account of wreck), 18 (sale list and account of wreck), 20 (account of wreck), 29 (enquiry into wreck) November, 20 December 1862
Lloyds Register of Shipping, 1862-63
Shipping Register, Cape Archives, C.C. 3/7/2/1

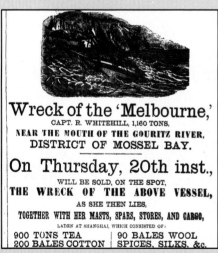

Wreck of the 'Melbourne,'
CAPT. R. WHITEHILL, 1,160 TONS,
NEAR THE MOUTH OF THE GOURITZ RIVER,
DISTRICT OF MOSSEL BAY.

On Thursday, 20th inst.,
WILL BE SOLD, ON THE SPOT,
THE WRECK OF THE ABOVE VESSEL,
AS SHE THEN LIES,
TOGETHER WITH HER MASTS, SPARS, STORES, AND CARGO,
LADEN AT SHANGHAI, WHICH CONSISTED OF:
900 TONS TEA | 90 BALES WOOL
200 BALES COTTON | SPICES, SILKS, &c.

Cape Argus

'Soares Wreck' (unnamed)

On 22 April 1504 a fleet of 13 Portuguese vessels under the overall command of Lopo Soares d'Albergaria sailed from Lisbon on an expedition to bombard Calicut in India. On the return voyage the two fastest vessels were sent ahead to report on affairs in India. One of these vessels, under the command of Pero de Mendonca, ran ashore a little to the west of Mossel Bay in 1505. The disaster took place at night and the whole crew was lost. The vessel was heavily armed and carried a cargo of pepper. In November 1505 two vessels left Lisbon to take military supplies and stores to Sofala and also to search for possible survivors from the wreck. The vessels anchored in Mossel Bay and sent a convict and a ship's boy to search the coast; after three days' travelling along the coast they found only a mast and a skeleton.
Barros, João de, *Da Asia* 1-2, Lisbon, 1771
Theal, G.M., *History of South Africa*, Vol 2, 1922

Star of the East

British wooden ship of 1 219 tons, built in 1853 at New Brunswick, and commanded by Capt Alfred Grayston. Wrecked near Ystervark Point on 10 April 1861 while on a voyage from Bombay to Liverpool with a cargo of cotton, linseed, coir yarn, wool, seed and madder roots. No lives were lost.
Cape Argus, 16 April 1861 (sale notice)
Lloyds Register of Shipping, 1860-61
Shipping Register, Cape Archives, C.C. 3/7/2/1

23. Cape St Blaize to Walker Point

This stretch of coast is heavily populated and is a popular tourist venue. There are many contrasts, from long sandy beaches to steep cliff faces. The water is usually clear and warm, influenced by the Agulhas current which flows westward. The seabed is often visited by divers even though heavy surf usually prevails and divers must wait for good diving conditions. The reefs are sparsely vegetated, but reef fish are found in great abundance. The land is well populated and the vegetation consists of Cape fynbos. The most prominent settlements are Mossel Bay, a large town with a good harbour, and the centre of the offshore oil industry. The water in the bay is usually clear, with a small swell, and good diving can be had the year round. Seal Island in the bay is populated by Cape fur seals and Great White sharks are found in abundance around the island. The Wilderness is a favourite tourist resort with a wide expanse of sandy beach. The prevailing winds are south-east in summer and south-west in winter. The main commercial activities are farming, fishing and tourism. Santos Beach at Mossel Bay is named after the German schooner Santos *wrecked there in 1874.*

Annie Benn

Schooner of 50 tons, built in Knysna in 1867. Wrecked in Mossel Bay on 27 November 1872 during a south-east gale with a full cargo for the Cape.
Cape Argus, 28 November 1872
Graham's Town Journal, 27 November 1872
Shipping Register, Cape Archives, C.C. 3/7/2/2

Dennia

English brig of 180 tons, commanded by Capt Crimp. Wrecked at Mossel Bay on 19 October 1864 when her cables parted during a south-east gale after a voyage from London with a general cargo.
Shipping Register, Cape Archives, C.C. 3/7/2/1

Erin

Barque wrecked at Mossel Bay on 27 November 1872 during a south-east gale after she had loaded part of her cargo for London.
Cape Argus, 28 November 1872
Shipping Register, Cape Archives, C.C. 3/7/2/2

Galatea

British wooden brig of 223 tons, built in 1829 at Chepstow, and commanded by Capt T. Owen. Wrecked on the rocks at Mossel Bay at 02h00 on 10 October 1846 after her cables parted during a south-east gale. Four persons were drowned.
Cape of Good Hope and Port Natal Shipping and Mercantile Gazette, 23 October 1846
Lloyds Register of Shipping, 1846-47
Shipping Register, Cape Archives, C.C. 2/16

Galera
34° 10.30S, 22° 08.00E

Norwegian wooden barque of 446 tons, built in 1873, and commanded by Capt J. M. Abrahamsen. Wrecked in the big gully on the west side of Danger Point, Mossel Bay on 25 August 1892 during a south-east gale while on a voyage from the Friendly Isles to Marseilles with a cargo of copra. No lives were lost. She was dived on in 1983. Little is to be seen of her, as most of the site lies in sand.
Cape Times, 27 August 1892
Lloyds Register of Shipping, 1892-93

Kate

Schooner commanded by Capt Kirby. Wrecked in Mossel Bay on 16 July 1849 at night during a south-east gale. No lives were lost. She lies in the same spot as the *Mary* (1853).
Shipping Register, Cape Archives, C.C. 2/17

King Cenric
34° 09.50S, 22° 06.80E

Norwegian wooden sailing-ship of 1 519 tons, built in 1874 by J. K. Dunlop & Co, St Johns, and commanded by Capt A. Paulsen. Wrecked near Dias Beach in Mossel Bay on 14 November 1903 during a south-east gale while on a voyage from Frederikstad with a cargo of Baltic timber. No lives were lost; the crew were saved with rocket apparatus. She lies near the *Rosebud* (1888).
Cape Argus, 14 November 1903
Lloyds Register of Shipping, 1901-02

Kron Prinsess van Denmark

Danish East-Indiaman commanded by Capt Swen Finger. Put into Mossel Bay on 9 June 1752 after being damaged in a storm and was abandoned after the cargo had been saved.
Cape Archives, V.C. 27

Lady Pryse

British wooden brigantine of 286 tons, built in 1875 by Evans of Aberystwyth, and commanded by Capt E. L. Lloyd. Wrecked in Mossel Bay on 6 November 1880 when her cables parted during a south-east gale after a voyage from London with a general cargo. No lives were lost. She lies close to the *Louisa Dorothea* (1882).
Eastern Province Herald, 9 November 1880
Lloyds Register of Shipping, 1880-81
Shipping Register, Cape Archives, C.C. 3/7/2/3

Louisa Dorothea

German three-masted schooner of 227 tons. Wrecked in Mossel Bay on 29 May 1882 during a south-east gale after a voyage from Adelaide with a cargo of wheat and flour. Three crew members were drowned, but five were rescued by means of rocket apparatus. She lies near the *Lady Pryse* (1880).
Eastern Province Herald, 6 June 1882
Shipping Register, Cape Archives, C.C. 3/7/2/3

Martha

Brig commanded by Capt Boustead. Wrecked 3 km from the landing-place in Mossel Bay on 30 August 1845 in the evening during a south-east gale after having entered the bay because of the loss of her boats and the low state of her provisions while on a voyage from Sydney to Table Bay with 20 immigrants and a large mail, which was saved. No lives were lost.
Shipping Register, Cape Archives, C.C. 2/16
South African Commercial Advertiser, 6 September 1845

Mary

British ship of 547 tons, built in 1813 of teak, and commanded by Capt Ardlie. Wrecked in Mossel Bay on 9 July 1824 after putting in for water while on a voyage from Calcutta and Madras to London with a cargo including indigo and dye.
Cape Town Gazette and African Advertiser, 17 July 1824
Lloyds Register of Shipping, 1824

Mary

Schooner of 117 tons, commanded by Capt J. Wood. Wrecked in Mossel Bay on 16 February 1853 after her cables parted during a south-east gale. One seaman was drowned. She lies in the same place as the *Kate* (1849).
Shipping Register, Cape Archives, C.C. 2/18

Nancy

Schooner commanded by Capt T. Metcalf. Wrecked in Mossel Bay on 5 April 1848 during a south-east gale after most of her cargo had been landed. One seaman was drowned.
Cape Town Mail, 15 April 1848
Shipping Register, Cape Archives, C.C. 2/17

Nepaul

British wooden ship of 462 tons, built in 1842 in Greenock, Scotland, and commanded by Capt A. Mclean. Wrecked at the Swart River mouth near Gericke Point, Sedgefield, on 11 February 1850 during a south-west gale while on a voyage from China and Bombay to London with a cargo of cotton and Indian produce. Three men drowned. She had anchored inside Gericke Point to shelter from a storm and ran ashore on a pinnacle while trying to leave the bay.
Lloyds Register of Shipping, 1850-51
Shipping Register, Cape Archives, C.C. 2/17
South African Commercial Advertiser, 20 February 1850

Philia

British wooden snow of 236 tons, built in 1862 by Mills, Sunderland, and commanded by Capt J. Edwards. Wrecked at Mossel Bay on 11 January 1880 during a south-east gale with a general cargo, most of which had been discharged, and included the material to build the Little Brak River bridge. No lives were lost.
Cape Argus, 13 January 1880
Lloyds Register of Shipping, 1879-80
Shipping Register, Cape Archives, C.C. 3/7/2/3

Poseidon

Norwegian wooden barque of 606 tons, built in 1890 at Arendal, and commanded by Capt C. Clausen. Wrecked in Mossel Bay on 2 September 1902 at night during a south-east gale with a cargo of 1 500 bags of coffee. No lives were lost.
Eastern Province Herald, 2 September 1902
Lloyds Register of Shipping, 1901-02

Rosebud
34° 09.80S, 22° 06.70E

British three-masted wooden schooner of 341 tons, built in 1876 by Carnegie, Peterhead, and commanded by Capt J. Collie. Wrecked on Dias beach at Mossel Bay on 30 August 1888 during a south-east gale while on a voyage from Calcutta to London via Mossel Bay and Cape Town with a general cargo. No lives were lost.
Lloyds Register of Shipping, 1888-89
Shipping Register, Cape Archives, C.C. 3/7/2/4

Ruby (ex *Figilante*)

British schooner of 75 tons. Wrecked at Mossel Bay on 13 January 1866 during a strong south-east wind while on a voyage from Algoa Bay to Cape Town via Mossel Bay with a cargo of rice, salt and general merchandise. No lives were lost. She was formerly the *Figilante*, which went ashore in Table Bay on 17 May 1865.
Eastern Province Herald, 9 February 1866
Shipping Register, Cape Archives, C.C. 3/7/2/1

Santos

German schooner of 163 tons, commanded by Capt Thaysen. Wrecked on Santos Beach at Mossel Bay on 18 July 1874 during a heavy swell after her cables parted with a full cargo of skins, dried fruit and wool for Cape Town. No lives were lost.
Shipping Register, Cape Archives, C.C. 3/7/2/2

Seagull
34° 10.30S, 22° 07.50E

Norwegian three-masted wooden schooner of 373 tons, built in 1886, and commanded by Capt C. Christensen. Wrecked on the beach below the 'Bakke' at Mossel Bay on 11 March 1894 during a south-east gale after a voyage from Rio de Janeiro via Table Bay with a cargo of coffee. The crew were saved by means of rocket apparatus. She was dived on in 1983 and many timbers, copper nails and iron knees can be seen protruding from the sand. Her anchor and chain are still clearly visible.
Cape Argus, 12 March 1894
Lloyds Register of Shipping, 1893-94

Susan Pardew

British wooden barque of 378 tons, built in 1863 by Hardie, Sunderland. Wrecked at Mossel Bay on 28 April 1872. No lives were lost.
Lloyds Register of Shipping, 1871-72
Shipping Register, Cape Archives, C.C. 3/7/2/2

Wilhelmine

German schooner commanded by Capt Rane. Wrecked at Mossel Bay on 17 March 1880 when her cables parted during a south-east gale after a voyage from Rio de Janeiro with a cargo of 1 500 bags of coffee. The vessel and her cargo were sold for £75 000.
Shipping Register, Cape Archives, C.C. 3/7/2/3

24. Walker Point to Cape Seal (Robberg)

Dominated by the Knysna lagoon, this stretch of coast is a popular tourist area and is often visited by divers. The coastline consists of steep cliffs cloaked in Cape fynbos, including many species of proteas and heather. The water is clear and warm due to the Agulhas current, but the shore is usually pounded by heavy ground swells. The reefs are sparsely vegetated but reef fish are found in great abundance. The most prominent settlement is Knysna, which is situated on an estuary and is a popular tourist venue. The main commercial activities are farming, fishing, timber and tourism. The prevailing winds are south-east in summer and south-west in winter. Emu Rock at the Knysna Heads is named after the British transport Emu which struck it in 1817.

Adolphus

Coasting brig commanded by Andrew Carr. Wrecked at Knysna in December 1819. She was engaged in the coasting trade between Knysna and Cape Town.
Cape Town Gazette, 8 January 1820

Emu
34° 04.40S, 23° 03.60E

British Navy transport brig, commanded by Lieut G. B. Forster. Run ashore in the Knysna Lagoon after hitting Emu Rock on 11 February 1817. She is the first recorded wreck at Knysna and had been sent there from Simon's Town, leaving on 8 February 1817, to test the navigability of the lagoon and to collect timber. A cast iron cannon was recovered from this wreck, which lies buried in the sand.
Cape Town Gazette, 26 July 1817 (sale notice), 28 February 1818

Cape Town Gazette

Fairholme
34° 05.00S, 23° 02.60E

British iron ship of 1 706 tons, built in 1885 by Richardson, Duck & Co, Stockton. Wrecked on the east side of Buffalo Bay on 1 April 1888 after being abandoned on fire off Cape Agulhas while on a voyage from Calcutta to New York with a cargo of jute.
Lloyds Register of Shipping, 1888-89
Shipping Register, Cape Archives, C.C. 3/7/2/4

Fredheim
34° 04.80S, 23° 03.80E

Norwegian wooden barque of 491 tons, built in 1875 by Strenge & Sohn, Hamelwarden. Wrecked at Coney Glen at the Knysna Heads on 23 June

1897 during a north-west wind after a voyage from Hull with a cargo of creosote for the timber industry. The sailmaker died.
Eastern Province Herald, 25 June 1897
Lloyds Register of Shipping, 1897-98

Harmony

British snow of 168 tons, built in 1817, and commanded by Capt R. Butler. Wrecked on 13 March 1826 while leaving the Knysna Heads. No lives were lost.
Lloyds Register of Shipping, 1826
South African Commercial Advertiser, 22, 29 March 1826

Helen

Cape wooden brigantine of 130 tons, built in 1854 at Newcastle, and commanded by Capt J. Burstal. Struck the inner bar at Knysna and was wrecked on the Coney Glen Rocks on 11 September 1858 with a cargo of timber for Table Bay. No lives were lost.
Cape Argus, 21 September, 14 October 1858
Cape of Good Hope Shipping and Mercantile Gazette, 15 October 1858
Lloyds Register of Shipping, 1858-59
Shipping Register, Cape Archives, C.C. 2/18

Louise

Norwegian barque from Blyth, commanded by Capt Martuisen. Wrecked a little east of the Knysna Heads on 17 October 1901 during a south-west wind after a voyage from Cape Town with a cargo of creosote and coal for Thesens & Co. She had been waiting outside the Knysna Heads for favourable weather to enter the lagoon, but on 13 October she sprang a leak and for three days the crew had to work the pumps. No lives were lost.
George and Knysna Herald, 7, 23 October 1901

Luna

British brig of 201 tons, built in 1818, and commanded by Capt R. Knox. Wrecked on the Brenton shore at Knysna on 27 June 1830 while leaving the port.
Lloyds Register of Shipping, 1830
Shipping Register, Cape Archives, C.C. 2/12

Magnolia

British wooden brig of 240 tons, built in 1840 at Plymouth. Struck a rock off Black Rock Point in the Knysna Heads opposite the white beacon (where the *Paquita* sank in 1903) on 24 July 1859 while leaving Knysna. Her crew jumped ashore from the bowsprit and she broke up immediately.
Cape Argus, 30 July 1859
Lloyds Register of Shipping, 1859-60

Munster Lass

Schooner of 52 tons, commanded by Capt Roper. Wrecked on the east side of the Knysna Heads on 19 April 1863 at the start of a voyage from Knysna to Cape Town with a cargo of railway sleepers. No lives were lost.
Shipping Register, Cape Archives, C.C. 3/7/2/1

Paquita (ex *Irma*, ex *Maggie Leslie*)
34° 04.60S, 23° 03.60E

German iron barque of 484 tons, built in 1862 by A. Leslie & Co, Newcastle, and commanded by Capt R. Wanke. Ran ashore below the white beacon at the Knysna Heads on 19 October 1903 after having offloaded creosote in Knysna and having taken on sand ballast. She plied between Gothenburg and Guam with timber. She is often dived on and is in a fairly good state of preservation. Her bows lie on a sand-bank in shallow water and her stern lies on a rocky bank in deeper water.
Eastern Province Herald, 21 October 1903
Lloyds Register of Shipping, 1901-02
Shipping Register, Cape Archives, C.C. 3/7/2/6

Phoénix

French three-masted schooner of 145 tons. Abandoned at sea and washed ashore at the Noetzie River mouth, 7 km east of the Knysna Heads, on 5 April 1881 while on a voyage from Réunion.
Cape Argus, 7 April 1881

Seier

Norwegian wooden barque of 491 tons, built in 1885 by T. Taraldsen, Risör, and commanded by Peder Larsen. Beached in the surf in Buffalo Bay, west of the Knysna Heads, on 23 May 1910 while on a voyage from Goole, near Hull, to Knysna with a cargo of 2 528 barrels of creosote and 40 tons of coal. She had struck a rock west of Walker Point.
Cape Argus, 26 May 1910
Lloyds Register of Shipping, 1909-10

Sovereign

Commanded by Capt I. Ancker. Wrecked while leaving Knysna on 29 December 1841. No lives were lost.
Graham's Town Journal, 20 January 1842
Shipping Register, Cape Archives, C.C. 2/15

25. Cape Seal to Storms River mouth

Dominated by the premier Cape resort of Plettenberg Bay, this stretch of coast is one of the most beautiful places in the world. It enjoys a large tourist turnover and the seabed is often visited by divers. The coastline consists of steep cliffs cloaked in Cape fynbos and temperate

forest. The reefs are well covered in marine growth and fish are abundant. The water is warm and clear due to the influence of the Agulhas current, but the shore is usually pounded by heavy ground swells. The most prominent features are Robberg Point and the thriving holiday and residential town of Plettenberg Bay. This bay is protected to some degree from the heavy swells and diving is good the year round, the best diving being had on the blinders off Beacon Island. Keurbooms River is another popular resort, as is Nature's Valley. From Nature's Valley westward to Storms River mouth the coastline is part of the Tsitsikamma Coastal National Park. The prevailing winds are south-east in summer and south-west in winter.

Active

British wooden schooner of 86 tons, built in 1787 at Chester, and commanded by Capt J. Bruce. Run ashore in Plettenberg Bay on 9 September 1845 while on a voyage from Knysna to Table Bay. No lives were lost. She was old and had put into the bay after springing a leak.
Lloyds Register of Shipping, 1845-46
Shipping Register, Cape Archives, C.C. 2/16
South African Commercial Advertiser, 20 September 1845

Agnes

Cape wooden schooner of 94 tons, built in 1868 by Arbroath Shipbuilding Co, Arbroath, and commanded by Capt Needham. Wrecked at Plettenberg Bay on 28 May 1882 after her cables parted. No lives were lost.
Cape Argus, 31 May 1882
Lloyds Register of Shipping, 1882-83
Shipping Register, Cape Archives, C.C. 3/7/2/3

MFV Athina (ex *Rosa Vlassi*, ex *Galaxidi*)
34° 05.60S, 23° 22.90E

Greek stern factory trawler of 814 tons, launched

in 1941, and commanded by Capt John Katsiaris. Run aground on Robberg Beach in Plettenberg Bay on 1 August 1967 at night after hitting Whale Rock and holing the engine-room while on a voyage home with a full cargo of 1 000 tons of fish caught in the Indian Ocean; the Suez Canal was closed and the coast was unfamiliar. No lives were lost. She was run ashore in front of the survivors' camp of the *São Gonçalo* (1630). Her hull is still visible (1987).
Cape Argus, 1 August 1967
Cape Times, 2 August 1967 (photograph)
Lloyds Register of Shipping, 1966-67

Christina

Cape wooden brigantine of 196 tons, built in 1874 by Leary, New Brunswick, and commanded by Capt G. Love. Wrecked at Plettenberg Bay on 28 May 1882.
Cape Argus, 31 May 1882
Lloyds Register of Shipping, 1882-83
Shipping Register, Cape Archives, C.C. 3/7/2/3

Diadem

Brig of 158 tons, built in 1824, and commanded by Capt J. Caithness. Wrecked in Plettenberg Bay on 4 December 1851 after her cables parted during a south-east gale. No lives were lost.
Lloyds Register of Shipping, 1851-52
Shipping Register, Cape Archives, C.C. 2/17

Dorothys

British brig of 167 tons, commanded by Capt Newbold. Wrecked at Plettenberg Bay at 07h00 on 14 July 1836. No lives were lost.
Lloyds Register of Shipping, 1836-37
South African Commercial Advertiser, 23 July 1836

Athina.

George Henry Harrison

Schooner of 136 tons, commanded by Capt J. Shannon. Wrecked on the rocks at Plettenberg Bay on 15 September 1851 while leaving the bay during a south-east gale. No lives were lost.
Cape Monitor, 1 October 1851
Shipping Register, Cape Archives, C.C. 2/17

Jane
34° 00.20S, 23° 29.30E

British wooden barquentine of 256 tons, built in 1878 by W. Pickersgill, Sunderland, and commanded by Capt R. Evans. Wrecked near Matjes River on 27 August 1888 during a south-east gale while on a voyage from Port Elizabeth to the West Indies in ballast. No lives were lost. She lies in a gully near Forest Hall and little is to be seen at the site besides a rusty anchor and other badly corroded pieces of iron.
Lloyds Register of Shipping, 1888-89
Shipping Register, Cape Archives, C.C. 3/7/2/4

Magneten
34° 03.40S, 23° 22.80E

Norwegian brig of 205 tons, commanded by Capt Berentsen. Driven ashore between the old timber shed and Beacon Isle in Plettenberg Bay on 29 November 1872 during a south-east gale after a voyage from Table Bay. No lives were lost.
Cape Argus, 3 December 1872

Maria

Dutch flute of 908 tons on hire to the Amsterdam Chamber of the Dutch East India Company. Ran ashore near Robberg in Plettenberg Bay on 23 August 1788 after being driven from her anchorage by a south-east gale while on a homeward-bound voyage from Ceylon (Sri Lanka), which she had left on 8 December 1787 with a cargo of saltpetre, coffee and pepper. The crew was ill with scurvy. No lives were lost. Part of her cargo was saved and taken over by the outward-bound *Jonge Frank* and homeward-bound *Duifje*.
Cape Archives, V.C. 34
Dutch-Asiatic Shipping Homeward Voyages, 1597-1795, The Hague, 1979

Midge

British wooden schooner of 61 tons, built in 1861 by Hall, Arbryth, and commanded by Capt Bernstein. Wrecked at Plettenberg Bay on 19 November 1874 after her starboard anchor-chain parted during a south-east gale. The chain was found to be badly corroded and the captain was found guilty of incompetence.
Cape of Good Hope Government Gazette, 25 December 1874
Lloyds Register of Shipping, 1874-75

Prince Albert

Brig commanded by Capt W. Dolly. Wrecked at Plettenberg Bay at 20h00 on 24 August 1844 after her cables parted during a south-east gale. No lives were lost. Her cargo was saved.
Shipping Register, Cape Archives, C.C. 2/16
South African Commercial Advertiser, 2 September 1844

São Gonçalo

Portuguese East-Indiaman commanded by Fernão Lobo de Meneses. Wrecked at the Piesang River mouth in Plettenberg Bay in July 1630 during a storm while on a homeward-bound voyage from Goa, which she had left on 4 March 1630, to Lisbon with a cargo of spices, rice and Chinese porcelain. She had sprung a leak in mid-ocean and put into the bay for repairs. After battling for 50 days to effect repairs, a south-east gale blew her ashore and 133 persons died. The survivors built two pinnaces; one went to Delagoa Bay, arriving safely, and the other made for Angola. This boat was picked up by a passing homeward-bound Portuguese East-Indiaman, the *Santo Ignacio Loyola*, which was wrecked on the bar at Lisbon, drowning most of the survivors. What is believed to have been the survivors' shore camp was found during building operations on Mr Jerling's plot next to the Robberg in 1981. This site lies directly in front of the site of the *Athina* (1967).
De Faria Y Sousa, Manuel, *Asia Portuguesa*, Vol 3, Lisbon, 1675. Partial text and English translation in Theal, G.M., *Records of South Eastern Africa*, Vol 6, pp 411-421

St Helena

Schooner of 142 tons, commanded by Capt J. Lewis. Wrecked in Plettenberg Bay on 13 September 1851 during a south-east gale. No lives were lost.
Shipping Register, Cape Archives, C.C. 2/17

Susan Crisp

British wooden barque of 261 tons, built in 1838 at Yarmouth, and commanded by Capt E. R. Kersey. Wrecked in Plettenberg Bay on 28 September 1857 during a south-east gale after a voyage from Algoa Bay to collect the cargo from the wrecked brig *William Bayley* (1857). Five men were lost.
Cape Argus, 7 October 1857
Lloyds Register of Shipping, 1857-58
Shipping Register, Cape Archives, C.C. 2/18

Swiftsure

Schooner commanded by Capt J. F. Sewell. Wrecked in Plettenberg Bay on 8 August 1847 at night during a north-north-west gale. No lives were lost.

Shipping Register, Cape Archives, C.C. 2/16
South African Commercial Advertiser, 14 August 1847

Waif

British brigantine commanded by Capt Brown. Wrecked at Plettenberg Bay on 25 March 1874.
Mossel Bay Advertiser, 1 April 1874

William Bayley

British wooden brig of 198 tons, built in 1840 at Ipswich, and commanded by Capt J. McGreen. Run ashore and wrecked at Plettenberg Bay on 11 July 1857 after her cargo caught fire by spontaneous combustion while on a voyage from Algoa Bay to London with a cargo of wool, hides, horns, ivory, aloes, ostrich feathers, spermaceti, beads and sugar, most of which was saved. The *Susan Crisp* was sent from Algoa Bay to fetch the cargo, but was also wrecked at Plettenberg Bay on 28 September 1857.
Cape Argus, 22, 25 (sale notice) July 1857
Lloyds Register of Shipping, 1857-58

26. Storms River mouth to Klippen Point

This stretch of coast is extremely inaccessible and is rarely visited by divers. The shoreline consists of steep cliffs and ravines choked with temperate forests and Cape fynbos, though the area from Tsitsikamma Point is flatter. The water is clear and warm due to the influence of the Agulhas current, but the shore is usually pounded by heavy ground swells. The stretch from Storms River mouth to Grootrivier (Oubos) is part of the Tsitsikamma Coastal National Park. The reefs are well covered in marine growth and fish life is abundant. The prevailing winds are south-east in summer and south-west in winter. After a prolonged period of south-east wind cold water wells up, the sea becomes ice-cold and discoloured, and fish are often stunned and wash ashore. Wreck Point, west of Klippen Point, is named after the British ship Runnymede *which was wrecked there in 1866.*

Berwick

British ship of 454 tons, built in 1795. Wrecked near Algoa Bay (possibly near the Tsitsikamma River) on 30 June 1827. Her cargo of cotton was saved and shipped to Cape Town from Algoa Bay.
Cape of Good Hope Government Gazette, 27 July 1827
Lloyds Register of Shipping, 1827

SS Bosphorus
34° 10.50S, 24° 32.30E

British steam screw and sailing ship of 2 116 tons, commanded by Capt Alexander. Wrecked near Tsitsikamma Point at 01h00 on 21 October 1867 during a strong west gale while two days

out on a voyage from Simon's Town to Bombay. She broke up within three hours and only 40 people out of 88 were saved. She was on hire to the Navy and was one of 14 vessels despatched to transport troops from Bombay to Abyssinia to help in the Abyssinian Campaign against Theodora.
Cape Argus, 24, 26, 29 October, 7, 19 November (enquiry) 1867
Shipping Register, Cape Archives, C.C. 3/7/2/2

British Duke
34° 11.02S, 24° 34.50E

British iron barque of 1 420 tons, built in 1875 by Barrow Shipbuilding Co, registered in Liverpool, and commanded by Capt T. Fairfield. Wrecked about 2,5 km west of Klippen Point on 13 November 1888 while on a voyage from Calcutta to London with a general cargo of grain, saltpetre and cotton waste. The 27 crew members were saved by the *Urms Anglican*.
Eastern Province Herald, 19 November 1888
Lloyds Register of Shipping, 1888-89
Shipping Register, Cape Archives, C.C. 3/7/2/4

MV Evdokia (ex *Atlantic Darby*, ex *Himeji Maru*)
34° 03.00S, 24° 06.00E

Greek cargo vessel of 7 144 tons, built in 1956 by Harima Zosensho, registered in Piraeus, owned by Nicopan Shipping, and commanded by Capt Anatasias Patsiatzis. Wrecked a little east of the Storms River mouth in the Tsitsikamma Coastal National Park on 12 June 1979 during a south-west gale while on a voyage from Durban and East London to Rio de Janeiro with a cargo of 1 974 tons of copper in 118-kg ingots, 90 tons of nickel plates, newsprint and rolls of tinplate. The wreck broke up immediately and six crew members died. Four hundred tons of copper were salvaged, but when thick sand covered the cargo, efforts ceased. The cargo was then bought by another group of salvors who to date have recovered a further 600 tons of copper.
Eastern Province Herald, 13 June 1979
Lloyds Register of Shipping, 1979-80

Copper from the Evdokia.

PS **Hope**

Schooner-rigged paddle-wheel coaster of 194 tons, built by Scott, Sinclair & Co, Greenock, and commanded by Capt J. Baddely. Wrecked about 250 m from the shore in the vicinity of Tsitsikamma Point on 11 March 1840 in fog while on a voyage from Cape Town. The vessel caught fire, but no lives were lost. She plied between Algoa Bay and Cape Town, and was the first steamer wrecked on the coast of South Africa. She lies about 300 m from the *Queen of the West* (1850).
Graham's Town Journal, 2 April 1840
South African Commercial Advertiser, 21, 25, 28 March 1840

L'Aigle
34° 10.70S, 24° 33.20E

French barque of 700 tons, commanded by Capt Du Bergue. Wrecked about 4 km west of Klippen Point near Cape St Francis on 16 June 1850 during a south-west gale after being disabled while on a voyage from Sumatra to Marseilles with a cargo of pepper, malacca canes, rattans, coffee and 2 000 blocks of tin (70 tons). Ten people died, including the captain, supercargo and a Spanish governor from Manila; the mate and nine men reached the shore. Searle & Co of Port Elizabeth tried to recover the tin in the 1880s, but it was finally salvaged only in 1981. She lies 5 km east of the *Queen of the West*, which was wrecked during the same gale.
Cape Town Mail, 29 June, 6 July 1850
Eastern Province Herald, 22 June 1850
Port Elizabeth Telegraph, 27 June 1850
Sam Sly's African Journal, 4 July 1850
Shipping Register, Cape Archives, C.C. 2/17
South African Commercial Advertiser, 29 June 1850
South African Library Manuscript Collection, M.S.B. 190

SS **Lyngenfjord** (ex *Nidaros*, ex *Santa Cecelia*, ex *Colusa*)
34° 08.50S, 24° 26.50E

Norwegian cargo steamer of 5 627 tons, built in 1913 by W. Hamilton & Co, Port Glasgow, and owned by the Norwegian American Line, Oslo. Wrecked at the Tsitsikamma River mouth on 14 January 1938 in thick fog while on a voyage from France to Madagascar with a mixed cargo

Lyngenfjord. *(Frank Neave)*

including 8 000 bags of cement, dates, stoves, paint, fertilisers, matches, enamelware, timber and liquor. She also carried a spare manganese bronze propeller. Very little cargo was saved. She lies in extremely shallow water directly below a steep hill, and has been worked on.
Eastern Province Herald, 15 January 1938
Lloyds Register of Shipping, 1937-38

Milford (ex *Montreal*)

British wooden ship of 1 046 tons, built in 1869 by Julian, Quebec, and commanded by Capt D. Simpson. Wrecked close to Tsitsikamma Point on 12 October 1875 after springing a leak and being abandoned 8 km off Cape St Francis while on a voyage from Calcutta with a cargo of linseed. She had a crew of 21. She lies close to the *Bosphorus* (1867).
Eastern Province Herald, 15, 19 October 1875
Lloyds Register of Shipping, 1875-76

Nederlandsche Vlag

Dutch ship of 600 tons, commanded by Capt Van der Broek Humurie. Wrecked near Tsitsikamma Point on 22 July 1870 during a south-west gale while on a voyage from Macassar to Amsterdam with a cargo of coffee, gutta-percha, cajaput, macassar oil, rattans, gum, cork and spices, worth £200 000, The captain and twelve men were drowned. She lies within a few metres of the *Bosphorus* (1867).
Cape Argus, 23, 26, 28 July, 2, 4 August 1870
Shipping Register, Cape Archives, C.C. 3/7/2/2

President Reitz. *The arrow points to a warning to salvors to keep off.*

SS **President Reitz** (ex *Segundo Ruiz-Belvis*)
34° 09.60S, 24° 28.00E

South African liberty ship of 7 176 tons, built in 1943 by the Oregon Shipbuilding Corporation, Portland, owned by the Southern Steamship Co, and commanded by Capt George Hamilton. Wrecked a little west of Tsitsikamma Point on 27 November 1947 in dense fog while on a voyage from Cape Town to Durban in ballast to load coal for Malta. No lives were lost. Her stern is still intact, but her midships and bow section are badly broken up (1987). She lies within sight of the *Panaghia* (1938) to the east and the *Lyngenfjord* (1938) to the west.
Cape Argus, 27, 28 November 1947
Lloyds Register of Shipping, 1946-47

Panaghia. *(John Munnik)*

SS **Panaghia** (ex *Temple Lane*)
34° 10.00S, 24° 29.40E

Greek cargo vessel of 4 289 tons, built in 1928 by W. Hamilton & Co, Port Glasgow. Wrecked about a kilometre east of Tsitsikamma Point on 17 February 1938 in fog while on a voyage from the River Plate to Australia in ballast. No lives were lost. She lies in extremely shallow water and at low tide her boilers stick half out of the water. Her propeller was salvaged at the time and little of value remains. She lies within sight of the *Lyngenfjord* (1938) and a little east of the *President Reitz* (1947).
Eastern Province Herald, 18, 19 February 1938
Lloyds Register of Shipping, 1937-38

Queen of the West
34° 10.20S, 24° 32.20E

British wooden ship of 1 160 tons, built in 1848 in Quebec, and commanded by Capt Webster. Wrecked on the rocks west of Wreck Point on the Tsitsikamma coast on 16 June 1850 during a south-west gale while on a voyage from Bombay to London with a cargo of cotton, cochineal, wool, coconut oil and coir rope. All lives were lost; 30 bodies washed up and were buried in the vicinity. She lies about 5 km west of the *L'Aigle*, wrecked during the same gale, and close to the *Hope* (1840).
Cape Town Mail, 29 June 1850
Eastern Province Herald, 22 June 1850

Lloyds Register of Shipping, 1850-51
Sam Sly's African Journal, 4 July 1850
Shipping Register, Cape Archives, C.C. 2/17
South African Commercial Advertiser, 29 June
  1850

Runnymede
34° 10.90S, 24° 34.40E

British wooden ship of 720 tons, built in 1854 at Sunderland, and commanded by Capt J. Little. Wrecked on Wreck Point, a little west of Klippen Point, on 6 February 1866. She had sprung a leak off Mauritius and was abandoned off Plettenberg Bay on 2 February while on a voyage from Wallaroo to Swansea with a cargo of copper ore. The crew reached Algoa Bay in boats.
Eastern Province Herald, 6 February 1866
Lloyds Register of Shipping, 1865-66

27. Klippen Point to Seal Point

This stretch of coast is rarely visited by divers. The shore consists of low hills covered in Cape fynbos and small patches of coastal bush. The water is warm and clear due to the Agulhas current, but heavy ground swells usually pound the coast. The reefs are well covered in marine growth and fish life is abundant. The most prominent feature of the coast is Oyster Bay with its small resident population and long sandy beach. Few tourists visit Oyster Bay, however, most of them preferring Seal Point. The prevailing winds are south-east in summer and south-west in winter.

SS **Cape Recife** (ex *Hohenfels*)
34° 12.70S, 24° 50.10E

British steam cargo vessel of 5 394 tons, built in 1898 by Wigham, Richardson & Co, Newcastle, and commanded by Capt. Bradley. Wrecked a little west of the Cape St Francis lighthouse on 20 February 1929 in fog while on a voyage from Cape Town to Durban in ballast. No lives were lost. Her bronze propeller was removed by salvors in the 1970s.
Eastern Province Herald, 21 February (photographs), 8 March (enquiry), 9 March (photographs) 1929
Lloyds Register of Shipping, 1928-29

Derby
34° 11.20S, 24° 43.90E

Norwegian wooden barque of 1 137 tons, built in 1855 in the USA, and commanded by Capt M. Abrahamsen. Run ashore in Thys Bay 10 km west of Cape St Francis on 27 April 1895 after sustaining damage during a storm while on a voyage from Algoa Bay to New South Wales in ballast. Four seamen were lost after they had come ashore, had returned to the vessel and were then washed overboard.
Eastern Province Herald, 29 April 1895
Lloyds Register of Shipping, 1895-96

Cape Recife. *(Frank Neave)*

Eliza and Alice
34° 12.30S, 24° 48.60E

Barque commanded by Capt Dan Hayes. Wrecked at Mosterts Hoek, a little west of Cape St Francis, on 21 September 1870 while on a voyage from Sundsvall, Sweden, to Algoa Bay with a cargo of timber. No lives were lost.
Cape Argus, 28 September 1870
Kaffrarian Watchman, 3 October 1870
Shipping Register, Cape Archives, C.C. 3/7/2/2

L'August

French ship of 500 tons, commanded by Capt Gerrard. Wrecked near Cape St Francis on 22 January 1858 during a gale while on her maiden voyage from Réunion to Marseilles with a cargo of sugar. Eight lives were lost.
Cape Argus, 30 January 1858
Shipping Register, Cape Archives, C.C. 2/18

Niagara

French full-rigged ship, commanded by Capt Sicard. Run ashore at the Slang River mouth in Oyster Bay on 4 September 1872 after springing a leak while on a voyage from Mozambique to Marseilles.
Graham's Town Journal, 6 September 1872
Shipping Register, Cape Archives, C.C. 3/7/2/2

Noord(ster)

Dutch galiot of 90 tons, built in 1686 at the Amsterdam Yard for the Amsterdam Chamber of the Dutch East India Company, and commanded by Pieter Timmerman. Wrecked 25 km west of Cape St Francis (Klippen Point) on 16 January 1690 while on a voyage of survey, with the aim of purchasing Algoa Bay and the Bay of Natal from the native tribes. At low tide the crew of 18 were able to walk ashore; they then set off on foot for Cape Town, but only four made it. She was on a homeward-bound voyage to the Cape after having purchased the Bay of Natal; after a stop at Algoa Bay the windswept bay was not considered worth purchasing.
Cape Archives, V.C. 12
Dutch-Asiatic Shipping, 1595-1795, The Hague, 1979
Moodie, D., *The Record,* Part 1, pp 445-446

HMS **Osprey**
34° 12.05S, 24° 48,20E

British wooden steam screw gunboat of 682 bm, built in 1856 by Fletcher, Limehouse, and commanded by Capt W. Menzies. Wrecked about 3 km west of the Cape St Francis lighthouse on 30 May 1867 early in the morning during a westerly storm while on a voyage from the China Seas to England. Only one life was lost. She carried three large cast iron guns (1 x 110 pdr, 2 x 68 pdr) and one small bronze gun. She lies in a shallow gully and has been extensively worked on over the years; many interesting artefacts have been recovered, including the bronze gun, the twin-bladed bronze propeller, Japanese coins, silver dollars and silverware.
Eastern Province Herald, 7, 11 (sale notice), 14 June 1867
Illustrated London News, 29 September 1866
Shipping Register, Cape Archives, C.C. 3/7/2/2

28. Seal Point to the Port Elizabeth harbour

This stretch of coast is dominated by the wide expanse of St Francis Bay and consists mainly of long sandy beaches and sand dunes. The water is warm due to the Agulhas current, but is usually turbid due to the Kromme and Gamtoos rivers which empty into the bay. The main settlement is Jeffrey's Bay, world famous for its surfing waves. The area is well populated and is a favourite holiday venue for many; it is also often visited by divers. The most prominent feature of the coast is Cape Recife and the treacherous Thunderbolt Reef, which dominates the approach to Algoa Bay, a wide bay in which the water is ususally turbid due to the Swartkops and Sundays rivers which empty into the bay. In the bight of Algoa Bay surf is usually non-existent, except after storms or during south-east gales, which cause huge seas to break in the bay. Port Elizabeth is a large industrial city and the second largest city in the Cape Province. The bay is a transitional area between the temperate south coast and the subtropical east coast; from here the coast cuts away sharply to the north-east and the climate changes dramatically. The prevailing winds are south-east in summer and south-west in winter. Place names associated with wrecks are Cannon Bay, named after the bronze cannon from the Portuguese East-Indiaman Santissimo Sacramento (wrecked there in 1647) which used to lie in a rock pool in the bay; Holland Reef, named after the Dutch corvette Zeepaard wrecked there in 1823; and Thunderbolt Reef, named after the British paddle-wheeler Thunderbolt, which struck it in 1847.

Abeona

British iron barque of 1 004 tons, built in 1867 by A. Stephen & Sons, Glasgow, and commanded by Capt McCorkindale. Wrecked on Thunderbolt Reef off Cape Recife on 4 September 1900 while on a voyage to Algoa Bay with a cargo of 1 468 tons of coal for the railways. She had on board a crew of nineteen.
Eastern Province Herald, 6 September 1900
Lloyds Register of Shipping, 1900-01

Colonial Empire
34° 02.00S, 25° 42.30E

British steel barque of 2 436 tons, built in 1902 by J. Reid & Co, Glasgow, owned by the Anglo American Oil Company, and commanded by Capt Sanders. Run ashore near the Cape Recife lighthouse on 27 September 1917 after striking Thunderbolt Reef while on a voyage from New York to Delagoa Bay via Algoa Bay with a cargo of paraffin oil in tins. The wreck was dynamited at the time to flatten her. She was the last sailing cargo vessel to be wrecked on the coast of South Africa.
Eastern Province Herald, 28 September 1917
Lloyds Register of Shipping, 1917-18

RMS Dane

Iron screw steamer of 530 tons, built in 1855 by Lungley, London, owned by the Union Company, and commanded by Capt Waldeck. Wrecked on Thunderbolt Reef off Cape Recife on 1 December 1865 during a south-west wind while on a voyage from Table Bay to Zanzibar. No lives were lost. She had been chartered by the Admiralty to convey stores to Zanzibar for naval forces who were suppressing the slave trade. She took the inner passage between Thunderbolt Reef and the mainland and stranded inside the wreck of the *L'Imperatrice Eugenie* (1867).
Lloyds Register of Shipping, 1865-66
Shipping Register, Cape Archives, C.C. 3/7/2/1
South African Advertiser and Mail, 2 December 1865

SS Fidela
34° 00.60S, 25° 42.00E

British steel screw steamer of 714 tons, commanded by Capt H. Swainstone. Wrecked 1,7 km north of the Cape Recife lighthouse on 7 April 1873 in thick fog while on a voyage from Cape Town to Mauritius via Algoa Bay. No lives were lost. She was a new vessel, intended for the mail service between Melbourne and New Zealand. During WW II she was used as a practice target by bombers using dummy concrete bombs, which are still clearly visible on the site. Her engine block is still visible in the surf (1987). She lies close to the *Galloway* (1882).
Cape Argus, 7, 12 April 1873
Kaffrarian Watchman, 12 April 1873
Shipping Register, Cape Archives, C.C. 3/7/2/2

Fountain

Schooner. Wrecked on Thunderbolt Reef on 20 March 1872 while on a voyage from Algoa Bay to East London. No lives were lost.
Shipping Register, Cape Archives, C.C. 3/7/2/2

Freeman Clarke

American ship of 1 336 tons, commanded by Capt J.S. Dwight. Drifted ashore near the Gamtoos River mouth on 18 July 1883 after catching fire and being abandoned while on a voyage from Calcutta to New York with a cargo of 3 800 bales of jute cuttings. The captain and several seamen were reported missing in their boat, but later arrived in Algoa Bay.
Eastern Province Herald, 20, 23 July 1883
Shipping Register, Cape Archives, C.C. 3/7/2/3

Galloway

British ship of 1 329 tons, built in 1863 in New Brunswick, and commanded by Capt Stenhouse. Wrecked a little north of the Cape Recife lighthouse at 22h00 on 11 October 1882 while on a voyage from Cardiff with a cargo of coal for the railways. She lies close to the *Fidela* (1873).

Eastern Province Herald, 13 October 1882 (sale notice)
Lloyds Register of Shipping, 1882-83
Shipping Register, Cape Archives, C.C. 3/7/2/3

Harmonie

Norwegian wooden barque of 406 tons, built in 1873 at Arendal. Wrecked near the Cape Recife lighthouse on 22 October 1891 while on a voyage from Frederikstad to Algoa Bay with a cargo of deals.
Eastern Province Herald, 23 October 1891
Lloyds Register of Shipping, 1891-92

Hotbank

British wooden snow of 249 tons, built in 1866 by Chilton, Sunderland, and commanded by Capt James Binet. Run ashore at the Shark River in Algoa Bay on 25 April 1873 after striking an object off Cape Recife and developing a leak while on a voyage from London to Algoa Bay with a cargo of coal and bar iron.
Eastern Province Herald, 29 April 1873 (sale notice)
Lloyds Register of Shipping, 1873-74
Shipping Register, Cape Archives, C.C. 3/7/2/2

SS Itzehoe
34° 01.30S, 25° 42.20E

German Australian Line twin-funnelled screw steamer of 4 487 tons, built in 1899 in Flensburg, Germany, and commanded by Capt F. Kirstein. Ran aground a little north of the Cape Recife lighthouse on 24 May 1911 on a moonlit night after striking Thunderbolt Reef while on a voyage from Hamburg to Australia with 8 000 tons of cargo, including pianos and soft goods, most of which was saved by means of lighters. The captain fell from the bridge when she struck and was injured. The crew put on their best clothes and waited calmly to be rescued.
Eastern Province Herald, 26, 27 May 1911
Lloyds Register of Shipping, 1911-12

Itzehoe. *(P.E. Public Library)*

Josephine

Schooner of 99 tons, commanded by Capt A.

Equino. Wrecked on the rocks 16 km west of Cape Recife on 17 May 1855.
Port Elizabeth Telegraph, 24 May 1855
Shipping Register, Cape Archives, C.C. 2/18

MV **Kapodistrias**
34° 02.40S, 25° 42.10E

Greek bulk carrier of 29 185 tons, built in 1972 by Hakodate Dock Co, Muroran, and commanded by Capt N. Liodis. Ran ashore on the eastern end of Thunderbolt Reef off Cape Recife on 29 July 1985 in calm weather while leaving Algoa Bay on a voyage to Montreal with a full cargo of 7 500 tons of manganese ore, 27 653 tons of sugar, zirconium sand and rutile. No lives were lost. The wreck was bought by two Port Elizabeth businessmen and the cargo by a Cape Town salvor.
Eastern Province Herald, 30, 31 July 1985
Lloyds Register of Shipping, 1985-86

L'Imperatrice Eugenie

British iron barque of 308 tons, built in 1854 at Greenock, owned by J.T. Rennie of Aberdeen, and commanded by Capt Robinson. Wrecked on Thunderbolt Reef, about 1 km offshore, on 6 February 1867 while on a voyage from Algoa Bay to London with a cargo of wool, most of which was saved. No lives were lost. She lies close to the *Dane* (1865).
Eastern Province Herald, 8 February 1867
Lloyds Register of Shipping, 1867-68
Shipping Register, Cape Archives, C.C. 3/7/2/2

L'Uranie

French ship of 50 tons. Run ashore at the Seekoei River mouth in early October 1800 with a cargo of 300 bags of coffee. Her crew had been without food for almost five days.
Cape Town Gazette, 25 October 1800

Lady Head

British wooden ship of 868 tons, built in 1852 at New Brunswick. Wrecked on rocks close to the Kromme River mouth in St Francis Bay on 26 April 1859 while on a voyage from Rangoon to Liverpool with a cargo of rice. Only three out of the 26 people on board are known to have survived. A population of swans which were found on the Kromme River estuary are believed to have originated from this wreck.
Lloyds Register of Shipping, 1859-60
Shipping Register, Cape Archives, C.C. 2/18

Lady Leith

Brig commanded by Capt J. Caithness. Wrecked on Thunderbolt Reef off Cape Recife on 27 February 1848 during a south-east gale while entering Algoa Bay after a voyage from Waterloo Bay in ballast. No lives were lost.

Cape Town Mail, 11 March 1848
Shipping Register, Cape Archives, C.C. 2/17

Lakmé

Norwegian wooden barque of 668 tons, built in 1871 by Lawrence, Novia Scotia, and commanded by Capt E. Bache. Struck Thunderbolt Reef off Cape Recife and sank immediately in 20 m of water on 2 September 1896 while on a voyage from Sunderland to Algoa Bay with a cargo of 698 tons of coal. One man was drowned.
Eastern Province Herald, 4 September 1896
Lloyds Register of Shipping, 1896-97

Lebu

Norwegian iron barque of 762 tons, built in 1868 by Gourlay Bros, Dundee, and commanded by Capt Mathisen. Struck Thunderbolt Reef and sank a little west in 55 m of water on 17 May 1899 while on a voyage from Christiania to Algoa Bay with a cargo of timber. The crew were taken off by the tug *Sir Frederick*.
Eastern Province Herald, 18 May 1899
Lloyds Register of Shipping, 1899-1900

SS Ourimbah
34° 02.90S, 25° 37.60E

British steel screw steamer of 696 tons, built in 1909 by the Ardrossan Dry Dock & Shipbuilding Co, and commanded by Capt R. Stewart. Wrecked at Chelsea Point near Cape Recife on

Ourimbah. (Eastern Province Herald)

Pati. *(Evert Smith)*

26 November 1909 in fog while on her maiden voyage from Ardrossan, Scotland, to Sydney via Natal in ballast. The crew of 24 were all saved by the tug *Sir Frederick*. She was intended for coastal trade in Australia. She lies scattered in a shallow gully directly inshore from the *Queenmoor* (1934).
Eastern Province Herald, 27 November 1909
Lloyds Register of Shipping, 1909-10
Shipping Register, Cape Archives, C.C. 3/7/2/7

MV Pati (ex *Kate*, ex *Ajana*)
34° 02.45S, 25° 41.40E

Cypriot cargo vessel of 5 623 tons, built in 1950 by William Hamilton & Co, and commanded by Capt Costas Hardialias. Wrecked on Thunderbolt Reef off Cape Recife on 29 February 1976 in dense fog while on a voyage from the Ivory Coast to the Persian Gulf with a cargo of cement. She broke up rapidly, but her engine block can still be seen at low tide (1987).
Eastern Province Herald, 1, 2 March 1976 (photographs)
Lloyds Register of Shipping, 1976-77

Port Douglas

British steel ship of 1 662 tons, built in 1889 by Russell & Co, Port Glasgow, and commanded by Capt J.H. Trask. Wrecked on Cape Recife on 19 June 1897 at night while entering Algoa Bay. No lives were lost.
Eastern Province Herald, 21, 23, 25 (sale notice) June 1897
Lloyds Register of Shipping, 1897-98

Prince of the Seas
34° 02.60S, 25° 32.60E

British wooden barque of 414 tons, built in 1855 at Sunderland, and commanded by Capt H. le Gresley. Wrecked 13 km west of Cape Recife on 18 April 1866 at night during a westerly gale

while on a voyage from London to East London via Port Elizabeth with a general cargo and military stores. Seven men died. A sale was held at the 'Duine', 6,5 km west of Wyatts Mill.
Eastern Province Herald, 20 April 1866 (sale notice)
Lloyds Register of Shipping, 1865-66

SS **Queenmoor**
34° 03.15S, 25° 37.60E

British cargo steamer of 4 863 tons, built in 1924 by J. Redhead & Sons, Southshields, and commanded by Capt E. Edwards. Wrecked on Chelsea Point, west of Cape Recife, on 7 September 1934 in fog after striking an offshore reef while on a voyage from Finland to East London and Beira with a cargo of 7 000 tons of Baltic timber.
Eastern Province Herald, 8, 10 September 1934
Lloyds Register of Shipping, 1934-35

Queenmoor.

Sabina
34° 01.90S, 25° 42.20E

Spanish ship of 700 tons, commanded by Capt B. Mateu. Wrecked at Cape Recife on 7 August 1842 early in the morning while on a voyage from Manila to Cadiz with a cargo including tobacco, hides, sugar, coffee, dye-wood, rope, indigo, silk and 30 000 Spanish dollars in specie, valued at £90 000. Out of a crew of 72, 22 lives were lost. The wreck was sold for £550. In 1982 she was found and worked on; silver coins (8-reales from the reign of Ferdinand), nails and crockery were recovered.
Cape of Good Hope Government Gazette, 19 August 1842
Shipping Register, Cape Archives, C.C. 2/15
South African Commercial Advertiser, 20, 27, 31 August 1842

Santissimo Sacramento
34° 02.15S, 25° 31.20E

Portuguese East-Indiaman (*não*) of 1 000 tons, built of teak at Bassein, India, by Rui Dias da Cunha. Wrecked in Cannon Bay, a little west of Schoenmakerskop, on 1 July 1647 after her rudder broke while on a homeward-bound voyage from Goa to Lisbon in the company of the *Nossa Senhora de Atalaia* (which was wrecked at the Cefane River mouth shortly before) with the commander of the fleet, Luis de Miranda Hen-

riques, on board, as well as a cargo of pepper, diamonds, spices, Chinese porcelain and bronze cannon from the foundry of Bocarro in Macao. More than 40 bronze cannon were recovered from the site in 1977, but about 17 cast iron cannon still remain. The survivors walked to Delagoa Bay.
Allen, G. and D., *The Guns of Sacramento*, 1978
Axelson, E., *Dias & his successors*, 1988
Feyo, Bento Teyxeyra, *Relacam do Naufragio que fizeram as Nãos Sacramento & nossa Senhora da Atalaya vindo da India para o Reyno, no Cabo de Boa Esperança*, Lisbon, 1650. Translated into English in Theal, G.M., *Records of South Eastern Africa*, Vol 8, pp 295-360

Shepherdess

British wooden barque of 331 tons, built in 1850 in Aberdeen, and commanded by Capt George Urquhart. Wrecked on Thunderbolt Reef off Cape Recife on 30 May 1859 while on a voyage from London to Algoa Bay with a general cargo. Only two men were saved.
Lloyds Register of Shipping, 1859-60
Shipping Register, Cape Archives, C.C. 2/18

Spy

British wooden brigantine of 193 tons, built in 1837 at Shoreham, and commanded by Capt J. Draper. Wrecked in St Francis Bay on 21 August 1851 after her cables parted during a south-east gale. She had landed her cargo after having arrived from Algoa Bay, and was busy loading a large cargo of timber. No lives were lost.
Lloyds Register of Shipping, 1851-52
Shipping Register, Cape Archives, C.C. 2/17

SS **Strathblane**
34° 02.90S, 25° 37.75E

British screw steamer of 2 341 tons, built in 1888 by Russell & Co, Port Glasgow, and commanded by Capt J. Nimmo. Beached a little east of Chelsea Point, west of Cape Recife, on 23 January

1890 after striking a rock while on a voyage from London to Natal with a general cargo including sleepers and gold-mining equipment. No lives were lost.
Eastern Province Herald, 24 January 1890
Lloyds Register of Shipping, 1890-91
Shipping Register, Cape Archives, C.C. 3/7/2/4

Swallow

British schooner of 179 tons, commanded by Capt Scott. Wrecked near the Van Stadens River mouth 32 km west of Cape Recife on 26 November 1863 while on a voyage from Table Bay to Shanghai with a cargo of coal. No lives were lost.
Shipping Register, Cape Archives, C.C. 3/7/2/1

HMS **Thunderbolt**
33° 57.90S, 25° 38.00E

Wooden paddle-wheeled sloop of 1 085 bm, built in 1842 at Portsmouth, and commanded by Capt Boyle. Run ashore at the Baakens River mouth in Algoa Bay on 3 February 1847 after striking Thunderbolt Reef (Roman Rock) while on a voyage from Simon's Town to Algoa Bay. No lives were lost. She was later blown up to flatten her. She lies buried beneath reclaimed land.
Graham's Town Journal, 6 February 1847
Shipping Register, Cape Archives, C.C. 2/16, 2/24

SS **Western Knight**
34° 03.20S, 25° 35.00E

American cargo vessel of 5 779 tons, built in 1919 by the Ames Shipbuilding & Dry Dock Co, Seattle, for the United States Shipping Board, owned by the American South African Line, and commanded by Capt Morgan. Wrecked between The Willows and Schoenmakerskop west of Cape Recife on 8 April 1929 in thick mist while on a voyage from the USA to Algoa Bay with a 2 000-ton general cargo including cars, spares and machinery, most of which was salvaged at

Western Knight. *(Frank Neave)*

the time by Capt Van Delden. No lives were lost. Her bronze screw was salvaged in the 1970s.
Eastern Province Herald, 9 April 1929 (photograph)
Lloyds Register of Shipping, 1928-29

William Forster

Schooner of 175 tons, commanded by Capt E. Hutchons. Wrecked on Thunderbolt Reef off Cape Recife at 21h00 on 17 July 1851 while on a voyage from Table Bay to Algoa Bay. No lives were lost.
Eastern Province News, 19 July 1851
Lloyds Register of Shipping, 1850-51
Shipping Register, Cape Archives, C.C. 2/17

HNMS **Zeepaard**
34° 02.20S, 25° 29.80E

Dutch corvette of 20 guns, built in 1817 by P. Schuyt at the Admiralty Yard, Amsterdam, and commanded by Capt Reynes. Wrecked on Holland Reef at Sardinia Bay, Port Elizabeth on 29 March 1823 at night in fog while on a homeward-bound voyage from Batavia with 180 men on board. Seven lives were lost. The explorer Theunissen was on board and as a result of this wreck did his well-documented trip overland to Cape Town. The site was discovered in the 1960s. A few bronze carronades have been recovered, and one is in the Port Elizabeth Museum. A helicopter was used to recover a bronze carronade in 1978. Many divers have visited the site and have recovered muskets, pistols, ceramic bottles, silverware and the ship's bell.
Shipping Register, Cape Archives, C.C. 2/10
Theunissen, J.B.N., *Aantekeningen eener Reis door de Binnenland van Zuid-Afrika*, 1824

29. Port Elizabeth harbour to the Sundays River mouth

Within Algoa Bay, which is dominated by the large industrial city of Port Elizabeth, the water is warm, due to the influence of the Agulhas current which sweeps into the bay, but usually turbid, due to the great volume of water which empties into the bay from the Swartkops and Sundays rivers, and this restricts visits by divers. The most prominent feature along this coast is the St Croix Island group, which consists of St Croix, Jaheel and Brenton islands. St Croix is home to a large population of jackass penguins. Many of the shipwrecks in Algoa Bay lie buried beneath harbour development. The prevailing winds are south-east in summer and south-west in winter. Amsterdam Hoek is named after the Dutch man-of-war Amsterdam, run ashore here in 1817.

Abbotsford

British emigrant barque of 328 tons, built in 1838 at Sunderland, and commanded by Capt E. Pigon. Wrecked in Algoa Bay at 14h00 on 12 Oc-

tober 1843 when her cables parted during a south-east gale. No lives were lost, as the crew were landed in a surf-boat. Although the vessel was new, her chains were badly corroded.
Graham's Town Journal, 26 October 1843
Lloyds Register of Shipping, 1843-44
Shipping Register, Cape Archives, C.C. 2/16

Abdul Medjid

British iron barque of 402 tons, built in 1854 in Glasgow, and owned by H.T. Vanner. Wrecked in the bight of Algoa Bay on 20 February 1871 when her cables parted during a south-east gale with a cargo of 580 bales of wool for Montreal; these were landed in a damaged state. No lives were lost.
Eastern Province Herald, 24 February 1871 (sale notice)
Lloyds Register of Shipping, 1870-71
Shipping Register, Cape Archives, C.C. 3/7/2/2

Agostino Rombo
33° 56.30S, 25° 36.80E

Italian wooden barque of 827 tons, built in 1882 at Sestri Ponente, and commanded by Capt Guiseppe Vasallo. Wrecked in Algoa Bay on 1 September 1902 during a south-east gale after a voyage from Buenos Aires with a cargo of mealies. Eight people died. She struck the sunken hulk of the *Queen Victoria* (1896) and was smashed to pieces.
Eastern Province Herald, 2 September 1902
Lloyds Register of Shipping, 1901-02

Albatross

German barque of 348 tons, commanded by Capt L. Kranest. Wrecked near the bight of Algoa Bay on 16 December 1881 during a south-east gale after a voyage from Cape Town with a general cargo. The crew were landed safely in the boat.
Eastern Province Herald, 20 December 1881
Shipping Register, Cape Archives, C.C. 3/7/2/3

Albinia

British wooden brigantine of 169 tons, built in 1840 at New Brunswick, and commanded by Capt J. Coulthard. Wrecked in Algoa Bay on 13 September 1851 when her cables parted during a south-east gale after a voyage from Natal. No lives were lost.
Lloyds Register of Shipping, 1851-52
Shipping Register, Cape Archives, C.C. 2/17, 2/24

Alert

New schooner. Wrecked in Algoa Bay on 4 September 1840 when her cables parted during a south-east gale. No lives were lost.
Graham's Town Journal, 17 September 1840
Shipping Register, Cape Archives, C.C. 2/15

Alma

German schooner of 128 tons, commanded by Capt P.H. Grahn. Wrecked in Algoa Bay on 23 August 1877 during a south-east gale after a voyage from Rio de Janeiro with a cargo of coffee; she had taken on board 500 bales of wool for London.
Eastern Province Herald, 24 August 1877

Almira Coombs

American barque of 362 tons, commanded by Capt G.S. Paine. Wrecked in Algoa Bay on 16 July 1878 during a south-east gale after a voyage from Boston with a general cargo. No lives were lost.
Eastern Province Herald, 19 July 1878 (sale notice)
Graham's Town Journal, 17 July 1878
Shipping Register, Cape Archives, C.C. 3/7/2/3

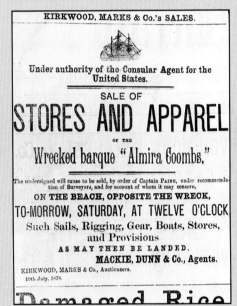

Eastern Province Herald

Amelia Mulholland

British wooden barque of 220 tons, built in 1837 in Newport, and commanded by Capt J. Forrest. Wrecked in Algoa Bay on 16 February 1850 when her cables parted during a south-east gale. No lives were lost.
Eastern Province Herald, 23 February 1850
Lloyds Register of Shipping, 1850-51
Shipping Register, Cape Archives, C.C. 2/17

HNMS **Amsterdam**
33° 51.90S, 25° 38.10E

Dutch man-of-war, commanded by Capt Hofmeyr. Run ashore at Amsterdam Hoek in Algoa Bay on 16 December 1817 after developing a leak while on a voyage from Batavia to Holland with a cargo including some rare treasures from Java for the king of the Netherlands; these were lost. Three men were drowned.
Cape Town Gazette, 7 March 1818

Amwell

Brig of 235 tons, built in 1835 at Shoreham, and commanded by Capt J. Mansfield. Wrecked in Algoa Bay on 14 August 1852 when her cables parted during a south-east gale after a voyage from the Downs, off south-east Kent. No lives were lost.
Lloyds Register of Shipping, 1852-53
Shipping Register, Cape Archives, C.C. 2/18, C.C. 2/24

Andreas Riis

Norwegian wooden barque of 577 tons, built in 1875 by J. Bang, Grimstad, and commanded by Capt T. Jensen. Wrecked in Algoa Bay on 30 August 1888 when her cables parted during a south-east gale after a voyage from Grimsby. Her cargo had been discharged.
Eastern Province Herald, 31 August 1888
Lloyds Universal Register of Shipping, 1888-89
Shipping Register, Cape Archives, C.C. 3/7/2/4

Anne Marie.

Anne Marie

French barque of 406 tons, built in 1854, and commanded by Capt Eugene Endel. Wrecked between the Swartkops River and Smelly Creek in Algoa Bay on 27 November 1872 during a south-east gale after a voyage from London with a general cargo. No lives were lost.
Eastern Province Herald, 29 November 1872 (sale notice)
Graham's Town Journal, 29 November 1872
Shipping Register, Cape Archives, C.C. 3/7/2/2

Arabian

Schooner of 91 tons, commanded by Capt F. Henry. Wrecked in Algoa Bay on 16 October 1859 during a south-east gale with a cargo of timber. No lives were lost. She came up against the *Governess* (1859) and the *Chasseur* (1859).
Shipping Register, Cape Archives, C.C. 2/18

Araminta

British wooden barque of 747 tons, built in 1870 by Harvie, Nova Scotia, and commanded by Capt H. Svendson. Wrecked on the North End beach in Algoa Bay at 21h00 on 19 January 1889 during a south-east gale after a voyage from Swansea with a cargo of coal, which had been partly discharged. She struck between the wrecks of the *Lada* (1888) and the *Jane Harvey* (1888). No lives were lost, as the crew were rescued by a lifeboat.
Eastern Province Herald, 21 January 1889
Lloyds Register of Shipping, 1889-90

Argali

Cape wooden barque of 254 tons, built in 1864 by Follett, Dartmouth, and commanded by Capt S. Milner. Wrecked in Algoa Bay on 19 September 1869 during a south-east gale. No lives were lost.
Eastern Province Herald, 21 September 1869
Lloyds Register of Shipping, 1869-70
Shipping Register, Cape Archives, C.C. 3/7/2/2

Arnold (ex *Eugénie*)
33° 56.90S, 25° 36.80E

German iron barque of 854 tons, built in 1868 by Forges & Co, La Seyne, and commanded by Capt Ahlers. Wrecked on the North End beach in Algoa Bay on 1 September 1902 during a south-east gale after a voyage from London with a cargo of sleepers.
Eastern Province Herald, 2 September 1902
Lloyds Register of Shipping, 1901-02

Arnold. *(P.E. Public Library)*

Asiatic

British wooden barque of 406 tons, built in 1841 at Sunderland, and commanded by Capt A. Waddell. Went ashore in Algoa Bay on 9 June 1850 when her cables parted during a south-east gale.

She was on a voyage from Adelaide to London with a cargo of 400 tons of copper ore and wool and had put into the bay because of damage and leaks. No lives were lost.
Cape Town Mail, 22 June 1850
Lloyds Register of Shipping, 1850-51
Shipping Register, Cape Archives, C.C. 2/17, 2/24

Atlantic

British brig of 130 tons, built in 1817, and commanded by Capt J. Barber. Wrecked in Algoa Bay at 22h00 on 1 October 1835 during a south-east gale with a cargo of tallow, aloes and hides. One man was drowned.
Graham's Town Journal, 8 October 1835
Lloyds Register of Shipping, 1835-36
Shipping Register, Cape Archives, C.C. 2/13

Ballarat

British wooden barque of 464 tons, built in 1852 at Sunderland, and commanded by Capt R. Davison. Wrecked in Algoa Bay at 22h30 on 19 October 1864 during a south-east gale with a cargo of coal for the Diamond Steamship Company. No lives were lost, as the crew of 13 were taken off by lifeboat.
King William's Town Gazette, 27 October 1864
Lloyds Register of Shipping, 1864-65
Shipping Register, Cape Archives, C.C. 3/7/2/1

Barbadoes

British wooden barque of 279 tons, built in 1860 by Green, Grimsby. Wrecked in Algoa Bay on 12 September 1861 when her anchor cable parted during a south gale while loading cargo for London. No lives were lost.
Eastern Province Herald, 13 September 1861
Lloyds Register of Shipping, 1861-62

Basileia

British snow of 248 tons, built in 1854 at Sunderland, and commanded by Capt W. J. Roberts. Wrecked in Algoa Bay on 3 October 1859 when her cables parted during a south-east gale.
Eastern Province Herald, 4, 7 (sale notice) October 1859
Lloyds Register of Shipping, 1859-60

Blackaller

British snow of 137 tons, built in 1831 at Sunderland, and commanded by Capt J. Watson. Wrecked in Algoa Bay on 25 March 1846 during a south-east gale while loading cargo for London. No lives were lost.
Cape of Good Hope and Port Natal Shipping and Mercantile Gazette, 3 April 1846
Lloyds Register of Shipping, 1846-47
Shipping Register, Cape Archives, C.C. 2/16

Brilliant

German brigantine of 147 tons, commanded by Capt Mattmann. Wrecked near the gas works in Algoa Bay on 5 May 1880 when her cables parted during a south-east breeze after a voyage from Rio de Janeiro with a cargo of coffee, which had been landed. The vessel was eventually sold for £193 13s.
Eastern Province Herald, 7 May 1880
Shipping Register, Cape Archives, C.C. 3/7/2/3

C. Boschetto

Italian wooden barque of 723 tons, built in 1875 by D. Cravioto, Varazze, and commanded by Capt B. Marini. Wrecked in Algoa Bay on 30 August 1888 during a south-east gale after having put into the bay for repairs while on a voyage from Rangoon to Greenwich with a cargo of teak.
Eastern Province Herald, 31 August 1888
Lloyds Universal Register of Shipping, 1888-89
Shipping Register, Cape Archives, C.C. 3/7/2/4

C. Boschetto. *(P.E. Public Library)*

Cape Breton

British brig of 122 tons, built in 1812 at Cape Breton. Wrecked in Algoa Bay on 1 October 1835 during a south-east gale.
Graham's Town Journal, 8 October 1835
Lloyds Register of Shipping, 1835-36

Caprera

American barque of 674 tons, commanded by Capt Hichhem. Wrecked in Algoa Bay on 23 August 1884 when her cables parted during a south-east gale. No lives were lost. Her cargo of rice had been discharged.
Shipping Register, Cape Archives, C.C. 3/7/2/3

Catherine

German brig of 281 tons, commanded by Capt H. Oltmann. Wrecked on the North End beach in Algoa Bay on 25 October 1883 when her cables parted during a south-east gale after a voyage from Calcutta with a cargo of rice, which had been discharged. She was in ballast, cleared for St Thomas. No lives were lost.
East London Dispatch, 31 October 1883
Eastern Province Herald, 26 October 1883
Shipping Register, Cape Archives, C.C. 3/7/2/3

Catherine Scott

British wooden barque of 309 tons, built in 1864 by Gardner, Sunderland, and commanded by Capt Baillie. Wrecked in Algoa Bay on 8 April 1878 when her cables parted after a voyage from Rio de Janeiro with a cargo of coffee.
Lloyds Register of Shipping, 1878-79
Shipping Register, Cape Archives, C.C. 3/7/2/3

Cavalieri Michelle Russo
33° 56.35S, 25° 36.80E

Italian steel ship of 1 529 tons, built in 1875 by T. R. Oswald, Sunderland, and commanded by Capt F. Russo. Wrecked on the North End beach in Algoa Bay on 1 September 1902 during a south-east gale while on a voyage from Newcastle to New South Wales with a cargo of coal. Of the crew of 20, only three survived.
Eastern Province Herald, 2 September 1902

Charlotte
33° 57.60S, 25° 37.60E

British wooden three-masted transport ship of 450 tons, built in 1844 at Liverpool, and commanded by Capt R. D. Affleck. Wrecked at the foot of Jetty Street in Algoa Bay on 20 September 1854 when her cables parted during a south-east gale after having put into the bay for water the day before while on a voyage from Cork to Calcutta with 163 soldiers and 5 officers of the 27th Regiment, 16 women and 26 children. 110 people died: 62 soldiers, 11 women, 26 children and 11 crew. The lifeboat sent to the wreck was driven on to the rocks. She lies buried beneath reclaimed land.
Lloyds Register of Shipping, 1854-55
Shipping Register, Cape Archives, C.C. 2/18, C.C. 2/24

Charlotte A. Morrison

American ship. Lost in Algoa Bay on 3 August 1862 at night when her cargo of rice caught fire by spontaneous combustion after she had put into the bay for repairs while on a voyage from Akyab to Falmouth.
Eastern Province Herald, 5 August 1862
Shipping Register, Cape Archives, C.C. 3/7/2/1
South African Commercial Advertiser and Mail, 7 August 1862

Chasseur

French barque of 198 tons, commanded by Capt E. Blanc. Wrecked in Algoa Bay on 3 October 1859 during a south-east gale after a voyage from Mozambique. No lives were lost. She lies next to the *Governess* (1859).
Eastern Province Herald, 4, 11 (sale notice) October 1859

Eastern Province Herald

Clara

American barque of 524 tons, commanded by Capt E.P. Nichols. Wrecked opposite the gasworks in Algoa Bay on 5 November 1880 when her cables parted during a south-east gale and she collided with the brig *Minora* and the *Vevera* after a voyage from Boston with a general cargo. No lives were lost. She lies close to the *Flying Scud* (1880).
Eastern Province Herald, 9, 10 (sale notice) November 1880
Shipping Register, Cape Archives, C.C. 3/7/2/3

Clara. *(P.E. Public Library)*

Constant
33° 56.60S, 25° 36.80E

Norwegian wooden barque of 292 tons, built in 1886 at Stavanger, owned by K. S. Bertelsen, and commanded by Capt A. Jacobson. Wrecked on North End beach in Algoa Bay on 1 September 1902 during a south-east gale after a voyage from Rio de Janeiro with a cargo of coffee.
Eastern Province Herald, 2 September 1902
Lloyds Register of Shipping, 1901-02

Constant. *(Frank Neave)*

Content
33° 56.36S, 25° 36.80E

Norwegian wooden barque of 547 tons, built in 1891 by G. Berntsen, Tvedestrand, owned by J. M. A. Marcussen, and commanded by Capt L. A. Gustavsen. Wrecked next to the *Emmanuel* (1902) on North End beach in Algoa Bay on 1 September 1902 during a south-east gale after a voyage from East London with a cargo of teak.
Eastern Province Herald, 2 September 1902
Lloyds Register of Shipping, 1901-02

County of Pembroke

British iron barque of 1 098 tons, built in 1881 by W. Doxford & Sons, Sunderland, and commanded by Capt J. Parry. Wrecked in Algoa Bay on 14 November 1903 during a south-east gale after a voyage from London with a general cargo. No lives were lost.
Eastern Province Herald, 20 November 1903 (sale notice)
Lloyds Register of Shipping, 1901-02

Cruiser

British wooden barque of 347 tons, built in 1862 by Robinson, Sunderland, and commanded by Capt S. Bull. Wrecked near the *Taurus* and the *E.B. Lohe* (1872) in Algoa Bay on 27 November 1872 during a south-east gale after a voyage from Table Bay in ballast. No lives were lost.

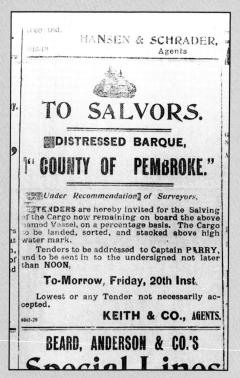

HANSEN & SCHRADER, Agents.

TO SALVORS.

DISTRESSED BARQUE, "COUNTY OF PEMBROKE."

Under Recommendation of Surveyors.

TENDERS are hereby invited for the Salving of the Cargo now remaining on board the above named Vessel, on a percentage basis. The Cargo to be landed, sorted, and stacked above high water mark.

Tenders to be addressed to Captain PARRY, and to be sent in to the undersigned not later than NOON,

To-Morrow, Friday, 20th Inst.

Lowest or any Tender not necessarily accepted.

KEITH & CO., AGENTS.

BEARD, ANDERSON & CO.'S
Special Lines

Eastern Province Herald

Eastern Province Herald, 29 November 1872 (sale notice)
Lloyds Register of Shipping, 1872-73
Shipping Register, Cape Archives, C.C. 3/7/2/2

Delhi

British barque of 276 tons, built in 1838 at Shoreham, and commanded by Capt H. Byron. Wrecked in Algoa Bay at 02h30 on 25 August 1843 after her cables parted during a south-east gale with a cargo of rice. One man was drowned.
Graham's Town Journal, 31 August 1843
Lloyds Register of Shipping, 1843-44
Shipping Register, Cape Archives, C.C. 2/16

Doris

Brig of 196 tons, commanded by Capt J. Reid. Wrecked in Algoa Bay on 17 October 1850 during a south-east gale after a voyage from Port Beaufort. No lives were lost.
Eastern Province Herald, 19 October 1850
Shipping Register, Cape Archives, C.C. 2/17, C.C. 2/24

Dorthea

Danish wooden brig of 171 tons, built in 1870 in Norway, and commanded by Capt Christensen. Wrecked in Algoa Bay on 30 August 1888 during a south-east gale after a voyage from Hamburg with a general cargo which was still being discharged.
Eastern Province Herald, 31 August 1888
Lloyds Universal Register of Shipping, 1888-89
Shipping Register, Cape Archives, C.C. 3/7/2/4

Drei Emmas (ex *Egmont & Hoorn*)

Belgian wooden barque of 657 tons, built in 1865 at St Johns, New Brunswick, and commanded by Capt R. Nicholass. Wrecked in Algoa Bay on 30 August 1888 during a south-east gale after a voyage from Cardiff. She was still discharging her cargo. She grounded next to the *Wolseley* (1888).
Eastern Province Herald, 31 August 1888
Lloyds Universal Register of Shipping, 1888-89
Shipping Register, Cape Archives, C.C. 3/7/2/4

E.B. Lohe

German brig of 234 tons. Wrecked in Algoa Bay on 27 November 1872 near the *Cruiser* (1872) and the *Taurus* (1872) during a south-east gale after a voyage from Rio de Janeiro. No lives were lost.
Eastern Province Herald, 29 November 1872
Graham's Town Journal, 27 November 1872
Shipping Register, Cape Archives, C.C. 3/7/2/2

East London Packet

Schooner of 29 tons, built in East London in 1854 for the coasting trade. Wrecked in Algoa Bay on 24 October 1855.
Cape of Good Hope Almanac, 1856

Elda (ex *Musca*)

Norwegian iron barque of 714 tons, built in 1878 by H. F. Ulrichs, Vegesack, and commanded by Capt G. Guldbrandsen. Wrecked in Algoa Bay on 14 November 1903 during a south-east gale after a voyage from Buenos Aires with a full cargo of 100 bags of flour and 15 600 bags of mealies. No lives were lost.
Eastern Province Herald, 19 November 1903 (sale notice)
Lloyds Register of Shipping, 1901-02

Elda. *(Frank Neave)*

Elizabeth Brown

British wooden snow of 234 tons, built in 1854 in Perth. Wrecked in Algoa Bay on 31 December 1872 when her cables parted during a south-east gale with a cargo of 500 bales of wool. No lives were lost.
Lloyds Register of Shipping, 1872-73
Shipping Register, Cape Archives, C.C. 3/7/2/2

Emmanuel

Oakworth

Iris

Constant

Elizabeth Rowell

British snow of 288 tons, built in 1839 at Sunderland, and commanded by Capt C. M. Wake. Wrecked in Algoa Bay at 04h00 on 25 August 1843 when her cables parted during a south-east gale and she smashed through the jetty with a cargo of butter and oats for Mauritius. No lives were lost.
Cape of Good Hope Government Gazette, 1 September 1843
Graham's Town Journal, 31 August 1843
Lloyds Register of Shipping, 1843-44
Shipping Register, Cape Archives, C.C. 2/16

Elizabeth Stevens

British wooden barquentine of 198 tons, built in 1871 by Bayley, Ipswich, and commanded by Capt J. Strike. Wrecked in Algoa Bay on 30 August 1888 during a south-east gale after a voyage from Cape Town with a cargo of 3 400 bags of wheat, none of which had been discharged.
Eastern Province Herald, 31 August 1888
Lloyds Register of Shipping, 1888-89
Shipping Register, Cape Archives, C.C. 3/7/2/4

Emilia

Portuguese composite wood and iron barque of 712 tons, built in 1868 by Denton Gray & Co, Hartlepool, and commanded by Capt L. D'Almeida. Sank in Algoa Bay at 10h00 on 17 July 1898 after having struck Thunderbolt Reef early in the morning the day before and being towed by tug into the anchorage in Algoa Bay

in a leaking condition. She was on a voyage from Delagoa Bay to Barbadoes in ballast to pick up a charter.
Eastern Province Herald, 18 July 1898
Lloyds Register of Shipping, 1898-99

Emmanuel (ex *Kinderdijk*)
33° 56.36S, 25° 36.80E

German iron barque of 1 147 tons, built in 1876 by J. K. Smit, Kinderdijk, and commanded by Capt J. Tuitzer. Wrecked on the North End beach in Algoa Bay on 1 September 1902 during a south-east gale after a voyage from Port Pirie with a cargo of wheat and flour. She was wrecked next to the *Content* (1902).
Eastern Province Herald, 2 September 1902
Lloyds Register of Shipping, 1901-02

England

British oak barque of 361 tons, built in 1863 by Pearson, Sunderland, and commanded by Capt E.B. Fulham. Wrecked opposite the lifeboat house in Algoa Bay on 18 September 1869 during a south-east gale with a cargo of 800 bales of wool and skins.
Eastern Province Herald, 21 September, 5 October (sale notice) 1869
Lloyds Register of Shipping, 1869-70
Shipping Register, Cape Archives, C.C. 3/7/2/2

Essex

British whaling ship of 300 tons, built in 1808.

The Great Gale, 1902.

SALE AT PORT ELIZABETH.

By Order of the Agents for the condemned Bark ESSEX, Whaler.

ON THURSDAY, the 5th July next, will be sold by Public Auction, to the Highest Bidder, the Hull of the condemned bark *Essex*, together with her Masts, Spars, running and standing Rigging, Sails, Blocks, and Tackling. Whaling Gear, consisting of Harpoons, Lances, Spades, Blubber Hooks, Fry Pots, Looper Coolers, Whale Line, and every thing requisite for establishing a Whale Fishery, for which the vessel is excellently calculated. Also Anchors, Cables, Muskets, Cutlasses, &c. &c. together with a few remnants of Stores, damaged Biscuit, &c. &c.
NB. The Sale to commence at 11 o'clock in the morning, precisely, and the first lot sold to be the Hull, with Lower Masts and standing Rigging.
Uitenhage, 20 June. J. H. BREHM, Auctioneer.

Graham's Town Journal

Wrecked in Algoa Bay on 22 June 1832.
Graham's Town Journal, 29 June 1832 (sale notice)
Lloyds Register of Shipping, 1832

Eurydice

British wooden brig of 210 tons, built in 1845 at Greenock, and commanded by Capt H. J. Falkner. Wrecked in Algoa Bay on 17 February 1857 when her cables parted during a south-east gale after a voyage from London via Table Bay. She struck the barque *Alexandrina* before wrecking.
Cape Argus, 25 February, 2 May 1857
Lloyds Register of Shipping, 1856-57
Shipping Register, Cape Archives, C.C. 2/18

Feejee

British three-masted schooner of 171 tons, built in 1827 at Workington, and commanded by Capt W. Bewley. Wrecked in Algoa Bay on 10 August 1837 during a south-east wind. No lives were lost.
Graham's Town Journal, 24 August 1837
Lloyds Register of Shipping, 1837-38

Flash

Brigantine of 110 tons, commanded by Capt A. R. Doane. Wrecked in Algoa Bay on 19 September 1869 when her cables parted during a south-east gale after a voyage from Melbourne with a cargo of rams. No lives were lost.
Eastern Province Herald, 21 September, 5 October (sale of rams) 1869
Shipping Register, Cape Archives, C.C. 3/7/2/2

Flora

Barque of 246 tons, commanded by Capt S. Robinson. Wrecked in Algoa Bay on 30 December 1854 when her cables parted during a south-east gale after a voyage from London.
Shipping Register, Cape Archives, C.C. 2/18, 2/24

Flying Scud

British wooden barque of 349 tons, built in 1863 by Thompson, Sunderland, and commanded by Capt W. Pick. Wrecked opposite the gas-works in Algoa Bay close to the *Clara* (1880) on 1 September 1880 when her cables parted during a south-east gale while on a voyage from Quadalpore to London with a general cargo. She had put into the bay for shelter. Four lives were lost.
Graham's Town Journal, 3 September 1880
Lloyds Register of Shipping, 1880-81
Shipping Register, Cape Archives, C.C. 3/7/2/3

Eastern Province Herald

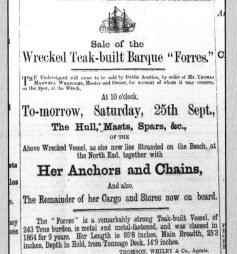

Sale of the
Wrecked Teak-built Barque "Forres."

THE Undersigned will cause to be sold by Public Auction, by order of Mr. THOMAS MAXWELL WRANGLES, Master and Owner, for account of whom it may concern, on the Spot, at the Wreck,

At 10 o'clock,
To-morrow, Saturday, 25th Sept.,
The Hull, Masts, Spars, &c.,
OF THE
Above Wrecked Vessel, as she now lies Stranded on the Beach, at the North End, together with

Her Anchors and Chains,
And also,
The Remainder of her Cargo and Stores now on board.

The "Forres" is a remarkably strong Teak-built Vessel, of 243 Tons burden, is metal and metal-fastened, and was classed in 1864 for 9 years. Her Length is 95.8 inches, Main Breadth, 25.3 inches, Depth in Hold, from Tonnage Deck, 14.9 inches.
THOMSON, WHILEY & Co., Agents.

J. S. KIRKWOOD, Auctioneer.
24th September, 1869.

Forres

British wooden ship of 243 tons, built in 1851 of teak in Maulmein, Burma, and commanded by Capt T. M. Wrangles. Wrecked in Algoa Bay on 18 September 1869 during a south-east gale. She was pulled off, but once more ran ashore.
Eastern Province Herald, 21, 24 September (sale notice) 1869
Lloyds Register of Shipping, 1869-70
Shipping Register, Cape Archives, C.C. 3/7/2/2

Frances Burn

British wooden barque of 248 tons, built in 1838 in Glasgow, and commanded by Capt W. Woolley. Wrecked in Algoa Bay at 23h00 on 25 March 1849 during a south-east gale. No lives were lost.
Cape of Good Hope and Port Natal Shipping and Mercantile Gazette, 6 April 1849
Lloyds Register of Shipping, 1849-50

Frances Watson

British brig of 333 tons, built in 1825, and commanded by Capt S. Bragg. Wrecked in Algoa Bay on 13 January 1830 during a south-east gale. Her cargo had been landed the day before.
Lloyds Register of Shipping, 1830
Shipping Register, Cape Archives, C.C. 2/12
South African Commercial Advertiser, 23 January 1830

Gabrielle
33° 57.00S, 25° 36.80E

British schooner of 78 tons, commanded by Capt A. de la Roche. Wrecked on North End beach in Algoa Bay on 1 September 1902 during a south-east gale after a voyage from Mauritius with a cargo of sugar, most of which had been discharged.
Eastern Province Herald, 2 September 1902

Gabrielle.

SS Gambia
33° 57.60S, 25° 37.70E

Cape and Natal Line iron screw steamer of 1 167 tons, built in 1860 by Leslie, Newcastle, and commanded by Capt A. Owen. Wrecked at the foot of Jetty Street in Algoa Bay on 27 May 1871 after her screw was entangled in a warp while helping a sailing-vessel. No lives were lost. She lies buried beneath reclaimed land.

Gambia. *(P.E. Public Library)*

Graham's Town Journal, 2 June 1871
Lloyds Register of Shipping, 1870-71
Shipping Register, Cape Archives, C.C. 3/7/2/2

Gerhardine

German wooden barque of 303 tons, built in 1869 by C.D. Oltmann, Neuronnebeck, and commanded by Capt Schmitzer. Ran ashore on a reef at the Coega River mouth in Algoa Bay on 8 May 1888 when her cables parted while on a voyage to the Celebes via Algoa Bay with a cargo of explosives. Three men died; the captain was killed by a falling spar as the vessel touched the beach, and the carpenter and cook were drowned.
Eastern Province Herald, 9 May 1888
Lloyds Universal Register of Shipping, 1888-89
Shipping Register, Cape Archives, C.C. 3/7/2/4

Gilbert Henderson
33° 58.01S, 25° 37.60E

British emigrant barque of 427 tons, built in 1837 at Sunderland, and commanded by Capt J. Tweedie. Wrecked opposite the Old Jetty in Algoa Bay on 16 March 1847 when her cables parted during a south-east gale. No lives were lost. She lies buried beneath reclaimed land.
Lloyds Register of Shipping, 1847-48
Shipping Register, Cape Archives, C.C. 2/16
South African Commercial Advertiser, 27 March 1847

Good Hope

Coasting brig. Wrecked in Algoa Bay on 30 August 1819 during a south-east gale. No lives were lost.
Cape Town Gazette, 25 September 1819
Shipping Register, Cape Archives, C.C. 2/9

Governess

Brig of 185 tons, commanded by Capt A. Henderson. Wrecked in Algoa Bay on 16 October 1859 during a south-east gale while on a voyage from Maulmein, Burma, with a cargo of teak.

No lives were lost. She was hit by the *Arabian* and ran against the *Chasseur*.
Cape Weekly Chronicle, 21 October 1859
Shipping Register, Cape Archives, C.C. 2/18

Gowan

British snow of 143 tons, built in 1815. Wrecked in Algoa Bay on 9 October 1830 during a south-east gale.
Lloyds Register of Shipping, 1830
Shipping Register, Cape Archives, C.C. 2/12
South African Commercial Advertiser, 23 October 1830

Gustaf

Swedish wooden barque of 382 tons, built in 1858 in Sweden, and commanded by Capt F. Schutt. Wrecked in Algoa Bay on 19 September 1869 during a south-east gale after having put into the bay for repairs with a cargo of 50 tons of lead. No lives were lost.
Eastern Province Herald, 21 September 1869
Lloyds Register of Shipping, 1869-70
Shipping Register, Cape Archives, C.C. 3/7/2/2

Hans Wagner (ex *Lobo*)
33° 55.80S, 25° 36.90E

German iron barque of 938 tons, built in 1877 by Osbourne, Graham & Co, Sunderland, and commanded by J. Müllmann. Wrecked on North End beach in Algoa Bay on 1 September 1902 when her cables parted during a south-east gale after a voyage from Melbourne with a cargo of wheat, flour and butter. No lives were lost. She was wrecked next to the *Coriolanus* (later refloated), and was struck by the *Nautilus* (1902).
Eastern Province Herald, 2 September 1902
Lloyds Register of Shipping, 1901-02

Hans Wagner (l), Coriolanus (r). (P.E. Public Library)

Hermann

Danish barque of 362 tons, commanded by Capt J. Walloe. Grounded opposite Barkers brickkilns in Algoa Bay on 11 September 1874 when her cables parted during a south-east gale while on a voyage from Mauritius with a cargo of coconuts, cigars, sugar and molasses. No lives were lost. The captain was ashore at the time. The wreck and cargo were sold for £310.
Eastern Province Herald, 15 September 1874

Hermanos
33° 56.30S, 25° 36.80E

Norwegian wooden barque of 498 tons, built in 1891 at Grimstad, and commanded by Capt G.M. Gundersen. Wrecked in Algoa Bay on 1 September 1902 when her cables parted during a south-east gale after a voyage from Bombay with a cargo of sleepers. Two men died, but the rest of the crew were rescued by means of rocket apparatus. She struck the sunken hulk of the *Queen Victoria* (1896).
Eastern Province Herald, 2 September 1902
Lloyds Register of Shipping, 1901-02

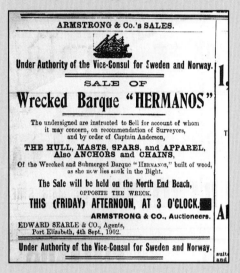

Eastern Province Herald

Hero

American whaling barque of 213 tons, commanded by Capt E. B. Hussey. Wrecked at the bight near the creek in Algoa Bay on 3 February 1861 when her cables parted during a south-east gale while on a voyage from New Bedford. The crew and most of the cargo were saved.
Shipping Register, Cape Archives, C.C. 3/7/2/1

Heworth

British snow of 236 tons, built in 1818, and commanded by Capt W. Beachcroft. Wrecked in Algoa Bay on 18 March 1823 when she parted from the government moorings after a voyage from London via Table Bay with a cargo including flour, most of which was saved. No lives were lost.
Cape Town Gazette and African Advertiser, 29 March, 5 April (sale notice) 1823
Lloyds Register of Shipping, 1822
Shipping Register, Cape Archives, C.C. 2/10

Horwood

British brig of 163 tons, built in 1829 at Southampton, and commanded by Capt J. Gales. Wrecked in Algoa Bay on 27 March 1845 when her cables parted during a south-east gale. No lives were lost. She was bound for London.

Cape of Good Hope and Port Natal Shipping and Mercantile Gazette, 4 April 1845
Lloyds Register of Shipping, 1845-46
Shipping Register, Cape Archives, C.C. 2/16

Ilva
33° 58.00S, 25° 38.00E

British wooden barque of 300 tons, built in 1865 by Pearson, Sunderland. Wrecked in Algoa Bay on the south side of the Port Elizabeth Boating Company jetty on 16 August 1866 while loading for London; she had 600-700 bales of wool on board at the time. She lies buried beneath reclaimed land.
Eastern Province Herald, 17 August 1866
Lloyds Register of Shipping, 1866-67

Inchcape Rock
33° 56.00S, 25° 37.10E

British full-rigged iron ship of 1 599 tons, built in 1886 by Russell & Co, Port Glasgow, and commanded by Capt A. Ferguson. Wrecked in Algoa Bay on 2 September 1902 when her cables parted during a south-east gale after a voyage from Portland, USA, with a cargo of wheat. No lives were lost. The bowsprit sticking out of the water near Darling Street (1987) is part of a well-preserved wreck which is almost certainly the *Inchcape Rock*.
Eastern Province Herald, 2 September 1902
Lloyds Register of Shipping, 1901-02

Iris (ex *Criffel*)
33° 56.36S, 25° 36.80E

German three-masted iron schooner of 522 tons, built in 1863 by R. Williamson & Son, Harrington, and commanded by Capt O. Berthelsen. Wrecked on North End beach in Algoa Bay on 1 September 1902 when her cables parted during a south-east gale after a voyage from Buenos Aires with a cargo of mealies. The crew were taken off by lifeboat.
Eastern Province Herald, 2 September 1902
Lloyds Register of Shipping, 1901-02

Isabel

Brazilian slaving barque, commanded by Lieut Alexander (RN). Wrecked in Algoa Bay at 21h00 on 21 August 1844 when her cables parted during a south-east gale. No lives were lost. She had been detained by HMS *Cleopatra*.
Graham's Town Journal, 29 August 1844
Shipping Register, Cape Archives, C.C. 2/16

Jack Tar

Brig. Wrecked in Algoa Bay on 12 January 1840 during a south-east gale. No lives were lost.
Graham's Town Journal, 23, 30 January (sale notice) 1840
Shipping Register, Cape Archives, C.C. 2/15

Jane Harvey
33° 57.10S, 25° 37.00E

British wooden barque of 347 tons, built in 1872 by Harvey, Littlehampton, and commanded by Capt J. Stevens. Wrecked in front of the gasworks in Algoa Bay on 30 August 1888 during a south-east gale while on a voyage from Cape Town to London via Algoa Bay with a cargo of wool and skins.
Eastern Province Herald, 31 August 1888
Lloyds Register of Shipping, 1888-89
Shipping Register, Cape Archives, C.C. 3/7/2/4

Jim Crow

British schooner of 187 tons, built in 1838 at Cork, and commanded by Capt G. Geere. Wrecked in Algoa Bay at 21h00 on 25 March 1846 during a south-east gale. No lives were lost. She had almost completed loading cargo for London.
Eastern Province Herald, 28 March 1846
Lloyds Register of Shipping, 1846-47
Shipping Register, Cape Archives, C.C. 2/16

Johanna

British wooden barque of 274 tons, built in 1843 at Newcastle, and commanded by Capt W. Falconer. Wrecked in Algoa Bay on 5 April 1848 when her cables parted during a south-east gale. No lives were lost.
Eastern Province Herald, 8 April 1848
Lloyds Register of Shipping, 1848-49
Shipping Register, Cape Archives, C.C. 2/17

Johanna

Dutch schooner of 198 tons, commanded by Capt A. Kamphuis. Wrecked in Algoa Bay on 15 February 1881 when her cables parted during a south-east gale with part of her original cargo of mealies loaded at Rosario, and a cargo of breadstuffs loaded at Cape Town. No lives were lost.
Grocott's Penny Mail, 18 February 1881
Shipping Register, Cape Archives, C.C. 3/7/2/3

John Witt

British wooden barque of 378 tons, built in 1840, and commanded by Capt J. Donavan. Wrecked in Algoa Bay on 17 October 1850 when her cables parted during a south-east gale after a voyage from Gothenburg. No lives were lost.
Eastern Province Herald, 19 October 1850
Lloyds Register of Shipping, 1850-51
Shipping Register, Cape Archives, C.C. 2/17, C.C. 2/24

Jorawur (ex HMS *Vulcan*)

Iron ship (hulk) of 1 736 tons, built in 1854 by C. J. Mare, London. Wrecked on North End

beach in Algoa Bay on 2 February 1887 during a south-east gale. Her bell is in the Port Elizabeth Museum.
Eastern Province Herald, 4 February 1887
Lloyds Register of Shipping, 1887-88

Kate

Coasting schooner commanded by Capt E. Cattell. Wrecked in Algoa Bay on 5 October 1834 during a south-east gale after a voyage from Table Bay with a general cargo.
South African Commercial Advertiser, 18 October 1834

Krimpenerward
33° 58.00S, 25° 37.60E

Dutch barque of 612 tons, commanded by Capt H. P. Klutt. Ran ashore near the Baakens River mouth on 12 August 1867 when her cables parted during a south-east gale after having put into the bay for repairs while on a voyage from Batavia to Rotterdam with a cargo of coffee, sugar and tin. No lives were lost. She lies buried beneath reclaimed land.
Eastern Province Herald, 13 August 1867 (sale notice)
Shipping Register, Cape Archives, C.C. 3/7/2/2

Eastern Province Herald

Lada

Austrian wooden barque of 544 tons, built in 1871 by Rosa, Fiume, and commanded by Capt L. Medanich. Wrecked in Algoa Bay on 30 August 1888 during a south-east gale. She was partly laden with a cargo of wool and skins for London.
Eastern Province Herald, 31 August 1888
Lloyds Register of Shipping, 1888-89
Shipping Register, Cape Archives, C.C. 3/7/2/4

Lady McDonald

British wooden barque of 593 tons, built in 1847 of teak in Maulmein, Burma, and commanded by Capt J. Hinks. Wrecked in Algoa Bay on 9 February 1876 after a voyage from London with a general cargo, including ironwork intended for the last span of the Sundays River railway bridge. No lives were lost.
Eastern Province Herald, 11 February 1876
Lloyds Register of Shipping, 1876-77
Shipping Register, Cape Archives, C.C. 3/7/2/2

Laura

British snow of 184 tons, built in 1824, and commanded by Capt Crockley. Wrecked in Algoa Bay on 25 August 1843 when her cables parted during a south-east gale with a cargo of sugar. She hit the *Sea Gull* (1843). Five crew members were drowned.
Graham's Town Journal, 31 August 1843
Lloyds Register of Shipping, 1843-44
Shipping Register, Cape Archives, C.C. 2/16

Ligonier

Cape cutter commanded by Capt W. Sexton. Wrecked in Algoa Bay on 2 March 1842 when her cables parted during a south-east gale. She was proceeding from the Kowie River to Mauritius to load sugar and was waiting in Algoa Bay for clearance. No lives were lost.
Graham's Town Journal, 10 March 1842
Shipping Register, Cape Archives, C.C. 2/15

Limari
33° 56.30S, 25° 36.80E

Swedish iron barque of 617 tons, built in 1867 by A. Stephen & Sons, Glasgow, and commanded by Capt C. A. Sundvall. Wrecked in Algoa Bay on 1 September 1902 during a south-east gale while on a voyage from Albany with a cargo of jarrah wood. She struck the sunken hulk of the *Queen Victoria* (1896) while being driven to the beach and was smashed to pieces. Eight people died. Her bell was found close to the *Queen Victoria*.
Eastern Province Herald, 6 September 1902
Lloyds Register of Shipping, 1901-02

Lyme Regis

British wooden barque of 250 tons, built in 1849 at Lyme, and commanded by Capt R. Hodder. Wrecked in Algoa Bay on 16 October 1859 when her cables parted during a south-east gale. No lives were lost.
Lloyds Register of Shipping, 1859-60
Shipping Register, Cape Archives, C.C. 2/18

Lyttelton

New Zealand barque of 585 tons, commanded by Capt W. C. Hosmer. Wrecked in Algoa Bay on

Lyttelton. *(Cape Archives, E5201)*

19 November 1874 when her anchor cables parted during a south-east gale after a voyage from Boston. The master was on shore. Most of her cargo, worth £7 000, had been discharged, and only recently loaded wool and skins were on board.
Eastern Province Herald, 20, 27 November (enquiry) 1874

Margareth
33° 56.60S, 25° 37.90E

Schooner commanded by Capt S. Drake. Wrecked opposite Jetty Street in Algoa Bay on 29 October 1846 during a south-east gale. She was loaded with government stores for Waterloo Bay. No lives were lost. She lies buried beneath reclaimed land.
Eastern Province Herald, 31 October 1846
Shipping Register, Cape Archives, C.C. 2/16

Maria

British brig of 159 tons, built in 1825 at Teignmouth, and commanded by Capt J. Burton. Wrecked in Algoa Bay during a south-east gale on 11 March 1837 when her windlass broke and she came ashore on the rockiest part of the bay. No lives were lost.
Graham's Town Journal, 16 March 1837
Lloyds Register of Shipping, 1837-38

Martha

British snow of 279 tons, built in 1838 at Sunderland, and commanded by Capt W. Woolley. Wrecked in Algoa Bay during a south-east gale on 5 April 1848 after a voyage from London. No lives were lost.
Eastern Province Herald, 8 April 1848
Lloyds Register of Shipping, 1848-49
Shipping Register, Cape Archives, C.C. 2/17, 2/24

Mary

Schooner commanded by Capt J. Caithness. Wrecked in Algoa Bay on 4 March 1844 when her cables parted during a south-east gale after a voyage from Mauritius with a cargo of sugar, rice and dates, which was saved. No lives were lost.
Shipping Register, Cape Archives, C.C. 2/16

Mary Ann

British wooden brig of 201 tons, built in 1838 at Ipswich, and commanded by Capt J. Guy. Wrecked in Algoa Bay on 17 October 1850 during a south-east gale after a voyage from London. No lives were lost.
Eastern Province Herald, 19 October 1850
Lloyds Register of Shipping, 1850-51
Shipping Register, Cape Archives, C.C. 2/17, C.C. 2/24

Mary Ann

British wooden barque of 313 tons, built in 1869 by J. Barkes, Sunderland, and commanded by Capt Enon. Wrecked in Algoa Bay on 12 January 1888 when her cables parted while on a voyage from Swansea to Natal. She had put into the bay for medical aid for the captain. No lives were lost.
Lloyds Register of Shipping, 1888-89
Shipping Register, Cape Archives, C.C. 3/7/2/4

Meg Merriles

British condemned wooden barque. Came ashore in Algoa Bay close to the *Sarah Black* (1869) on 19 September 1869 during a south-east gale when she broke from her moorings.
Eastern Province Herald, 21 September 1869
Lloyds Register of Shipping, 1869-70
Shipping Register, Cape Archives, C.C. 3/7/2/2

Modesta

Norwegian wooden schooner of 273 tons, built in 1875 by K. Jensenaes, Bergen, and commanded by Capt J. Simonsen. Wrecked opposite the Roburite factory in Algoa Bay on 26 August 1892 when her cables parted during a strong southeast gale after a voyage from Natal with a cargo of sugar and coal, most of which had been discharged. No lives were lost.
Eastern Province Herald, 29 August 1892
Lloyds Register of Shipping, 1892-93

Mona
33° 58.01S, 25° 37.60E

Barque commanded by Capt P. Sayers. Wrecked opposite the boating company stores in Algoa Bay on 28 October 1846 during a south-east gale. No lives were lost.
Eastern Province Herald, 31 October 1846

Natal

Swedish wooden brigantine of 335 tons, built in 1878, and commanded by Capt H. O. Breggen. Wrecked in Algoa Bay on 30 August 1888 during a south-east gale after a voyage from New York with a general cargo, very little of which had been discharged.
Eastern Province Herald, 31 August 1888
Lloyds Universal Register of Shipping, 1888-89
Shipping Register, Cape Archives, C.C. 3/7/2/8

Nautilus
33° 55.60S, 25° 37.00E

German iron barque of 747 tons, built in 1878 in Hamburg, and commanded by Capt J. J. Assing. Wrecked on North End beach in Algoa Bay on 1 September 1902 during a south-east gale after a voyage from Adelaide with a cargo of wheat and flour. She struck the *Hans Wagner* (1902), the sunken hulk of the *Queen Victoria* (1896) and the *Limari* (1902). Only three of her crew were saved, by jumping onto the *Hans Wagner*.
Eastern Province Herald, 2 September 1902
Lloyds Register of Shipping, 1901-02

Nicoline

German three-masted schooner. Wrecked in Algoa Bay on 23 December 1875 when her cables parted during a south-east gale while on a voyage from Hamburg to East London via Algoa Bay with a cargo of liquor. No lives were lost.
Eastern Province Herald, 24, 28 (sale notice) December 1875

Oaklands

British wooden barque of 424 tons, built in 1858, registered in London, and commanded by Capt J. Winn. Wrecked near the Coega River mouth in Algoa Bay on 20 March 1860 after a voyage from London with a general cargo. No lives were lost.
Lloyds Register of Shipping, 1860-61
Shipping Register, Cape Archives, C.C. 3/7/2/1

Oakworth
33° 56.36S, 25° 36.80E

British iron ship of 1 242 tons, built in 1874 by W. Hamilton & Co, Port Glasgow, and commanded by Capt J. Davies. Wrecked on North End beach in Algoa Bay on 1 September 1902 during a south-east gale with a cargo of wheat from Port Pirie.
Eastern Province Herald, 2 September 1902
Lloyds Register of Shipping, 1901-02

Orange Grove

Schooner. Wrecked in Algoa Bay on 11 November 1829 at night during a south-east gale. The cargo was saved.
Shipping Register, Cape Archives, C.C. 2/12

Orchomene

British iron ship of 1 586 tons, built in 1881 by W. H. Potter & Son, Liverpool, and commanded by Capt G. Thomas. Struck Roman Rock and was beached in the bight in Algoa Bay on 9 January 1892 after a voyage from Cardiff with a cargo of coal.
Eastern Province Herald, 11, 13, 18 January 1892
Lloyds Register of Shipping, 1891-92

Palestine

Brig commanded by Capt W. Collier. Wrecked on the rocks in Algoa Bay on 28 October 1846 when her cables parted during a south-east gale with government stores for Waterloo Bay. No lives were lost. Her crew were ill and could not handle her.
Eastern Province Herald, 31 October 1846
Shipping Register, Cape Archives, C.C. 2/16

SS **Paris Maru**
33° 55.20S, 25° 39.70E

Japanese cargo vessel of 7 197 tons, built in 1921 by Cammell Laird & Co, Birkenhead, owned by the Osaka Shosen Kaisha Line, and commanded by Capt K. Yugeta. Sank off North End beach in Algoa Bay on 15 January 1934 during a southeast gale while on a voyage from Japan to Cape Town with a cargo of general merchandise, including silk stockings and paraffin in tins. She had struck Roman Rock soon after leaving the harbour and was bought back into the bay in a sinking condition. She lies directly north of the mouth to the Port Elizabeth Harbour and is clearly marked on charts. She was blown up to flatten her.
Eastern Province Herald, 16, 17 January 1934 (photographs)
Lloyds Register of Shipping, 1934-35

Paris Maru. *(P.E. Public Library)*

Paz

British wooden barque of 290 tons, built in 1871 at Bilbao, and commanded by Capt Hoseason. Wrecked in Algoa Bay on 8 October 1884 when her cables parted during a south-east gale. No lives were lost.
Lloyds Register of Shipping, 1884-85
Shipping Register, Cape Archives, C.C. 3/7/2/3

Petronella

Dutch wooden barque of 500 tons, built in 1854 in the Netherlands, and commanded by Capt W. de Jong. Wrecked in Algoa Bay on 16 July 1878 during a south-east gale while on a voyage from Macassar to Amsterdam with a cargo of rattans, pearl shells, gum copal, tortoise-shell, coffee, tobacco and india-rubber. She had put into the bay in distress. No lives were lost.
Eastern Province Herald, 19 July 1878 (sale notice)
Lloyds Register of Shipping, 1878-79
Shipping Register, Cape Archives, C.C. 3/7/2/3

Philip Dundas

Brig. Wrecked near the landing-place in Algoa Bay on 16 August 1828 during a south-east gale. Two crew members were drowned.
Cape of Good Hope Government Gazette, 29 August 1828
Shipping Register, Cape Archives, C.C. 2/12

Portsmouth

American brig of 203 tons, commanded by Capt Lynch. Wrecked close to the Coega River mouth in Algoa Bay on 14 March 1866 when her cables parted during a north-west gale after a voyage from New York with a cargo of 2 500 barrels of flour. The cook was drowned while swimming ashore.
Eastern Province Herald, 16 March 1866

Poseidon

Norwegian wooden barque of 386 tons, built in 1867 at Tvedestrand, and commanded by Capt G. Terjesen. Wrecked in Algoa Bay on 30 October 1889 during a south-east gale after a voyage from Sundsvall with a cargo of deals, none of which had been discharged. No lives were lost.
Eastern Province Herald, 1 November 1889
Lloyds Universal Register of Shipping, 1889-90
Shipping Register, Cape Archives, C.C. 3/7/2/4

Prince Woronzoff

British wooden snow of 236 tons, built in 1851 at Sunderland, and commanded by Capt P. Clarke. Wrecked in Algoa Bay on 16 October 1859 during a south-east gale with a cargo of seed and cotton. No lives were lost.
Lloyds Register of Shipping, 1859-60
Shipping Register, Cape Archives, C.C. 2/18

Cape Times

SS **Queen Victoria**
33° 56.20S, 25° 37.10E

British steel screw steamer of 2 312 tons, built in 1887 by A. Stephen & Sons, Glasgow, chartered by the Clan Line, and commanded by Capt E. J. Heno. Struck Thunderbolt Reef on 21 April 1896 while on a voyage from Britain to Algoa Bay with a general cargo and was brought into the bay for repairs. Was beached off Humewood but later moved to North End beach, where she was run aground on 18 August 1896 to facilitate repairs. After heavy south-east gales she was declared a wreck. She lies near the foot of Darling Street and is fairly well preserved. This wreck was responsible for many deaths during the 1902 gale when the *Limari*, *Agostino Rombo*, *Waimea*, *Hermanos* and *Nautilus* struck her and broke up rapidly.
Cape Times, 8 May 1896 (advertisement for tenders to raise)
Eastern Province Herald, 24 April, 19, 21 August 1896
Lloyds Register of Shipping, 1895-96

Reistad (ex *Anni*, ex *Garibaldi*)

Norwegian full-rigged wooden ship of 1 422 tons, built in 1860 by Maxon & Fish, Mystic, Connecticut. Wrecked in the bight in Algoa Bay on 31 January 1897 when her anchor cables parted during a south-east wind and she collided with the barque *Arnguda* after a voyage from Sundsvall with a cargo of timber. No lives were lost, as the crew were rescued by the port boat.

Eastern Province Herald, 1, 3, 8 (sale notice)
  February 1897
Lloyds Register of Shipping, 1896-97

Resolution

Barque commanded by Capt J. Clark. Wrecked in Algoa Bay on 29 October 1846 during a south-east gale while on a voyage to Waterloo Bay with a cargo of Government stores, most of which was recovered. No lives were lost.
Eastern Province Herald, 31 October 1846
Shipping Register, Cape Archives, C.C. 2/16

San Antonio

Italian iron barque of 502 tons, commanded by Capt Astarita. Wrecked in Algoa Bay on 14 November 1903 during a south-east gale after a voyage from Marseilles with a cargo of bricks, tiles, cement and vermouth. No lives were lost.
Daily Telegraph, Port Elizabeth, 14 November 1903
Eastern Province Herald, 19 November 1903 (sale notice)

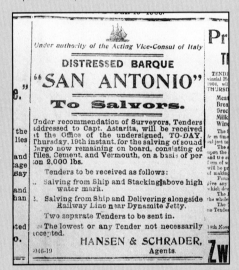

Eastern Province Herald

Sarah Black
33° 57.30S, 25° 37.00E

British wooden barque of 315 tons, built in 1858 at Sunderland, and commanded by Capt R. Hutchinson. Wrecked near the gas-works on North End beach at Port Elizabeth at 22h00 on 18 September 1869 during a south-east gale while loading cargo for East London. No lives were lost.
Eastern Province Herald, 21 September 1869
Lloyds Register of Shipping, 1869-70
Shipping Register, Cape Archives, C.C. 3/7/2/2

Sayre
33° 55.40S, 25° 36.90E

British wooden barque of 735 tons, built in 1890 by F. E. Sayre at St Johns, New Brunswick,

owned by E. E. Hutchings, and commanded by Capt W. H. Matheson. Wrecked on North End beach in Algoa Bay on 1 September 1902 during a south-east gale after a voyage from New York with a general cargo.
Eastern Province Herald, 2 September 1902
Lloyds Register of Shipping, 1901-02

Sea Gull

British brig of 258 tons, built in 1841, and commanded by Capt J. Murray. Wrecked in Algoa Bay on 25 August 1843 when her cables parted during a south-east gale with a cargo of rice. She hit the jetty and the *Laura* while drifting towards the beach. Five people were drowned.
Lloyds Register of Shipping, 1843-44
Shipping Register, Cape Archives, C.C. 2/16

Sea Snake

Swedish barque of 437 tons, commanded by Capt Christophersen. Wrecked to the north of the sea wall in Algoa Bay on 19 September 1869 when her cables parted during a south-east gale while on a voyage from Shanghai to Falmouth. She had put into the bay after springing a leak. Nine crew members were drowned.
Eastern Province Herald, 21 September 1869
Shipping Register, Cape Archives, C.C. 3/7/2/2

Sedwell Jane

British wooden barquentine of 201 tons, built in 1868 by Rolle Canal Co, Bideford, and commanded by Capt W. Tulloch. Wrecked in Algoa Bay half a kilometre south of the *Jorawur* (1887) on 2 October 1893 when she dragged her anchors during a south-east gale after a voyage from Port

Sayre. *(Frank Neave)*

Pirie with a cargo of flour. No lives were lost.
Eastern Province Herald, 4 October 1893
Lloyds Register of Shipping, 1893-94

Simon

Wooden brig of 223 tons, built in 1860 by Griffiths, Nevin, and commanded by Capt T. Volk. Wrecked near the gas-works in Algoa Bay on 13 January 1871 during a south-east gale after a voyage from Hong Kong. She had loaded 400 bales of wool for Sandy Hook. No lives were lost.
Eastern Province Herald, 17 January 1871
Lloyds Register of Shipping, 1870-71
Shipping Register, Cape Archives, C.C. 3/7/2/2

Sophia

Schooner commanded by Capt J. Sillands. Wrecked in Algoa Bay on 29 October 1846 when her cables parted during a south-east gale before a voyage to the Fish River. No lives were lost. In 1843 she had run ashore with the *Sir John S. Aubyn* at the Kowie River.
Eastern Province Herald, 31 October 1846
Shipping Register, Cape Archives, C.C. 2/16

Star of the East

Barque of 357 tons, commanded by Capt N. Tyack. Wrecked in Algoa Bay on 16 October 1859 during a south-east gale with a cargo of wool, hides, skins, and indigo. No lives were lost.
Eastern Province Herald, 22 November 1859 (sale notice and inquiry)
Shipping Register, Cape Archives, C.C. 2/18

Stella

Norwegian barque of 383 tons, wrecked in Algoa Bay on 18 September 1876 when her cables parted during a south-east gale after a voyage from Boston with a cargo of lumber.
East London Dispatch, 19 September 1876
Eastern Province Herald, 19, 22 (sale notice) September 1876

Susan

British barque of 573 tons, built in 1813 in Calcutta, and commanded by Capt H. Ager. Wrecked in Algoa Bay at 22h00 on 25 March 1846 when her cables parted during a south-east gale while loading a cargo for Mauritius. One man was drowned.
Eastern Province Herald, 28 March 1846
Lloyds Register of Shipping, 1846-47
Shipping Register, Cape Archives, C.C. 2/16

Taurus

French barque of 300 tons, built in 1859. Wrecked in Algoa Bay near the *Cruiser* (1872) and the *E. B. Lohe* (1872) on 27 November 1872 during a south-east gale after a voyage from Buenos Aires in ballast. No lives were lost.
Eastern Province Herald, 29 November 1872 (sale notice)
Shipping Register, Cape Archives, C.C. 3/7/2/2

Tentonia

North German barque of 853 tons, commanded by Capt Helsing. Wrecked in Algoa Bay on 7 August 1869 when her cables parted with a cargo of rice. Some of her cargo was salvaged by the barque *Major Van Safft*, which ran ashore in 1869 but was later refloated. No lives were lost.
Shipping Register, Cape Archives, C.C. 3/7/2/2

Thekla

33° 55.20S, 25° 37.00E

German wooden three-masted schooner of 350 tons, built in 1897 by the owners, A. Beckmann, Papenburg, and commanded by Capt R. Schnieders. Wrecked in Algoa Bay on 1 September 1902 during a south-east gale after a voyage from Mauritius with a cargo of sugar, which had been discharged.
Eastern Province Herald, 2 September 1902
Lloyds Register of Shipping, 1901-02

Trekboer

Schooner commanded by Capt T. Cobern. Wrecked in Algoa Bay between 22h00 and 23h00 on 21 August 1844 when her cables parted during a south-east gale after a voyage from Ceylon with a cargo of coir rope. One boy was drowned.
Graham's Town Journal, 29 August 1844
Shipping Register, Cape Archives, C.C. 2/16

Under authority of Vice-Consul for Sweden and Norway.
DISTRESSED BARQUE
"TWO BROTHERS."
TO SALVORS.
Upon recommendation of Surveyors, Tenders addressed to Capt. Johannsen, will be received at the Office of the undersigned up to Noon, THURSDAY, 19th Instant, for the Salving of the Cargo now remaining on board, Sorting and stacking above high water mark.
Lowest Tender not necessarily accepted.
EDWARD SEARLE & Co.,
AGENTS.

Daily Telegraph

Two Brothers (ex *City Camp*)

Norwegian wooden barque of 951 tons, built in 1870 by S. J. King, St Johns, and commanded by Capt Johannesen. Wrecked in Algoa Bay on 14 November 1903 during a south-east gale after a voyage from Sundsvall with a cargo of deals. No lives were lost.
Daily Telegraph, Port Elizabeth, 14 November 1903
Lloyds Register of Shipping, 1901-02

Uitenhage Packet

Coaster. Wrecked in Algoa Bay on 30 August 1819 during a south-east gale. No lives were lost.
Cape Town Gazette, 25 September 1819
Shipping Register, Cape Archives, C.C. 2/9

Univers

33° 57.00S, 25° 37.00E

French barque of 369 tons, commanded by Capt F. le Cart. Wrecked 50 m north of the gas-works in Algoa Bay on 23 August 1877 when her cables parted during a south-east gale after a voyage from London with a general cargo, including iron for the Colesberg bridge. No lives were lost. While drifting towards the beach she struck the *Hydra*, sustaining severe damage.
Eastern Province Herald, 24 August 1877

Urania

Cape Town-based brig of 132 tons, built in 1827 at Yarmouth. Wrecked in Algoa Bay on 1 October 1835 at night when her cables parted during a south-east gale with a cargo of iron.
Graham's Town Journal, 8 October 1835
Lloyds Register of Shipping, 1835-36

Ville D'Obéron

French barque of 236 tons, commanded by Capt M. Olivier. Wrecked in Algoa Bay on 9 October 1854 while on a voyage from Réunion to Mar-

seilles. She was in a sinking state and was run ashore on purpose.
Shipping Register, Cape Archives, C.C. 2/18, C.C. 2/24

Vilora H. Hopkins

American wooden barque of 977 tons, built in 1877 by E. Young, Millbridge, Maine, and commanded by Capt J. Wakeley. Wrecked on New Brighton beach next to the dynamite jetty in Algoa Bay on 7 February 1897 when her cables parted during a south-east gale after a voyage from New York with a general cargo including 1 094 cases of explosives, which had been discharged.
Eastern Province Herald, 8, 10, 19 (sale notice) February 1897
Lloyds Register of Shipping, 1896-97

Vilora H. Hopkins. *(Africana Museum)*

Waimea (ex *Dorette*)

33° 56.30S, 25° 36.80E

Norwegian iron barque of 874 tons, built in 1868 by Godeffroy, Hamburg, and commanded by Capt P. Ordrop. Wrecked on North End beach in Algoa Bay on 1 September 1902 during a south-east gale after a voyage from Fremantle with a cargo of jarrah wood. She struck the sunken hulk of the SS *Queen Victoria* (1896) on her way in. Eight crew were drowned. The wreck lies inshore of the *Inchcape Rock* (1902).
Eastern Province Herald, 2 September 1902
Lloyds Register of Shipping, 1901-02

Wayfarer

Norwegian wooden barque of 658 tons, built in 1874 at Digby, and commanded by Capt H. Petersen. Wrecked in Algoa Bay on 14 November 1903 during a south-east gale after a voyage from Gothenburg with a cargo of deals. No lives were lost.
Daily Telegraph, Port Elizabeth, 14 November 1903
Eastern Province Herald, 20 November 1903 (sale notice)
Lloyds Register of Shipping, 1901-02

West Indian

British wooden barque of 328 tons, built in 1829

at Bristol, and commanded by Capt R. Howlett. Wrecked in Algoa Bay on 4 December 1851 when her cables parted during a south-east gale while on a voyage from Madras to Table Bay. No lives were lost.
Eastern Province News, 13 December 1851
Lloyds Register of Shipping, 1851-52
Shipping Register, Cape Archives, C.C. 2/17, C.C. 2/24

Wheatlandside

British wooden full-rigged ship of 1 136 tons, built in 1872 in Quebec, and commanded by Capt D. Smith. Run ashore 1,6 km north of the gas-works in Algoa Bay on 30 January 1878 when she struck a reef during a south-east gale after a voyage from London with a cargo of sleepers and iron rails.
Eastern Province Herald, 1 February 1878 (sale notice)
Lloyds Register of Shipping, 1877-78

Wigrams

British ship of 286 tons, built in 1843 of teak in Maulmein, Burma, and commanded by Capt R. H. Dixon. Wrecked in Algoa Bay on 16 October 1859 when her cables parted during a south-east gale after a voyage from East London for repairs. No lives were lost.
Lloyds Register of Shipping, 1859-60
Shipping Register, Cape Archives, C.C. 2/18

Witch of the Waves

Schooner of 95 tons, commanded by Capt J. Phillips. Wrecked in Algoa Bay on 3 October 1859 at night during a south-east gale after a voyage from Rio de Janeiro with a cargo of coffee. One man was lost.
Eastern Province Herald, 4 October 1859
Shipping Register, Cape Archives, C.C. 2/18

Wolseley

British iron barque of 341 tons, built in 1876 by J. E. Scott, Greenock, and commanded by Capt A. Digman. Wrecked in Algoa Bay next to the *Drei Emmas* (1888) on 30 August 1888 during a south-east gale after a voyage from Cape Town with a cargo of 3 429 bags of grain.
Eastern Province Herald, 31 August 1888
Lloyds Register of Shipping, 1888-89
Shipping Register, Cape Archives, C.C. 3/7/2/4

Zephyr

Norwegian barque of 357 tons, commanded by Capt A. Neilsen. Wrecked in Algoa Bay on 16 October 1889 during a south-east gale after a voyage from Frederikstad in Norway with a cargo of deals. No lives were lost.
Eastern Province Herald, 18 October 1889
Shipping Register, Cape Archives, C.C. 3/7/2/4

30. Sundays River mouth to the Kariega River mouth

The area from the Sundays River mouth to Cape Padrone is one of the most desolate stretches of coast in South Africa. The beach is totally isolated from the nearest vegetation by large tracts of drifting sand dunes and in places no sign of greenery is visible. The sea is warm due to the Agulhas current which flows into the bay, but the water is turbid due to the discoloured water which pours into the bay from the Sundays River. Divers rarely visit this area. The most prominent feature of this stretch of coast is Woody Cape, a long stretch of high sandstone cliffs which form the eastern boundary of Algoa Bay. The tops of these cliffs are heavily wooded and form an oasis in a sea of sand. The coast from Cape Padrone eastward cuts away rapidly to the north-east and the vegetation takes on a sub-tropical appearance with huge green trees and fields of green grass, where dairy farming is practiced. The prominent features of this stretch of coast are Kwaaihoek, where Bartolomeu Dias planted a padrão, and the Bushmans River and Kariega River holiday resorts. Cannon Rocks are named after cast iron cannons from a wreck found here.

Ann and Eliza

British vessel commanded by Capt Haldene. Wrecked between the Swartkops and Bushmans rivers in Algoa Bay in April 1796 while on a voyage from Bengal to England via Table Bay with a cargo of rice and arrack. The captain and 35 of the crew were drowned; 5 were saved. The wreck was plundered by the inhabitants of Bruintjieshoogte.
Cape Archives, B.O. 146

Betsy and Sara

Dutch barque of 900 tons. Wrecked a little to the west of the Bushmans River near Cannon Rocks on 19 April 1839 while on a voyage from Batavia to Amsterdam with a cargo of coffee, arrack, tin and sugar. Nineteen lives were lost and 32 saved. Her captain, Captain Blaauwpot, had died at sea.
Graham's Town Journal, 25 April, 9 May (sale notice) 1839
South African Commercial Advertiser, 8, 11, 15 May 1839

Cambusnethan

British steel barque of 1 458 tons, built in 1891 by Russell & Co, Port Glasgow, owned by the Cambus Nethan Sailing Ship Co, Glasgow, and commanded by Capt Hugh Hughes. Wrecked near Woody Cape in Algoa Bay on 5 May 1897 in the early morning during a south-west gale at the start of a voyage to New York in ballast. No lives were lost among her crew of 23. She lies about 6,5 km east of the *R.A.C. Smith* (1898).
Eastern Province Herald, 10 May 1897
Lloyds Register of Shipping, 1896-97

Gladiator

British wooden ship of 1 502 tons, built in 1856 in Quebec, and commanded by Capt Jeffares. Wrecked between Cape Padrone and the Bushmans River on 12 November 1860 while on a voyage from Bombay to Liverpool with a cargo of cotton and seeds. Two crew members were drowned.
Cape Argus, 29 November 1860
Lloyds Register of Shipping, 1860-61
Shipping Register, Cape Archives, C.C. 3/7/2/1

Jupiter T.
33° 46.00S, 26° 30.30E

Austrian barque of 689 tons, commanded by Guiseppe Luigi Ivancich. Wrecked 3 km east of Cape Padrone and 1 km from the shore on 19 April 1875 at night in fog while on a voyage from Singapore to New York with a cargo of 6 500 bags of pepper, 200 boxes (400 tons) of nutmeg, 492 boxes (47 tons) of gum copal, 2 914 bundles (16,5 tons) of rattans, 1 361 buffalo hides, 1 810 bales (25 tons) of gambier and 277 tons of tin in the form of 5 330 slabs weighing between 48 and 50 kg each, worth £40 000. One man was lost. Tin worth £12 000 was recovered at the time and shipped to England; more tin was recovered in 1980. She lies close to the *Roma* (1892).
Cape Argus, 11 May 1875 (sale report)
Eastern Province Herald, 29 July 1879, 11 January 1881 (report on court case on salvage)
Graham's Town Journal, 23 April, 23 July (sale notice) 1875

Graham's Town Journal

Noatun

Norwegian wooden barque of 522 tons, built in 1881 by H. A. Weber, Grimstad, and commanded by Capt L. Rodland. Wrecked at Grootvley Beach, between Woody Cape and Cape Padrone, on 22 June 1892 during a westerly storm at the start of a voyage to Barbadoes in ballast after she had discharged her cargo in Algoa Bay.
Eastern Province Herald, 8 July 1892
Lloyds Register of Shipping, 1892-93

R.A.C. Smith
33° 42.60S, 26° 04.00E

American wooden barquentine of 662 tons, built in 1889 by G. A. Gilchrist, Belfast, Maine, owned by Swan & Son, and commanded by Capt H. B. Hooper. Wrecked 13 km east of the Sundays River mouth in Algoa Bay on 16 May 1898 at night after being dismasted during a storm while on a voyage from Mauritius to New York with a cargo of sugar. The captain and second mate were drowned. The wreck lies about 6,5 km west of the *Cambusnethan* (1897).
Eastern Province Herald, 18, 19, 20 May 1898
Lloyds Register of Shipping, 1898-99

Roma

British iron barque of 642 tons, built in 1865 by A. Stephen & Sons, Glasgow, and commanded by Capt J. Ewing. Ran ashore near Cape Padrone close to the *Jupiter T.* (1875) on 19 August 1892 at night while on a voyage from Bombay to Hull with a cargo of palm-nut oil. All lives were lost.
Eastern Province Herald, 24 August 1892
Lloyds Register of Shipping, 1892-93

São João Baptista

Portuguese East-Indiaman (*não*) commanded by Capt Pedro de Moraes Sarmento. Ran ashore near the Fish River in October 1622 while on a homeward-bound voyage from Goa, which she had left on 1 March 1622 with a cargo of diamonds, Chinese porcelain, cloth, carpets and pepper in the company of the flagship *Nossa Senhora do Paraiso*. She had been involved in a fight with two outward-bound Dutch East-Indiamen and was in a sinking condition. The crew, passengers and trade goods were landed, but 18 lives were lost. The survivors set fire to the hulk and walked to Inhambane in Mozambique, leaving many women and children at native kraals along the way. Chinese porcelain shards are found opposite a wreck site at Cannon Rocks, which may be the site of this wreck.
Dutch-Asiatic Shipping Outward Voyages, 1595-1794, The Hague, 1979
Almada, Francisco Vaz d', *Tratado do sucesso que teve a não Sam Ioam Baptista*, Lisbon, 1625. Translated into English in Theal, G.M., *Records of South Eastern Africa*, Vol 8, pp 69-137

Tevere

British barque of 326 tons, built in 1862 at Recco, and commanded by Capt E. S. Hill. Wrecked 48 km east of Algoa Bay near Woody Cape on 12 October 1878 when her anchor cables parted in Algoa Bay during a south-west gale after a voyage from Cardiff with a cargo of coal. No lives were lost.
Lloyds Register of Shipping, 1878-79
Shipping Register, Cape Archives, C.C. 3/7/2/3

Volo

Norwegian wooden barque of 616 tons, built in 1891 at Arendal. Wrecked between the Bushmans and Kariega rivers on 6 March 1896. Twelve people were saved.
Cape Times, 7 March 1896
Lloyds Register of Shipping, 1895-96

Volo.

31. Bird Island group

A group of low islands lying 4 nautical miles (8 km) off Woody Cape and consisting of Bird, Stag and Seal islands. Bird Island is home to a large population of gannets and is an important source of guano. Seal Island supports a large group of Cape fur seals and Great White sharks are found in abundance around the islands. The water is warm due to the Agulhas current which flows south-westwards, and is usually clear, but divers rarely visit the area due to the inaccessibility and the sharks. Doddington Rock is named after the English East-Indiaman Dodington, *wrecked on the island in 1755.*

SS Ashlands

British steel screw steamer of 2 303 tons, built in 1890 by E. Withy & Co, West Hartlepool, and commanded by Capt Gourley. Wrecked on Doddington Rock, Bird Island, on 5 July 1900 on a moonlit night while on a voyage from Hull to Natal with a cargo of coal. No lives were lost.
East London Daily Dispatch, 6, 9, 16 July 1900
Eastern Province Herald, 7 July 1900
Lloyds Register of Shipping, 1899-1900

Buffon

French brig commanded by Capt Guiod. Wrecked on the east point of Roman Rock, Bird Island, on 26 February 1858 with a cargo of guano. No lives were lost.
Cape Argus, 10 March 1858
Shipping Register, Cape Archives, C.C. 2/18

Charles

Schooner commanded by Capt G. Guilbert. Struck a sunken rock at Bird Island and sank in 37 m of water on 15 November 1845 with a cargo of 140 tons of guano. No lives were lost.

Eastern Province Herald, 3 December 1845
Shipping Register, Cape Archives, C.C. 2/16

SS Crusader

British steel screw steamer of 4 249 tons, built in 1901 by Sunderland Shipbuilding Co, and commanded by Capt Charles Richardson Hird. Wrecked near East Reef off Bird Island at 19h30 on 25 February 1910 while on a voyage from Norfolk, USA, to Manila with 7 200 tons of coal. No lives were lost.
Eastern Province Herald, 2, 8 (enquiry) March 1910
Lloyds Register of Shipping, 1909-10

Dodington
33° 50.06S, 26° 17.40E

British ship of 499 tons and 26 guns on hire to the English East India Company, and commanded by Capt James Sampson. Wrecked on the south-east corner of Bird Island on 17 July 1755 at night during a south-west gale while on an outward-bound voyage from England to Fort St George in India. Of the 270 crew, only 23 were saved. The survivors sailed to Delagoa Bay in a vessel called *The Happy Deliverance* which they had made out of timber from the wreck. The site was worked by divers from Port Elizabeth in 1977 and many silver Mexican pillar dollars and four bronze field-guns were recovered, together with 30 tons of copper plates and pigs. John Lethbridge, the English diver, unsuccessfully applied for permission to dive on her in 1757.
Allen, G. and D., *Clive's Lost Treasure*, 1978
Hardy, Charles, *A Register of Ships in the Service of the English East India Company*, 1800
Plaisted, Bartholomew, *A Journal from Calcutta* and *A Journal of the Proceedings of the Doddington East Indiaman*, London, 1758

Edith Smith

Cape wooden brig of 171 tons, built in 1862 by Gough, Bridgewater, and owned by I. O. Smith, Cape of Good Hope. Wrecked on the North Patch on Bird Island on 2 December 1871 while on a voyage from East London to Algoa Bay with a cargo of 340 bales of wool, some hides and 30 tons of mealies. She had called at the island to land provisions for the guano party.
Graham's Town Journal, 6 December 1871
Lloyds Register of Shipping, 1871-72
Shipping Register, Cape Archives, C.C. 3/7/2/2

Florence

British schooner of 67 tons, commanded by Capt W. Carstens. Wrecked on the north-east side of Stag Island, off Bird Island, on 19 April 1883 when she drifted from her anchorage after a voyage from Port Elizabeth to load guano. No lives were lost, as the crew landed on the island in the lifeboat.
Eastern Province Herald, 4 May 1883

Forest Grove

British wooden barque of 347 tons, built in 1867 by W. H. Pearson, jr, Sunderland, and commanded by Capt T. Simonds. Wrecked on Doddington Rock at Bird Island on 13 January 1887 while on a voyage from Algoa Bay to East London. No lives were lost.
Cape Argus Weekly, 19 January 1887
Lloyds Register of Shipping, 1887-88
Shipping Register, Cape Archives, C.C. 3/7/2/4

Katherine Gwladys

British wooden schooner of 161 tons, built in 1851 at Poole, and commanded by Capt M. Abell. Wrecked on Bird Island on 27 February 1854 after shifting her berth with a cargo of guano. No lives were lost.
Lloyds Register of Shipping, 1853-54
Shipping Register, Cape Archives, C.C. 2/18

Norfolk

Wooden schooner of 132 tons, built in 1841 at Yarmouth, owned by J. O. Smith, Algoa Bay, and commanded by Capt P. H. Watts. Wrecked on Seal Island, off Bird Island, on 23 September 1850 while waiting to load a cargo of guano for Mauritius. No lives were lost.
Cape Town Mail, 5 October 1850
Lloyds Register of Shipping, 1850-51
Shipping Register, Cape Archives, C.C. 2/17, C.C. 2/24

SS Westenhope

British steamer of 750 tons, owned by Payne & Co, and commanded by Capt James Mackay. Wrecked on Seal Island, off Bird Island, on 1 January 1871 on a moonlit night while on a voyage from Algoa Bay to Natal. No lives were lost.
Eastern Province Herald, 6, 10, 17 January 1871
Shipping Register, Cape Archives, C.C. 3/7/2/2

32. Kariega River to Hood Point

A long stretch of coast consisting mainly of long sandy beaches interspersed with rocky points, as well as many river mouths and estuaries. The water is warm due to the Agulhas current, but is turbid due to the many rivers which discharge into the sea, especially in the summer months. The climate is warm and humid in summer and the vegetation on land consists of thick coastal bush. The coast is popular and many holiday-makers flock to the many resorts, the main pastime being fishing. The most prominent features of the coast are Port Alfred, a thriving seaside town on the Kowie River, the Great Fish River, the Keiskamma River, with the small settlement of Hamburg nearby, and Cove Rock. Madagascar Reef is named after the steamer SS Madagascar which was wrecked there in 1858, and Waterloo Bay after the Cape schooner Waterloo wrecked in Cawoods Bay in 1848.

Africaine
33° 35.80S, 26° 54.80E

Schooner of 80 tons, owned by Cock and Hodgkin, and commanded by Capt E. Salmond. Wrecked on the rocks 1 km east of the Kowie River on 5 May 1841. No lives were lost and most of her cargo was saved. She had been specially built for the Kowie trade and was the first vessel to enter the Kowie through the west entrance.
Graham's Town Journal, 13 May 1841
Shipping Register, Cape Archives, C.C. 2/15

African Belle
33° 36.30S, 26° 54.00E

Cape brigantine of 122 tons, built in 1871, and commanded by Capt W. C. Turner. Wrecked on the west side of the Kowie River on 12 September 1873. She was later blown up to clear the channel for shipping.
Cape Argus, 16 September 1873
Lloyds Register of Shipping, 1873-74
Shipping Register, Cape Archives, C.C. 3/7/2/2

Amana

British full-rigged iron sailing ship of 1 299 tons, built in 1875 by A. Stephen & Sons, Glasgow, and commanded by Capt A. Becket. Wrecked 1,6 km north-east of the Fish River mouth on 25 September 1889 while on a voyage from Rangoon to Rio de Janeiro with a cargo of rice. One seaman was lost.
Eastern Province Herald, 27 September 1889
Lloyds Register of Shipping, 1889-90
Shipping Register, Cape Archives, C.C. 3/7/2/4

SS Ashmount

British steel screw steamer of 3 109 tons, built in 1904 by A. Rodger & Co, Port Glasgow, and commanded by Capt J. D. McDowall. Wrecked between Fish Point light and Stalwart Point on 5 April 1905 while on a voyage from Sydney to Liverpool with a cargo of sugar. Eight lives were lost.
Eastern Province Herald, 8 April 1905
Lloyds Register of Shipping, 1904-05

Bennebroek

Dutch ship of 800 tons, built in 1708 at the Amsterdam Yard for the Amsterdam Chamber of the Dutch East India Company, and commanded by Jan Hes. Wrecked on the coast south-west of Hamburg near the Mtana River on 16 February 1713 while homeward-bound from Ceylon, which she had left on 22 September 1712. The vessel broke up immediately and many lives were lost. The survivors tried to walk to Cape Town, but only one Indian reached this goal; a further four were rescued by an English boat. The wreck was discovered by Peter Sachs of East London in 1985, and many broken and a few intact pieces of Chinese porcelain were recovered.

Bronze breech-loading swivel-guns bearing the Amsterdam crest were also found.
Cape Archives, V.C. 20. Translated into English in *Précis of the Archives of the Cape of Good Hope, Journal, 1699-1732*, H. C. V. Leibbrandt, 1896
Dutch-Asiatic Shipping Homeward Voyages, 1597-1795, The Hague, 1979

SS Bismarck

German iron screw steam-coaster of 497 tons, built in 1868 by Henderson, Renfrew, owned by Lippert & Co, Hamburg, and commanded by Capt Staats. Wrecked on a reef (Madagascar Reef) 14 km south-west of the Keiskamma River on 31 January 1873 in fog. No lives were lost. She plied between Cape Town and Durban and was the first steamer to cross the bar and enter the Buffalo River. She rescued the passengers and crew of the *Jane Davie* near East London in 1872. Her bell is in the East London Museum.
Lloyds Register of Shipping, 1872-73
Shipping Register, Cape Archives, C.C. 3/7/2/2

Briseis
33° 36.20S, 26° 55.30E

British wooden ship of 1 180 tons, built in 1852 in St Johns, and commanded by Capt John Adams. Wrecked on Fountain Rocks east of the Kowie River mouth on 16 March 1859 while on a voyage from Bombay to London with a general cargo including coir, sperm-oil, cotton and ivory. She had been abandoned off Cape Padrone, where her cargo of 250 elephant tusks and her crew were transshipped to the *Royal Arthur*. No lives were lost.
Cape Weekly Chronicle, 17, 25 March 1859
Lloyds Register of Shipping, 1859-60
Shipping Register, Cape Archives, C.C. 2/18

PS Buffalo
33° 35.25S, 26° 53.00E

Iron paddle-wheel tug of 36 tons, commanded by Capt R. M. Cells. Struck a sand bar up the Kowie River and sank on 19 July 1889. She can be seen at low tide about 3 km up the river (1987).
Eastern Province Herald, 24 July 1889
Shipping Register, Cape Archives, C.C. 3/7/2/4

SS Cariboo
33° 25.40S, 27° 17.40E

British steamer of 7 275 tons, built in 1924 by J. Brown & Co, Clydebank, owned by the Elder Dempster Line, on charter to the Union Castle Line, and commanded by Capt Michell. Was holed and sank a little east of Stalwart Point about 1,5 nautical miles (3 km) from the shore in about 36 m of water on 24 November 1928 while on a voyage from East Africa to New York with a cargo of chrome ore, wool, hides, wattle bark and 1 400 tons of blister copper, most of which was salvaged at the time by the *Kate* (a

coaster and former dredger). In 1981 Peter Sachs, Terrence Roebert and the late Sean Mitchley from East London salvaged a large amount of copper ingots from the wreck.
Cape Argus, 24 November 1928
Lloyds Register of Shipping, 1928-29

Catherine

British wooden barque of 234 tons, built in 1837 at Aberdeen, and commanded by Capt A. Brown. Wrecked about 1 km east of the landing-place at Waterloo Bay, near the Fish River mouth, on 3 October 1846 when her cables parted during a south-west gale with a cargo of provisions, which was lost. No lives were lost.
Graham's Town Journal, 10 October 1846
Lloyds Register of Shipping, 1846-47
Shipping Register, Cape Archives, C.C. 2/16

Chanticleer

Iron schooner, owned by the Kowie Shipping Association, and commanded by Capt A. Fenton. Struck a rock on the east bank of the Kowie River on 1 March 1848 while entering the river with a cargo of sugar. No lives were lost.
Graham's Town Journal, 4 March 1848
Shipping Register, Cape Archives, C.C. 2/17

SS Craigellachie

British steel screw steamer of 3 271 tons, built in 1899 by A. Rodger & Co, Port Glasgow. Wrecked a little east of Riet Point, 16 km east of the Kowie River near Three Sisters Rocks on 10 May 1900 while on a voyage from Hull to Durban with a cargo of coal. No lives were lost.
Eastern Province Herald, 11, 12, 14 (enquiry) May 1900
Lloyds Register of Shipping, 1899-1900

Elite
33° 35.80S, 26° 54.30E

German brig of 206 tons, commanded by Capt Behrman. Beached while being towed into the Kowie River on 26 June 1870. No lives were lost.
Kaffrarian Watchman, 27 June 1870
Shipping Register, Cape Archives, C.C. 3/7/2/2

Elizabeth

British ship of 366 tons, built in 1824 at Liverpool, and commanded by Capt R. Highat. Wrecked near the Bira River mouth, south of East London, on 8 November 1839 at night. No lives were lost, and part of the cargo was saved.
Graham's Town Journal, 14 November 1839
Lloyds Register of Shipping, 1839-40

Emma

Norwegian wooden barque of 292 tons, built in

1875 in Barcelona, and commanded by Capt Isaachsen. Wrecked at the Mpekweni River in the Peddie district on 31 March 1888 while on a voyage from Liverpool to Natal with a cargo of coal. No lives were lost.
Lloyds Universal Register of Shipping, 1888-89
Shipping Register, Cape Archives, C.C. 3/7/2/4

Esterias
33° 36.00S, 26° 54.40E

Barque of 400 tons, commanded by Capt Shaptor. Wrecked on the east side of the Kowie River mouth on 4 December 1865 at the start of a voyage to London with a full cargo of 700 bales of wool, most of which was saved. No lives were lost.
Cape Argus, 7 December 1865
Shipping Register, Cape Archives, C.C. 3/7/2/1

SS Finland

Steel screw steamer of 1 363 tons, built in 1886 at Dumbarton, owned by the Union Line, and commanded by Capt J. Freebody. Wrecked between Kleinmond and Great Fish Point on 26 April 1887 while on a voyage from Cape Town to coast ports and Mauritius with a full general cargo, including machinery for the goldfields and a box containing 2 000 sovereigns to pay the Army. No lives were lost, as the passengers and crew took to the boats. The cargo was saved.
Eastern Province Herald, 29 April, 2 May 1887
Lloyds Register of Shipping, 1887-88

Finland. *(Cape Archives, J489)*

SS Frontier (ex *Echo*, ex *Empire Convoy*, ex *Levensau*, ex *Finkenau*, ex *Cattaro*)
33° 10.50S, 27° 39.80E

Single-screw steam-coaster of 998 tons, built in 1923 by Lindenau & Co, Memel, Prussia, owned by African Coasters, Durban, and commanded by Captain S. O'Brien. Wrecked near Kidd's Beach 32 km south-west of East London on 27 September 1957 while on a voyage from Durban to Cape Town via Mossel Bay with a general cargo of 450 tons and 1 000 tons of sugar. No lives were lost.
Cape Times, 28 September 1957 (photograph)
Lloyds Register of Shipping, 1957-58

Frontier. *(George Young)*

Hercules

American ship commanded by Capt Benjamin Stout. Wrecked near the Bira River mouth (possibly near Madagascar Reef) in Kaffraria on 16 June 1796 during a violent storm while on a homeward-bound voyage from India to London with a cargo of 9 000 bags of rice for the English East India Company. She was leaking badly and was run ashore on purpose. No lives were lost. The name 'Hercules' appears on maps of the area and possibly derives from this wreck.
Stout, Benjamin, *Narrative of the Loss of the Ship Hercules*, 1798

Justitia

Schooner commanded by Capt J. Simpson. Wrecked in Waterloo Bay near the Fish River mouth on 28 September 1848 with a part-cargo. No lives were lost.
Cape Town Mail, 14 October 1848
Shipping Register, Cape Archives, C.C. 2/17

SS Kilbrennan
33° 33.50S, 27° 02.00E

British steel screw-steamer of 3 640 tons, built in 1903 by C. Connell & Co, Glasgow, owned by Napier & Connell, Glasgow. Struck a reef off Riet Point near the Fish River mouth and sank in 18 m of water close to the Three Sisters Rocks east of Kowie on 28 March 1907 while on a voyage from Barry to Diego Suarez, Madagascar, with 6 000 tons of coal. Three seamen were lost.
Eastern Province Herald, 29 March, 2 April 1907
Lloyds Register of Shipping, 1906-07

Laetitia

German schooner of 154 tons, commanded by Capt Hörder. Wrecked near Fountain Rocks at Port Alfred on 18 July 1874 when her cables parted during a heavy swell. No lives were lost.
Shipping Register, Cape Archives, C.C. 3/7/2/2

Lilla

British schooner of 80 tons. Wrecked inside the East Pier at Port Alfred on 28 November 1897 after a voyage from Mossel Bay in ballast to take on a cargo of Government stores for East Lon-

don. The launch *Victoria* was trying to tow her into the river in good weather, but the tow-rope was rotten, and broke. No lives were lost.
Graham's Town Journal, 30 November 1897

SS **Losna** (ex *Admiral Börresen*)

Norwegian screw steamer of 4 187 tons, built in 1904 by Sir Raylton Dixon & Co. Wrecked east of the Fish River on 28 November 1921 while on a voyage from Cape Town to Durban with a cargo of timber, most of which was salvaged by the *Flora*. (The *Flora* was renamed *Rusholme* and was wrecked south of Port Nolloth in 1923.)
Eastern Province Herald, 29 November 1921
Lloyds Register of Shipping, 1921-22

Losna. *(George Young)*

SS **Madagascar**

Screw steam-coaster of 321 tons, launched in 1855 at Scotts Greenock Yard, owned by Rennies, and commanded by Capt J. McKenzie. Struck Madagascar Reef near East London and was beached at the Bira River mouth at 24h00 on 4 December 1858 while on a voyage to Algoa Bay. No lives were lost. She plied between Durban and Cape Town with mail and was a sister ship to the *Waldensian*, wrecked on Struis Point in 1862.
Shipping Register, Cape Archives, C.C. 2/18

Martlet
33° 36.00S, 26° 54.40E

British wooden brig of 228 tons, built in 1866 by Metcalfe, South Shields, owned by Maddock and Co, Newcastle, and commanded by Capt Whitehouse. Wrecked on the rocks at the end of the eastern pier at Port Alfred on 12 August 1870 at dusk after a voyage from London with a large general cargo including cloth, ironmongery, hardware, candles, sugar and deals. The captain was impatient and had tried to enter the river without a pilot.
Graham's Town Journal, 15, 17, 19 (sale notice) August 1870
Lloyds Register of Shipping, 1870-71
Shipping Register, Cape Archives, C.C. 3/7/2/2

Memento

British wooden barque of 464 tons, built in 1860.

Wrecked near Shelly Beach on 5 February 1876 when her cables parted during a south-east wind at East London. She collided with the *Notre Dame de la Garde*, was badly damaged and was to have been run ashore on the west bank opposite the cemetery, but she drifted away towards Cove Rock.
East London Dispatch, 8 February 1876 (sale notice)
Lloyds Register of Shipping, 1876-77
Shipping Register, Cape Archives, C.C. 3/7/2/2

Rosalie

Brig. Wrecked on the West Beach at Port Alfred on 30 January 1881. No lives were lost.
Graham's Town Journal, 1 February 1881 (sale notice)

Rubia (ex *Etha Rickmers*)

Norwegian wooden barque of 1 072 tons, built in 1871 by R. C. Rickmers, Geestemünde. Wrecked on 4 May 1901 near the Nqculura River while on a voyage from East London to Port Elizabeth in ballast. Seven people lost their lives.
Eastern Province Herald, 20 May 1901
Lloyds Register of Shipping, 1901-02

Saint Austell

British wooden schooner of 136 tons, built in 1866 by Harvey, Hayle, and commanded by Capt E. Scott. Wrecked at Port Alfred on 2 May 1870 during a gale after a voyage from Mauritius with a cargo of sugar. No lives were lost.
Eastern Province Herald, 13 May 1870
Lloyds Register of Shipping, 1869-70
Shipping Register, Cape Archives, C.C. 3/7/2/2

Seaforth

British schooner of 172 tons, built in 1834 in Scotland, and commanded by Capt Greengrass. Wrecked on the east side of the Kowie River on 18 August 1844 when the wind dropped as she was leaving the river. No lives were lost.
Lloyds Register of Shipping, 1844-45
Shipping Register, Cape Archives, C.C. 2/16
South African Commercial Advertiser, 31 August 1844

PS **Sir John S. Aubyn**
33° 36.00S, 26° 54.40E

Paddle-wheel steam vessel of 175 tons. Wrecked at the Kowie River on 31 January 1843 while towing the *Sophia* across the bar. The tow-cable snapped and the two vessels fouled; the *Sophia* survived but was wrecked in Algoa Bay in 1846. No lives were lost. She was the replacement vessel for the *Hope*, which was wrecked at Tsitsikamma Point in 1840.
Shipping Register, Cape Archives, C.C. 2/15

Snorre Straulassen

Norwegian brig. Wrecked 6,5 km west of Port Alfred on the rocks at Freshwater Point on 15 July 1875 when her anchor cables parted off Port Alfred during a south-west gale with a cargo of timber and bridge repair parts, some of which was saved. No lives were lost, as her crew were saved by means of rocket apparatus.
Graham's Town Journal, 16, 21, 23 (sale notice) July 1875

Graham's Town Journal

SS **Umvolosi**

British steamer of 1 775 tons, built in 1889 by J. Laing, Sunderland, owned by Bullard King and Co, and commanded by Capt H. Clarke. Wrecked 300 m east of the Kleinmond River mouth on 12 April 1890 while on a voyage to Natal with a cargo of six railway coaches, sleepers, deals and mining machinery. The crew and two passengers were safely landed. She traded between London and Natal.
Lloyds Register of Shipping, 1890-91
Shipping Register, Cape Archives, C.C. 3/7/2/4

Waterloo

Cape iron schooner, commanded by Capt R. Wood. Wrecked in Cawoods Bay near the Fish River mouth on 5 April 1848 at night during a south-east gale. The master and the second mate were drowned. Waterloo Bay on Dassen Island is named after her, as this vessel often loaded penguin eggs here. Waterloo Bay near the Fish River is likewise named after her, as she often off-loaded supplies for the frontier there.
Cape Town Mail, 15 April 1848
Shipping Register, Cape Archives, C.C. 2/17

SS **Welcombe**

British iron steam vessel of 2 166 tons, built in

1883 by R. Dixon & Co, and commanded by Capt W. R. Corfield (part owner). Wrecked on a reef 8 km east of Great Fish Point on 16 November 1885 while on a voyage from East London to Algoa Bay with a cargo of wool and skins, most of which was saved by the tug *Buffalo*.
Eastern Province Herald, 20, 23 November 1885
Lloyds Register of Shipping, 1885-86
Shipping Register, Cape Archives, C.C. 3/7/2/3

33. Hood Point to the Gonubie River mouth

This stretch of coast is densely populated and is dominated by the Buffalo River which forms the harbour for the Cape's third largest city, East London, a large industrial town. The water is warm due to the Agulhas current, but is usually turbid due to the large amount of water discharged by the rivers in the area. Divers are very active in the area, but heavy surf usually breaks along the coast. The climate is warm and humid in the summer months. The coast is popular with tourists and holiday-makers who flock to the many holiday resorts, the main pastime being fishing. Place names associated with shipwrecks are Bonanza Street in East London, named after the barque Bonanza wrecked on Orient Beach in 1894; the Kennaway Hotel, named after the Lady Kennaway wrecked in 1857; and Orient Beach named after the Russian ship Orient wrecked there in 1907.

Albert Juhl
33° 01.50S, 27° 55.00E

Three-masted schooner commanded by Capt Ruchholts. Wrecked on Orient Beach, East London, on 4 February 1876. No lives were lost. A rocket line was fired, but the crew did not know how to attach it; eventually a basket was rigged up.
East London Dispatch, 8 February 1876 (sale notice)
Shipping Register, Cape Archives, C.C. 3/7/2/2

Alma

German schooner of 152 tons, commanded by Capt Tierhand. Went ashore near the Gonubie River mouth on 26 October 1878 when her cables parted at East London during a strong south-west gale after a voyage from Gothenburg with a cargo of deals. No lives were lost.
Graham's Town Journal, 30 October 1878
Shipping Register, Cape Archives, C.C. 3/7/2/3

Amatola

Iron schooner of 60 tons, commanded by Capt J. Cameron. Wrecked on a ridge of rocks called the Blinders on 28 May 1852 while entering the Buffalo River mouth at East London. No lives were lost.
Eastern Province News, 8 June 1852
Shipping Register, Cape Archives, C.C. 2/18

Ann Staniland

British wooden schooner of 192 tons, built in 1857 by Whaley, Thorne, and commanded by Capt John Richards. Wrecked at East London on 28 November 1876 with a cargo of rails and sleepers. She was under arrest because of debt, and hit the eastern wall while being towed in by the tug *London*, after having been damaged in a collision with the *Euterpe* (1876).
East London Dispatch, 1, 8, 11 December 1876
Lloyds Register of Shipping, 1876-77

Annie S.

British wooden brigantine of 121 tons, built in 1868 by Gillis, Prince Edward Island, and commanded by Capt S. B. Avery. Wrecked at the west wall in East London on 11 December 1875 after a voyage from Cape Town with a cargo of coal and railway material (including a locomotive). She took ground opposite the Old Customs House on the west bank at East London while entering the port under tow by the tug *Buffalo* and then drifted to the west wall.
East London Dispatch, 14, 21 (sale notice), 28 (enquiry) December 1875
Lloyds Register of Shipping, 1875-76

Antonie

German brig of 134 tons, commanded by Capt F. M. Scholz. Wrecked at East London at 23h00 on 18 October 1864 when her anchor cables parted during a south-east gale after a voyage from Cape Town with a general cargo including coffee, liquor and flour, most of which had been discharged. No lives were lost. She came ashore about 100 m west of the lighthouse.
King William's Town Gazette, 24, 27 (sale notice) October 1864

Atbara (ex *Thomas S. Stowe*)

Norwegian iron barque of 686 tons, built in 1863 by T. R. Oswald, Pallion, and commanded by

Capt P. T. Pettersen. Wrecked on the rocks below the Beach Hotel, Marina Beach, East London, on 10 June 1902 during a south-east gale while on a voyage from Hamburg to Natal with a general cargo including cement. Eight lives were lost. She had called at East London for orders.
Eastern Province Herald, 16 June 1902
Lloyds Register of Shipping, 1901-02

Aurora
33° 00.40S, 27° 55.80E

Swedish wooden barque of 592 tons, built in 1877 by Fr. Hagglund, Nordmaling, and commanded by Capt A. Nilssen. Wrecked 50 m east of the *Elise Linck* (1902) at the Blind River, East London, on 10 June 1902 during a south-east gale after a voyage from Sweden with a cargo of deals, matches and trellis-work.
Eastern Province Herald, 16 June 1902
Lloyds Register of Shipping, 1901-02

Bierstadt

American barque of 585 tons. Wrecked at Nahoon Point, East London, on 3 February 1877 when her cables parted during a north-west gale. No lives were lost. Her general cargo had been discharged; she was in ballast and due to leave on an easterly voyage.
East London Dispatch, 5, 6 (sale notice) February 1877

Bonanza
33° 01.50S, 27° 55.00E

American wooden barque of 1 356 tons, built in 1875 by W. Rogers, Bath, Maine, owned by Puget Sound Commercial Co, and commanded by Capt W. F. Stetson. Wrecked on Orient Beach at East London on 22 December 1894 while entering the river. Most of her cargo was saved.
East London Standard, 28 December 1894
Lloyds Register of Shipping, 1894-95

Aurora (l), Elise Linck (r). (East London Museum)

Bonanza. *(East London Museum)*

Brighton

British barque of 407 tons. Wrecked at Nahoon Point in East London on 25 July 1881 when her cables parted during a south-west gale after a voyage from London. Only two people were saved. The captain was on shore at the time.
Eastern Province Herald, 2 August 1881
Shipping Register, Cape Archives, C. C. 3/7/2/3

Carl zu den Drei Greiffen

German brig of 300 tons. Wrecked opposite the West Bank Cemetery in East London on 16 October 1875 when her anchors dragged during a south-east wind. All the crew were saved by the rocket brigade.
Graham's Town Journal, 18 October 1875
East London Dispatch, 19 October 1875 (sale notice)

Carrie Wyman

American wooden barque of 436 tons, built in 1869 at Bangor, Maine, and commanded by Capt McNeil. Wrecked at the East Wall, East London, on 14 August 1886 when her cables parted after a voyage from New York with a general cargo for East London and Algoa Bay. The crew were landed by means of rocket apparatus.
Argus Weekly, 25 August 1886
Lloyds Universal Register of Shipping, 1886-87
Shipping Register, Cape Archives, C.C. 3/7/2/4

Clansman

British wooden brigantine of 382 tons, built in 1870 by Kinloch, Kingston. Ran ashore at East London west of the lighthouse opposite the cemetery, in the same spot as the *Dauntless* (1883), on 31 May 1882 when her cables parted during a south-east gale.
Eastern Province Herald, 2 June 1882
Lloyds Register of Shipping, 1882-83

Clymping

British wooden barque of 342 tons, built in 1871 by Harvey, Littlehampton, and commanded by Capt Evans. Wrecked on the East Beach at East London on 25 July 1881 when her cables parted during a south-west gale after a voyage from Cardiff. Only one life was saved. The captain was ashore at the time.
Eastern Province Herald, 2 August 1881
Lloyds Register of Shipping, 1881-82
Shipping Register, Cape Archives, C.C. 3/7/2/3

Columba

Russian barque of 346 tons, commanded by Capt Trojan. Wrecked at East London on 5 November 1880 when her cables parted during a south-east gale after a voyage from Cardiff. No lives were lost.
Shipping Register, Cape Archives, C.C. 3/7/2/3

Compage

British wooden schooner of 91 tons, built in 1864 by Cato, Liverpool. Wrecked at East London a little east of the *Coquette* (1874) on 5 December 1874 during a south-west gale. No lives were lost.
East London Dispatch, 8 December 1874
Lloyds Register of Shipping, 1874-75

Constantia

British wooden barque of 337 tons, built in 1866 by Barrick, Whitby, and commanded by Capt Laws. Wrecked at East London on rocks close to the *Crusader* and *Nundeeps* (1868) on 20 July 1868 when her cables parted during a south-west gale.
Cape Standard, 4 August 1868
Lloyds Register of Shipping, 1868-69
Shipping Register, Cape Archives, C.C. 3/7/2/2

Coquette

Wrecked at East London a little east of the steamer *Quanza* (1872) on the Esplanade rocks on 5 December 1874 when her anchors dragged during a south-west gale. No lives were lost.
East London Dispatch, 8 December 1874

Countess of Dudley
33° 01.50S, 27° 55.00E

Australian wooden brig of 257 tons, built in 1866 in Perth, Australia, and commanded by the mate, Hans Johnson. Wrecked on Orient Beach in East London on 23 August 1877 when her cables parted during a light easterly breeze and she collided with the *Smyrniote* after a voyage from London with a general cargo, half of which had been discharged. The crew were landed by means of rocket apparatus. Her captain had died shortly after her arrival.

East London Dispatch, 23, 30 August 1877
Lloyds Register of Shipping, 1877-78

Crixea

British wooden barque of 347 tons, built in 1863 by Haswell, Sunderland, and commanded by Capt Osborne. Wrecked on the west bank of the Buffalo River, East London (west of the lighthouse), on 27 November 1872 when her cables parted during a south-east gale after a voyage from London with a general cargo. No lives were lost. Her bell is in the East London Museum.
East London Dispatch, 3 December 1872
Lloyds Register of Shipping, 1872-73
Shipping Register, Cape Archives, C.C. 3/7/2/2

Crusader

Barque of 446 tons. Wrecked at East London on the rocks close to the *Constantia* and the *Nundeeps* (1868) on 29 August 1868 during a south-east gale after she had loaded 1 300 bales of wool for London. No lives were lost.
Cape Standard, 1 September 1868
Shipping Register, Cape Archives, C.C. 3/7/2/2

Dauntless

American ship of 995 tons. Wrecked opposite the West Bank Cemetery at East London on 28 September 1883 when her cables parted during a south-east breeze after a voyage from Boston with a full general cargo including building materials, tobacco, paraffin and foodstuffs, only 42 tons of which had been landed. No lives were lost, as the crew were saved by rocket apparatus. She was wrecked on the same spot as the *Clansman* (1882).
Eastern Province Herald, 3 October 1883
Shipping Register, Cape Archives, C.C. 3/7/2/3

Dauntless. *(Africana Museum)*

Die Heimath

Barque of 341 tons. Wrecked beyond Bats Cave at East London on 25 July 1881 when her cables parted during a south-west gale after a voyage from Newcastle. There were no survivors. The captain was ashore at the time.
Eastern Province Herald, 2 August 1881
Shipping Register, Cape Archives, C.C. 3/7/2/3

Elaine

British iron brig of 195 tons, built in 1867 by Marshall, Newcastle. Wrecked to the east of the Buffalo River, East London, at 10h00 on 26 May 1872 during a south-east gale.
Eastern Province Herald, 31 May, 7 June (sale notice) 1872
Lloyds Register of Shipping, 1871-72

Elise

German barque of 347 tons, commanded by Capt Bargmann. Wrecked at East London on 16 February 1878 at night when her cables parted during a southerly gale. No lives were lost.
Shipping Register, Cape Archives, C.C. 3/7/2/3

Elise Linck

33° 00.40S, 27° 55.80E

German wooden barque of 530 tons, built in 1879 by J. W. Klawitter, Danzig, and commanded by Capt G. Staatsmann. Wrecked at the Blind River, East London, on 10 June 1902 during a south-east gale while on a voyage from Geestemünde to Natal with a cargo of timber. No lives were lost. She had called at East London for orders.
Eastern Province Herald, 16 June 1902
Lloyds Register of Shipping, 1901-02

Ellen Browse

33° 01.50S, 27° 55.00E

German wooden barque of 352 tons, built in 1865 by Naizby, Sunderland. Struck Orient Beach at East London close to the *Countess of Dudley* (1877) on 26 October 1877 when her cables parted during a south-east gale after a voyage from London. No lives were lost. She had discharged most of her cargo. Her captain had been killed a few days previously in a surf-boat accident.
East London Dispatch, 29 October 1877
Lloyds Register of Shipping, 1877-78

Elpida

Norwegian wooden barque of 590 tons, built in 1890 at Grimstad, and commanded by Capt A. J. Henriksen. Wrecked 1,5 km northeast of the Buffalo River, East London, on 29 September 1893 after a voyage from the Baltic with a cargo of deals. No lives were lost, as the crew were rescued by means of rocket apparatus.
Eastern Province Herald, 2 October 1893
Lloyds Register of Shipping, 1893-94

Emile Marie

Barque of 250 tons. Wrecked a little north-east of East London on 7 December 1874 during a south-west gale after a voyage from Saigon with a cargo of 12 235 bags of rice. No lives were lost.

She lies close to the *Jane Davie* (1872).
East London Dispatch, 8 December 1874

Emma

Brig. Wrecked on the east side of the Buffalo River, East London, on 26 May 1872 during a south-east gale.
Eastern Province Herald, 31 May 1872

Emma

German brig of 173 tons, commanded by Capt J. Jesselsen. Wrecked at the Blind River, East London, on 18 November 1880 during a south-west gale after a voyage from Cape Town with a general cargo and breadstuffs.
Shipping Register, Cape Archives, C.C. 3/7/2/3

Euterpe

British wooden brig of 250 tons, built in 1864 by Stewart, Prince Edward Island. Wrecked at Eastern Beach, East London, on 1 November 1876 during a south-west gale after colliding with the *Stirling*. No lives were lost.
East London Dispatch, 7, 14 (enquiry) November 1876
Lloyds Register of Shipping, 1876-77

Fingoe

Cape iron barque of 488 tons, built in 1869 by Pile, Sunderland, and commanded by Capt James Williams. Wrecked at the Blind River mouth, East London, on 19 July 1874 during a gale. No lives were lost. She had previously run ashore on 18 September 1869 during a south-east gale in Algoa Bay while on her maiden voyage.

Eastern Province Herald

SALE OF
Damaged Cargo,
Ex Stranded Barque "Fingoe."
At half-past 2 o'clock To-morrow,
(Wednesday), 29th September,
On the Spot, at the Wreck, North-End Beach,
Mr. Kirkwood will sell, by Auction,
For account of whom it may concern, by order of Captain
E. McGREGOR,
SUNDRY BALES OF WOOL,
Cases and Casks of Gum, &c., &c.
More or less damaged by Sea Water,
And the Interest of Cargo remaining on Board,
COMPRISING
89 Bags of Shells, each 500
12 do. Shank Bones, weighing 495 lbs.
2 do. Giraffe Shank Bones, weighing 391 lbs.
500 do. Rice, Bill of Lading Weight 100,000 lbs.
Cases Old Brass
SAVAGE & HILL, Agents.
Port Elizabeth, Sept. 28, 1869.

Florie

British wooden barque of 273 tons, built in 1862 by Parkes, Chester. Wrecked near the Blind River, East London, on 6 December 1874 during a south-west gale. One sailor was washed overboard and drowned.
East London Dispatch, 8 December 1874
Lloyds Register of Shipping, 1874-75

Flower of the Arun

British wooden brigantine of 157 tons, built in 1861 by Harvey, and commanded by Capt Whitburn. Wrecked at East London on 31 October 1870 during a south-east gale after a voyage from London. No lives were lost. Her cargo had been partly discharged. Her figurehead is on display at the East London Museum.
Kaffrarian Watchman, 2 November 1870
Lloyds Register of Shipping, 1870-71
Shipping Register, Cape Archives, C.C. 3/7/2/2

Foam

British wooden schooner of 95 tons, built in 1846 at Montrose, and commanded by Capt J. Burnet. Wrecked on the eastern side of the Buffalo River at East London, close to the *Ghika* (1847), on 13 September 1851 when her cables parted during a heavy south-west swell and an easterly wind with a cargo of wine, blankets, sperm candles and ironmongery. No lives were lost.
Graham's Town Journal, 23 September 1851
Lloyds Register of Shipping, 1851-52
Shipping Register, Cape Archives, C.C. 2/17

Francisca

33° 01.50S, 27° 55.00E

Italian wooden barque of 692 tons, built in 1873 by Tapani, Genoa. Beached off Orient Beach, East London by order of the captain on 12 May 1882 after having sprung a leak while on a voyage from Akyab, Burma, to the English Channel with a cargo of rice.
Lloyds Register of Shipping, 1881-82
Shipping Register, Cape Archives, C.C. 3/7/2/3

General Nott

33° 00.30S, 27° 55.80E

British wooden brig of 298 tons, built in 1865 by Lister, South Hamilton. Wrecked at the Blind River, East London, on 10 December 1876 during a north-west gale with a general cargo. No lives were lost.
East London Dispatch, 18, 23, 30 December 1876
Eastern Province Herald, 19 December 1876

Cape Argus, 21 July 1874
Lloyds Register of Shipping, 1874-75
Shipping Register, Cape Archives, C.C. 3/7/2/2

Lloyds Register of Shipping, 1876-77
Shipping Register, Cape Archives, C.C. 3/7/2/2

Ghika

Cape wooden schooner of 122 tons, built in 1836 at Ipswich, and commanded by Capt W. Frowde. Wrecked on the Esplanade rocks, East London, on 17 October 1847 after her cables parted. Nineteen men died, including the captain. She struck the *Harriet* on her way in.
Graham's Town Journal, 23 October 1847
Lloyds Register of Shipping, 1847-48
Shipping Register, Cape Archives, C.C. 2/16

Helene
33° 01.00S, 27° 55.00E

Iron hulk. Ran ashore a little east of Orient Beach, East London, on 10 October 1905 at night during a storm.
East London Daily Dispatch, 12 October 1905

Henry Douse

British wooden brigantine of 197 tons, built in 1865 by Douse, Prince Edward Island. Wrecked at East London on 12 August 1867 during a south-east gale while on a voyage from London. No lives were lost.
Lloyds Register of Shipping, 1867-68
Shipping Register, Cape Archives, C.C. 3/7/2/2

Hohenzollern
33° 00.30S, 27° 55.80E

German barque commanded by Capt Stindt. Wrecked at the Blind River, East London, on 1 November 1876 during a south-west gale and heavy rain after a voyage from London with a cargo of beer, soap and deals. One man was drowned. A diver named Bartlett who was under the influence of liquor died while trying to dive on the wreck on 2 November 1876.
East London Dispatch, 7 November 1876

Hope

Barque of 371 tons, commanded by Capt Rumble. Wrecked at East London on 5 November 1880 when her cables parted during a south-east gale after a voyage from London with a general cargo. No lives were lost.
East London Dispatch, 10 November 1880
Shipping Register, Cape Archives, C.C. 3/7/2/3

Huma

Schooner of 97 tons. Wrecked at East London on 27 October 1855.
Shipping Register, Cape Archives, C.C. 2/18

Imogen

British wooden barque of 302 tons, built in 1854 at Aberdeen, and commanded by Capt J. Goodridge. Wrecked at East London at 06h30 on 20 November 1867 during a south-east gale after a voyage from Algoa Bay with a general cargo. No lives were lost.
Cape Standard, 26 November 1867
Lloyds Register of Shipping, 1867-68
Shipping Register, Cape Archives, C.C. 3/7/2/2

Jane Davie
32° 58.30S, 27° 59.20E

British iron schooner of 799 tons, built in 1868 by Duncan, Port Glasgow, and commanded by Capt P. le Gallais. Wrecked on a reef near Bonza Bay north-east of the Buffalo River close to the *Emile Marie* (1874) on 26 May 1872 during a south-east gale while on a voyage from Rangoon to Liverpool with a cargo of rice and cotton. One sailor was drowned. The captain's pregnant wife and child were roped together and tied to a stanchion to prevent their being washed overboard, staying like this for three nights. The passengers and crew were saved by Capt George Walker, the harbour master at East London, and taken on board the steamer *Bismarck*, which was wrecked south of East London in 1873.
East London Dispatch, 31 May, 2 June 1872
Lloyds Register of Shipping, 1872-73
Shipping Register, Cape Archives, C.C. 3/7/2/2

Johan
33° 01.50S, 27° 55.00E

Swedish barque. Wrecked on Orient Beach, East London, on 20 February 1882 when her cables parted during a south-east gale after a voyage from the Baltic with a cargo of deals. No lives were lost. All except 30 tons of her cargo had been discharged.
Shipping Register, Cape Archives, C.C. 3/7/2/3

SS Kaffir

British iron steamer of 309 tons, built in 1883 by Mordey, Carney & Co, Newport, and commanded by Capt W. Reimer. Ran ashore on a sandy spit on 7 December 1890 after having hit the west wall while entering the Buffalo River, East London, and holing herself badly. She was later moved up-river, where her cargo was removed.
Eastern Province Herald, 10 December 1890
Lloyds Register of Shipping, 1890-91

SS King Cadwallon (ex *Stathis*)
33° 01.10S, 27° 55.50E

British screw steamer of 5 119 tons, built in 1920 by the Hong Kong & Whampoa Dock Co, Hong Kong, owned by the King Line, and commanded by Capt A. W. Wheeler. Ran onto the rocks below the Esplanade, East London, and burnt out on shore on 11 September 1929 during a gale; she

had caught fire 11 km out of Durban while on a voyage from Menthil, Fifeshire, to Adelaide with a cargo of coal, and was abandoned on 12 July 1929. After drifting for 41 days she was sighted off East London; the Port Captain towed her in on 20 August 1929. Her bell is in the East London Museum.
East London Daily Dispatch, 12, 13 September 1929 (photograph)
Lloyds Register of Shipping, 1929-30

Lady Kennaway
33° 01.80S, 27° 54.85E

British emigrant ship of 584 tons, built in 1817 in Calcutta, and commanded by Capt Michael Santry. Wrecked on a sandy spit at the mouth of the Buffalo River, East London, 300-400 m east of the lighthouse, on 25 November 1857 during a south-east gale. No lives were lost; she had just completed offloading passengers. She was later partly blown up to clear the channel. The Kennaway Hotel is named after her.
Cape Archives, B.K. 41 (diagram)
Cape Argus, 5, 30 December (enquiry) 1857
Lloyds Register of Shipping, 1857-58
Shipping Register, Cape Archives, C.C. 2/18

Lockett

British wooden barque of 556 tons, built in 1852 at Liverpool, and commanded by Capt Stockton. Wrecked on the west bank at East London on 4 January 1884 during a south-east gale after a voyage from Cardiff with a cargo of coal, which had been discharged. No lives were lost.
Eastern Province Herald, 7 January 1884
Lloyds Register of Shipping, 1884-85
Shipping Register, Cape Archives, C.C. 3/7/2/3

Lord of the Isles

Brig of 147 tons, commanded by Capt R. Jeary. Wrecked east of the Buffalo River, East London, on 26 October 1873 after a voyage from Cape Town. No lives were lost.
Shipping Register, Cape Archives, C.C. 3/7/2/2

Lunaria

British wooden barque of 206 tons, built in 1855 in Wales, and commanded by Capt W. Edwards. Wrecked near the lighthouse on the west bank at East London at 03h30 on 12 September 1861 when her cables parted during a south gale while on a voyage from London to Mauritius with a cargo including deals, foodstuffs, coal, liquor, clothing and crockery. No lives were lost.
King William's Town Gazette, 13, 17 September (sale notice) 1861
Lloyds Register of Shipping, 1861-62

Marengo

British wooden barque of 314 tons, built in 1860

by Haswell, Sunderland, and commanded by Capt James Fell. Wrecked at East London on 19 October 1876 during a south-east wind after a voyage from England with a cargo of railway iron.
East London Dispatch, 24, 31 (enquiry) October 1876
Lloyds Register of Shipping, 1876-77

Maron Neil
33° 01.50S, 27° 55.00E

Barque of 407 tons, commanded by Capt Wilkins. Wrecked on Orient Beach, East London, on 5 September 1885 when her cables parted after a voyage from London with a general cargo. No lives were lost.
Shipping Register, Cape Archives, C.C. 3/7/2/3

Martha

Brig of 191 tons. Wrecked on the east side of the Buffalo River, East London, on 26 May 1872 during a south-east gale.
Eastern Province Herald, 31 May, 7 June (sale notice) 1872

Medusa

British wooden barque of 211 tons, built in 1861 by Gray, Newhaven, and commanded by Capt W. Lancaster. Wrecked on the eastern side of the Buffalo River, East London, on 10 November 1863 after a voyage from London.
Lloyds Register of Shipping, 1863-64
Shipping Register, Cape Archives, C.C. 3/7/2/1

Nant-Y-Glo

British wooden snow of 264 tons, built in 1866 by Mills, Sunderland. Wrecked on the east side of the Buffalo River, East London, on 26 April 1872 during a south-east gale. No lives were lost.
Lloyds Register of Shipping, 1871-72
Shipping Register, Cape Archives, C.C. 3/7/2/2

Natal Star

British wooden barque of 366 tons, built in 1862 by Hall, Aberdeen, and commanded by Capt F. Airth. Wrecked at East London on 19 July 1874 during a gale. No lives were lost.
Lloyds Register of Shipping, 1874-75
Shipping Register, Cape Archives, C.C. 3/7/2/2

Nundeeps

British wooden schooner of 178 tons, built in 1849 at Scilly. Wrecked on the rocks at East London, close to the *Crusader* (1868) and the *Constantia* (1868) on 29 August 1868 during a south-east gale after having loaded 250 bales of wool for London. No lives were lost.
Lloyds Register of Shipping, 1868-69
Shipping Register, Cape Archives, C.C. 3/7/2/2

Olive

British wooden barque of 374 tons, built in 1871 by Gibbon, Sunderland, and commanded by Capt Jurgensen. Wrecked at East London on 16 February 1878 at night during a southerly gale. Six crew were drowned as she struck and broke up a long way off-shore.
Lloyds Register of Shipping, 1878-79
Shipping Register, Cape Archives, C.C. 3/7/2/3

Orient
33° 01.60S, 27° 55.00E

Russian full-rigged steel ship, fitted with auxiliary steam power, of 1 647 tons, built in 1889 by C. Connell & Co, Glasgow. Wrecked on Orient Beach, East London on 29 July 1907 with a cargo of 2 600 tons of wheat from Geelong, Australia. No lives were lost among her crew of 26.
East London Daily Dispatch, 30, 31 July 1907
Lloyds Register of Shipping, 1901-02

Orient. *(East London Museum)*

Osprey

British schooner of 60 tons, commmanded by Capt Roper. Wrecked on the east side of the Buffalo River, East London, on 23 September 1865 during a south-east gale after a voyage from Table Bay with a general cargo. No lives were lost.
Shipping Register, Cape Archives, C.C. 3/7/2/1

SS Palatinia
33° 00.50S, 27° 56.00E

British steel four-masted steamer of 3 620 tons, built in 1899 by Furness Withy & Co, West Hartlepool, and commanded by Capt E. Lawson. Beached off the east beach, East London, on 7 March 1911 after striking a sunken object 48 km south-west of East London while on a voyage from Tampa to Kobe, Japan, with a cargo of phosphates.
Cape Argus, 8, 10 March 1911
Lloyds Register of Shipping, 1910-11

Palatinia. *(Africana Museum)*

SS Quanza
33° 01.40S, 27° 55.00E

Four-masted steamer of 1 000 tons. Wrecked at Quanza Beach, on the east side of the Buffalo River mouth, East London, at 05h00 on 26 May 1872 during a south-east gale with a cargo of 1 000 bales of wool. No lives were lost.
Eastern Province Herald, 31 May, 7 June (sale notice) 1872

> ## WRECKS AT EAST LONDON.
> ### A STEAMER AND FOUR VESSELS ASHORE.
> Disastrous intelligence has been received this morning from East London by Mr. Sidney Hill, who has just received the following telegram from Messrs. J. J. Irvine & Co.:—
> Steamer *Quanza* ashore, as well as brig *Sharp*, which arrived yesterday. Weather very bad.

Eastern Province Herald

Queen of May

British wooden barque of 314 tons, built in 1856 at Harrington. Wrecked on the rocky shore to the west of the Buffalo River, East London, at 08h30 on 26 May 1872 during a south-east gale. One boy was drowned.
Eastern Province Herald, 31 May, 7 June (sale notice) 1872
Lloyds Register of Shipping, 1871-72

Queen of Nations

British wooden ship of 1 462 tons, built in 1863 at St Johns, New Brunswick, and commanded by Capt Pahlesis. Wrecked at Bats Cave, East London on 8 June 1889 after her cables parted. She had been towed in by the SS *Clan Alpine* on 6 June 1889, having been abandoned, disabled, off the Kowie River by her crew of 21 while on a voyage from Point de Galle, Ceylon, to New York with a cargo of coconut oil.
Lloyds Register of Shipping, 1889-90
Shipping Register, Cape Archives, C.C. 3/7/2/4

Refuge

British wooden barque of 272 tons, built in 1856 at Brixham. Wrecked on the east side of the Buffalo River, East London, on 26 May 1872 after her cables parted during a south-east gale.
Eastern Province Herald, 31 May, 7 June (sale notice) 1872
Lloyds Register of Shipping 1871-72

MV SA Oranjeland (ex Oranjeland)
33° 01.25S, 27° 55.50E

South African freighter of 15 790 tons, built in 1969 by Blohm & Voss, Hamburg, and commanded by Capt U. Weidner. Wrecked a little east of Orient Beach, East London, close to the *Valdivia* (1908), on 13 August 1974, during a north-east gale after leaving the harbour on a voyage to Europe with a cargo of 7 500 tons of general cargo. She had put ashore the crew of the *Produce* (1974), wrecked on Aliwal Shoal.
Cape Times, 14 August 1974
Lloyds Register of Shipping, 1974-75

Sandvik

Swedish wooden barque of 593 tons, built in 1873 by O. Jonsson, Umea, and commanded by Capt Pehrsson. Wrecked at East London on 26 March 1888 after a voyage from London with a general cargo, including 300 tons of coal and cement. No lives were lost.
Lloyds Universal Register of Shipping, 1888-89
Shipping Register, Cape Archives, C.C. 3/7/2/4

Santa Maria Madre de Deus

Small Portuguese vessel (naveta) under the command of Dom Luis de Castelbranco. Wrecked on the south-east coast of South Africa, possibly near Bonza Bay, East London, in 1643 while on a homeward-bound voyage from Goa, which she had left in March 1643 with a cargo of silk, spices and Chinese porcelain; broken shards of porcelain dating from this period often wash up in Bonza Bay. Many lives were lost. The survivors walked overland to Cape Correntes.
Axelson, E. *Dias & his successors*, 1988
Feyo, Bento Teyxeyra, *Ralacam do Naufragio que fizeram as Naos Sacramento & nossa Senhora da Atalaya vindo da India para o Reyno, no Cabo de Boa Esperanca*, Lisbon, 1650. Translated into English in Theal, G.M., *Records of South Eastern Africa*, Vol 8, pp 295-360

Sarah Phillips

British wooden brig of 181 tons, built in 1864 by Jones, Aberystwyth, and commanded by Capt David Jenkins. Wrecked on the east side of the Buffalo River, East London, on 15 October 1871 after a voyage from London to Kaffraria with a cargo of sundries. No lives were lost.
Eastern Province Herald, 20 October 1871
Lloyds Register of Shipping, 1871-72
Shipping Register, Cape Archives, C.C. 3/7/2/2

Schmayl
33° 01.50S, 27° 55.00E

American barque of 406 tons, commanded by Capt Hammond. Wrecked at Orient Beach, East London, on 24 October 1883 when her cables parted during a south-east gale after a voyage from Savannah with a cargo of pitch pine, which had been landed with the exception of 100 tons. No lives were lost.
Eastern Province Herald, 26 October 1883
Shipping Register, Cape Archives, C.C. 3/7/2/3

Sea Rover

British wooden barque of 212 tons, built in 1855, and commanded by Capt Froud. Wrecked at East London on 20 July 1868 when her cables parted during a south-west gale after a voyage from London with a general cargo. No lives were lost.
Lloyds Register of Shipping, 1868-69
Shipping Register, Cape Archives, C.C. 3/7/2/2

Sea Wave

British wooden barque of 389 tons, built in 1858 at Sunderland, and commanded by Capt H. Edwards. Wrecked on the rocks on the west bank at East London at 22h00 on 8 October 1879 during a gale after a voyage from Milford with a cargo of 450 tons of steam coal, 350 tons of which had been discharged. She had taken on ballast. No lives were lost: the captain was ashore and the crew saved themselves in a boat.
East London Dispatch, 11 October 1879 (sale notice)
Lloyds Register of Shipping, 1879-80

Seafield

British wooden barque of 616 tons, built in 1861 by Tay Shipbuilding Co, Dundee, and commanded by Capt W. Seward. Wrecked at Bats Cave, East London, on 29 May 1882 during a south-west gale when she collided with the SS *Roxburgh Castle* after a voyage from London with a cargo of coal, most of which had been discharged. The captain was ashore.
Eastern Province Herald, 13 June 1882 (judgement)
Lloyds Register of Shipping, 1882-83
Shipping Register, Cape Archives, C.C. 3/7/2/3

Shantung

British wooden barque of 311 tons, built in 1858 at Sunderland, and commanded by Capt J. Parker. Wrecked at East London on 20 July 1868 when her cables parted during a south-west gale while loading a cargo of wool for London.
Lloyds Register of Shipping, 1868-69
Shipping Register, Cape Archives, C.C. 3/7/2/2

Sharp

British wooden brig of 204 tons, built in 1869 by McLaine, Belfast. Wrecked at East London at 06h00 on 26 May 1872 during a south-east gale. One man was killed by a falling block.

Eastern Province Herald, 31 May 1872
Lloyds Register of Shipping, 1872-73

South Easter

British iron barque of 303 tons, built in 1863 by Hill, Port Glasgow. Wrecked at East London, east of the *Quanza* (1872), on 29 June 1872 with a cargo of 15 000 bags of rice. Five men were drowned. Her bell was recovered in 1967.
Lloyds Register of Shipping, 1872-73
Shipping Register, Cape Archives, C.C. 3/7/2/2

Star Beam

Barque of 377 tons, commanded by Capt Peter Webster. Wrecked at East London on 4 November 1880 when her cables parted during a south-east gale after a voyage from Newport. No lives were lost.
Shipping Register, Cape Archives, C.C. 3/7/2/3

Star Beam. *(Africana Museum)*

SS Stuart Star
33° 02.50S, 27° 54.70E

Blue Star refrigerated twin-screw steamer of 11 928 tons, built in 1926 by Palmers, Newcastle, and commanded by Capt Sinclair. Wrecked at Hood Point south-west of East London at 09h00 on 17 December 1937 in dense fog after a voyage from Algoa Bay with 15 passengers and a crew of 93.
Eastern Province Herald, 18, 20, 21 (photographs) December 1937
Lloyds Register of Shipping, 1937-38

Stuart Star. *(P.E. Public Library)*

Therese

Cape Town-based schooner commanded by Capt A. Bertinette. Wrecked near the lighthouse on the west bank of the Buffalo River, East London, at 03h00 on 12 September 1861 when her cables parted during a southerly gale after a voyage from Table Bay with a general cargo including liquor, coffee, sugar, soap, candles, rice, coal and meal. No lives were lost.

King William's Town Gazette, 13, 17 (sale notice) September 1861

SS **Valdivia**
33° 01.10S, 27° 55.45E

British steel screw steamer of 4 952 tons, built in 1906 by Russell & Co, Port Glasgow. Sank at her moorings off East Beach, East London, on 2 October 1908 after striking off Stalwart Point and holing her bottom while on a voyage from New York to Che-Foo on the Shan-Tung Peninsula in China with a cargo of 40 000 tins of paraffin. Attempts to pump her out failed. She had a crew of 40. The *SA Oranjeland* (1974) was wrecked close to her. Her bell is in the East London Museum.

East London Daily Dispatch, 1, 2, 3 October 1908
Lloyds Register of Shipping, 1908-09
Shipping Register, Cape Archives, C.C. 3/7/2/6

Valdivia. *(East London Museum)*

Verulam

British wooden barque of 312 tons, built in 1865 by Wray. Wrecked on the west side of the Buffalo River, East London, close to the cemetery, on 7 December 1874 during a south-west gale while on a voyage from Penang to London with a cargo of sugar, coffee, pepper, rattans and hides. No lives were lost.

East London Dispatch, 8 December 1874
Lloyds Register of Shipping, 1874-75

Vigilant

British wooden snow of 304 tons, built in 1846 at Southshields, and commanded by Capt W. Stewart. Ran ashore at East London on 11 December 1853 when her cables parted during a strong south-east gale.

Lloyds Register of Shipping, 1853-54
Shipping Register, Cape Archives, C.C. 2/18

Western Star
33° 01.40S, 27° 55.00E

British wooden brig of 207 tons, built in 1862 by Johnson, Bideford. Ran ashore on the corner of Orient Beach, East London, west of the *Coquette* (1874), on 5 December 1874 after dragging her anchors during a south-west gale. No lives were lost.

East London Dispatch, 8 December 1874
Lloyds Register of Shipping, 1874-75

Wild Rose
33° 01.50S, 27° 55.00E

British wooden barque of 295 tons, built in 1856 at Whitby, and commanded by Capt John Holman. Wrecked on Orient Beach, East London, between the *Elaine* (1872) and the *Emma* (1872), on 25 September 1872 during a south-east gale after a voyage from Cape Town with a general cargo. No lives were lost, as the crew were saved in the whale boat, the line thrown by the rocket apparatus having parted.

East London Dispatch, 1, 8 October 1872
Lloyds Register of Shipping, 1872-73

34. Gonubie River mouth to the Kei River

A rocky stretch of coast interspersed with sandy beaches. The water is warm due to the Agulhas current, but is usually turbid due to the many rivers discharging into the sea. The coast is pounded by heavy surf and is popular with tourists, the main pastime being fishing. The climate is warm and humid and the vegetation on land consists of thick coastal bush.

Asphodel

British wooden barque of 305 tons, built in 1862 by Hardie, Sunderland, and commanded by Capt E. R. Stone. Ran ashore 48 km north-east of East London, near Cape Morgan, on 15 October 1878 when her cables parted at East London during a strong south-west gale after a voyage from London with a general cargo. No lives were lost.

Graham's Town Journal, 16 October 1878
Lloyds Register of Shipping, 1878-79
Shipping Register, Cape Archives, C.C. 3/7/2/3

James Gibson

British wooden barque of 323 tons, built in 1857 at Sunderland. Wrecked 32 km north-east of East London, near Cape Henderson, on 7 December 1874 during a south-west gale.

East London Dispatch, 15 December 1874
Graham's Town Journal, 25 January 1875
Lloyds Register of Shipping, 1874-75

SS **Khedive**

German steamer of 5 106 tons, built in 1906 by Bremer Vulkan, Vegesack, and owned by the German East Africa Line. Wrecked off Cape Morgan near the Kei River mouth on 16 August 1910 while on a voyage from Antwerp to Durban with a cargo of cement, machinery and timber. The third officer was drowned.

Eastern Province Herald, 17, 22 August 1910
Lloyds Register of Shipping, 1910-11

Nossa Senhora de Atalaia do Pinheiro
32° 48.60S, 28° 08.70E

Portuguese East-Indiaman (*não*), built in Portugal of pine sheathed in lead, and commanded by Capt Antonio de Camara de Noronha. Wrecked near the Cefane River 30 km north-east of East London in June 1647 while on a homeward-bound voyage from Goa to Lisbon in the company of the *Santissimo Sacramento* (which was wrecked at Schoenmakerskop near Port Elizabeth), with a cargo of pepper, diamonds, spices, Chinese porcelain and bronze cannon from the Bocarro Foundry in Macao. She had sprung a leak in mid-ocean after firing a seven-gun salute in honour of the commodore and was later parted from the *Sacramento* during a westerly gale; she was anchored near the shore, and later went to pieces. Many lives were lost during the wrecking. The survivors walked to Lourenço Marques (Maputo) and were joined by the survivors of the *Sacramento*. The wreck was discovered in 1980 and 23 bronze cannon, an anchor and cast iron gun were recovered.

Feyo, Bento Teyxeyra, *Relacam do Naufragio que fizeram as Naos Sacramento & nossa Senhora da Atalaya vindo da India para o Reyno, no Cabo de Boa Esperanca*, Lisbon, 1650. Translated into English in Theal, G.M., *Records of South Eastern Africa*, Vol 8, pp 295-360

Nuovo Abele

Italian wooden barque of 690 tons, built in 1873 by Rolla, Ravenna, and commanded by Capt Cuneo Francisco. Wrecked at the Cintsa River mouth in the East London area on 6 December 1874 during a south-west gale while on a voyage from Batavia to London with a cargo of sugar. A courageous rescue was carried out by a certain Sargeant Kelly, who swam a line out to the wreck.

East London Dispatch, 15 December 1874
Lloyds Register of Shipping, 1874-75

Santo Alberto

Portuguese East-Indiaman (não) commanded by Capt Julião de Faria Cerveira. Wrecked, presumably near East London, on 24 March 1593 while on a homeward-bound voyage from Cochin, which she had left on 21 January 1593 with a cargo of spices, silks and Chinese porcelain. She was leaking, as her hull was in an extremely rotten state, and was beached to prevent her from sinking. The survivors, 125 Portuguese and 160 slaves, walked to Delagoa Bay; 28 Portuguese and 34 slaves were drowned. A cast iron cannon and broken Chinese porcelain found at Sunrise-on-Sea are thought to come from this wreck.

Lavanha, João Baptista, *Naufragio da não S. Alberto no penedo das fontes no anno de 1593* (compiled 1597). Translated into English in Theal, G.M., *Records of South Eastern Africa*, Vol 2, pp 283-346

Santo Espiritu

Portuguese East-Indiaman. Wrecked, presumably near Haga Haga, a little north-east of the site of the *Nossa Senhora de Atalaia* (1647), in 1608 while on a homeward-bound voyage with a cargo of silk, spices and Chinese porcelain.The survivors made boats from the wreckage and sailed away from the wreck site to Delagoa Bay (Maputo). Broken shards of Chinese porcelain wash ashore near Haga Haga and have been dated to this period.

Sousa, A. Botelho de, *Subsídios para a historia Marítima da India* (1585-1669) II, Lisbon, 1930

35. Kei River mouth to Port Edward

This beautiful, unspoilt stretch of coast, also known as the Wild Coast, is the traditional tribal home of the Xhosa and Pondo people. It is a long, rocky coast interspersed with sandy beaches, river mouths and estuaries. The sea is warm due to the Agulhas current, but the shore is usually pounded by heavy ground swells. The coast is a popular tourist venue noted for its unspoilt character, and spearfishermen and fishermen visit regularly. The climate is warm and humid and the vegetation on land is lush. The only major settlement along the coast is Port St Johns, a popular holiday resort situated at the Mzimvubu River mouth. The river cuts through a deep ravine cloaked with sub-tropical vegetation before spilling out into the sea on a wide sandy beach. Place names associated with shipwrecks are Agate Terrace at Port St Johns, named after the trade beads from the Nossa Senhora de Belem (1635) which wash up there; Clan Lindsay Rocks at Mazeppa Bay, named after the steamer Clan Lindsay wrecked there in 1898; Port Grosvenor on the Pondoland coast, the supposed but incorrect spot of the wrecking of the Grosvenor in 1782; and Twine Point near the Xora River, named after the cargo of hemp which washed ashore from the wreck of the Calcutta in 1881.

SS Alfredia

Screw steamer of 39 tons. Wrecked at Port St Johns on 10 July 1887 after crossing the bar while on a voyage from Natal to East London via Port St Johns with a cargo of 1 026 pockets of sugar. No lives were lost.
Eastern Province Herald, 13 July 1887
Shipping Register, Cape Archives, C.C. 3/7/2/4

Alice Smith

Cape schooner of 60 tons, built in 1855 at Newhaven, sheathed with zinc, and owned by J. O. Smith, Algoa Bay. Wrecked on the rocks at Port St Johns on 21 December 1861 when the wind failed her while coming out of the river. No lives were lost.
Graham's Town Journal, 4 January 1862
King William's Town Gazette, 31 December 1861
Lloyds Register of Shipping, 1861-62
Shipping Register, Cape Archives, C.C. 3/7/2/1

Calcutta
32° 10.00S, 28° 59.00E

American ship of 843 tons, owned by Edward Lawrence of Boston, and commanded by Capt Andrew J. Smith. Wrecked a little south-west of the Xora River mouth in the Transkei on 28 July 1881 while on a voyage from Cebu in the Philippines to Boston with a cargo of flax, sugar and manila hemp. The captain and 12 crew were drowned; three were saved. The vessel was wrecked at Twine Point, named after the hemp (twine) which washed ashore.
Eastern Province Herald, 9 August 1881
Shipping Register Cape Archives, C.C. 3/7/2/3

Circassia

Norwegian wooden barque of 487 tons, built in 1873 by Oliver, Quebec, and commanded by Capt C. Gundersen. Wrecked near the Qora River mouth in Transkei on 10 November 1894. No lives were lost.
Argus Annual, 1895
Lloyds Register of Shipping, 1894-95

SS Clan Lindsay
32° 28.80S, 28° 39.30E

Clan Line steamer of 2 668 tons, built in 1896 by Naval Construction & Armament Co, Barrow, and commanded by Capt J. Schofield. Wrecked at Clan Lindsay Rocks in Mazeppa Bay on the Transkei coast on 20 March 1898 while on a voyage to Mauritius. No lives were lost.
Cape Times, 23, 24 March 1898
Lloyds Register of Shipping 1897-98

Conch

Schooner commanded by Capt W. Moses.

Clan Lindsay. *(John Lamprecht)*

Wrecked on the bar at Port St Johns on 7 November 1847 after the wind had failed. No lives were lost.
Shipping Register, Cape Archives, C.C. 2/16

MV Forresbank
31° 51.00S, 29° 17.00E

British twin screw freighter of 5 155 tons, built in 1925 by Harland & Wolff, Glasgow, owned by the Bank Line, and commanded by Capt B. T. Symmonds. Wrecked a little north-east of the Mtakatye River in Transkei on 10 November 1958 after catching fire while on a voyage from Cape Town to Durban to load 1 000 tons of anthracite for the Far East. One man died.
Cape Argus, 10 November 1958 (photograph)
Lloyds Register of Shipping, 1958-59

Forresbank. (Cape Argus)

SS Frontier I (ex *Limpopo*)

South African twin-screw steamer of 191 tons, built in 1896 by Ramage & Ferguson, Leith, Scotland, and commanded by Capt A.V. Buuren. Wrecked at Port St Johns on 20 November 1926 with a general cargo including 100 pigs, which swam ashore. No lives were lost among her crew of 13.
Eastern Province Herald, 23 November 1926
Lloyds Register of Shipping, 1925-26

MV Frontier II (ex *Kornhaus I*)
32° 24.00S, 28° 44.40E

Twin-screw motor vessel of 163 tons, built in 1921 by Berninghaus, Duisberg, Germany, and commanded by Capt Plough. Wrecked on Shixina Point on the Transkei coast on 7 April 1938.
Cape Times, 7 April 1938
Lloyds Register of Shipping, 1937-38

Grosvenor.

SS **Meliskerk** (ex *Cesario*, ex *D.A.D.G. 76*)
31° 36.80S, 29° 34.50E

Dutch cargo vessel of 6 045 tons, built in 1919 by Blohm & Voss, Hamburg, managed by the Holland Afrika Line, and commanded by Capt B. Brouwer. Wrecked on a reef a few kilometres north-east of Port St Johns on 10 January 1943 with an 11 000-ton cargo of ammunition, tanks and aircraft. Captain Van Delden was involved in the salvage of the cargo; one day, shortly after he had left the vessel during a heavy swell, she blew up, pieces landing on the shore.
Van Delden, Gertrude, *I Have a Plan*
Lloyds Register of Shipping, 1942-43

Meliskerk. *(George Young)*

Grosvenor
31° 22.40S, 29° 55.00E

British vessel of 729 tons in the service of the English East India Company, commanded by Capt John Coxon. Wrecked in the big gully to the north-east of the Tezani Stream, near Port Grosvenor in Pondoland, on 4 August 1782 at night during a south-west gale while on a homeward-bound voyage from Trincomalee in Ceylon (Sri Lanka). Of the 150 people on board, 128 set out on an epic journey to the Cape through native territory. The vessel was reputed to carry a fortune of gold. Captain Sydney Turner recovered cast iron cannon and gold and silver coins in 1880. Iron ballast and cannon are evident on the site.
Barrow, John, *An Account of Travels into the Interior of South Africa*, Vol 2, 1804
Cape Archives, V.C. 550 (Report of William Hubberley)
Dalrymple, Alexander, *An Account of the Loss of the Grosvenor Indiaman*, London, 1783
Hardy, Charles, *A Register of Ships in the Service of the English East India Company*, 1800
Kirby, P.R., *Source Book on the Wreck of the Grosvenor*, V.R.S. 34, 1953
Natal Mercury, 21 May 1880 (report of salvage by Captain Sydney Turner)

MV **Horizon** (ex *Lydia*, ex *Lombardia*)
31° 40.50S, 29° 28.90E

Durban-owned coaster of 2 081 tons, built in 1954, and commanded by Capt W. F. Nicholls. Wrecked 8 km south-west of Port St Johns near the Mngazi River on 12 May 1967 while on a voyage from Cape Town to Mauritius via Durban with a cargo of cement, fruit and general cargo including liquor.
Cape Argus, 12 May 1967
Lloyds Register of Shipping, 1966-67

Idomene
32° 26.50S, 28° 41.00E

British iron ship of 1 390 tons, built in 1874 by T. R. Oswald, Sunderland, and commanded by Capt William Roy. Wrecked at the Qora River in Transkei on 14 November 1887 at night while on a voyage from Rangoon to London with a cargo of rice. The captain and 12 seamen were drowned and buried at Qora River. Eleven other crew members were saved and taken to East London by ox-wagon.
Cape Argus, 23 November 1887
Lloyds Register of Shipping, 1887-88
Shipping Register, Cape Archives, C.C. 3/7/2/4

MV **Jacaranda** (ex *Sloman Malaga*, ex *Malaga*, ex *August Sartori*, ex *Götaland*)
32° 37.40S, 29° 28.00E

Greek freighter of 1 591 tons, built in 1953, and commanded by Capt Kokkios Paulos. Wrecked a little south-west of the Kabonqaba River, a few kilometres north-east of the Kei River mouth, on 18 September 1971 after experiencing engine trouble while on a voyage from East London to Durban in ballast. She lies high and dry in a gully (1987).
Argus, 20 September 1971
Lloyds Register of Shipping, 1971-72

L'Éole

French ship commanded by Capt Vidette. Wrecked 48 km south-west of the Bashee River on 12 April 1829 while on a voyage from Calcutta and Réunion. Twelve men, including the captain, were drowned.
South African Commercial Advertiser, 9 May 1829

Nossa Senhora de Belem
31° 37.00S, 29° 34.00E

Portuguese East-Indiaman (*não*), commanded by Capt Joseph de Cabreyra (Admiral of the Fleet). Wrecked a little north-east of Port St Johns on 24 July 1635 while on a homeward-bound voyage from Goa to Lisbon with a cargo of Eastern goods and pepper. Her crew of 145 men were ill with scurvy and the ship was unsound. No lives were lost; the crew stayed at the wreck site for six months and built two boats, the *Nossa Senhora da Natividade* and the *Nossa Senhora da Boa Viagem*; the one boat reached Luanda 48 days later, but the other was lost.
Cabreyra, Joseph de, *Naufragio da Não. N. Senhora de Belem*, Lisbon, 1636. Translated into English in Theal, G.M., *Records of South Eastern Africa*, Vol 8, pp 187-234

SS **Obell** (ex *Concadoro*, ex *Umlazi*)
32° 17.00S, 28° 52.80E

British vessel of 1 797 tons, built in 1888 by J. Laing, Sunderland. Wrecked a little south-west of the Bashee River mouth on 29 December 1916 while on a voyage from Madagascar to England.
Cape Argus, 10 January 1917
Lloyds Register of Shipping, 1916-17

São Bento
31° 19.60S, 29° 59.00E

Portuguese East-Indiaman (*não*) of 22 guns, commanded by Fernão D'Alvares Cabral. Wrecked at the mouth of a gully on the seaward side of the island at the Msikaba River mouth

on the Pondoland Coast after being disabled in a storm on 21 April 1554 while on a homeward-bound voyage from Cochin, India, which she had left on 15 February 1554 with a cargo including pepper, cotton, Chinese porcelain, coconuts, silk and spices packed in 72 crates. Forty-four Portuguese and over 100 slaves lost their lives; 98 Portuguese (including Manuel de Mesquita Perestrelo), and 224 slaves landed safely and travelled overland to Delagoa Bay (Maputo) but only a few made it. They passed the *São João* wreck (1552) on the way. A great deal of broken Chinese porcelain has been found scattered on the island. Eighteen bronze cannon have been recovered; many lead cannon-balls were also found.
Annals of the Natal Museum, 1982, Vol 25, Part 1, pp 1-39
De Mesquita Perestrelo, Manuel, *Relacão Do Naufragio Da Não S. Bento*. Translated into English in Theal, G.M., *Records of South Eastern Africa*, Vol 1, pp 218-285

William Shaw

Schooner of 39 tons, owned by Mr Stoffels of Port St Johns, and commanded by Capt Davis. Wrecked in the Mzimvubu River mouth at Port St Johns on 9 December 1873 after a voyage from Durban. Unknown to her captain the sandbanks in the river mouth had changed and she was wrecked while trying to enter the river. She was employed in the coasting trade between Port St Johns and Durban.
Natal Mercury, 18 December 1873

36. Port Edward to the South Pier, Durban, and the Aliwal Shoal

This densely populated stretch of coast is the most popular tourist venue in South Africa. The coastline consists of many sandy beaches, estuaries and river mouths interspersed with rocky headlands. The sea is warm due to the Mozambique current, but the shore is usually pounded by heavy ground swells.
Spearfishermen and fishermen visit the coast regularly, but sharks are a very real danger and many of the holiday resorts have installed anti-shark nets. The climate is sub-tropical and the vegetation on land is lush. Aliwal Shoal is a large, submerged reef lying offshore. It is a popular spearfishing and diving venue and the water is usually clear. Tropical fish can be found on the reefs. The coast has many small settlements, the most important being Port Edward, Southbroom, Ramsgate, Margate, Uvongo, Shelly Beach, Port Shepstone, Umtentweni, Sea Park, Southport, Anerley, Sunwich Port, Sezela, Park Rynie, Scottburgh, Umkomaas, Kingsburgh, Amanzimtoti, Umbogintwini and Isipingo Beach. Place names associated with shipwrecks are Ivy Point, named after the British barque Ivy wrecked there in 1878; and Winkelspruit, named after the shop Capt Sydney Turner set up to sell the cargo of the British schooner Tonga, wrecked in 1875, which he had bought.

Ambleside
30° 43.00S, 30° 28.80E

British wooden barque of 535 tons, built in 1864 by Sherwood, Quebec. Wrecked between the Mtentweni and Mzimkulu river mouths on the Natal South Coast on 30 August 1868 during a south-east wind while on a voyage from Kurrachee to Liverpool with a cargo of cotton, wool and linseed oil, of which only a little was saved. No lives were lost. She came ashore about 1 km south of the *Defiance* (1871).
Lloyds Register of Shipping, 1868-69
Shipping Register, Cape Archives, C.C. 3/7/2/2

Defiance
30° 42.20S, 30° 29.50E

British iron full-rigged ship of 1 001 tons, built in 1857 at Liverpool, and commanded by Capt Langlois. Wrecked on the Natal South Coast 3 km north of the Mzimkulu River on 6 October 1871 during fog while on a voyage from Bombay to Liverpool with a cargo of 5 000 bales of cotton, buffalo and rhino horns, jute and wool. No lives were lost. She lies 1 km north of the *Ambleside* (1868).
Lloyds Register of Shipping, 1871-72
Shipping Register, Cape Archives, C.C. 3/7/2/2

Defiance. *(Local History Museum, Durban)*

Espero (ex *Pietá*, ex *Thorbecke VII*)
30° 38.50S, 30° 32.10E

Italian wooden barque of 909 tons, built in 1885 by A. H. Meursing, and commanded by Capt Stefano Graviolto. Ran ashore 11 km north of Port Shepstone on 19 August 1902 while on a voyage from Java to Cape Town with a cargo of 1 200 tons of sleepers. She had encountered a heavy westerly storm off Cape Agulhas and had run before it. No lives were lost.
Lloyds Register of Shipping, 1901-02
Natal Mercury, 20, 21, 22 August 1902

Fairfield

British wooden ship of 434 tons, built in 1833 at Hull, and commanded by Capt J. Hornwell. Wrecked about 130 km south of Durban, south

of the Mzimkulu River, on 7 September 1852 while on a voyage from Calcutta to Liverpool. The captain and 16 of the crew of 24 were drowned.
Lloyds Register of Shipping, 1852-53
Shipping Register, Cape Archives, C.C. 2/18

Fascadale
30° 54.80S, 30° 20.20E

British steel barque of 2 083 tons, built in 1890 by A. Stephen & Sons, Glasgow, and commanded by Capt B. J. Gillespie. Wrecked on the rocks south of the Mbizane River, 32 km south of Port Shepstone, on 7 February 1895 at night while on a voyage from Java to Liverpool with a cargo of sugar. Her captain had been left sick in Java. Out of the crew of 28 only 18 were saved by a boat manned by Frank Whitehead, chief officer of the *Norham Castle*, which had come to their aid. The settlement Fascadale appears on maps of the area and its name is most probably derived from this wreck.
Lloyds Register of Shipping, 1894-95
Natal Mercury, 8 February 1895

Fidia D.
30° 09.90S, 30° 49.40E

Italian wooden barque of 749 tons, built in 1875 at Sestri Ponente. Wrecked 5 km north of the Mkomaas River on the Natal South Coast on 18 July 1889 during an easterly gale after sustaining storm damage while on a voyage from Rangoon to Falmouth with a cargo of rice and teak. Two men, including the captain, were drowned.
Lloyds Register of Shipping, 1889-90
Shipping Register, Cape Archives, C.C. 3/7/2/4

Fusilier

British ship of 1 088 tons, commanded by Capt Carhap. Wrecked on the Bluff Rocks at the south entrance to the harbour at Durban on 25 May 1865 during a north-east wind while on a voyage from Calcutta to Demerara (British Guiana), with Indian workers. Twenty lives were lost.
Shipping Register, Cape Archives, C.C. 3/7/2/1
South African Advertiser and Mail, 8 June 1865

Harry Mundahl
30° 43.40S, 30° 28.80E

Cape wooden dandy of 122 tons, built in 1882 by C.C.A. Dreyer, Hamburg, owned by the Port Shepstone Shipping Co, and commanded by Capt Jacobson. Wrecked in 'Anchor Bay' about 5 km north of Port Shepstone on the Natal South Coast on 31 January 1901 at daybreak at the start of a voyage with a cargo of lime and sugar, all of which was lost. No lives were lost, as all the crew were saved by the rocket brigade. She was employed in trade between Port Shepstone and Durban.
Lloyds Register of Shipping, 1899-1900
Natal Mercury, 1 February 1901

Hector

British wooden barque of 293 tons, built in 1824 at Bristol, and commanded by Capt M. Brook. Wrecked 90 km south of Durban, between the Mtwalume and Mzumbe rivers, on 27 July 1852 after springing a leak while on a voyage from Batavia to London with a cargo of rice, sugar and sapan-wood. Five members of the crew were drowned.
Lloyds Register of Shipping, 1852-53
Shipping Register, Cape Archives, C.C. 2/18

Ivy
31° 02.30S, 30° 14.40E

British wooden barque of 319 tons, built in 1865 by Richard, Quebec, and commanded by Capt C. Orr. Wrecked 6 km north of the Mtamvuna River, 161 km from Durban, on 27 March 1878 while on a voyage from London to Durban with a cargo of liquor. One man was lost.
Lloyds Register of Shipping, 1878-79
Shipping Register, Cape Archives, C.C. 3/7/2/3

Leading Star

British wooden brig of 249 tons, built in 1868 by Barkes, Sunderland, and commanded by Capt T. Grenfell. Wrecked on the rocks near the Mzimkulu River mouth on 6 November 1880 at night while on a voyage from Christiania, Norway, to Durban with a cargo of timber. Four members of the crew, including the captain, were drowned.
Lloyds Register of Shipping, 1880-81
Natal Mercury, 11, 13 November 1880

Minerva

British wooden ship (a former East-Indiaman) of 987 tons, built in 1812 in Bombay, and commanded by Capt J. Moir. Wrecked on the rocks at the Point of the Bluff, Durban, at 23h00 on 4 July 1850 when her cables parted after a voyage to bring a party of settlers and general cargo to Durban. No lives were lost.
Cape Town Mail, 27 July 1850
Lloyds Register of Shipping, 1850-51
Shipping Register, Cape Archives, C.C. 2/17

SS Nebo
30° 15.20S, 30° 49.00E

British iron steamer of 2 067 tons, built in 1884 by J. Laing, Sunderland, and commanded by Capt Powell. Struck Aliwal Shoal off the south coast of Durban on 20 May 1884 in good weather and sank immediately while on a voyage from Sunderland, Durham, to Natal with a cargo of 4 500 tons of railway material. No lives were lost. She lies intact, bottom up.
Lloyds Register of Shipping, 1884-85
Natal Mercury, 21 May 1884
Shipping Register, Cape Archives, C.C. 3/7/2/3

Onaway
29° 52.40S, 31° 03.70E

British wooden barque of 441 tons, built in 1877 by E. W. Ogden, Sackville, and commanded by Capt Casey. Wrecked under the lighthouse against the south pier at Durban at 22h00 on 3 February 1892 after a voyage from New York to Durban with a general cargo, including 'Yankee notions' (patent medicines) and paraffin.
Lloyds Register of Shipping, 1891-92
Natal Mercury, 5 February 1892

Onaway. *(Local History Museum, Durban)*

MV Produce
30° 15.00S, 30° 49.30E

Norwegian bulk carrier of 13 358 tons, built in 1960 by Burmeister & Wain, and commanded by Capt Tormod Boge. Struck Aliwal Shoal and sank about 3 km off the Mkomaas River on the Natal South Coast on 11 August 1974 while on a voyage from Durban to the United Kingdom with a full cargo of 18 863 tons of molasses. No lives were lost, as the crew were rescued by the Safmarine freighter *SA Oranjeland*, which was wrecked at East London on 13 August 1974.
Cape Times, 12 August 1974 (photographs)
Lloyds Register of Shipping, 1974-75

Produce. (Daily News)

São João
31° 02.00S, 30° 14.20E

Portuguese East-Indiaman (galleon) commanded by Manuel de Sousa Sepulvida. Wrecked on the Natal South Coast north of the Mtamvuna River on 11 June 1552 after being disabled during a storm while on a homeward-bound voyage from Cochin, India, in the company of the *São Jeronymo*, which was wrecked on the Zululand Coast. Of the more than 200 Portuguese and more than 400 slaves on board, over 100 were drowned. The survivors walked to Delagoa Bay (Maputo) and were later rescued by boat and taken to Mozambique. The *São Bento* survivors claim to have passed the wreck site in 1554. *Relacão Do Naufragio Do Galeão Grande S. João Na Terra Do Natal No Anno De 1552.* Translated into English in Theal, G.M., *Records of South Eastern Africa*, Vol 1, pp 128-149

Stavenisse

Dutch flute of 544 tons, built in 1681 at the Zeeland Yard for the Amsterdam Chamber of the Dutch East India Company, and commanded by Willem Kuif. Ran aground near the mouth of the Mzimkulu River, just north of Port Shepstone, on 16 February 1686 while on a homeward-bound voyage from Bengal. Eleven people drowned and 60 reached shore.
Daghregister Gehouden in't Vaartuygh De Centaurus Zeylende Van D'Caap Na't Land Van Terra De Natal (Cape Archives, V.C. 94)
Dutch-Asiatic Shipping Homeward Voyages, 1597-1795, The Hague, 1979
Moodie, D., *The Record*, Part 1, pp 415-430, 443-446

Tonga

British wooden schooner of 299 tons, built in 1874 by Gibbon, Sunderland, and commanded by Capt W. P. Armitage. Wrecked on the rocks at Winkelspruit 2,5 km north of the Lovu River on 16 May 1875 during a north-east wind while on a voyage from London to Natal with a general cargo. No lives were lost. Her cargo was bought by Capt Sydney Turner and sold on the spot, hence the name Winkelspruit (Shop Creek).
Lloyds Register of Shipping, 1875-76
Natal Mercury, 20 May 1875

Trichera (ex *Nanny*, ex *Jane Porter*)
30° 17.30S, 30° 45.60E

Swedish iron barquentine of 1 003 tons, built in 1860 by Harland & Wolff, Belfast, and commanded by Capt Hermans. Wrecked 1,5 km south of the old lighthouse at Scottburgh, Natal, at 22h00 on 1 June 1905 while on a voyage from Western Australia to East London with a cargo of sleepers. The captain and eight crew members were drowned.
Lloyds Register of Shipping, 1904-05
Natal Mercury, 3 June 1905

37. Durban North Pier to Umhlanga Rocks

The most densely populated coastal area in South Africa. Durban is a large city attracting large numbers of inland residents to its beaches. The hot, humid, sub-tropical climate and proximity to the Witwatersrand ensure a constant flow of holiday-makers. The water is warm due to the Mozambique current, but the shore is usually pounded by heavy swells.

Pollution is a problem and shark nets have been installed at all the main beaches after many serious shark attacks. Divers and fishermen regulary visit the reefs in the area and many tropical fish are to be seen. Annabella Bank, Durban, is named after the British barque Annabella wrecked there in 1856.

Adelaide

British wooden barque of 640 tons, built in 1832 in Calcutta. Wrecked at Durban on 8 February 1866 during a strong east gale after a voyage from Madras with Indian immigrants. Several men were drowned.
Lloyds Register of Shipping, 1865-66
Natal Mercury, 8 February 1866
Shipping Register, Cape Archives, C.C. 3/7/2/1

African Adventure

Portuguese sloop of 120 tons. Ran ashore at Durban in January 1830 with a cargo of slaves.
Fynn, Henry Francis, *Diary,* pp 178-179
Isaaks, Nathaniel, *Travels and Adventures in Eastern Africa,* Vol 1, pp 10-12

Annabella

British barque of 199 tons, built in 1834 in Port Glasgow, and commanded by Capt J. Wilson. Wrecked on what is now known as Annabella Bank at Durban on 21 January 1856 with a general cargo. No lives were lost.
Lloyds Register of Shipping, 1855-56
Natal Harbour Board, 1866

Ariosto
29° 51.80S, 31° 03.00E

American barque commanded by Capt Balch. Wrecked on the Back Beach at Durban on 31 July 1854 while on a voyage from Sumatra to Boston with a cargo of pepper. No lives were lost.
Shipping Register, Cape Archives, C.C. 2/18

Breidablik
29° 51.20S, 31° 02.50E

Norwegian schooner of 147 tons, commanded by Capt Somme. Wrecked near the foot of West Street, Durban, on 31 July 1872 during a northeast gale after a voyage from Gothenburg with a cargo of timber.
Natal Mercury, 1 August 1872

Bridgetown
29° 51.20S, 31° 02.50E

British wooden barque of 370 tons, built in 1857 at Newhaven, and commanded by Capt F. H. Cornish. Wrecked on the Back Beach at Durban, just north of Vetches Pier, on 28 June 1882 during a north-east wind with a cargo of coal. No

lives were lost, as a heroic rescue was undertaken by the port lifeboat.
Lloyds Register of Shipping, 1882-83
Natal Mercury, 29 June 1882

Bridgetown. *(Local History Museum, Durban)*

British Tar
29° 51.80S, 31° 03.00E

British barque of 282 tons, built in 1845 at Sunderland, and commanded by Capt S. Down. Wrecked on the Back Beach at Durban on 29 September 1850 during an east-north-east gale with a general cargo. No lives were lost.
Cape Town Mail, 19 October 1850
Lloyds Register of Shipping, 1850-51
Shipping Register, Cape Archives, C.C. 2/17

Burnham

British schooner of 84 tons, built in 1838 at Gosport, and commanded by Capt G. Bowles. Wrecked at Durban on 29 May 1840 with a cargo of 400 muids of grain. No lives were lost.
Cape of Good Hope Almanac, 1852
Lloyds Register of Shipping, 1840-41
Shipping Register, Cape Archives, C.C. 2/15

Charles Jackson
29° 51.20S, 31° 02.50E

British wooden barque of 327 tons, built in 1852 at Maryport, and commanded by Capt J. L. Champion. Wrecked on the Back Beach at Durban on 26 August 1884 after a voyage from Liverpool with a general cargo including salt. No lives were lost.
Lloyds Register of Shipping, 1884-85
Natal Mercury, 27 August 1884

City of Lima

British barque of 353 tons, built in 1861 by Willmott, Newport, and commanded by Capt Gool. Wrecked on Bar Ridge 1 km from the beach

at Durban on 21 July 1883 during an east-north-east wind after a voyage from Garston on the Mersey with a cargo of coal. No lives were lost.
Lloyds Register of Shipping, 1883-84
Natal Mercury, 23 July 1883

Congune

Schooner. Sank while at anchor at Durban on 16 October 1872 with a full cargo of sugar for East London. No lives were lost.
Shipping Register, Cape Archives, C.C. 3/7/2/2

Courier

British barque of 187 tons, commanded by Capt Billins. Wrecked on the bar at Durban on 27 August 1846 during a west wind at the start of a voyage to Mauritius with a cargo of cattle. No lives were lost.
Natal Witness, 1 September 1846
Shipping Register, Cape Archives, C.C. 2/16

Draga
29° 51.20S, 31° 02.50E

Austro-Hungarian brigantine of 320 tons, commanded by Capt Viderlick. Run ashore on the Back Beach at Durban on 1 November 1880 during a north-east wind after springing a leak while on a voyage from Boston with a cargo of flour and oats. No lives were lost.
Natal Mercury, 2, 3 (sale notice) November 1880

Earl of Hardwicke
29° 51.80S, 31° 03.00E

British wooden ship of 903 tons, built in 1838 in London, owned by Greens Co, and commanded by Capt Maddison. Wrecked on the Back Beach at Durban on 26 September 1863 during a north-east gale after a voyage from Madras with a cargo of Indian immigrants. No lives were lost.
Lloyds Register of Shipping, 1863-64
Shipping Register, Cape Archives, C.C. 3/7/2/1

Eastern Star

British wooden brig of 209 tons, built in 1864 by Johnson, Bideford, and commanded by Capt Davis. Wrecked on the north side of the breakwater at Durban on 25 August 1880 when her cables parted during an easterly gale after a voyage from London with a general cargo. No lives were lost.
Lloyds Register of Shipping, 1880-81
Natal Mercury, 26, 27 August, 4 September (sale notice) 1880

Eleanor

Schooner. Wrecked on the Inner Bank at Durban on 28 July 1839. No lives were lost.
Shipping Register, Cape Archives, C.C. 2/15

Enfants Nantais
29° 51.20S, 31° 02.50E

French barque of 316 tons, commanded by Capt Lefrano. Wrecked on the Back Beach at Durban on 14 September 1876 when her cables parted during an east-north-east wind after a voyage from Adelaide with a cargo of flour. No lives were lost.
Natal Mercury, 16 September 1876

Fratelli Arecco
29° 51.21S, 31° 02.55E

Italian wooden barque of 953 tons, built in 1875 by Craviotto, Varazze, and commanded by Capt B. Arecco. Wrecked on the Back Beach at the foot of West Street, Durban, abreast of the rocket-house, on 22 August 1883 at night when her cables parted during an east-north-east wind after a voyage from Akyab, Burma, with a cargo of rice. No lives were lost.
Lloyds Register of Shipping, 1883-84
Natal Mercury, 23, 24 August 1883

Gazelle
29° 51.15S, 31° 02.50E

American brig of 326 tons, commanded by Capt Dickson. Wrecked on the Back Beach at Durban on 13 March 1879 during a north-east gale after a voyage from Table Bay with a cargo of mealies and rice. No lives were lost.
Natal Mercury, 17 March 1879
Shipping Register, Cape Archives, C.C. 3/7/2/3

Good Hope

English ketch of 50 tons and six guns, commanded by Capt John Adams. Wrecked on the Point of the Bay of Natal (Durban) on 17 May 1685. She was from Gravesend and had been trading along the coast for ivory and slaves. Of her crew of 24, 10 sailed on a slaving expedition to Madagascar via Delagoa Bay (Maputo) in a boat they had built.
Cape Archives, C. 332 (old number)
Moodie, D., *The Record*, Part 1, pp 416-424

Grace Peile
29° 51.80S, 31° 03.00E

British wooden barque of 321 tons, built in 1858 at Liverpool. Wrecked on the Back Beach at Durban on 30 July 1872 during a north-east gale with a cargo of mules. No lives were lost.
Lloyds Register of Shipping, 1872-73
Natal Mercury, 1 August 1872
Shipping Register, Cape Archives, C.C. 3/7/2/2

Graf Wedell
29° 51.20S, 31° 02.51E

German brig of 290 tons, commanded by Capt Mannick. Wrecked on the Back Beach at Dur-

Natal Mercury

ban on 24 October 1880 at night during an east wind after a voyage from Gothenburg, Sweden, with a cargo of timber. Four lives were lost.
Natal Mercury, 26 October 1880 (sale notice)

H.D. Storer
29° 51.22S, 31° 02.51E

American barque of 381 tons, commanded by Capt Patten. Wrecked on the Back Beach at Durban on 2 August 1878 when her cables parted during an east-north-east gale after a voyage from New York with a general cargo. The crew were saved by means of rocket apparatus.
Shipping Register, Cape Archives, C.C. 3/7/2/3

Hawthorn
29° 51.50S, 31° 02.70E

British wooden barquentine of 621 tons, built in 1874 by Rowan, St John, and commanded by Capt Chapman. Wrecked between the Point and the rocket-house at Durban (200 m south of West Street) on 19 August 1889 during a north-east gale after a voyage from New York with a general cargo. The crew were saved by means of rocket apparatus.
Lloyds Register of Shipping, 1889-90
Natal Mercury, 20 August 1889
Shipping Register, Cape Archives, C.C. 3/7/2/4

Hydra

German brig of 178 tons, commanded by Capt Spiering. Wrecked on the bar at Durban on 13 December 1867 when her cables parted during a south-west gale after a voyage from Algoa Bay in ballast. Seven lives were lost.
Shipping Register, Cape Archives, C.C. 3/7/2/2

James Gaddarn
29° 51.20S, 31° 02.50E

British wooden barque of 379 tons, built in 1868 by Gaddarn, Neyland, and commanded by Capt Jones. Wrecked on the Back Beach at Durban on 27 January 1882 when her cables parted during an east-north-east wind after a voyage from Mobile, Alabama, with a cargo of timber, which

had been offloaded. She was in ballast. No lives were lost.
Lloyds Register of Shipping, 1881-82
Natal Mercury, 28 January 1882

Le Paquebot Bordelais

French barque of 233 tons, commanded by Capt J. T. Libadey. Wrecked on the bar at Durban on 28 June 1847 at the start of a voyage to Réunion with a cargo of cattle. No lives were lost.
Shipping Register, Cape Archives, C.C. 2/16

Lola
29° 51.20S, 31° 02.50E

Swedish barque of 326 tons, commanded by Capt Nilsen. Wrecked below West Street at Durban on 30 March 1879 during a north-east wind after a voyage from Gothenburg with a cargo of deals. No lives were lost.
Natal Mercury, 31 March 1879

Lord George Bentinck
29° 51.80S, 31° 03.00E

British wooden barque of 592 tons, built in 1848 at Sunderland, and commanded by Capt George Case. Wrecked on the Back Beach at Durban, close to the *Queen* (1863), on 3 January 1861 during a north-east wind after a voyage from Madras with a cargo of Indian immigrants. No lives were lost.
Lloyds Register of Shipping, 1860-61
Natal Mercury, 10 January 1861

Luna
29° 51.22S, 31° 02.50E

British brig of 184 tons, built in 1837 at Sunderland, and commanded by Capt Grube. Wrecked on the Back Beach at Durban on 2 September 1880 when her cables parted during a south-east gale after a voyage from London with a general cargo. No lives were lost, as the crew were saved by means of rocket apparatus.
Lloyds Register of Shipping, 1880-81
Natal Mercury, 3 September 1880

Luna. *(Africana Museum)*

Mabel
29° 51.20S, 31° 02.50E

British wooden barque of 299 tons, built in 1871

Natal Mercury

by Bourke, Prince Edward Island, and commanded by Capt Richards. Wrecked at the foot of West Street, Durban, on 26 October 1877 during an east-north-east gale after a voyage from Glasgow with a general cargo. The captain and three men were lost.
Lloyds Register of Shipping, 1877-78
Natal Mercury, 27, 30 October 1877, 24 August 1880 (sale notice)

Mary
29° 52.20S, 31° 03.15E

British brig commanded by Lieut King. Wrecked on the bar on 1 October 1825 while entering the bay at Durban under the command of the mate, John Hatton, after a voyage from Britain. No lives were lost. Lieut King and most of the crew stayed on to build a boat, while the mate made it to Algoa Bay in the longboat. On his arrival at Cape Town he asked for assistance for the men left in Port Natal. Lieut King was a former Royal Navy officer who was intending to embark in trade with the natives on the East Coast of Africa.
Cape Archives, C.O. 293 (Letter from Hatton to the Secretary of the Government)

Mary Emily
29° 51.20S, 31° 02.52E

German wooden barque of 461 tons, built in 1872 by Harvey, Littlehampton, and commanded by Capt Burmeister. Wrecked near the foot of West Street, near Vetches Pier, Durban on 29 August 1889 at night when her cables parted during an easterly gale after a voyage from Cardiff with a cargo of coal. The tug *Churchill* went to her aid but turned back when she was told that assistance was not needed. Her entire crew of ten was lost.
Lloyds Register of Shipping, 1889-90
Natal Mercury, 31 August 1889
Shipping Register, Cape Archives, C.C. 3/7/2/4

North-Wester

Wrecked at Durban on 31 May 1839. No lives were lost.
Cape of Good Hope Almanac, 1852

SS Ovington Court (ex *Amblestone*)
29° 51.50S, 31° 02.70E

British steel cargo vessel of 6 095 tons, built in 1924 by Richardson, Duck & Co, Stockton, owned by the Court Line, and commanded by Capt G. O. Lindsell. Wrecked on South Beach, Durban, on 25 November 1940 during a north-east gale after a voyage from Mauritius with a cargo of sugar, which was saved. Four men drowned. She lies a little west of the West Street groin.
Lloyds Register of Shipping, 1940-41
Natal Mercury, 5 December 1940

Peusamento

Portuguese brig of 279 tons, commanded by Capt Castro. Wrecked at Durban on 19 October 1879. She was anchored in the Bluff Channel, waiting to proceed to Mozambique, when she developed a leak and broke her back after bumping on the bar. No lives were lost. Her cargo was saved.
Natal Mercury, 20 October 1879

Pioneer
29° 51.80S, 31° 03.00E

British barque of 453 tons, commanded by Capt Scott. Wrecked on the Back Beach near Annabella Bank at Durban on 23 October 1862 when her cables parted after a voyage from London with a cargo of timber for the harbour works. No lives were lost.
Natal Mercury, 24, 28 October 1862

Ponda Chief

Clipper Line wooden barque of 397 tons, built in 1875 by Fellows, Yarmouth, and commanded by Capt C. Warren. Wrecked at Durban on 3 March 1878 when her cables parted after a voyage from London. No lives were lost. Most of her cargo was saved.
Eastern Province Herald, 22 March 1878
Lloyds Register of Shipping, 1878-79

Princess Alice

British three-masted wooden schooner of 190 tons, built in 1861 by Hall, Arbryth. Wrecked at Durban on 31 July 1872 during a north-east gale after a voyage from Gothenburg with a cargo of timber. No lives were lost.
Lloyds Register of Shipping, 1872-73
Natal Mercury, 1 August 1872
Shipping Register, Cape Archives, C.C. 3/7/2/2

Queen
29° 51.80S, 31° 03.00E

British brig of 198 tons, commanded by Capt Easson. Wrecked near Vetches Pier at Durban on 16 August 1863 when her cables parted during a

Possibly the Queen. *(Africana Museum)*

north-east wind after a voyage from London. No lives were lost. She lies close to the *Lord George Bentinck* (1861).
Natal Mercury, 18 August 1863

Queen of Ceylon
29° 51.20S, 31° 02.50E

British wooden barque of 422 tons, built in 1863 by W. Naizby, Sunderland, and commanded by Capt J. Hamilton. Wrecked on the Back Beach at Durban on 3 March 1882 during a north-east wind after a voyage from Grimsby with a cargo of coal. No lives were lost.
Lloyds Register of Shipping, 1881-82
Natal Mercury, 6 March 1882

Saint Clare
29° 51.80S, 31° 03.00E

British wooden barque of 318 tons, built in 1868. Wrecked on the Back Beach at Durban on 20 October 1871 during a north-east wind with a general cargo. One life was lost.
Lloyds Register of Shipping, 1871-72
Shipping Register, Cape Archives, C.C. 3/7/2/2

Sebastian
29° 51.80S, 31° 03.00E

British wooden barque of 364 tons, built in 1855 at Sunderland, and commanded by Capt F. Little. Wrecked on the Back Beach at Durban on 26 September 1863 during a north-east gale after a voyage from London with immigrants and a general cargo. No lives were lost.
Lloyds Register of Shipping, 1863-64
Shipping Register, Cape Archives, C.C. 3/7/2/1

Seenymphe
29° 51.80S, 31° 03.00E

German schooner of 191 tons, commanded by Capt Loser. Wrecked a little north of Vetches Pier at Durban at 24h00 on 12 December 1885 during a fresh east wind after a voyage from Mozambique with a cargo of salt and corn. No lives were lost.
Natal Mercury, 14 December 1885

Southport
29° 51.80S, 31° 03.00E

British wooden barque of 359 tons, built in 1857 at Sunderland, and commanded by Capt S. Cripps. Wrecked on the Back Beach at Durban on 23 August 1878 during an east-north-east gale after a voyage from East London. No lives were lost.
Lloyds Register of Shipping, 1878-79
Shipping Register, Cape Archives, C.C. 3/7/2/3

Star of Wales

British wooden brig of 185 tons, built in 1866 by Jones. Wrecked 2,5 km south of the Mgeni River, Durban, near the *Transvaal* (1874), on 7 December 1874 during a south gale while on a voyage from Adelaide with a cargo of flour. Three lives were lost.
Lloyds Register of Shipping, 1874-75
Natal Mercury, 10 December 1874

Suffren

French barque of 293 tons, commanded by Capt Weisbrod. Wrecked at Durban on 17 December 1845 when her cables parted during a north-east gale after a voyage from Réunion in ballast to load a cargo of cattle. No lives were lost.
Shipping Register, Cape Archives, C.C. 2/16
South African Commercial Advertiser, 3 January 1846

Surprise
29° 51.80S, 31° 03.00E

Norwegian barque of 427 tons, commanded by Capt Larsen. Wrecked on the Back Beach at Durban on 25 August 1880 when her cables parted during an east gale after a voyage from Gothenburg with a cargo of timber. No lives were lost.
Natal Mercury, 26, 27 August, 4 September (sale notice) 1880

Natal Mercury

HMSAS Sydostlandet (T33)

South African seaward patrol vessel of 259 tons, built in 1932 in Sandefjord. Wrecked about 8 km south of Umhlanga Rocks on 6 April 1942 at night during a gale. She was formerly a whaler owned by the Kerguelen Sealing and Whaling Co, Cape Town.
Lloyds Register of Shipping, 1941-42

Sydostlandet. *(George Young)*

Tancred

British wooden brigantine of 199 tons, built in 1877 by Duncan, Prince Edward Island, and commanded by Capt Vincent. Wrecked at Durban on 2 May 1879 during an east wind after a voyage from London. No lives were lost.
Argus Annual, 1889
Lloyds Register of Shipping, 1879-80

Theresina
29° 51.80S, 31° 03.00E

British wooden brigantine of 294 tons, built in 1862 by Steele, Greenock, and commanded by Capt E. Christian. Wrecked on the Back Beach at Durban on 9 April 1878 during an east-north-east gale after a voyage from London with a general cargo. The crew were saved by means of rocket apparatus.
Lloyds Register of Shipping, 1878-79
Shipping Register, Cape Archives, C.C. 3/7/2/3

Transvaal

British wooden barque of 370 tons, built in 1874 by Crown, Sunderland, and commanded by Capt Bolton. Wrecked about 2,5 km south of the Mgeni River at Durban on 8 December 1874 when her cables parted during a south gale after her maiden voyage from London with a general cargo worth £35 000. Twelve lives were lost. The captain was on shore at the time. She lies close to the *Star of Wales* (1874).
Lloyds Register of Shipping, 1874-75
Natal Mercury, 8 December 1874

Tugela
29° 51.20S, 31° 02.50E

British wooden ship of 475 tons, built in 1864 by Hall, Aberdeen, and commanded by Capt G. Stewart. Wrecked on the Back Beach below West Street, Durban, on 3 February 1868 at night in fine weather when a chain unshackled and she drifted. No lives were lost. She was in ballast.
Lloyds Register of Shipping, 1867-68
Shipping Register, Cape Archives, C.C. 3/7/2/2

Vigor
29° 51.20S, 31° 02.50E

Norwegian wooden brig of 179 tons, built in 1874 in Sandefjord, and commanded by Capt Johannessen. Wrecked on the Back Beach at Durban on 9 June 1884 during an east wind after a voyage from Drammen, Norway, with a cargo of timber. No lives were lost, as her crew were saved by lifeboat.
Lloyds Universal Register of Shipping, 1886-87
Natal Mercury, 10 June 1884

Tugela. *(Africana Museum)*

Wagrien

German schooner of 170 tons. Wrecked at Durban on 8 December 1874 during a south gale after a voyage from London with a general cargo. All the crew members lost their lives.
Natal Mercury, 10 December 1874

Zambesi
29° 51.20S, 31° 02.50E

Dutch wooden schooner of 130 tons, commanded by Capt Schloemer. Wrecked on the Back Beach at Durban on 10 December 1882 when her cables parted during an east wind after a voyage from Delagoa Bay with a general cargo. No lives were lost. She was in quarantine.
Natal Mercury, 11, 28 (enquiry) December 1882

Zennia
29° 51.80S, 31° 03.00E

Irish wooden barque of 316 tons, built in 1867 by

O'Brien, Bathurst, and commanded by Capt D. Bowen. Wrecked on Annabella Bank at Durban on 21 July 1880 at night during a south wind after a voyage from Newcastle with a cargo of coal. No lives were lost. She later drifted on to the Back Beach.
Lloyds Register of Shipping, 1880-81
Natal Mercury, 22, 27 (sale notice) July 1880

Ziba
29° 51.70S, 31° 03.00E

American schooner of 425 tons, commanded by Capt Gaskin. Wrecked at Durban on 13 March 1879 during a north-east gale after a voyage from Buenos Aires with a cargo of maize. No lives were lost.
Natal Mercury, 17 March 1879
Shipping Register, Cape Archives, C.C. 3/7/2/3

38. Umhlanga Rocks to Ponta do Ouro

Known as the Natal North Coast, this stretch of coast consists of long sandy beaches. The water is warm due to the Mozambique current; in the north it is usually clear, and the first signs of tropical coral appear on the reefs. The coast is a popular tourist venue and is often visited by divers and spearfishermen. Sharks are a very real danger. The climate is sub-tropical, with an extremely high humidity. The main settlements along the coast are Compensation, Stanger, Mtunzini, Port Durnford and Richards Bay, which has developed into a large port. The main features are the large St Lucia Estuary, which is home to hippos, crocodiles and many other species of animal, Cape Vidal, Leven Point, Sordwana Bay National Park and Kosi Bay National Park. There are many inland bodies of water along the coast, and malaria is a serious problem. There is a restricted military zone just north of Cape Vidal. Ponta do Ouro demarcates the border between South Africa and Mozambique.

Bonaventura

English ketch of 20 tons, commanded by Capt John Gilford. Wrecked in St Lucia Bay on 25 December 1686 after a voyage from the Downs, off south-east Kent, to Natal. One crew member was lost; the remaining nine intended to walk overland to the Cape, but at Durban met some other shipwrecked survivors who were building a boat, and joined up with them.
Cape Archives, C. 332 (old number), C. 1895
Moodie, D., *The Record*, Part 1, pp 417-419

SS **Clan Gordon**
28° 57.40S, 31° 50.20E

Clan Line iron screw brig of 2 117 tons, built in 1879 by A. Stephen & Sons, Glasgow, and commanded by Capt Wakeford. Wrecked on the south end of Tenedos Reef in Zululand on 17 Oc-

tober 1897 while on a voyage to Mozambique with a general cargo. No lives were lost.
Cape Argus, 19, 20, 21 October 1897
Lloyds Register of Shipping, 1897-98

Dorothea (ex *Ernestine*)
28° 07.40S, 32° 33.80E

American-registered wooden barque of 851 tons, built in 1884 by J. Jürgens, Elsfleth, and commanded by Capt Harold Mathisson. Wrecked at Cape Vidal on the Zululand Coast on 31 January 1898 after she began sinking and the crew abandoned her. She is reputed to have been carrying Transvaal gold (amalgam) loaded at Lourenço Marques (Maputo) and cemented under her fore-hold.
Cape Argus, 31 July, 1 August (report on salvage) 1899
Cape Times, 2 August 1899 (report on salvage)
Lloyds Register of Shipping, 1896-97
Natal Mercury, 3 February 1898

SS **Newark Castle**
28° 48.30S, 32° 05.10E

Union Castle Line extra steamer of 5 093 tons, built in 1902 by Barclay Curle, Glasgow, and commanded by Capt Neilson. Wrecked in the mouth of Richards Bay on 12 March 1908 while on a voyage from London to Mauritius with draftees for the garrison at Mauritius and a general cargo, including a large amount of paper money. Three people lost their lives when the vessel grounded and was abandoned; thereafter she drifted 11 km before running ashore.
Lloyds Register of Shipping, 1901-02
Shipping Register, Cape Archives, C.C. 3/7/2/6

SS **Octopus**
29° 33.00S, 31° 12.60E

British-registered steel twin-screw hopper-dredger of 969 tons, built in 1895 by W. Simons & Co, Renfrew, and commanded by Capt Thomas Ogilvie. Ran ashore a little south of Ballito Bay on the Natal North Coast on 15 October 1906. She had been sold by her former owners, the Natal Government, to the Administration of Geelong in Australia and had been working in Durban for many years. She was being delivered to her new owners in Australia and was heavily laden with 780 tons of coal for the voyage. Shortly after leaving Durban harbour she experienced heavy weather and began taking in water, which extinguished her furnaces. She was abandoned by her crew after they had released a messenger pigeon, and then ran ashore.
Lloyds Register of Shipping, 1899-1900
Natal Mercury, 16 October 1906

São Jeronymo

Portuguese East-Indiaman. Wrecked on the Zululand Coast, north of Richards Bay, in June

1552 while on a homeward-bound voyage from Cochin, India, to Lisbon in the Company of the *São João*, which was wrecked a little north-east of the Mtamvuna River in June 1552. There were no survivors.
De Couto, Diogo, *Da Asia de Diogo de Couto dos feitos, que os Portuguezes fizeram na conquista, e descrubimento das terras, e mares do Oriente*, Lisbon, Regia Officina Typografica, 1778-1788, Vol 3, Part 2

São João de Bescoinho

Portuguese East-Indiaman commanded by Lopo de Sousa. Wrecked near Ponta do Ouro in 1551 while on a homeward-bound voyage from India to Lisbon with a cargo of silks, spices and Chinese porcelain. There were no survivors. The survivors of the *São Bento* found her remains during their march to Delagoa Bay (Maputo) in 1554.
De Mesquita Perestrelo, Manuel, *Relacão do Naufragio da Não S. Bento*. Translated into English in Theal, G.M., *Records of South Eastern Africa*, Vol 1

SS **Saxon**
26° 55.60S, 32° 53.20E

Portuguese iron screw steamer of 462 tons, built in 1887 by Oswald, Mordaunt & Co, Southampton. Wrecked on a reef 1 km south of the mouth of Kosi Bay near the Mozambique border on 29 January 1896 while on a voyage from Durban to Maputo. The crew and passengers landed safely in Delagoa Bay in the lifeboats. This wreck is the most northerly on the coast of South Africa and is a popular diving venue.
Lloyds Register of Shipping, 1895-96
Natal Mercury, 31 January 1896

SS **Timavo**
32° 36.50E, 27° 52.00S

Italian cargo vessel of 7 549 tons, built in 1920 by Cantiere San Rocco, Trieste, and owned by Lloyd Triestino. Beached a few kilometres north of Leven Point in Zululand in June 1940. She had slipped out of Durban harbour after Italy had declared war on the Allies, and was making her way up the coast when she was forced ashore by Air Force aircraft. She lies 200 m offshore in the sand.
Lloyds Register of Shipping, 1940-41
Van Delden, G., *I Have a Plan*

Trygve (ex *Centaur*)

Norwegian wooden barque of 476 tons, built in 1875 by J. Paulsen, Apenrade, and commanded by Capt S. Isaaksen. Wrecked near the Zinkwazi River on 10 June 1897 while on a voyage from Pensacola to Durban with a cargo of pitch pine. Seven crew members were drowned.
Lloyds Register of Shipping, 1897-98
Natal Mercury, 11 June 1897

Bibliography

Main Sources
Archives of the Batavian Republic, Cape Archives
Archives of the Colonial Office, Cape Archives
Archives of the Council of Policy, Cape Archives
Argus Annual and South African Gazeteer, The
Cape of Good Hope Almanac and Annual Register, The
Diving Records, Malcolm Turner
East India Office, London
Kennedy, R. F.: *Shipwrecks On and Off the Coasts of Southern Africa,* 1955
Lloyds Register of British and Foreign Shipping, London
The Hague Archives
Theal, G. M.: *Chronicles of Cape Commanders*
Theal, G. M.: *Records of the Cape Colony*
Theal, G. M.: *Records of South-Eastern Africa*
Various South African Newspapers

Select Bibliography
Addison, A. C.: *The Story of the Birkenhead,* Simpkin, Marshall, Hamilton, Kent & Co, London, 1902.
Addison, A. C. and Matthews, W. H.: *A Deathless Story,* Hutchinson, London, 1906.
Allen, G. and Allen, D.: *Clive's Lost Treasure,* Robin Garton, London 1978.
Allen, G. and Allen, D.: *The Guns of Sacramento,* Robin Garton, London, 1978.
Axelson, E. (Ed): *Dias & His Successors,* Saayman & Weber, Cape Town, 1988.
Bevan, D.: *Drums of the Birkenhead,* Purnell, Cape Town, 1972.
Bulpin, T. V.: *Shaka's Country,* Howard Timmins, Cape Town, 1952.
Burman, J. L.: *Great Shipwrecks off the Coast of Southern Africa,* C. Struik, Cape Town, 1967.
Burman, J. L.: *Strange Shipwrecks of the Southern Seas,* C. Struik, Cape Town, 1968.
Burton, A. W.: *Sparks from the Border Anvil,* Provincial Publishing Co, King William's Town, 1950.
Carter, G.: *A Narrative of the Loss of the Grosvenor East-Indiaman,* J. Murray & William Lane, London, 1791.

Colvin, I. D.: *The Cape of Adventure,* T. C. & E. C. Jack, Edinburgh, 1912.
Green, L. G.: *South African Beachcomber,* Howard Timmins, Cape Town, 1958.
Green. L. G.: *Something Rich and Strange,* Howard Timmins, Cape Town, 1962.
Green, L. G.: *Almost Forgotten, Never Told,* Howard Timmins, Cape Town, 1965.
Hale, J. R.: *Age of Exploration,* Time-Life International, 1966.
Humble, R.: *Captain Bligh,* Arthur Barker, London, 1976.
Kirby, P. R.: *A Source Book on the Wreck of the Grosvenor East-Indiaman,* The Van Riebeeck Society, Cape Town, 1953.
Lighton, C.: *Sisters of the South,* Howard Timmins, Cape Town, 1951.
Mackeurtan, G.: *The Cradle Days of Natal, 1497-1845,* Longmans, Green & Co., London, 1930.
Murray, M.: *Ships and South Africa,* Humphrey Milford, London, 1933.
Murray, M.: *Union-Castle Chronicle, 1853-1953,* Longmans, Green & Co, London, 1953.
Narrative of the Loss of the Sceptre Man of War of 64 Guns, Capt Valentine Edwards, John Fairburn, London. (Written by one of the survivors.)
Parry, J. H.: *Europe and a Wider World, 1415-1715,* Hutchinson University Library, London, 1969.
Rosenthal, E.: *The Hinges Creaked,* Howard Timmins, Cape Town, 1951.
Sparrman, A.: *A Voyage to the Cape of Good Hope,* G. G. J. & J. Robinson, London, 1785.
Speight, W. L.: *Swept by Wind and Wave,* Howard Timmins, Cape Town, n.d.
Steedman, A.: *Wanderings and Adventures in the Interior of Southern Africa,* Longmans, London, 1835.
Stout, B.: *Narrative of the Loss of the Ship Hercules,* J. Johnson, London, 1798.
Thompson, G.: *Travels and Adventures in Southern Africa,* Henry Colburn, London, 1827.
Valentyn, F.: *Oud en Nieuw Oost-Indiën,* Joannes van Braam, Dordrecht, 1726.
Van Delden, G.: *I Have a Plan,* Howard Timmins, Cape Town, 1950.
Wexham, B.: *Shipwrecks of the Western Cape,* Howard Timmins, Cape Town, n.d.
Willcox, A. R.: *Shipwreck and Survival on the South-East Coast of Africa,* Drakensberg Publications, Winterton, 1984.

Thermopylae. *(Cape Archives, J 5198)*

Index